SPLIT

DECISIONS

Janet Halley

SPLIT

DECISIONS

How and Why to Take
a Break from Feminism

PRINCETON UNIVERSITY PRESS
Princeton and Oxford

Copyright ©2006 by Princeton University Press

Published by Princeton University Press, 41 William Street,

Princeton, New Jersey 08540

In the United Kingdom: Princeton University Press, 3 Market Place,

Woodstock, Oxfordshire OX20 1SY

All Rights Reserved

Library of Congress Cataloging-in-Publication Data

Halley, Janet E., 1952–

Split decisions : how and why to take a break from feminism / Janey Halley.

p.   cm.

Includes bibliographical references and index.

ISBN-13: 978-0-691-12737-8 (hardcover : alk. paper)

ISBN-10: 0-691-12737-9 (hardcover : alk. paper)

1. Feminist theory. 2. Feminism. 3. Sex—Philosophy. 4. Sex—Social aspects.

5. Sex role. 6. Sexual orientation. I. Title.

HQ1190.H345 2006

306.701—dc22   2005038028

British Library Cataloging-in-Publication Data is available

This book has been composed in Minion

Printed on acid-free paper. ∞

pup.princeton.edu

Printed in the United States of America

10 9 8 7 6 5 4 3 2 1

To David and Duncan

Contents

PART THREE
How and Why to
Take a Break from Feminism

Acknowledgments

The moment of saying "thank you" is always a pleasure. Paul Brest, Mark Kelman, Barbara Fried, and Richard Thompson Ford made it possible for me to be an academic—Paul by hiring me against all odds; and all four of them by making my years at Stanford an encounter with rigorous critical thought. Since coming to Harvard Law School I have enjoyed the critical incitement of Lama Abu-Odeh, Libby Adler, Nathaniel Berman, Yishai Blank, David Charny, Brenda Cossman, Dan Danielsen, Karen L. Engle, Aeyal Gross, Tracy Higgins, Karen Knop, Joel Paul, Kerry Rittich, Hani Sayed, Amr Shalakany, Chantal Thomas, Robert Wai, and Robyn Wiegman. My experience of the genealogy set forth in Part Two of the book—we are talking here about twenty-five years of work in politics, conflict, friendship, and love—has been enriched by Thomas Bass, Wendy Brown, Judith Butler, Jonathan Goldberg, Roberta Krueger, Michael Moon, Andrew Parker, Elizabeth Faye Potter, Eve Kosofsky Sedgwick, Nancy Sorkin Rabinowitz, and Michael Warner. Dan Danielsen persistently helped me to remember that the disciplinary divides among all these interlocutors were enticing—not somehow blocking. Countless intense conferences, collaborations, and moments of sharp anxiety—what is about to happen??!!—with many people contributed to my work: I particularly want to thank Bruce Ackerman, Henry Abelove, Tal Arbal, Leo Bersani, Peter Brooks, Soo Choi, Natalie Zemon Davis, Christine Desan, Carolyn Dinshaw, Mary L. Dudziak, Martha Albertson Fineman, Katherine M. Franke, Karla Freccero, Gerald E. Frug, Phillip Brian Harper, Hendrik Hartog, Sarah Jain, Christine A. Littleton, Maria Rosaria Marella, Sylvia Niccolai, Julie Peters, Richard Rambuss, David A. J. Richards, Teemu Ruskola, Jed Rubenfeld, Vicki

Schultz, Reva B. Siegel, Anna Marie Smith, Bianca Gardella Tedeschi, Kendall Thomas, Lucie E. White, and Amalia Ziv. I am enduringly grateful to Libby Adler, Brenda Cossman, and Duncan Kennedy for intense and thrilling collaborations with the Harvard Law School's Program on Law and Social Thought. And I treasure the discussions I have had through teaching. Kerry Abrams, Yael Aridor Bar-Ilan, Noa Ben Asher, Amy Cohen, Eyal Diskin, Pascale Fournier, Havva Guney, Isabel Jaramillo, Prabha Kotiswaran, Fernanda G. Nicola, Bernie Meyler, Zinaida Miller, Tanya Monforte, Rober Pao, Moria Paz, Rachel Rebouche, Anna di Robilant, Nathaniel Brishen Rogers, Talha Sayed, Hila Shamir, Ruth E. Sternglantz, Jeannie Suk, Madhavi Sunder, Ziona Tanzer, Philomila Tsoukala, and Raef Zreik, and many others, have made a mark on my work that I hope they will be able to detect. I will always be grateful to Jan Schreiber for her myriad contributions to all this work.

I have been lucky to have had wonderful opportunities to learn by teaching, at Stanford Law School, Harvard Law School, the University of Toronto Faculty of Law, the Tel Aviv University's Bachman Faculty of Law, and the European University Institute of the Academy of European Law in Florence. Coteaching has significantly changed my argument: I particularly want to thank Judith Butler, Andrew Parker, and Dori Spivak for that.

Work like this—many years of circulating and reading manuscripts, cooking for interlocutors, throwing conferences aimed at figuring it all out—depends on many kinds of help. I am grateful for the contributions of my librarians at Stanford, especially Paul Lomio and Erica Wayne, and the dedicated librarians at Harvard, including the amazing Melinda Kent; of my assistants Pat Adan, Judy Dearing, Deenie Stevens, Anne Marie Calareso, Judith Walcott, and Terry Cyr; of my party-giving stalwarts Tania Lima and Doreen McGuirk; of Information Technology Services at both schools, and particularly Elizabeth McManus, who rescued me at the last minute from Microsoft Word; and of research assistants Kerry Abrams, Eric Bakilana, Jessie Brown, Ashwin Krishnan, and Hila Shamir.

Conferences, lectureships, and guest teaching engagements have been equally important. Organizers and audiences in Canada, Egypt, Israel, Italy, and all over the United States helped me find the boundaries and content of my argument, and I am grateful to them all—even, or rather especially, when the engagement felt fracturous and risky. I am grateful for invitations: at the American University in Cairo, to the Graduate Law Program's Legal Theory seminar taught by Amr Shalakany, to the Human Rights Program lecture series, and to consult with the Women's Studies Program; at the University of California at Irvine, to the Chancellor's Distinguished Fellowship series, the Humanities Institute Residential Group, "Interdisciplinary Queer Studies," and the Research Seminar on Law and Sexuality; at the University of California at Los Angeles, to the Williams Project lecture series, and to the Lesbian, Gay, Bisexual and Transgender Studies Program and Women's Studies Program lecture series; at the University of California at San Diego, to the Women's Studies/Critical Gender Studies Colloquium; at the University of Chicago, to the Franke Institute for the Humanities final Sawyer Conference, "Hatred: Confronting the Other"; at the Columbia University Law School, to the *Columbia Journal of Gender and Law*'s conference, "Why a Women's Law Journal?" and a fabulous opportunity to compare approaches with Dan Danielsen, Brenda Cossman, and Tracy Higgins, and to the Center for the Study of Law and Culture lecture series; at Cornell University, to serve as a Messenger Lecturer; at the Davis/McGeorge Law Schools, to the Legal Theory Workshop; at Duke University, to the Women's Studies Program lecture series; at Duke University School of Law, to serve as a Brainerd Currie Memorial Lecturer; at Emory University, for a lecture jointly sponsored by the Women's Studies Program, the

Feminism and Legal Theory Project, and the Law School; to the
Fondazione Basso, Rome, to speak in its lecture series; at Ford-
ham Law School, to the Legal Theory Workshop; at Harvard University's Barker Center, to make several presentations to the
Workshop on Feminist Theory (the latter cosponsored by the
Committee on Degrees in Women's, Gender, and Sexuality Studies), including a fabulous opportunity to compare approaches
with Robyn Wiegman; at Harvard Law School, to the Faculty
Workshop, several times, and to speak at the European Law Research Center's "Colloquium on Structural Bias and Identity"; at
Johns Hopkins University, to speak to the Interdisciplinary Seminar offered by the Program for the Study of Women, Gender &
Sexuality; to New York University's Center for the Study of Gender and Sexuality, for several opportunities to speak in its lecture
series; at New York University Law School, to the Graduate Studies Program Conference and the Legal Theory Workshop; at University of Pennsylvania School of Law, to the Penn Lambda Law
lecture series; at the University of Perugia Faculty of Law, to the
Feminist Legal Theory course taught by Maria Rosaria Marella;
at Princeton University, to the Woodrow Wilson School's Program in Law and Public Affairs Faculty Workshop; at Stanford
Law School, to the Redistribution Seminar offered by Barbara
Fried and Thomas C. Grey, and the Status and Subordination
Seminar offered by Richard Thompson Ford; at the University of
Southern California Law School, to the Legal Theory Workshop;
at Tel Aviv University, to the Conference on Gay and Lesbian
Studies and Queer Theory, organized by the university's Women
Studies Forum and the Gay & Lesbian and Queer Theory Forum,
to the Women's Studies Conference, and to the Queer Theory
Reading Group, as well as, within the Bachman Faculty of Law,
to the Faculty Workshop and the course on Legal Theory taught
by Yishai Blank, Roy Kreitner, and Shai Lavi; to the University of
Texas School of Law's conference, "Subversive Legacies," and a

fabulous opportunity, organized and moderated by Karen Engle, to compare approaches with Nathaniel Berman, Adrienne Davis, Vicki Schultz, and Elizabeth Schneider; at the University of Torino Faculty of Law, to the Faculty Workshop; at the University of Toronto, to consult with the Women's Studies Program; and at the University of Toronto Faculty of Law, to the Feminism and Law Workshop, several times; at the Wesleyan University Humanities Center, to its lecture series and colloquium; to the Western New England Law School Conference on Feminist Legal Theory for a fabulous opportunity to compare approaches with Vicki Schultz and Duncan Kennedy; at Yale University, to Whitney Humanities Center conferences, "Sexuality, Modernity, and Social Theory," and "Postmodernism/Postmodernity: Politics, Law, Culture, Aesthetics"; at Yale Law School, to the Legal Theory Workshop; at York University, to serve as the Or Emet Lecturer in Osgood Hall.

Four deans—Paul Brest, Kathleen Sullivan, Robert Clark, and Elena Kagan—provided crucial support, as did the National Endowment for the Humanities, the Robert E. Paradise Faculty Fellowship at Stanford, and Ric Wieland, also during my Stanford years.

Catharine A. MacKinnon generously provided substantive criticism of some pages; and Lauren Berlant was the absolute dream reader of the manuscript as it went up for approval for publication. Thanks to Duncan Kennedy and Leo Bersani for reading the parts of the manuscript relating to their own work, and to Jerry Frug for finding the Abelardo Morell that adorns the jacket. Ian Malcolm has been a simply wonderful editor.

Editors of many kinds have worked hard on this book, making it better. Has there ever been a better text editor than Lauren Lepow? I doubt it. Several parts of this book were first published in journals and anthologies, and appear here in revised form. I am grateful to all the editors of these articles and essays for their work: "The Politics of Injury: A Review of Robin West's *Caring for Justice*," in *unbound* (Spring 2005), at http://www .law.harvard.edu/students/orgs/unbound/; "Take a Break from Feminism?" in *Gender and Human Rights*, ed. Karen Knop (Oxford: Oxford University Press, 2004); "Gender, Sexuality and Power—Is Feminist Theory Enough?" with Brenda Cossman, Dan Danielsen, and Tracy Higgins, in *Why a Feminist Law Journal?*, a special issue of the *Columbia Journal of Gender and Law* 12 (2004): 601; "Queer Theory by Men," nominally by Ian Halley, *Duke Journal of Gender, Law & Policy* 11 (2004): 7; "Sexuality Harassment," in *Left Legalism/Left Critique*, coedited with Wendy Brown (Durham: Duke University Press, 2002), 80–104; "Sexuality Harassment" (a somewhat different version) in *Directions in Sexual Harassment Law*, ed. Catharine A. MacKinnon and Reva B. Siegel (New Haven: Yale University Press, 2004), 182–200. I also wish to thank all the journals and publishers just listed for recognizing my "right" to reprint, whether by leaving copyright in my hands, by contract terms to that effect, or by express permission (the last recognition is due to *unbound*).

For all my indebtedness to so many, no one mentioned here bears any responsibility for any errors I have made, of judgment or execution.

I dedicate this book to David Kennedy and Duncan Kennedy in profound gratitude for their world-making energy, their will to engage critique with politics, and their deep capacity for intelligent friendship.

Cambridge and Dighton, Massachusetts
December 2005

PART ONE

TAKING A BREAK FROM FEMINISM

THE ARGUMENT

Over the last twenty-five years the U.S. Left has produced a rich range of theories of sexuality. These theories differ a lot, partly because they were made by people involved in a context of deep internal critique, debates so intense that they were sometimes experienced as "war." The result is a wide array of incommensurate theories of sexuality and of power.

This book argues that the splits between the theories are part of their value. It proposes an alternative to the normative demand to harmonize them, reconcile them, and smooth out their clashes. I argue here for a politics *of* theoretic incommensurability. I think it will be better for the Left—we will make better decisions about what we want, and possibly even win more conflicts with the Right—if we lavish attention and appreciation on the capacity of our theory making to reveal the world as a normatively fraught, contradictory, conflictual place, a place where interests differ, change over time, and come into zero-sum conflicts, a place where all our decisions—even our decisions to abstain from deciding—shift social goods among highly contingent but pressing, urgent, vital interests.

As part of this argument, I also argue that theory making has been crucial to left-of-center politics of sexuality. What people have done theoretically has changed reality for them, has changed them so deeply it has shifted their very beings; and it has changed their political situations. And as their political life has changed, the demands they bring to theory have shifted; the desire for theory has been a political desire.

I assume here that human beings operate according to the maxim "I'll see it when I believe it"—or perhaps more accurately, "I'll see it when I can and do theorize it." And so I'll argue that our different theories about sexuality are useful to the extent that they throw into visibility different stakes which we then distribute when we act politically and legally. Theory produces reality not only by making it visible, moreover, but by shifting the available terms for consciousness, desire, and thus interest. And so theory is part of how we distribute social goods toward and away from various constituencies and interests. Inasmuch as we are *all* legal decision makers when we decide what political aims to pursue and resist, when to engage and when to hang out on the sidelines, the perceivability and ethical urgency of various social interests are deeply contingent on the theories we have developed and on our selection of some of them in favor of others.

This book argues that, at least when it comes to sexuality, the responsible way to engage in a politics that depends on theory and that produces it—a politics that shifts social resources toward and away from safety and risk, men and women, gay men and lesbians, pleasure and danger (etc., etc., etc.) in part by rendering them theoretically salient, culturally productive, and thus phe-nomenologically accessible—is to decide in the splits between theories and between the interests they make visible, produce, and narrate. That's how this book got the title *Split Decisions*.

The book got its subtitle because one of the chief impediments to my being able to persuade people to take the attitude I've just described (that is, to desire it) lies in the particular place that feminism occupies at the moment in left-of-center U.S. sexual politics. Three commitments that attend feminism today are in-volved here. The first seems always to be part of feminism today in the United States: it is persistently a subordination theory set by default to seek the social welfare of women, femininity, and/ or female or feminine gender by undoing some part or all of their subordination to men, masculinity, and/or male or masculine gender. That is, there are three parts to this first part: a distinction between something m and something f; a commitment to be a theory about, and a practice about, the subordination of f to m; and a commitment to work against that subordination on behalf of f. In my shorthand throughout this book, these three parts are m/f, m > f, and carrying a brief for f. It's not necessary for feminism to hold to these three points, but my experience is that so far, in the United States, it always does.

The second is the deeply held but entirely dispensable view that feminism is an indispensable element, if not the overarching structure, of any adequate theory of sexuality, gender, m/f, and associated matters.

And the third is a series of interconnected assumptions that almost all feminists share with almost all left-of-center theorists of sexuality in the tradition I study here: that one theory is better than many; that integrating alternative theories together is the goal of our work; that reality must come fully into line with, be engulfed by, theory; that theory will tell us all the crucial things we *need* to know about moral value and emancipation. I'll call this the prescriptive deployment of theory. The consequence of thinking this way, in the debates I examine in this book, is a pervasive consensus that any particular theory is a compact, dense mass of valid description, correct normative judgment, and indispensable emancipatory aspiration.

The story of feminism that I tell here is the story of people setting some of these commitments aside. First, feminism has been highly productive both as a social force and as an idea generator for the Left; and some of its offspring are not feminist. That is, many important strands of left-of-center thought and practice about sexuality don't posit feminism as an indispensable element of what they think and do, and thus don't hold to a theory of social subordination in which emancipation is figured as the release of women, femininity, and/or female or feminine gender from its subordination to men, masculinity, and/or male or masculine gender. Of course these splits have been highly controversial, painful, and life-changing for those involved in making them. I argue here that they should also be remembered for the sheer joy that they made possible, both inside feminism and in its prodigals. They have multiplied the desires and interests that we can see and articulate, and among which we distribute social goods. I think that has been a good thing, most of the time. I tell a story here in which the very vitality and usefulness of feminism as a social theory seems to have waxed when the commitment to its omnipresence wanes, and vice versa.

Finally, I think some of the agony of split decisions, both at the theoretical and at the political and legal levels, arises from the assumption that feminist theory—or a particular feminist theory, or a competitor of feminist theory—is inevitably aspirational and normative even when it operates at the level of description, that it *must* be deployed prescriptively. Most of the theories that I present in this book deploy theory in order to map a moral universe of good and bad sex and of sexual emancipation and sexual oppression, and to produce from that map a morally valid political plan for getting people more of the former and less of the latter. This is a compelling project, and we all do it. But sometimes we deploy the theory that results prescriptively: we stipulate that it does or must describe reality *and* explain why different aspects of it are good or bad, *and* point the only way to emancipation. Our practice of theory then presupposes that the theory that does all of this will necessarily either enfold into itself or invalidate other, incommensurate theories. When we're behaving this way, we're set by default to say that if anyone takes a break from our theory, she becomes incapable of noticing or caring about real-world moments when theory's constituents are oppressed, injured, exploited, harmed in sexuality.

I don't want to see theory that way. I want to see it as the effort to form hypotheses about what is happening in the world and about the various social goods and bads that are being distributed among people. Instead of working to defend, protect, and maximize theory as an account of the world and program for the world, I am trying to see it as theory fragments lying about that we can use quite instrumentally, pragmatically, and disloyally to deal with problems we perceive and want to do something about. Let's imagine that you are working on a problem. My hunch is that, during most of your work, your sense of the real is very contingent, can shift, is itself fragmented, not coherent; and that your sense of your goal will often be very loose, even just an impulse or a desire; it could be an ideological predisposition or taste. In any event, you are shuttling between interpretations of the world and formulations of your objective, reforming each in light of the other.

Of course it can be quite otherwise—there are moments when everything begins to gel; a consolidated theory meets a preternaturally clearly ordered reality—and that can be a moment of wonderful energy, power, and effectiveness. A bold total theory can startle you out of worn-out habits of mind, enable you to see newly and act creatively. But in my experience—yours, too?—it's horrifying to live that way too long: when reality presents you with experiences that don't fit, the paranoia you feel can be intense; and as theory hardens into dogma, you attract the wrong sort of people to work with you. Suddenly you're surrounded not by adventurous lively people but by complainers and bullies. So even in the times of consolidation, my desire is for a pragmatic posture, a sense of being *in relation to* problem seeing and problem solving; and for an existentialist attitude that understands being as just the appearance of phenomena to a being. My desire is a posture, an attitude, a practice, of being in the problem, not being in the theory.

Almost any theory can "receive" this attitude. Even a theory devised by someone aiming to deploy it prescriptively can be cannibalized in fragments; opted for and against on the grounds not of its truth but of its usefulness; lived, loved, and set aside in the pragmatic, existentialist attitude that, in writing this book, I am trying to seduce you to want for yourself.[1]

If we work with this attitude, it makes a lot of sense to say that we can have a whole lot of different theories of sexuality. Feminism is one, and it's got really important contributions to make. If I'm right that feminism as it is practiced in the United States today is dedicated to thinking in terms of male and female (masculine and feminine, etc.), noticing instances of male power and female subordination, and working on behalf of subordinated female interests, we can convert these aspirational and prescriptive commitments to hypotheses, and then take a break from them and try to see other arrangements of m and f and other kinds of power. And we can elect to "be for" other interests (we can aspire and moralize differently) *without losing access to feminist theory.* Any one person can "flicker" in and out of feminism—the term is Denise Riley's; she was writing about how one flickers in and out even of being a woman[2]—without feminism's being destroyed or even rendered theoretically inaccessible; and across our debates about what the Left should aim for in its politics of sexuality, leftists can vary in the same way. We might even try to see sexuality in terms that don't refer to male and female at all. Feminism would still be there for us to resort to if this effort to understand things differently seemed not to correspond to the world and our political aims. Sustaining competing theories for describing the same social arrangements can expand our sense of the stakes at stake when we make our choices about what to see as a social good and a social bad, how to understand their distribution, what to think of as normatively bad, and what to aspire to. We can become more responsible.

If we deploy feminist theory (or any other social theory of sexuality) prescriptively—if it is *itself* emancipatory—then taking a break from it is to give up on emancipation. If it's not—if it's about hypothesis formation and about seeking to "see the world" politically—taking a break from one hypothesis might expose you others, and so to new insights into power that are different, clashing perhaps, but possibly also emancipatory. You might face a split decision about what to think and do then, but that would be a vital and engaged moment.

Perhaps my ultimate point is that we can't make decisions about what to do with legal power in its many forms responsibly without taking into account as many interests, constituencies, and uncertainties as we can acknowledge. To wield power responsibly, we need to fess up to the fact that, in deciding to advocate, negotiate, legislate, adjudicate, or administer one way or another, we spread both benefits and harms across social and ideological life—and that some of these benefits and costs, however real, may be constituted by our very practices of accounting for and attempting to redress them. One of the consequences of thinking that we "see it when we believe it" is having to face, moreover, a situation of persistent theoretic incommensurability and conflict: as long as that is our situation, uncertainty is an inescapable condition of deciding. Thus I argue, finally, for an integration of critical thought into the work of deciding.

So I hope to elicit your desire to think that no one theory, no one political engagement, is nearly as valuable as the invitation to critique that is issued by the simultaneous incommensurate presence of many theories (past, present, and still to be made). We decide immense questions of social distribution and social welfare—substantive, strategic, and tactical—when we commit to one of these theories over another. I am promoting a left-of-center political consciousness that makes such commitment perpetually contingent on redecision at the level of theory. I am urging us to indulge—precisely because we love justice but don't know what it is—in the hedonics of critique.

To do that we (or at least some of us) have to be willing to Take a Break from Feminism. Not kill it, supersede it, abandon it; immure, immolate, or bury it—merely spend some time outside it exploring theories of sexuality, inhabiting realities, and imagining political goals that do not fall within its terms. Because it is so very difficult for so many people on the left in the United States to think in these terms, this book has the subtitle *How and Why to Take a Break from Feminism*.

MY COMPLETE AND TOTAL LACK OF OBJECTIVITY

It is widely (but by no means universally) thought that left/progressive theoretical, political, and erotic work in sexuality today, in the United States, will always, at root or ultimately, be *feminist*. I argue here, to the contrary, that feminism is not a universal advocacy project for all sexual interests that left/progressive/liberal intellectuals and advocates have constructed, inhabited, defended, and advanced. In the United States over the last twenty years, we have seen a range of political and theoretical incursions, all indicatively "left" of center, and all adding significantly different analyses and agendas. These projects—gay-identity thought and politics, sex-positive feminism, antiracist, postcolonial, and socialist feminisms that are willing to diverge from feminist priorities, postmodernizing feminism, queer theory with and without feminism—have been *competing* with various feminisms—some of them compete with feminism *tout court*—for intellectual authority and political fealty among left, progressive, liberal people. Feminism is not our only word on women's or human sexual welfare; on power, subordination, and gender; on power in erotic experience.

Outsiders to these debates may be surprised to hear that these claims are seriously controversial. Within left/progressive theory and politics on sexuality, the fact of conflict among the various constituencies and understandings and aims of the Left has been experienced as a *problem*. In particular it is understood to be a problem for feminism, because feminists facing the challenge of "postfeminism" so often insist that there are only two possible outcomes: either feminism is reinstated as the pervasive ground commitment of *all* left sexuality projects, or it is buried alive. To say that there is something other than feminism is to say that feminism is dead, post, over.

I hope that I won't promote any of the contestants of feminism against it—but I will celebrate the distinctive contours of their constituencies, their theories, their entailments for political and legal action. I will situate various feminisms in a genealogy with other left sexuality projects it has spawned in order to find out the differences between the parent and its offspring and to make the stakes involved in those differences clear.

To inhabit this scene without automatically "picking sides" is to embrace a seriously discomfited political position. The subject matter of this contestation is highly intimate, involving our capacity to intensify and relax forms of life that give us intense pleasure and intense shame, near-complete merger into others and near-perfect separation from them. Much is at stake. Moreover, the questions posed by these theoretical divergences—over, say, whether anal penetration is an act of dignified categorical-imperative love (this is the idea we see promoted in cultural-feminist-inflected gay-identity politics) or a longed-for threat to the intact self (this is the reality promoted by shame-affirming queer theory)—arise not only between theories, constituencies, groups, but also *within* many of us. This inconsistency, ambivalence, and paradoxicality can be how each of us lives.

I suspect it can be a good thing to be internally riven: Teiresias was a prophet, after all, not the village idiot. But even if it's bad to be internally riven, many of us (the postmodernists) just are. There's no putting that genie back in the bottle. And the genie has mischievous ways of providing the thrill of liberation from the self. A certain politics (and a certain hedonics) of the complexly constituted erotic self have arisen for me as the writer of these pages. I have held every position I describe in this book; I have abandoned many of them, often with cries of pain but also with swoops of joy. (Or at least I claim I have; the ressentiment with which I describe cultural feminism suggests that it retains some peculiar, painful hold *inside* me.) And there have been the pleasures of being wrong and changing my mind: if the project began as an effort to beat back the influence of Catharine A. MacKinnon in left thought and practice about sexuality, it has brought me to a vital new respect for her early, radical, and even critical work and a wish to promote and disseminate it. I look back with yearning on her early antinormativity, her profound appetite for epistemological crisis, and her somewhat inchoate critique of rights, and I wonder: where have they gone? I have often said of this book, "I need to finish it before I change my mind"—only to change my mind and set in motion a round of revisions equally humiliating and exhilarating. And if I could click my heels and become "a gay man" or "a straight white male middle-class radical," I would do it in an instant—wouldn't you? Even if certain identity strictures forbid me to claim actually to *be* Leo Bersani or Duncan Kennedy—my examples, in this book, of these two points of erotic and political articulation—the erotic interests that they put on the map are, to me, virtually my own.

On the downside, that means that I can easily come into conflict with myself. As a gay man I could want some things that could hurt me in my life as a woman. I'm acquiring a deep sense that the resulting inner cacophony is fun. The project for me, then, has been to find a *politics* of internal-riven-ness—a discomfited politics—that is equally fun.

But even if I can't convince a single reader to admit to a complex identification of the sort I've just confessed is mine (ahem), I think it is simply uncontestable that *feminism itself* is internally riven and has seen parts of itself break off and become—not merely diverse parts of feminism but—something else. I will argue that several of the intellectual/political projects that have resulted bring hypotheses about sexual life and power which are inconsistent with any version of feminism currently on offer. Certainly these alternative projects have constituencies that can't be described as f. That is, there is a political struggle going on right now among a range of constituencies and within many of their members—elements that promote various theories of sexuality, explore various theories of power, advocate various ways of sexual life. Each would imagine and thus wield power differently; each would govern differently; each would precipitate different sexual possibilities and realities; each would distribute status and authority to different bodies, different acts, different relationships—and (let's face it) *take* status and authority from different bodies, acts, relationships.

Apprehending this is, it seems to me, a simple predicate of responsible power wielding. And here I come up against the profound commitment of so many participants in the politics that engage me in this book—not merely feminist ones; gay ones, queer ones, trans ones also—to an understanding of themselves as *utterly without power*. The intellectual, institutional, and affective trends contributing to this attitude are many: the proliferation on the left of minoritizing identity-based vocabularies in which high-priority political and moral claims can be made only by the "marginalized" and the "silenced"; the subordination-theoretical assumption that power is always bad; the fact that so many intellectually and politically productive contributors to this politics work in humanities departments, and that these departments are in a deep crisis, experienced as powerlessness, about their place in the university; the seeming inability of most participants in these politics to move beyond a certain sentimental and moralistic view of law and legal action in which nothing short of complete and total moral vindication by the *Supreme* Court *is* legal power. I hope this book will sketch at least some ways out of at least some of these habits of mind.

Meanwhile, there is the question of my objectivity. It's nonexistent. Put another way: do I have a dog in this fight? I do, several in fact, and I try to be forthcoming about exactly what they are. I am a sex-positive postmodernist, only rarely and intermittently feminist, a skeptic about identity politics, with a strong attraction to "queer" revelations of the strangeness and unknowability of social and sexual life, and a deep distrust of slave-moralistic pretensions to identity-political "powerlessness." I don't think my preferences on these points can be argued conclusively, but I also think it would be dishonest to write a book like this that hid them. They animate the whole project for me, but I know they may not matter much, may even be strongly aversive, to you. I try to make the "take-it-or-leave-it" status of these preferences clear. I'd like to persuade you to share them; but I've tried to make it possible for you to crisply identify them and disengage yourself from them. I admit it's impossible to get this right.

TAXONOMIES AND TERMS

This book sets out a genealogy of theories of sexuality, developed left-of-center, in the United States, between 1980 and 2000. It is a genealogy for two reasons: as the people making the theories worked, they worked in the context created by their predecessors and self-consciously engaged them; and it is perceivable as a going-forward narrative only because of the active work of retrospection and desire—my desire.

All the theories have in them an image of power. And all of them have implications for how power can and should be used. Though few of them are *legal* theories, all of them have implications for law, and many of them have successfully implanted themselves in law, broadly construed.

The genealogy runs from the early 1980s, videlicet Catharine A. MacKinnon's early work and the forms of cultural feminism simultaneously then thriving, forward to the highly successful engagement of both of these kinds of radical feminism with liberal feminism (transforming all of them and producing the very powerful legal enterprise I designate the "late MacKinnon"), then on to their resistance by sex-positive feminism, the emergence of gay-identity theory and politics, and the encounter of both of *those* with postmodernism, and on forward to queer theory, trans theory, governance feminism, postfeminism, and the other characters that occupy today's stage. The table of contents shows my idea of that genealogy, and Part Two is a book-by-book, article-by-article narration and mapping of its evolving claims.

In the rest of Part One I try to provide some basics for the whole discussion. This chapter lays out some of the terms that I've devised to help me keep a whole range of highly diverse vocabularies about sex in touch with each other. The next chapter is a thumbnail statement of the whole genealogy. And the final chapter of this introductory part returns to my polemic.

m/f, m > f, and Carrying a Brief for f

In part because I am arguing that left projects about sexuality and power do, and should, occasionally, Take a Break from Feminism, I have tried to understand feminism as capaciously as possible. This seemed to me only right, given an objection I met with often, one that seemed important. The objection was that, when I pointed out the possibility and promise of a certain departure from feminism, I was merely objecting to a specific pathology *in* feminism—a habit of thought to which other strands of feminism were not prone, to which they might indeed be antagonistic. These feminists argued that I must be seeking to bury feminism alive, get rid of it, if I wasn't eager to share their work of purging it of error from within. Since I was not aiming to end feminism, I took this objection seriously. What *is* necessary for a certain thought project, or political project, or normative project, to *be feminist?* What is the *absolute minimum* of elements such a project must have? A minimalist definition would have to encompass the broadest possible range of feminisms precisely so that it would be as hard as possible to argue (as I intend to do) that Taking a Break from Feminism is both possible and desirable.

I think, as a descriptive matter, that current U.S. projects are always feminist if they have three characteristics, and never feminist if they don't have them. They are these.

First, to be feminism, a position must make a distinction between m and f. Different feminisms do this differently: some see men and women, some see male and female, some see masculine and feminine. While "men" and "women" will almost always be imagined as distinct human "groups," the other paired terms can

describe many different things: traits, narratives, introjects. However a particular feminism manages these subsidiary questions, it
is not "a feminism" unless it turns in some central or core way
on a distinction between m and f.

Second, to be a feminism in the United States today, a position
must posit some kind of subordination as between m and f, in
which f is the disadvantaged or subordinated element. At this
point feminism is descriptive and not normative: m > f.

And third (here is the normative turn), feminism opposes the
subordination of f. It typically frames this not as a raw preference
or as the self-interest of women, but as a matter of justice or
emancipation. As between m and f, and possibly because m > f,
feminism carries a brief for f.

I think these attributes are noticeable in virtually every form
of feminism in the United States today, and will treat them as
definitional—as essential in an Aristotelian sense. That is, I am
not claiming that these attributes are essential in the sense that
they are absolute or natural; rather that they are essential in the
sense that current conventions seem to require them as a disciplinary matter.

In the remainder of this section I will defend this list of essential elements from expert feminist attacks; if you aren't interested
in those (yet?), you can skip on to the next section.

In an exchange for which I continue to be grateful for this and
other reasons, Tracy Higgins and Brenda Cossman (both working
at that moment as feminists) convinced me that the current range
of feminist possibility includes projects that turn on m/f and that
carry a brief for f, but that are not subordination projects and
that therefore don't definitionally require their proponents to
claim that m > f. Liberal feminisms that celebrate "women's
agency" often come close to doing something like this. You could
think that Queen Elizabeth—the one who ruled England in the
sixteenth century—was a woman and thus that she was not like

men in some important ways (or that she practiced masculinity in some ways that differentiated it importantly from femininity, or from the masculinity of men); and your power politics or moral assessment could be "for" her in these differentiations. You could do all of that without justifying the distinction or your political or moral engagement by a claim that she suffered, vindicated, resisted, or undid the subordination of f. You could love Queen Elizabeth for her sheer gender-y[1] power and never once mention—not even think or feel!—that you loved her partly because she was such a relief from the otherwise wall-to-wall subordination of women.

You could do it—but I have to tell you: in my voracious but admittedly partial reading, you haven't. I've always found, in any actual instance, that, for the feminist whose work supposedly disposed of m > f, the decisions to focus on m and f and to carry a brief for f are always somewhere justified, and may well be motivated, by the idea that somewhere, in an important even if intermittent way, m > f.

Or you can imagine a feminism that is *against m/f*. Postmodernizing feminists often claim that they do more than anyone to deconstruct, question, threaten, mobilize, and effervesce the m/f distinction. I think that they find my deduction of the feminist minima from their work to be an example of sheer ingratitude. Most noticeably in the genealogy examined here, Judith Butler has put forward a "sexual difference" feminism that, she argues, can evade m/f.[2] She has argued, for instance, that through Lacanian psychoanalysis we can posit that the feminine has distinct etiological sources from the masculine; does not emerge as its opposite; and is neither subordinate to it nor its equal. At least as far as I have been able to tell (and in order to defend these minima I've done a lot of sympathetic reading!), no U.S. postmodernizing feminist has gone further. But as I try to show in Part Two through a close reading of Butler's intervention, the very book in which she advances sexual difference feminism also manifests her strong will to pair f with m as a relevant opposition, to insist that coming untethered from it reinstates male dominance, and to keep vigil against the subordination of f.

And finally, what I'll describe below as the "hybrid" feminisms—socialist, antiracist, and postcolonial feminisms—are often claimed to depart from the three essential characteristics I'm offering here. I agree that they sometimes do this; but I contend that they do so only by diverging from and thus suspending their feminism. That is, they Take a Break from Feminism. To enable myself to explain this, I define convergentist and divergentist feminism in one of these definitional sections, just a few pages further on.

So: things could change; feminism could evolve away from these commitments. My point is that it hasn't, not that it can't.

Governance Feminism

If you look around the United States, Canada, the European Union, the human rights establishment, even the World Bank, you see plenty of places where feminism, far from operating from underground, is running things. Sex harassment, child sexual abuse, pornography, sexual violence, antiprostitution and antitrafficking regimes, prosecutable marital rape, rape shield rules: these feminist justice projects have moved off the street and into the state. In family law alone, feminism has scored numerous victories that prefer the wife to the husband and the mother to the father: the presumption that young children must spend substantial time with their mothers, the rise of alimony, the shift in common-law-property states to equitable division of property upon divorce, the replacement of "cruelty" with "domestic violence" as a fault grounds for divorce, the revitalization of intimate

torts like alienation of affections, criminal conversation, and se-
duction as *women's* lawsuits.

It would be a mistake to think that governance issues only from
that combination of courts, legislatures, and police which constitutes the everyday image of "the state." Employers, schools, health
care institutions, and a whole range of entities, often formally "private," govern too—and feminism has substantial parts of them
under its control. Just think of the tremendous effort that U.S.
employers and schools must devote to the regulation of sexual conduct at work, through sexual harassment policies that have produced a sexual harassment bureaucracy with its own cadre of professionals and its own legal character. And many feminist policy
campaigns take power in the form of ideological shifts within state
and nonstate entities that don't turn explicitly on m/f. Consider, as
a possible example, that one result of feminist rape activism is the
elevation of child sexual abuse as a serious enforcement priority
complete with "zero tolerance" enforcement attitudes; other kinds
of child neglect and abuse, other kinds of adult/adult interpersonal
violence, lack the charisma of the sexual offenses. They fall into the
background. And this is an effect of governance feminism.

Feminists have learned how to participate in what is often
called "the new governance." Ask any group of U.S. Women's
Studies majors what they intend to do with their degree: many
will say that they intend to "work in an NGO." Global governance
and local governance are often done through informal, opaque,
ideologically committed "nongovernmental organizations" that
strategize hard—sometimes successfully—to become indispensable when major new fluidities in formal power emerge. A classic
example is the highly effective feminist activism aimed at the ad
hoc criminal courts formed by the United Nations to prosecute
war crimes in Rwanda and the former Yugoslavia: feminist and
legal players have written that this effort substantially changed
the rules.[3] By positing themselves as *experts* on women, sexuality,
motherhood, and so on, feminists walk the halls of power.[4]

And feminism exerts itself in the culture wars as a real force to be contended with. It has convinced lots of men that the "new man" must defer to feminism on questions relating to women's welfare in sex and reproduction. In the United States, the only left-of-center locales where male masculinity is worshiped anymore are gay and male. The Vatican has noticed the cultural diffusion of feminist consciousness and is worried: its Congregation for the Doctrine of the Faith, presided over by Joseph Cardinal Ratzinger (since installed as Pope Benedict XVI), has issued an important dogmatic letter specifically to refute feminism, complete with a concentrated attack on the ideas that biological sex and cultural gender are distinct and independently variable, and that foundational biological difference between m and f should not be a source of social norms.[5] That is to say, the current pope has devoted a substantial portion of his time to refuting feminism. *He* takes Butler's *Gender Trouble* seriously as a political danger. A battle for hearts and minds is under way, and feminism is one of the contenders.

In some important senses, then, feminism rules. Governance feminism.

Not only that, it *wants* to rule. It has a will to power.

And not only *that*, it has a will to power—and it has actual *power*—that extends from the White House and the corporate boardroom through to the minute power dynamics that Foucault included in his theory of the governance of the self. Feminism may face powers greater than its own in its constant involvement with its opponents; but it deals with them in the very terms *of* power.

Feminism, Sexual and Reproductive

This book takes it as a fait accompli that feminists often divide their labor between sexuality, on one hand, and reproduction, on the other, as distinct domains of feminist concern.

There are important reasons not to comply with this division. Socialist feminism, for instance, when it was a very active element of U.S. feminism, persistently aimed for formulations that understood sexuality and reproduction to be profoundly linked. And it may well be that the arguments advanced here would be useful on the reproduction side: in family law, which for feminism has been primarily a domain for theories focused on how m/f, m > f, and carrying a brief for f are crucial because of f's distinctive reproductive role, the classroom payoff of Taking a Break from Feminism can be breathtakingly immediate. On the other hand, I'm not sure whether the impulse to Take a Break would be so strong if the two sides hadn't developed as semiautonomous domains, or if there were a strong theoretic and political practice of merging them. Those are questions I'll leave on the table for future work.

To justify taxonomic location of the present project, I'll just say that most feminist work over the last several decades has given great prominence to sexuality *or* reproduction as the key term for articulating m/f, m > f, and carrying a brief for f; that work in the genealogy examined in this book is largely, indeed almost exclusively, preoccupied with sexuality; that a genealogy of the kind offered here, but of feminist work on reproduction, would be lovely to have in hand but as far as I know does not exist;[6] and that I make no claim that the arguments advanced here would necessarily work on the reproduction side. *This* book—it's about sex.

A Sex Lexicon

The genealogy examined in Part Two of this book involves some highly expert terminological struggles. In order to get access to those, and to make my readings intelligible on their own terms, I will use a sex lexicon that I derived from them but that I invented for this book. Here are the terms:

Sex1. By sex1, I will mean the purported bodily difference between men and women. The supposedly irreducible fact of biological dimorphism. "Is it a boy or a girl?" Penis or vagina, testicles or ovaries, testosterone or estrogen, and so forth.

Gender. By gender, I mean everything else that differentiates all men from all women, or most men from most women, or "real" men from "defective" or "deviant" men and "real women" from "defective" or "deviant" women, or this man "as a man" from that woman "as a woman." Gender is sometimes understood to be equivalent to "masculine or feminine traits"—let's say, aggression is an element of "masculine gender" and altruism a feature of "feminine gender"; or "short hair" is a trait of men and "long hair" is a trait of women. In that version, gender tends to come with the idea that some binarized *traits* are *appropriate* to men and not to women, and vice versa. But there is a deeper sense in which some U.S. feminists use the term gender: to indicate not a checklist of trait pairs and their "appropriate" allocation to masculinity and femininity or men and women, but the whole system of social meaning that holds the masculine to be different from the feminine, *tout court*, and that places the differentiation in *any relation* to sex1.

Sex2. By sex2, I mean everything that turns us on. The erotic. The paradigm image here is "fucking," but it could be (for you) the vibration of your car or your unconscious wish to sleep with your mother and kill your father.

Sexual orientation. By sexual orientation, I mean the idea that, for a particular person, there can be some temporally durable object of erotic desire. You could want to be turned on by the vibration of your car *one more time.* That could be your sexual orientation. We happen not to use the term in such a broad-ranging, open-ended way in the United States, alas. What we usually mean by it is your temporarily durable desiring relationship to persons of a masculine or feminine sex1/gender. And we don't even admit the full range of possibility implied in that formulation; we tend vastly predominantly to mean the permanent, characterological, lifelong direction of your sexual desire to *men* or *women.* Thus "sexual orientation" tends to mean "homosexual or heterosexual." I will make it clear when I am using this term in its less conventional, but I think more adequate, sense.

Sexuality. In this book, sexuality means "some arrangement of most of the foregoing terms." It is the most general term of all those listed here, and I use it to designate a psychic, social, political phenomenon the nature of which is subject to deep political contestation.

Convergentism and Divergentism

A person framing a conceptual, descriptive, normative, and/or political project that involves a discontinuity between two theories of power, two descriptions of the world, two normative aims, two invoked constituencies, and so on ... can choose between *converging* and *diverging* them. We could, for instance, decide that normatively it would be terrible to have a theory of homosexuality that was not ultimately feminist, or a feminism that did not wholly encompass our theory of homosexuality; we would then be aiming for complete convergence. Or we could say that it is better for some reason to have some division or autonomy or even conflict between the two projects; we would then be aiming for some degree of divergence.

What I'll call convergentist feminism insists that feminism mediate whatever comes into conflict, harmonizing it into a *feminist* frame. In its divergentist forms, feminism is prepared to see political splits and split decisions, *within its feminism.* Such a project Takes a Break from Feminism, according to me, whenever it decides that feminism need not be the normative or political measure of the goodness of the results; that feminism need not be the ultimate form of the product; that f need not be the constituency on whose behalf it works; and so on.

The hybrid feminisms are constantly forced by their very hybridity to take either convergentist or divergentist attitudes. But sexual-subordination feminism, sex-positive feminism, gay-identity politics, and pro-sex postmodernism—and pro-sex activism generally—have been made to confront the decision whether to converge or diverge. So the question of the value of divergence runs through all the debates in the genealogy I present here.

A STORY OF
SEXUAL-SUBORDINATION
FEMINISM AND ITS OTHERS

Here I offer a story of how feminism (along with several other forces) produced its others during the last two decades of thought and activism relating to sexuality in the United States. It is a violently foreshortened version of what you have, in lavish textual detail, in Part Two.

By far the most brilliant and forceful thinker about sexuality in U.S. feminist legal theory for the last twenty-five years has been Catharine A. MacKinnon. Her formulation—which for short-hand I will call power feminism—has become the paradigmatic understanding of sexuality in sexual-subordination feminism in the United States. The chief alternative source of descriptive and normative insights is cultural feminism.

It took me a long time to realize that MacKinnon is not a cultural feminist in the sense most people use that term. I attempt to locate the chief commonalities and differences between her mode of feminism and cultural feminism below; for now it should suffice to note one fact about cultural feminism and two important differences between it and power feminism.

Though cultural feminism is roughly half of the time devoted to the cultural revaluation of women's distinctive relationship to care, the rest of the time it is concerned about women's distinctive engagement in sexuality. That part of cultural feminism agrees with power feminism in characterizing male sexuality as a vast social problem. But while MacKinnon focuses on the unjust male domination of women through power, cultural feminism empha-sizes the unjust male derogation of women's traits or points of view through male-ascendant normative value judgments. And the early MacKinnon regarded male *and female* sex, gender, and sexuality to be fully constituted by the eroticization of male domination; whereas cultural feminism reserved a special place for the redemptive normative insights that women derive from their sexuality and their role as mothers.

For all their differences, however, power feminism and cultural feminism turn strongly on m/f, they are subordination theories in which the problem is m > f, and they carry a brief for f, with a vengeance. Women are the client base of these feminisms, and women are the people they would help first if they had to pick. They support identity politics *of women.*

At the same time that these sexual-subordination feminisms were developing themselves as important elements in U.S. legal thought and practice, another identity-based sexuality movement became important in the United States: homosexuals. They (we, actually) borrowed a lot of ideas about how to have an identity movement from the black civil rights movement (as did feminism), but the focus of my story here is the way the gay movement borrowed ideas from feminism about how to have a *subordinated-sexuality movement.* Roughly speaking, gay-identity politics in the United States can be construed to take forms resembling the common elements of sexual-subordination feminism: homosexuals are a real social group subordinated in sexuality to heterosexuals; justice requires ending that form of social ranking. Moreover, gay-identity movements tend to take either a MacKinnon-like form, looking with a wary eye for traces everywhere of heterosexual dominance and seeking its overthrow; or a cultural-feminist-like form, emphasizing the moral virtues of homosexuals and seeking their normative inclusion in the center.

To be almost unbearably reductive, three things happened "then." First, AIDS. In the United States, AIDS first emerged as an epidemic among gay men. For about ten years starting in the early 1980s the death toll—affecting a youthful population then fomenting an ecstatic politics of sexual liberation and otherwise expecting to live for decades—was a huge social fact. Social conservatives and defenders of heterosexual virtue quickly stigmatized the epidemic as the product of "gay male promiscuity"—a move that put to gay-identity movements the question whether they could continue to affirm sexual liberation as a defining goal.

Second, power feminists and cultural feminists began in the early 1980s to identify some fairly specific targets of activism—rape and other forms of direct violence, pornography, intergenerational sex, commercial sex, sex between social unequals (e.g., boss/secretary, teacher/student), sex in public—as leverage points for the desubordination of women. They formed important alliances with social and religious conservatives morally opposed to these practices, and made significant progress in articulating and enforcing legal sanctions against them. This simultaneous turn "to the state" and "against sex2 and sexuality" broke alliances between power and cultural feminists on the one hand and radical, sexual-liberationist feminists on the other. The latter precipitated abruptly and with great energy *out* of these feminist movements, forming a distinct "sex-positive" feminism specifically in struggle with power and cultural feminism.

And third, postmodernism arrived on the U.S. intellectual scene, bringing with it a whole array of new (to the left/liberal U.S. intelligentsia) brainwaves. The antifoundational, libertine, irrationalist, ecstatic, antimoralistic tendencies in postmodernism led many power and cultural feminists to wonder what had come over them. The postmodern critique of the Enlightenment subject brought the already-uneasy fit between identity politics and liberal individualism into question. The postmodern emphasis on subject formation rather than brute domination as the really trenchant application of power to persons called into question the subordination paradigm. The Dark Side appeared everywhere. Things needed to be rethought, right away.

These three events were highly productive for left-of-center thought and politics on sexuality in the United States. Gay/lesbian politics, postmodern feminism, sex-positive feminism, feminist queer theory: these and many other *feminist* others emerged. But many of the sequelae are not primarily feminist: gay-identity politics, transgender and transsexual politics, sex liberationism that is not primarily feminist, and some queer theory. That is, some of these projects have remained feminist through and through; others have Taken a very durable Break from Feminism; others "flickered."

Finally, starting way before the story I tell here, and extending well beyond the borders of feminism however broadly conceived, feminism has encountered *other* subordination politics, most notably those sounding in "class," race, and imperial/postimperial power. Very frequently feminists have responded to these encounters by developing deep, sustained, and often very conflictual theoretical, practical, coalitional, and political engagements. The result has been the vast array of projects we are accustomed to describing as socialist, antiracist, and postcolonial feminism. These hybrid feminisms set out to examine (at least) two incommensurate modalities of power at once.

And once again, some of these projects have remained resolutely feminist; others have Taken a Break from Feminism.

LIBERATION AND
RESPONSIBILITY

Over the course of the splits involved in this story, ideas changed, politics changed, groups changed, research projects changed, identities changed, political consciousnesses changed. Keywords in the debate—male domination, "women," "pleasure"—changed their meanings. There was a no-going-back quality to it all; each intervention had a path-dependent effect on what was then possible; the constraints of the debate also provided its intensity and its capacity to produce new work. People Took a Break from Feminism; feminism reacted; and things changed again.

Feminism emerges from this story not as a transhistorical truth—a brooding omnipresence in the sky—that suffers one or the other incarnation but remains transcendently pure "up there," but as an evolving historical practice continually conditioned by its own preceding gestures.

One of the more regrettable of these gestures is the manifestation of anguish at the departure of its prodigals. For feminism has been highly productive of "others"—of prodigal sons and daughters who have wandered off to do other things. Inside feminism, there has been intense dysphoria about these departures. Each of them has been experienced as an abandonment, as live burial. Feminists have tried to bring the prodigals back home; they have struggled hard to prevent anyone from Taking a Break. These struggles often pulled tight a cinch of crisscrossing demands; in the face of them feminists (like Buridan's ass) often felt *paralyzed*. Feminist work addressed to this experience—the bibliography from the 1990s is voluminous[1]—is laced with anger, pain, mourning, resentment, and fear. Faith also: the saving remnant has often been invoked.

As I see it, the diagnoses of feminist paralysis, live burial, and so on were exactly wrong: feminism *experienced itself* as paralyzed (etc.), but it *wasn't.* The 1990s was the decade par excellence of the emergence of governance feminism; and it was, as I try to show in Part Two, a time of intense theoretical productivity among feminists. If anything needs diagnosis here, it is the profound rupture between the actual, real-world and theoretical power that feminism was exercising, and its experience of theoretic and institutional powerlessness.

Let me say, loud and clear, that governance feminism has been, in manifold ways, a good thing. Many feminist governance projects address social reality at points where its theory of sexuality— we all believe—aptly describes what is happening between men and women: men *do* rape women; they *do* commit reprehensible acts in sexual life that cause intense suffering for individual women and put women across the board at a bargaining disadvantage in sexual life, economic life, and elsewhere. Feminist theory has been immensely productive in making these realities visible; and governance feminism that has changed these circumstances, even marginally, has surely made life better for real, actual women. It has made life better for me.

But surely even a beneficiary of governance feminism can question the good faith of feminists who persistently represent feminism as unequivocally a political underdog, as lacking governance ambitions and effects, and as pushed into the grave by every upstart prodigal theory. Perhaps we can instead acknowledge that feminism has a will to power, and thrill to the ferocity with which it sometimes wields the power it has won.

Of course acknowledging feminism to be a governance project has a dark side, and it is important to face it. That dark side includes its vanquished, its prisoners of war, the interests that pay the taxes it has levied and owe the rents it has imposed. Feminism with blood on its hands.

Any force as powerful as feminism must find itself occasionally looking down at its own bloody hands. And any force as powerful as feminism will occasionally impose itself on its own constituent elements. Prodigal theory often emerges to represent sexual subjects, sexual possibilities, sexual realities, acts, bodies, relationships onto which feminism has been willing to shift the sometimes very acute costs of feminist victories in governance. I think this is an inevitable, not a bad consequence of feminism's ascension to some governance powers. But when governance feminism/feminist theory pretends it is always the underdog, and when feminists insist that the prodigals must be converged back into feminism *or feminism will die*, it wages power without owning it. Feminism then has governance capacity to change social life, but it also avoids acknowledging the full range of its effects.

This is perhaps the apogee of feminists' prescriptive deployment of feminist theory. And it is a very dangerous moment. When feminist theory refuses to own its will to power, when it insists that the prodigals must be converged back into feminism, it commits itself to a theoretical stance that makes it hard for feminists to see around corners of their own construction. Unless it Takes a Break from itself, it can't see injury to men. It can't see injury to men by women. It can't see other interests, other forms of power, other justice projects. It insists that all justice projects will track a subordination model. And this refusal to see, sustained while feminism imposes costs on interests and projects outside its purview, gives us a textbook case of bad faith.

This bad faith is a highly contingent element of feminism; feminism could give it up. But as long as it closes its eyes to the effects of its power on neighboring but different theoretical/political projects and constituencies, on its prodigal sons and daughters, they will—and I think they should—prolong their sojourn away.

If feminism were more ready to acknowledge these costs, more gracious about admitting that, like any governor, it has blood on its hands, the requisite that new sexual theories give themselves birth by Taking a Break from Feminism might not be nearly so acute, and the motives that produce the brain drain from feminist theory and practice might weaken.

Of course the convergentist ambitions of feminism might eventually prevail and bring the prodigals back home. I have to say, it's hard for me to imagine it happening. The day that feminism provides a fully adequate theory and advocacy agenda for, say, heterosexual men or masturbation will be the day that the interests of heterosexual men or masturbators have lost/gained, respectively, a certain relationship to m/f that is not "in" them now. But it could happen. Or feminism could let go of m/f, m > f, and carrying a brief for f and become the theory *of* the alternatives to those commitments, the place one finds the best ways of managing their relationships. Maybe feminism could do this; and maybe it should. I'll leave that possibility aside, for others to explore.

My argument is focused elsewhere: on how divergence in left-of-center thinking about sexuality and power can not only get us some conceptual gains that seem unavailable from convergence; it can also get us analyses that seem crucial to a responsible involvement in governance. So I argue here that left-of-center politics in the United States should welcome, at least provisionally, formations—theoretical, political, legal—in which feminism is occasionally suspended, interrupted, set aside.

Prodigal theories, of course, have their own will to power; and when they get anywhere with it, they, too, get blood on their hands. I'm not promoting them as innocent underdogs rising up against oppressive Father Feminism. As we'll see, they often carry forward the tradition, now so familiar in feminism and visible in much prodigal theory to date, of deploying theory prescriptively; when they do, they become convergentist too, threaten to wield power while denying it, and strive to distribute myriad social goods and bads without taking into account any but the most rudimentary ones presupposed by their own theories. Again, I offer the emergence of prodigal theory here not because any one instance of it is "right," but because its continual emergence asks us to learn how to take a break from any hegemonic theory, and how to split the decisions we must make to govern responsibly.

PART TWO

THE
POLITICAL/
THEORETICAL
STRUGGLE
OVER TAKING
A BREAK

I present here a genealogy of a single protracted debate among feminist, gay-positive, postmodernizing, and "queer" theorists of sexuality, taking specific crucial texts up for close comparative reading. The upside of this approach: it allows me to hew very closely to the actual texture of argumentation as it developed over the years. The downside: the texts I've selected might not seem as decisive and exemplary to everyone as they seemed to me. Overall, I've preferred depth over breadth; this approach always omits things arbitrarily.

The feminist bibliography spans almost two decades, from MacKinnon's 1982–83 *Signs* articles (which I'll call First and Second *Signs*) to Elisabeth Bronfen's and Misha Kavka's 2001 anthology of feminist essays, *Feminist Consequences*. It includes Robin West's *Caring for Justice* as its example of cultural feminism; *The Combahee River Collective Statement* and Gayatri Spivak's "Can the Subaltern Speak?" as its examples of convergentist and divergentist hybrid feminisms; Judith Butler's *Gender Trouble* and an essay she published soon thereafter as its examples of queer, postmodernizing feminism; and a series of feminist anthologies—Marianne Hirsch and Evelyn Fox Keller's *Conflicts in Feminism*, Kavka and Bronfen's *Feminist Consequences*, Butler and Joan W. Scott's *Feminists Theorize the Political*, the collectively produced volume by Seyla Benhabib, Butler, Drucilla Cornell, and Nancy Fraser, *Feminist Contentions*, and *feminism meets queer theory*, edited by Elizabeth Weed and Naomi Schor, and particularly one of Butler's contributions to that last volume, "Against Proper Objects"—as its examples of feminism responding to the onset of postmodernism and of hybrid and queer work that Took a Break. The full citation to each of these books and essays appears in the note.[1]

But a lot of the work examined here Takes a Break. Gayle Rubin's 1984 essay "Thinking Sex" can serve as our evidence that the project of Taking a Break had begun. I examine some classics in the Taking a Break project: the introductory volume of Michel

Foucault's *History of Sexuality* (I'll refer to it as *Volume One*), Eve Kosofsky Sedgwick's *Epistemology of the Closet* and *Tendencies*, Leo Bersani's "Is the Rectum a Grave?", Duncan Kennedy's "Sexy Dressing," Henry Abelove, Michèle Aina Barale, and David M. Halperin's anthology, *The Lesbian and Gay Studies Reader*, Michael Warner's *Fear of a Queer Planet*, and Jay Prosser's *Second Skins* are my examples. I argue also that Scott's own contribution to *Feminists Theorize the Political* and the divergentist impulses in "Can the Subaltern Speak?" Take a Break, though neither piece manifests any sense that this would become a controversial thing to do. I am particularly grateful for Elizabeth Weed and Naomi Schor's volume *feminism meets queer theory*, as it provides an energetic example of feminists responding to many of the texts examined in my genealogy. Of particular interest in that volume is Butler's interview with Rubin, "Sexual Traffic: *Interview*" (I'll use "*Interview*" for short), which gives us their diverging retrospect on "Thinking Sex." Again, I collect the citations to all these materials here.[2]

I read these texts as closely and sympathetically as I can in sections marked ❦. When it seems useful to compare them to ascertain their convergences and divergences, I offer sections marked ✂.

BEFORE THE BREAK:
SOME FEMINIST PRIORS

Two important kinds of sexual-subordination feminism, each of them radical, have infiltrated liberal-feminist thought and engaged deeply in governance over the last twenty-five years: MacKinnon's power feminism and cultural feminism. During the same period, the hybrid feminisms—socialist, antiracist, and postcolonial—produced a major eruption of controversy within feminism, and provide my first examples of divergentism within and from feminism.

Power Feminism

Cards-on-the-table moment: MacKinnon's focus on power—her quite self-conscious deployment of it—is one of the things I love about her work. I find the cultural-feminist alternative—moralism—repellent. That's just my taste, I know. I am going to try to talk you into sharing it, but it's not crucial to the overall claim that it might sometimes be good to Take a Break from *both* forms of feminism.

❦ *Catharine A. MacKinnon, Early and Late*

Without question, MacKinnon's two articles bearing the umbrella title "Feminism, Marxism, Method and the State," published in *Signs* in 1982 and 1983, are classics in feminist social and legal theory. MacKinnon revised them in later publications, a practice that allows a close reader to watch her changing her mind over time. Indeed, as we will see, there are even important differences between her 1982 and 1983 articulations of feminism. I will call the feminist who "speaks" these papers "the early MacKinnon." She was breathtakingly radical.

In the first *Signs* article we find the following, now-classic, statement of sexual-subordination feminism:

> Sexuality, then, is a form of power. Gender, as socially constructed, embodies it, not the reverse. Women and men are divided by gender, made into the sexes as we know them, by the social requirements of heterosexuality, which institutionalizes male sexual dominance and female sexual submission. If this is true, sexuality is the linchpin of gender inequality. (533)

At its crux, MacKinnon's theory is a *power* theory. As a form of power, gender promulgates sex hierarchy as what men and women *are*; it produces rather than reflects sex1.[1] This is one of the most radical elements of MacKinnon's theory. The reality of sex1—the very idea that men and women exist and are bodily dimorphically different—and the consciousness in which that reality seems real, natural, and inevitable, are *effects* of power.

In this articulation, every single important term in my lexicon of sexuality is resolutely ordered by m/f and m > f.[2] Sex1, sex2, gender, and (as we will see) sexual orientation are *all* manifestations of the domination of f by m: that is what sexuality *is*.

I will call this set of ideas "power feminism." In MacKinnon's hands, it is a neat, tight system; indeed, for all its constructedness and contingency, it is total, structural, complete.[3] Purportedly operating on the ground of sex1 but actually producing it, men use sex2 to make themselves superordinate, and that is their gender; and to make women subordinate, and that is our gender.

MacKinnon deployed theory prescriptively from the start. Here is a classic statement of this attitude to theoretical work, appearing in the first *Signs* article:

> The challenge [for feminist theory] is to demonstrate that feminism systematically converges upon a central explanation of sex inequality through an approach distinctive to its subject yet applicable to the whole of social life, including class. (528)

Like other radical American social theories of the time, MacKinnon's theory is a *consciousness* theory.[4] Power produces consciousness; it recruits all its subjects to the production of domination across the whole expanse of human life. Sex hierarchy is ontologically and epistemologically "nearly perfect":[5] by producing both its own reality and our every mode of apprehending that reality, it almost completely occupies the horizon of possibility.

Radical theories like this one pose a deep challenge to anyone seeking emancipation: the very consciousness with which women perceive their being, the very wellspring of their desire, is male domination. Only a transformation of consciousness—of women, by women, and for women working utterly without leverage from any emancipatory "outside"—can possibly give any hope of release from m > f. This is why the word "*consciousness-*raising" described MacKinnon's emancipatory method.

The link between consciousness-raising and legal reform is where the early MacKinnon's radicalism is eclipsed by the late MacKinnon's dogmatism. In Second *Signs*, published in 1983, MacKinnon fully embraced the problem that women's knowledge of their reality, their ability to see male dominance and to object to it for themselves, was relentlessly situated *in* male dominance. Boldly, she refused to explain the problem away on grounds of false consciousness ("my consciousness is true, yours false, never mind why") or of the verity of any biological woman's experience ("I know I am right because it feels right to me, never mind why"), attributing the paired objections to the object/subject polarity that feminism detects at the heart of male power (637–38 n. 5). This is a profoundly critical move, and it makes the early MacKinnon's feminism highly paradoxical. The dilemma is not feminism's fault; it arises from the historical capture of objectivity for, and as, the male point of view, and the resulting object*ification* of women, the rendering of their powerlessness *as* their subjectivity. Thus true feminism, "feminism unmodified," MacKinnon argued, must be radical: "Women's situation offers no outside to stand on or gaze at, no inside to escape to, too much urgency to wait, no place else to go, and nothing to use but the twisted tools that have been shoved down our throats. If feminism is revolutionary, this is why" (638–39).

Hence the centrality of *method* in the *Signs* articles: feminism does not *have* the truth of women, but rather seeks an unprecedented disruption in the conceptual and social order by untying women's experience from the subject/object, objectivity/subjectivity, truth/feeling dyads that are the epistemology of male power: "The project is to uncover and claim as valid the experience of women, the major content of which is the devalidation of women's experience."[6] "The pursuit of consciousness becomes a form of political practice."[7] And within that political practice, the radical project is "the claim of feminism *to* women's perspective, not from it."[8]

In First *Signs*, MacKinnon partially derailed this radicalism, however, when she invoked women's experience as the source of authority for the claim that sexuality is a form of power generating male superordination and female subordination. The derailment occurs in stages. MacKinnon was at first frank that her own interpretive inductions led to the claim: "*I think* that feminism fundamentally identifies sexuality as the primary social sphere of male power. The centrality of sexuality emerges . . . from *feminist practice* on diverse issues, including abortion, birth control, sterilization abuse" (529, emphasis added). How did feminist practice—much of it by practitioners who would have resisted MacKinnon's assessment of sexual injury and of sexuality—provide this insight? "If the literature on sex roles and the investigations of particular issues are read in light of each other, each element of the female *gender* stereotype is revealed as, in fact, *sexual*" (530). Passive verbs: a bad sign for agency and *pleine aire* interpretation. But pay no attention to the man behind the curtain, for he is about to emerge as women asserting their experience of sexuality as subordination: "*Women experience* the sexual events these issues codify as a cohesive whole. . . . The defining theme of that whole is the male pursuit of control over women's sexuality" (532, emphasis added). MacKinnon's interpretive insight has become the meaning of feminist practice across the board and, ultimately, the substantive centrality of sexual subordination to women's experience of gender (and thus sex1). Sexuality is sex discrimination. QED.

The dogmatism of the late MacKinnon therefore emerged within the critical and radical practice of the early MacKinnon. In Second *Signs* the sexual subordination idea had become so central to MacKinnon's reasoning that it could be induced and deduced in the same gesture: male dominance provides the substantive, social context for construing the meaning to women of particular sexual encounters—and the meaning to women of particular sexual encounters reveals that male dominance is their substantive, social context. This circularity may explain the remarkable grammatical stability of the meaning of sexual encounters from women's point of view. "[T]he injury of rape lies in the meaning of the act to its victims" (652)—that is, surely, all women—and we know what that is:

> The law distinguishes rape from intercourse by the woman's lack of consent coupled with a man's (usually) knowing disregard of it. A feminist distinction between rape and intercourse, to hazard a beginning approach, lies instead in the *meaning* of the act from women's point of view. What is wrong with rape is that it is an act of the subordination of women to men. (651–52)

Note the exclusive article ("*the* meaning"): MacKinnon concludes that the subordination of women to men is structural. And note the rhetorical posture MacKinnon assumes, of hearing "the meaning" emerge "*from*" "*women's* point of view": she warrants her finding by its real authorship in the collectivity of women. Remarkably, the formulation is no longer "to" but "from" women's point of view—precisely what had been disavowed the year before. MacKinnon's 1983 confidence in her inferences was so strong that she could affirm that particular women, interpreting particular sexual encounters, always have access to this meaning: "the only difference between assault and (what is socially considered) noninjury is *the meaning* of the encounter *to the woman*" (652, emphasis added).

For all the fixity of MacKinnon's power feminism as women's point of view, in 1983 MacKinnon was unready to suggest that, because "the woman" knows "the meaning," the rules governing rape (her primary example in Second *Signs*) should be altered to affirm her experience and disaffirm his. This reticence arises in part from a bold conclusion that the state, its law, and the rule of law are male. MacKinnon "propose[d] that the state is male in the feminist sense" not only because it pursued and protected men's interests in sexual control over women by adopting particular rules (which presumably could be rewritten), but because, "[f]ormally, the state is male in that objectivity is its norm." The very "rule form . . . institutionalizes the objective stance as jurisprudence," which, in liberalism, is "the law of law" (644–45). Asking the law, rather than women, to speak the meaning of sexuality from women's point of view would be a hopelessly contradictory undertaking. And so rewriting the rules of rape adjudication to make women's subjective experience decisive would merely reinscribe the terms of male dominance into the feminist project:

> [E]ven though the rape law oscillates between subjective tests and more objective standards invoking social reasonableness, it uniformly presumes a single underlying reality, not a reality split by divergent meanings, such as those inequality produces. . . . One-sidedly erasing women's violation or dissolving the presumptions into the subjectivity *of either side* are alternatives dictated by the terms of the object/subject split respectively. These are alternatives that will only retrace that split until its terms are confronted as gendered to the ground. (652, 654–55, emphasis added)

This at least suggests what the *Signs* articles repeatedly affirm, that women's subjective experience, no less than men's, is part of the epistemological dilemma posed by male dominance. To move "toward a feminist jurisprudence," for the MacKinnon of 1983, was to critique that dilemma as an opening for a feminist consciousness currently unattainable in its terms. And so, just after affirming, in the passage quoted above, that "[w]hat is wrong with rape is that it is an act of the subordination of women to men," MacKinnon turned, from law and rape, to the system of meaning in which they are embedded: "the issue is not so much what rape 'is' as the way its social conception is shaped to interpret particular encounters" (652).

It seems quite fitting, then, that Second *Signs* ends in the mode of critique. The last section warns that "making and enforcing certain acts as illegal reinforces a structure of subordination," catalogs the dilemmas posed for her feminist project by liberal and left jurisprudence, insists in its last line that "[j]ustice" would require something quite "new"—and avoids any effort to reconcile the idea of a particular woman's charge of rape or cause of action for sex harassment with the problematic relationship that may obtain between her understanding and "women's point of view" (655–58). Here is a third trace of her early radicalism; the *legal* moves she makes here are characteristic of critical legal studies (an attitude toward law that she was later to denounce).

In *Toward a Feminist Theory of the State*, a 1989 volume collecting and revising much of her earlier work including First and Second *Signs*, MacKinnon seeks a synthesis between her early theoretical work and two decades of her feminist law reform activism. By then she was ready to draw conclusions about law that are quite different from those we see in the *Signs* articles. Consider this revision of the passage on rape quoted just above:

> [W]hen an accused wrongly but sincerely believes that a woman he sexually forced consented, he may have a defense of mistaken belief in consent or fail to satisfy the mental requirement of knowingly proceeding against her will. Sometimes his knowing disregard is measured by what a reasonable man would disregard. This is considered an objective test. Sometimes the disregard need not be reasonable so long as it is sincere. This is considered a subjective test. A feminist inquiry into the distinction between rape and intercourse, by contrast, would inquire into the meaning of the act from women's point of view, which is neither. What is wrong with rape in this view is that it is an act of subordination of women to men. It expresses and reinforces women's inequality to men. Rape with legal impunity makes women second-class citizens.[9]

The changes are subtle but substantial. MacKinnon is no longer seeking to establish a feminist distinction; instead she now aims to frame the question for feminist inquiry. And while she doesn't suggest that she wants *courts* to ask this question, her 1983 reticence to do so has been revised away. She addresses "the act"—a particular, not a general one; there is a particular accused; and we will understand his act critically, if not legally, by inquiring into "the meaning of the act from women's point of view." Moreover, that point of view is no longer dangerously merged into the subjectivity that male dominance has assigned women: in a remarkable shift, to inquire after it is to avoid the twin falsities of objective and subjective tests. The truth of rape's wrong is the same—"it is an act of subordination of women to men"—but MacKinnon now replaces her 1983 invitation to critique with a denunciation of "[r]ape with legal impunity." Legal punishment of rape apprehended from women's point of view would be a *feminist* project.[10]

Once again she insists that the male point of view is not only male superordination but also the objectivity of the law, its neutrality, and the very substance of its idea of equality.[11] But now she also insists that, confronting this impenetrable system from within it, there can be "feminist law":

> Abstract rights authoritize [*sic*] the male experience of the world. Substantive rights for women would not. Their authority would be the currently unthinkable: nondominant authority, the authority of excluded truth, the voice of silence.[12]

An individual woman who suffers sex harassment at work thereby exemplifies, in her sexual injury, women's gender. As long as her legal cause of action for sex harassment performs the perspective produced by *women's point of view*, it will allow her to interrupt the ontological seamlessness joining male superordination with the law, enabling her to make not only her injury but the injury of all women visible, audible, and interruptable.

The idea that the legal claim of one woman flawlessly reveals the injury that male superordination and female subordination inflict on all women seems quite foreign to the radicalism and the critical stance of MacKinnon's *Signs* articles, but nevertheless pervades her practice of legal remediation. Almost luckily, rape and sex harassment are especially concentrated forms of sex2. Just like myriad other rituals of heterosexual interaction, but with particular force and clarity, rape and sex harassment give men and women gender (that is, make them men and women), which, for MacKinnon, means their relative place in a m/f hierarchy. And here is where MacKinnon places her Archimedes' lever. According to MacKinnon's theory of legal remediation, the laws of rape and of sex harassment, when they provide a remedy for the injury of sex2 *based on a woman's claim to women's point of view,* provide ways of exposing this terrible mistake, interrupting the ontological and epistemological seamlessness of sex2, and enlisting the energies of the state in the project of justice.[13]

Perhaps the apogee of this development in her thought is the famous antipornography ordinance that MacKinnon and Andrea Dworkin together drafted, and which they actually persuaded several municipalities to adopt. And because the controversy within feminism over the ordinance was such an important moment in the encounter of sexual-subordination feminism with sex-positive feminism—sometimes described as "the sex wars" and sharply focused on pornography—I think it might be helpful to spell out what the ordinance actually would have done to make "women's point of view" legally manifest.

The MacKinnon/Dworkin antipornography ordinance would have allowed an individual woman to obtain an injunction against "trafficking" in "pornography," acting "as a woman acting against the subordination of women."[14] Though MacKinnon and others frequently defended the ordinance on the grounds that an individual woman would have to "prove injury,"[15] that is precisely what women complainants seeking to enjoin "trafficking" in pornography were *not* required to do. Instead, the ordinance would have allowed one woman to act for all women, without any showing of actual harm to herself or anyone else, by enjoining the production, sale, exhibition, and distribution of a wide array of "pornography," even against defendants who thought in good faith that the materials were not subordinating to women. Here's how.

I'll take the Indianapolis ordinance as my example. Famously, the ordinance defined pornography as the "graphic sexually explicit subordination of women," and specified six second-order criteria defining what materials had this subordinating effect:

(1) [w]omen are presented as sexual objects who enjoy pain or humiliation; or (2) [w]omen are presented as sexual objects who experience sexual pleasure in being raped; or (3) [w]omen are presented as sexual objects tied up or cut up or mutilated or bruised or physically hurt, or as dismembered or truncated or fragmented or severed into body parts; or (4) [w]omen are presented as being penetrated by objects or animals; or (5) [w]omen are presented in scenarios of degradation, injury, abasement, torture, shown as filthy or inferior, bleeding, bruised or hurt in a context that makes these conditions sexual; or (6) [w]omen are presented as sexual objects for domination, conquest, violation, exploitation, possession or use, or through postures or positions of servility or submission or display.[16]

No complainant would be required to demonstrate that material that met one of these six second-order criteria also *was* the graphic sexually explicit subordination of women: that question had been settled in the ordinance's findings, which stipulated that "[p]ornography is a systematic practice of exploitation and subordination based on sex which differentially harms women." As

MacKinnon put it, "The hearings establish the harm. The definition sets the standard."[17] And she was right: "Women's point of
view" that pornography is sex2 as it is represented in MacKinnon's theory is built into the definition of pornography. The legislative hearings that produced the definition were the last time,
under the ordinance, when the question of fact whether pornography is a discriminatory practice based on sex imposing differential harms on women would be "tried."

The mechanism of enforcement would have reintroduced the
question of actual harm in some claims but not in the one that
lay closest to the theoretical commitments of MacKinnon's construction of "women's point of view." The ordinance created a
private right of action as well as regulatory proceedings against
four uses of pornography. It was an act of sex discrimination
to traffic in pornography (defined to include producing, selling,
exhibiting, and distributing it); to coerce a person into "performing for pornography" (where the resulting pornography was
then actually distributed or sold); to "forc[e] pornography on a
person" in public or in private; or to assault, physically attack,
or injure a person "in a way that is directly caused by specific
pornography." The last three of these all posited an injured person—someone at least nominally coerced, forced, or assaulted.
The first, however, does not: "trafficking" *sounds* bad, but the
underlying conduct could just as accurately be described in the
language of manufacture, display, gift, and market exchange.

The power to initiate a complaint about any of these activities,
including trafficking, was granted to "any person claiming to be
aggrieved by the practice" or by officials on the city's Equal Opportunity Advisory Board. Courts might have construed "aggrieved" broadly to permit claims by anyone who believed a violation had occurred; or narrowly to permit claims only by those
who could show that a violation had not only occurred but had
harmed them personally. But in actions targeting trafficking, the

ordinance provided that "*any woman* may file a complaint as *a woman acting against the subordination of women.*" Courts might have refused to enforce this provision fully, invoking limits on the judicial role lodged in standing doctrine, but it seems clear that otherwise the ordinance would have invited *any* woman to complain on behalf of *all women.* Moreover, it seems clear that this broad claim is based on MacKinnon's theory that each woman must necessarily share the injury of women's sexual subordination and women's point of view on it: the same provision gave men, children, and transsexuals standing to bring a trafficking claim, but they had to prove injury in fact. Indeed, the injury they had to prove was that they were injured "in the same way that a woman is injured."

To be sure, the trafficking claim was narrowed on two other dimensions. Materials that met the sixth (arguably the broadest) but none of the other second-order criteria could not be subject to a trafficking claim. And remedies differed. The ordinance provided for injunctive, preliminary injunctive, and monetary remedies—orders to stop offending the substantive law and possibly to do something positive to make things better, orders to stop doing something or to do something pending trial, and orders to pay money to the plaintiff. The only exception: sellers, exhibitors, and distributors (but not producers)—these would be the traffickers—could avoid *damages* if they showed that they did not know the materials were pornography. They could still be enjoined, even with that showing.

Taken all together, these provisions would have allowed one woman to act for all women, without any showing of actual harm to herself or anyone else, by enjoining the production, sale, exhibition, and distribution of pornography that met any of the first five second-order criteria, even against defendants who thought in good faith that the materials were not subordinating to women.

Nor was MacKinnon's aim providing recompense to injured individuals or securing a locale in which those seeking to avoid pornography could do so; at least in the Minneapolis phase of their activism, MacKinnon and Dworkin urged the municipal Zoning and Planning Commission to reject a zoning approach and to adopt the private right of action not because the latter would recognize harm to individual women but because any pornography anywhere is sex discrimination. As MacKinnon told the commission, "I do not admit that pornography has to exist."[18]

An astonishing analogue of the antipornography ordinance appears in MacKinnon's thinking on sex discrimination lawsuits in the workplace setting. There, MacKinnon has advocated removing any requirement that an individual woman prove that her employer fired her with any intent to disadvantage her because of her sex; "[s]tatistical proofs of disparity would be conclusive."[19] Inside statutory antidiscrimination law, such a reform would mean that a woman plaintiff who could show any m/f disparity in her workforce—caused by *any*thing—could always successfully sue. MacKinnon would not say this unless she thought that *any* harm to one individual woman is the 100 percent pure distillate of the harm suffered by all women.

Or consider MacKinnon's assimilation of male/male sexual violence to her feminism. Here we see the convergentist energy of MacKinnon's structuralism working at top speed.[20] My example will be a brief that MacKinnon submitted to the U.S. Supreme Court in 1997 for a group of amici committed to stopping violence by and against men. The case was entitled *Oncale v. Sundowner Offshore Services, Inc.*,[21] and it involved Joseph Oncale's claim that he had been sexually harassed by other men while working on an oil rig. The allegations were of sexual assault and sexual ridicule. To prevail, Oncale had to convince the Court that he had suffered *sex* discrimination.[22] MacKinnon's brief[23] shows concisely how her structural theory of sexuality as male dominance works when it incorporates three new elements: men's sub-ordination *of a man*, male/male *sex2*, and thus *sexuality* re-construed as the social dimension not of male/female sex2 but of sex2 more generally. Basically, it converges them fully into m/f, m > f, and carrying a brief for f.

According to MacKinnon's brief, Joseph Oncale suffered sex discrimination because he was injured *as a man*. He and other male victims of male sexual aggression are "victimized through their masculinity, violated in their minds and bodies as individual members of their gender" (7). This happens because they are given not only the *worse* gender, but the *wrong* one:

> They are feminized: made to serve the function and play the role customarily assigned to women as men's social inferi-ors. . . . For a man to be sexually attacked, by placing him in a woman's role, demeans his masculinity; he loses it, so to speak. This cannot be done to a woman. What he loses, he loses through gender, as a man. (10)

What is utterly remarkable about this formulation is the endorse-ment it offers to a rigid, monolithic association of male bodies with male gender and superordination, and of female bodies with female gender and subordination. This endorsement is even nor-mative to the extent that it maintains MacKinnon's project of articulating "the authority of excluded truth, the voice of silence." Adopting the perspective of male victims of male sexual violence requires us to recognize that they are persecuted by other men because they fail to represent dominant masculinity seamlessly. Here the brief seems to detach sex1 from gender, to recognize a moral project of loosening the stringencies of masculinity. But the brief's articulation of the wrong suffered by Oncale also re-quires us to acknowledge that his primary, definitional injury is the loss of masculine superordination. How can this be a com-pensable loss in a feminist theory of injury?

The answer lies in the structural character—the totalism, if you will—of MacKinnon's power feminism. Like the *Signs* articles, MacKinnon's *Oncale* brief formulates the male domination not as natural—it is, *au contraire*, a historical contingency that the law can resist (11)—but as total. This is unequivocally clear for women: a woman has no masculinity to lose. Men, however, can endure gender downward mobility. Though the brief is careful to flag the socially constructed quality of male gender, it is equally insistent that a man who loses masculinity is necessarily feminized: *there is nowhere else for him to go*. Thus men who lose their masculinity do so in "their gender, as gender is socially defined" (7), but there is nothing socially negotiable about their fate "as men": because of the harassment they "*are* feminized" (10, emphasis added). Similarly, the brief posits that the attacks on Oncale "violat[ed] (what is conventionally considered) his manhood" (25). This would be a nice recognition of the social negotiability of that outcome except for the parentheses, which give us the option of reading the violation as real: the attacks "violat[ed] . . . his manhood." Whether it's conventional or not, his manhood is all Joseph Oncale has got that is properly his. Take it away, and he is wronged.

The MacKinnon brief reveals the structural ambitions, the totalism, of MacKinnon's theory again when it insists that homoeroticism and homosexuality are fully explained inside feminism. The latter are subsumed into the former. The MacKinnon brief achieves this by arguing that the question of homosexuality is both irrelevant to the question of sex discrimination and fundamentally identical with it. It is irrelevant because a homosexual harassing a person of his or her own sex is acting just like a heterosexual harassing a member of what the brief calls "the opposite sex" (1, 24), and because victims of sex harassment are victims whether they are straight or gay (25). Harassment is harassment no matter who does it to whom; it always reproduces the paradigm of male/

female harassment; and thus we need not take into account anything distinctive about the same-sex-ness of the parties. But at
the same time homosexuality is really fundamentally male/female
gender all over again: the sex of one's sexual object choice is a
"powerful constituent" of one's gender, and antigay discrimination fundamentally disadvantages people for deviating from gender expectations (26–27). As MacKinnon wrote on her own behalf
in 1989, "Since sexuality largely defines gender, discrimination
based on sexuality is discrimination based on gender."[24]

I think it would be fair to call the late MacKinnon a structuralist. By a historical accident, but everywhere, human beings produce the meaning and the reality of male domination one single
way. *Everything* about the relationship of m to f manifests domination and subordination. *Every* woman suffers—however differently—the same thing. Women have a point of view on this, and
feminism unmodified speaks it. Any woman can transfer this
truth from feminism to law; if she succeeds in obtaining redress
for sexual injury, she does so on behalf of all women everywhere.
Homosexuality, male gender, and male/male sex2 can be fully
explicated within the terms of sexuality, which *is* m/f and m > f.

Feminist critics of MacKinnon's theory of gender, and of her
prescription for using law to undo gender, have objected to this
reification of all women in the body and speech of the one who
happens to file a claim. The totalism of the model, the idea that
women have a single point of view, and the idea that joining these
to the institutional system of rights adjudication and enforcement
will liberate women from power, have all been contested *by
women*. Wendy Brown asks some of the crucial questions:

> [I]f MacKinnon aims to write "women's experience into
> law," precisely which "women's experience(s)," drawn from
> which historical moments, and which culture, racial, and
> class strata, is MacKinnon writing? . . . [W]hat does it mean

to write historically and culturally circumscribed experience into an ahistorical discourse, the universalist discourse of the law? What happens when "experience" becomes ontology, when "perspective" becomes truth, and when both become unified in the Subject of Woman and encoded in law as women's rights?[25]

It will be part of the argument of this book to show that these questions can be extended further, through the problem of male victimization, to require at least some of us to Take a Break from Feminism if we are to answer them well at all.

But it would also be fair to describe the *early* MacKinnon as a structuralist. In a way, that MacKinnon was a deeper, darker structuralist: for her, male domination—top-down power— structures not only the entire human population in the particular domain that is sexuality, but our very terms for apprehending social life, for having desires, for experiencing ourselves as em- bodied. The system is loaded heavily to prevent its own detection; most of its elements (law especially) are so permeated by male domination that they cannot be used against it. People—women included—often object that such a theory offers no exit. But if it is *true*, the theory itself would be the only hope of finding an exit from the world it describes. If it's *true*, moreover, its design with- out exit would be a virtue. Oddly, Taking a Break from Feminism is *more* possible if feminist structuralism takes the form given to it by the early, rather than by the late, MacKinnon.

Cultural Feminism

Cultural feminism holds that women have a distinct conscious- ness and/or culture. In some versions, this distinctiveness derives from their biological situation; in others, it emerges from their historical oppression by men. Some versions emphasize women's reproductive experience; others focus on their situation in sexuality. Thus we have seen cultural-feminist arguments that women's capacity for maternal care generates their special insight into issues like war; these take both "essentialist" forms (women are naturally maternal) and "social constructionist" ones (men made women do all the mothering). And we have seen cultural-feminist arguments that women's sexuality is naturally receptive, soft, and interactive while men's is naturally dominating, objectifying, and selfish (essentialism) or that men and women historically incurred these positions in sex2 (social constructionism). For feminist legal theory, a lot less turns on the essentialist/social constructionist controversy in cultural feminism than you would suppose from the amazing amount of ink that has been spilled on the question. We can have a sensible policy agenda for or against human activities and attitudes that are biological; for instance, we are against death and have many policies that push against this inevitable, gruesomely embodied, natural event. And if we regard some historically constructed elements in human life as structural, it might be quixotic to seek to change or eliminate them: recall how difficult it was for MacKinnon in her most radical, most structuralist mode to articulate a progress narrative for feminism. The important thing that makes a feminism *cultural* feminist is not its position on the essentialist/social constructivist divide, but its dedication to the propositions that women's feminine attributes amount to a consciousness or culture, that their consciousness or culture is improperly devalued, and that the reform goal is to revalue it upward.

I think I'd better put my cards on the table once again, before attempting the following exposition of cultural feminism. I was a cultural feminist for years, a fact that I confess with considerable shame. Somehow, now, cultural feminism is a deep embarrassment to me. I think that's because I lived the world described by cultural feminism for several years. It was a time of intense misery in my life—misery that I then attributed to patriarchy but that I now attribute to my cultural feminism.[26] And it was a wrenching and painful—also liberating and joyful—process to move into a different metaphysics, a different epistemology, a different politics, and a different ethics about sex1, sex2, gender, sexual orientation, and sexuality. That is to say, my writing, teaching, gender sensibility, politics, intimacies, and sex life were all deeply embued with cultural feminism, and now (I hope) they are not. Today cultural feminism is *the* mode of feminist thought and action that makes me feel most warlike, most vigilant, most aggressively oppositional, and most threatened. Compared to the early MacKinnon, whose breathtakingly radical version of feminist theory fills me with awe—I hereby go down on my knees to the *Signs* articles—cultural feminism and I are simply in opposition.

I think a lot of sex-positive and postmodernizing feminists could honestly say everything in that last paragraph (except the obeisance to the early MacKinnon, whom they don't distinguish, by and large, from the late). But I think their disavowal of cultural feminism is tinged sometimes with bad faith: you can detect in their work large chunks of *cultural-feminist reasons* to adhere persistently to m/f, m > f, and carrying a brief for f. To persuade them that I'm right, and to make sure I can later describe exactly how cultural feminism in its governance mode wants to rule the world, I want to give the most sympathetic account of cultural feminism I can.

❦ *Robin West,* Caring for Justice

If I *were* a cultural feminist, the book I hope I would have written instead of this one is Robin West's 1997 *Caring for Justice.* It is the grand statement of one of the legal academy's most articulate and theoretically astute cultural feminists. What does it say?

First, there is such a thing as patriarchy—"the social system in which men's interests trump women's whenever they conflict" (132). West's patriarchy varies in intensity through time and space, but "no society is utterly free of it, including this one" (132). When it deintensifies, when feminism (also, apparently, an irrepressible human reality) and that aspect of legalism which is autonomous of patriarchy can exert themselves, we have the opportunity to learn how patriarchy might be further curtailed, even ended (138–39).

West nevertheless figures patriarchy in staggeringly structural terms: it is "a very general power matrix . . . which exists across time and culture": the "masculine self" that it produces is not a liberal but a "patriarchal construct, the origin of which transcends and predates particular social forms" (282). So this cultural feminism is structuralist.

The early MacKinnon does not make positive historical claims on that scale, though the late one does, and the early MacKinnon would have disagreed strongly with the proposition that anything in legalism is outside of male domination—but otherwise she would pretty much go along with this basic framing of the problem to which feminism addresses itself. The distinctively *cultural-*feminist character of West's project—and the place where we *know* MacKinnon would not go with her—is the pervasive *moral* character of patriarchy and of feminism. MacKinnon's theory attributes sex inequality to *power*—male domination, for her, is "not a moral issue."[27] For cultural feminism, though, female values have been depressed and male values elevated in a profound moral error that can be corrected only by feminism. Perhaps the locus classicus for this idea is Virginia Woolf's *A Room of One's Own*: "[I]t is obvious that the values of women differ very often from the values which have been made by the other sex. . . . Yet it is the masculine values that prevail." [28] Fully within this tradition, West takes it as axiomatic that

> women, as a group, have been *subordinated* in this culture, rather than simply 'discriminated against' by the state. One (but not the only) consequence of that subordination, is that *all* women's work, distinctive attributes, experiences, perspectives and sensibilities have been **undervalued**: such attributes, perspectives, and sensibilities must be, in order to sustain the **moral justification** for women's lesser status and lesser lives. (7–8, italics in original; bold emphases added)

The emphasis on an "ethic of care" as the crucial source of feminist emancipatory insight is the "positive" phase of this moral framing.

West is clearly happiest when she can say that what is true for women is true also, exactly but in reverse, for men. I will call this her drive to diametricality. It manifests itself at the most general level when she argues that the very sites of women's most acute harms are *also* the wellsprings of their most authentic and indigenous generation of an *ethic of care*, which, if joined legally and culturally to an ethic of justice, would "heal[] the world" (280). Thus there are two diametric sexes—men and women—and they produce two diametric moral effects *in women*: women have been *harmed* by men in the very aspects of their lives that they infuse with their *superior values*. Sex and reproduction (domesticity, motherhood, etc.) are the domains in which this harm happens and this superior ethical style develops.

West argues that "the concept of harm" is central both to the feminist understanding of women's experience in patriarchy and to the optimal approach of feminism to law. I'll consider her legal arguments in Part Three;[29] here I'll restrict myself to the problem of women's experience in what MacKinnon would call male domination and what West calls patriarchy. She sets out a four-part

catalog of the "gendered harms" that women suffer at the hands
of men: the "harms of invasion," the harms of "private altruism,"
the "harms of separation," and the "patriarchal harms" (100–
138). These pages offer an elaborated taxonomy of the "gendered
harms" that women suffer *and men don't* (diametricality), each
element of which manifests itself in women's experience of sex
and domestic life in two forms: the vast phenomenology of patriarchy's spirit-murdering violence on one hand, and the generation of women's moral virtue on the other (diametricality again).

So how do women's harms and women's capacity to produce
superior values meet diametrically? Let's follow the "harms of
invasion"—rape, unwanted impregnation, sexual harassment,
street harassment, incest (100–103)—through West's argument.
Violent rape produces a "shattering of selfhood so profound and
traumatic as to echo throughout a lifetime" (107); "in extreme
cases" these harms result in "the death of subjectivity" (109). The
threat of violent rape can do the same; and so can the individual
and collected array of other harms of invasion, whether actual or
threatened. The most devastating consequences of these harms,
for West, are not the physical and material injury they cause but
the breakdown of selfhood that they produce. Unlike generic assaults, these harms occupy a woman's interior body and turn her
sexuality against herself. They cut women off from themselves;
make it impossible for them to align desire, pleasure, and action;
unmoor them in liberal individualism. For all women, who suffer
a "much larger number" of invasive harms than men, the liberal
self is consequently more foreign. And when the invasive harms
do happen to men, those men are (here West tracks MacKinnon)
feminized: "*Feminine* men are also subordinated *along gender
lines*" (18, emphasis added).

For all that—and here West departs from MacKinnon and also
from many other cultural feminists—her cultural feminism does
not see (hetero)sexuality as a wall-to-wall domain of male super-

ordination—but that's because (unlike MacKinnon) she knows a difference between morally good and morally bad sex. Virtuous sexuality is *feminine* sexuality, and it has a decidedly infantile, lesbian, and caring shape.

West relies on Adrienne Rich's decisive 1980 article "Compulsory Heterosexuality and Lesbian Existence"[30] to derive a redemptive feminist, intrinsically lesbian, sexuality from the "woman-to-woman bond" of a girl with her mother and other girls. As West put it, "a young girl's natural, early, fierce, loving, erotic and caring identification with women and girls is shattered by the pervasive patriarchal institution of compulsory heterosexuality" (286). It is nevertheless there to be recovered through feminism, and West renders it as infinitely redemptive. Embodied childhood innocence—female variety—is the reference point for adult sexual morality.

The details are beautifully embedded in West's example. It comes from the autobiographical reflections of Ellen Bass, the coeditor of an important feminist anthology on incest who had become a stripper (for men) in her effort to grapple with the way in which "our pornographic, incestuous, and sexually abusive culture shatters women's natural, playful and affective eroticism" (287). West traces the breaking point in Bass's infantile development to a moment when she eagerly disrobed for a trusted doctor, only to face her mother's and doctor's collusive joke objectifying her *as a* destined stripper. Equally decisive was her subsequent encounter (child's-eye perspective) with a calendar showing a housewife struggling with grocery bags as her shirt was blown upward and her panties fell to her ankles, "her rosy buttocks exposed": "Notice," admonishes Bass, "next time you are shopping, the covers of magazines at children's eye level."[31] Feminist consciousness-raising, implies West, enabled Bass to discover, or rather *recover*, a redeemed sexuality: "*the original desire*, that of sharing who I truly am with my lover, both as a gift and as an affirmation of myself."[32] That is the sexuality which West's cultural feminism validates and diametrically opposes to the harms of invasion: it is original, innocent, mutual, sharing, giving, affirming.

This is a highly distinctive formulation of the authenticity of feminine sexuality. Many, perhaps most, producers of feminist legal theory, given the chance, would say something else. But West's formulation has a feature that I regard as widely characteristic of feminist legal theory today and highly puzzling, if not downright inexplicable: a pervasive lack of interest in women's erotic yearning for men and a foreclosure of theoretic space for an affirmation of men's erotic yearning *for them*. Though many of the chief producers of Unitedstatesean feminism are women with husbands, women with boyfriends, women who have sex with men, and women with sons, some of whom will have sex with women and some of whom, whatever they do with their alloeroticism, will want to be *masculine* in it—West herself may be no exception—there seems to be no urgent need in their feminism to understand *women's* version of what Leo Bersani, writing on behalf of *gay men*, has called "[gay male] love of the cock."[33] Writing this book I have encountered thick theories and thick descriptions of lesbian love (butch/femme, femme/femme, butch/ butch), gay male erotic genders of all kinds, and transsexual crossings back and through all of that: but I have not found *anyone* determined to produce a theory or politics of *women's heterosexual desire for masculinity in men*. It's just missing. Inside feminism I've found affirmations of female femininity, female masculinity, and male femininity (we've seen MacKinnon's and West's)—but no affirmations of *male masculinity*. That, too, is just missing. I think West's redemptive sexuality provides the pattern for this gap, so strongly so that I would also argue that the gap shows the trace of cultural feminism's oft-denied power in left sexuality theory and politics today—even in those feminisms, gay-identity formulations, queer theories, and trans politics that purport to have departed from it.

However that may be, the erect penis circulates in West's book as a paradigm image of the acquisitive, self-interested, monadic liberal self—the agent of the invasive harms—that feminism must not so much resist as *replace*: the "ejaculatory, self-imposing, world-conquering, nature-taming, capitalistic, commodifica-tionist . . . masculine self" is decidedly part of the problem, not part of the solution (108). By contrast, West's peroration includes a long quotation from Luce Irigaray's *This Sex Which Is Not One*, in which the French thinker describes what West reveres as "women's internal, prelingual, and even presymbolic sense of ourselves" (289):

> What claim to raise ourselves up in a worthier discourse? Erection is no business of ours: we are at home in the flat-lands. . . . Stretching upwards, reaching higher, you pull yourself away from the limitless realm of your body. Don't make yourself erect; you'll leave us. The sky isn't up there: it's between us. . . .
> . . . Our bodies are nourished by our mutual pleasures . . . our exchanges are without terms, without end.[34]

This is a *lesbian* sensibility, and an entirely *feminine* sexual ethics. Perhaps I can diametricalize a little myself: just as West's theory of sexual harm deletes women's capacity to injure men, so her theory of sexual virtue deletes women's desire for phallic mascu-linity in men; just as her theory of sexual harm deletes men's mas-culine capacity to nurture women, so her redemptive sexuality deletes the possibly vital and life-affirming dimensions of men's bodily immediacy, phallic drive, and aggression. It's virtually a mandate to men who want to sleep with feminists: become lesbi-ans. Not that there's anything wrong with being a lesbian, I hasten to add—that (in addition to gay male love of the cock and femme versions of the same, not to mention certain attitudes about my car, and so on . . .) has been one of my favorite sexual orientations, and I've admired it in many male friends. But it's just odd, striking, puzzling, that cultural feminism (and all the liberal feminisms, postmodern feminisms, queer theories, gay and lesbian sexual theories, and trans theories that hew to its limits) have not been asked to explain how they can excuse or affirm precisely the male desire that they do desire, and why so many feminists who interdict it ethically seem to keep going back for more of it.

OK. So the bottom line is that West's cultural feminism *has* a sexual ethics for everybody, derived from women's vital, infantile, and generative sexual experience. The naive expressiveness of the aboriginal self, the erotic disposition to give and receive in mutuality, the happy embodiedness of the unshamed female form and of the idyllic symbiosis originally experienced by mother and daughter—this is the stuff of ethically good sex. It's got everything that the invasive harms would erase. And if everyone had sex this way, the invasive harms would disappear from the face of the earth.

West produces a diametrical relationship as well between the second kind of harm—that of "*private altruism*"—and its cancellation in women's *maternal* being. She argues that the invasive harms deeply construct the lives even of the very few women who are never personally subject to them: rape, street harassment, incest are lurking out there, threatening all women all the time, and producing fear. In their fear, in their desperate but mostly covert quest for security, women decide on altruism: they are not forced to do this; instead, they *consent to it.* They do it in sex and in the domestic sphere of nurturance, and especially in reproduction (114).

Almost better, West laments, that they were outright *forced* to have sex with men, to become pregnant, and to mother their children: at least then they would not suffer this distortion of the very capacity to consent, that definitive feature of selfhood. But instead the "harms of private altruism"—all the sex a woman will have, the children she will bear, the nurturing she will do, the sacrifice of market-earning power she will make, out of *fear*—cumulate, cutting her off from liberal individualism yet again, and subjecting her to dependency on the very people she serves, dependency that then ratifies her fears of abandonment and produces another round of voluntary servility (109–27). "It is indeed possible for an entire adulthood to be spent in such a state of duress" (120).

Women performing altruistically in the shadow of fear—and that is all women—suffer intense, invisible, silent misery, misery that constitutes a moral injury to their very selfhood:

> The altruistic acts [of domesticity] are exhausting and not particularly pleasurable—menial domestic labor, and a good deal of child care as well, is repetitive, understimulating, physically demanding work. It is boring. It is also, of course, enraging to know that one is doing considerably more than one's fair share and to know that the consequence of insisting on domestic justice for oneself will very likely be child neglect and an unacceptable degree of filth. Rage, particularly impotent rage, is not carried lightly. And it is exhausting to live with the knowledge, even if buried, of dependency—that disaster is around the corner should one's life partner choose to desert. But most important, the damaged "giving self" that is constituted so as to ward off the boredom of the work, the rage at the injustice, and the fear of abandonment also sustains distinctive *moral* wounds—wounds to self-possession, integrity, autonomy, and self-assertiveness. (126, emphasis added)

The precise valence of West's move here might be clearer if we set it in the context of debates between cultural feminists and

power feminists in the 1980s. West's overall thesis depends heavily on Carol Gilligan's 1982 cultural-feminist classic, *In a Different
Voice*, in which Gilligan argued that then-prevalent theories of
moral development, based as they were on psychological studies
of boys and men, silenced the "different voice" in which girls and
women talk about moral problems.[35] *In a Different Voice* argued
that the field's representation of men's moral development—teleologically aimed toward an ethic of justice predicated on an understanding of human beings as individuated and separate, on
the rule of logic and the rule of law—was diametrically opposed
to the "ethic of care" (30) that Gilligan observed in the moral
development of girls and women. Girls and women saw the world
as made up not of separated, self-seeking individuals, but of inter-
relationships, connections webbing everyone together in communities of concern; Gilligan claimed that they made moral decisions not through abstract reasoning from rules but by balancing
the infinitesimal and acute needs of everybody concerned (25–
63). The great stumbling block for women as they grow morally,
Gilligan found, is learning to acknowledge *oneself* as one among
the many whose needs, wants, and welfare must be taken into
account: the "maternal morality that seeks to ensure care for the
dependent and unequal" becomes fully mature when it has
"sort[ed] out the confusion between self-sacrifice and care inherent in the conventions of feminine goodness" (74).

   Here we can map West and MacKinnon into an alliance *against*
Gilligan, in a way that highlights the structuralist commitments
of these feminists. MacKinnon of course objected vigorously to
Gilligan's translation of feminism into moral rather than power
terms, and in particular to her representation of women's capacity for care—in sex, in reproduction—as anything but an element
in the eroticization of domination: the self-sacrifice of women is
no mere stumbling block but a chronic feature of women's existence as such, an effect of male power, and the antifeminist kernel

of every act of care that they perform.[36] As we shall soon see, West grounds her feminism precisely in women's distinctive experience of altruistic concern and the "ethic of care" that emerges from it: this is what makes women's values so valuable; and it is redemptive, capable of profoundly interrupting male dominance. To be sure, maintaining women's maternal virtue as a ground is a move that MacKinnon would never make, but West *also* makes a partial concession to MacKinnon's structuralism when she grants the "altruistic harms" as an effect of male power in a way that Gilligan, as far as I know, never did. For West, women chronically choose altruism—the actual caring work that they really do do in sex and in the family—out of fear. And this fear—of the invasive harms, of abandonment—is their particular lot in patriarchy. In MacKinnon's thought, you don't *outgrow* patriarchy. West agrees. When West insists that women's very voluntary altruism is a devastating harm inflicted on them by patriarchy, she incorporates elements of MacKinnon's thought into Gilligan's cultural-feminist framework.

Just as the invasive harms are diametrically opposed by the eroticism of innocent mutuality to which girls, in the symbiotic prehistory of maternal love, have special access, however, the altruistic harms are diametrically opposed by the care of the "powerful mother" who nurtures not out of fear but out of an almost prediscursive love. Rejecting social theories in which hierarchical power is (supposedly) always figured as oppressive—and departing massively, once again, from MacKinnon—West says women (that is, women who are mothers) *know better:*

> [I]t is simply not true—it is *emphatically* not true—as many women know . . . that oppressive "power" in *any* of its manifestations is the necessary consequence of inequality and hierarchy, and that the end of hierarchy is therefore the necessary root of morality. Women of *all* cultures routinely,

though not always, respond to their utterly unequal and hierarchic relationships with their infants and children with
nurturance, care, and love rather than power, narcissism,
and the imposition for the sake of ego gratification of the
stronger's will upon the weaker's fate. . . . The physically unequal mother *in all cultures* typically breast-feeds and protects, rather than bullies or browbeats, the vulnerable infant
and child. The powerful mother nurtures so as to give life
and create growth in the weak. She does not impose so as to
inscribe her will. (277)

Not only moral theory but legal theory should be shifted to rest
on this new foundation, the ethic of care:

For it is these straightforward but overlooked experiences—
experiences of breast-feeding, nurturing, caring for, and loving the weak so as to make the weak healthy—that could
ultimately form the foundation of a feminist, maternalist
(and humanist) moral theory—and therefore a legal theory—which is grounded neither in the Enlightenment ideals
of rationality and objectivity, nor in a post-Enlightenment
glorification of power, but instead in an intersubjective sensitivity to the needs of others. . . . If we are right to trust
our nurturant response within the natural inequality of the
mother-infant relationship, then we are also right to suspect
that hierarchic relationships such as parent-child, teacher-
student, judge-litigant, and legislator-constituent could and
should be infused *neither* with false claims of equality, objectivity, or a distanced and alienating respect, nor with levers
by which the hierarchy can be smashed. Rather, those relationships can be infused, simply, with care. (277–78)

This is the happy face of cultural feminism: the love shared in
mutuality by mother and infant can be the model for sexual love

between adults, and a redeemed adult sexuality becomes imaginable (if possibly necessarily lesbian); the altruistic care almost organically bestowed by the powerful mother on the infant and on the child can become the model of *every* hierarchical relationship throughout social life. Nothing could be less like MacKinnon's dark vision of wall-to-wall domination than West's ready access to a core of pure ethical goodness, and her optimism that modeling the rest of life upon it is an imaginable—indeed, possibly a doable—project.

To get there West has to indulge in some pretty extreme female supremacist thinking. When altruism escapes the context of patriarchally induced fear, it becomes not just one among many but a sublime human good, one capable of being "*the* foundation" of moral and legal theory. And this exceptional human good can be seen only "from a truly woman- and child-centered perspective" (277). *Only a woman* can give suck, *only a woman* can remember being the daughter of a mother, and thus *only women* can "form the foundation of a feminist, maternalist (and humanist) moral theory" (277) or recall the innocent mutuality of redeemed sexuality. Though West has argued that a fully complete human ethics can arise only in the "overlap" of justice with care (38, 88–93, and everything in between), the population capable of excising from justice the detritus of patriarchy is going to be the population capable of—possibly also experienced in—maternity.

West here resolves for herself an ambivalence that divides *In a Different Voice* and that caused a controversy which, to my mind at any rate, Gilligan never resolved. How does cultural feminism imagine its aim? Is the redeemed ethical universe that it envisions one in which feminine values, so long devalued, are finally allowed to take their stand on a par with masculine ones—or are they superior, destined in a fully ethical world to *rule*?

Gilligan's great synthetic passages provide one utopian vision and her great denunciatory ones another, and I just don't see

anyplace in *In a Different Voice* that resolves their differences.
When she pulls out all the stops to play the justice organ to full
crescendo, Gilligan announces the dynamic integration of male
with female ethics in a new fully *human* ethics: the book's last
page envisions "a *marriage* between adult development as it is
currently portrayed and women's development as it begins to be
seen could lead to a changed understanding of human development and a more *generative* view of human life" (174, emphases
added).[37] But it is far more characteristic of Gilligan's argument
to trace horrifying social pathologies to men's vision of social
reality and their ethical style:[38] in particular Gilligan finds "the
origins of aggression"—understood always to be morally defective—in the characteristically male "failure of connection" (173).
The ethic of care is not yin to the yang of the ethic of justice; it
is its rebuke and the exclusive teleological aim of ethics *tout court*:

> The different voice . . . is a relational voice: a voice that in-
> sists on staying in connection and most centrally staying in
> connection with women, so that psychological separations
> which have long been justified in the name of autonomy,
> selfhood, and freedom no longer appear as the *sine qua non*
> of human development *but as a human problem*.[39]

Half the time—and *only* half the time—Gilligan returns to an
integrationist stance and a centrist, humanist politics.

West marks her radicalism when she falls solidly on one side—
the female supremecist side—of Gilligan's apparent ambivalence.
The conclusion of her reflections on the "powerful mother"
promises that the distinctive altruism of mothers can become suffused into *the human*, fully occupying its ethical space, and reach-
ing for total governance over all the subjects of justice. It's a complex passage, warranting a close reading:

> If feminist legal theorists are **to share** in healing the world,
> we will have to . . . remember, remain true to, and draw upon

the naturalism and quietness that have always been central to what has been and still is most admirable **in women's moral lives**. There is surely no way to know with any certainty whether **women** have privileged access to a way of life that is more nurturant, more connected, more natural, more loving, and thereby more moral than the principled lives which **both men and women** presently pursue in the public sphere, including the legal sphere of legal practice, theory, and pedagogy. But it does seem that whether by reason of sociological role, psychological upbringing, or biology, **women are** *closer* **to such a life**: if it is but a memory, then **for women it is a more vivid memory**; if it is a utopian dream, then for **women it is a dream we have never fully denied** and from which we routinely draw sustenance and guidance. For those of us (**men and women**) for whom principled, reasoned morality has come to seem a thinly veiled excuse for cruelty ... the suggestion that **women—and therefore the human community—can and should respond in a more nurturant, caring, and natural way to the needs of those who are weaker**, is both more and less than a "contestable, empirical claim": it is, rather, in the nature of a promise. **It is one promise, among others, that the human community can be reconstituted in a way that will salvage the planet as well as save the species**. (280, italics in original; bold emphases added)

This remarkable passage begins and ends with gestures in the direction of power sharing ("share in healing the world"; "one promise, among others"); and indeed throughout the book West seeks in liberalism, in utilitarianism, in legalism, and in postmodernism for ideas originating outside feminism that can help her search for and build justice. But West's basic argumentative protocol is to ensure that *not one element of any of them is left standing* if she is able to find it complicit with patriarchy or inconsistent with her feminism. These nonfeminist traditions persistently draw her attention, earn her respect, and appear—castrated, however—in her agenda.

That adjudicatory position of feminism with respect to liberalism, utilitarianism, legalism, and postmodernism is reduplicated inside the utopian passage just quoted. It achieves this though a persistent if incremental shift of *women* into the position of *the human community*. Here's the logic of this shift, step by step. Feminist legal theorists—a pretty small fragment of humanity, surely—have unique access to "what . . . is most admirable in women's lives" because only their theories can place the proper—sublime—value on it. Why do *women*, in turn, have access to the ethically sublime nurturant life? West does not know. It could be biology; it could be history: all possibilities are open, and to the supposedly crucial question "essence or construction?" West demurs. What really matters is that ("it seems that," a proviso that is blown away by the climax that follows) "*women are* closer to such a life." The "we" of the operation now shifts. "We" are no longer feminist legal theorists or women but "men and women" who see through the patriarchal ruse of principled morality—that is to say, the allied feminist and critical male Left. "We" men *and* women can expand the reach of "what . . . is most admirable in *women's* lives" by making "*women—and therefore the human community*" more nurturant. The origin, medium, and teleological aim of this moral project is *women*: men can assist by promoting *women's* moral authority and the scope of *women's* values; but their gender in the utopian vision is erased under the general humanity of "the human community." Diametricality again: *whereas* patriarchy in its liberal mode installed abstraction, logic, objectivity at the pinnacle of justice and as the image of fully realized humanity, a feminist ethic of care, fully empowered to redeem all justice, will install embodiedness, care, and women's point of view as the panoptic decider and the full expression of humanness.

Not only is West's political project female-, feminine-, women-and-girls-, maternal-, and feminist-supremecist; not only is it total in its aim to "heal the world" through that supremacy; it is "total" as well in the intimate depth of the moral changes it seeks to achieve. "[S]ociety won't" "take gendered harms seriously until women's interests are weighted equally with men's"—that is, until patriarchy ceases to happen—and "[t]hat in turn will not occur until women are viewed as of coequal importance, and that, finally, is *a political and moral*, not a legal or intellectual[,] *transformation of the heart*" (165, emphasis added). West's cultural feminism would *rule*, from horizon to horizon and from the pinnacles of institutional power to the smallest, deepest stirrings of the human spirit.

✂ MacKinnon/West

So: How does cultural feminism differ from and repeat power feminism as MacKinnon articulates it? First, West's patriarchy is a contingent, not metaphysical structure; male domination is far from "nearly perfect." Women escape dominance much or some of the time, have agency, are authentic, and so on. Indeed, women have more of every kind of virtue than men, including the epistemological and ontological ones of knowledge and existence. But her theory is structural nonetheless: all human life defaults to patriarchy, its timeless affliction. The immemorial but interrupted character of this patriarchy enables cultural feminism to make nonstructural accounts that are impossible in the thought of the early MacKinnon.

Second, while MacKinnon's theory is a *power* theory, cultural feminism is intensely moralistic. Women's subordination is a moral error, and it has produced women's moral superiority to men.

These two differences produce very different takes on sex2 and on law. Sex2 first. Whereas MacKinnon's theory makes it impossible to know the difference between normal heterosexual intercourse and rape, cultural feminism (when it is about sexuality, not maternity) knows a lot about what good sex2 between men and women looks like. It has the virtues that have been, at least since the late nineteenth century in the West, associated with women. Good sex is intersubjective, caring, respectful, alert to human dignity, human values, human sensibilities, human sensitivities. Good sex involves taking one's pleasure in the pleasure of the other, or at least only on the condition of the pleasure of the other. Good sex is expressive; it respects, reflects, and/or constitutes personhood. In the name of these ideals, good sex, to be good, must depress masculinity in either partner and promote femininity in both.

And the differences between power and cultural feminism produce a very different relation to liberal feminism and a different approach to legal reform. Unlike MacKinnon's theory, cultural feminism has a firm grasp on the categorical imperative in sex2. It can speak to liberalism about human dignity in a way MacKinnon cannot. There are people on the planet—women—who are doing life right; we can all model ourselves on them. This is why cultural feminism (though, as we have seen, it has its apocalyptic moments) basically has a sunny disposition. If we could let women run things, or convert men to femininity, things would be better. Women's oppression is episodic; there is almost always light at the end of the tunnel.

Cultural feminism thus fits into liberal feminism without all the angst that attends MacKinnon's relation to it. It has permeated feminist *legal* theory, I think, because it is good at designing incremental reforms and maintaining faith in them, and because liberal feminism is hospitable about half of the time to special treatment.

For all that, though, cultural feminism shares a lot with power feminism. When it is about sexuality, not maternity, it is a sexual dominance theory. That is, it holds that sexuality is central to women's subordination and that women's subordination is the central fact in sexuality; that masculinity is dominance and objectification; that femininity is its opposite; that masculinity belongs to men and femininity to women; that this formula states the relevant alternatives so exclusively that, if a man is sexually subordinated, he must be understood to be feminized;[40] and that whenever in sexuality we find dominance, it is masculine and morally erroneous.

And the moralism of cultural feminism makes it just as radical as MacKinnon's theory, though in a very different way. MacKinnon would like to get them by the balls because she doesn't believe their minds and hearts *can* follow; whereas cultural feminism has detailed plans for their hearts and minds. It is a fighting faith seeking the moral conversion of a little less than half the human race. The emphasis on values in cultural feminism has led it to have reform aspirations that are at once minute and diffuse; it knows things like "lesbians should not wear strap-ons" and "people having sex should be required to ask permission for every new intimate touch" and "a husband who introduces his penis into the vagina of his sleeping wife has raped her and should be prosecuted." It can't stand to listen to Randy Newman's "You Can Leave Your Hat On." It thinks that a man who would joke to a female subordinate at work about pubic hairs appearing on his Coke can has shown himself unfit for high office. It's easily offended; it is schoolmarmish, judgmental, self-righteous. And here it begins to look not like a species of liberal feminism but like an alien infiltrator in it: we have seen it seeking to clear the airwaves of all endorsements of values it thinks are bad; we have seen it thinking that *referring* to a value is *endorsing* it.[41] It can insist that people not only do the right thing but do it with the right spirit. In short, cultural-feminist moralism can trend toward totalitarian regulatory projects. Opposing it makes one sound like a libertarian.

Liberal Feminism

Liberalism (as opposed to feudalism or communism) being the mode in which all our politics are waged, every currently articulable feminist position is liberal in some way, though some aspire more than others to a critical relationship to their own inevitable importation of liberal tenets. "Liberal feminism" holds no such aspirations; instead, it stumbles into a critical relationship with liberalism. Here is how.

Liberal feminism is characterized by a view that women and men are, for all legitimate purposes, the same; equality is its central social and legal goal. For liberal feminists, the hard part is deciding what constitutes a legitimate purpose. In recurrent ambivalence on this question, liberal feminism has veered from equal treatment to special treatment; from formal equality to substantive equality; from empty theories of gender to particularized ones. The more closely it hews to the classic liberal view that the state has no business forming strong views of the good life and good ways of being human, the less it has to say about gender, the more likely it is to take libertarian forms, and the more likely it is to want to stop at formal equality. The more detailed is its vision of what equality between the sexes would look like, the more it is willing to see the state as an appropriate vehicle for promoting the good life, and the more substantive its specifications for equality. Because this latter swing of the pendulum— toward, let us say, a "thick" agenda for the state and a "thick" description of gender—puts liberal feminism at risk of entering into a critical relationship with liberalism, it recurrently produces the energies that result in a return to its "thinner" mode.[42]

Liberal feminism has policy reform projects in all the domains where it observes that women are at a disadvantage, whether in the family, reproduction, sexuality, access to education and employment, access to political power. It does not always need a theory of sex1, sex2, gender, sexuality, sexual orientation, and the rest. As long as it can say that there aren't enough women in Congress without having to say how that came about or why it's bad, it can avoid a thick description of gender. But inasmuch as liberal feminism eventually always *does* have to say how that came about and why it's bad, it contains, even in its "thin" mode, the impulse toward its "thick" one; and inasmuch as the latter does need to have things to say about gender, it is highly permeable to theories of sex1, sex2, gender, sexuality, sexual orientation, and the rest.

MacKinnon's best work is a withering critique of this oscillation both in liberal equality models and in liberal feminism. The very idea that justice for women depends on a comparison of their life situation with that of men limits equality theories to the terms set by male dominance; and indeed, the oscillation from equal to special treatment and back again is a classic symptom not of women's interests but of the way in which they are trapped in the double binds of feminine subordination within abstract justice. Cultural feminism, with its strong affirmation of women as they now exist as sources of valid models of justice and goodness, tends to find special treatment perfectly hospitable. Within feminist projects that are more characteristically *liberal*, however, the oscillation continues, and there, both power and cultural feminism have been astonishingly successful at smuggling themselves in at moments of theoretic need. Male domination, and the centrality of sexuality to its establishment and maintenance, are the default terms in which liberal feminism describes sex1, sex2, gender, sexuality, and sexual orientation, when it has to describe them at all.

Convergentist and Divergentist Hybrid Feminism

Various strands of feminist thought and action base themselves on the hypothesis that something conceptually *outside* sex1, sex2, sexuality, gender, and sexual orientation nevertheless fundamentally inflects one or more of these elements of the sexuality complex. The most substantial hybrid feminist projects focus on class, race, and nation as simultaneous modes of ordering.

Socialist feminism is, today, in the United States, like a patient etherized upon a table. My examples of hybrid feminism in what follows will be drawn from the antiracist and postcolonial projects.

Work in these quite disparate traditions aims to find ways in which class hierarchy, racial subordination, and postcolonial trauma can be understood to have consequences inside gender, sexuality, and so on. As I've suggested in Part One, these consequences can *converge* with feminism or *diverge* from it.

Strongly convergentist work has a very pronounced telos: the various forms of subordination that it takes into account are hypothesized or assumed to act *together.* Socialist feminism hypothesizes that causal priority in women's subordination goes to capitalism; when we see women losing out to men in sexuality, we should understand that to result from the disadvantage with which they emerge from market relations. Similarly, critical-race and postcolonial feminisms see some element in the sexuality complex as taking the bad—and woman-disadvantaging—forms it does because of something in racism or something in the history of the postcolonial nation. Racism and nationalism are *gendered*; are *eroticized*; etc.

It is not always possible, however, to converge. Consider the problem of interracial rape. Antiracist feminism has noticed in considerable historical detail the ways in which American racial slavery found justifications for slave owners' rape of their women slaves and for their punitive control of black male slaves' sexuality that sound with harmonious convergence in gender and race terms. Racial and sexual oppression worked hand in hand, in *convergence*, to produce a complex but integrated system of oppression that could be fully described and opposed by antiracist feminism. But work in this genre frequently encounters moments when this convergence cannot be analytically imagined, descriptively maintained, or normatively endorsed. A classic example would be the simultaneous possibility that a white woman, operating in the racial and gender system just described, might accuse a black man of rape because he raped her (in which case the *gender* injustice of *disbelieving* her is acute and firmly embedded in the history of *sexism*) or because they had had illicit sex that she solicited and enjoyed a lot but needed to disavow (in which case the *racial* injustice of *believing* her is acute and firmly embedded in the history of *racism*). That is, the differences between race and sex, or racism and sexism, might produce a divergence. How antiracist (or postcolonial or socialist) feminism handles this divergence has been at the crux of the hybrid feminist project.

The convergentist vision, and the logic that drives convergentist hybrid feminisms very reluctantly to divergence, are exemplified here by the manifesto of the Combahee River Collective, written by black feminists in 1977 and first published for mainstream consumption in 1983.[43] The divergentist impulse enjoys a particularly rigorous workout in Gayatri Chakravorty Spivak's "Can the Subaltern Speak?" published in 1988.

❦ The Combahee River Collective Statement

A collective of unnamed black feminists produced this classic text in U.S. antiracist feminism in the late 1970s. It is cited again and again for this almost perfect statement of the convergentist agenda:

> The most general statement of our politics at the present time would be that we are actively committed to struggling against racial, sexual, heterosexual, and class oppression, and see as our particular task the development of integrated analysis and practice based upon the fact that the major systems of oppression are interlocking. The synthesis of these oppressions creates the conditions of our lives. As Black women we see Black feminism as the logical political movement to combat the manifold and simultaneous oppressions that all women of color face. (264)

To restate: the goal of the Collective's intellectual work is to elaborate the already-known fact that power takes the form of *systems of oppression* that *interlock* so seamlessly that they are *synthesized*: they are *manifold, simultaneous, and integrated*. A successful piece of convergentist analysis or activism will show how multiplicity and hybridity produce not fracturing and splitting but harmony: racism and sexism, or market power and male attitudes toward sex2, intersect, converge, reinforce one another, provide the meanings and moments for one another's success. The systematic quality of this convergence has particular meaning for those who are subordinated at its nexus: the *conditions of the lives* of *black women*—or even of *all women of color*—are shared among them, and can be illuminated through consciousness-raising that focuses not only on sexism but also on class and racism. Failures to produce convergence are, in this genre of feminist work, understood to reinstate the oppressive norms belonging to the unconverged system of oppression: if gender is not fully *racialized*, the analysis is complicit with *racism*; if race is not fully *gendered*, the analysis is complicit with *heterosexism*.

As the Combahee River manifesto proceeds, it attempts to merge its framing of oppression as unitary (though complex and multiple) with a similarly unitary conception of the Collective's black lesbian socialist feminist aim:

> Above all else, our politics initially sprang from the shared belief that Black women are inherently valuable, that our liberation is a necessity not as an adjunct to someone else's but because of our need as human persons for autonomy. . . .
>
> . . . To be recognized as human, levelly human, is enough. (266–67)

The assumption that oppression is seamlessly systematic emerges again, reversed, in this vision of emancipation in the undifferentiated and universalizing language of liberal humanism. Indeed, the Collective's almost privileged position at the subordinated end of all interlocking oppressions gives it a hope of access to an unmediatedly alternative social vision:

> The major source of difficulty in our political work is that we are not just trying to fight oppression on one front or even two, but instead to address a whole range of oppressions. We do not have racial, sexual, heterosexual or class privilege to rely upon, nor do we have even the minimal access to resources and power that groups who possess any one of these types of privilege have. . . .
>
> . . . We might use *our position at the bottom*, however, to make a *clear leap* into revolutionary action. (269–70, emphases added)

Many U.S. feminists of my generation first encountered the term "identity politics"[44] in *The Combahee River Collective Statement*, so it is remarkable how precisely the text enacts some of the complex ramifications that ensued when strongly convergentist feminism retained a commitment to the universal and converged telos of particularized identity *and* to the elaboration of nonconverged forms of power and oppression. The result, to be blunt, was the unwilling production of divergence.

The trajectory can be traced from the first paragraph of the Statement to the last. As we've seen, the Collective launches its Statement with a bid to speak "[a]s Black women" for "all women of color"; however deep and difficult their struggle (and the Statement relates many reformulations of the group, its personnel, and its practice), the consolidated image of black feminism corresponds (as we've also seen) to an image of black women as deeply unified in political experience. The rub seems really to come when the Statement affirms that black feminism must maintain "solidarity with progressive Black men" (267). Doing so produces a rejection of lesbian separatism, then in its brief heyday, for "leav[ing] out far too much and too many people, particularly Black men, women and children" (269).

This asymmetry—splitting from lesbian separatist feminists, allying with black men and children—reappears as the Statement elaborates the Collective's positions with respect to racism in white feminists and sexism in black men. Compare the terms of affiliation and disaffiliation in the following elements of the position:

> We *struggle together with* Black men against racism, while we also *struggle with* Black men about sexism. (267, emphases added)

> *Eliminating racism* in the *white women's movement* is by definition *work for white women* to do, but we will continue to *speak to and demand accountability on this issue.* (273, emphases added)

The elision from "struggle together with" to "struggle with" emphasizes the solidarity within difference that the Collective wishes to maintain vis-à-vis black (or, in an earlier moment quoted above, "progressive Black") men; the temporality imagined for the project is open-ended; the stance is strategic; and "while" suggests both contradiction and simultaneity. By contrast, the Collective addresses white feminists as Others who have their own distinct project (one that they manage without aid from black feminist women and for which they can be held accountable); the temporality of the encounter is imagined to have a blunt ending, a telos of perfection rather than of ongoing relationship; the encounter is what it is "by definition," not because of the speakers' strategic, situated judgment; and "but" expresses contradiction *simpliciter*. Though the Statement does not explain why it imagines two such different practices for black feminism, this asymmetry strongly suggests that some theoretical, historical, or other difference obtains between sexism and racism; that some profound pragmatic and/or conceptual conditions emerge for black feminists confronting white ones that do not arise when they confront black men (and vice versa). Divergentist impulses are working their way to the surface of the text here.

By the end of the Statement, these differences have driven it firmly away from the convergentist vocabulary with which it begins. The trend becomes pronounced when the Statement rebukes essentialist cultural and power feminists who had adopted the view that male dominance is biologically based (a view that was widely held, though not uncontroversial, among lesbian separatists). The Collective objects, and not only because such biologism corroborates (racist) theories of biological superiority and inferiority:

> We have a great deal of criticism and loathing for what men have been socialized to be in this society: what they support, how they act, and how they oppress. But we do not have the misguided notion that it is their maleness, per se—i.e., their biological maleness—that makes them what they are. (269)

The Statement authors knew how to specify black men when they wanted to, so I take it as indicative, not accidental, that here they refer to men and their maleness in generic terms. Rejection of biological essentialism seems, then, to entail an insistence that there are human and redemptive possibilities *for white men.* The loathability of *all men* is historical, is contingent; *all men* could emerge from sexism redeemed; *for them too,* the text implies, "to . . . [live] as human, levelly human, [would be] enough."

This visionary humanism, the temporality of struggle, the uncertainty of identity affiliation in the process, and the longed-for vision of human redemption—all of these produce a conclusion that is stylistically quite different from the formulations with which the Statement begins. Here are the last passages in full:

> In the practice of our politics we do not believe that the end always justifies the means. Many reactionary and destructive acts have been done in the name of achieving "correct" political goals. As feminists we do not want to mess over people in the name of politics. We believe in collective process and a nonhierarchical distribution of power within our own group and in our vision of a revolutionary society. We are committed to a continual examination of our politics as they develop through criticism and self-criticism as an essential aspect of our practice. In her introduction to *Sisterhood is Powerful* Robin Morgan writes:
>
> > I haven't the faintest notion what possible revolutionary role white heterosexual men could fulfill, since they are the very embodiment of reactionary-vested-interest-power.
>
> As Black feminists and Lesbians we know that we have a very definite revolutionary task to perform and we are ready for the lifetime of work and struggle before us. (273)

Finis.

This is a seriously ambiguous passage. Robin Morgan justifies her categorical disaffiliation from white men by invoking their *embodiment* of dominant power, a basis that the Statement has just rejected. There must be some distance between the quotation, then, and the series of gestures that present it; exactly what this distance implies is left unarticulated. Moreover, the Statement's own affirmations refer to a future of uncertain possibility and explicitly disavow a judgmental and knowing politics. One can read Morgan's assertion that she "ha[s]n't the faintest notion" as an ironic and dismissive equivalent of the statement "I can't imagine it because it cannot be real"; if the Statement adopts that formulation, it has to be as a more direct and even wistful confession that it is hard to imagine what a revolutionary future might bring. The conclusion provides us with an oblique, tentative, even dimly visionary moment, all the more striking in its delicacy as it follows immediately upon the stern promise to hold white feminists accountable for their racism.

So the concluding paragraphs constitute political reality as temporal, largely *future*, and knowable only with visionary apprehension; the voice is tentative, uncertain, and somewhat melancholy, reflective, self-doubting; and the moral reach of its aspiration is encompassing. All of this *un*performs elements in the convergentist opening statement of purpose quoted above: there, reality is consolidated and apprehended as a matter of fact; the voice already knows exactly what it is going to find out if it looks at the social world; and the moral rigor of the tone is militant and even a bit ruthless.

The Combahee River Collective Statement is widely regarded inside various Unitedstatesean feminisms as a canonical statement, even an ur-text, for many strands of hybrid convergentist feminism. Its basic convergentist vocabulary ("manifold, simultaneous and integrated," etc.) is by now widespread and familiar. This should remind us that the hybrid feminisms, even in their convergentist modes, have been willing to see tensions, conflicts, contradictions, and outright war between the two (or more) forms of dominance each tradition takes into view.

✄ THE COMBAHEE RIVER COLLECTIVE STATEMENT/
THE COMBAHEE RIVER COLLECTIVE STATEMENT

Cards on the table moment. I think the incoherence of *The Combahee River Collective Statement* is a good thing for left politics. In anticipation of my arguments in that direction in Part Three, I'll say a bit here about why.

The divergentist analytics displayed at the end of the Statement have a number of virtues that the convergentist attitude forgoes. First, the convergentist statement with which the Collective begins is a moral *dictat,* an *assumption* about the world, which it is part of the Collective's *moral* project to maintain. This is a deployment of theory as normative in the sense that aspirational and normative commitments are attributed to its very hypotheses about social reality and morally *must* remain there. Of course, to the extent that racism and sexism (for example) *can be understood* to exist in hybrid form—to the extent that that is a productive way to understand what is happening in social life—the hypothesis that they *will do so* brings their joint operation within the range of description and activist engagement. As hypothesis, a convergentist formula can be extremely useful. But the ontological promotion of a convergentist formula—*any* theoretic formula—from hypothesis to moralized assumption is a convergentist move: it closes the project from seeing otherwise.

Not accidentally, I think, the Statement's divergentist ideas gradually return theory to hypothesis. I think this is a good thing. The divergentist mode allows its users to notice ways in which the world does not submit to convergentist monolithism.

The divergentist impulse in hybrid feminism has other serious advantages. For anyone who has misgivings about the more structuralist dimensions of power feminism and cultural feminism *as a set of understandings of sex1, sex2, sexuality, and gender*, diverging can be quite powerfully capacitating. Because work in the hybrid traditions is, ex hypothesi, committed to the idea that differences between women can be just as important as their commonalities, it cannot maintain the structuralist design of m/f and m > f as MacKinnon deploys them. And it finds it difficult to sustain the moralism about men that we see in cultural feminism; after all, it sees men, as well as women, as victimized by market relations, racism, and imperium. As a result work in these traditions is much more open to complex and nuanced, even contradictory, hypotheses about women, men, sex1, sex2, gender, and sexuality than unhybridized sexual dominance feminism.

When, as in the opening moves of *The Combahee River Collective Statement*, the convergentist idea is promoted from a hypothesis to an assumption, belief, or demand, however, it works to preclude its true believers from articulating divergentist events. The punishment for doing so can be severe: all of us who have worked in hybrid feminist settings know that moralism about women, particularly women inside feminism, for failing to produce convergence, is a pretty frequent concomitant of convergentist ambitions. Moreover, failure to see divergentist events in its own project can make convergentist work seem magic realist: it can seem more interested in a world of its own making than in the worlds under construction by others. The ideas that power is seamless, that oppression is monolithic, that the "most multiply oppressed" share an identity and undivided interests and experiences that bestow on them unique and unassailable epistemic powers and political authority—all of these are strongly defended when convergentist hybrid feminism produces its theoretic moralism, and don't (in my view) deserve nearly as much protection as they get in feminism as it has been and still is practiced in the United States.

❦ Gayatri Spivak, "Can the Subaltern Speak?"

Hybrid feminism sometimes avoids or minimizes these costs, most obviously when it affirms rather than suppresses its tendencies to divergence. The possibilities here—merely suggested in *The Combahee River Collective Statement*—are exemplified in Gayatri Chakravorty Spivak's essay "Can the Subaltern Speak?" This is a classic text in postcolonial feminism; it is a classic text in *postmodernizing* postcolonial feminism; and it is also relentlessly difficult. I will attempt to "restate" it here, noting of course that my own desires for its coherence may exceed what the text itself can possibly provide.

Spivak begins with a formulation of the relationship between the "masses" and left/critical "intellectuals" offered by Foucault and Giles Deleuze in a 1972 "Conversation."[45] Spivak quotes Foucault in a disavowal of all responsibility to "voice" prisoners, the proletariat, or any other subordinated class, saying instead that "the masses *know* perfectly well, clearly . . . they know far better than [the intellectual] and they certainly say it very well" (274). Spivak wanted to reject both the idea that "the masses" are known to themselves and able to make their interests manifest politically, *and* the idea that intellectuals can fulfill their political responsibility by standing back and allowing this self-sufficient display to occur.

The Combahee River Collective, if asked, would surely have rejected the stance attributed to Foucault here. They would have sought intellectual adoption of the masses' consciousness. Spivak produces some very distinctive countermoves by turning not to consciousness-raising but to Marx, then to Derrida, to locate theoretical matériel for establishing a distinctively elite protocol for political engagement. And she wanted it to include a socialist *and* postmodernizing version of divergentist postcolonial feminism.

Spivak observes, in Marx's analysis of small peasant proprietors in *The Eighteenth Brumaire*, a delicate but decisive toggle between two German verbs that differently describe the "representative" capacities of this crucial class. *Vertreten* she associates with *political* representation, as in "my representative in Congress" or "the union representing the workers"; while *darstellen* she aligns with *aesthetic* representation, as in "Van Gogh's representation of a Starry Night" or the pictorial capacities of a claim, for instance, that "the small proprietor class suffers exploitation." The difference could be described as that between "proxy" and "portrait" (276), between the work (and here she addresses them in reverse order) of "the poet and the sophist, the actor and the orator," and more generally between "representation . . . as tropology and persuasion." These are profound binaries, foundational to Western philosophy at least since Plato's attacks on the Sophists, and of crucial importance to (yes, you can see where this is tending) the thought and, Spivak is soon to insist, the specifically *political* practice of Derridean deconstruction.

The Derridean Marx of *The Eighteenth Brumaire*—Spivak's Marx—refuses to attribute to the small peasant proprietors an "undivided subject where desire and interest coincide." Such an "essentialist, utopian" understanding of them "run[s] together" *vertreten* (their voice as the subject of economic and political *interests*) and *darstellen* (the *depiction* of them as the subject of a coherent *desire*) "in order to say that 'beyond both is where oppressed subjects speak, act, and know *for themselves*' " (272).

By this moment in the essay, Spivak has assembled a nested set of binarisms: *vertreten/darstellen*, proxy/portrait, voice/picture, oratory/poetry, interest/desire. I think Spivak, if confronted with the opening manifesto-like statement of the Combahee River Collective, would observe that (however much the Collective would repudiate the allocations of political responsibility set forth by Foucault and Deleuze) its authors had reproduced the

Foucaultian/Deleuzian "essentialist, utopian" modeling of the subaltern as fully unitary along all the dimensions suggested by these binarisms.

By contrast, Spivak's divergentism rifts this consolidated "subject" at least twice, and attributes both splits not only to the small peasant proprietors faced with a historical need to generate a political consciousness, but also to intellectuals apprehending and representing them as a class with an actual political consciousness or the capacity for one. First, her (Derridean) Marx insists that, though the small peasant proprietors are a class in the sense that they share an intelligible antagonism that cuts them off from all other classes, they are also *not* a class inasmuch as they are not conscious of their shared experience of this antagonism: "In so far as millions of families live under economic conditions of existence that separate their mode of life . . . *they form a class.* In so far as . . . the identity of their interests fails to produce a feeling of community . . . *they do not form a class.*"[46] This split between their status as a class in the sense that they are "cut off [in] their mode of life" from "those of the other classes," on one hand, and their capacity to form an image of themselves so situated, on the other—the split between their situation in economic life and their consciousness of it—belongs to "representation" in the sense allocated to *vertreten.* In that sense, their existence as a class is not a reification but a "staging, or signification." And this doubleness has a consequence for representation in the sense allocated to *vertreten*: "they cannot represent themselves; they must be represented." And here a new split appears: "Their representative must appear simultaneously as their master, as an authority over them, as unrestricted governmental power that protects them from the other classes." Not only is this "class" riven within its own existence; a second rift divides the small peasant proprietors imagined as a class from the proxy who can imagine and speak their interests: this servant is a master, and functions not to dissolve but to consolidate the antagonism with which the class confronts the social world.

So the very possibility of perceiving the political life of the small peasant proprietor class rests on our ability not only to distinguish *darstellen* from *vertreten*, but also to see the ways in which the division between them is reproduced within them. In a climactic moment in the analysis, Spivak concludes: "The complicity of *Vertreten* and *Darstellen*, their identity-in-difference as the place of practice . . . is precisely what Marxists must expose" (277).

Against this background Spivak poses the question that gives her essay its title: "*can the subaltern speak?*" (283). And her answer is a classic example of divergentist hybrid feminist practice, post-colonial mood. She specifically insists on the incapacity of the European intellectual to decide this question ("It is impossible for contemporary French intellectuals to imagine the kind of Power and Desire that would inhabit the unnamed subject of the Other of Europe" (280). She situates herself as a postcolonial in-tellectual who would resist any implication that she, by contrast, has unmediated access to the "lost roots of my own identity" (280). And she proceeds on a course of analysis which concludes that, even in her hands, the genealogy of the subaltern she investi-gates (the precolonial, colonial, and postcolonial Indian woman) cannot integrate *vertreten* with *darstellen*.

In the final sections of the essay, Spivak reproduces these splits within and between *darstellen* and *vertreten* in two parallel read-ings of the Indian woman: first, a construal of the many widows who sacrificed themselves, in the practice designated *sati*, on the funeral pyres of their husbands; and, second, a more concise read-ing of the suicide by hanging of Bhuvaneswari Bhaduri in Cal-cutta in 1926. The latter reading recapitulates the former.

As Spivak tells us, the practice of widow sacrifice emerges as an object of knowledge for her through two textual traditions, one Western, the other precolonial Indian, specifically Hindu. In the Western textual genealogy it emerges as its prohibition by the Raj. This was, she indicates, an instance of "White men . . . saving brown women from brown men." And against that, she poses the "Indian nativist argument" (297) that eulogizes the "purity, strength, and love of these self-sacrificing women" (301) and that insists, to support this representation, that "[t]he women actually wanted to die" (297). Both formulations, she suggests, create a crisis for her own genealogical desire to recover the subjectivity of these lost women. Threading her way through the documents that constitute this history, looking for signs of the desire or will of the women on one hand, and for the problem of their "being spoken for" on the other, Spivak encounters a dense pattern of violences, together leading her eventually to the conclusion that "[t]here is no space from which the sexed subaltern subject can speak" (307).

Tracing first the Western route into this problematic, Spivak notes that the only Hindu law on the subject is actually imperial British legislation "carried through without the assent of a single Hindu" (298). Spivak herself admires the prohibition of a practice so obviously detrimental to the interests of Indian widows (298–99) but notes that it simultaneously validates "[i]mperialism's image as the establisher of the good society . . . marked by the espousal of the woman as *object* of protection from her own kind" (299). Nor was this objectification and erasure simply Western or absolute: imperial administrators "collaborated and consulted with learned Brahmans to judge whether *suttee* was legal," making the precolonial Hindu tradition part of the colonial ban (301); and they created the only actual records of specific women who immolated themselves, though their notation of names reflects mostly their comically skewed misunderstanding of Indian forms of personal identification (297, 306). Most crucially, perhaps, under this prohibition, widows who declined to immolate themselves performed a compliance with Western law: they became not only objects of Western solicitude but subjects of colonial rule when they (freely?) chose to survive their husbands.

Not much hope for discovering the voice of the subaltern there. Spivak turns next to classic Hindu texts—the *Dharmasāstra* and the *Rig-veda*—and finds in them a seriously torqued iteration of this problematic. Like the nostalgic nativist insistence that "[t]he women really wanted to die," the *Dharmasāstra* floods the self-immolating woman with will. So much so that it almost excludes her from the narrow zone of permissible suicides. Whereas, according to the text, men can permissibly end their lives if they come to such a knowledge of the insubstantiality of truth that their bodies are no longer really proper elements of their identity, and whereas gods can commit suicide on the far less reasoned grounds that they do so upon a sacred place, widows immolate themselves upon a sacred space precisely *because* the death of their bodies is of crucial importance. The justified male suicide is not suicide at all; the justified divine suicide is beyond the reach of ethical judgment; and the widow's self-immolation—perhaps excused but certainly not required—is permissible only because she freely chooses to do it. It is justified by almost nothing but her sheer will. So when she does choose it, we must think of her as free. Through *sati* she must truly speak "her own desire" (300).

Spivak turns abruptly from this spiritual crescendo to note that widow sacrifice, within Hindu society at the time of its imperial/Hindu prohibition, was "an ideological battleground" fought out on the mesh of background rules of family inheritance (300). The pressure to do it was surely far greater, she imagines—it might even have been no choice at all but *enforced* (303)—for those widows who, if they lived, would step into their husband's rights over joint family property; the husband's family could recoup these property rights only if the widow died (300). So it's not about desire but about interest; and *within the indigenous under-*

standing of it the will of the widow to sacrifice herself suddenly appears subject to rhetorical pressures and possibly coercions of the most intense kinds.

Coercion and freedom now have symmetric and equally paradoxical purchase within both genealogical projects; the complicity of *vertreten* with *darstellen*, both in the formulation "White men saving brown women from brown men" and in its "opposite," "The women really wanted to die," has been at least partially exposed. Spivak is now ready to grind down the possibility that we could escape this problematic by recourse to an indigenous, originalist understanding of widow sacrifice. She vectors into the ancient texts through Raghunandana, a fifteenth/sixteenth-century legalist thought to be an authority on them (Spivak's text does not indicate who gave him this authoritative status—quite possibly the colonial administrators already referred to), and who insisted that widow sacrifice was not only permissible but *required*. Spivak then arrives at *his* authorizing text in the *Rig-Veda—only to discover there a foundational misreading*. Nor is it even clear what the misreading *is*. Raghunandana construed the passage to say of the widows: "Let them first ascend the *fluid abode* . . . , O fire [or of fire]." Spivak finds that P. V. Kane, "the authority on the history of the Dharmasastra," deduces that this "probably mean[s] 'may fire be to them as cool as water,'" but she herself wonders, "Why should one accept that . . . ?" (304; brackets in Spivak's original).[47] And it is apparently *Kane* who reveals that the text, translated accurately, actually (?) addresses not the widow but the women of the dead man's household whose husbands were still living, urging them: "Let these whose husbands are worthy and are living enter the house with clarified butter in their eyes. Let these wives first step into the house, tearless, healthy, and well adorned." If so, it is more likely that it "means" something quite unlike "required widow self-immolation"; rather, perhaps, something like what the next passage (according to Kane) recommends: *celibacy* for the widow, unless one of her husband's kinsmen marries her (304). (Kane is, incidentally, Spivak's authority for the argument from inheritance rules that widows were required not spiritually but economically to sacrifice themselves.)

Note that Spivak has by now rendered the "originary" text accessible only through a highly ambiguous reading offered by a precolonial Indian authority *read—and undermined—by* a postcolonial Indian one bearing an English last name, writing in English for the Bhandarkar Oriental Research Institute! But *if* the passage permits (requires?) widows to immolate themselves, it also constructs widow sacrifice (again) in terms of the sexed subaltern subject's desire. Let us return to the celibacy required of widows who survive their husbands and don't remarry. Spivak reads the textual chain to indicate that they were consigned to a celibacy that corresponded to that of unmarried girls. They were thought to be deeply enmeshed in their bodies, inescapably committed to life "in the cycle of births," and so to be foreclosed from the fully achieved celibacy (accessible to living men) of "laying aside." But if they died on the pyre, they would both enjoy a fully celestial sensuality—"she . . . sports with her husband as long as fourteen Indras rule"—*and* they would release themselves from the "cycle of births" that *is* the female body. So it's not about interest but about desire, desire that both floods the woman with sensual possibility and eliminates not only the physical but even the conceptual ground for it.

Finally, Spivak deconstructs the historiographical ground even for supposing that *sati* is *sati*, that is, widow sacrifice. She gives an etymology of the term tracing it back to *sat*, which she understands to designate "being" on a register that transcends gender. "It is the present participle of the verb 'to be' and as such means not only being but the True, the Good, the Right. In the sacred texts it is essence, universal spirit. . . . *Sati*, the feminine of this word, simply means 'good wife' " (305). So *sati* simultaneously liberates its subjects (women) from the duty, or virtue, of self-destruction and constrains them to approach "essence" and "the True" through good wifehood—through heterosexual marital monogamy. A highly compromised liberation. And then Spivak trains her sights on the imperial "grammatical error" that conflated "the burning of the *sati*," the burning *of* the good wife—a formulation that locates her virtue in her marital posture and leaves her immolation ethically unconstrued—into *sati*, the goodness of the wife *as* her burning. So when "White men save brown women from brown men," they also condemn them to an "absolute[] identifi[cation], *within discursive practice*, [of] good-wifehood with self-immolation on the husband's pyre" (305). And so the celebratory nativist formulation is genealogically traced to empire!

Spivak then turns to a more contemporary problem in construing the Indian woman's desire. Bhuvaneswari Bhaduri, she tells us, committed suicide by hanging in Calcutta in 1926. Spivak seeks to figure out why—she attempts to find the desire that brought a modern Indian woman to self-inflicted death—and her answers progress from certain pronouncements about Bhuvaneswari's intention (transparent records of her transparent desire) to a very complex splitting between *vertreten* and *darstellen*. From transparency and certainty, Spivak moves to depiction without imitation; speaking-for without an utterance to speak. Here's how the interpretive process proceeds.

First, Spivak knows what Bhuvaneswari's suicide means. At the time of her death no one could understand her motive, because she had been menstruating when she died and therefore could not have decided to kill herself to avoid the consequences of an illicit pregnancy. (Note already the burrowing back from sign to sign, from supposition to supposition, from representation to representation.) This initial reading was, Spivak suggests, definitively supplanted when, nearly a decade after Bhuvaneswari's death, "it was discovered" (trenchant use of the passive voice—we don't know by whom, how, or how plausibly) that she had belonged to a "group[] involved in the armed struggle for Indian independence" and had been assigned to commit an assassination. And now comes a sentence purporting to state an immutable historical fact: "Unable to confront the task and yet aware of the practical need for trust, she killed herself." Says Spivak—stating Bhuvaneswari's desire as a fact fully accessible to her own consciousness and to Spivak's as well, and voicing Spivak as its perfectly transparent proxy. Any attentive reader of the essay will note this conflation of *vertreten* with *darstellen* and will anticipate its imminent unraveling.

The next paragraph begins with Spivak still voicing herself as a complacent knower and transparent proxy, but she also begins to stretch her historical claims over more speculative material. Spivak imagines Bhuvaneswari as a devious manipulator of the sign of her own dead body; now Spivak knows that Bhuvaneswari sought to *delude* interpreters by *waiting* to commit suicide until she was menstruating. The *sati*-widow could not commit suicide while she was menstruating; the modern single Indian woman who commits suicide while menstruating is negating the first supposition people will make about her motive: against these interpretive backgrounds, to commit suicide while bleeding was boldly indicative and marked a strong will. "Perhaps," Spivak speculates (the gap between representations begins to open with this tentative mark of interpretive supposition and uncertainty), Bhuvaneswari "rewrote the social text of *sati*-suicide in an interventionist way." The uncertainty of this offering immediately surges forward, in the form of a parenthesized explanation that contradicts all the possibilities set forth so far and threatens to collapse Spivak's effort to heroize Bhuvaneswari: maybe she committed suicide because she was too old to be unmarried; apparently someone knew that her brother-in-law had been teasing her about her spinster status. If so, Spivak promptly speculates, her suicide while menstruating would signify not solidarity with the clandestine politics of the anticolonial group but stern freedom from bodily occupation by the "legitimate passion of a single male."

Spivak's next paragraph designates all that has been presented so far as "this reading," forcing the two inconsistent narratives to stand as one; announces the homology between it and the genealogy she has offered of widow sacrifice, and concludes: "The subaltern as female cannot be heard or read."

You would expect it to end there. But the last paragraph of this amazing interpretive tour de force begins (astonishingly, ironically, self-displacingly), "*I know.*" It reads:

> I know of Bhuvaneswari's life and death through family connections. Before investigating them more thoroughly, I asked a Bengali woman, a philosopher and Sanskritist whose early intellectual production is almost identical to mine, to start the process. Two responses: (a) Why, when her two sisters, Saileswari and Răseswari, led such full and wonderful lives, are you interested in the hapless Bhuvaneswari? (b) I asked her nieces. It appears that it was a case of illicit love. (308)

Finis (of the Bhuvaneswari coda).

The paragraph is a montage of grammatically structured evasions. Spivak knows not *about* but *of* Bhuvaneswari's life. She knows of it through family connections—but we are not sure whose, Spivak's or Bhuvaneswari's. And Spivak deferred seeking information through them in order to start with a woman "almost identical" to herself. This slightly displaced self gives two responses, one of which actually comes from someone's nieces. (It is not clear whether these are the nieces of the philosopher or of Bhuvaneswari.) Especially since the latter is grammatically possible, the failure of parallelism between (a) and (b) defeats our effort to make this paragraph chronological. Meanwhile the first response displaces the "full" life of Indian womanhood onto other women we know nothing about. The strong implication, but it is only that, is that these women married and had children—involved themselves completely in the "cycle of births"— and are recommended as objects of admiration precisely at the expense of every effort, political and erotic, that Spivak has made to heroize Bhuvaneswari. And the second response, the final word, proposes as explanatory the "appear[ance]" of precisely the explanation that was jettisoned from the start. The trajectory runs from knowledge to appearance, and from Spivak's voice to the spectral voice of a temporally and nominally dislocated speaker. Perhaps we should recall here a conclusion Spivak offered while trying to find the desire of Indian women somewhere in the record of *sati*: "There is no itinerary we can retrace here" (302).

✄ MacKinnon/West/Combahee River Collective/Spivak

I have proposed that divergentist hybrid antiracist/postcolonial/ socialist feminist work is willing to hypothesize and describe the "subjects" of male and racial/imperial/economic dominance as incommensurate, and can imagine progressive politics on those terms. Spivak's "Can the Subaltern Speak?" does that and more. She locates, in the juncture of feminism and postcolonialism, as she apprehends the two projects, an almost endlessly split relation to representation. The Indian woman has the social intelligibility, to herself and to others, of Marx's small peasant proprietors— with the Derridean superaddition that Spivak herself is part of the Indian woman's problematic.

And Spivak identifies the conditions that the Combahee River Collective imagined as necessary to political engagement—the search for firm, self-transparent identity, the premium placed on univocal self-articulation and self-expression, and the priority given to moralized demands for a coherentist picture of social power and of resistance—as precisely inimical to it. For Spivak, these are the errors that lead one to Foucault's abdication of responsibility. Instead, revealing and working with the violence of representation—precisely the continual teasing apart of *vertreten* from *darstellen*—replaces "the subaltern (herself)" as the ethically obligatory focus of the Western intellectual's work.

Here are three passages that any reader of the essay will highlight, as each states with some specificity both what Spivak's project is not and what it is. Each time the contrast is between the emptiness, paralysis, and vacuity of a politics tied to the authentic, transparent, and solidaristic voice, and the agonized but active splitting that belongs to a divergentist politics of representation:

> Between patriarchy and imperialism, subject-constitution and object-formation, the figure of the woman disappears, not into a pristine nothingness, but into a violent shuttling which is the displaced figuration of the "third-world woman" caught between tradition and modernization. (306)

> The case of *suttee* as exemplum of the woman-in-imperialism would challenge and deconstruct this opposition between subject (law) and object-of-knowledge (repression) and mark the place of "disappearance" with something other than silence and nonexistence, a violent aporia between subject and object status. (306)

> Derrida marks radical critique with the danger of appropriating the other by assimilation. He reads catachresis at the origin. (308)

This is the crux in postmodernizing divergentist hybrid feminism that feminists like West understand to "deny the existence of women."[48] Nothing of the kind is happening here, however: rather, we could attribute to Spivak the deepest longing for a direct, unmediated, and plenitudinous apprehension of the subaltern woman who cannot speak, and we could see her as running—hard—into the resistant matter of representation. And in that matter, the subaltern woman both exists *and doesn't*. She "disappears, *not* into a pristine nothingness" but into "a violent shuttling"—a "violent aporia"—a "catachresis"—a state of being riven between her actuality and her representation, her status as a subject and her formation as an object, her tortured representational place between inauthentic tradition and forceful modernization. Catachresis is a rhetorical figure in which a word is used "incorrectly" to force the most intense paradox into the smallest verbal space possible: Milton's denunciation of the priests in "Lycidas"—"Blind mouths!"—is the classic English-language dictionary example.[49] Spivak's Derrida counsels her to look for precisely such constitutive contradiction in the very origin of the existence of woman, and of course in the beloved but unattainable reality of the subaltern woman.

Spivak further construes this bitter encounter of desire with impossibility, of the reality of the subaltern woman with her disappearance into representation, as *hard work* that it is "the female intellectual['s]" *responsibility* to undertake. The essay's short coda reads:

> The subaltern cannot speak. There is no virtue in global laundry lists with 'woman' as a pious item. Representation has not withered away. The female intellectual as intellectual has a circumscribed task which she must not disown with a flourish. (308)

It is Deleuze and and Foucault—and the Combahee feminists in their convergentist demands, and West and MacKinnon in their confident voicing of "women"—who, in Spivak's formulation, act irresponsibly, who amass "global laundry lists" piously voicing "woman." Painfully piecing together the violently torn fragments of the subaltern woman's existence is a task that "the female as intellectual . . . *disowns*" in these magic invocations.

Finally, note that Spivak does not repeat, in her coda, her earlier formulation, that "[t]he *sexed* subaltern subject can[not] speak"; the formulation she uses instead, thanks to the genderlessness of English nouns, is perfectly capable of referring as well to "brown men." Though she insists throughout these readings that she is engaged in a feminist project, and relentlessly notes the specific cruxes that crisscross the female figure, she also manifests that characteristic note of divergentist hybrid feminism, a willingness to be *indifferent to* the foundational binarism, m/f, of feminism.

Cards-on-the-table moment: I am really sorry she merely suggested the possibility and didn't carry through with it.

THE BREAK

Divergentist antiracist and postcolonial feminisms verge on Taking a Break from Feminism, but they maintain feminist aims. When they suspend those, in current academic practice, they are received into long-running traditions of antiracist and anticolonial thought and practice and disappear from feminist reading lists. (I see this as a pathology not of the work but of the lists.) Something different is happening in the generation of gay identity, a politics of "sexual minorities," and queer theory: so far at least, even when Taking a Break they have stayed in close discursive and political contact with feminism. There could be lots of reasons for this: feminists have been among the most prolific producers of these ancillary projects; the projects are new and don't have many other places to go; and feminists have felt much more confident in their authority to demand that these breakaway projects maintain some accountability to feminism. With the hybrid feminisms, somehow, it is the other way around. This demand for accountability produced in the prodigals the need to say why they would not *be feminist* 24/7. The confrontation has been gripping.

I've decided not to extend my genealogy back into the fascinating and substantial elaboration of gay-identity theories and politics in the United States: the first genuine contact this book makes with that story will be in the emergence of pro-gay queer theory, videlicet Leo Bersani's "Is the Rectum a Grave?" This was an arbitrary decision, determined by the need to put some limits on this book's length. So I'll pause for a moment here to consider in general terms the relations among gay-identity articulation, feminism, and queer theory. This thumbnail introduction is heavily

loaded with my own conclusions from years of work in this domain and is therefore "interested."

✄ Gay Identity/Feminism/Queer Theory

As a social movement, gay identity is springloaded with opportunities for divergence. To see how, let's assume that the basic distinction of sex1 is in place; that is, let's agree that most people
are either men or women. You could say that, whenever a man
has sex2 by physical contact with a man, you have a homosexual
act, an instance of "homosexuality." You might even say, you have
at least one homosexual. The jump from the first deduction (that
there is something generalizable about male/male sex acts) to the
second (that there is something generalizable about the kind of
people who do such acts) has been repeatedly problematic for
gay-identity movements in the United States.

What kind of person *does* want to have sex2 with someone of
the same sex1? The question whether this question is empirical
or ideological or perhaps even constitutive of the very identities
into which it purports merely to inquire has been coextensive
with the existence of an active, political gay-identity movement
in the United States. Some people have a subjective experience
of complete, lifelong, wall-to-wall homosexual orientation; there
never was a day when the idea of heterosexual sex2 had any appeal
to them. They are numerically pretty rare, however; no one has
identified any etiological feature that could explain their distinctiveness; it remains highly plausible that their experience and self-
description represent a deployment rather than a validation of
the idea that homosexual orientation constitutes a human type.
Even if we take this subset of the professed homosexual population in the United States to be its paradigmatic core, it's by no
means clear what their "homosexual orientation" orients them

to. Is it to the sex acts that are possible only with a certain combination of sex1'd bodies? To some configuration of gender that is associated with male or female bodies? To the transgressive or secretive possibilities of really really wanting something society doesn't want you to have? Do the answers to those questions lead us to think that "gay men" and "lesbians" are really different human types? Just imagine how the possible answers to those questions proliferate, and generate new questions, if you posit (as I do) that lifers should not be regarded as the paradigm homosexuals—and that any theory of the identity needs to take into account people who have same-sex fantasies but no history of homosexual social practices; who engage in same-sex sex2 while heterosexually married; who have demonstrated their ability to have sex with men *and* women; who love homosexual culture and identify with it but don't have sex with anyone; and so forth.

Similar complexities affect gay identity as the product of movement politics. Keeping this identity going socially is a bit of a high-wire act. Some homosexuals are men; others are women; and what makes them homosexuals is a decision to avoid (for some life purposes) people who aren't of their own sex1, and thus to avoid (for those life purposes) approximately half of the existing homosexuals, who, it happens, are simultaneously involved in the reciprocal avoidance. Nationalist thought, with all its homeland-origin worship, isn't much help: homosexuals tend not to be born to homosexuals; far more commonly the people they grew up with—parents, siblings, neighborhood, "community"—would be horrified if they knew what little Jeffy was going to end up doing with his dick. Though they may move to gay ghettos, and gain some purchase on local concentration as a means of social and political cohesion, those locales tend quickly to become so chic that infiltration by "heterosexuals" is the next big real estate trend. Nothing in one's capacity to have sex with a person of one's own sex1 seems to have an indigenous "politics":

you can be for and against the Democrats or the Republicans, or for or against "ending welfare as we know it" without its having much effect on your qualifications for or capacity for a same-sex quickie or long-term same-sex pair bonding. Some homosexuals are black, some are white; some are rich, some are poor; some love having sex with homosexuals just like them in these and other respects; others get turned on by big differences. Some are celibate, never even engaging in "the acts" upon which the whole thing is supposedly based; others are homosexuals in desire but heterosexual in act ("lie back and think—not of England—but of Betsy"); others engage in same-sex1 sex2 pretty regularly but don't think of it as "sex" or, because of something in their understanding of the act/identity polarity, don't think their activities have any bearing on their heterosexual personhood. Moreover, all these people care very, very deeply about their sexual selves, and deeply resent any identity project that "misrepresents" them—often even though they themselves, when asked, could not say anything very snappy or coherent about what their sexual orientation *really* is. It's a confusing array of elements for an identity movement to bind together.

Gay-identity movements have attempted to suppress and overcome those problems by a number of stratagems. One of the chief ones has been rhetorical, a "borrowing" of the identity and rights articulation of the black civil rights movement, so that homosexuals are articulated as an oppressed group "like blacks"; homophobia is the unfair animus that causes their oppression and is "like racism"; fairness to homosexuals is a matter of equal dignity and equal rights, "like black civil rights." There are many upsides and downsides to this approach, which I have described elsewhere.[1] As a way of papering over the problematics of the idea of "gay identity" it has been pretty patently futile.

Another approach has been to borrow, fairly systematically, from feminism. Sexual-subordination feminism has some facilities that make it an excellent source of such borrowings.

MacKinnon's feminism, early and late, strongly supports the view that heterosexuality is a deeply oppressive system. It stipulates that heterosexuality *is* the eroticization of domination. Her structural subordination model, with a little tweaking, can enable one to draw a social picture in which—though neither heterosexuals nor homosexuals constitute natural human categories—the capture of social power by heterosexuals from homosexuals reifies while ranking the two human groups, and permits an endless ontological validation of heterosexual desire at the expense of its necessary homo counterpart. Homosexual love may not be able to escape the horizonless perfection of this structure, but it is at least not explicitly committed to repeating it. It is a path to liberation, if not liberat*ed*.

Of course there are problems with adapting power feminism to the organizational demands of gay-identity projects. Most of the impedances come under the headings *men* and *gender*. MacKinnon's model, in which men, masculinity, and male erotic desire are by definition dominant, has to be wrenched around a bit to represent (homosexual) men as subordinate. MacKinnon herself manages this by articulating (some) gay men as sexually oppressed in the same way that women are, by being feminized. It's hard to keep masculine gay men (at least those without a significant masochistic streak) interested in the resulting political formulation. And many lesbians have objected that they feel more political solidarity with gay men, including and often especially the "masculine" ones, than with the vast array of men who are currently so eager to disavow male dominance. Another method has been—well, not to be male at all. Lesbian separatism and lesbian exceptionalism have drawn a lot of energy from power feminism. But a movement of lesbians only has been almost impossible to sustain in U.S. culture. Maybe it's just that we (they?) don't make enough money, or do too much care work, to have the resources to sustain a separate political sphere just for women. But I rather suspect it's because too many women like too many men too much—their sons, their fathers or the fathers they wish they'd had, the gay men they don't have to sleep with, fully half of their best students, the macho hunks they wish they were or wish would spank them every now and then. And also because they like themselves pretty well: too many women are too masculine to keep faith with MacKinnon's derogation of the whole gender.

Cultural feminism has provided more portable assets. Its amenability to episodic rather than structural accounts of subordination makes it more adaptable all round. Its affirmative attitude toward women's sexuality provides a handy antidote to the shame many people who love having sex2 with people of their own sex1 feel about it. It's much easier to march under the banner Gay *Pride* if you are forming your homosexual identity on a cultural-feminist idea that the oppressed sexuality is not merely "unfairly worse off" but "morally better" than the oppressor one. Cultural feminism, with its righteous indignation about the depredations wrought by men in their masculinity, its idea of itself as "moral tutor to the world," and its strong theme tying good sexual love to the values of permanency, monogamy, sensitivity, and care, is a good source of rhetorical moves for the social conservative and bourgeois centrist parts of gay culture, where outdoing heterosexuals at marital and parental virtue has become a kind of cultural sweepstakes, and where one hears credulous and self-congratulatory assertions that same-sex coupling will by definition be more "equal," and pave the way to liberation, because it provides no preassigned "husband" or, especially, "wife." Finally, as I have noted, cultural feminism speaks in the language of human dignity and the categorical imperative, and thus has many more direct contact points with liberalism than radical theories like MacKinnon's early formulation of the relation between m and f as *constitutive* domination. Borrowing from cultural feminism makes it much easier to imagine what your Washington, D.C., staffers are going to *say* to Senator Biden.

There have been problems with the cultural-feminist model of course. The sticking points seem to be *masculinity* and *sex2*. Producing and celebrating masculinity is an important part of gay male culture in the United States, as is enacting and eroticizing female masculinity among lesbians and women. Ruthlessness, selfishness, and phallic vigor are seen as good things, either because they turn you on or because you value them in yourself. Cultural feminism has validated women's masculinity but not men's—apparently on some thesis that "inauthentic" masculinity is less morally problematic than the "indigenous" kind, or maybe even an idea that women's masculinity is mere playacting and wouldn't hurt a fly. Some branches of pro-gay thinking have (as we shall see) decided to grant no such safe harbor to ideas of authenticity and of one's "proper" gender. And (again, as we shall see) the moral tenor of cultural feminism's idea of good sex, especially combined with the moralistic fervor with which cultural feminists claim to exemplify it, has produced wave after wave of left resistance: gay liberation, sex liberation, libertine, libertarian, sadomasochist, and shame-affirmative impulses; participants in sex publics, kinship and friendship networks intended to trump the tyranny of the couple; single and child-free, polyamorous, and autoerotic enthusiasms—all of these have emerged within gay-identity movements and, under intellectual and political conditions that I will describe below, have wondered whether they would thrive best outside them. They've simultaneously emerged inside feminism.

Queer theory—feminist and non-—has emerged as a search for ways to do work on same-sex desire and erotic life more generally, without recourse to these problematic models. Here are some places where queer theory diverges from gay-identity politics. As they have confronted each other so far, gay-identity theories and queer theory seek the welfare of different sexual subjects. A gay-identity approach posits that some people are homosexual and that the stigma attached to this kind of person should be removed. It is receptive to claims that homosexuality is biologically caused, and frequently manifests itself in assertions that lesbians and gay men are very different. It is a minoritizing identity-based project; it sports a subordination theory; and it seeks equality. By contrast, a queer approach regards the homosexual/heterosexual distinction with skepticism and even resentment, building arguments that it is historically contingent and is itself oppressive. It regards gender with the same skepticism. Producers of queer theory tend to think they expose and erode strong identity differentiations between gay men and lesbians or between men and women generally. A gay-identity approach fosters specifically gay culture and gay ghettos, and engages in loyalty projects like "outing" and the denunciation of homosexuals who "convert" to heterosexuality. Conversely, a queer approach thinks it is fine to be "queer in the streets, straight in the sheets"; encourages contingent and alterable sexual identification along dimensions other than the sex of one's sexual object choice, such as the object's gender or particular sexual acts; and takes within its purview not only same-sex love that does not express itself in sexual acts, but also cross-sex love that does.

Thus a gay-identity analytic thinks that there *are* homosexuals just as women's-subordination feminisms think that there *are* women; they object to the social subordination of these discrete constituencies; and they at least tend to, if not need to, maintain the discreteness of the identities on whose behalf they labor in order to present themselves as coherent.

Queer work, by contrast, wants to be anti-identitarian. It tries to dissociate male bodies, masculinity, and superordination from each other, rendering sexuality a domain in which sex1, gender, and power are highly mobile. The masculinity of women (Judith

Butler's reflections on the lesbian phallus; Judith Halberstam's on female masculinity) and the appetitive sexual abjection of men (Richard Rambuss's machinehead and Leo Bersani's homos)[2] could not be noticed in the vocabulary of MacKinnon's theory of gender and would be decried as morally defective by cultural feminism. Queer thinking agrees with MacKinnon and cultural feminism that sexuality is shot through with power, but it is much more open to the idea that the result is only episodically, not structurally, domination.

Oddly, though, the actual theory that people think is queer theory remains, often, homo-supremacist and gender-mobility-supremacist. The symptom of this return to feminist terms, which I will note whenever it appears, is its failure, so far anyway, to produce interesting nondismissive and normatively unfraught work on the queerness of masculine male heterosexual desire for the sexy femininity of women. And it is in love with the edge, implying contempt for the average, the everyday, the reassuringly persistent. One of the polemics I offer below, in the section entitled "Feminism from Its Outside: Queer Theory by Men," is that queer theory often falls into step with the commitment to m/f, m > f, and carrying a brief for f, to the convergentism, the structuralism, the identitarianism, and the prescriptive deployment of theory that I think have so eroded feminism and gay-identity theory as seedgrounds for critical work.

❦ Gayle Rubin, "Thinking Sex"

Let's go back to 1975, when Gayle Rubin published a widely influential article entitled "The Traffic in Women."[3] This article is the locus classicus of the crucial feminist idea—I rely heavily on it in this book, and so does everyone in this lineage from here on out—that sex1 and gender are distinguishable. Rubin powerfully demonstrated that the distinction would give feminism a remarkable new range of explanatory powers. Her immediate project was to argue that women are subordinated in sexuality and kinship by the forced differentiation of the two genders and a sexual division of labor that required heterosexual affiliation; that their subordination through gender in erotic and family life was historically contingent but primary in relation to their place in economic and political life; and that women's interests must be to evade and undo gender so constituted. Drawing on Lévi-Strauss's *Elementary Structures of Kinship*, she interpreted culture as a "sex/gender system": a systematic structure of meanings and practices that takes the "givens" of sex—sex1 and the rudiments of sex2 necessary for reproduction—and transforms them into gender. Gender in this reading became the cultural.[4]

By 1984, when Rubin published her next landmark article, "Thinking Sex," a lot had happened in feminism. Just a few of the high points that have been relevant to my genealogy: MacKinnon had published her *Signs* articles; her work on sex harassment had helped convince the U.S. Supreme Court that unwanted sex at work could be sex discrimination against women; MacKinnon and Andrea Dworkin had injected their antipornography ordinance into local politics across the country; and feminists had encountered postmodernism, including Foucault. And a lot had happened outside feminism: a major, complex, "out" pro-gay movement had emerged; it had fostered myriad social projects that Michael Warner aptly calls "sex publics"; and AIDS was becoming an epidemic with the power to change the terms on which gay men participated in public life.

An amazing thing then happened in feminism. We saw a mobilization of self-described sex radicals or "sex-positive feminists"—women who wanted to resist MacKinnon's theoretical point that all of sexuality was structured by male dominance and female submission. These feminists set out to fight regulatory projects like the MacKinnon/Dworkin pornography ordinance. A major impetus for this mobilization came from an already existing sex-liberationist radical-feminist tradition from which MacKinnon's theory had emerged[5] and which it had almost completely eclipsed, but there were many new elements, especially among younger participants. The sense that feminism was "at war" with itself was something new.[6] Lesbian sadomasochism, which MacKinnon derided as a pale, utterly bad-faith, and co-opted imitation of the dominance/submission pattern of heterosexuality, was one important mode in which this movement articulated itself. A long-running U.S. tradition of lesbians' forming relationships in which one woman enacted a "butch" sensibility—that is, accumulated all the masculinity for herself, while the other became the "femme"—came out of the closet and strutted itself in archival research and on the street. Lesbians broke away from their cultural-feminist taboo on the penis and started using strap-on dildos to fuck their girlfriends. Women made pornography and opened stores devoted to sex toys and erotica. An important cultural-feminist newspaper entitled *Off Our Backs* got a mocking reply when women published its pornographic counterpart *On Our Backs*. On campus, the defection of feminist intellectuals from Women's Studies programs began.

In the ferocious conflict between the sexuality-as-male-dominance and cultural feminists, on one hand, and the sex-radical feminists, on the other, accusations of bad faith and collaboration with the enemy became endemic. To some, the fight seemed to be over feminism itself. But some sex radicals—Rubin is my example here, but she had lots of company—looked around and thought something like this: "Gosh, I have less in common with the women who are promoting MacKinnon's agenda than I have with gay male sadomasochists, men being arrested for having sex with other men in public parks, drag queens, women working in prostitution or pornography, and"—as Rubin put it in "Thinking

Sex"—"unapologetic heterosexuals" (303). We're not all women and so we aren't primarily feminists—we're perverts. *We're queer.*

"Thinking Sex" was published in one of the most important books to emerge from the sex-radical side of this conflict. Its title—*Pleasure and Danger*—carries a double point about this movement. First, we are asked to read "and" as a term of contrast, as stating alternatives (as in "up and down"). Contributors to the volume affirmed that women sometimes are subjected to sexual injury by men, and that sex is a place where harmful dominance and submission can happen. Danger is real, and really bad. But they tended to say that it is bad not because it realizes male dominance, but because it deters women from being sexually adventurous, from seeking and finding pleasure. And second, the title puts pleasure and danger into conjunction (as in "salt and pepper"). It affirmed that sex has a dark side, is a domain of experience in which passion, power, shame, loss of boundary, violent vitality assume erotic dimensions and can give pleasure. Here the contributors to *Pleasure and Danger* tended to say that danger is intrinsic to physical and emotional intimacy, and at least potentially part of what one seeks in them. Of what *women* seek in them.

Pleasure and Danger was a *feminist* book. But in it, Rubin made a move that opened a new, separate road for theoretical and political—and I would add, legal—work on sex1, sex2, gender, sexual orientation, and sexuality. After a polemic directed at MacKinnon and the antipornography campaign, and after a critique of moderate feminists who tried to "split the difference" between MacKinnon and the sex radical feminists by tolerating rather than condemning or affirming their pervert sisters, Rubin wrote this:

> I want to challenge the assumption that feminism is or should be the privileged site of a theory of sexuality. Feminism is the theory of gender oppression. To automatically

assume that this makes it the theory of sexual oppression is to fail to distinguish between gender, on the one hand, and erotic desire, on the other. (307)

For the Rubin of "Thinking Sex," both sex1 and sex2 have social dimensions best described in terms of gender—and to describe those, she would turn to feminism. (Note that she maintains the assumption that gender involves masculine dominance and feminine oppression or inequality.) But she argued that sex1 and sex2 should *also* be understood to refer to "sexual activity, lust, intercourse, and arousal"—and to assess those, *where they don't overlap with gender,* she claimed, feminist analysis "becomes misleading and often irrelevant." Rubin thus proposed that gender and sexuality have "separate social existence" and need separate explanatory lexicons and activist engagements. "In the long run," she said, the study of sexuality and the study of gender could contribute to one another or even be reincorporated. But meanwhile, and to make that convergence politically desirable, "an *autonomous* theory and politics specific to sexuality must be developed."

Note that Rubin assumes here that the purpose of developing a theory and politics of sexuality is to understand the sexual *oppression* of sexual *minorities,* "systems of power" that encourage some forms of sexual life while "punishing and suppressing others." Though she relies on Foucault's *History of Sexuality, Volume One* for the idea that kinship does not capture all of sexuality, and elsewhere describes that book as crucial to her framing of feminism in the late 1970s and early 1980s—what she adorably said was "I was really, just totally hot for that book"[7]—in "Thinking Sex" she does not adopt his understanding of power. Rubin assumed that a left progressive pro-sex movement must think and act on the basis of a subordination theory. That assumption has been very hard to shake. In the following pages I'll try to shake it.

Receiving French Social Theory

Volume One of Michel Foucault's *History of Sexuality* was read and read again by feminists, gay activists, and emerging queer theory makers. No one could be indifferent to this book.

❦ *Michel Foucault,* Volume One

In *Volume One,* Foucault set out the hypothesis that sexuality understood and experienced as a distinct element of life had a long slow emergence in European thought and patterns of living. He traced it back to the Christian confessional tradition: the practice of acknowledging and disclosing the truth of one's innermost self by articulating in minute detail the attachment of desire to bodily functions. He wanted to refute an idea sometimes attributed to Freud, that sex desire is a natural, indigenously human urge—the unedited *real thing* about us—which law and power punish and repress. Thus he resisted the idea that derepressing sexual desire would be liberating. Foucault wanted us to see that sexuality in the modern era is no underdog, and that being "on its side" doesn't put you in a revolutionary position against power. Instead, sex desire is rampant everywhere, and wherever it appears it is the *product* of power, one of its effects.

Already it is possible to map an important difference between Foucault and MacKinnon. Both of them see sexuality as domains primarily of power. But for MacKinnon power is a "top-down" matter; hers is a *subordination* theory. Foucault had a different idea. Power is not *puissance* but *pouvoir*[8]—the capacity to produce effects—and if at one time it could install itself only in high places whence it lorded itself over low ones, that time is over. According to the Foucault of *Volume One,* at the onset of the modern age power learned to move from high centers to the population, to the whole social array as it is regulated by itself. Though he persistently maintained that power never forgot how to dominate, he thought the characteristically *modern* form of power would answer his hypothesis that it took the form of "technologies" by which the population produces regularity in the sense recognized by social statistics: not sameness, but regular, patterned arrays. In the production of sexuality, he was most sure of four technologies of this kind: the hysterization of women, the sexualization of childhood, the psychiatrization of perversions, and the socialization of reproductive behavior (146–47).

Within those technologies of sexuality, then, Foucault tries to imagine power not as an external violence or a top-down imposition but as an open-ended series of reciprocally constitutive *relations*. He repudiated as a misreading of his work the logic "Foucault says power is everywhere, so there is no point of resistance, no possibility of freedom," saying, "The idea that power is a system of domination that controls everything and leaves no room for freedom cannot be attributed to me." "I scarcely use the word *power*, and if I use it on occasion it is simply as shorthand for the expression I generally use: *relations of power*."[9] And *relations of power* are by definition movable: as he put the idea in *Volume One*, "one is dealing with mobile and transitory points of resistance, producing cleavages in a society that shift about" (96).

Thus when Foucault writes of the hysterization of women, his idea seems not to be that psychiatry made women feel and act hysterical, and thus oppressed them, but that, in myriad ways, the entire social array—including the women in it—produced and managed the conception of women as distinctively embodied around reproductive functions; that the temporal interplay of all these social responses—some minuscule, some quite dramatic—is "power"; that power is thus diffuse, mobile, immanent everywhere, and exerted on all by all; and that it produces as its *effects* not only hysterical women and the practices of medical science fitted to notice them as such, but every feature of social life bearing on the importance of reproductive mental hygiene.

Similarly, the "sexualization of children" did not involve the oppression of children. Instead, Foucault seems to have wanted to see how *everyone* participated in producing anxiety about the eroticism of children—and thus participated in the eroticism. The modern child is the subject (in both senses of the word) of this anxious sexuality not because, in him, nature in the form of oedipal instincts meets the prohibitive Law of the Father, but because of a vast battery of big and minute forces intent on *knowing* him as such. In an arresting image, Foucault asks us to picture "the body of the child, under surveillance, surrounded in his cradle, his bed, or his room by an entire watch-crew of parents, nurses, servants, educators and doctors, all attentive to the least manifestation of his sex" (98)—that is, all acting not to repress it but to bring it into knowledge.

Both of these technologies show the importance for Foucault of normalization, subjectivity, and knowledge as effects of power. Normalization seems to work two ways: it arranges social differences around an average, and it implicitly confirms that the average is also good. As François Ewald suggested, "[t]he norm is the group's observation of itself. . . . A norm is a self-referential standard of measurement for a given group."[10] But the idea of the average depends on deviation; normalcy can be articulated as such only if it has outliers. Unlike subordination theories, Foucault's seems to posit that power applies with equal force—with equal productivity—to generate both average and deviant subjects. If we had to articulate Foucault's idea here in the vocabulary of a subordination theory, we would have to say that both are equally "oppressed."

But it would be much more Foucaultian to say that both are equally *subjected.* The idea of *asujetissement* in *Volume One* contains a paradox: power as I have been describing it sets the terms by which human beings attain subjectivity—become persons, individuals, selves; have consciousness, will; are capable of action, choice, freedom—so that human beings become subjects through a subjection. We have seen this idea before, in MacKinnon's proposal that male dominance produces female consciousness without horizon. But for MacKinnon the paradox, and the attendant "problem of agency," arises for women and is their subordination; for Foucault it is a foundational problematic for everyone and is what both capacitates and subjects us all.

Let me rehearse these ideas by retelling Foucault's idea of the psychiatrization of perversions. The psychiatrization of perversions was not the medical oppression of a preexisting population of perverts or the medical production of a social category thenceforward doomed to suffer subordination. Rather, it was a societywide set of practices that brought the whole population into collective compliance with a distribution of normalcies and deviances and that thus subjected—*and thus animated*—everyone. Foucault thought it was extremely important that the history of medical knowledge at one point produced the human categories "fetishist" and "homosexual," but not because that involved oppressing fetishists and homosexuals, and not only because it involved producing fetishist and homosexual subjects in the paradoxical sense of *asujetissement* that I set out just above, but because, in the normalization that attended this function of power—and that involved players across the social scene, not just medical knowers and doers—it *also* produced *as normal* everyone who avoided these wayward desires, and thus also subjected them in the same paradoxical sense.

I would like now to call attention to the fact that we have had four pages of very interesting—I think quite plausible—propositions about sexuality that make no use of m/f sex1, m/f sex2, gender, or dominance! At the end of *Volume One*, Foucault acknowledges that his entire interpretive apparatus is not merely indifferent to but *opposed* to the idea that sexuality is grounded in the distinction between m and f. For MacKinnon m/f is primary, and sex2's erotic interpersonal appeals are (almost?) always the tools of producing gender, which, understood as a social system, is sexuality. For Foucault, by contrast, both sex1 and sex2 are merely categorical accidents produced by the historical situation in which "sexuality" places us.

This is so counterintuitive that it's worth pausing to think about it for a moment. Foucault proposed that we think of ourselves as men and women; that we think of erotic/procreative activities as distinctive, and normatively more problematic than, say, eating; and that we give all of these foundational importance of the sort we see in MacKinnon's work, because of a subjection. He proposes that the primum mobile may instead be sexuality, which operates in the modern period along dimensions that involve sex1, sex2, and even gender only in the most epiphenomenal ways. The entire domain of the sexual is primary; and it has emerged more causally in the sexualization of children, the hysterization of women, the psychiatrization of perversions, and the socialization of procreative behavior than in any particular requirement about how men and women are related to one another. And so sexuality is not indigenously or naturally human. It is historical. Various highly decentralized technologies of sexuality produce the *idea*, the *notion* that sex1 and sex2 are primary, and catch us up in the job of trying to understand who we are in terms of them (what do I really desire? how can I find and reveal my real desire?) when we should be thinking about how sexuality organizes our lives in unfree ways:

> [T]he notion of "sex" [sex1 amalgamated with sex2, I think] made it possible to group together, in an artificial unity, anatomical elements, biological functions, conducts, sensations, and pleasures, and it enabled one to make use of this ficti-

tious unity as a causal principle, an omnipresent meaning, a secret to be discovered everywhere: sex was thus able to function as a unique signifier and as a universal signified. . . . Sex—that agency which appears to dominate us and that secret which seems to underlie all that we are, that point which enthralls us through the . . . power it manifests and the meaning it conceals, and which we ask to reveal what we are and to free us from what defines us—is doubtless but an ideal point made necessary by the deployment of sexuality. . . . We must not make the mistake of thinking that sex is an autonomous agency which secondarily produces manifold effects of sexuality over the entire length of its surface of contact with power. On the contrary, sex is the most speculative, most ideal, and most internal element in a deployment of sexuality organized by power in its grip on bodies and their materiality, their forces, energies, sensations, and pleasures. (154–55)

✂ FOUCAULT/MACKINNON/WEST/GAY-IDENTITY POLITICS

The hypotheses offered by Foucault in *Volume One* posed a profound challenge to Unitedstatesean feminist ideas. Indeed, it is hard to imagine a theory less hospitable to feminism as it is framed by MacKinnon or the American cultural feminists. Foucault sets aside here the very m/f distinction that is so crucial to both of those projects. If we think what Foucault seems to have thought when he wrote *Volume One*, these feminisms can only produce us as compliant subjects of sexuality. In short, we have the surprising idea that these feminisms may assist in producing the very social formation they purport to critique and dismantle.

And there is trouble for feminist legal theory as well. To the extent that feminist theory in its law reform modes takes sexual subordination of women by men to be the crux of the problem, it selects reform projects that would promote women's sexual equality. Since male dominance is the form of power that it sees as unfreeing, it understands that sex equality would be liberty. This formulation produces a certain indifference to possible tensions between equality and liberty that may help to explain the totalitarian trend visible in some feminist law reform proposals. But from a Foucaultian perspective these projects appear not as rules of justice but as regulatory practices. They are as powerful as any deployment of institutional forces in the management of knowledge and subject formation. From a Foucaultian perspective their credentials for promoting liberty will *always* be in question.

And so: both MacKinnon and West, on one hand, and Foucault, on the other, offer us theories of sexuality in which it is a dark power. Neither MacKinnon nor Foucault, moreover, imagines it to be redeemable or a source of redemption. For MacKinnon this is because sexuality is pervasively structured by male dominance and female subordination, and for Foucault it is because, in modernity, it is such a crucial mode for the entry of bodies and their capacity for pleasure into the social. Even for West sexuality is pervasively the site of women's moral injury at the hands of men though also, diametrically, their moral victory over men.

For both the early MacKinnon and Foucault, moreover, this structural reach has the effect of setting the conditions under which knowledge is possible. Thus we must confront the alliance of the early MacKinnon *with* Foucault, and the alliance of the late MacKinnon and West against him. The MacKinnon of the *Signs* articles resembles Foucault much more closely than does the MacKinnon of the *Oncale* brief, the antipornography ordinance, and *Toward a Feminist Theory of the State*. As I indicated above, Foucault thought normalization, subjectivity, *and knowledge* are effects of power. The early MacKinnon thought this too: "*Power to create the world from one's own point of view is power in its male form.* The male epistemological stance, which corresponds to the world it creates, is objectivity."[11] More subtly, he thought of knowledge as a *mode* of power. The early MacKinnon thought this too: "Objectivity, the epistemological stance of which objectification is the social process, creates the reality it apprehends by defining as knowledge the reality it creates through its way of apprehending it."[12]

But then Foucault and the early MacKinnon begin to diverge. Foucault sought to develop genealogies of knowledge—to find out how a human will to know had produced shapely and powerful knowledges. His *Volume One* traced modern sexuality back to the Christian confessional to argue that sex has been "constituted as a problem of truth" (56). Foucault sought out the conditions of this knowledge. He thought that power/knowledge posited its products as Truth; so that knowing the Truth would subject one to it; while seeking to *know knowledge* enabled one to seek to avoid or disrupt this equation. Hence Foucault's persistent appetite for undoing his own knowledge. The second volume of the *History of Sexuality*, for example, begins with an announcement that his research program (taking the genealogy back to classical and late antiquity) had utterly dislocated his ideas, had required a complete reframing of the problem, and had delayed publication of the new work for years. And he gave no apology: "As to those to whom to work hard, to begin again and again, to attempt and be mistaken, to go back and rework everything from top to bottom, and still find reason to hesitate from one step to the next—as to those, in short, for whom to work in the midst of uncertainty and apprehension is tantamount to failure, all I can say is that clearly we are not from the same planet."[13] And finally, since knowledge produces subjects (that is to say, is a power that has the effect of *asujetissement*), he relished the way in which such disruptions produced a new Michel Foucault: "When I write, I do it above all to change myself and not to think the same thing as before."[14]

Foucault was thus deeply irrationalist. By comparison, the later MacKinnon and certainly West are strong rational positivists. I've already parsed MacKinnon's transition from the *Signs* articles, published in 1982 and 1983, to her 1989 book *Toward a Feminist Theory of the State*, to show a shift from affirming both the necessity and the impossibility of knowing "women's point of view," to a claim to speak unproblematically from it. Surely not accidentally MacKinnon the Certain Knower reached her apotheosis in a 2000 paper, "Points against Postmodernism," where she resists precisely the irrationalism I've attributed to Foucault (she attributes it to postmodernism generally) by claiming, for herself and for feminism, positive knowledge of reality as it is experienced by women:

> Gender . . . was what was **found there, by women, in women's lives**. Piece by bloody piece, in **articulating direct experiences**, in resisting the disclosed particulars, in trying to make women's status *be* different than it was, a theory of the status of women was forged, and with it a theory of the method that could be adequate to it: *how* **we had to know in order to know** *this*.
>
> . . . **In and from the experience of woman after woman** emerged a systematic, systemic, organized, structured, newly coherent picture of the relations between women and men that discernibly extended from intimacy throughout the social order and the state. Our minds **could know it was real** because our bodies, collectively, lived through it. . . .
>
> My own work provides just one illustration of how this philosophical approach of theory from-the-ground-up has been productive in practice. . . .
>
> Feminism made a bold claim in Western philosophy: **women can access our own reality because we live it**; slightly more broadly, that living a subordinated status can

give one access to its reality. . . . We . . . claimed **the reality of women's experience as a ground to stand on and move from**, as a basis for conscious political action. . . . Women turned the realities of powerlessness into a form of power: credibility. And reality supported us. **What we said was credible because it was real.**[15]

We have here a way to explain MacKinnon's good fit with liberal law reform projects: at a certain point she started to know whose interests to advance, and to know what to do. For all the radical darkness of her theory, it has produced in her work a breathtaking certainty, a certain Enlightenment clarity. And with those came an increasing conviction that male control over the episteme could be interrupted by the reality of women spoken by women. MacKinnon lost her suspicion that the audible, the credible, could be (to use Foucault's terms) an effect of power.

We are witnessing the collapse of perfectly useful theoretical hypotheses into descriptive and normative *dictats*. In First *Signs*, in 1982, she had set herself the goal of showing that, for feminism, "the personal is epistemologically the political, and its epistemology is its politics. Feminism, on this level, is the theory of women's point of view" (535). By the time she'd completed her conflation of theory with reality and feminism with truth, MacKinnon was ripe for the most acute rights-reductionism. As we've seen, she always deployed theory prescriptively; the late, unlike the early, MacKinnon extends that prescription to the very horizon of the real.

For her part, West sees postmodernism, and particularly Foucault's thought, as an insidious threat to women and feminism, second only to patriarchy in undermining the conditions of their well-being.[16] She devotes the last chapter of *Caring for Justice* to diverging cultural feminism from postmodernism, and makes Foucault's radical critique of knowledge one of her four chief targets. For West, because women's suffering and their genuine altruism are prediscursive, nondiscursive, and silent, the heuristic that will reveal them will decidedly not be one that emphasizes the discursive production of knowledge. Women have direct, embodied experience of the world; their epistemic stance has priority over patriarchy's (and thus Foucault's) belated chattiness:

> In marked contrast to the postmodern social theorist's certitude that language, speech, and discourse generate all else, *women know* that there is a nonlingual domestic world of human needs that compels fulfillment—a world of bodies, of babies, of babies sucking milk, of babies' shit, of babies' sleeplessness, of children, of children's needs, of children's appetites—lurking beneath. *We know* about this nondiscursive world because we live there. (269, emphases added)

Women's embodied, prediscursive knowledge can be extremely dysphoric, a component of the harm they suffer in being primarily responsible for human beings' embodied needs, for their shit. But the great maternal peroration with which *Caring for Justice* closes also (diametrically) sees that same knowledge as the possible "foundation of a feminist, maternalist (and humanist) moral theory," one that (once again) can dispense not only with maleness and all its enlightenment but also with postmodernist chatter:

> We might [West is actually arguing that we *should*] conclude that morality is grounded in the experience of being cared for in symbiosis with a protective and nurturant other rather than in our later experiences of disciplined, disciplining, and verbose authority. We might conclude that moral ideals and moral inclinations derive from the quiet love of the mother rather than from the discursive guidance of the father. (279)

Note the "rather than": West marks her radicalism, as against Gilligan's liberal humanism, once again.

Foucault would have seen these claims to truth, to knowledge, and to the concrete, foundational reality of experience, as a particularly acute, regulatory form of power/knowledge. In the formulation of *Volume One*, all four "real" technologies of sexuality—the hysterization of women, the sexualization of childhood, the psychiatrization of perversions, and the socialization of reproductive behavior—produce human beings who *think* that if they could only know and express their real sexuality they would be liberated. Feminists like the late MacKinnon and like West are, from this perspective, a particularly intense symptom of, and producers of, sexuality in its modern form.

Nor would Foucault share these feminists' subordination-theory-based figuration of liberation as an *escape from* or *overthrow of* power. To be sure, he fully acknowledged that domination of the sort MacKinnon describes does happen. But in a 1984 interview he posited that domination is something different from power relations—something like their cessation: "When an individual or social group succeeds in blocking a field of power relations, immobilizing them and preventing any reversibility of movement by economic, political, or military means, one is faced with what might be called a state of domination."[17] Such fixities are very rare. The typical, typically modern, form of power is not domination but relations of power that are by definition movable: normally, almost always, "one is dealing with mobile and transitory points of resistance, producing cleavages in a society that shift about."[18]

Thus Foucault hypothesized that distinctively modern power is both fixed and mobile. Roughly speaking, in his late writing, the lexically appropriate way to figure resistance to "domination," power in its most "fixed" form, is "liberation," while "relations of power" instead located resistance in a "strategic situation," in "tactics," and in "practices of freedom." But he also frequently indicated that domination itself was shot through with relations of power. Whether domination shared the character of mobile power or stood apart from it, throughout his discussion of these matters Foucault guarded himself constantly from figuring the utopian project as a yearning for "liberation" from "power."[19]

Thus though the terms resistance, struggle, and freedom have important utopian allure in Foucault's vocabulary, he does not give them the valence they have in subordination theories committed to the prescription that confronting and overthrowing power are what the oppressed must do. Because Foucault's lead hypothesis about power is that it is not "on top" but "everywhere," he imagines as emancipatory those projects that *engage* rather than *oppose* it. "[B]etween a relationship of power and a strategy of struggle there is a reciprocal appeal, a perpetual linking and a perpetual reversal."[20] Foucault imagines that a "strategy of struggle"—a term probably synonymous with *Volume One*'s "practice of freedom"—reverses while repeating a "relation of power"; and the appeal between them is reciprocal, so that a "relation of power" both repels and invokes the "strategy of struggle." Strategy, struggle, and practices of freedom are not only not opposed to power; they are also intrinsic to it and involve one in it. No Nietzsche's *Of the Genealogy of Morals*, no Foucault.

These trends in his understanding of power put Foucault in an important disagreement as well with gay-identity liberationism. His agenda for liberation maintains uncertainty, tentativeness, open-endedness, and mobility as virtues not because they are freedom itself, but because they bring resistance into a full engagement with power. Sex itself, not being repressed, is not the underdog we need to liberate. As he put it in *Volume One*:

> We must not place sex on the side of reality, and sexuality on that of confused ideas and illusions; sexuality is a very real historical formation; it is what gave rise to the notion of sex, as a speculative element necessary to its operation.

We must not think that by saying yes to sex, one says no to
power; on the contrary one tracks along the course laid out
by the general deployment of sexuality. It is the agency of
sex that we must break away from, if we aim—through a
tactical reversal of the various mechanisms of sexuality—to
counter the grips of power with the claims of bodies, pleasures, and knowledges, in their multiplicity and their possibility of resistance. The rallying point for the counterattack
against the deployment of sexuality ought not to be sex-
desire, but bodies and pleasures. (157)

Not surprisingly, then, Foucault maintained a highly ambivalent
attitude toward gay male identity. Wherever gay male liberation
projects appeared in highly identitarian terms—vaunting themselves as the emerging historical form for repressed and forbidden
sexual subjectivities, pushing themselves into the light, illuminat-
ing the darkness imposed by the prohibitive heterosexual law, and
so on—he detected in them a return to sexual liberation of the
most dominated kind. When such projects took experimental,
uncertain social forms—sadomasochism was probably less important to him than friendship and solitary practices of self-discipline—he detected in them the rudimentary essentials of a practice of freedom. This tension has its own bibliography, and the
temptation to genealogize it here is strong, but I will desist.

The Split, from Feminism and within It

We now come to the uncanny coincidence that Eve Kosofsky
Sedgwick and Judith Butler came up, separately, with the same
idea in the late 1980s, and that in 1990 they published it in books
that did, and that didn't, respectively, Take a Break from Feminism. They might have done exactly the same amazing thing even

if Rubin had never published "Thinking Sex" and even if—each of them arriving at the late 1980s with strong appetites for subordination models of power—they had not felt the full body blow of *Volume One*, but I don't think so. I think that "Thinking Sex" and *Volume One* made *Epistemology of the Closet* and *Gender Trouble* possible.

❦ *Eve Kosofsky Sedgwick,* Epistemology of the Closet

Rubin's invitation to conduct *some, not all* thought and activism relating to sexuality without feminism can be intelligibly taken up only if you want to be able to say that there are, or think that there are, elements of sexuality that don't overlap with m/f. Eve Kosofsky Sedgwick's *Epistemology of the Closet*, published in 1990, proposed that she had found some.

Sedgwick relied much more directly and fully on Foucault than Rubin did. One thing she borrowed was his idea that modern sexuality, far from repressing sex feelings and censoring all discussion of them, produced sex desire and fostered a profusion of sexual discourses. She also made amazing amounts of analytical hay out of Foucault's proposition that, in those discourses, silence might be not an absence (a void created by repression) but a *practice* (a positive power/knowledge). She relied on the following suggestion in *Volume One*:

> Silence itself—the things one declines to say, or is forbidden to name, the discretion that is required between different speakers—is less the absolute limit of discourse, the other side from which it is separated by a strict boundary, than an element that functions alongside the things said, with them and in relation to them within over-all strategies. There is no binary division to be made between what one says and

what one does not say; we must try to determine the different ways of not saying such things, how those who can and those who cannot speak of them are distributed, which type of discourse is authorized, or which form of discretion is required in either case. There is not one but many silences, and they are an integral part of the strategies that underlie and permeate discourses. (27)

It was the closet inhabited by male homosexuals and male/male erotic feeling that Sedgwick selected for particular study. She argued that it corresponded in dense ways to a modern concern with knowledge-in-a-world-of-representations that is repeatedly structured in dyads like known/unknown, open/closed, patent/secret, apparent/real, public/private, outer/inner, subject/object, and infamy/"the love that dare not speak its name." Hence her title—*Epistemology of the Closet*. Sedgwick argued that the driving problem of male/male homosexuality in the modern era concerns not male and female, not masculinity and femininity—not m/f—but dimensions of experience and practices of power that, at least on first articulation, have nothing to do with them.

In the introductory chapter of *Epistemology of the Closet* Sedgwick argued for a suspension of feminism not only in order to inaugurate a distinctively antihomophobic or gay-affirmative inquiry, but to let elements of sexuality that do not sound in m/f or gay/straight terms get some attention. She gave some fairly gripping new reasons for wanting to do this. Let me address her desire to suspend gay/straight first, as it rests more directly on Rubin's formulation in "Thinking Sex." Though Sedgwick admits that we could not have the concept *homosexual* without the concept *gender*—how could we have the idea of *same*-sex love if we didn't also have an idea of which sexes were the same? (31)—sexuality as erotic desire attaches itself all the time to objects that don't have sexes: "desires attaching to mouth, anus, breast, feet";

desires animated by the nonhuman status of the love object (animal, fetish), or by generational distance from it, or by the scriptedness or spontaneity of sexual encounters; desires that can thrive only in masturbation or in fantasy; and so on (35). These can all be sexual orientations, and in phenomenological gravity—in explanatory and appetitive and social-ordering importance—they probably swamp sex1-of-object-choice.

And it's not only that the homosexual/heterosexual distinction is often irrelevant; Sedgwick hypothesizes that, vastly predominantly since the emergence of modern "sexual orientation," it has been *antigay* discourses which insist that everyone and everything line up under the label "gay" or the label "straight."

Her critique does not rest at pointing out this baneful pedigree: she argues, further, that to presuppose that this distinction tells us everything about sexual orientation or sexuality is to make it impossible to explore how it came to be so mandatory or to measure its constraints (31). And so though *Epistemology of the Closet* devoted itself to representational problems affecting male/male desire, Sedgwick insisted on that desire's extension throughout the modern world, refusing any formulation that would "park" it in gay men.

That is the move from Gay and Lesbian Studies to queer theory. Note several Foucaultian elements. Sedgwick actually has things to say about bodies, sensations, and pleasures. She is talking not about prohibition but about production. Power is assumed to be exercised not (or not only) on lines of subordination, oppression, and the creation of punished minorities, but through distinctions, modes of knowing, and idea clusters that map the social and experiential field. Identity politics are going to be hard to keep going if we limit ourselves to these terms of discussion: implicitly, Sedgwick has said that a gay man who insists on the centrality to his psychic and social being of his homosexuality has just reiterated an *antigay* definitional move.

All of these elements of *Epistemology of the Closet* were part of a complex detachment of queer from gay politics. More controversial within feminism was Sedgwick's argument for suspending gender. Note that she doesn't understand gender as embodied domination and submission (MacKinnon) or as a list of traits and ethical capacities (cultural feminism), but as a *distinction*. It is, moreover, a *diacritical* distinction: the meaning of "male" depends on its not being "female," and the meaning of "female" depends on its not being "male"—just as a green light doesn't mean anything by itself but depends, to say "go," on *not being* a red light. And she suggests that referring all discussion of sexuality to what she calls the "diacritical frontier between different genders. . . . gives heterosocial and heterosexual relations a conceptual privilege of incalculable consequence" (31). That is, to insist that gender tell the whole story of sexuality is to presuppose that sexuality is always already structured as heterosexuality. "It may be . . . that a damaging bias toward heterosocial or heterosexist assumptions inheres unavoidably in the very concept of gender" (31). An antihomophobic inquiry could not want that.

Inasmuch as Sedgwick thinks of feminism as dedicated to gender, then, she is saying that feminism may be foundationally and definitionally biased toward heterosocial and heterosexist assumptions.

That's serious.

❦ *Judith Butler,* Gender Trouble

The same year that Sedgwick published *Epistemology of the Closet*, Judith Butler published *Gender Trouble*. In *Gender Trouble* Butler makes the very same point that Sedgwick made in *Epistemology of the Closet*, that any feminism devoted to analyzing gender in terms of a male/female distinction affirmed heterosexuality as a primary concept. Compulsory heterosexuality produces not only heterosexuals, but also men and women: "The institution of a compulsory and naturalized heterosexuality requires and regulates gender as a binary relation in which the masculine term is differentiated from a feminine term, and this differentiation is accomplished through the practices of heterosexual desire" (22–23). Feminism that accepts the binary structure of gender helps to naturalize and mandate heterosexuality.

So far, Butler's formulation resembles Sedgwick's. But she turns back to Rubin's distinction in "Traffic in Women," between sex1 and gender, and pursues a critique of the very idea that there are women:

> Is the construction of the category of women as a coherent and stable subject an unwitting regulation and reification of gender relations? And is not such a reification precisely contrary to feminist aims? (5)

Crucially unlike Rubin and Sedgwick, Butler declined to respond to the problem of feminism's definitional heterosexuality by bracketing gender and suspending feminism. Instead, she insisted that, however powerfully the male/female distinction subtends heterosexuality, it was inescapable—both for people existing in the world, and for feminism. It was an infliction—a law—that one was doomed to repeat again, and again, and again, whether in becoming a girl or a woman, or in becoming a boy or a man, or in loving people who were becoming boys or girls or women or men.

Thus though Butler's work should be reassuring for feminism in some ways—it insists that we should develop feminism rather than seek an understanding of sexuality outside of it—it should also be (and has been) quite disconcerting. The very existence of women depends on the male/female distinction and thus dooms women to a dependence on the existence of men; the very infu-

sion of parental love and erotic desire into that matrix dooms all
subjects to the loss of same-sex parental intimacy and same-sex
adult sexual love; the very subject of feminism—women—commits it to struggle with an internal affirmation of the priority of
heterosexuality in our conceptual and social orders. The seemingly natural occurrence of women emerges in Butler's formulation as the problem to which feminism must address itself.

Butler urged feminism to develop ways to assail the category
of "women." In a utopian world, one would burn down gender.
But inasmuch as Butler regarded that as impossible—no more
than MacKinnon could she imagine life outside its terms—feminism should promote *gender trouble.* And how could gender be
troubled? We can't not repeat it, but we could seek to repeat it
wrong. And she sought that not because she thought that the law
of gender restricts both men and women to certain gender traits
from which they should be free to deviate, but because if we repeat gender wrong—classically, in *Gender Trouble,* if we engage
in drag—we might reveal that gender produces the illusion that
male and female bodies exist in nature and are our bodies and in
some legitimate or inevitable way set the terms for our introit into
sexuality (and thus dedicate us teleologically to heterosexuality).

Revealing the fictional status of gender doesn't make it unreal
or less of a law, but it does open up room for what Foucault
thought of as resistance or practices of freedom (typically described in *Gender Trouble* as subversion). Feminism should thus
apply all its corrosive powers not to male dominance but to sex1
itself. If Sedgwick liberated gay-positive and queer theory from
feminism, setting up the conditions for their antagonism, Butler
set feminism against its own defining dyad, introducing the antagonism into feminism itself. *Gender Trouble* and *Epistemology
of the Closet* are thus queer theoretic (and Foucaultian) in much
the same way, but *Gender Trouble* maps the possibility of *feminist*
queer theory.

✂ Butler/MacKinnon

It may be helpful at this point to check in once again with Mac-Kinnon's thought. For MacKinnon, male dominance lines male/female sex1 up with male/female sex2 to produce sexuality, which is (surprise!) the eroticization of male domination. Sex1—the bodily truth of men's difference from women—is, for all we know (we who have no way out of sexuality as male dominance), a fiction. But since the problem is the eroticization of male dominance, the early MacKinnon didn't need to know whether sex1 is a natural given or an effect of male dominance. For Butler, however, it is centrally problematic that the law of gender stipulates male/female sex1 as the ground upon which it operates and the foundation whence it launches elaborate regulations of desire. Thus, while for MacKinnon nothing much turns on the question whether male and female bodies exist in nature, for Butler the materiality and inevitability of sex1 figured as a rigid duality is possibly the crucial ruse of the law of gender:

> Gender ought not to be conceived merely as the cultural inscription of meaning on a pregiven sex (a juridical conception); gender must also designate the very apparatus of production whereby the sexes themselves are established. As a result, gender is not to culture as sex is to nature; gender is also the discursive/cultural means by which "sexed nature" or "a natural sex" is produced and established as "prediscursive," prior to culture, a politically neutral surface *on which* culture acts. (7)

Dislodging sex1 from nature might also produce mobilities in the gaps between sex1 and sex2, sex2 and desire, any of those and gender, and all the above and sexual orientation:

> Gender can denote a *unity* of experience, of sex, gender, and desire, only when sex [I think she means sex1] can be under-

stood in some sense to necessitate gender—where gender is a psychic and/or cultural designation of the self—and desire—where desire is heterosexual and therefore differentiates itself through an oppositional relation to that other gender it desires. The internal coherence or unity of either gender, man or woman, thereby requires both a stable and oppositional heterosexuality. That institutional heterosexuality both requires and produces the univocity of each of the gendered terms that constitute the limit of gendered possibilities within an oppositional, binary gender system. (22)

Thus, for MacKinnon, sex1, sex2, gender, and sexuality become rigidly homologous because they all take the form of female submission and male dominance; for Butler it is the rigid homology, and the practices which ground them all in sex1, that are the problem. That is to say, Butler's *feminism* objects to MacKinnon's formulation of gender as *itself* (with many other things, of course) constitutive of women's oppression. Butler is deeply involved here in developing a Foucaultian feminism, and so it makes sense that she performs at this point the turn we derived from *Volume One*: in her critique of m/f, she detects in feminism the capacity to produce the reality of women's domination by men. And not accidentally, gender trouble as a tactic within sexuality envisioned as the field of power seeks not a liberation or overthrow but a mode of temporal engagement much like Foucault's "practices of freedom."

❦ Butler, "Imitation"

Butler's characteristic vocabulary for describing this tactic—and engagements with other discursive powers as well—sounds in *(re)iteration*. In an essay published the year after *Gender Trouble* and contemplating the problem not of "woman" but of "lesbian," Butler offered what is by now one of the canonical queer critiques of identity. In "Imitation and Gender Insubordination," she cannily refused to tie the overnight crescendo of excitement and even adulation that greeted *Gender Trouble* to gay-identity politics (which had moved very promptly and vigorously to appropriate it), asking instead what it would mean to "theorize as a lesbian":

> I'm permanently troubled by identity categories, consider them to be invariable stumbling blocks, and understand them, even promote them, as sites of necessary trouble. (14)

Noting that any gesture of "coming out"—by ostensibly clarifying the identity of its performer and liberating her from darkness and enclosure—instantly implies a new spatial zone to be "in," a new regulated domain, and a new set of strictures for the self, Butler construes lesbian identity as fully dependent on its erasure: "For being 'out' always depends to some extent on being 'in'; it gains its meaning only within that polarity" (16). The dynamic in which identity grounds itself on a reiteration that both *repeats* and *deviates from* its original belongs not only to the identity "lesbian" but to heterosexuality.

In "Imitation" Butler is preoccupied with the dismissive charge that homosexuality is a pale imitation of the valid sexual orientation, its "opposite," compulsory heterosexuality. She gradually flips this disauthorizing etiology without making the gay-identity-affirmative move that would authorize homosexuality. Rather, both heterosexuality and homosexuality, in their mutually reiterative embrace, reveal themselves to be no more authentic than drag (actually, to be nothing other than drag). The "first" step goes like this:

> As a young person, I suffered for a long time, and I suspect many people have, from being told, explicitly or implicitly,

that what I "am" is a copy, an imitation, a derivative example, a shadow of the real. Compulsory heterosexuality sets
itself up as the original, the true, the authentic; the norm
that determines the real implies that "being" lesbian is always a kind of miming, a vain effort to participate in the
phantasmatic plenitude of naturalized heterosexuality which
will always and only fail. (20)

And so compulsory heterosexuality repeats itself and is ultimately
in that sense no different from lesbian identity:

[T]he naturalistic effects of heterosexualized genders are
produced through imitative strategies; what they imitate is
a phantasmatic ideal of heterosexual identity, one that is
produced by the imitation as its effect. In this sense, the
'reality' of heterosexual identities is performatively constituted through an imitation that sets itself up as the original
and the ground of all imitations. In other words, heterosexuality is always in the process of imitating and approximating
its own phantasmatic idealization of itself—and *failing*. (21)

Imitation repeats and is therefore *not* the same. And so if lesbianism incorporates in itself heterosexual norms, it does not dupli-
cate but perverts them: "*imitation* does not copy that which is
prior, but produces and *inverts* the very terms of priority and
derivativeness" (22). This is why Butler finds lesbian identity to
be a stumbling block that she would promote; why she persistently insists on the subversive *and* reinstitutive effects of imitative performances (they "reiterate and . . . oppose" (17)); why she
sees gay and lesbian performativity as both a "recapitulation of
straightness" and "a site in which all sorts of resignifying and
parodic repetitions become possible" (23); and why the "need for
repetition" compels identity "to be instituted again and again,
which is to say that it runs the risk of becoming *de*instituted at
every interval" (22).

Lest this seem completely abstruse, perhaps we should contextualize the argument in the very intense, even sometimes searing conflict that flared up in the late 1980s and early 1990s between sexual-subordination feminists, on one hand, and pro-sex feminists and the producers of queer theory (feminist and non-), on the other. This period saw a dramatic burst of interest in lesbian sadomasochism, frequently construed as a set of practices that women could fully share with gay men; the emergence of a politics of acts; and a strong resurgence of very "gender-y"[21] lesbian styles, particularly a celebration of the butch/femme relationships of the pre-Stonewall era and a reinvigoration of masculine and feminine gender play between women who were having sex with each other. *Gender Trouble* was the bible for this movement, even and perhaps especially "on the street." Power feminists and cultural feminists resisted: the former understood these developments in sex-positive feminism as a fully reactionary embrace of the eroticization of male dominance; cultural feminists saw them as a morally defective reproduction of masculinity by the very people best situated to elide the male and the masculine altogether. Feminism was splitting up and transforming itself from within.

In this conflict, Butler's theory of imitation took sides. When she extended the concept of (re)iteration from lesbian identity to *gender,* she produced a virtually complete reversal of MacKinnon's formulation:

[S]exuality may be said to exceed any definitive narrativization. Sexuality is never fully "expressed" in a performance or practice; there will be passive and butchy femmes, femmy and aggressive butches, and both of those, and more, will turn out to describe more or less anatomically stable "males" and "females." *There are no direct expressive or causal lines between sex, gender, gender presentation, sexual practice, fan-*

tasy and sexuality. None of those terms captures or determines the rest. (25, emphasis added)

For MacKinnon, power organizes male/female sex1, male/female sex2 to produce gender, which is the existence of women as dominated and men as dominant, and sexuality, which is the eroticization of this highly stable binarized pattern. For Butler, by contrast, power is deployed in the *unstable* and *fractured* relationships among the same elements. It is highly distinctive of queer theory to insist on the possibility for slippage between "sex, gender, gender presentation, sexual practice, fantasy and sexuality." Whereas for MacKinnon power is a top-down affair, for Butler it has the mobility of Foucault's *micropouvoir*. But while in *Volume One* Foucault sought out a number of highly incommensurable discourses—the hysterization of women, the psychiatrization of perversions, and so forth—to characterize the invention of sexuality, Butler returns repeatedly to pairs: masculine and feminine, heterosexual and homosexual, male and female bodies, original and copy, rule and subversion. In a way, Butler gives us Foucault's "practices of freedom" played out in the tight constraints of a dazzlingly complex series of nested, deconstructively mobile binarisms committed to m/f.

Butler's idea that feminism should devote itself to troubling gender has been accused of "paralyzing" feminism by putting its organizing feature—woman—in crisis. Assuming that's what it did, "Imitation" would pass the virus to gay-identity politics. But seen from a Foucaultian perspective, her theory insists on the ample range and perpetual openness of political engagement. And it critically engaged as well with the dimension of the late MacKinnon that *knows* the reality of women. The very knowledge effect that MacKinnon produces, Butler implies, *is the problem.*

Thus there is a warning in Butler's argument, much like the one Foucault issued when he intimated that the idea of liberating "our sex" may be a terrible trap. Fully occupying sex1, sexual identity, and gender may be precisely the recipe for a new institutionalization of compulsory heterosexuality:

> Although compulsory heterosexuality often presumes that there is first a sex [that would be sex1] that is expressed through a gender and then through a sexuality [here, "sexual orientation, gay or straight"], it may now be necessary fully to invert and displace that operation of thought. . . . It may be that the very categories of sex, of sexual identity, of gender are produced or maintained in the *effects* of this compulsory performance, effects which are disingenuously renamed as causes, origins, disingenuously lined up within a causal or expressive sequence that the heterosexual norm produces to legitimate itself as the origin of all sex. How then to expose the causal lines as retrospectively and performatively produced fabrications? Perhaps this will be a matter of working sexuality *against identity*, **even against gender**, and of letting that which cannot fully appear in any performance persist in its disruptive promise. (29, italics in original; bold emphasis added)

Here Butler almost puts her foot on the track taken by Sedgwick: in imagining sexuality deployed *against* gender, she suggests that it might be subversive to step outside the characteristic language of feminism altogether. As we will see, she was soon to refuse this opportunity and to insist instead that feminism, with its distinctive analytic purchase on gender, must remain the domain in which to "work sexuality against identity, even against gender." Let us assume that is the stance we should attribute to the Butler of "Imitation" as well. The feminist queer politics she recommends—and we could do it in bed, as a man or as a woman, with men or women, or through intellectual work, or through activism of every kind—would work to reveal the fabricated quality of our most profound sexual givens, the very ideas that our bodies are sexed, have sexual orientations, are gendered. She asks us to experience the most social and the most isolating dimension of our humanity—our eroticism—not though but *against* these supposed givens. And I think it is precisely because of the deconstructive element in her thought that she can cancel Foucault's effort to transcend sexuality through bodies and pleasures: instead, we comply *and* resist by repeating with a difference.

❦ *Rubin,* "Interview"

In the "*Interview*" with Judith Butler first published in 1994, Rubin recalls that she wrote "Thinking Sex" both to contest several trends in feminist theory and politics that I've been describing as inessential to feminism; and also to propose that theory and politics about sexuality might have to Take a Break from Feminism even minimally defined in order to articulate certain related but distinct, equally urgent, projects. This retrospection, written after many sequelae of the Rubin/Butler/Sedgwick nexus had been elaborated, adds two further alternative approaches to those already put in place.

In the "*Interview*" Rubin recalls from a distance of ten years several projects that she had been seeking to contest *within* feminism: the ascendency of feminist antipornography activism, including MacKinnon's variant (77) and its alliance with a strong, new-right effort to repress gay male public sex (78); the feminist move that Rubin recalls that she unlearned with some dismay, in which women's prostitution exemplifies women's oppression (79–80); the ascendency, under the aegis of Rich's "Compulsory Heterosexuality," of a feminist understanding of lesbianism as fully defined by female solidarity and female/female sentimental affectivity (as opposed to carnal, erotic, sex2-saturated engage-

ments) (80–82); feminist condemnation of gay male sexual culture—"drag and cross-dressing, gay public sex, gay male promiscuity, gay male masculinity, gay leather, gay fist-fucking, gay
cruising, and just about anything else gay men did" and anything
else in lesbianism that resembled them—as exemplary, again, of
male domination; and feminist condemnation of "perversion,
sexual deviance, sexual variance, or sexual diversity"—"[t]ran-
sexuality, male homosexuality, public sex, tranvestism, fetishism,
and sadomasochism"—as the same. "Somehow, these poor sexual
deviations were suddenly the ultimate expression of patriarchal
domination" (83). But she also remembered a number of emergent projects relating to sexuality that were not indigenous to
feminism—projects that Rubin understood to have emerged
from outside it and to have found articulation without reference
to it—which she wanted to participate in and develop: the critical
impact of *Volume One* (78, 91); the emergence of a political and
theoretical literature about gay male sexuality that "evaluated gay
male sexual behavior in its own terms, rather than appealing to
feminism for either justification or condemnation" (83); within
that project the emerging possibility that masculinity could undergo sexual subordination without being transformed into femininity (103); and an emergent sense that the erotics and politics
attending sexual practices, and the existence of "diverse sexual
content" in the political surround of sexual politics (72), required
distinct articulation.

Rubber, leather, fetish, sadomasochism—these were under oppression. Rubin invoked them in her 1994 "*Interview*," as she had
in "Thinking Sex," as subordinated. But she added something in
the 1994 interview that was not evident in "Thinking Sex": an
interest in the "ethnogenesis" of social forms to create the social
nexus—especially the urban nexus—for the continuing elaboration of sexual practices: "I want to know about the topograph*ies*
and political econom*ies* of erotic signification" (101, 85, emphases

added). This framing presupposes not domination and subordination, but ongoing social productivity across an open-ended frontier of social possibilities. It is receptive to an understanding of power much more like Foucault's than like MacKinnon's.

Rubin's "*Interview*" also deviates from Sedgwick's and Butler's motives for placing critical pressure on the essential status of m/f in feminism. Recall that, for Sedgwick, one reason to attempt a study of gay male sexuality from outside feminism was that "[i]t may well be . . . that a damaging bias toward heterosocial or heterosexist assumptions inheres unavoidably in the very concept of gender";[22] and that for Butler the reinscription of heteronormative assumptions by the feminist insistence on m/f was an important reason to turn feminism toward its own internal critique. These formulations left an important question on the table: to what extent should either project posit that the heterosexual *is* heterosexist. Rubin's 1994 articulation of her motive silently declined to engage this question; but it also offered a motive that significantly routes her project away from its implicit subordination-model normativity. For her, by then, the *binary form* of m/f—not its complicity with heterosexual supremacy—was its weakness; in that way it was no different from the hetero/homo presumption of pro-gay argumentation; and the problem they both posed for continuing sexual politics was not normative but conceptual. Feminism's commitment to m/f, and the pro-gay political commitment to "a simple hetero-homo opposition" (76), advance hypotheses that take binary form over others that might provide other hypothetical resources for the social study of "sexual practices":

> I think these binary models seemed to work better for gender, because our usual understandings posit gender as in some ways binary; even the continuums of gender differences often seem structured by a primary binary opposition.

> But as soon as you get away from the presumptions of het-
> erosexuality, or a simple hetero-homo opposition, differ-
> ences in sexual conduct are not very intelligible in terms of
> binary models. Even the notion of a continuum is not a good
> model for sexual variations; one needs one of those mathe-
> matical models they do now with strange topologies and
> convoluted shapes. (76–77)

That is, not only are there topics in the sociology of sexual life
that do not seem assimilable to m/f or homo/hetero; the very
presumption of binarized difference that m/f and homo/hetero
both bring with them backgrounds, at the moment of framing
exploratory hypotheses, *other* framings of difference that might
make visible *other* distributions of power. Once again, Rubin's
thinking by 1994 had moved from MacKinnon's focus on group
dominance and subordination, toward an interest in social forms
more like those imaginable under the rubric of Foucault's idea of
biopower.

To see the stakes of Rubin's shift in her 1994 interview with
Butler, consider, finally, this objection to it offered by Butler and
published in the same volume:

> If sexuality is conceived as liberated from gender, then the
> sexuality that is "liberated" from feminism will be one which
> suspends the reference to masculine and feminine, reenforc-
> ing the refusal to mark that difference, *which is the conven-*
> *tional way in which the masculine has achieved the status of*
> *the "sex" which is one.* (23, emphasis added)

Unlike Rubin, Butler remains committed to a queered *feminism.*
The binary of gender remains primary; to fail to mark it is to
reproduce it under the sign of its erasure, *and that is precisely to*
reinstate the conditions of a masculinist consciousness and thus to
reproduce and ratify male dominance. m/f, m > f, and carrying a
brief for f.

Oddly enough, MacKinnon could have said exactly the same thing.[23]

Feminism from Its Outside: Queer Theory by Men

What is possible in left work on sexuality that does not accept feminism as its overarching rubric? To explore this question I examine, in this section, two interventions by men into the feminist/postmodernist/gay/queer debate about how to theorize sexuality. I have selected them because they both borrow from and struggle with feminism but ultimately are not feminist. Both have been crucial in my own evolving understanding of what a "queer theoretic" project, especially one involved with the state, might look like. In the following pages I'll try to spell out (as I have been trying to do for forms of feminism) exactly where these projects depend on, and exactly where they depart from, feminism, and to count up the analytic openings that the departures produce.

I've selected two otherwise quite different texts, one anticipating *Epistemology of the Closet* and *Gender Trouble* by three years, the other published two years after their appearance and everywhere showing the marks of a serious encounter with *Gender Trouble*. Both were written specifically from the point of view of male authors who insist on their sexual interests in the face of feminist denunciation; the homologies between them are even more remarkable given the facts that one articulates a gay male, the other a heterosexual male, sex-positive position, and that one is structured around a crisis in normativity while the other reveals a crisis in decision. I am referring of course to Leo Bersani's 1987 essay "Is the Rectum a Grave?" and Duncan Kennedy's 1992 article "Sexual Abuse, Sexy Dressing, and the Eroticization of Domination." The former is widely read as canonical queer theory;

the latter is—sorry, folks!—the only sophisticated *legal* analysis of American sexual regulation that I am tempted to call queer.

🍒 *Leo Bersani, "Is the Rectum a Grave?"*

In "Is the Rectum a Grave?" Bersani reconfigured Stonewall-era gay male sexual liberation for the era of gay-male AIDS.[24] He asked gay men whether their exposure—at the time overwhelmingly distinctive—to the epidemic would lead them in the direction of gay-identity liberalism—marriage, monogamy, and equality as equal respect—or back to the bathhouse. Gay male thinking faced a split in the road before it: it could disavow or find new affirmations of male/male promiscuity, what Bersani would later call male "love of the cock,"[25] gay men's yearning for male/male anal sodomy, and the peculiarly intense new association of sex with death. Bersani urged the second, sex-affirmative option.

In affirming sex, however, Bersani performed an unusually strong-minded embrace of abjection. The essay begins[26] with angry reflections on the intense homophobic mobilization against gay men that attended the early years of the AIDS epidemic in the United States (it is helpful to remember that people seriously proposed "chemical castration" and quarantine of gay men to protect "the general population" from the virus), and finds both in them *and* in gay male sexual desire a homophobic and misogynist association of gay male anal receptivity with female sexual subordination. Bersani is interested to show that, in misogyny, in anti-gay-male homophobia, *and* in gay male erotic longing, the vagina and the anus are figured as sexually insatiable and as animated erotically by a desire for annihilation. He observes an agreement between Foucault, who at one point, *Volume One* notwithstanding, affirmed that "[m]en think that women can only experience pleasure in recognizing men as masters," and

MacKinnon, who decried "the male supremacist definition of female sexuality as lust for self-annihilation."[27] He then adds his own affirmation that this lust is an aspect of gay male eroticism. In these moves, Bersani takes MacKinnon's gay-male-feminization argument to fever pitch.[28] He fully accepts—as a *pro-gay-male description* of "the hygienics of social power"—the proposition that "*[t]o be penetrated is to abdicate power*" (212).

That acceptance manifests a decided appetite for paradox and the problematic. Bersani admires in MacKinnon's thought precisely her "indictment against sex itself" (214). He treasures in her work a capacity to hold the power in sex2 under a steady, unblinking gaze:

> [MacKinnon and Dworkin in their antipornography analysis and activism] have given us the reasons why pornography must be multiplied and not abandoned, and, more profoundly, the reasons for defending, for cherishing the very sex they find so hateful. Their indictment of sex—their refusal to prettify it, to romanticize it, to maintain that fucking has anything to do with community or love—has had the immensely desirable effect of publicizing, of lucidly laying out for us, the inestimable value of sex as—at least in certain of its ineradicable aspects—anticommunal, antiegalitarian, antinurturing, antiloving.[29]

What could Bersani be thinking? How could one have a normative vision of human life (or any part of it) that *wants it to be* "anticommunal, antiegalitarian, antinurturing, antiloving"?

The argument is both descriptive and prescriptive, and I will attempt to lay it out as if these were distinct parts, even though the essay does not distinguish them. The descriptive argument has wonderful simplicity. Bersani claims that we all already do have such a vision, that it animates an important part of our erotic desires, that it cuts sex2 off from politics-as-usual in a deeply radical way, and that we shouldn't shoot the messenger. To anchor this argument, Bersani draws from Freud the idea that the very possibility of human selfhood emerges in the "shifting experience that every human being has of his or her body's capacity, or failure, to control and to manipulate the world beyond the self" (216). And it runs even deeper than that: the "human being" who aspires to a relationship of control over "the world beyond the self" experiences "his or her body" as ambiguously the self and/or the world: "the sexual . . . involv[es] . . . the source and locus of every individual's original experience of power (and of powerlessness) in the world: the human body" (221). Sexuality broadly conceived is a special domain of human experience, one in which a profoundly inchoate, constitutive, infantile, but inescapable narrative of the unstable wish for both mastery and dissolution is continually in play, never subject to closure. And in it the penis has a distinctive symbolic relation to mastery. It does not bestow mastery on men—far from it; "the idea of penis envy describes how men feel about having one" (216)—but rather presents, for gay male and heterosexual interactions at least, a bodily correlate especially capable of representing (perhaps sometimes by mocking) the desire of every self for mastery over the body and of every embodied self for mastery over the world.

And yet (or should I say, perhaps, "and so"?) there is also dissolution, and that is a distinctive part of sexual experience. The "*jouissance* of exploded limits," the deep savoring of "that sexual pleasure [which] occurs whenever a certain threshold of intensity is reached, when the organization of the self is momentarily disturbed by sensations or affective processes somehow 'beyond' those connected with psychic organization"—for Bersani these are so characteristic of the orgasmic aim that he is led to propose that "[s]exuality . . . may be a tautology for masochism" (217). It is precisely phallocentrism that has engineered discursive limits which make it almost impossible for our publicly respectable selves to do anything with that last sentence but disavow it:

> Phallocentrism is ... not primarily the denial of power to women (although it has obviously also led to that, everywhere and at all times) but above all the denial of the *value* of powerlessness in both men and women. I don't mean the value of gentleness, or nonaggressiveness, or even of passivity, but rather of a more radical disintegration and humiliation of the self. (217)

Obviously this argument depends heavily on and to some extent reenacts strongly structuralist feminist theories of the eroticization of m/f and m > f. Most explicitly, Bersani lays hold of MacKinnon as to a lifeline. On sexuality, on dominance, and on desire, he is MacKinnon all over again: he fully embraces her theory of sexuality *as* power, and as constitutive of the self not through the modalities of Kantian subjectivity but through and as sheer domination; he pushes us back to her early idea that in the eroticization of domination we experience the unspeakable thrill of encountering our own metaphysical and experiential dissolution. He does not see *gender* in anything like the same way, however: the strong link he draws between the penetrable vagina and the penetrable anus leaves implicit one feature of gay male sex2 that escapes MacKinnon's resentful analysis of gay male eroticism: for Bersani the "love of the cock" (the cock that one has, that one wishes one had, that that man over there has or might have) simply never goes away. And MacKinnon is a subordination-theory structuralist throughout her work, early and late, whereas for Bersani the project is to fracture the structural totalism of her *descriptio* and, picking among the pieces, to redeem for euphoria some of the most apparently irredeemably dysphoric elements of her sexual world. I have been tempted to say Bersani "flips" MacKinnon's social/normative vision, but, because of this fracturing, his procedure is something more akin to bricolage.[30] Still, within that fractured frame, we could say Bersani offers us a classic example of the "perverse" in queer argumentation: there is a peculiar torque, a strong and nasty reversal, in Bersani's agreement that phallocentrism is a social calamity because it blocks *men's* access to the "humiliation of the self" *enjoyed* by women.[31] But even if fragmentary and self-consciously paradoxical, his affirmation of MacKinnon's feminist analysis of the eroticization of domination always reverses (and thus reveals) a normative judgment: not bad but good.

Though initially, therefore, "Is the Rectum a Grave?" seems utterly opposed to and "outside" cultural feminism—one of the pleasures of reading it, for me, is imagining the indignation and offense it probably arouses in cultural-feminist readers—it does repeat the central move of cultural-feminist moralism. There is something good in sex, something that has been devalued, and the reform project is to revalue it back "up"—if not "over" the currently triumphal but "bad" value, at least "equal" to it. That is, cultural feminism and Bersani are engaged in serious combat over the value of degradation and human erasure in sex: cultural feminism says they have been overvalued because they have been allocated exclusively to women; Bersani replies that they have been vastly undervalued through their association with women. But they agree, it seems, that the combat is waged on the field of "value"—a field that MacKinnon pushed over and beyond the horizon of her understanding.

Is there anything left that is "not feminist" in Bersani's invocation of sexual erasure? I can think of two things. First, "Is the Rectum a Grave?" intervenes in a specifically *gay male* political crisis, to push interests that are not necessarily those of women, gay or straight. These are the interests of gay men: on their behalf, Bersani reproached Foucault for leaching gay male identity of its sexual specificity. It really does matter for Bersani whether one is

a man or a woman, gay or straight; this is not because these identities are a source of authenticity and dignity, but because they
provide distinctive inroads into the dissolution of the very self
that would bear them.[32] Thus although Bersani concedes that
male masculinity may be "socially determined," he insists that it
is nevertheless of crucial importance to the projects of male sexual
desire and, even more to the point, of male/male sexual desire
(209); it provides for men a peculiarly intense vocabulary in
which to seek the frenzy of dissolution. So "Is the Rectum a
Grave?" Takes a Break from Feminism in the everyday political
sense that it is not primarily "for" women.

Nevertheless, as we have seen, at every crucial turn its theory of
sexuality is claimed for "men *and* women" (222). We have already
encountered the virtual equation, in his psychic economy of dissolution, of the gay male anus with the heterosexual female vagina. Gay men, and men generally, have full psychic and political
access to the abjection in sexuality that feminists attribute (Bersani would say, with veracity, and enviably) to women (though
men reach it through broken denial and women through denied
appetite), because access to that abjection is a distinctive virtue of
sexuality generally. He conversely also insists that women, heterosexual men, and gay men too, have access to the will to dominate
that introduces the self into its being. The crux of the theory—
one he derives from his most important nonfeminist theoretic
source, Freud—seems to be the infantile psyche confronting not
a sexed or gendered body but "the" body as an object of erotically
crucial but unsustainable mastery, and the embodied self confronting "the world" with the same anxious need. "[T]he sexual
. . . involv[es] . . . the source and locus of *every individual's* original experience of power (and of powerlessness) in the world: *the
human body*" (221, emphasis added). In this narrative gender is
temporally and analytically secondary; primacy is given to a complex string of mobile dyads including at least self/body, embodied

self/outside world, mastery/dissolution, and existence/annihilation; and annihilation through the anus or the vagina is annihilation still. This formulation definitely Takes a Break from Feminism in the sense that it stakes sexuality to something *other than* male/female difference.

My exposition of Bersani's argument thus far has limited itself to its affirmation of a shamed desire and a shamed pleasure because they *are* a desire and a pleasure: implicitly, he's arguing, "We desire it, and love it when we get it, so it's good." But Bersani goes further, to lay out a moral politics that *justifies* this desire. This will seem paradoxical to readers familiar with the essay, because in one sense Bersani offers a dark view of the value of sexual desire precisely in order to renounce any possibility of its smooth incorporation into liberal politics and into subordination-theory identity politics of all kinds (feminist, gay, and race-based). In this Bersani is an extreme divergentist, insisting that the form and value of power in sexual abjection are unique to it, nonhomologous to and analytically nontransferrable to other forms of power. The central goal of "Is the Rectum a Grave?"—as Bersani persistently notes—is to figure out "the extremely obscure process by which sexual pleasure *generates* politics" (208). Gay-subordination theories of the sexual he rejects precisely for their convergentism. He is particularly anxious to scotch gay utopian dreams that "sexual inequalities are predominantly, perhaps exclusively, displaced social inequalities" (220): because sexual experience is primordially about the struggle of the self for mastery over the body and the world, it cannot derive its paradoxes of power from the social subordinations, "as if . . . [it] were, so to speak, belatedly contaminated by power from elsewhere" (221).

Bersani thus argues that the power which infuses sexuality is quite discontinuous with social power of the sort emphasized in left multicultural subordination theories. The dark side of sexual experience, especially perhaps male/male sexual experience, *is dif-*

ferent. He takes it as evident that blacks as a group, women as a group, and the poor as a group are socially subordinated to whites, men, and those with material means; he affirms as his own the normative ambition to resist these social hierarchies. But he carefully unperforms what has become a classic convergentist trope, of asserting that he writes on behalf of sexual minorities implicitly "like" blacks, women, and the poor and thus is smoothly solidarized with them. In the course of this refusal he achieves an unusually high number of politically incorrect bons mots: far from serving as an example of "Whitmanesque democracy," gay male bathhouses are (were?) "one of the most ruthlessly ranked, hierarchized, and competitive environments imaginable" (206); the parody of women and femininity that pervades gay male camp, far from subverting gender norms, is "a way of giving vent to the hostility toward women that probably afflicts every male" (208). Male homosexual pleasure does not track directly into antisubordination politics: "To want sex with another man is not exactly a credential for political radicalism"; AIDS surprised gay men, the vast majority of whom otherwise expected to live their lives "without modifying one bit their proud middle-class consciousness or even their racism." In suggesting otherwise "we have been telling a few lies" (205–6).

Instead, Bersani forces to its limit the split between the social and the sexual:

> "AIDS," [Simon] Watney writes, "offers a new sign for the symbolic machinery of repression, making the rectum a grave." But if the rectum is the grave in which the masculine ideal (an ideal shared—differently—by men *and* women) of proud subjectivity is buried, then it should be celebrated for its very potential for death.[33]

Wow—the rectum—it's *dark* in there. So dark that Bersani launches a critique of Foucault and MacKinnon for being too sunny! In MacKinnon's utter and complete disaffirmation of the power that constitutes male dominance, female submission, and their subsumption in and as the sexual, Bersani sees an implicit affirmation of sex without it: "What bothers me about MacKinnon and Dworkin is not their analysis of sexuality, but rather the pastoralizing, redemptive intentions that support the analysis" (215). And he rejects Foucault's "bodies and pleasures" ambitions as no less pastoral, recommending instead an enthusiastic plunge into the specific intensities of those eroticized parts of the body— especially the penis, anus, and vagina—from which Foucault wished to "untie" sexuality (215, 219–20). I think Bersani here misses the horizonlessness of male dominance in MacKinnon's *Signs* articles, the critique of consciousness there, in sum the radicalness of the theory (though he would be right if the only MacKinnon on offer were the late MacKinnon); and also misses the procedural, almost heuristic, quality of the "bodies and pleasures" agenda suggested by Foucault in his own deep critique of consciousness at the end of *Volume One* (though he rightly captures Foucault in some quite complacent formulations published in the gay press).

That is to say, I don't really think that what's bugging Bersani at this point is usefully attributable to Foucault and MacKinnon. Much more plausibly the pastoralizing models of sexuality he's concerned about come from the gay-identity project in its cultural-feminist mode. There and in some early-sex-wars defenders of lesbian sadomasochistic sex, Bersani locates "a hidden agreement about sexuality as being, in its essence, less disturbing, less socially abrasive, less violent, more respectful of 'personhood' than it has been in a male-dominated, phallocentric culture" (215).

The flip side of Bersani's inattentiveness to the deeply critical stance that I think we find in the early MacKinnon and *Volume One* is his indifference to his own repetition of the basic argumentative trope of cultural-feminist gay-identity arguments, the argu-

ment that homosexual sexuality, however despised and subordinated, is actually a site of equal, possibly superior, *virtue*.
Bersani's essay pervasively argues in just this way. The shattered
self strives to capture political virtue, a paradoxical argumentative
trajectory that produces Bersani's feminism at its most sublime.
Here's how it happens.

The self-shattering that Bersani finds in our sexual intensities
is to be valued as a political project because it gestures to a state
of being in which the self/other structure of social life is suspended and the political will to dominate rendered inarticulate
and helpless. The social and the political inevitably involve domination or at least the struggle for it, but sexuality has a fleeting
existence prior to and free of them: "For it is perhaps primarily
*the degeneration of the sexual into a relationship that condemns
sexuality to becoming a struggle for power*" (218). Social power is
puissance, not pouvoir; bad, not neutral (or good); MacKinnon,
not Foucault (or Nietzsche). In seizing it, the self inserts itself
inescapably into the mutually constitutive pairing of purity and
brutality, virtue and sheer domination, arrogating one and alienating the other. Whereas we could try to see "[t]he self [as] . . .
a [mere] practical convenience," instead we allow it to be "promoted to the status of an ethical ideal, [where] it is a sanction for
violence" (222). The basic structure of this idea is deconstructive:
in the articulation of brutality through its opposite (purity), of
domination through its opposite (virtue), and vice versa, the self
makes itself both a moral force and a deadly one.

But as we have seen, that deadly force is precisely what Bersani
proposes we should grant his dark vision of sexual *jouissance* and
his own moral advocacy for it. He argues that the very self-respect
which, in liberal theory, is supposed to check social subordinations in the sexual domain—homophobia, misogyny, and sexual
moralism being his examples—actually produces them and every
form of power struggle. They can be traced not to mastery or

submission but to the self that would transcend its own relentless problematic. Sexual abjection with its momentary disorientation of the self offers to interrupt this generation of social dominance through the self, and constitutes a vast critique of political and social power. Indeed, gay male abjection is situated with enviable precision exactly at the nexus of masculinity and *heterosexism* and thus may offer redemption not only from homophobia but also from sexism:

> An authentic gay male political identity therefore implies a struggle not only against definitions of maleness and of homosexuality as they are reiterated and imposed in a heterosexist social discourse, but also against those very same definitions so seductively and so faithfully reflected by those (in large part culturally invented and elaborated) male bodies that we carry within us as permanently renewable sources of excitement. (209)

The claim is only ostensibly gay supremecist; more accurately it is abjection-supremacist and ultimately convergentist at the highest level. It bids to be a sweeping critique of social dominance, of which male dominance of women becomes only one example; and thus to be more feminist than feminism.

This explains why Bersani's critique of social violence does not undermine even a little his own deployment of social violence. His analysis of homophobia, racism, sexism, and pastoralism are full of certainties, moral denunciations, and mandatory affirmations. The convergence of the political with the moral becomes important early in the essay and introduces a certain cultural-feminist style of political antisubordination thinking.[34] The essay's moralistic violence begins early, as Bersani attempts to evade the strictly paradoxical implications of his delightful first line: "There is a big secret about sex: most people don't like it" (197). Later in the essay he will need all the paradoxical power of Freud's theory of the self, constituted in the tension between mastery and dissolution, to explain the aversion packed into desire. But here in the opening pages, Bersani attempts to distinguish benign from malignant aversion to sex: we should affirm our own dysphoric experience of sex, especially male/male homosexual sex, because it is benign; and condemn the social manifestation of it in antigay sentiment, because, although propositionally identical, the latter is malignant (198).

A more critical engagement with this problem would admit, I think, that the very distinction between benign and malignant is constitutive of sexual moralism and cannot be relied upon to resolve the problematics of shamed desire. But that is not Bersani's approach here. Instead, he proceeds as though, faced with the homophobia that animated "the general population" in the early days of the AIDS crisis, one can easily decide what to condemn and why: "morally, the only *necessary* response to all of this is rage" (201). Gay men in the HIV crisis are "[f]requently on the side of power, but powerless; frequently affluent, but politically destitute; frequently articulate, but with *nothing but a moral argument* . . . to keep themselves . . . out of the quarantine camps" (205). Bersani never actually articulates the moral argument, but the indignant urgency of his tone strongly suggests he doesn't have to because it's obvious. Implicit in this kind of argumentation is a threat: if you don't also already know the moral argument, you must be *very, very* antigay.

Bersani also collapses into a single monolithic oppression quite disparate and possibly distinguishable political events. (This would be a good time to recall the affiliation of moralism with convergentism in *The Combahee River Collective Statement.*) Bersani argues, for example, that, when federal public health officials proposed mandatory reporting and registration of the name of anyone who tested positive for HIV, they demonstrated that they "might not find the murder of a gay man with AIDS (or without

AIDS?) intolerable or unbearable"; and that makes them *just like* German citizens who, in the run-up to the Holocaust, "failed to find the idea of the holocaust unbearable"; and that makes mandatory registration of HIV-positive patients or, indeed, any other policy initiative regulating rather than benefiting the HIV-positive population *just like* the Holocaust: "by relegating the protection of people infected with HIV to local authorities, [officials] are telling those authorities that anything goes, that the federal government does not find the idea of camps—or worse—intolerable" (201–2, emphasis omitted). Let us leave aside the Holocaust analogy, which is a convergentist trope to be sure, but not exactly my focus just now. The thing I'm interested in is what Sharon Marcus called the "collapsed continuum," what Butler with a wicked twist called the *copula*,[35] within pro-gay-male argumentation. Along that axis, a policy decision to have local rather than federal officials decide HIV policy *is the same as* a policy decision to establish a registry (a federal one, we might note) listing people who test positive for HIV *is the same as* a willingness to murder an HIV-positive gay man *is the same as* a willingness to murder any gay man *is the same as* a willingness to put all gay men in camps and thus *is the same as* a willingness to kill them all in a genocidal paroxysm.

This instance sounds hectic today only because the panic that produced it has subsided: however maladroit it would now seem to deploy the copula in this way on behalf of American gay men, the trope is still very much in vogue in some feminist and some antiracist circles, and may even have migrated with HIV to Africa and Asia to affect some postcolonial discursive projects. Quite visibly, in retrospect, the copula here forgoes all the descriptive, political, and strategic advantages of dissolving rather than massifying and structuralizing oppression; and of imagining power in the social world, at least by hypothesis, to be as complex as it is in really good sadomasochistic sex.

What Bersani's political descriptions borrow from feminism, they also return to it, affirming representations of gender and power that, I have argued, were soon to be contested by sex-positive, sex-radical, postmodernizing, and queer feminisms (and that are not endorsed in *Homos*, where Bersani explicitly engaged Butler and Monique Wittig and their postmodernizing explosion of the female subject).[36] The main gesture here is to put outside the reach of critique not only subordination-theory, minoritizing framings of gay male existence in the AIDS crisis but similar representations of women's existence under male domination.[37] One form of it is what you might call an a priori gesture that "times" political subordination theory so that its conclusions have been reached *before* the present analysis begins: "I mention these [examples of malignant homophobia] . . . simply as a *reminder* of where our analytical inquiry *starts*" (199, emphasis added). Another is to state one's claims as obvious: it would "*of course* be obscene" to claim that gay men are more oppressed than poor blacks (204, emphasis added). With respect to women and feminism, this "obviousness" gesture produces an affirmation of the complete, wall-to-wall domination of women by men *as an assumption that is also true*: "the hostility towards women that probably afflicts every male (and which male heterosexuals have *of course* expressed in infinitely nastier and more effective ways)" (208, emphases added); phallocentrism, though "not primarily the denial of power to women[,] . . . has *obviously* also led to that, *everywhere and at all times*" (217, emphasis added); gay men should not imitate heterosexual monogamy, that "*unrelenting* warfare between men and women, *which nothing has ever changed*" (218, emphasis added).

Listening to that 1987 voice now, I have to say how glad I am that its social authority in left sexuality theory has been so substantially eroded.

That sense of relief, however, leaves me with a hard question. What *are* the politics of queer theory when they don't do these convergentist things? How could "Is the Rectum a Grave?" be rewritten today?

✄ Bersani/Taking a Break

My own idea is that the distinctively queer features of Bersani's paper—its willingness to affirm sexuality as carrying an appetite for deep threats to integrated selfhood, its willingness to lose touch with propositional ethical logic to do so, its plunge into a profoundly irresolvable problematic of desire, and its fragmentation not only of the self but of the gendered self—*can* be maintained in politically acute work.

In order to move, ever so tentatively, in the direction of this object, I'd like to extrapolate from the "queer" dimension of "Is the Rectum a Grave?" some representations of sex2, gender, and power that might lodge well under the descriptors "queer feminism" and "queer thought that Takes a Break from Feminism."

Queer feminism might claim, without *necessarily* denouncing or romanticizing it, to be the theory of women's subordination in the eroticization of domination. It might suspend normative judgment and merely descriptively insist that it's there. This could lead to a descriptive rereversal of gender: female masculinity could become just as crucial as the feminine abandon Bersani attributes to a gay man, "legs high in the air, unable to refuse the suicidal ecstasy of being a woman" (212)—oops, I mean, of being a gay man. The status of female femininity with respect to power could become quite uncertain; female masochism, furthermore, could be understood sometimes to be "on top." If this logic were part of lesbian sexual politics, it would necessarily involve an exploration of the degree to which female masculinity is drag or deadly serious. Perhaps even more so if it were part of heterosexual women's engagement with men. In either case, it might well contribute to the program for feminism that Butler sets out, in italics, in "Against Proper Objects": *"when and where feminism refuses to derive gender from sex or from sexuality, feminism appears to be part of the very critical practice that contests the heterosexual matrix."*[38] There would be some clear splits from MacKinnon and West: the attribution to women, as to men, of the psychic stamina to sustain experience this challenging could be deployed against the feminist and social conservative images of women as "always rapable," structurally vulnerable, and perpetually in need of some kind of protective custody. Whether the representation of women's relationship to power in sex would be uniformly "good for them" would be really hard to decide, however. So much would depend on so much.

Let's try the same thought experiment in a queer mode that Takes a Break from Feminism. Here, what is erotic is the confrontation of the self with its embodiment, with its will to power over and its ultimate lack of control over that object, the body—its pleasurable and frightening ability to wield itself as embodied to control the world, and the persistent fragility and reversability of that project (the world against the body, against the self). Both assertion and dissolution are compellingly familiar, mutually contingent, and constantly yielding to one another in the body's very capacity to experience itself as human. Gender is secondary, derivative, and (however highly useful as a vocabulary) definitive of exactly nothing in the tremulous project of the self. Indeed, if the implicit masochism of the orgasmic aim involves a will to be shattered, disoriented, erased, then gender could be one of the things that one lost track of. This hypothesis could help explain lots of things that don't make much sense under the descriptive mandates of sexual-subordination feminism of any kind: for example, the fact that masculinity *and* femininity have fairly rich vocabularies for "getting wasted" in this way, and the hunch that male and female persons probably have, at least in theory, equal access to the power and danger of such experience. It, too, would seem to deliver on Butler's agenda—*"when and where feminism refuses to derive gender from sex or from sexuality, feminism appears to be part of the very critical practice that contests the heterosexual matrix"*—without the need to be feminist. Whether it would connect to other politics in good ways would depend on whose welfare you cared about, and (given the deep problematic into which the theory places the very idea of sexual welfare) what you would do about the vast increase in uncertainty.

Something like that. At this point the queer theoretic contribution of Bersani's gripping essay to a reformulation of the politics of sex and power kind of runs out. My next example, Duncan Kennedy's "Sexy Dressing," comes at some of the same issues in sexuality from an explicitly regulatory and legalistic perspective and with the aid of Butler's postmodernizing feminism.

❦ *Duncan Kennedy, "Sexy Dressing"*

Duncan Kennedy dedicated "Sexy Dressing" to Mary Joe Frug, a legal scholar murdered in 1991 as she was finishing her distinctively pro-sex, postmodernizing, and feminist book *Postmodern Legal Feminism*.[39] By all accounts Frug was a very sexy dresser.

Moreover, Kennedy wrote "Sexy Dressing" after and, in a sense, into, a decisive rupture among left intellectuals in legal studies that Robin West had described six years earlier as the "CLS-Fem Split."[40] Critical legal studies, or CLS, lives of course; this book is an example of it. But the CLS *conference* is dead. Active in the late 1970s and early 1980s, the CLS conference was, I'm told (I was elsewhere at the time), a vital and internally riven intellectual and social movement among left law teachers; both Kennedy and West played prominent roles in it. As I've suggested in my genealogy of intrafeminist conflict so far, at about this time across many domains of feminist encounter, and certainly within CLS, power feminism and cultural feminism took the turn away from radicalism and critique and toward law, certainty, and the rigorous regulation of sexual life in the name of women; and sex-positive and postmodernizing feminism emerged to resist this turn. Toward the end of her life, I understand, Frug was a powerful figure mediating the conflict. Well before her death, West and Kennedy had come to represent it.

In 1985 Kennedy published a short essay entitled "Psycho-Social CLS" in which he analyzed the relationship between erotic desire and intellectual politics inside the CLS conference.[41] He said some things in that paper which West thought to be so bad that, unless he retracted (and other men in CLS renounced) them, CLS could no longer be thought "a congenial atmosphere for feminist work, nor . . . a healthy environment for women, and women should therefore get out."[42] Here are the things Kennedy said:

> First, there is desire—between men and women and also between men and between women. . . .
> Second, there is the historical fact of the oppression of women by men. . . .
> Third, there is feminism, a self-conscious reaction against the oppression of women. . . .
> . . . [T]he internal structure of the [CLS] conference is unmistakably reflective of the larger patriarchy.[43]

Kennedy then addressed one consequence, as it were, of these three parts: in CLS, more powerful men and less powerful women had erotic relations, relations of desire, often in the roles of mentor/mentee; and the feminism of many women in the conference was, from the perspective of the men, both a welcome and a frightening element of those relations.

West's criticism of Kennedy's 1985 paper in her essay on the "CLS/Fem Split" is a short classic in cultural feminism. She construed Kennedy's "First, there is desire" as a claim that heterosexual desire is natural and thus beyond political criticism, and as a claim that, because it is reciprocal it is also equal, and thus (again) beyond political criticism (87–88). Against those claims (not directly observable in Kennedy's argument), she proposed that desire is movable, and that men and women in CLS should direct theirs outside the conference: "We can, after all, eroticize *other* things" (91). And she predicated this call on a counterclaim that heterosexual desire in the conference, far from being equal, was seamlessly of a piece with patriarchal domination. The erotic desire of more powerful men and less powerful women for one another in CLS was an eroticization of domination precisely fitted to repeat male domination everywhere:

> The societal and institutional commitment to the notion that powerless women naturally desire powerful men—that heterosexual desire is reciprocal, symmetrical and natural even though it is between *concededly* unequal partners—accounts for this society's inability to "see" marital rape as rape rather than as "bad sex." It accounts for the societal belief that women who don't desire men are "frigid." It accounts for the societal inability to see that sexual harassment in the workplace is indeed harassment rather than the soft "personal" touch of an office. It accounts for the societal inability to even consider the possibility that teenage pregnancy is a function of teenage male coercion rather than a breaking of societal "taboos" against "natural" promiscuity. It accounts for the belief that rape victims asked for it. It accounts for the belief that pornography causes no harm other than an imagined and illusory offense to a Victorian sensibility. It accounts for the belief that wolf whistles and

sexual jeers on the streets are compliments rather than assaults. (88–89)

Indeed, it accounts for Kennedy's ability "to bemoan the demise
of behavior which many feminists and many more women
now understand to be sexual harassment on the job, plain and
simple" (90).

West here offers us a convenient synopsis of the cultural-
feminist politics against which "Sexy Dressing" was written. She
categorically precludes, largely on moral grounds, any possibility
of women's thriving in their subordinated desire for men who
have power over them; she seamlessly merges the resulting power
hierarchy into an m > f structure; she knows exactly what wom-
en's interests in that situation are and announces them with indignant finality. "Sexy Dressing" is in one sense a response to
every element of West's denunciation of Kennedy for his actual
historical engagement in intellectual politics as a powerful heterosexual man.

"Sexy Dressing" takes women's sexy dress as a semiotic system
that registers, in subtle and dynamic ways, the degree to which
women are able to enter as strong self-interested bargainers into
sex and sexually fun symbolic play with other women and with
men. He argues from a position of highly identified "erotic interests"—his own—which he bluntly characterizes as those of a heterosexual white middle-class male who wants there to be women
(on the street, in the media, at work) who can afford to be erotically thrilling *to him*. And he attempts to design an algorithm
for deciding how to regulate sexual abuse (rape, sex harassment,
domestic violence, date rape, sexual intimidation of women by
men) to maximize women's safe, and minimize their endangered,
engagement in sexy dressing, sexually meaningful play, and sex
with men. The project is unequivocally pro-sex.

To me, moreover, "Sexy Dressing" is distinctly queer in its analysis of sexuality, power, and knowledge. It fragments and "flips" MacKinnon's structural model of male dominance in a way that is highly reminiscent of Bersani's operation in "Is the Rectum a Grave?"; but in part because its reasons for doing so emerge not from Freud but from social theory, the resulting pattern of sexual complexities is more explicitly political. Even more than Bersani's partisanship on behalf of gay men, to which most feminists defer out of a convergentist sympathy with minoritized, subordination-theory formations generally, Kennedy's stance has been scandalous among feminists; it is difficult to get feminist students even to read the essay. His decisions to write explicitly from the standpoint of "a straight white male middle-class radical" (126), to take into account the erotic interests of a person so situated, to turn postmodernizing feminism against power feminism while nevertheless declaring that "I do not think of myself as a feminist" (129) are, severally or together, somehow absolutely disauthorizing in many feminist circles. So be it. It's not feminist. It Takes a Break from Feminism. Moreover, seeing it as queer instead—*because* of its embrace of male heterosexual erotic interests—provides deep satisfaction to my own ambition that queer work would be able to Take a Break not only from these feminist strictures, but also from the homo- and bi-supremacy that more or less go with the term so far.

Like Bersani, Kennedy embraces power feminism, relying heavily, again like Bersani, on MacKinnon for a set of understandings of sexuality and power. He affirms that men (even those who don't abuse women) eroticize women's subordination; suspects that women do too; and acknowledges multiple male interests in the underenforcement of rules against men's sexual abuse of women. (These include not only the free range some men find within this margin of underenforcement—the "tolerated residuum" of abuse—to abuse women; but also the reduction, for all men, of the risk that they will be falsely or mistakenly accused of abuse, and the considerable cultural repose and bargaining advantage all men gain by being able to shift the burden of taking precautions regarding abuse to women.)[44] He shares MacKinnon's view that the eroticization of domination provides a pervasive language and power form for the relations between men and women. He takes it as a given (and also as a personal observation) that women suffer wide-reaching social subordination because some men abuse some women.

But Kennedy departs substantially from the structuralist premise of MacKinnon's power feminism. Recall what that structuralism means in MacKinnon's thought. The eroticization of domination precipitates women as women and men as men; it produces women as subordinated to men, *by definition*. In MacKinnon's early work, this is not only a social but also a metaphysical and ontological achievement, so that no human consciousness is free of it. Sexuality as women's subordination and men's superordination pervades human reality, such that rape is merely the paradigmatic form of heterosexual interaction; and it pervades human consciousness, such that no one is in a position to say for sure that a given act of "voluntary" or "ordinary" heterosexual intercourse (or watercooler flirtation) is not precisely homologous to what we call rape. In this worldview, it makes sense to attribute to the woman who files a complaint the "truth" of all women.

Kennedy splits from MacKinnon by substituting politics imagined in economic terms for what he would later call the "paranoid structuralism" characteristic of her strain of radical thought.[45] There are several moving parts to the resulting analytic approach, many of which are central to my own argument but unimportant to the vanishing point in the queer canon and in liberal-feminist work, so I will attempt to spell them out in some detail.

First, law in Kennedy's formulation is not nearly as mystified, monolithic, temporally smooth, unilaterally productive, or normative as it is in MacKinnon's power feminism or in West's cultural feminism. Rules governing sexual abuse are embedded in noisy enforcement systems that produce some punishment of abusers, some punishment of perfectly innocent men, and the tolerated residuum of abuse (134–38). The deterrent effects of the rules are therefore seriously complicated. These arise not only from the "hits" but also from the "misses"—indeed, they arise as well from the *perception* of the *ratio* of hits to misses. The deterrent effects arise, moreover, not only from the real circumstances that lead some instances of actual abuse to become "hits" and others to become "misses," but also from ideologically saturated "causation" narratives ("she was asking for it"; "frat boys are suave rapists"), the descriptive power of which is itself an object of political struggle. The properly *legal* question is how to design and enforce rules that get the "right" balance among punishments, immunities, and deterrences, but this is going to be hard. (More on "deciding under conditions of extreme difficulty" at the end of this section.)

This idea of law is almost entirely foreign to any current work that commits itself to power-feminist or to cultural-feminist tenets; it is even more unknown in queer theoretic work. There, the institutional noisiness of legal enforcement is usually blinked, in favor of an idea of law as a prohibition or a right that is vindicated in some sense merely by existing. In MacKinnon's more radical early work, law imagined this way becomes the "maleness" of law: the capacity of its very neutrality and abstraction to vindicate male interests in a highly mystified way.[46] In her "rights" phase, it becomes the capacity of a legal prohibition or a right to instantiate, more or less unilaterally, "women's point of view." In cultural feminism, the tolerated residuum is a male right to be morally wrong; women's right to be free of abuse, and the reform goal of completely and seamlessly effective prohibition of abuse, would reformulate law as the complete realization of feminist moralism: every rule change is seen as a moral *dictat*. Even where queer theoretic texts question the monolithic picture of power and of norms that these understandings provide, they almost never put into question the accompanying picture of law.

Kennedy's understanding of law is, as we will see, much more capacious for a postmodernizing fragmentation of reality than the idea, typically assumed in left humanities work on sexuality, of "the law" as a consolidated entity imposing its norms unilaterally on a social world made up simply of obedient and disobedient subjects. His whole approach to law springs not from feminist or queer theoretic precursors but from the quite different ones of American legal realism.[47] It is central, core, vital to my argument that this shift to legal realism is necessary for anyone who wants to split decisions and think responsibly about the legal dimension of governance feminism.

Second, the real action is not in law per se but in wildly differently interested players who participate in wildly complex social interactions, calibrating their own activities according to their perception of the balance of punishments, immunities, and deterrences that the rules, as enforced, happen to produce. They engage in cost-benefit calculations and then engage in social interactions with other people doing the same. This *mutual* calculatedness can be imagined as *bargaining*, and the players can be imagined as *bargaining in the shadow of the law*. This phrase, taken from the title of a key contribution to legal studies by Robert Mnookin and Lewis Kornhauser,[48] carries the idea that social interactions happening far, far away from the scene of legal enforcement—conceptually, geographically, and narratively—are pervasively informed by the parties' sense of what the law, with all its hits and misses, means for their pursuits.

Kennedy uses the idea of bargaining in the shadow of the law to notice, for instance, that, if a woman perceives the tolerated residuum of abuse to expose her to the possibility of abuse without protection ever, even once, that perception weakens her bargaining position with *this man now* in myriad ways. Sometimes—possibly on average, and not necessarily in any single case, but surely more often than she would if the tolerated residuum were smaller—this loss of bargaining power will induce her to dread being single more than men do; to take less desirable lovers than she otherwise would; to concede more to her partners during relationships than she otherwise would, and than her partners concede in return; to regard breaking relationships off as more costly to her than she otherwise would, and than her partners do in turn; to "pay more" for a breakup than she otherwise would, or than her partners do; and so on (146–47). The tolerated residuum strengthens the bargaining position of abusive husbands, of course, but also of perfectly lovely ones. It alters the amount of battering that women take at home from bad men (upward), and the amount of the housework they can extract from all men (downward).

Something like this analysis has been important in radical feminism and cultural feminism for a long time. It has produced formulations like "the state as a male protection racket" and "the lesbian continuum"—the ideas that the threat of rape benefits all men at the expense of all women by requiring each woman to secure a single committed man to protect her from all the other men;[49] and that, faced with a life structured by bargaining from a position of overdetermined weakness, women have more in common with each other, and against all men, than they do with their supposedly dearest heterosexual love objects.[50] Even for feminists who balk at or pay no attention to MacKinnon's expansive ontological and metaphysical claims for male dominance, this form of subordination-theory structuralism makes her description of the world seem basically "right."

Kennedy drops some flies into the feminist ointment, however, when he posits (my words, not his) that wildly differently interested players participate in wildly complex social interactions. As we've seen, the feminist penchant for convergence means that, when feminism thinks about bargaining in the shadow of the law, it persistently sees women and men, discretely, as consolidated social groups with fairly smooth, uninterrupted, and, *inter sese*, opposed interests. Kennedy punctures this smoothness, first, by insisting that some, many, men have an interest in reducing the tolerated residuum—not because they are good converts to cultural-feminist normativity who would sleep better at night if they knew that all human beings were safer, but because they are erotically self-interested heterosexual men who could be more restless at night if women knew it was safer to be sexy *to them* (138, 208–13). Reducing the tolerated residuum would not only create conflicts of interest among men by requiring more of them to side with women against other men; it would also retilt the playing field in an already existing conflict of interest among men, one in which the abusers are extracting the social goods of women's sexual safety not only from women but from men (144).

The next fly draws its pedigree from postmodern, pro-sex feminism, most explicitly the work of Butler and Frug and thus indirectly from Foucault (183). Here, Kennedy agrees that the eroticization of domination has "taken" in the sense that human heterosexual life seems unimaginable without it, definitely in the sense that this involves all men and all women in a highly dangerous and oppressive sexual system. But the "seamless quality" of that system as it is described by the structuralist feminisms cannot account for "the fissures of gendered existence within liberal patriarchy" (157). They miss three "puzzling aspects of eroticized hierarchy": the overdetermined quality of male dominance (it does not seem to *need* sexuality to secure its place—here we have a brief nod in the direction of socialist feminism); the capacity even for strong critics of male dominance to affirm the "egalitarian and even redemptive" quality of some heterosexual experience *within the vocabulary of eroticized domination*;[51] and "the persistence of resistance, compromise, and opportunism as strategies for negotiating the regime, rather than buying into it without reserve, so that the image of a fully rationalized, totalitarian gender system seems paranoid" (157).

Let us take stock in passing of the way in which this frames an anti-identitarian project. Like Bersani, Kennedy insists that there are, in politics and in sexual life, a huge variety of highly particularized and interested sexual positions that are male, and he places (or performs?) himself directly in one of them. Both Bersani and Kennedy stake themselves very definitely to identity positions. But also like Bersani, Kennedy insists that sexuality produces politics without sustaining simple identitarian framings like "gay men" and "heterosexual men." In pretending otherwise, Bersani intones, "we have been telling a few lies"; in supposing that men (e.g., social conservative and sexually libertine heterosexual men), or women (e.g., social conservative women and butch lesbians), have undifferentiated stakes in the regulation of sexual abuse, Kennedy concludes, feminism mistakes its own interests (181–85). And like Bersani, Kennedy deploys this fragmentation of identitarian interests not only against group consolidation (*wildly differently interested players*) but also against the simple consolidation of an interested self (*participate in wildly complex social interactions*). At this point both Bersani and Kennedy draw upon social theoretical resources of high modernism—Freud, and, in Kennedy's case, Saussure as well[52]—to produce a postmodernist explosion of the self and a highly paradoxical account of human sexual interests and welfare.

We can see this fracturing if we follow Kennedy as he multiplies the possible meanings of women's sexy dress. He defines sexy dress semiotically, so that, for instance, a particular pair of women's shoes might signal sexiness at a family dinner party or a church prayer meeting but not at a nightclub or even at work, and so that, if dress is sexy at all, it refers ultimately (let's face it) to fucking. The "meaning" of a particular act of sexy dressing is deeply contingent on the semiotics of locale and male/female performativity in which it occurs, as those are understood (that is, intended, experienced, *and* interpreted) by the men and women involved (163–208).

Kennedy agrees with MacKinnon and cultural feminists that a woman's sexy dress can indicate her vulnerability to sexual abuse by men; indeed, in traditional conservative sexual morality, a woman who dresses sexy and is abused is *actually* understood to have "asked for it." Kennedy goes further, and affirms that sexy dress invokes women's and men's capacity to be sexually excited by the possibility of abuse (194). But to follow convergentist, structuralist power feminism or cultural feminism at this point, and hold sexy dress to a monolithic meaning (women's sexual objectification and subordination)—to attach it unilaterally to the eroticization of women's actual, chronologically unbroken sexual subordination—is both "speculative and paranoid": "not," he is careful to add, "that it *couldn't* be true," but it *need not* be (196).

So women's sexy dress can "mean" sexual objectification and vulnerability in ways that are substantively related to women's subordination. But Kennedy construes Madonna's *Open Your Heart* video to discover in sexy dress a splendid fissuring of power and gender.

Here is a summary of his reading of the music video's representation of sexy dress and the powers it organizes. *For men*, it can refer to the erotic imagery that men deploy in masturbation, and thus, along with excitement, can produce in them a whole range of feelings that do not sound in domination—dirtiness, shame, secrecy, confusion, guilt, fear, embarrassment, and anxiety about getting caught. It can refer to locales (red-light districts, tough urban settings) with working-class and racial associations and thus produce in middle- and upper-class men, and with specific effects if they are white, not only excitement but the dread of getting hurt there. It can refer to, or even make possible, a direct exercise of women's sexual power *over* men—a power to grant and withhold, a power to overpower, a power to "drive men crazy." And it can refer to or enact out-and-out female defiance of patriarchal sexual codes, indifference to male needs and fears, male powers and threats: female sexiness as female sexual autonomy and invulnerability. Of course, female sexual autonomy and invulnerability are modes of female existence that are highly prized in sex-positive feminism, so their emergence in the analysis provides Kennedy with a moment for convergence not only with sex-positivity but with feminism. But he sticks to his identity position within male heterosexual interests by insisting that erotically dominant women might well provoke in some men, sometimes, a will to dominate or retaliate, while they might just also, for some men sometimes, provoke a sense of powerlessness, fear, doom, envy, or disorientation. And they provide also to men the basis for pleasurable fantasies that are not exactly what MacKinnon or West attributes to them, for instance, the fantasy of setting down the good man's burden of being careful and protective; the fantasy of being absolved from worry about whether the woman really wanted it, had a good time, came; the fantasy of a borrowed self, of an introjected powerful female other, a self that is as narcissistic and as powerfully embodied as the sexy-dressing woman. Of course the very same act of sexy dressing might actually mean, *to the woman*, that she has failed to produce those happy outcomes:

it might be "shadowed by the possibility that no one, not one person, experiences it as she would want—that the whole audience consists of 'dirty old men,' abusers lying in wait, and critics who think she is a slut or politically incorrect or too old or not pretty enough or doesn't really know how to do it right" (206).

Shame is deeply embroidered into this image of erotic life. It has the place in Kennedy's queered analysis that abjection does in Bersani's. And again like Bersani, though Kennedy acknowledges the pain that shame involves, he nevertheless represents it as intrinsic to female *and* male hetero-eroticism; and wherever it appears it *reverses* the basic presupposition of m > f—the basic idea in feminism that, in the eroticization of domination, men and masculinity dominate women and femininity. Men responding erotically to sexy dress that refers to pornography may experience not only a will to dominate women but also loss of control, direct humiliation, and a relinquishment of erotic responsibility—and all of these can produce the allure of subordination, a highly pleasurable eroticization of *female* domination; while women dressing sexy in order to accrue the corresponding powers may experience humiliation not because they are eroticized by men but because they aren't.

At this point Kennedy *almost* produces the uncertainty and will to paradoxical irresolution that are crucial to Bersani's most queer analytic moment:

> I think nonetheless that some of the time, some sexy dressers and some of their audience are engaged in pleasure/ resistance in the interstices of the regime. They are eroticising female autonomy. . . .
>
> This must be always an uncertain form of politics because the signifying woman may be doing more harm than good, feeding the conventional view in which the tease deserves what she gets and men get off on woman-wanting mixed

with woman-hating. For both men and women, the experience is compromised because it occurs within, is indeed dependent for its meaning on, the larger web of references to male sexual abuse of woman and male degradation in relation to them. *It is never just "the truth" . . . that the experience is indeed pleasure/resistance rather than something else, something bad, instead.* (206, emphasis added)

Kennedy's idea that some male/female interactions—even though they refer, through sexy dress, to male abuse of women—nevertheless involve not domination but "pleasure/resistance in the interstices of the regime" is a Foucaultian one, drawing directly on the vocabulary of *Volume One.*[53] As he explores the "fissures of gendered existence," Kennedy here turns (quite appropriately, it seems to me) from MacKinnon's top-down model of power to an idea of its "interstitial" form, and even to the formulation of "pleasure/resistance" operating not against power from below, but from within it. Moreover, he posits as the basic linguistic dichotomy against which male/female sexual semiotics are played out, not male sexual abuse of women and *women's subordination,* but male sexual abuse of women and *male degradation in relation to it.* In such a context, finally, "It is never just 'the truth' " that an act of sexy dressing achieves pleasure/resistance or confirms women's subordination in the eroticization of domination: Kennedy affirms "uncertain[ty]" in the form of an open-textured hypothetical stance toward a reality anticipated to be complex and contradictory, at exactly the point in his argument where MacKinnon would *know.*

✄ KENNEDY/TAKING A BREAK

I note with a certain reluctance that Kennedy (again and finally, like Bersani) draws back from the not-feminist implications of his formulation, cutting feminism and knowingness some slack that his own argument would, if followed through, deny them. Here I push the argument more decisively into an engagement with the *un*knowing dimension of postmodernist thought, and further into the trajectory toward Taking a Break from Feminism.

The basic legal algorithm of Kennedy's paper, as I've suggested, is cost-benefit policy analysis. Determining that we want one legal rule about sexual abuse rather than another involves minimizing the tolerated residuum of sexual abuse and discouraging sexy dress, on one hand, and maintaining the tolerated residuum of abuse while engaging in sexy dress and eroticizing, it on the other, until we "do more harm than good." As I've suggested, the resulting fracturing of the legal project is highly amenable to the postmodernizing complexification that sexual regulation, I think, requires. But Kennedy doesn't go all the way. The paper takes us carefully through the ways in which bargaining in the shadow of the law between men and women, performed as it is against the background of the tolerated residuum, starts from women's weaker bargaining position and thus, not structurally but on average and over the whole range of bargains men and women strike, produces their subordination. I summarized that analysis above. It is grippingly convincing. But Kennedy does not return to this calculus after establishing the ambiguities of male/female power. If he had, he might have had to add that, if heterosexual men experience women's sexual autonomy as a threat—not only through their power to deny men something they want very much, but also through their ability, in providing it, to humiliate, disorient, and abject them—then there is a second tolerated residuum of abuse to take into account: men's. And he would have had to acknowledge that women can secure a bargaining advantage whenever men want them to produce the effect of bold, indifferent female sexual autonomy and are willing to make concessions to get it. On this side of the ledger, if Kennedy had filled it in, he would have said that men not only come into bargaining with women with a distinct source of bargaining disadvantage but also seek complex erotic goods, so that they might, over the full range of bargains that they make with women, find *themselves* in subordination.

How would we ever know how to add it all up, balance it all out? By putting "the truth" in scare quotes, and mockingly demoting it as "*just* 'the truth,' " Kennedy strongly suggests that we may be on the verge of an epistemic crisis here. Too bad that Kennedy uses feminism to draw back from the brink. Consider the passage just quoted. It posits a heterosexual interaction in which a woman's sexy dress is experienced by her and perhaps even taken up by one or more men as "pleasure/resistance." Kennedy is right to say that it may also, elsewhere presumably, "feed[ ] the conventional view" that she "deserves what she gets" and ratifies male erotic misogyny. If that happens, Kennedy suggests, she may be "doing more harm than good." You could not reach this judgment about relative values without covert recourse to feminist sexual-subordination premises; *somewhere* in the analysis Kennedy must be thinking of sexuality in terms of m > f and carrying a brief for f. And as the passage draws to a close, Kennedy seems to endorse those premises: "It is never just 'the truth' ... that the experience *is indeed* pleasure/resistance *rather than* something else, something bad, instead." In this formulation, the feminist construal can cast doubt on the Foucaultian one, but not the other way around. The gesture hinges on "rather"—only one *or* the other can be true—and, within that dichotomy, if the harm occurs, the event was "instead" and "indeed" not pleasure/resistance in the first place.

The not-feminist queer theoretic move, I think, is to insist that these two understandings cast profound doubt *on each other.*

Thus also the not-feminist queer theoretic project, willing to Take a clear Break, would resist the way in which here, in petit point, and throughout the paper's concluding arguments, m > f and carrying a brief for f produce "facts" for policy balancing, while the claim that heterosexual interactions produce pleasure/ resistance occupies the slippery grammatical status of hypothesis and evanescent speculation. It would see a failure of follow-through when, at points involving a contest between feminist and Foucaultian construals of power as it plays out between men and women, the normative and epistemic weight ends up on the side of m > f and carrying a brief for f. Indeed, it would see that Kennedy lost an opportunity to explore the "fissures of gendered existence" when he didn't ask whether the erotic/power dynamics between "men" and "women" arise outside gender *tout court.*

So let me gather together the various strands of Kennedy's analysis of the "dark side" of sexy dressing and the semiotics of heterosexual desire, and say what I think he would have said if he hadn't been working overtime to stay in alliance with Frug's effort to mediate the conflict between sexual-subordination feminists and sex-positive/postmodernizing ones. As long as the semiotics of sexiness makes every sign contingent on all other signs in an ever-shifting set of cross-references; as long as "meaning" resides problematically in intention, experience, *and* uptake; as long as men and women do find intense pleasure inside the eroticization of domination; as long as pleasure sometimes takes the form of pain, and pain of pleasure; as long as desire can extend its reach to shame; as long as gender as power-over is subject to complex psychic reversals; as long as the resulting highly volatile system is understood to provide the raw material *both* for domination *and* for "resistance, compromise, and opportunism"—as long as all of these hypotheses about our life in sexuality hold— it could never be "just 'the truth'" that the scenario we are construing was only pleasure/resistance and not something bad as well, or only something bad and not pleasure/resistance as well. Under these hypotheses, "the truth" and "the real" are not the ground upon which we can base our cost-benefit assessments, but *effects* in a sexual semiosis that is pervasively riven with paradox and knowable only through the murky epistemes of desire and politics.

Approaching questions of sexual politics and sexual regulation with those hypotheses would lead us strongly away from the equality-is-freedom, victim's-truth model of legal reform advanced by the late MacKinnon, and would alienate us quite completely from the legal moralism that characterizes cultural feminism. A much better fit, it seems to me, is the neorealist picture of law Kennedy also sets out in "Sexy Dressing": a complex system of legal rules sustaining a tolerated residuum of abuse, plenty of false-positive accusations and convictions, strategic actors politically engaged in the system at all levels—in all a legal system that looks more like a social semiotics than a mandate for the vindication of any single Truth. To be sure, single Truths can inhabit the system: conservative women want to constrain the social space for all women's sexy dress; they know why they want to do this; and they work hard to get what they want. Queer anti-identitarians want everyone's gender to fall apart—but they paradoxically thereby emphasize and intensify gender. Constraining sexy dress intensifies its signals. And sexual abuse, sexual suffering, sexual harm are distributed across this system in patterned but uneven ways: prohibition can deter, but it can also become permission, and even intensify the value of rape to rapists.

Elsewhere Kennedy describes a consciousness that can grasp hold of this complexity and *do* things with it, a kind of decisionism.[54] Here is a decisionist sentence: making decisions about what legal rule we want to use in the domain of sexual abuse—or even which political direction to go in—is hard. Hard because sexuality is dark, unknown to us, riven by paradox and reversal. Hard because legal rules operate in social contexts not only of subordination-theory puissance but also of Foucaultian pouvoir. We might have to decide without knowing that our understanding of the situation is right, without knowing how our decision will play out, and even convinced that, in a system in which any decision will transfer some social goods from, say, women to men or men to women, there *is* no decision that we could possibly make that will not hurt vast numbers of real, actual people, possibly the very people on whose behalf we think we are acting. One reason to bracket feminism as we struggle to decide is suggested by the gesture of queer theoretic yearning that Kennedy makes, and then interrupts in the name of feminism, in "Sexy Dressing": presupposing power-feminist or cultural-feminist "takes" on sexual abuse, insisting in advance on their ubiquitous utility, refusing to Take a Break from Feminism—indeed, refusing to Take a Break from any single model of reality, truth, and justice, queer theory included—is precisely to decide by *not* deciding.

FEMINISM AND ITS OTHERS

This is a story of the consequences of the Break, as they unfolded over the 1990s.

Feminist "Paralysis"

Feminist theorists and activists repeatedly generate a profound misreading of *Gender Trouble* and Butler's postmodernizing, specifically deconstructive, feminism. One encounters again and again feminists who say: "But how can we seriously entertain Butler's deconstruction of woman? For does it not deny the social existence of women, disable us from organizing on behalf of women, and lead to paralysis?"

Similarly, feminist theory often runs onto the rocks of despair over hybrid feminist divergentism. The multiplicity of women; their relation to each other through racial, colonial, and class differences; their divided loyalties to one another and to men within and across these differences; the incommensurabilities that drive class and race into discourses unlike and in tension with those attributed to sex1, sex2, gender, and sexuality: all of these are often thought to incapacitate feminism, to disauthorize it, to render it so incoherent that it cannot serve as a mode of intellectual or political articulation. Faced with this threat, feminists wreak upon fellow feminists highly moralistic denunciations for failing to produce convergence.

The bibliography of this despair—this impasse, this paralysis, this crisis, this error, this moral failure—is very considerable, and some of the most interesting and most reticulated discussions within feminist theory are about how to explain it, narrate it, conceptualize it, and imagine a way out of it.[1] Major splits in feminism—the pragmatists against the postmodernists, the materialists against the theory-heads, women of color against white feminists, and "real women" against the "gender troubled"—are organized around the very common view that, at least for the pragmatists, the materialists, some women of color, and "real women," postmodernizing divergentism and/or hybrid feminist divergentism *are the problem*.

But I wonder. I wonder whether the experience of paralysis arises instead from two related commitments that are highly salient among those who fear and decry postmodernist feminism for its paralyzing force and divergentist hybrid feminism for its paralyzing force *and* its racism, classism, imperialism: paranoid structuralism and the moralized mandate to converge.

In this section I first explain what I mean by paranoid structuralism and the moralized mandate to converge, and show why I think they have produced in feminists the experience of paralysis; and then I offer a thought experiment asking you to ponder whether and when you find paranoid structuralist writing to be empowering or paralyzing.

❦ Paranoid Structuralism and the Moralized Mandate to Converge

It may be that *any* social/theoretical movement has the experience of paralysis at times when its power is not actually growing. I don't think that this is such a time for many forms of feminism, however. Instead, we see feminism moving into state and statelike power in the United States and globally (not everywhere of course). Rather, I'll propose here that structural and convergentist feminist projects may be producing for themselves the experience of paralysis. Postmodernizing feminism might be responsible only to the extent that it has undermined feminists' confidence in their own work. If this is the right way to see their resistance, then their injunction that feminists must continue to produce feminism—even when they have lost faith in its defining concept, representative authority, and ability to identify political goals— has led to a collective life within feminism that gives bad faith the upper hand. That, too, would be a very paralyzing experience for a political/theoretical effort so committed to finding and denouncing bad faith in its opponents. Query whether they might feel less paralyzed if they could take periodic trips not only into postmodernizing feminism, but out of feminism altogether.

Of course it is no longer acceptable to "be a structuralist" in the strongest sense—that would seem hopelessly naive, almost as bad as being "essentialist"—and almost no one does either any more if he or she can help it. Nevertheless subordination theories across the board, feminist ones being no exception, continue to have persistent recourse to an attitude of paranoid structuralism.[2]

Feminist paranoid structuralism either hypothesizes or presupposes (big difference) that, although things in the world *seem* to be organized in a way that does not invoke m/f and m > f, or require us to carry a brief for f, this perception is probably a deep error, and profoundly counterintuitive investigation will eventually reveal that, yep, it's m > f all over again.

I am a huge fan of hypothetical paranoid structuralism. It is a crucial element of every radical theory that regards the very consciousness of those propounding it to be one of the "powers" against which it works. I love it also for how hard it works: it takes nothing for granted; it is a persistent incitement to critique. I love its love of the covert, its need for highly astute interpretive practices, and its constant yearning for a radical transformation of consciousness.

And sometimes it really does find things in the world that it can describe powerfully. Consider, as an example of what it can achieve, Elizabeth Potter's recent tour de force study entitled *Gen-*

der and Boyle's Law of Gases.[3] Yes, that was not a typo. Potter shows—I think persuasively to the point of near conclusiveness— that the first law of modern physics was no better at explaining the "relevant facts" as they then existed than was another proposal, one that was, at the time, in equally wide circulation and that (until the contest between them was resolved in favor of Boyle's Law) had an equally valid claim for scientific legitimacy.

Boyle presupposed a world made up of physical laws operating on dead matter; the competing model presupposed a world of animated matter involved in constant relational rearrangements. Both were equally good at explaining the seventeenth-century equivalent of the thermometer. When this happens in science (and it does, apparently, very often), we are (Potter argues) entitled to seek *social* reasons for the triumph of one rule over the other, the designation of one as "true" and the other as "magic and superstition." And in this case those reasons can be found in the rich historical record, painstakingly assembled by Potter, showing that Boyle and his contemporaries saw that the "dead matter" thesis presupposed a hierarchical and gendered physical order, a hierarchical and gendered social order, and a gendered experimental scientist in which m could $> $ f—whereas the "live matter" theory would have supposed a more contingent and indeterminate physical, social, and epistemological scheme (and was, not coincidentally, favored by feminists, social and religious radicals, and antirationalists).

It takes a long, long time to work out a thesis as counterintuitive as Potter's. You have to stare at the record that you have been taught to read as exemplifying the triumph of objective science, patiently waiting to see whether the pattern you've been taught will fade and be replaced by another that actually fits your hypothesis. And it's unequivocally thrilling when the work pays off. But will it always do so? Will we need (for instance) a feminist explanation for the timing with which asteroids have hit the earth? Maybe,

maybe not. *Presupposing* the covert importance of one's favorite paranoid idea—or claiming to see it precisely *because of* its seeming absence—can have the big downside of being, well, paranoid. It can lead you to miss noticing other things that *are* going on, things that just can't, and even if they can probably shouldn't, be forced into the vocabulary of m > f. If you can't Take a Break from Feminism—if your attitude to your feminism requires you to deploy its ideas prescriptively—you are going to feel stuck. Paralyzed.

Even more than paranoid structuralism, convergentism has been elevated in too many contemporary feminisms to the status of a moral demand. For convergentists, racism and sexism are seamless, interlocking, synthesized, and integrated systems that intersect, converge, and reinforce one another; that produce conditions of existence and of consciousness of those subordinated by them that both are and must be understood as unified in the form of identity; that give the subordinated unique epistemic purchase on their oppression; and that are reinscribed and reinforced whenever their seamlessness becomes unapparent or, worse, whenever it is denied.

As a set of hypotheses, convergentist models are crucial: without them, how would we notice when we really *do* want to see the world as they imagine it? But the *moralized mandate* to converge has almost no upsides that I can think of. Its moralism makes it prescriptive. The social forms that have accumulated around this particular prescription are particularly ferocious and are themselves a reason to reconsider. But the epistemic politics of this style of feminist thought, even without them, seems to me to impose tragic costs.

Of course it is very, very hard to produce intelligible convergentist accounts at the required level of seamlessness. The moment of default is a very jealously guarded one in feminist thought. When it comes up, there is always a great deal of tension in the room. If you're the feminist who hasn't successfully converged, you run the risk of being held responsible for reiterating or even performing domination. Finely honed knives of self- and mutual blame lie on the table, ready for use: *someone* must pick one of them up; *someone* must make a confession or a denunciation. Oddly enough, it sometimes seems the animating demand of these moments is that feminism will stand accused of *racism* or *orientalism* if it does not posit its ambition to "top" both anti-racism and anti-imperialism by emerging, when all is said and done, as their ultimate conceptual, normative, and political reference point. Structuralist ambitions figure in these gestures as an ultimate fealty to a transcendence, a utopia, or a harmonic convergence that, if we were only smart and good enough, we would be able to produce out of the terrible conflictual material we have to work with.

So it's not just that the "race, class . . ." mantra, deployed prescriptively, often obscures rather than illuminates the complexity of power in the social world. The moralized crisis that sustains it is so ritualized—is performed again and again with such Kabuki-like precision—that one could call it a deadlock in feminism. Paralysis again.

❦ An Experiment in Political Stylistics (do try this at home)

The following experiment works from the assumption that political ideas have prose styles, and that you can find out something about your political libido by feeling for whether you are turned on or off by a political idea's way of addressing itself to you. It is here to help you see whether, at some noncognitive level like taste or desire, you are drawn to or repelled by strong structuralist and convergentist statements.

I offer here a series of lists. The list is a time-honored rhetorical form—think of the lists in the *Iliad* or *Paradise Lost.* Here I compare some lists that, I think, produce highly distinct affects among different types of feminists and queer theory mavens. The affects I'm trying to test for are the feeling-state of loving paranoid structuralism and the moralized mandate to converge, or finding them to be paralyzed and paralyzing; the feeling-state of loving the exploded list with its lush expansiveness, or rage (or some other emotion) at its irresponsible diffuse shapelessness, nausea in the face of its sheer aporetic openness, or even disappointment when its hidden structural tenets come to light. I'm invoking a politics of style, in which structural feminists present consolidated, compact, unified lists and queer theory replies with exploded ones.

Prescriptive paranoid structuralism insists that, in the world of experience, a vast array of apparently distinct events are actually, when fully revealed, the same. And so people producing this politics are strongly drawn to the word "and," grammatical parallelism, and the rhetorical trope *anaphora*.[4] Rape *and* pornography *and* sexual harassment *and* domestic abuse *and* prostitution *and* sex work (actually, it would be "trafficking in women")—*and* marriage *and* makeup *and* the Boy Scouts—they are all mere *instances* of the structure of male dominance and are basically all alike. Following Butler, I will designate this collection of stylistic strategies the *copula*.[5]

The copula is the rhetorical form of many of MacKinnon's most breathtaking statements. Consider this: "Socially, femaleness *means* femininity, which *means* attractiveness to men, which *means* sexual attractiveness, which *means* sexual availability on male terms. What defines woman as such *is* what turns men on."[6] The tendency is, if anything, more pronounced in her later work. For instance: "*[T]he way* subordination *is done in* pornography is *the way it is done in* prostitution *is the way it is done in* the rest of the world: *rape, battering, sexual abuse of children, sexual harassment, and murder* are sold in *prostitution* and are the acts out of which *pornography* is made."[7] To make distinctions is to be fooled by male domination.

Or reconsider this passage, from Robin West's essay "The CLS/Fem Split":

> The societal and institutional commitment to the notion that powerless women naturally desire powerful men—that heterosexual desire is reciprocal, symmetrical and natural even though it is between *concededly* unequal partners—**accounts for** this society's inability to "see" marital rape as rape rather than as "bad sex." **It accounts for** the societal inability to see that sexual harassment in the workplace is indeed harassment rather than the soft "personal" touch of an office. **It accounts for** the societal inability to even consider the possibility that teenage pregnancy is a function of teenage male coercion rather than a breaking of societal "taboos" against "natural" promiscuity. **It accounts for** the belief that rape victims asked for it. **It accounts for** the belief that pornography causes no harm other than an imagined and illusory offense to a Victorian sensibility. **It accounts for** the belief that wolf whistles and sexual jeers on the streets are compliments rather than assaults. (89, italics in original; bold emphases added)

West captures perfectly here the sense that all of these features of the social world are so overwhelmingly identical, so uniformly hostile to women's consolidated interests, and ultimately so boring (feminists have known all this all along) that there is a special moral affront in her having to reveal it all *once again.*

How do these lists make you feel? If you see the world as they describe it, the feelings they produce will be energized, emboldened, fortified. You probably feel indignant and determined. For some political moments and some political sensibilities, the copula can guide, even galvanize political and intellectual energy. But it might also be the other way around: you might love the feelings produced by these examples of the feminist copula, and for that reason see the world as they describe it.

But if you don't see the listed elements as the same, if you're interested in the differences between them, if you actually treasure any element in the list's parade of horribles, the copula produces almost musically the experience of stasis, historical atemporality, ceaseless numbing repetition. Paralysis. Again, its hammering insistence, its righteous wrath, will sound to you like scary, even crazed zeal. And it might also be the other way around: these subverbal libidinal aversions might tell your political brain not to see the world as these examples describe it.

My next example is the ur-list of third-wave radical feminism, Adrienne Rich's rendering of a catalog of the eight characteristics of male power propounded by Kathleen Gough in 1975.[8] In her classic essay "Compulsory Heterosexuality and Lesbian Existence," Rich gave Gough's list in italics and added in brackets examples showing the breathtaking historical and cultural scope of male power. Gough's list had aimed to show how m/f sex inequality is produced; Rich's amended version aimed also to show that its animating core is not merely m > f but m > f *in the form of* compulsory heterosexuality for women.

Do you like the ur-list of structuralist feminism? Or does it make you feel paralyzed? Take your time; really read it slowly; read it the way you would a poem by Gertrude Stein:

Characteristics of male power include:

the power of men

1. *to deny women* [our own] *sexuality*
   [by means of clitoridectomy and infibulation; chastity belts; punishment, including death, for female adultery; punishment, including death, for lesbian sexuality; psychoanalytic denial of the clitoris; strictures against mas-

turbation; denial of maternal and postmenopausal sensuality; unnecessary hysterectomy; pseudolesbian images in media and literature; closing of archives and destruction of documents relating to lesbian existence];

2. *or to force it* [male sexuality] *upon them*
   [by means of rape (including marital rape) and wife beating; father-daughter, brother-sister incest; the socialization of women to feel that male sexual "drive" amounts to a right; idealization of heterosexual romance in art, literature, media, advertising, etc., child marriage; arranged marriage; prostitution; the harem; psychoanalytic doctrines of frigidity and vaginal orgasm; pornographic depictions of women responding pleasurably to sexual violence and humiliation (a subliminal message being that sadistic heterosexuality is more "normal" than sensuality between women)];

3. *to command or exploit their labor to control their produce*
   [by means of the institutions of marriage and motherhood as unpaid production; the horizontal segregation of women in paid employment; the decoy of the upwardly mobile token woman; male control of abortion, contraception, and childbirth; enforced sterilization; pimping; female infanticide, which robs mothers of daughters and contributes to generalized devaluation of women];

4. *to control or rob them of their children*
   [by means of father-right and "legal kidnapping"; enforced sterilization; systematized infanticide; seizure of children from lesbian mothers by the courts; the malpractice of male obstetrics; use of the mother as "token torturer" in genital mutilation or in binding the daughter's feet (or mind) to fit her for marriage];

5. *to confine them physically and prevent their movement*
   [by means of rape as terrorism, keeping women off the

streets; purdah; foot-binding; atrophying of women's athletic capabilities; haute couture, "feminine" dress codes; the veil, sexual harassment on the streets; horizontal segregation of women in employment; prescriptions for "full-time" mothering; enforced economic dependence of wives];

6. *to use them as objects in male transactions*
[use of women as "gifts"; bride-price; pimping; arranged marriage; use of women as entertainers to facilitate male deals, e.g., wife-hostess, cocktail waitress required to dress for male sexual titillation, call girls, "bunnies," geisha, *kisaeng* prostitutes, secretaries];

7. *to cramp their creativeness*
[witch persecutions against midwives and female healers and as pogrom against independent, "unassimilated" women; definition of male pursuits as more valuable than female within any culture, so that cultural values become embodiment of male subjectivity; restriction of female self-fulfillment to marriage and motherhood; sexual exploitation of women by male artists and teachers; the social and economic disruption of women's creative aspirations; erasure of female tradition]; and

8. *to withhold from them large areas of the society's knowledge and cultural attainments*
[by means of noneducation of females (60% of the world's illiterates are women); the "Great Silence" regarding women and particularly lesbian existence in history and culture; sex-role stereotyping which deflects women from science, technology, and other "masculine" pursuits; male social/professional bonding which excludes women; discrimination against women in the professions].[9]

If you yield to it enough, this list is horrifying, suffocating. This intense dysphoria is not in itself a good reason to dislike it. It might be unpleasant for you, but urgent and even good for you, to face up to a reality this bad. Indeed, aversion to such lists because they are depressing runs a huge risk of bad faith, magic realism, and what E.M.W. Tillyard, working in quite another context, called "triviality of mind."[10] But it can be deeply delusional, intensely paranoid, utterly paralyzing to approach a highly varied, complex world with nothing more than the descriptive capacities of Rich's list to help you understand it.

The copula need not always yoke together an infinite array of oppressions; it can also marshal the myriad sparkling forces of rebellion and resistance. Rich, like West—and indeed, serving as one of West's primary models—thought that the sheer monolithically multiplied unity of male domination has a counterweight; and as for West, it is the lesbian capacity of all women. The "pervasive cluster of forces [constituting male power], ranging from physical brutality to control of consciousness . . . suggests that an enormous potential counterforce is having to be restrained" (640). That force is the "lesbian continuum":

> I mean the term *lesbian continuum* to include a range— through each woman's life and throughout history—of woman-identified experience; not simply the fact that a woman has had or consciously desired genital sexual experience with another woman. If we expand it to embrace many more forms of primary intensity between and among women, including the sharing of a rich inner life, the bonding against male tyranny, the giving and receiving of practical and political support; if we can also hear in it such associations as *marriage resistance* and the "haggard" behavior identified by Mary Daly (obsolete meanings: "intractable," "willful," "wanton," and "unchaste" . . . "a woman reluctant

to yield to wooing")—we begin to grasp breadths of female history and psychology which have lain out of reach. (648–49, footnote deleted)

That sounds like a lot more fun. But there are possible downsides even here. For all its expansiveness and infinite reach, this list is fixed tightly at the top to the idea of a lesbian continuum. Emancipation is structural too. Many, many feminists have objected to this move: some to Rich's lesbian exceptionalism; others to her assimilation of all women's resistance transhistorically to a specific historical moment in female same-sex love; some to the resulting de-emphasis on lesbian lust. Her raw point-of-view-ism. She leaves out men. She leaves out gay men. A gay man might hate it because it's pastoralizing. And so on.

Postmodernizing feminists have objected to this style and its politics as being instrumentally *bad for women*. Contributing to one of the feminist anthologies that we'll examine below, Sharon Marcus calls it the *collapsed* continuum, and argues that it produces in women an unvaried and thus vulnerable stance toward the world. She argues that it makes women more helpless, for instance, in the face of rape by

> [l]ink[ing] language and rape in a way that can be taken to mean that representations of rape, obscene remarks, threats and other forms of harassment should be considered equivalent to rape. . . . In a "continuum" theory which makes one type of action, a verbal threat, immediately substitutable for another type of action, sexual assault, the time and space between these two actions collapse and . . . rape has always already occurred. . . . [But] occlud[ing] the gap between the threat and the rape . . . [risks closing] the gap in which women can try to intervene, overpower and deflect the threatened action.[11]

Paralysis again.

Work that Takes a Break seems to have a very different hedonics of the list. The early years of queer theory produced lists following Foucault, who began *The Order of Things* with Borges's list of incommensurables and thus signaled the postmodern and critical will to put the practice of taxonomy in question. Borges purported to have found in "a certain Chinese encyclopedia" an entry providing that

> animals are divided into: (a) belonging to the Emperor, (b) embalmed, (c) tame, (d) sucking pigs, (e) sirens, (f) fabulous, (g) stray dogs, (h) included in the present classification, (i) frenzied, (j) innumerable, (k) drawn with a very fine camelhair brush, (l) *et cetera*, (m) having just broken the water pitcher, (n) that from a long way off look like flies.[12]

Here's how Foucault described his affective uptake of Borges's exploded list:

> This book first arose out of a passage in Borges, out of the laughter that shattered, as I read the passage, all the familiar landmarks of my thought. . . . In the wonderment of this taxonomy, the thing we apprehend in one great leap, the thing that, by means of the fable, is demonstrated as the exotic charm of another system of thought, is the limitation of our own, the stark impossibility of thinking *that.*[13]

Pursuing this hedonics, queer theory produces lists that emphasize not repetition, homology, analogy, and sameness, but variety, incommensurability, and endless difference—and it seeks something like Foucault's sense of surprise, wonder, comedy, and the frisson of epistemic disorientation.

We've already seen one such list: in her 1994 "*Interview*" with Butler, Rubin remembers a plethora of heterogeneous sexual-political projects as making up the motivating context in which she had written "Thinking Sex." Recall also that she wanted not to study a single social structure but sexual communities working out "political econom*ies*" of sex2 over time; she wanted to back-burner the binary as her primary hypothetical form and shift to the "continuum" and toward "those mathematical models they do now with strange topologies and convoluted shapes."[14] I take two contributions to queer theory in the early 1990s to exemplify this desire: they are Michael Warner's *Fear of a Queer Planet* and Sedgwick's *Tendencies*. As we will see, they deliberately open queer theory up to the possibility of exceeding and abandoning all of its categorical commitments. What's amazing is how hard it is to pull off that effect, and how persistently their lists fall back into uses of the copula from which they seem, otherwise, to be struggling to depart. When queer theory makes lists, it flips the political emotions that I've attributed to the feminist copula: loss of taxonomic control is libidinally animating, while the "click" of the copula feels like the snapping shut of the same old trap.

In his introduction Warner sets out the research program of queer theory:

> The essays in this volume suggest that political struggles over sexuality ramify in an unimaginably large number of directions. . . . Every person who comes to a queer self-understanding knows in one way or another that her stigmatization is connected with gender, the family, notions of individual freedom, the state, public speech, consumption and desire, nature and culture, maturation, reproductive politics, racial and national fantasy, class identity, truth and trust, censorship, intimate life and social display, terror and violence, health care, and deep cultural norms about the bearing of the body. (xii–xiii)

One affect: the world-encompassing range of this list, and the sheer variety of its elements, produces a sense of opening, expansion, exploration. Warner seems to want to recruit us to Foucault's sense of wonder: we are invited to marvel with him that the concerns of queer theory "ramify in an unimaginably large number of directions." Ramification and wonder: each root travels in a different direction, probing different domains of human life; nothing is irrelevant, and everything promises to surprise. But the list can produce another affect: everything is tethered at the top, as in Rich's euphoric list, to the stipulation that queer people exist and that every one of them knows that his or her stigmatization finds its causes in every conceivable social form. Warner leaves out the normal, the everyday, the unqueer. Paranoid structuralism too: queers are oppressed by *everything*. Political paralysis or political energy? Which is it for you?

In *Tendencies*, Sedgwick produces a list polemically aimed against MacKinnon's and Rich's deployments of the copula. Asking herself "What's queer?" she offers us "one train of thought about it." (Other trains are running on other tracks, she implies, and are just as good, though they go quite elsewhere. For Sedgwick, a network of trains traveling all over; for Warner, a tree with roots spreading all over.) Indicating then that her own "ruling intuition" is to "*dis*articulate" the elements of her life one from the other, she asks us to

> think of all the elements that are condensed in the notion of sexual identity, something that the common sense of our time presents as a unitary category. Yet, exerting any pressure at all on "sexual identity," you see that its elements include
>
> > your biological (e.g., chromosomal) sex, male or female;
> > your self-perceived gender assignment, male or female (supposed to be the same as your biological sex);
> > the preponderance of your traits of personality and appearance, masculine or feminine (supposed to correspond to your sex and gender);
> > the biological sex of your preferred partner;

the gender assignment of your preferred partner (supposed to be the same as her/his biological sex);

the masculinity or femininity of your preferred partner
(supposed to be the opposite of your own);

your self-perception as gay or straight (supposed to correspond to whether your preferred partner is your sex or
the opposite);

your preferred partner's self-perception as gay or straight
(supposed to be the same as yours);

your procreative choice (supposed to be yes if straight, no
if gay);

your preferred sexual act(s) (supposed to be insertive if
you are male or masculine, receptive if you are female
or feminine);

your most eroticized sexual organs (supposed to correspond to the procreative capabilities of your sex, and to
your insertive/receptive assignment);

your sexual fantasies (supposed to be highly congruent
with your sexual practice, but stronger in intensity);

your main locus of emotional bonds (supposed to reside
in your preferred sexual partner);

your enjoyment of power in sexual relations (supposed to
be low if you are female or feminine, high if you are
male or masculine);

the people from whom you learn about your own gender
and sex (supposed to correspond to yourself in both
respects);

your community of cultural and political identification
(supposed to correspond to your own identity);

and—again—many more. (6–8, footnote omitted)

Two disaggregative strategies are at work here. Sedgwick has broken "sexual identity" up into independent fragments and stacked

them vertically as items on an infinitely expandable list. Each of these vertically disarticulated elements comes with a parenthetical aside, the horizontal dimension, which reveals it to be less onto-logical—less a new "fact" about sexual identity that has to be added to our understanding of its reality—than ideological, a supposition, a funny idea we have and could probably ditch.

Recall that MacKinnon and West understand that male gender, male bodies, male will to penetrate, and male will to dominate stack up with frightening "fit" and meet feminine gender, female bodies, female will to be penetrated, and female will to submit with enraging persistence, and that these constitute—for Mac-Kinnon the structure; for cultural feminism the mistake—of the heterosexual mandate. We have seen that this binary structure of gender is so total for MacKinnon that, if a man rapes a man, the latter can only be understood to have been feminized. Sedgwick's vertical fracturing of "sexual identity" suggests that for any indi-vidual, any element that feminism regards as m could switch to f, any element pinned to f could switch to m—and that could happen without predetermining the outcome (m or f?) for the next element. If structural feminism is transfixed by the "male masculine heterosexual insertive procreative power-appetitive man," Sedgwick's idea is to look around for mix-and-match events: the masculine male receptive procreative man, the mascu-line female lesbian who likes to sleep with men, the gender-labile man who describes himself as a lesbian trapped in a woman's body. "And—again—many more": the possibilities are endless; they "ramify in an unimaginably large number of directions."

Sedgwick also contests here the structural feminist ideas that, for any given person, it's either m or f all the way down, and that each and every element in the gender system is ultimately des-tined to dock in m/f somewhere. Sedgwick's bemused attitude and the light irony of her list suggest that these ideas are a bit absurd, daft, imaginary. Working horizontally, we continually encounter ironic asides suggesting that each micro-stack of gender elements—the coherence of your gender and your sex1; the oppositeness of your sex1 and that of your preferred partner; the simultaneous oppositeness of your preferred partner's gender, etc., etc., etc.—is purely suppositional. Wink—get it?—readers in the know have not been fooled; they *already know* that all the strongly binarized patterning of erotic affairs, particularly its limitation to m and f, is ideological. Maybe we know, or are, people whose "sexual identity" doesn't even refer to the m/f sex1 or m/f gender of the preferred partner; we may be people who derive our sexual identities not from the sex1 of the person we like to have sex with but from our friends; perhaps we are gay men who persistently yearn for sex with women because they have money now; perhaps we are lesbians who yearn for sex with men because they fall asleep so fast afterward . . .

What affects do these queer exploded lists provoke? The form launches an open-ended trajectory ending with implicit ellipses leading out to infinity; it multiplies taxonomies. It invites emotions of childish exploration, delighted surprise, hushed anticipation that one has found an analytic antimortality strategy.

This queer affect provokes intense resentment in many feminists. Queer theory's claims to infinite mobility are read as elite confidence that queer theory will be perpetually apropos, and to suggest that uncool stuck feminism, with its pathetic commitment to the superseded category of women, is fighting a rearguard action against intellectual adventure and academic omnipresence. To be sure, the invitation to ramify everywhere has been invoked to authorize dizzyingly random scholarly efforts and to ratify as high politics private hedonic projects that utterly fail to face up to the challenges posed by the social violence in which we live. The tone of queer theory when it does this is bratty, smug, and unserious. The feminists have a point.

But there's nothing in either Warner's or Sedgwick's list to endorse those sequels: Warner's is about the almost infinite forms of (bad) sexual domination; and Sedgwick's is about the almost infinite forms of erotic cathexis on and indifference to gender. Within the exploded confines of either, m > f can still happen and can still be said to be a bad social outcome warranting a political response. And, as we'll see below, Warner's essay amply indicates that he would look to feminism for the best ideas about what his response would be. Finally, there's nothing in feminism that *requires* the copula and its stuckness: again, query whether some feminists' experience of pathetic stuckness is self-induced.

A more fully critical engagement with queer theory's exploded list would note that, even when it ramifies all over and multiplies possibilities to infinity, it is nevertheless a list. At the top is a structuralist tether: all queers, all sexuality, all the time. Sedgwick's has an armature of sameness—a Fordist mechanical operativeness—that exceeds even that of Rich's. Her list is, moreover and by her own admission, written at the behest of a *ruling* intuition. As we will see, neither Sedgwick nor Warner desired this effect: it's almost as though it crept in structurally. But these lists can produce the difficult-to-describe feeling of being disconcerted, disappointed, even a little confused—perhaps the feeling Sedgwick once described to me as her own emotion when faced with a bumper sticker ordering her to "Question Authority."

Mandated multiplicity, dissolved identity, mix-and-match all the way down—these might, moreover, not make everyone feel good. Any leftist with a serious heterosexual fetish for the erotic connection between masculine men and feminine women is going to discover in Sedgwick's list a certain limit: its ambitions to infinitude, and her relegation of that desire, that personhood even, to "and so on . . . ," might make such a person feel . . . a bit forlorn, left out of the party.

The future of Foucault's laugh is a bit uncertain. For myself, Taking a Break from Feminism in order to decide mixes the sense of delicious wonder at the profound uncertainty of all our knowledge, the steep, almost delirious complexity of sexuality as it is so variously lived, with the grim resolution that the structural feminists, in all their consolidated knowledge, produce through the copula. I like this mix better than the segregated euphorias and dysphorias of the copula and the exploded list. I hope you will too.

1990–2000: From Political to Ethical Feminism

In 1990 Marianne Hirsch and Evelyn Fox Keller published *Conflicts in Feminism*. Just a little over ten years later Elisabeth Bronfen and Misha Kavka published *Feminist Consequences: Theory for the New Century*. Each is a brilliantly apt performance of the feminist political and intellectual possibility of its moment. And they are formally alike: coedited, medium-length anthologies of essays stating the art in feminism as it attempts to render itself coherent under the pressures of the moment, and bidding for a feminist future in which those pressures would strengthen rather than weaken feminism. Both volumes grapple with critiques arising from socialist-feminist, antiracist-feminist, and anticolonial-feminist projects. One mark of the decade that intervened, in which the feminist experience of paralysis had its crescendo, is that the challenges of postmodernizing feminism, though quite peripheral for *Conflicts in Feminism*, are taken to be definitive for *Feminist Consequences*. What can we learn about the consequences of the Break *inside feminism* by comparing them?

❦ *Marianne Hirsch and Evelyn Fox Keller,* Conflicts in Feminism, *and Elisabeth Bronfen and Misha Kavka,* Feminist Consequences

Here are some striking differences between the two books. *Conflicts in Feminism* explicitly placed its contributors into political engagement with one another, fully incorporated the feminist authority of a man (and its hot denunciation), and encompassed a range of different responses to the moralized mandate to converge feminism with antiracism;[15] while *Feminist Consequences* insulates the authors from one another, elides the question of men in feminism, and produces as a very strong effect the ethical mandate to merge feminism with antiracism and indeed with universalized humanism.[16] *Conflicts* is prepostmodern; *Consequences* is postmodernizing and ethical.

The formal composition of the two books makes some of these differences visible. *Conflicts* begins and ends with essays coauthored by the coeditors; the introduction is titled by its date of completion, marking it as a temporal intervention for "now"; and the conclusion taxonomizes the various essays' style of managing conflicts in feminism, specifying their differences *inter sese.* More—the editors' conclusion eventually splits itself into two parallel columns that voice two distinct analyses independently, implying that the editors, too, are "in conflict" either between or within themselves.

Consequences begins with an introduction by only one of the editors (Kavka); there is no indication why Bronfen did not sign on. The volume closes with the transcript of an interview, conducted by both editors, with Drucilla Cornell. It is clear from the interview and from the editors' essays published in the volume that Kavka and Bronfen had distinct projects, but Cornell more or less adopts what they say and fits it as well as she can into her own articulation of feminism, and they don't object. Any tensions among the three feminists are muted into an overall harmonic convergence.

It seems that ethics has arrived and works at the expense of politics.

Conflicts addresses "those issues that seemed to be most critically divisive" for people attempting to " 'do' theory as feminists." These included "race and class, pornography, the 'Sears' case, the 'Baby M' case" (3). This means that the editors directly engage the antiracist critique; the "sex wars"; the problem for feminism posed by the fact that working-class women employed by Sears *preferred* sex-segregated, lower-wage employment; and splits among feminists and between women and men about reproduction. Clearly the place of postmodernism in feminism had not become centrally problematic; this book, published the same year as *Gender Trouble* and *Epistemology of the Closet*, is not structurally worried about Foucault.[17] Though the word "pain" occurs a lot in the introduction and the conclusion, the editors and contributors model a great deal of stamina for confronting each other and for managing and observing themselves as managers of conflict. Indeed, "mapping" these conflicts is a persistent concern of the editors and the authors: several classic taxonomies of feminisms appear here. Most basically, perhaps, all of the "conflicts" and all of the participants in them were understood to be "in feminism." Feminism itself is not defined, and is assumed to be there as an ongoing political and intellectual project for all the contributors.

By contrast, *Consequences* is continually worried about what feminism is and whether it's in OK shape. In the interview with Cornell, Kavka asks: "What would you say has become of the political project that was once feminism? Or has feminist politics perhaps taken on a different resonance?" (437). Kavka's introduction poses as its central problem the unintelligibility, the incoherence, and even the possible death of feminism as a theoretical *and* political project:

> [F]eminist work of the "long" 1980's (read late 1970's to early 1990's), in refining from ever-proliferating positions the objects, goals, and definitions of feminism, has had the effect of splintering what had been a recognizable feminist project into unrecognizability, even into a paradoxical state of visible invisibility. . . .
>
> . . . Most important, the very terms through which we might now seek to define feminism have been refined, pluralized, displaced, and/or deconstructed to the point where they hardly seem available any more, certainly not if one claims to be defining feminism on behalf of "women." Which brings us to the paradox of being involved in a political practice that can no longer define itself as a practice, let alone define its goals. (ix–x)

Paralysis. Against it, the task of the book is to find that "different resonance" which will make feminism continuingly possible.

For both Kavka and Cornell, this search amounts to a yearning for an ideal—Justice—and an actual social practice of ethics. Both the ideal and the ethical design of the project will enable feminists to maintain their relationships across difference. How? Both the ideal and the practices it inspires have a proleptic structure, a future orientation, which itself is invoked to guarantee feminism against essentialism and denial of difference. They become overarching universals reconverging feminism above the divergentism introduced by *The Combahee River Collective Statement, Gender Trouble,* "Can the Subaltern Speak?" and their likes. Temporality, justice, and ethics become the media into which racial difference and the postmodernizing critique of the subject disperse, lose their cutting edge, and reconfigure as compatible elements of a new convergentism. The whole design of the project proposes that it is not difference within "woman" or among women that has been "paralyzing" for these feminists; it is divergentism.

Let's take a moment to see, in some detail, how Kavka accomplishes this new configuration of feminist convergentism. She first desubstantivizes feminism by making it a temporality. Feminism, she argues, has no intrinsic social commitments; rather it is the ever-evolving congeries of human projects that inject themselves into the historical context of other projects that have been understood to be feminist.[18] Feminism *is* its consequences, in the strong sense that it has almost no present but rather an ever-receding past into which ever-new futures intervene. We can tell that a project is feminist not because of anything internal to it, but because it is willing to enter into the ever-forward movement of feminism's soon-to-be-past future.

This is a somewhat tautological definition of feminism: feminism is anything that intervenes into feminism as feminism. If Kavka stopped there, I would have to classify her feminism as an escapee from the definitional minima I have deduced in U.S. feminism today (m/f, m > f, and carrying a brief for f), though of course I would also have to point out that it managed its escape through the expedient of imagining feminism as the empty repetition of its own name. In three steps, however, Kavka adds substance to the project, substance that introduces convergentism in a very sublime form. They add at least m/f and carrying a brief for f; I think m > f too.

The first substantivizing move is to further define feminism as participation in highly differentiated social projects that are nevertheless oriented toward the universal goal of social justice. "Feminism is not . . . the object of a singular history but, rather, a term under which people have in different times and places invested in a more general struggle for social justice and in so doing have participated in and produced multiple histories" (xii). Because Justice is not known or fixed but visionary ("Justice"

itself "lies outside feminist history and propels its continued unfolding" [xxiv]), this prolepsis is both temporally propelling and
rich in meaning.

At least two taxonomic questions are raised by Kavka's proposed definition, of course. If "feminism" is "a term under which
. . . a more general struggle for social justice" is undertaken, what
are the other terms and how are they distinct from "feminism"?
And how "general" *is* "a more general struggle for social justice"?
Does it include (for instance) struggles for social justice that see
female domesticity as a sublime human good? Kavka, aware no
doubt that more definitional work was needed, provides an additional defining characteristic of feminism: ethics.

> The difficulty that has now developed is the question of rela-
> tionality, or how we understand and effect relations with one
> another that manifest a sense of social responsibility beyond
> the limits of the group based on a set of shared differences.
> In order to address the problem of how to do politics in an
> age of "different differences," feminism has turned to face
> the multivalent problem of ethics. (xvi)

Kavka's tone now becomes rhapsodic, registering a release from
paralysis and a resurgence of vitality. She senses that the "tide is
turning"; the "we" of feminism may be united in an effort to
"broach the issue of ethical relations for feminism as a way of
making contact with one another without assuming each other
to be all the same" (xxiii). Ethics at the top makes feminism a way
of *relating* to and through difference; at that level, "the diversified
feminist project [note the singular] is moving [note the present
progressive tense] toward re-claiming universalism, though in
such a way as to radically redefine 'universalism' itself" (xx). Similarly, no one feminist project has captured justice; rather justice
itself is a desire arching over and out of time. And this, in turn,
enables the temporal framing: "Feminism has—perhaps—been

through the era of differences, learned its lessons, and is moving on" (xxiii). The last words of the introduction are these: "feminism lives" (xxiv).

For all its abstraction and its present-progressive temporality, Kavka's vision is convergentist. Feminists in conflict, feminists diverging over some aspect of hybrid feminism, feminists reduced to those who "share differences" are nevertheless merged into a new "universalism" in which "justice" is the shared goal and "ethics" the shared mode of relating across difference. The teleology of this is, if you will, a poststructuralist structuralism: "it indicates an extension of feminist history into further (what would have once been called 'other') theories, objects, methodologies" (xxi). That which is not feminism becomes feminism's future and eventually will be feminism. This vision of feminism, for all its prolepsis, is just as structuralist in its ultimate vision as MacKinnon's and West's feminisms are in their descriptions of our everyday reality. Futurity has replaced present-tense description; beyond that, only the dysphoria and the attendant paranoia are missing.

But why is it *feminist?* Kavka might think that relatedness and nondeontological ethics are distinctively feminine. This would be a classic Gilliganian cultural-feminist move; but strikingly, Kavka doesn't make it. Instead, she concludes by recuperating postfeminism, and all that is not feminism, to feminism, a firm return to m/f—even to women!—and to feminism as a project that carries a brief for f.

> [F]eminist work cannot be differentiated from "postfeminist" work precisely because postfeminism can only be understood in terms of the various histories in which feminism has provided its adherents with a sense of political agency. This means that feminist thinking may now stretch beyond "women" or even gender as categories and as delimiting objects of investigation; it does not, however, mean leaving

these categories behind. Rather, as Biddy Martin suggests, the idea is to "suspend or defer questions about what [other objects, methodologies, or technologies] have to do with women or gender long enough to make our analyses of gender and sexuality new again and supple enough to help us intervene usefully in those developments." Postfeminism, in this sense, refers not to the end of a politics or practice but, rather, to a suspension within it that allows such a politics to remain vital and relevant to contexts of social change.[19]

The "contexts of social change" remain describable in the nested terms of gender, sexuality, and woman; the "suspension" recommended by Rubin and Sedgwick originates and ends in m/f; divergence emerges not between but within. Temporality, Justice, and Ethics are feminist not only because of their sublime place in the scale of adjudicatory values, but also because they remain committed to contemporary feminism's essential characteristics.

For all those harmonics in the introduction, it would have been plausible to give the volume as a whole the title *Conflicts in Feminism*, and to introduce it with a Hirsch-and-Keller-like mapping of the frictions it presents. For example, although Kavka, as we have seen, assimilates Biddy Martin's essay to her vision of feminism, Martin's essay itself concentrates on the "failures" implicit in Women's Studies' "success." We read there that Women's Studies "has reached a point of stasis," "has lost much of its intellectual and political vigor," and is "stultifying" (353–54). "To be exciting again," the field "would have to" engage (354) (no promise here that it will, or can, engage, and certainly no assertion that it is already engaging) with "developments in the field with no immediately apparent relationship to 'women' or 'gender'" (356), and especially it would have to confront the disciplinary crisis that splits the sciences of the body off from the sciences of thought (357–58); it would have to accept responsibility for its own implication in academic authority and the competitive energies it incites (355); and it would have to be willing to accept a stance as an almost empty "placeholder" while "some of our liveliest scholarship and teaching is conducted outside its official parameters" and while "a healthy ambivalence" exposes its "limits" (378–79).

Martin wants to Take a Break. Kavka's introductory invocation of her essay emphasizes Martin's hope that departure from feminist terms might enable "us" to "make our analyses of gender and sexuality new again"; but Kavka invests a confidence in that teleology, and a will to converge it firmly back into feminism, that are simply absent from Martin's essay.

Another split. Kavka's introduction lets "Justice" do the work that domination does for MacKinnon and West, and it carries such a slight hint of m > f that I sometimes wonder whether it's even there. And the contributors seem split whether to take the Foucaultian break from the presumption that power is subordination. Martin, on one hand, reassures us that her agenda "is not a way to unknow what we already know about forms of oppression, subordination and discrimination" (368); while Lauren Berlant's essay questions even that: "*the psychic pain experienced by subordinated populations must be treated as ideology* not as prelapsarian knowledge or a condensed comprehensive social theory."[20]

Or consider the way in which the concluding section of the volume—titled "Where to Feminism?"—contains and sublimes away a conflict inside feminism about feminist paralysis. Mieke Bal adopts an attitude that Judith Butler explicitly rejects,[21] and it remains for Cornell, in her interview with the editors, to find the harmonic convergence between them. Here's how it goes.

Bal regrets the "tragic fate of feminism in the 1990s" (323); Butler acknowledges that "for many of us it is a sad time for feminism, even a defeated time" (418). Their remedial ideas differ dramatically. Bal stipulates that "[t]he worst waste of energy for feminists is to fight other feminists on the ground of a difference of opinion" (323), and invokes women's solidarized experience as ground; while Butler welcomes hard times as an invitation to "submi[t] to the demand for rearticulation" (418).

Bal thinks in terms that should be familiar to us from *Caring for Justice*. She argues that the "fact" that "a woman" made Louise Bourgeois's *Femme Maison* series "does matter" because "the experience of bodily confinement in the mud of housewifery called motherhood can only be so acutely yet humorously rendered if one knows the experience from one's own body" (336). I think Bal would say that she avoids the reifying implications of this astonishing conflation of "woman" into the maternal, and the prepostmodern invocation of experience as ground, by insisting on the metaphoric and "folded" quality of gender as she imagines it. But the structural tendency of her feminism—and its firm stance against differences in opinion—produce this reflection on one of several artworks by Doris Salcedo addressing the memory of victims of political violence in Columbia:

> The dead whose violation is actualized are women and men. Does this mean that gender is no longer an issue, that other, more burning problems require our attention?
>
> Allow me to refrain from answering this question, which accepts no either/or. There is a small difference, though, that is neither ontological nor epistemological but enfolded in both. *The Orphan's Tunic* is made of human hair, and the silk from a dress a little girl wore day in and day out when the artist was working in the village where the little girl lived. Her mother had made the dress for her. Then the mother was killed. The dress, the material presence of it in Salcedo's work, remains stubbornly gendered in a multiplicity of ways. Faced with this work, you can't even question if it matters whether the artist, the little girl, or the viewer is female or male. (347)

I gather you can't question whether it matters because *you know it does.*

Butler, on the other hand, lays out differences of opinion between and among feminists, Lesbian and Gay Studies proponents, the vanguardists of queer theory, *and the Vatican!* about the ever-varying capacities of "sex," "gender," and "sexual difference" to enter into signifying relation to each other and to various justice projects. Asking, "Why is it that posing a question about a term is considered the same as effecting a prohibition against its use?" (422), Butler proposes that

> It makes no sense, I would argue, to hold fast to theoretical paradigms and preferred terminologies, to make the case for feminism on the basis of sexual difference, or to defend that notion against the claims of gender, the claims of sexuality, the claims of race, or the umbrella claims of cultural studies. . . . Sexual difference is not a given, not a premise, not a basis on which to build a feminism; it is not that which we have already encountered and come to know; rather, as *a question* that prompts feminist inquiry, it is something that cannot quite be stated, that troubles the grammar of the statement, and that remains, more or less permanently, to interrogate. (418)

"You can't even question" / "Sexual difference is . . . a question. . . ." Women are a distinct social group unified in experience and suffused with immanent feminine knowledge / sexual difference is a critical distinction to which feminism remains dedicated even when it is utterly riven about what it distinguishes. Dogmatic truth / inquiry, rearticulation, and critique within the constraints of sexual difference. By 2001, these two paths in feminism had diverged almost completely. It is especially striking that Kavka's introduction makes no reference to the *actual* differences that animate her authors.

Into this quite profound divergence, Cornell intervenes to assert that feminism—defined now *as* feminist ethics—is an overarching definitive ethos. The design is unmistakably convergentist.

Renouncing any "master narrative" for feminism, Cornell says: "[W]hat I would look for is what I have called 'ethical feminism,' which would try to examine the components of feminist theory, and its relationship to a feminist practice, in terms of the relationship between the aesthetic, the ethical, the political, the moral, and the legal" (438). "[F]or the last seven or eight years, since I've been asked to give a name to my feminism, I've called it ethical feminism" (449).

Cornell's ethical feminism is postmodernizing. It incorporates as a redemptive project the relationship of women to gender that Butler described in the early 1990s as both a historical calamity and a constant opportunity for resistance. But Cornell offers an important translation of Butler's idea. For Cornell, ethical feminism would be the mode of working out the insight that everyone has a right to *claim* personhood (and, more specifically, in the subdomain of sexuality, "a sexuate being"), to move toward these, to imagine them for him- or herself, and to construct them in the course of living (439–41). This is Cornell's "imaginary domain." It is an extremely deft incorporation into a humanistic, even a rights, vocabulary of postmodern intuitions that the "sovereign subject" is fragmented, split, temporal.[22]

In Cornell's ethical universalism, as in Kavka's, feminism insinuates itself into and over otherwise divergent justice projects as their shared future, and thus o'erleaps their present otherness. To be sure, Cornell's postmodernism fractures identity, insisting instead that we are all ethically engaged in a project of identification: indeed, "it's precisely because our identities are not captured by any set of identifications that we are engaged in ethics when we do make identifications" (451). But for anyone asking "whether an identification is one that should be taken up, or needs to be reappropriated, renegotiated, or re-represented," "ethics is the ultimate criterion by which we judge" (451).

Cornell asserts at least three times that she has an ethical obligation to identify as white and Anglo (441–42) and describes her inability to speak Spanish (which she treats as homologous to her identification as white and Anglo) as "a disability" (442). This identification—though performed, not given, and thus undertaken responsibly (441)—is just as fixed and static as the prepostmodern forms of white (and black) feminist identification imagined in the early passages of *The Combahee River Collective Statement*. In Cornell's racial world, some spaces are proper to some racial subjects:

> As a white, Anglo woman, I am not going to be renegotiating the meaning of "Latina"; my daughter might, but I'm not. That's not my "place." (442)

What would Spivak say to this? Something like this, I think: *of course* Cornell's gesture "renegotiat[es] the meaning of 'Latina.' " In any important deconstructive binary, a change in the meanings of one term brings about a change in the meanings of the other, so that Cornell's disavowal of any effect on Latina identity would *of course* have profound effects on Latina identity. If anyone is persuaded by Cornell's point, she has helped to make Latina identity more embodied, more distinct to its holders, less Anglo, less white, and more disavowable by bearers of Anglo, white identity than it was before. Cornell's ethically self-congratulatory renunciation of any participation in Latina identity reiterates Foucault's more carefree renunciation of representational responsibility for prisoners and the working class. And the racial "place" so powerfully temporalized by Cornell is precisely what Spivak, after much agonized searching, did not find. Though Cornell would not use the Combahee Statement's convergentist terms (synthesis, simultaneity, integration, and so on), she reconstitutes its allocation of social otherness based on identity, while moving feminism into place as the ultimate ground on which otherness, as a human problem, will be redeemed.

Cornell would take *feminist* responsibility for justice projects and social constituencies that divergentist hybrid feminism would at some point conceptualize as intersecting with but distinct from feminism. She traces her feminism to formative years in which she "saw national difference, ethnic difference, and class struggle as being at the very heart of what feminism was about and I never thought of feminism or gender separately from these issues" (436). In "the imaginary domain," where the project of identification proceeds, she frames "a shared project of legal reform that would include the transgendered, transsexuals, gays, and lesbians, and also, in a very different arena, would allow us to make claims for language rights" (442–43). Borrowing David Richards's convergentist framing of subordination, in which he homologized racial, sexual, sexual-orientation, and class subordination as "moral servitude,"[23] Cornell concludes:

> It seems to me that all of us, because we have the right to lay claim to our own person, can join together in the struggle against moral servitude and make that struggle the heart of a meaningful platform of legal reform. (443)

Clearly some elements of postmodernizing feminism can be incorporated into a strong articulation of feminism going forward in a convergentist mode. The split self can be turned into a reconstructive project, aiming for an ever-deferred but beloved coherence; and can place itself in relationship to other very different selves through the sublime media of universal justice and ethics.

Whether the result is a more or less energized politics probably depends on what turns you on. For myself I will say that the formal characteristics of *Consequences* bespeak a kind of political (dis)engagement that is quite apt to the program laid out for feminism—sublime, ideal, postmaterial, and virtuous with respect to everyone—in Kavka's introduction and in Cornell's interview. And note that, if my reading of these two anthologies convinces anyone, then I have also probably made my case that postmodernism and hybrid divergentism are not necessarily paralyzing for feminism; not only does *Consequences* present feminism as alive and well, but it appears that Sublime Liberal Feminism can incorporate them and keep moving. Whether you want to move along with it is another question.

1990–95: Getting to Deadlock

We return now to our chronological genealogy, starting in the early 1990s. This section looks closely at the emergence of a specific "deadlock" inside feminism.

❦ *Judith Butler and Joan W. Scott,* Feminists Theorize the Political, *and Seyla Benhabib et al.,* Feminist Contentions

In *Feminist Contentions*, Seyla Benhabib warned that "[t]he postmodernist position(s) thought through to their conclusions may eliminate not only the specificity of feminist theory but place in question the very emancipatory ideals of the women's movements altogether."[24] Paralysis. *Feminists Theorize the Political* is a partisan entry, opposed to Benhabib's position. Both books register the high degree of political engagement that the paralysis critique provoked.

Judith Butler was involved in both books. She and Joan Scott edited *Feminists Theorize the Political.* It represents the state of the art, circa 1992, of the feminist critique of woman. It emphasizes the poststructuralist inquiry into gender and sexuality, the poststructuralist/psychoanalytic ditto, and some more-and/or-less divergentist hybrid feminist projects that continue them. In their cowritten introduction, Butler and Scott provide the fifteen questions that they addressed to their contributors. Here is the first question:

> There appears to be a belief that without an ontologically grounded feminist subject there can be no politics. Here, politics is understood as a representational discourse that presumes a fixed or ready-made subject, usually conceived through the category of "women." As a result, analysis of the political construction and regulation of this category is summarily foreclosed. What are the political consequences of such foreclosure? And what political possibilities does a critique of identity categories make possible? (xiv)

The claim that postmodernizing feminism precludes feminist politics is reduced here to a "belief" that "appears" to exist. Describing your opponents' actual position as either illusory or an illusion is not very nice, but it has the thrill of good sarcasm and performs the editors' confidence in their alternative-world-making powers. The title *Feminists Theorize the Political,* moreover, puts theory and politics into an intimate relationship and points out that different feminist*s*—not femin*ism*—are its agents. Indeed, the title is a sentence with an active verb in the present tense: there is something of the manifesto in its tone.

Note also the lovely paradox that Benhabib's claim, that postmodernizing feminism precludes politics on behalf of women and feminism, is countered by Butler and Scott's claim that Benhabib's claim, if honored, would preclude politics within feminism about women and feminism. Everyone is for politics, with the postmodernizing feminists regarding their "paralysis" objectors as willing their own immobility. There is a conflict in feminism.

There is no hint *Feminists Theorize the Political* of the onset of queer theory as a carrier of the postmodernizing-feminist virus, or as an alternative to feminist theory for left politics about sexuality. Rubin's "Thinking Sex" and Sedgwick's *Epistemology of the Closet* don't come up for discussion. But the idea that work outside feminism can be crucial to and critical of feminism has pride of place in the collection—unacknowledged, however—in the form of coeditor Scott's own essay.

Scott's " 'Experience,' "[25] is a critique—indeed, it's *the* classic critique—of arguments from experience. Scott saw all around her—in historiographical debates, in the practice of social historians, and in then-contemporary social-movement politics—a wave of arguments giving foundational epistemic authority to claims from experience. Many kinds of claims, she argues, do indeed garner our respect because they arise from experience. But experience in its turn arises on the ground of already-consolidated effects of preexisting historical and political knowledge. She operates from the Foucaultian hypothesis that discursive forms, theoretical and political, both arise from and produce experience; so that a fully historical understanding of these dynamics would require a genealogical examination of the very concept and practice of the phenomenon of (it's time to bring in her scare quotes) "experience."

Scott's essay has an important place in the bibliography of the "new historicism"; it also offered itself as a reflection on "identity politics" across the board. What's interesting for our purposes here is that feminist materials are entirely subsidiary to these broader engagements and appear not as the subject of her examination but as mere examples. To be sure, feminist texts—drawn (inter alia) from work by MacKinnon—provide some of her clearest instances of arguments from unmediated, transparently perceived and represented "experience"; but other feminist texts—by Spivak, Denise Riley, Chandra Tapalde Mohanty, Katie King, and others—serve as counterexamples. And to be sure, feminists in a wide array of convergentist feminist projects have taken exception to Scott's argument: they clearly saw that, if its critique were accepted, it would disable arguments resting on the epistemic authority claimed for "women's experience" in so much of MacKinnon's work and its moral authority in cultural feminism; and it would destabilize the presumptive status of "black women's experience" as both consolidated and politically radical in the opening articulations of *The Combahee River Collective Statement.* Instead, Scott's essay assists in the project I have deduced from Foucault, of inquiring whether and when feminism creates the discursive conditions for women's existence and suffering.[26]

But feminism is not Scott's subject matter or professed mode of proceeding. Instead, the structure of Scott's argument bears a certain uncanny similarity to that of *Epistemology of the Closet* as I've described it. Scott's "set text"—the text that she reads and rereads at least three times in the course of the essay as a way of working out the consequences of conceding and resisting the "authority of experience"—is an autobiography of a gay man and his gay maleness. Scott opens and closes her argument with readings of Samuel R. Delaney's narration, in his 1988 book *The Motion of Light in Water,* of an ecstatic moment in 1963 when he stood in a crowded gay male bathhouse and gazed in near delirium at the "undulating mass of naked male bodies, spread wall to wall" in the blue light. He claims to have had at that moment the involuntary aperçu, the direct, unmediated, and ecstatic perception—the *experience*—of homosexuals as a population with a historical purpose and of himself *as* a homosexual socially tied by experience to others.[27] Scott's procedure is first to insist on this direct invocation of the "authority of experience" and then to deconstruct it, word by word, until the very same text serves as the perfect example of her genealogical and new-historicist undertaking. As a series of rereadings, this is a tour de force.

Perhaps not coincidentally, Scott's essay first appeared one year after the publication of *Epistemology of the Closet*. The two texts were presumably being written at about the same time. They both show us feminism capable of producing and cohabiting with an "outside"—capable, in my terms here, of Taking a Break from itself. But Scott's essay seems quite complacent about the value of such a departure. This complacency was not secure. Like Sedgwick, Scott took a lot of heat for presuming to write about an experience "not her own" and for defecting—in an essay that would offer important critiques of many specific feminist projects—from the rich sources of "properly" women's experience; of course these criticisms missed the point of the essay entirely. Instead, like Sedgwick, she seems to have gained some critical purchase on an important problem in then-contemporary feminism by Taking a Break from its identitarian terms. Unlike Sedgwick, however, Scott, and *Feminists Theorize the Political* generally, do not mark this departure from the terms of feminism to be particularly problematic, to require theoretical reflection, or to constitute one of the volume's militancies. The edginess of this possibility has a history, it seems.

Meanwhile, Benhabib, Butler, Drucilla Cornell, and Nancy Fraser were working on *Feminist Contentions*. Like *Conflicts in Feminism*, this is an intensely engaged performance, and one that emphasizes the temporal contingency of politically engaged thought. All four feminists coauthor the volume as a whole; it has no "editor." Each contributes her own essay and a response to all the others. The date of "publication" is similarly multiple: the exchange started as a face-to-face event in 1990; the essays were published in German in 1993; and the English edition, with the

responses, was not printed until 1995. Butler even dates the segments of her response (February 1993, March 1994).

Unlike *Conflicts in Feminism*, however, *Feminist Contentions* disavows any effort to represent feminism generally (2); instead, each
contributor elaborates her own position inside feminist theory
and specifically inside feminist philosophy. Benhabib, Butler, Cornell, and Fraser address the relationship among feminism, postmodernism, poststructuralism, and critical theory; the status of
the subject, of history, of agency, of the political world as envisioned by and for feminism; and the place of theory in that world.
None of their positions can be imagined arising outside their
four-way exchange. It is internal critique in a highly disciplinary
mode. If *Conflicts in Feminism, Feminist Consequences*, and *Feminists Theorize the Political* are Feminism 210, *Feminist Contentions*
is Feminism 430.

The exchanges are blunt and even bitter. Benhabib opens with
the argument that "[t]he postmodernist position(s)," taken seriously and to their logical ends, disable feminist theory, stifle the
articulation of feminist emancipatory ideals, and render women's
social movements incoherent. She concludes by invoking for feminism a return to utopian and ethical projects that can ground it
politically in the search for women's emancipation. Butler argues—specifically against Benhabib—that the antifoundational
protocols of postmodernism (a term she uses with reservations)
are just as necessary as the terms they would require us to examine (woman, nation, etc.). Fraser prunes what she perceives as the
solecisms and errors from both essays in an effort to integrate
them into a stronger feminism; and Cornell offers an early version of the ethical feminism discussed above.[28] The four responses
are fascinating intensifications of the positions each author has
taken in the primary essays; except for Butler's puzzling adoption
of Cornell's position as harmonious with her own, each contribu-

tor seems more than willing to invalidate or reconstrue the contributions of the others as decisively as she can.

Overall, the pattern seems to be this: Benhabib and Butler work out strongly different feminisms on either side of a "postmodernist" divide, while the syncretic efforts of Cornell and Fraser (ethical and pragmatic, respectively) implicitly contradict one another by their sheer mutual incommensurability, while doing interpretive violence to Benhabib's and Butler's arguments precisely by striving so hard to make them fit into a single, overarching, harmonious feminism.

Butler's response concludes with "sadness" that "there is a deadlock that pervades this debate" (127)—a mournful invocation of the paralysis trope. But it seems more accurate to say that Benhabib and Butler represent the feminism espoused by each other to be *both* frighteningly frozen *and* alarmingly active; Butler's "deadlock" seems to seize not the individual programs for feminism that make up the book, and certainly not Fraser's and Cornell's voluble convergentisms, but Butler's own dashed hopes for convergence *with Benhabib*. This seems to me to be a distinctively *feminist* sadness. Typically, academic fields that produce the degree of highly articulate theoretic disagreement manifested in this book are understood to be productive, active, capacious, fraught with meaningful cruxes; alarming but also vital places to be.

Around 1993: Mapping Feminism and Queer Theory

The year 1993 was a big one.[29] Sedgwick published *Tendencies*, Michael Warner published *Fear of a Queer Planet*, and an A-team of lesbian and gay academic heavies published the *The Lesbian and Gay Studies Reader*. None of these is a feminist text. All of them Take a Break from Feminism in one way or another. They indicate that there was increasing pressure inside the left intelligentsia's politics of sexuality to *do something* about the Rubin/Sedgwick/Butler nexus in feminism, about the emergence of queer theory by men that was fully engaged with feminism but not feminist, and about the energies building up inside divergentist styles of feminism. In 1994 some feminists responded with an anthology aptly entitled *feminism meets queer theory*.

❧ *Henry Abelove, Michèle Aina Barale, and David M. Halperin,* The Lesbian and Gay Studies Reader

The Lesbian and Gay Studies Reader bears all the marks not only of a "state of the art" collection but even of what we might call a fieldifying encyclopedia or textbook. The book is large-format (seven by ten inches) and long (666 pages); the forty-two excerpts display and map an active, existing field. It includes a "User's Guide" showing how to teach Lesbian and Gay Studies within traditional academic disciplines or in a new separate field. The introduction announces that this new academic field already exists and argues for its institutionalization.

The editors claim that Lesbian and Gay Studies is distinct from feminism and Women's Studies. They propose that Lesbian and Gay Studies exceeds the study of lesbians and gay men just as Women's Studies exceeds the study of women; just as Women's Studies takes "gender as a fundamental category"—just as Women's Studies "treats gender (whether male or female) as a central category of analysis"—so Lesbian and Gay Studies has as its central subject "sex and sexuality" (xv). They aim to Take a Break from Feminism in a very bold, absolute way: gender, understood as subdivided into two kinds ("male *or* female"), is proposed to be conceptually and possibly descriptively distinct from sex and sexuality; the former is to be the intellectual focus of feminism and Women's Studies, while the latter concerns need to migrate to politics focused on advocacy for gay men and lesbians and against "homophobia and heterosexism." It was time for sex and sexuality, gay men and lesbians, and the intellectual branch of antihomophobic and antiheterosexist politics to close down their operations inside feminism and Women's Studies, and to open up new offices next door.

The editors confess that they forefronted "Lesbian and Gay" not to be "assimilationist" but merely "to acknowledge the force of current usage" (xvii); eventually Lesbian and Gay Studies would accede to the term "Queer Studies." This was where people would seek a sympathetic study of "many kinds of sexual non-conformity, including, for instance, bisexuality, trans-sexualism, and sadomasochism" (xvii)—the "sexual minorities" of "Thinking Sex." The result would be a consolidated new field with a broad subject matter mandate: it, and not, apparently, Women's Studies, would "focus[] intense scrutiny on the cultural production, dissemination, and vicissitudes of sexual meanings" (xvi).

To be sure, the new "field" would engage in "lively debate and ongoing negotiation" with Women's Studies over the "connections between sexuality and gender" and the "degree of overlap or distinctness between the fields" (xv–xvi). Though the editors nod in the direction of the eventual dissolution of their project—they dedicate the book to their students, who "will remake [it]—perhaps beyond recognition—in the years ahead" (xvii)—nothing in the introduction develops the tools for this work. The *Reader* marks Lesbian and Gay Studies as a new academic enterprise that is robust precisely because it is "consolidating" (xvi). There is a new kid on the block, Taking a Break and brimming with convergentist ambition.

The *Reader* fully replicates the habit, well entrenched in feminist work and in queer theory that Takes a Break, of deploying theory prescriptively, of collapsing its speculative descriptive and normative dimensions. That's how it could reify its subject matter and imagine itself to wrest its topic, *tout court, from* feminism; that's how it could imagine Lesbian and Gay Studies and Women's Studies flourishing as two contiguous domains of truth.

The volume claims the aegis of "Thinking Sex" and *Epistemology of the Closet* by including them as its inaugural entries.[30] It is a startlingly inappropriate invocation. Rubin and Sedgwick had proposed that sexual minorities and sexual oppression (Rubin) and "sexuality" (Sedgwick) might not yield all of their secrets to hypotheses staked decisively to m/f, m > f, and carrying a brief for f (Rubin) or gender (Sedgwick). They did not claim that feminism is out of a job when it comes to transsexualism or sadomasochism or homosexuality or heterosexism; or that feminism's explanatory power runs out before we reach the study of sexual minorities or sexuality. They certainly did not claim that gender can be divided into two distinct parts, male *or* female. The consolidating ambition of the *Reader*'s reified taxonomy and institutional agenda is quite unlike anything in either of the two texts that the *Reader*—and this book—both genealogize to inaugurate the queer Break.

❦ *Sedgwick,* Tendencies, *and Michael Warner,* Fear of a Queer Planet

Meanwhile, queer theory of a very different sort was happening all over, and some of it Took a Break. What were these intellectual sequelae of Rubin's and Sedgwick's interventions?

The central ambition of Warner's anthology *Fear of a Queer Planet*[31] is to bring queer theory and social theory into full body contact. In *Tendencies*, a collection of her own essays, Sedgwick returned to a hypothesis, articulated but mostly ignored in *Episte-*

mology of the Closet, that modern sexualities depend in intricate ways on "a double-binding but immensely productive incoherence about gender" (xii). Both try to Take a Break from Feminism and from gay identity by methods very different from those we see in the *Reader*. Both try to shed the structuralism and convergentism that, I've argued, have had such an important place in the production of the feminist experience of paralysis. Both go so far as to question whether the queer project should remain tethered to *anything* in the sexuality lexicon. The result is a significant, if incomplete, rethinking of a part of feminism that has remained unchallenged so far: >. In order to make this new attitude about subordination as clear as I can, I follow this section with a recap of MacKinnon's and Spivak's social thought as they differ from Warner's and Sedgwick's.

So how do Sedgwick and Warner position themselves vis-à-vis feminism? Warner's introduction acknowledges that feminism "has made gender a primary category of the social" and has revealed the contingency of gender on sexuality "in a way that makes queer social theory newly imaginable" (viii). He regards Rubin's argument "that sexuality is a partially separate field of inquiry and activism" (viii, footnote omitted) to emerge from inside her feminism. And he quotes in full Sedgwick's query whether "a damaging bias toward heterosocial or heterosexist assumptions inheres unavoidably in the very concept of gender" (xviii). Thus he gives pivotal status to the texts that the *Reader* also emphasizes. And he insists that queer theory and queer life are semiautonomous of feminism. But he both launches his queer undertaking *from* feminism and acknowledges that it has feminist participants and feminist projects (xxvii). So his queer project originates in feminism, is semiautonomous from it, overlaps with it, sometimes is feminist, but also sometimes isn't.

The jacket of *Tendencies* indicates that it should be shelved in "Gay and Lesbian studies / Cultural studies / Literary studies": no

mention of Women's Studies. The index devotes sixteen suben-
tries to "Gender," twenty-two to "Binary oppositions," eleven to
"Anal eroticism," and precisely none to "Feminism." Even turning her attention to gender, Sedgwick tacitly abandons the taxonomic and genealogical struggle to divide the goodies between
feminist and queer theory just right. She gives the question of the
relationship between gender and feminism, between the "queer"
and feminism, and so on, the same status as the question of the
relationship between queer theory and, say, quantum physics.
That is, the question does not come up.

What about gay and lesbian identity? Same difference. The
opening of Warner's introduction specifically invokes an audience of "lesbian and gay intellectuals" (vii), but, after making the
appeal at least once more (x), he turns gay identity against itself
in a way that is highly reminiscent of Butler's operation in "Imitation": "A lesbian and gay population . . . is defined by multiple
boundaries that make the question who is and is not 'one of them'
not merely ambiguous but rather a perpetually and necessarily
contested issue" (xxv). Warner is promoting gay-identity trouble.
To him, one virtue of the term "queer" is its at least temporary
capacity to dodge identity: "It is partly to avoid th[e] reduction
of the issues [that he associated with identity assertion] that so
many people in the last two or three years—including many of
the authors in this volume—have shifted their self-identification
from 'gay' to 'queer' " (xxvi). Warner's queer project is launched
not only from feminism but also from gay identity, and seeks to
depart in similar ways from both of them.

Sedgwick, on the other hand, includes some pretty ferocious
assertions on behalf of gay and lesbian identity. Here is one:

[A] lot of the way I have used ["queer"] . . . is to denote,
almost simply, same-sex sexual object choice, lesbian or gay,
whether or not it is organized around multiple criss-cross-

ings of definitional lines. And given the historical and contemporary force of the prohibitions against *every* same-sex
sexual expression, for anyone to disavow those meanings, or
to displace them from the term's definitional center, would
be to dematerialize any possibility of queerness itself. (8)

That is, Sedgwick is militantly pro-gay and lesbian, and insists on
the "central[ity]" of gayness to queerness, because she takes it as
morally mandatory to resist antigay political forces.[32] But when
she's describing the social world *she* sees and wants to see, the
militant assertion of gay identity gives way to something far more
labile, more playful, and more "organized around multiple criss-
crossings of definitional lines." Identities, including m/f ones,
don't dissolve; they may even intensify; but they do become mobile. Thus in "White Glasses," her elegiac essay mourning Michael
Lynch's death from AIDS, Sedgwick reflects on the "uncanny effects" she achieved when she wore the same queer glasses Lynch
wore—"effects that have been so formative of my—shall I call it
my identification? Dare I, after this half-decade, call it with all a
fat *woman's* defiance, my identity—as a gay man" (256).[33] We
have entered into the vocabulary of what Sedgwick calls "queer
performativity" (11).

Warner and Sedgwick also resist the moralized command to
converge sex, race, class, imperium. Sedgwick first:

[A] lot of the most exciting recent work around "queer"
spins the term outward along dimensions that can't be subsumed under gender or sexuality at all: the ways that race,
ethnicity, postcolonial nationality criss-cross with these *and
other* identity-constituting, identity fracturing discourses,
for example. (8–9)

The imagery is centrifugal: "queer" work by "intellectuals and
artists of color" is "spinning the term" "queer" out along new

dimensions heading *away* from gender and sexuality; when the trajectory of their work intersects with race, ethnicity, and the like, it encounters—it "criss-cross[es]" with—discourses that are both "identity-constituting" *and* "identity fracturing." Such work uses "the leverage of 'queer' to do a new kind of justice to the fractal intricacies of language, skin, migration, state" (9). Fracturing, fractal: queer work on race wants to disarticulate it in much the same way Sedgwick's list seeks to disarticulate gender. Note also how, in tracing the end point of the dispersing energies Sedgwick admires in this work, she forgoes "race, class, imperium" for "language, skin, migration, state." The queer move here—one we have seen Sedgwick make inside gender and sexuality, and that can be found as well where *Volume One* refocuses sexuality onto technologies that refer only secondarily to m/f—is to upend received taxonomic priority: perhaps *language* or *migration* is our topic, and *race* is a subsidiary element or an effect of it. But note finally that it is a *queer* move: convergentism has not gone away; rather, it has moved to a more general, more "meta" level in the project; it is more hypothetical and less moral, but it's still there.

While Sedgwick refuses the moralized mandate to converge only implicitly, Warner goes out of his way to rebuke it. He starts by emphasizing the unique character of antigay politics, rejecting the idea that it might be found to be *like* racial or gender or class politics: "There have always been moral prescriptions about how to be a woman or a worker or an Anglo-Saxon; but not about whether to be one" (xviii). This is small potatoes: most convergentists would be ready, indeed all too eager, to emphasize such differences, preparatory to a heroic convergence. But Warner proceeds to dismiss the "slogan 'race, class, and gender' " and the convergentist politics he uncharitably dubs "Rainbow Theory" (xix). His reasons: though "[t]here are many worse things in the world than Rainbow Theory," its ultimate political desire is "expressivist pluralism," an idea that justice will have arrived when everyone is recognized and nobody is left out. To that end it reifies identity, ratifies a norm of authentic identity, and construes both as properly embodied in minoritized subjects whose emancipation is cabined in the narrow liberal confines of expression, inclusion, and membership (xix). "[I]t will be necessary to break this frame if we are to see the potential alliances with movements that do not thematize identity in the same way" (xx). Note again, however, the return of the moralized mandate to converge at a more "meta" level: now we are morally obliged to find alliances with movements that *aren't* like the ones feminism and antiracism and socialism have imagined themselves to represent.

Finally, Sedgwick and Warner want to untether queer theory from sexuality as its proper domain. Sedgwick is persistently looking over the edge of gender and of sexuality to bring her project in contact with domains in human life—in erotic life— that matter a lot but that exceed them. It's not just that she wants " 'queer' [to] ... refer to: the open mesh of possibilities, gaps, overlaps, dissonances and resonances, lapses and excesses of meaning when the constituent elements of anyone's gender, of anyone's sexuality aren't made (or *can't* be made) to signify monolithically" (8). We need to be ready to bracket m/f and the very idea of gender:

> The binary calculus I'm describing here depends on the notion that the male and female sexes are each other's "opposites," but I do want to register a specific demurral against that bit of easy common sense. Under no matter what cultural construction, women and men are more like each other than chalk is like cheese, than ratiocination is like raisins, than up is like down, or than 1 is like 0. The biological, psychological, and cognitive attributes of men overlap with those of women by vastly more than they differ from them. (7 n. 6).

Maybe gender and sexuality aren't the terms in which we should be thinking:

> Even [her exploded] list[34] is remarkable for the silent presumptions it has to make about a given person's sexuality, presumptions that are true only to varying degrees, and for many people not true at all: that everyone "has a sexuality," for instance, and that it is implicated with each person's sense of overall identity in similar ways; that each person's most characteristic erotic expression will be oriented toward another person and not autoerotic; that if it is alloerotic, it will be oriented toward a single partner or kind of partner at a time; that its orientation will not change over time. (8)

To study sexuality on a hypothesis that some people might not have one at all is to study it with a will to Take a Break from the very terms from which one has started.

Warner addresses the institutional consequences for queer theory of this way of thinking.

> [Q]ueer theory is opening up in the way that feminism did when feminists began treating gender more and more as a primary category for understanding problems that did not initially look gender-specific. The prospect is that queer theory may require the same kinds of revision on the part of social-theoretical discourse that feminism did, though we do not know yet what it would be like to make sexuality a primary category for social analysis—if indeed "sexuality" is an adequate grounding concept for queer theory. (xiv–xv; see also xxiii)

Note the imagery of erotic penetration here: queer theory (like feminism before it) "open[s] up" to the loss of conceptual ground. *Not knowing* here ("we do not yet know") is an erotic event—risky, pleasurable, obliterating, full of promise. Warner is apparently prepared to relinquish precisely the taxonomic purchase on sexuality that the *Reader* claimed for Lesbian and Gay and/or Queer Studies.

Warner and Sedgwick were preparing to Take a Break from their own Queer Theory. It would have been really interesting to see what happened if they had actually done it *inside* these queer theoretic classics. For such a Break, we have to turn to their equally trenchant work in other academic domains.[35]

✄ MacKinnon/Spivak/Warner/Sedgwick

The difference between MacKinnon's and Foucault's representations of power presents a difficult question about emancipatory possibility. Where power is the subordination of one social group by another (m/f and m > f, for instance), then emancipation can be thought to be m = f, or f > m, or the dissolution m/f itself, and it makes eminent sense to carry a brief for f. But where power is productive rather than repressive, and transmits in myriad ways among social entities of highly contingent and evolving kinds, producing them and arranging them with equal though ever-variable force—if relations of power are inevitable, and to be productively engaged with them is to resist, not to liberate—then it does not make much sense to presume that one will carry a brief for f or even think about resistance in terms of subordination or of groups. But what does make sense, then? Warner's focus on social theory gives us a valuable opportunity to see what the queer break made it possible to say about this difficult question.

As we've seen, Warner understands that gay identity exists only on the condition of its own contestation. In subordination theories, this state of play is typically thought to be pathological and disabling. Paralysis. The idea is that, because the subordinated identity lacks definitional clarity and a congealed consciousness, it is more or distinctively subordinated. In subordination theories, the implicit political prescription is "more solidarity/more consciousness"; the implicit rights prescription is "more protection." These prescriptions have a complex trajectory. For my purposes here, it goes back to Marx, and forward to Spivak and Warner (and MacKinnon).

In First *Signs* MacKinnon drew on a classic Marxist trope when prescribing solidarity and consciousness for women:

> [A] women's movement exists whenever women identify collectively to resist/reclaim their determinants as such. This feminist redefinition of consciousness requires a corresponding redefinition of the process of mobilizing it: feminist *organizing*. The transformation from subordinate group to movement parallels Marx's distinction between a class "in itself" and a class "for itself."[36]

The "class-in-itself/class-for-itself" figure is firmly attached in the text MacKinnon cites—Marx's 1947 *The Poverty of Philosophy*—to another crucial figure for Marx, the proletariat. Together they imply a narrative: the proletariat exists persistently as a class but goes through a transformation. That is, it is a distinct group of humans sharing a common, exploited, relationship to the mode of production; it starts out as a class *in* itself (but merely so), and when it becomes conscious of this commonality, this exploitation, this relation, it is transformed, in a one-way no-going-back progression, into a class *for* itself. It is now ready to perform as an agent in class struggle. MacKinnon's use of the *in-itself/for-itself* figure directly imports this imagery into her structuralist vision of feminist consciousness-raising and collective feminist action.

Moreover, in *The Poverty of Philosophy*, Marx associates this transformation of the proletariat with a complete resolution of the problematic of representing it. Once the proletariat becomes a class for itself, it will produce such striking transformations in the entire social order that no "theoretician" attempting to speak for it can make any error in deciding what he should say:

> So long as the proletariat is not yet sufficiently developed to constitute itself as a class, and consequently so long as the struggle itself of the proletariat with the bourgeoisie has not yet assumed a political character, and the productive forces are not yet sufficiently developed in the bosom of the bourgeoisie itself to enable us to catch a glimpse of the material conditions necessary for the emancipation of the proletariat and for the formation of a new society, these theoreticians are merely utopians who, to meet the wants of the oppressed classes, improvise systems and go in search of a regenerating science. But in the measure that history moves forward, and with it the struggle of the proletariat assumes clearer outlines, they no longer need to seek science in their minds: they have only to take note of what is happening before their eyes and to become its mouthpiece. (125)

Not accidentally, perhaps, just a few pages after claiming that feminist consciousness-raising will produce women as a class *for* itself, MacKinnon also claims that feminism has completely abrogated the problem of representation: "Feminism is the first theory to emerge from those whose interests it affirms" (543). That is to say, for the early Marx, and in slightly different terms for the early MacKinnon, the *in-itself/for-itself* figure supports an idea that the oppressed class will be transparently and authentically present and the problem of its representation will wither away: the subaltern shall speak!

Etienne Balibar indicates that, by the time Marx wrote *Capital* (he completed the first volume in 1867),[37] he had almost completely abandoned the term "proletariat" and had developed a far more "dialectical" (or perhaps better said, paradoxical) range of figures for the complex historical process by which "the masses" enter into political and economic struggle as "a class."[38] And Andrew Parker and Balibar indicate that *The 18th Brumaire*, written and published in 1852, is a pivotal text in Marx's struggle to develop a theory that would accommodate the failure of history to deliver on the *in-itself/for-itself* narrative.[39]

Marx struggles throughout *The 18th Brumaire* with the collapse of the French Revolution into a systematically chaotic relation of fragmented, abject social classes to each other and to a farcically supreme state. The French proletariat had not transformed itself from a class-*in*-itself to a class-*for*-itself, had not acceded to the transparency that Marx had predicted for it and that MacKinnon would later claim for feminism, and was not driving class struggle toward the forgetting of class *tout court*. Lamenting with horror the coup of Louis Bonaparte on the anniversary (the 18th Brumaire is a *date*) of Napoleon Bonaparte's accession to power, and faced with the conspicuous failure of Marxist revolutionary history to have happened, Marx offers, as one part of his understanding of what happened instead, this rendering of the failure of the small peasant proprietors (not "the proletariat") to sustain the revolutionary potential they had performed in the collapse of feudal land tenure:

> In so far as millions of families live under economic conditions of existence that separate their mode of life, their interests and their culture from those of the other classes, and put them in a hostile opposition to the latter, *they form a class*. In so far as there is merely local interconnection among these small-holding peasants, and the identity of their interests begets no community, no national bond and no political organization among them, *they do not form a class*.[40]

Insofar as certain crucial facts pertain (and they do), the small peasant proprietors do *and* do not form a class.

If I'm right so far, the *in-itself/for-itself* figure posits a clear logical distinction between stages in the historical development of a coherent class (it is *always* a class), and thus also a crisp historical break, and thus finally an end-point moment in which the problems of vanguardism and representational practice dissolve in the face of the epistemic authority of the proletariat. By contrast, the *do/do not form a class* figure cedes before-and-after periodization to a present state of affairs divided along the lines of a sheer contradiction, and places in question the descriptive power of either of its terms. Taxonomy is replaced by paradox. And with the imagery of transformation goes any possibility that Marx, observing the historical developments in France, can aim to be objectively detached from them, to voice the proletariat transparently as it accedes in all inevitability to class consciousness. The epistemic authority and ontic transparency of the proletariat dissolve: though readings of *The 18th Brumaire* differ, no one can read it well without observing that the problem of representation is obsessively central to its thematics and its poetics.

Perhaps we can state the following analogy:

the *class-in-itself/class-for-itself* figure   is to   MacKinnon
                                                    as the
the *is/is not a class* figure   is to   Spivak.

I propose, further, that this framing gives us some purchase on Warner's decision to deploy of *both* figures (only to reject both of them for "queers"):

> Queer people are a kind of social group fundamentally unlike others, a status group only insofar as they are not a class. (xxv)

A subtle and complex gesture, indeed. Not homosexuals but "queer people." Whozzat? Well, they are a "social group fundamentally unlike others"—so seeing them using endowments derived from prior social formations is going to be a representational practice struggling to be critical of itself. And they are a

Weberian "status group" (and thus intelligible as a social force dealing individually and in small fragmented associations with the complex but unequal distribution of social honor)[41] only insofar as they are not a Marxian class (intelligible in terms of commonality of interest and an accession to shared consciousness). Precisely the judgment that, for Marx, explained the failure of the small peasant proprietors to act coherently in the run-up to the second, farcical 18th Brumaire—"they are not a class"—becomes for Warner the gauge of the extent to which "queer people" *have* access to social struggle à la Weber. The point of entry into politics that the early Marx announced for the proletariat, and that MacKinnon claimed for feminism—the class subordination paradigm—is not a solution for "queer people"; instead, splitting from it makes queer politics possible.

So here's something odd: Warner hints that his positive proposal turns on Weber's sociology of status groups, but he does nothing more with that suggestion in the introduction, and his next major intervention in the field, *The Trouble with Normal*, though it is a sustained attack on the shame/dignity framing of sexual politics in the United States, seems to be entirely devoid of any Weberian techniques.[42] Instead, the introduction to *Fear of a Queer Planet* argues that the problem faced by "queer people" is not domination or repression but the biopoweristic management of the social world to array around the "normal":

> The preference for "queer" represents, among other things, an aggressive impulse of generalization; it rejects a minoritizing logic of toleration or a simple political interest-representation in favor of a more thorough resistance to the regimes of the normal. (xxvi)

Warner suggests that a queered approach even to the interests of gay men and lesbians and surely to an adequate left understanding of sexual politics requires a direct engagement with social powers distributed so widely and ingrained so finely in the social world that minoritarian framings cannot adequately hypothesize them:

> Following Hannah Arendt, we might even say that queer politics opposes society itself. . . . If queers, incessantly told to alter their "behavior," can be understood as protesting not just the normal behavior of the social but the *idea* of normal behavior, they will bring skepticism to the methodologies founded on that idea. (xxvii)

To take this "aggressive impulse of generalization" to its apparent destination, you'd have to say that queer politics would work against regimes of the normal on behalf of *everyone*. That is, if, as we've seen, the direct implication of Foucault's biopower hypothesis is to see the psychiatrization of perversions, the hysterization of women, and so on, as operating with even constitutive and regulatory power on homosexuals and heterosexuals, on men and women, then a "resistance to regimes of the normal" would forgo the homo/hetero and m/f distinctions as much as possible in deciding what to do. In the register of desire, the (almost?) alloeroticism of Sedgwick's exploded list manifests this trend in queer thought. Warner gives it an explicitly political spin: "Even the concept of oppression has to be reevaluated here, because in queer politics the oppression of a class of person is only sometimes distinguishable from the repression of sexuality, and that in turn is a concept that has become difficult to contain since Foucault."[43] He doesn't draw any conclusions from this difficulty. It seems clear to me, though, that one consequence would be the proposal that, if sexuality *produces* rather than *represses* sexualities, including gay and lesbian ones—and if the resulting power relations are at least sometimes mobile, reciprocal, and forcefully

constitutive all 'round—then (once again) the "sexual minorities/
structural subordination" model (initiated in our genealogy by
Rubin) has been put in question.

Warner offers some new moves here. But it seems almost impossible for him to hold this alternative way of thinking open.
Even when he is working it out, even where he makes his clearest
statement that an opposition to the regimes of the normal would
be a good thing for queer politics to do, he also suggests that a
certain unnamed minoritized population has privileged epistemic purchase on how to do it: "If *queers*, incessantly *told to alter
their 'behavior,'* can be understood as protesting not just the normal behavior of the social but the idea of normal behavior, *they*
will bring skepticism" (xvii, all emphases added; original emphasis deleted). So, after all, queers are people who are targeted for
change by the prescriptions of normality; regimes of the normal
will be more repressive for them than for others; they are thus
not everyone but some subset of everyone; and they have at least
some of the epistemic advantages of a class-*for*-itself. To the extent
that Warner affirms these ideas for "queer people," he carries
forward the very ideas of subordination-theory identity politics
that I've associated in the last few pages with MacKinnon!

❦ *Elizabeth Weed and Naomi Schor,* feminism meets queer theory

Elizabeth Weed and Naomi Schor first published *feminism meets
queer theory* as a special issue of the postmodernizing-feminist
journal *differences* in 1994; it was reissued, with some changes, as
a book in 1997. Butler's "*Interview*" of Rubin appears here; the
book includes "Against Proper Objects," Butler's important critique of the idea that queer theory should proceed independent
of feminism; and Weed and Schor collect a wide range of highly

engaged, muscular work that draws from virtually every tradition (except that represented by Kennedy's legal realism) that I've identified in this genealogy.

This genealogy hasn't seen an anthology as politically engaged since *Conflicts in Feminism.* Many of the entries are interactive: there are call-and-response exchanges, two interviews, and a book review responded to by the book's author. Weed and Butler begin the volume with essays strongly objecting to the terms in which (they believe) queer theory proposes to encounter feminism.[44] In Butler's interview with Rosi Braidotti they disagree about how a Lacanian "sexual difference" feminism might respond to the queer break; in her interview with Rubin they disagree about the implications of "Thinking Sex."[45] Biddy Martin criticizes queer theory for repeating all the mistakes of misogyny with respect to femininity; Evelynn Hammonds, speaking this time as a black woman, criticizes queer theory for repeating all the mistakes of feminism in its encounter with race; Trevor Hope writes as a feminist gay man about gay male sexuality; Braidotti responds with an indignant feminist attack on his project for repeating all the mistakes made by feminism in its occlusion of lesbianism; and Hope provides an (ironically?) abject response.[46] The volume concludes with Elizabeth Grosz's comment on a new book by Teresa de Lauretis and de Lauretis's response. This exchange occurs largely outside feminism: de Lauretis describes her book as "not concerned with feminist theory, except insofar as feminist theory has concerned itself with lesbian sexuality"; Grosz proposes that, to detour certain impasses in that project, de Lauretis would have to Take a Break not only from feminism but from psychoanalysis as well.[47] Men are back: one of them works within feminism, while the other more or less ignores it, to work out some consequences for male gender and male sexuality with special reference to male/male eroticism.[48]

Taken as a whole, the book sets up at least three meetings between feminism and queer theory. There are struggles within feminism to make it more fully capacious to theorize sexuality as it is inflected by gender or sexual difference (Butler and Braidotti; Hope and Braidotti). There are struggles between feminism and queer theory to repair something rupturous for, or damaging to, f in the emergence of nonfeminist queer theory (Butler; Weed; Martin; Hammonds). And there is nonfeminist, queer theoretic work on sexuality, with or without gender, without or without reference to feminism (Rubin; Michasiw; Grosz and de Lauretis; Carole-Anne Tyler).[49] Feminism lives, in part because there is queer theory that's not feminist for it to engage.

Weed and Butler vehemently denounce queer theory's representation of feminism in essays that both exemplify that vitality and deny it. In the course of this work, they introduce several new forms of the paralysis trope. Queer theory's feminism is a "reduction," a "caricature" (Weed, xi; Butler, 2, 24). Weed's introduction depends on Butler's "Against Proper Objects," which in turn frames the meeting as bringing feminism face-to-face with its representation in the *Reader*. Looking in that mirror, these feminists do not recognize themselves *at all*. Weed puts the encounter this way:

> No matter how reluctant queer theory has been to pin itself down as a coherent set of theorizations, it has been consistent about one aspect of its project: considerations of sex and sexuality cannot be contained by the category of gender. This is not, in itself, a controversial proposition. The problem, as Judith Butler shows in her argument "Against Proper Objects," is that in this formulation gender becomes the property of feminist inquiry while the proper study of sex and sexuality is located elsewhere. . . .

... Queer theory's feminism is a strange feminism, stripped of its contentious elements, its internal contradictions, its multiplicity. ...

Our purpose was ... *to look squarely at the way the inter-section of feminism and queer theory has been rendered by queer theory.* On the one hand, there are queer thematics ... which seem to invite an obvious interplay between the two fields; on the other, there is an exclusionary logic that all but precludes such interplay. This move ... renders feminism's relationship to queer theory simultaneously inevitable and impossible. ... The feminism against which queer theory defines itself is a feminism reduced almost to caricature: a feminism tied to a concern for gender, bound to a regressive and monotonous binary opposition. That reduction of feminist critique calls for analysis. (viii–xi, footnotes omitted)

Butler's "Against Proper Objects" addresses this "reduction" in a long critique of the *Reader,* taken up as *the* instance of queer theory. Butler describes the triple move made in the *Reader*— reducing feminism to the terms of sex1, strictly associating gender with sex1, and dividing sex2, sexuality, sexual orientation, sexual practice, and sexual minorities from sex1, gender, and feminism for their allocation to Gay and Lesbian Studies and queer theory—as a profound "elision" of feminist complexity and ultimately a "refusal" of its work.

Butler tallies the malign effects that the *Reader's* Break will produce: it precludes the common concern of feminism and Lesbian and Gay/Queer Studies with sex2; limits feminism to sex1 and thus elides its power to make sex1 visible as a Foucaultian effect— problematic, historical, and political; elides feminism's sex-positive and sex-radical traditions, desolidarizing from them and denying their conceptual and political power; ditto feminism's concern with the interrelation of gender and sexuality; reduces sex2 by its division from gender and "sexual difference" *and* reduces gender to the m/f terms of sex2; seizes sexual practice as a subject for queer theory, and thus divides it from identity; profoundly reduces the massive feminist literature on the relation between sex1 and gender, including branches devoted to the status of the biological and of race in that relation, and thus simplifies the relation between the biological and the cultural; narrows the definition of both feminism and queer theory in such a way as to "rule[] out" "race" and "class" (4–9). The disaffiliation of queer theory from feminism a fortiori disaffiliates with the struggles in feminism against the "anti-pornography paradigm" (9), making them "barely legible as 'feminist' " (14). Butler assails the *Reader* for giving the rubric Lesbian and Gay Studies to the study of sexuality and the full range of the sexual minorities. This is, she indicates, a massive seizure by a capital figure incapable of generalizing the domain, one that promises to make some of the minorities—transsexuality, for instance—newly unintelligible (13–14). Her conclusion about the meeting thus understood: "Politically, the costs are too great to choose between feminism, on the one hand, and radical sexual theory, on the other" (18).

Butler further charges that the queer break from feminism not only distorts feminism; it reproduces the very normative evils that Butler's (and, I would add, MacKinnon's) feminisms exist to fight. In an introduction to "Against Proper Objects" that is new to the 1997 edition, Butler recounts the "rage" with which, while writing *Gender Trouble*, she had encountered feminists' commitment to the foundational dyad of "men" and "women": their resistance to adding "sexual practices" and "gender trouble" to their core agenda signaled, to Butler, hidden heterosexist presuppositions (2). The feminist desire to refuse *Gender Trouble*—to exile it to a remote domain, queer theory—manifested this very commitment to feminism's heterosexism. For queer theory to return the gesture—pushing gender back to feminism so as to study "sexual practice" without it—would, by this logic, reinstate the heterosexism of feminism and could well license the misogyny of queer theory. The two projects must be interimplicated in the mode of "internal critique" (1) to enable either to provide the tools against these normatively unacceptable commitments.

Why would these be bad outcomes? Because of m/f, m > f, and carrying a brief for f. To be sure, Butler continues to turn feminism against its foundational dyad:

> Where and when a feminist analysis accepts th[e] cultural presumption [that m and f are dyadically arrayed, in a predetermined way, across sex1, sex2, gender, and sexual practice], feminism actively recapitulates heterosexist hegemony. . . . *But when and where feminism refuses to derive gender from sex or from sexuality, feminism appears to be part of the very critical practice that contests the heterosexual matrix.* (12)

A theory of sexuality detached from gender recapitulates the very conceptual conditions of heterosexism. And it reinscribes male dominance as well:

> If sexuality is conceived as liberated from gender, then the sexuality that is "liberated" from feminism will be one which suspends the reference to masculine and feminine, reenforcing the refusal to mark that difference, which is the conventional way in which the masculine has achieved the status of the "sex" which is one. Such a "liberation" dovetails with mainstream conservatism and with male dominance in its many . . . forms. (23)

As I noted the first time we encountered this passage,[50] MacKinnon could have said that: m/f, m > f, and carrying a brief for f, with the addition of a full critique of m/f and m > f as creating the heterosexist matrix.[51]

If Butler is right, we should not Take a Break from Feminism.

But I think she's wrong. I offer my own tally of the downsides and upsides of Taking a Break in Part Three. There I take into account Butler's predictions of theoretical, social, and political damage to the interests held dear by her feminism. Many of them, I have to admit, would indeed be placed at risk; others can be vindicated only at sharp cost to interests articulated outside feminism. I'll argue that the dangers and the damage, though real, are worth the gains. But here I want to argue that Butler's (and Weed's) understanding of the relationship between feminism and queer theory is partial, omitting much in queer theory that could not possibly give rise to their objections; that it includes simple textual errors; and that some, perhaps many of the costs they worry about are produced by their own theoretic defenses.

Butler and Weed repeat the pathological scenario of feminist paralysis, complete with misdiagnosis and self-inflicted experience of deadlock. Oddly, the very same structuralism and moralized mandate to converge that, in my view, actually produce the feminist experience of paralysis, emerge in Butler's argument and, I think, are once again producing the unnecessary experience—this time—of feminism's elision, erasure, denial, foreclosure, refusal, and repudiation in some phases of the argument, and its supersession in others. Thanks to Rubin's "*Interview*" with Butler, *feminism meets queer theory* provides me with a concrete opportunity to argue that the prescriptive deployment of theory—*any* theory—along with not Taking a Break, is the pathogen.

I'll take up the experience of feminism's elision, erasure, denial, foreclosure, refusal, and repudiation first, and the concern about its supersession a bit further on.

You can find the words "elision," "erasure," "denial," "foreclosure," "refusal," or "repudiation" on almost every page of "Against Proper Objects." Butler reads the *Reader* to insist that the "common concern" of feminism and Lesbian and Gay Studies with sex "must be *denied*, through *elision*"; sex-positive sex-radical feminism "is *elided* in the articulation of lesbian/gay studies from feminist," a move that "is either *to deny* this important feminist contribution . . . or to argue, implicitly, that the feminist contributions to thinking sexuality culminate in the supersessions of feminism by lesbian and gay studies" (10–11, emphasis added). The *Reader*'s division of Lesbian and Gay Studies from feminism "*forecloses* the field of social differences from which both projects emerge" and "*rule[s] out*" the constitutive terms of "race" and "class" from "either field" (9, emphases added); "to the extent that lesbian and gay studies *refuses* the domain of gender, it *disqualifies itself* from the analysis of transgendered sexuality altogether" (13, emphasis added); "Insofar as lesbian and gay studies relies on [the *Reader*'s] notion of sex it appears to take as one of its grounds, its founding methodological claims, a *refusal* of sexual difference" (5, emphasis added). When Butler revised the essay for the 1997 edition, she shifted at two moments from the language of refusal and repudiation to that of erasure and elision, suggesting that there is some difference between these sets of terms, but typically, and even at the site of one of these revisions, elision *is* refusal.[52]

As we've seen, the "refusal" to mark "gender" is the very form of male abstraction, neutrality, and generality: if queer theory pursues this course, it reinvokes male epistemic power and reinstalls "male dominance."

On behalf of feminism, Butler refuses these refusals: the idea that "gender" is tied to the biologistic premise "male or female" is "refuse[d]" by almost all feminist work because, instead, it "calls into question the settled grounds of analysis" (8); and that refusal is what makes feminism capable of insisting on gender while critically untethering it from a presumption of heterosexuality. It's no accident, perhaps, that Butler italicizes her crucial refusal: "*But when and where feminism refuses to derive gender from sex or from sexuality, feminism appears to be part of the very critical practice that contests the heterosexual matrix.*" Queer theory's elisions foreclose, refuse, repudiate, and deny, while feminism's refusals become its most aspirational mode of operation.

Feminism is clearly on top here. It emerges from these strenuous sentences highly committed to some fundamental aims (against the heterosexual matrix; against masculinist unmarkedness). If queer theory works to elide or omit these normative commitments, or any of the analytic cruxes that support them, it is functioning to repudiate those aims, to refuse their importance, to deny their possibility, to foreclose them. Antiheterosexism and the unwinding of masculinist epistemic power have moved into a structural position. *All* work relating to *any* aspect of sex1, sex2, gender, sexual orientation, and sexuality *must* commit itself to these descriptive and aspirational goals. These commitments return Butler's feminism to the familiar structural—even prescriptive paranoid structural—form that she also *objects to* in MacKinnon's thought (9–10, 12). This is theory rendered fully prescriptive.

Not surprisingly, then, "Against Proper Objects" issues a mandate to converge that is at least as demanding as the moralized one that feminists issue when antiracism, postcolonial thought, and the like, threaten to operate independent of feminism. The study of all sexual subjectivities, all sexual minorities, all sexual practices, all configurations of sex1, sex2, gender, sexual orientation, and sexuality—all of it—is indivisible from feminism, "and it remains an open question whether 'queer' can achieve these same goals of inclusiveness."[53] The essay even whips queer theory for not producing full merger with antiracism (9)!

The feminist experience of paralysis is typically diagnosed as an effect of postmodernizing feminism; indeed, typically Butler's work is the diagnostician's pathogen of choice. But Butler manifests here not only a very similar experience but also a very similar diagnosis. And just as *Gender Trouble* didn't paralyze feminism—

the feminist experience of paralysis seems, from the outside anyway, to be delusional—Butler's feminism is in fact not elided,
erased, denied, and foreclosed by queer theory. I think we're faced
here with a historical event inside feminism much bigger than
the postmodern critique of woman, or the splits provoked by
divergentist feminism, or the emergence of queer theory that
Takes a Break. I think we're getting close to seeing clearly how
much paralysis, deadlock, elision, refusal, live burial, and so on,
have been produced inside feminism by its own refusal to counte-
nance anyone's Taking a Break, a refusal motivated or justified
and certainly performed as a prescriptive deployment of theory.

"Against Proper Objects" makes it clear that this strategy is
costly for feminism. First, Butler is enraged at the limitations imposed upon feminism there and is fighting back hard. The vitality
of her response is palpable. But the sense of powerlessness and of
elision is unjustified by the actual situation.

And there was no need for Butler or Weed to frame feminism's
encounter with queer theory as the *Reader* frames it. It is impossible to jibe Butler's and Weed's objections to the *Reader* with the
framings of queer theory proposed in *Fear of a Queer Planet* or
Tendencies, for instance. The many nonfeminist queer theoretic
moments in *feminism meets queer theory* itself, Bersani's "Is the
Rectum a Grave?" and Kennedy's "Sexy Dressing" don't attempt
any of the territorial reductions we find in the *Reader*'s introduction. These projects are not feminist; all of them forgo the rigid
taxonomic impulse of the *Reader;* all of them offer supple and
complex rearticulations of the relations between sex1, sex2, gender, sexual orientation, and sexuality. Why didn't Weed and Butler work harder to meet *them?*

To be sure, Weed and Butler acknowledge (mostly in passages
that they added in 1997) that feminism could step up to meet
plenty of queer theory that is quite innocent of the territorializing
taxonomic offenses of the *Reader.* Thus Weed recognizes that *fem-*

inism meets queer theory presents "not one but many meetings," including encounters "of feminists and queer theorists, of queer feminist theorists and feminist queer theorists."[54] She says, "This one move, the separation of gender from sex and sexuality, is by no means the only topic of conversation between feminism and queer theory—the essays in this volume address a number of other questions—but it is this move above all that makes the meeting of feminism and queer theory a strange one" (viii). Butler acknowledges that in *Tendencies* Sedgwick "make[s] rich and brilliant use of the problematic of cross-gendered identification and cross-sexual identification"—that is to say, brings together the subjects which the *Reader* would alienate into distinct fields.[55] Weed acknowledges that Rubin's proposal in "Thinking Sex"— that "considerations of sex and sexuality cannot be contained by the category of gender[—] . . . is not, in itself, a controversial proposition" (viii). Butler: the claim that it is "necess[ary to] . . . consider[] sexuality as having a distinct character as a regulatory regime . . . [is] true and right" (6).

None of these concessions have any effect, however, on the way Weed and Butler locate "the meeting" between feminism and queer theory. It must take place on the terms set by the *Reader.* Neither works out the consequences of the fact that the *Reader*'s reduction of gender to "male and female" and of feminism to gender, and the appropriation of sexuality for queer theory, which they take as definitive of queer theory, are actually not entailed in, and had already been unperformed in, much nonfeminist queer work.

Again, Weed and Butler have *opted for* the experience of feminist elision, erasure, refusal, repudiation, denial, and foreclosure. Feminism elided, erased, refused, repudiated, denied, foreclosed—like feminism paralyzed—suffers a self-inflicted wound.

Paralysis has a lot in common with elision, refusal, and the rest. The sense that feminism has been *superseded*—that its prodigals will replace it and leave us "post" feminism—is more specifically historiographical. It's a central concern of Butler and Weed. Butler worries that the *Reader*'s "sex" will "include and supersede the feminist sense" (5); that the *Reader* installs a "narrative of supersession" in which Gay and Lesbian Studies commits feminism to failure by outliving it; that the *Reader* dedicates feminism, through an act of "violence," to burial "in and through the funereal figure of the 'ground' " (7, 9). Denial and supersession are Butler's Scylla and Charybdis: the *Reader*'s elision of the sexual-radical tradition in feminism "is either to deny this important feminist contribution to the very sexual discourse in which lesbian and gay studies emerged or to argue, implicitly, that the feminist contributions to thinking sexuality culminate in the supersession of feminism by lesbian and gay studies" (10–11). Weed's introduction objects that queer theory, speeding ahead into the unbounded space of its exploded lists, represents feminism as "*tied* to a concern for gender, *bound* to a regressive and monotonous binary opposition" (xi).

It is wonderful, then, that in this volume, preoccupied as it is with the possibility that "Thinking Sex" had invoked work that now threatens feminism with supersession, Butler interviewed Rubin, and interviewed her about "Thinking Sex." This editorial move invites two crucial figures in the genealogy I am tracing to negotiate the extent and the terms of their struggle over beloved ground. The fact that this interview exists; the fact that in it Butler and Rubin enjoy so much rapport that twice, at very happy moments for both of them, they are reported to have spoken "in unison" (78, 90); the fact that they disagree persistently and with great precision and grace across its pages—these are facts that indicate, to me, that there is no deadlock, no paralysis, no burial, no supersession, here.

The "*Interview*" makes it evident that Rubin had read "Against Proper Objects" before she and Butler turned on the recording machine (95), so, to approach the former, we might start with Butler's reflections on Rubin's work in the latter. In "Against Proper Objects" Butler records her strong affiliations with, and deep fears about, "Thinking Sex." This friendly reading understands "Thinking Sex" to call, from within and for feminism, for a distinct effort to study sexuality outside it. Acknowledging that Rubin had proposed that we "conceptualiz[e] gender and sexuality as two separable domains of analysis," Butler thinks that "the separation of the two domains is to be contextualized within the effort" of feminists "to contest those efforts 'which treat sexuality as a derivation of gender' " (12). She emphasizes Rubin's prescription in "Thinking Sex" that "in the long run, feminism's critique of gender hierarchy must be incorporated into a radical theory of sex." You could read that as a proleptic concession to convergence deferred for years, perhaps decades, but Butler asks, "Has 'the Long Run' Arrived?" and answers with an unequivocal Yes (14, 18). Butler objects to the "appropriation" of "Thinking Sex" for the *Reader*'s queer theory (11); these passages claim it for feminism.

But in other arguments stated in "Against Proper Objects," and in the "*Interview*," Butler reverses this operation, worrying that "Thinking Sex" *did* perform the queer supersession of feminism. In the essay she worries that "Thinking Sex" quadruply supersedes "The Traffic in Women." First, whereas "Traffic" was a feminist structuralist analysis of kinship, drawing on Marx, Freud, and Lévi-Strauss (among others), "Thinking Sex" was a sex-radical, non- or poststructural analysis of sex2 drawing on Foucault. By shifting from one to the other, Butler fears, Rubin installs the later essay as the *replacement* of the first. This would imply that, with respect to our optimal object of study, kinship has been replaced by sex. It would also imply that, with respect to historical periods, premodern kinship has been replaced by modern sexuality. And, third, with respect to our optimal theoretical reference point, it would imply that Freud has been replaced by Foucault:

> The argument in "Thinking Sex" that posits the *anachronism* of kinship is supported by a Foucauldian historiography in which state-sponsored efforts at population control and the heightened medicalization of sexuality are figured as *replacing* kinship as the organizing structure of sexuality.
>
> In following Foucault's scheme, Rubin *severs* the newer deployment of sexuality from the *older regime* of kinship, *dropping* the psychoanalytic analysis offered in "Traffic" and offering *in its place* a regime-theory of sexuality, which would include psychoanalysis itself as one of its regulatory modes. (16, emphases added)

Thus a fourth supersession has occurred: Rubin has replaced feminism with queer theory.

For Butler the stakes at this point are high. We've already seen how she assesses the possible supersession of feminism by queer theory. Nor does she want kinship to recede into the analytic past. For Butler kinship is an important crux for work against marriage, "domestication," and other social forms enforcing the heterosexual matrix.[56] We see this project in "Against Proper Objects," where she invokes kinship as a "site of redefinition which can move beyond patrilineality, compulsory heterosexuality, and the symbolic overdetermination of biology" (17). She relies on Freud as much as she does on Foucault; and she has resisted the idea that Foucault's attack in *Volume One* on "the repressive hypothesis" ended the usefulness, for the study of sexuality, of Freud.[57]

When Butler proposes this quadruple supersession in the "*Interview*," Rubin firmly disavows it: "No. I don't mean to suggest that" (94). And the textual record is on her side. Here is what Rubin actually said in "Thinking Sex" about Foucault's periodization of a shift from kinship to sexuality: "As Foucault has pointed out, a system of sexuality has emerged out of earlier kinship forms and has acquired significant autonomy" (307). In the *"Interview,"* then, Rubin reflects on Butler's odd forgetfulness about this:

> You know, . . . many people seem to have overinterpreted the last few pages of "Thinking Sex." I was not arguing there that kinship, gender, feminism, or psychoanalysis no longer mattered in any way. Rather, I was arguing that there were systems other than kinship which had assumed some kind of relative autonomy and could not be reduced to kinship, at least in the Lévi-Straussian sense. When I wrote about that, I very much had in mind the section from the *History of Sexuality* where Foucault says, "Particularly from the eighteenth century onwards, Western societies created and deployed a new apparatus which was superimposed on the previous one[.]" . . . He never says it *replaces*, he says "superimposed."[58]

Rubin here launches into an exposition of *Volume One*, citing chapter and verse for approximately a page, all to the effect that, for Foucault, kinship and sexuality are distinct systems operating simultaneously, not mutually exclusive and crisply periodized structures. For instance (Rubin's italics): "One can imagine that one day it [sexuality] will have replaced it [kinship], but as things stand at present, . . . *it has neither obliterated the latter, nor rendered it useless. Moreover, historically it was around, and on the basis of the deployment of alliance* [i.e., kinship] *that the deployment of sexuality was constructed.*"[59]

The Foucault Rubin described in "Thinking Sex" and the Rubin Rubin described in the *"Interview"* saw sexuality and its biopoweristic management to emerge within a social world arranged by kinship, and then to work simultaneously alongside kinship, perhaps predominantly, not exclusively—"relatively autonomously"—to cocreate some of the discursive conditions for

social life relating to sex, gender, and so forth. In Rubin's formulation, sexuality does not supersede kinship; the modern does not
eclipse the premodern; Foucault does not supersede Freud; and
so queer theory does not eclipse or supersede feminism. Instead
the former terms become available as the objects or methods of
an alternative project; they work simultaneously to change
human conditions of existence and to generate hypotheses for
understanding them.

Rubin objects explicitly to Butler's idea that the *Reader*'s taxonomic approach is the only one worth noticing:

> As for this great methdological divide you are talking about,
> between feminism and gay/lesbian studies, I do not think I
> would accept that distribution of interests, activities, objects,
> and methods. I see no reason why feminism has to be limited
> to kinship and psychoanalysis, and I never said it should not
> work on sexuality. I only said it should not be seen as the
> privileged site for work on sexuality. I cannot imagine a gay
> and lesbian studies that is not interested in gender as well as
> sexuality and, as you note in your paper, there are many
> other sexualities to explore besides male homosexuality and
> lesbianism. But I am not persuaded that there is widespread
> acceptance of this division of intellectual labor between fem-
> inism, on the one hand, and gay and lesbian studies on the
> other. And it was certainly never my intention to establish a
> mutually exclusive disciplinary barrier between feminism
> and gay and lesbian studies. That was not an issue I was
> dealing with. I was trying to make some space for work on
> sexuality (and even gender) that did not presume feminism
> as the obligatory and sufficient approach. But I was not try-
> ing to found a field. (95)

I think that Rubin's reading of Foucault is the more adequate
one; that her representation of the relationship between "Traffic

in Women" and "Thinking Sex" is right; that she accurately distinguishes between her project in "Thinking Sex" and the one—derived from it, to be sure—of the *Reader*. It's an amazing moment: Rubin performs a *gotcha* at Butler's expense, and Butler prints it. Being wrong has achieved status as a political gesture in its own right. (But of course this is not new: recall Foucault's will to depart from himself at the beginning of *Volume Two*, and Warner's excited hope that every formulation he had achieved might be wrong.)

But let's face it: when Butler's kinship meets sexuality, when her Freud meets Foucault, when Weed's and Butler's feminisms meet queer theory, they produce their own supersession. Butler's and Weed's announcements of an unnecessary and even textually mistaken experience of feminism in supersession has a certain pathos. As of the moment *feminism meets queer theory* went to press, at any event, they seem to have been willing to hold that position because they could not imagine any place for feminism and its descriptive and normative commitments (to m/f, m > f, and carrying a brief for f, plus more) except that of structural centrality; could not imagine any place for theory except that of descriptive and normative mandate.

1998: Trans Theory Splits While Staying in Place

The first chapter of Jay Prosser's *Second Skins: The Body Narratives of Transsexuality* is a theoretic and political manifesto for transsexuality as it emerges from within but diverges from feminism, gay-identity politics, and queer theory. He writes from the "perspective[]" (58) of transgender projects that are also transsexual. "Thinking Sex," *Epistemology of the Closet*, *Gender Trouble*, *Tendencies*, and "Against Proper Objects" (along with some other texts by Sedgwick and Butler not examined here) provide the matrix, if you will, for Prosser's articulation of a new, transsexual project that breaks quite decisively from them in some ways and not in others. The next generation speaks.

And so the ways in which Taking a Break can be imagined and performed have moved to a new place. This is the last location to which I trace the project before putting in my oar for a new direction, in Part Three.

❦ *Jay Prosser,* Second Skins

The constituency "transsexuals" has been (as Prosser shows) a crucial figure in feminism and queer theory through the 1990s. The moralized mandate to converge has often accreted around it. We often hear that no feminist or queer theory is morally or conceptually adequate if it does not affirm and account for transsexuality. So efforts to build transsexuals into movements originating among women, gay men, lesbians, and "queers" have repeatedly produced substantial new breaks in the development of feminist, gay, and queer theory.

The pressure—both to converge and to break—grew as American sex politics saw an amazing insurgence of actual transsexuals and an emergence of explicitly transgender and transsexual politics. It wasn't just female masculinity, butch lesbians, gay male transvestite camp theater, and genderfuck: over the course of the 1990s ever more people engaged in sustained, everyday (not theatrical) cross-dressing; they pursued hormone treatment and surgery to change their sex1; the numbers grew large enough that small urban and collegiate enclaves of transsexuals emerged and became social forms. They asserted their social interests via minoritizing social-movement politics (modeled, once again, on the black civil rights movement and feminism, but also incorporating a critique of that modeling derived from the problems discovered in it at the gay/queer divide). At the same time emerged a distinct politics of intersexuality addressed to—better said, perhaps, attacking—the ubiquitous policy in U.S. hospitals of "assigning" infants born with gender-ambiguous genitals to one sex1 and gender or the other.

Though transsexuality, as we call it now, has been given historical roots dating well before these shifts of the 1990s,[60] that decade saw the coincidence and mutual incitement of this insurgency of young, bold transsexuals within the queer ranks (and outside them) with the queer turn in feminism, the queer suspension of feminism, and the intensification of feminist politics of sexuality. Decisively emergent "trans" movements were increasingly able to put new pressure—theoretic, political, practical, moral—on left sexuality politics to comprehend and articulate its claims.

It was never going to be easy. Some of the questions that seemed hard to answer: Would feminism advocate smoothly for the interests of pre-op m-to-f's: women with penises? How would feminist resistance to misogyny deal with the yearning of many female human beings to shed so many of their female attributes? How would the gay-affirmativity of left sexual politics deal with the evident fact that many transsexuals intended a heterosexual future for themselves, sometimes precisely to abandon the same-sex character of their relation to their preferred sexual object? What about their lovers, many of whom, in love and through desire, were also making a transition from homosexual to heterosexual? And what about the high value that queer gender (feminist and non-) placed on the "constructedness" of sex1 and on mix-and-match identifications across sex1, gender, and sexual orientation? (Recall Butler's insistence on the fluidity of all the elements of gender and sexuality vis-à-vis one another; recall Sedgwick's exploded list.) Given this theoretic desire, how would queer gender cope with the strong desire of many transsexuals to embody one gender or the other, *really*, and to consolidate themselves and their lovers as m or f all the way down?

Torquing across this vexed field was the apparently even more inconsistent politics of intersexuality. If the policy proposal of intersexuality is to make social space for gendered and sexual bodies that "fit" neither already-existing sex1—to find a celebratory or at least safe and affirmed life for people whose sex1 was neither male nor female but of some third (or fourth or fifth . . .) kind—how would left sexual politics accommodate *that* with the strong simultaneous push from many transsexuals to disambiguate their bodily sex and their social gender, to intensify the binary relation between m and f? If "choice" became liberalism's way of accommodating transsexuality, how would the resulting normative frame cope with the fact that a hugely tendentious decision about intersexed infants—whether to send them into infancy and childhood with ambiguous or surgically disambiguated genitals—must be made for them by adults long before they could possibly participate in deciding?

One of Prosser's answers to the convergentist quest packed into all these questions: Stop Trying. To be sure, he derives the very possibility of transsexual politics from feminism, and particularly from queer theory (feminist and non-):

> In closing, it needs emphasizing that it is precisely queer's investment in the figure of transgender in its own institutionalization—and above all the methodological and categorical crossings of Butler's queer feminism—that have made it possible to begin articulating the transsexual as a theoretical subject. (60)

But he also argues that neither theoretic resource is capable of sustaining several desiderata that are crucial to transsexuality:

> To resist queer's incorporation of trans identities and trans studies is not to refuse the value of institutional alliances

and coalitions (in the form of shared conferences, journals, courses and so on). But an alliance, unlike a corporation, suggests a provisional or strategic union between parties whose different interests ought not to be—indeed, cannot totally be—merged. (60)

The theory and politics of transsexuality, and perhaps whole quadrants of transgender, can thrive only if they Take a Break from feminism, gay-identity politics, *and* queer theory.

What is it in feminism and queer theory that Prosser thinks "ha[s] made it possible to begin articulating the transsexual as a theoretical subject"? Prosser answers this question through an intensive rereading of Rubin, Sedgwick, and Butler. And I mean intensive. If you don't understand all their contributions to my genealogy plus some others, and in minute detail, you won't understand these pages. Butler is both the chief capacitor of Prosser's vocabulary and method, and the chief blocking figure he confronts. Sedgwick's work enters in as a foil to Butler's; Rubin's too. When he needs a move that would allow him to find some distance from Butler, he seeks it in *Epistemology, Tendencies,* and a few other contributions of Sedgwick's, in "Thinking Sex," and in Rubin's "*Interview*" with Butler. I had drafted most of Part Two before reading *Second Skins* and was quite struck by the frequency with which Prosser deploys against Butler precisely the same moments in Sedgwick's and Rubin's work that I have described as points of departure between them. But it is Butler's contribution that is persistently being reworked, and it is being reworked by an oedipally murderous prodigal son who wants his father to approve the prodigal's depredations at the homestead.

Prosser's first chapter is titled "Judith Butler: Queer Feminism, Transgender, and the Transubstantiation of Sex." This act of entitling, if you will, ensured that the text's running head would be "Judith Butler"—an extraordinary reiteration of Butler's full name, page after page, inscribed *over* Prosser's text as a kind of preferred but inappropriate signature, as the "subject" of the chapter that, because it is the name of a human being, treats her also as its "object" of study. That Prosser's project depends upon but is not Judith Butler's is made graphic.

Not only is the relationship between Prosser and his "Judith Butler" intensely personal; he makes it clear that his very access to a livable life is at stake in it. At one point, for instance, Prosser assesses arguments that transsexual subjectivity is the artifact of medical management and therefore does not originate, authentically, from the transsexuals themselves. He quotes with full assent Carroll Riddell's reply to one contribution to this bibliography: "My living space is threatened by this book."[61] Later, having promised to read the life narratives of transsexuals as deeply riven by a contradictory desire—a desire both to lay claim to narrative, to representation, to visibility, to legibility *as transsexual* and to merge perfectly, silently, invisibly into one's new sexed being— Prosser has this: "In accounts of individual lives, outside its current theoretical figuration transition often proves a barely livable zone" (12). That is to say, theory is a *more livable zone* than autobiography—but, Prosser warns, we must never forget that theory, too, can threaten living space.

Prosser means this pretty literally. Consider his assessment of Butler's discussion of *Paris Is Burning*, in particular of the fact that Venus Xtravaganza, a non-op m-to-f who was a crucial figure in Jennie Livingston's documentary, was murdered during filming. He contrasts what he sees as Livington's and Butler's disdain for Xtravaganza's yearning for a bourgeois home, with his own horror at the likelihood that she died because she was engaged in prostitution to earn money for her operation and fell victim to a john who discovered her transitional embodiment: of course such a person is entitled to yearn for a hearth. And he suggests that

neither Livingston nor Butler really notices or cares why Xtravaganza died, or even that she died.[62]

This is a frightening and tendentious moment in the politics
of theory, one in which Prosser mimics the very feminism he
seeks to displace. The demand from a hybrid project that feminist
theory must either represent "a livable life" or threaten life itself
is a convergentist demand. The moral tenor of the demand is
intense. Theory appears here as fully descriptive, normative, aspirational, and mandatory—that is, fully prescriptive. Prosser's
project both Takes a Break and refuses feminism its independence. If past is prologue, the seeds of trans paralysis are planted
exactly here.

Prosser translates *Gender Trouble* into a series of descriptive
statements about the world that make his transsexual narrative,
and indeed his transsexual life, possible (I will compare them
with their sources in Part Three). Here are some: "the subject
does not precede but is an effect of the law; heterosexuality does
not precede but is an effect of the prohibition on homosexuality;
sex [both Prosser and Butler here mean sex1, I think] does not
precede but is an effect of the cultural construction of gender"
(26). Prosser's *Gender Trouble* "argues that *all* gender is performative—that 'man' and 'woman' are not expressions of prior internal essences but constituted, to paraphrase Butler, through the
repetition of culturally intelligible stylized acts" (28). The place
of transgender and transsexuality in *Gender Trouble*, Prosser concludes, is to "bring[] into relief" the fully patent fact of the constituted rather than grounded sexed body (28). To be a lot cruder
about it than Prosser ever is, *Gender Trouble* read this way makes
his transsexual project possible because it acknowledges that individual transsexuals can do a lot to produce their sex1 and gender
as *effects*, and because it insists that, in doing so, they are no less
authentically male or female than anyone else.

But inasmuch as the effect aimed for is not apparent, visible, self-deconstructing performativity but a natural, coherent man or woman fully embodied in his or her sex1, the very propositions attributed to *Gender Trouble* also *block* the trajectory of transsexual desire. Prosser deduces from *Gender Trouble* a "scheme" (31) in the form of a tightly yoked syllogism that is rife with impediments for his project. If I read him right, this syllogism goes like this:

1. Seeing the "trans" of gender reveals that gender *and sex1* are performative (not natural and not fixed).
2. Seeing the performative quality of gender and sex1 upsets the heterosexual presumption, which requires m and f to diverge and require each other in sex1, sex2, gender, and sexual orientation, both in nature and in law. Transgender thus unravels the heterosexual matrix and so is homosexual. This is the "queer" moment in gender.
3. "Queer" is therefore subversive of the claims of "nature" and of law.

What's wrong with this picture from Prosser's perspective? He starts: "In the first instance, transgendered subjectivity is not inevitably queer. That is, by no means are all transgendered subjects homosexual" (31). Even if one resists this conflation of the queer into the homosexual—even if "the queer" can be understood more capaciously as "a figure for the performative" so that it can migrate toward, even emanate from, heterosexual subjects—"by no means are all transgendered subjects queer even in this figurative, nonreferential sense" (32). More profoundly, the antifoundationalism of Butler's version of queer theory—its persistent effort to destabilize the ground of sexuality in sex1 by revealing it to be a "construct" or an "effect"—actively cancels from its project the very object of much transsexual desire:

[I]n fact there are transgendered trajectories, in particular *transsexual* trajectories, that aspire to that which this scheme devalues. Namely there are transsexuals who seek very pointedly to be nonperformative, to be constative,[63] quite simply, to *be*. What gets dropped from transgender in its queer deployment to signify subversive gender performativity is the value of the matter that often most concerns the transsexual: the *narrative* of becoming a biological man or a biological woman (as opposed to the performative of effecting one)—in brief and simple the materiality of the sexed body. (32)

And finally:

In the case of transsexuality there are substantive features that its trajectory often seeks out that queer has made its purpose to renounce: that is, not only reconciliation between sexed materiality and gendered identification but also assimilation, belonging in the body and in the world. . . . There is much about transexuality that must remain irreconcilable to queer: the specificity of transsexual experience; the importance of flesh to self; the difference between sex[1] and gender identity; the desire to pass as "real-ly gendered" in the world without trouble; perhaps above all . . . a particular experience of the body that can't simply transcend (or transubstantiate) the literal. (59)

So: Prosser reads *Gender Trouble* as strongly affirmative, even normative; as syllogistically, schematically propositional; as teleologically committed to certain objects of desire. Counter to that, he proposes transsexuality as equally affirmative and normative, equally propositional (not yet, perhaps, schematically so); and teleologically committed to objects of desire that are what feminist queer theory—his term is "queer feminism" (21, 59)—does not want.

Prosser has enacted a Break from Feminism precisely at one of the spots where Rubin, in "Thinking Sex," had proposed we might need one to "think sex" for diverse sexual minorities. It's a brilliant intervention. I want to close this genealogy with a few thoughts on the politics of this Break, first by considering its implicit shift in desiderata, and second, by looking at the relative place of affirmation and critique in it.

Assuming that the operation of theory is to affirm and disaffirm, to value and devalue, here are some of the oppositions Prosser draws between a queer feminist project and a transsexual one:

Feminist queer theory affirms:	*Transsexuality affirms:*
The body as effect	The body as material
The body as surface	The body as interior (43)
Seeing; the visible body	Feeling; the sensible body (43)
Sex1 as language	Sex1 as ground
Nature as law (to be subverted)	Nature as object of desire (to be sought)
Homosexual affirmativity	Rehabilitation of heterosexuality
"Social construction"	"Sexed realness, . . . embodied sex" (49)
Deconstructions of literality and referentiality	Literality and referentiality (13, 58)
Deconstruction of monolithic signifiers	Reconstruction of bodily integrity as the aim of transition (6)
The unraveling of identity	The consolidation of identity (6)
Iteration, performance	Narrative (beginning, middle, and desired end) (29)
Trouble	Safety

Feminist queer theory affirms:	*Transsexuality affirms:*
Performance	Passing
Affirmation of the perversions	Affirmation of the normal
Domesticity as law (to be resisted)	Domesticity as object of desire (to be sought) ("territory, belonging, creating homes" [56])
Differentiation	Assimilation

There's something thrilling in seeing these new objects of desire come into view—but if you are someone who desires the "old" ones, something alarming too. Of course transsexuals—in fact, all people—want safety, normality, domestic familiarity, a home; of course the experience of bodily integrity, and firm inhabitation of one's sex1, can provide extreme pleasure and settled comfort. But attaching normativity and coercive regulatory force to them is what liberalism, the regulatory family, and compulsory heterosexuality have been doing for centuries. Political and legal gains for transsexuals might well be losses for many feminist, gay, and queer projects. It might be time, in fact, to wonder whether those of us who play left/progressive sex-positive politics can learn to handle the tensions between transsexual politics, gay-identity politics, feminism, and queer theory better than feminism has handled its relationship with queer theory.

As we inch our way toward that encounter, Prosser's framing of the desire for narrative, which he opposes to the queer desire for performativity, may suggest how to get a critical purchase on it. Prosser begins his book with the story of a class he taught while also beginning "massive doses of testosterone": by the end of the semester, he says, "I was . . . able to begin living full-time as a man, documents all changed to reflect a new, unambivalent status" (1). The ensuing story completely fails to deliver unambivalence, however. Prosser tells about his agonized uncertainty throughout the semester about where he was in the transition from female to male, his anxious worry and hope that his shifting status was legible to his students, the silence surrounding it that he felt was compelled but which he also plainly orchestrated, the displacement of his thinking about transition onto a student also transitioning (between "Native, Spanish, and Irish cultural heritages" and "from college to . . . graduate school"), and her presentation to the class *on the theme of transition*. Three pages later: "transitioning is what transsexuals *do*" (4). The "unambivalent status" that Prosser yearns for and achieves is "transition."

Second Skins ends with an epilogue that reproduces the basic shape of this contradiction. Here Prosser examines photographic portraits of transsexuals to argue that "transsexuality is . . . bound to representation, dependent on its symbolization to be real" (209). The antepenultimate page reproduces an image from Del LaGrace's photographic sequence representing the somatic transition of Zachary Nataf from female to male: we see a completely familiar penis in all its strange and endearing embodiment, and alongside it a tape measure allowing us to "measure" it. Then comes Prosser's last written page, and then (the last page of the text) a full-page photograph of Prosser himself, his body silhouetted against a riverbank, half-land/half-water as his background (233–35). The last words of the book are Prosser's promise to "blow my cover [here], and embody my narrative with this photograph." Liminality everywhere. Prosser "comes out" both as a man and as a transsexual, a gesture that places him exactly at the crosshairs of the contradiction which, he argues, vexes transsexual narrativity. And he has trained us to be hyperalert to the way in which the image of a body emphasizes both its materiality and its "dependen[cy] on . . . symbolization to be real." The gesture both yearns for and defers, both presents and represents, that beloved referent, Prosser the man.

The first and last pages of the book—and most of the pages in between—don't so much reject the desiderata of feminist queer theory in favor of those of transsexuality, as place them into para-doxical tension. So: the body as effect *and* as material; sex1 as language *and* as ground; social construction *and* sexed realness; deconstruction of literality and referentiality *and* their assertion; deconstruction *and* reconstruction of bodily integrity as a mono-lithic signifier; unraveling *and* consolidation of identity; iteration *and* narrative; performance *and* passing; the postmodern critique of the subject *and* Kantian individuality. We are approaching a moment not of affirmation, of valuing and devaluing, but of cri-tique. That is to say, in the pages I've been reading, Prosser puts into critical relation the terms that he *also* poses as the alternative, indeed inconsistent, possibly opposed values of feminist queer theory and transsexual theory.

You can say something like that about his identity politics too. Prosser's first chapter is saturated with the basic moves of iden-tity-based social movements. Transsexual experience has speci-ficities that nontranssexuals cannot know (59); Prosser can come out as a genuine transsexual more capable of speaking transsexual experience than Butler (59); he insists that political work on the subject emerge from the "perspective[]" of transsexuality (58); misrecognition inflicts the injury of "stigmatization," and theory has a moral obligation to jettison its misrecognizing commit-ments in favor of those proposed by stigmatized subjects for themselves (8); until everyone gains the right understanding of transsexuality, transsexuals will remain a subordinated minority faced with an unlivable life (8–9); to that end the people who are transsexuals need to acknowledge that they have consolidated interests which are not those of the constituency of feminism and which must be articulated in a separate movement (58–59); and to *that* end feminism needs to let go (60). The class in itself must become a class for itself.

But at the same time, every single statement of transsexual sub-jectivity that I have examined unravels this formulation to offer another, in which "unambivalent status" becomes a term *within* "transition" and in which we are asked to see the critical relation between all the oppositions that divide feminist queer theory's desiderata from those of transsexuality. As Prosser himself puts it, "queer deconstruction" aims for "a third space, 'a stance, detached, calm, and free, from which the opposition as a whole and its attendant terms can be perceived and judged."[64] Prosser both unperforms and performs that stance, too. That is to say, his argument is riven between prescriptive deployments of theory and critical ones.

✂ Prosser/Butler/Rubin

I suppose it's good to feel paralyzed, buried alive, and murdered when in fact that's what has happened to you; but I am firmly convinced that it's bad to feel these ways when it hasn't. The story of feminism and its others that I have told here leads me think that you are more likely to feel these ways needlessly, indeed somewhat irresponsibly falsely, if you want your social theory (here, of sexuality and power) to be normative, descriptive, and aspirational; if you deploy it prescriptively. If that's how theory stands for you, you are going to want your theory to be total. Prescriptive paranoid structuralism and the moralized mandate to converge are symptoms of this attitude to theory.

My idea is that a different attitude to theory is possible. When theory is hypothetical, and also when it is critical, it is less hostile to the existence of inconsistent theories operating at top speed "over there." It is more capable of apprehending these theories as possible competitors, as producing different worlds, as articulating different social goods and bads, and as driving divergent political desires. It is more capable of splitting decisions.

I am assuming that we live in a world where gains for transsexuality might come at the expense of feminism. This can happen at the level of material distributions: safety and home for transsexuals might require the reaffirmation of precisely the social forms that have been deployed to make heterosexuality compulsory. And it can happen at the level of theory: thought practices that make transsexuality articulate might make intersexuality less intelligible, might make gender trouble less powerful as an idea. Real social goods, real social costs are being allocated here. But getting clear on what they are, and deciding more clearly what to do about them, are more possible, I argue, if we see our theories as sources of hypothetical and critical purchase than if we want them to be right all the time.

As we've seen, Prosser (like MacKinnon, Bersani, Kennedy, and Butler, and probably like all of us) operates sometimes in one of these modes, sometimes in the other. So, for all the critical ambivalence of transsexual identity as transition, he gets very uncritically "stuck" when he attributes to *Gender Trouble* a schematic syllogism the terms of which have a propositional, even positively descriptive valence and packed an affirmative normative wallop. And when working in this mode he also experiences Butler's inconsistent theory to threaten his living space, to be indifferent to the murder of a man he cherishes. But—just as Butler didn't have to see nonfeminist queer theory as foreclosing, denying, etc., feminism—Prosser didn't need to see *Gender Trouble* as threatening his living space. This reading of *Gender Trouble* makes Butler's book quite unnecessarily normative, descriptive, and aspirational. Something of the hypothetical, speculative, discursive, critical, and dysphoric texture of Butler's writing didn't survive into Prosser's reiteration of it. Some examples, taken from *Gender Trouble* and *Second Skins*:

> *Butler*: the "impersonation of women [by Divine] *implicitly suggests* that gender *is* a kind of persistent impersonation that passes as the real." (x, emphases added);
>
> *Prosser*: Butler is able to show that drag recapitulates straight

genders *"for all 'gender is* a kind of persistent impersonation that passes as the real.' "* (30, emphasis added)

Butler: "*If* 'the body is a situation,' as [Simone de Beauvoir] claims, ... sex, *by definition, will be shown to have been* gender all along." (8, emphases added);
Prosser: Transgender "allows Butler [to provide] a performative model where sex *can 'be shown to have been* gender all along.' " (33, emphasis added)

Prosser's Butler makes announcements about the world that aim for truth and judgment: *all* gender *is* an impersonation, *and that's good.* He strips off the conditionals, the modals, and the gestures acknowledging that she's producing interpretations, readings, representations. Butler's Butler is performing operations and ascertaining possibilities, contingent entailments. Prosser's Butler is describing and affirming.

Prosser makes things much much harder for himself—*he* constrains the transsexual subject's living space—when he reiterates Butler's critical hypotheses in this doubly positivized form. And the very positivity of trans theory in his formulation virtually commits it to see its relationship to feminist queer theory as paralyzed, buried alive, murdered, and impossible.

I don't mean to imply that Butler never shifts into the gear that Prosser thinks is her only one. *Au contraire,* as we've seen, her work often insists on the truth and judgment in feminism, and shifts out of her more hypothetical or critical mode. When it does so she, too, sets up the conditions for the feminist experience of paralysis.

Consider this formulation from "Against Proper Objects": "If sexual relations cannot be reduced to gender positions, which seems true enough, it does not follow that an analysis of sexual relations apart from an analysis of gender relations *is possible*" (11, emphasis added). Surely Butler does not mean that no one could write an analysis of sexual relations that did not turn on gender. For instance, let's suppose I set out to write an essay, "Two Orifices," on the erotic possibilities of the mouth and the anus that assumed these parts of the body to have a relative place in sexual practice that works without regard to gender. Surely I could emphasize, for instance, their location, as quite different sphincters, at either end of the alimentary canal. This binarized location is a fact about them that surely can be and often is experienced in gendered terms (anything from the association of food and diapers with Mom, to the relative slowness with which women's, as opposed to men's, anal eroticism, and men's, as opposed to women's, pleasure in giving fellatio, have emerged as topics of cultural activity or objects of left political solicitude). But comparing the two openings/closings might ask for other comparisons—loose/tight, clean/dirty, patent/hidden, acquisitive/relinquishing, and so forth—that aren't configured in terms of m and f. I can imagine that my essay "Two Orifices," focusing exclusively on those not-necessarily-gendered terms, could be very, very long and very, very fun to write.

I think that when Butler doubts that such an essay "is possible," she is concerned not with whether it could be written, but whether it would make sense, be adequate—and inasmuch as she is a feminist 24/7, her answer would have to be "no." This is not only because *her* interest in the topic would be left unaddressed (though that would indeed be the case), but also because—as we have seen—she regards the omission of gender as its elision: gender as m > f *must* be marked if we are to avoid recapitulating masculinist epistemology and reinstating male dominance.

Note that Butler now occupies the stance toward theory which Prosser takes in objecting to the tight, positive, descriptive, normative, and aspirational syllogism he deduces from *Gender Trouble, and which paralyzed feminists take in objecting that* Gender Trouble *dissolves the category "woman."* Theory about sexuality must resist the collaboration between the unsaid of gender and masculinist abstraction: theory itself is a crucial politics of gender; to do a good descriptive job *and* avoid moral error, you have to get your theory right. The feminist versions—both Butler's and those devised to oppose her critical work—commit feminism in advance to unmasking male dominance and toppling it from the apex of social value. They regard theory that doesn't at least try to do this to be impossible.

In her "*Interview*" with Butler Rubin directly disagrees with this attitude toward theory:

> For some, feminism had become the successor to Marxism and was supposed to be the next grand theory of all human misery. I am skeptical of any attempt to privilege one set of analytical tools over all others and of all such claims of theoretical and political omnipotence.
>
> I approach systems of thought as tools people make to get leverage and control over certain problems. I am skeptical of all universal tools. A tool may do one job brilliantly and be less helpful for another. I did not see feminism as the best tool for the job of getting leverage over issues of sexual variation. (97)

For Rubin, theories are tools that people invent in order to manage problems. Many problems, many theories. Grand theory is an impediment not because it is theory but because it is grand. Rubin argues that theories provide hypotheses that have value to her only insofar as they enable her to make politically and conceptually useful accounts of social life as it is lived by human beings. Faced with the theoretical exclusion of gender from "Two Orifices," Rubin would object to it, if at all, not on the grounds that it gets its theory wrong at the level of structure or totality; nor because, as a feminist, she wants constantly to learn more about m/f; and certainly not on the grounds that its elision of gender ratifies the abstraction of masculinist epistemologies and so collaborates with the dark forces of male domination. Her assessment would be more pragmatic: is "Two Orifices" "[more or] less helpful" to her, she would ask, in her effort to "get leverage and control over certain problems"? Depending on whether "Two" sharpened the tools of theoretic hypothesis formation about sexuality, or produced rich accounts of social life, and depending on what problems she was trying to get leverage over, she would either find my essay to be "brilliant" or "less helpful," banal or even quite harmful.

I think it's no coincidence that, in the "*Interview*" and in "Thinking Sex," Rubin has so much to say about gay male masculinity and includes "unapologetic heterosexuals" among her allies.[65] It's hard to be affirmative about these dimensions of human sexuality if you are precommitted to unmasking male dominance and toppling it from the apex of social value; it's especially hard if you think that abandoning these projects even for a moment reconfirms the unmarked abstraction that lies at the heart of masculinist epistemology and for that reason is a bad thing to do. This is probably why the elision of interest in and admiration for gay male masculinity and of "unapologetic heterosexuals" is such a strong signal of a feminist political style committed to the prescriptive deployment of theory.

But let's press on in a Foucaultian direction and beyond Rubin's formulation. What if our theories, though incommensurate and conflicting, are more productive than she supposes? What if a project deeply interested in promoting the welfare of masculine men or unapologetic heterosexuals really and truly does make it necessary for women to be more womanly, or abstraction to be more male dominant? What if writing "Two Orifices" takes away some of the shame attached to anal sex and makes it less exciting? What if picking a theory out of the theory tool kit does more than just illuminate the problem to which it alone is adequate; what if it also ratifies that problem, produces our experience of its reality, recruits people to suffer it? What if theory does more than illumine, hypothetically, real goods and bads that already exist in the world; what if it also produces their very intelligibility, their experience-ability, so that when we develop a theory, we distribute social harms and social gains? How would we even know something was a problem if we hadn't *already* picked out the theory for it? If these are the right questions, we live in a darker world than the one imagined by Rubin; one in which the very decision to opt for one theory and not another would be understood to have distributive consequences, some bad, some good. We would face split decisions all the time. Part Three tries to perform Taking a Break from Feminism in that dark world, precisely to make this condition of deciding under conditions of theoretic incommensurability and radical uncertainty one we can approach responsibly.

PART THREE

HOW AND WHY TO TAKE A BREAK FROM FEMINISM

Would it possibly be a good idea for feminists, and for people involved in related justice-seeking intellectual/activist enterprises, to learn to suspend feminism—indeed, to suspend antiracism, queer theory, trans theory, any theory—to interrupt it, to sustain its displacement by inconsistent hypotheses about power, hierarchy, and progressive struggle? I argue for the remainder of this book that it may well be. First, though, I want to show what I mean by Taking a Break from Feminism.

TAKING A BREAK TO
DECIDE (I)

I've divided this chapter in two, one portion appearing both here and at the end of Part Three, and thus at the very end of the book. In both segments I look at feminist and gay-identity legal issues: up front, the decisions to seek workplace accommodations for pregnant women and to make male/male sexual harassment actionable as sex discrimination, and later, the decision to regulate the sexual injury husbands impose on their wives by letting wives sue for money damages on the grounds that they've been emotionally harmed. The idea is to read (and reread, and reread . . .) these legal decisions in the mode of Taking a Break.

My first such effort, "The Costs of 'Making Difference Costless,'" is a rather abstract thought experiment, seeking to identify interests other than those of pregnant women that an emancipation- and equality-loving leftist might want to take into account, but which feminists have worked hard to omit from their policy calculus. The second and third subdivisions (one now, one later) involve actual legal victories, both via adjudication, won by feminists and gay-identity advocates suing in court. One of these has already been considered: we have examined *Oncale v. Sundowner Offshore Services* in order to understand MacKinnon's brief to the U.S. Supreme Court in that case;[1] here I revisit her factual and legal understandings of the case in order to compare them with those we can generate from cultural-feminist, gay-identity, and queer theoretic presuppositions. The third Taking a Break exercise is deferred until the end so that I can offer an intervening section surveying all the arguments I know of against Taking a Break and all the reasons to do it anyway. Only then will I attempt to read and reread *Twyman v. Twyman*[2] in the language of different social theories—feminist sexual-subordination social theory, feminist social subordination theory, Nietzsche's idea of the slave revolt in morals, and Foucault's *Volume One* idea of biopower—to ask whether we want divorcing wives to be able to sue their husbands for sexual injury during the marriage. If the section on *Oncale* is primarily about the adversity of interests among incommensurable social *constituencies*, several of which fall well outside the scope of feminist theory and advocacy, the rereadings of *Twyman* probe the adversity of interests suggested by incommensurable social *theories* of sexuality and power.

I stress that these readings are thought experiments. Since real living people are involved in both of the judicial opinions I look at, I must emphasize that I am not denying that the real actual plaintiffs involved in the real actual litigation were victims and suffered subordination of the sort that power feminism and cultural feminism (and gay-subordination theories tracking them) attribute to them. Maybe they, individually, are fully and only intelligible within the terms of those theories. But maybe they aren't. My rereadings attempt to explain all the facts we're given just as well as feminism does. I'm not merely agnostic but skeptical that we could learn anything more about these cases that would resolve this ambiguity as a matter of fact. And surely people who are not victims and are not subordinated in feminist terms will invoke these cases and obtain victories over their foes using them. If we are to evaluate the social effects that can be produced by a legal rule, a responsible approach—one tracking the methodology deployed by Kennedy in "Sexy Dressing"—includes scanning for its fragmented, disparate, and paradoxical consequences, not just its beauty as a statement of moral values. If these victories could allow social outcomes like those I describe in my rereadings, people on the left should be concerned. And we might have to Take a Break from Feminism, sometimes even from the feminist minima m/f, m > f, and carrying a brief for f, to see those possible consequences and decide whether we want to risk them.

My method here is to engage theory to make apparent some radically incommensurate patterns of the costs and benefits of legal decisions. My hope is that, for at least some readers, these rereadings will put in question their ideas of what a cost and a benefit *are*. Above all I hope this disorientation—however painful it might also be—will be pleasurable, erotically animating, and politically enabling.

The Costs of "Making Difference Costless"

What should we do with learning disabled kids in school? Mark Kelman and Gillian Lester have shown that our current answer sounds not in distributive terms, but in antidiscrimination.[3] In the last chapter of their brilliant book *Jumping the Queue*, Kelman and Lester reflect more broadly on the political and political-theoretical implications of similar framings all over the range of projects they describe as "left multiculturalism." By this they mean left-of-center advocacy framed on the subordination model of social power, seeking primarily equality for a wide range of subordinated social groups. Kelman and Lester observe that these projects persistently argue that desubordination requires not mere formal equality or abstract equal treatment but affirmative action, accommodation, and remedies not only against invidious and malicious treatment but also against disadvantageous outcomes. Almost all left feminist law reform efforts today sound in antidiscrimination, so Kelman and Lester's analysis is highly suggestive about their structure.

Kelman and Lester show that left multicultural subordination-theory remedial schemes relating to employment discrimination persistently yield the proposed rule that employees presenting "real" differences—real differences that we have decided to protect, specifically, against illegitimate "discrimination"—must be accommodated by the employer. The calculus that left-multicultural subordination theories advocate would require the employer to accommodate, ignore the costs of accommodation, ignore the employee's net, accommodated output, and take into account only the employee's gross output. To do otherwise is what it is *to discriminate*.

Let me translate that. Two people apply for an entry-level job in a law firm. They are exactly similar with the sole exception that one of them reads and writes more slowly because he has a mild learning disability. The remedial ideal of left-multicultural subordination theory would require the employer not to prefer the nondisabled applicant, but at minimum to toss a coin in deciding which one to hire, and maybe to go further and *prefer* the disabled employee. In doing so, the employer must embrace the following mode of economic thinking. The disabled applicant will need more time and/or more equipment, and/or a downward adjustment in his workload (those are "the accommodation"). Every unit of work he produces will cost me more (that is the net, accommodated output). But I must evaluate him on the basis of his *gross* output, which (once we've left out the additional time and the downward adjustment in workload) is identical to that of the nondisabled applicant. As a result, the costs of the disability (at least with respect to our employment relation) will fall entirely on me, the employer; and if I shift any of the costs in this calculus to my disabled employee (by not hiring him, or compensating him differently, or not promoting him), I am *discriminating*.

Many, many feminists think that this is the way the legal system should approach "women's difference" in employment. In Christine Littleton's phrase, our antidiscrimination paradigm should operate "to make [female] difference costless"[4]—costless, that is, to women. But, in the context of LD kids and equality in education, Kelman and Lester ask an important question: why should members of the subordinated group on whose behalf we have constructed our antidiscrimination regime be our only objects of solicitude when it comes time to spend education dollars? What about garden-variety slow learners—kids who could benefit, too, from the accommodations we give disabled kids, but who don't get them, sometimes even *because* we're spending those dollars on antidiscrimination?

Let's play that out in the context of the chief example Littleton is considering, pregnancy and work. Her argument is not only that the costs of remedying the disparate impact of workplace rules on pregnant workers, for instance, should be entirely shouldered by employers, so that these workers would experience no downturn in compensation, promotion, seniority, medical and other leave, quality of work assignment, and the like. It is also that such a remedial structure *eliminates* rather than *shifts* the costs of pregnancy.

This is of course magical thinking. As Kelman and Lester insist, the costs don't disappear; they go to the employer, who will then allocate them *some*where, possibly to places where they will hurt women; possibly to places where they will hurt men; maybe only blacks will shoulder them, or third-world workers; maybe they will go to places where no current subordination theory can find them. For many feminisms, that means they fall off the edge of the analytic universe. Bringing them back is seen as unfeminist.

So, as long as feminism feels that way, let's Take a Break from Feminism and see if we can imagine where the costs might go. Indeed, let's go further and see how far feminism, reduced to the definitional minima that I have attributed to it—m/f, m > f, and carrying a brief for f—can travel with us as we seek to follow the costs wherever they may go.

From outside feminism, it appears strange that feminism would be so bent on ignoring the first possibility—that *women* might end up shouldering all or some of the costs of pregnancy accommodations. Feminism seems at this point to have allied itself with maternalism; otherwise, ignoring the costs of pregnancy accommodation to unaccommodated women—the de facto transfer of social resources from nonreproducing women to pregnant ones—would be understood to breach any "duty of fair representation" that promulgators of the theory might bear to the entire constituent group. It may be a symptom of left multicultural/feminist flight from the politics of distribution that feminist conflicts about this trade-off get so nasty so fast.[5]

What if black or offshore workers end up bearing the costs? Convergentist feminist antiracism and feminist postcolonial work seek solutions that *merge* the interests of black workers, offshore workers, and pregnant women in the United States. And I agree that it is very important to seek possibilities of such merger, and to act on them politically. But even to see them clearly you have to be willing to see moments in which their interests don't converge, and you have to be ready to decide when to give up and do things for one group of workers at the expense of another. The thought experiment of a mostly-divergentist-but-ultimately-aspirationally-convergentist hybrid feminist project would have to pass through many, many moments in which it would try to see how protecting one group might harm another.

The potential adversity of interests between American working women who get pregnant, and black and brown workers at home, and all workers in "globalization" (some of whom will be men) can be illuminated only if we are willing to entertain divergentist antiracist and poco feminist hypotheses. But this brings us face-to-face with harm to men. I will argue below that feminists doing policy-oriented work in the United States today tend to have a strong commitment to a triad of descriptive assumptions: that m > f takes place as female innocence, female injury, *and male immunity.*[6] But even without that thought habit, the feminist minima m/f, m > f, and carrying a brief for f make it very difficult for feminists to imagine first-world women subordinating men in global markets—as they may well do if they preserve their pregnancy leaves.

And then let's go back home, and imagine the costs as allocated strictly between "men" and "women" workers there; let's imagine that pregnancy accommodations cost just enough to motivate a workforce reduction that happens to fall entirely on male workers, who are now without jobs. It could happen—and it could happen without the operation of sex discrimination against women by anyone. (To imagine that, picture this: the employer could decide to eliminate the least profitable segment of the workforce; and that could be a segment that became all-male because working conditions there were so grim that women, enjoying the superior bargaining power that they derive in low-wage employment markets from their productive roles as homemaker/ mothers and their ability to secure wage-earning men [that is, husbands] on whom to be wholly or partially dependent, did not seek to work there.) Here again, feminists have been seriously averse to hearing—from anyone, but especially from feminists— that the possibility of harm to men as such is any of its concern. This aversion is yet another symptom of the tight logic linking female injury, female innocence, and male immunity as mutually fixed terms in feminist argument. But the definitional criteria of feminism operate as well here: short of a new feminist politics of incommensurable political theories, we'd have to Take a Break from Feminism to notice and care about those laid-off men.

And let's take it one step further, and imagine that the costs of accommodating pregnancy fall diffusely but with a certain weight on the enterprise itself. Let's say it's the last straw in a troubled industry or economic downturn; the business fails. Theoretically, at least, all the workers could be laid off before feminists committed to "making difference costless" while tethering female injury to female innocence and male immunity could notice that women are sometimes not women but workers *simpliciter*, and that being permanently laid off is usually a bad outcome for a worker.

My observation has been that, at this point, feminists will reconfigure "a worker" as "a woman," and thus occlude the sheer workforce impact of joblessness in the high winds of late modern capitalism, in order to keep itself in a position of theoretic indispensability. But let's resist the temptation. At this point it's not clear what we should *do* about the resulting bad outcome. All the other straws "caused" it too; and there is no reason to think that pregnant women must cut back their demands in deference to them: it's the politics of distribution all the way down. But there's also no reason to think that pregnancy leaves are of such absolute and sublime importance that they primordially trump all the other costs and benefits at stake in the politics of a hypothetical business on the brink of failure. We might want to Take a Break from Feminism—not only specific, contingent feminisms with strong commitments to redistribution toward pregnant women, but even feminism in general, minimally defined by commitments to the m/f distinction and to carrying a brief for f—in order to assess and participate in those politics.

Oncale v. Sundowner Offshore Services

The facts alleged by Joseph Oncale are disturbing. Working on an oil rig in an all-male workforce, he was repeatedly menaced and assaulted by his supervisor and two coworkers. They threatened to rape him; twice they held him down while placing their penises up against his body; once they grabbed him in the shower and did something (one cannot be sure quite what) with a piece of soap. His complaints were ignored, and he quit under protest.

Oncale complained in federal court that he had suffered the form of employment discrimination under Title VII that we call "sexual harassment." In doing so he challenged a then-strong line of cases in federal trial and appellate courts holding that same-sex sexual harassment, though not a good idea or commendable practice, was not sex discrimination and therefore was not actionable under the federal employment discrimination statute. The Supreme Court reversed all these holdings when it ruled, on Oncale's appeal, that he could sue under Title VII.

The Court held that same-sex sexual harassment on the job could be found to be discrimination based on sex in two ways. First, where the plaintiff alleged "proposals of sexual activity," courts could inquire into whether the alleged harasser was homosexual: if so, they could return to an assumption they always make in cross-sex sexual-overture cases, that the sexual overture was targeted at the plaintiff "because of [his or her] sex." And second, a plaintiff could show that conduct not motivated by sexual desire was sex discrimination by showing an animus against members of his or her sex, a general practice of treating members of one sex worse than those of the other, or other equally circumstantial manifestations of discriminatory intent. "[M]ale-on-male horseplay [and] intersexual flirtation" would not be sanctionable, the Court held, because in all cases, the conduct had to be "severely or pervasively abusive," such that "a reasonable person in the plaintiff's position would find it hostile or abusive." The "common sense" of juries and judges, together with their "appropriate sensitivity to social context," would guarantee that they could "distinguish between simple teasing and roughhousing among members of the same sex" and illegal harassment.[7]

Let's read the facts and the outcome from inside the hypotheses of power feminism, cultural feminism, gay-identity politics, and queer theory. Wherever they could converge, I'll try to split them.

As we've seen, MacKinnon was able to construe the sexual violence and sexual ridicule alleged by Oncale as male dominance and female submission, and thus sexual harassment, because she said that Oncale had been feminized. The same-sex or homosexual dimension of the case presented no mysteries to her: she maintained the ontological supremacy of feminism by simultaneously evacuating sexual orientation of any distinct components and flooding it with gender understood as male superordination and female subordination. She converged.

Cultural feminists like West would want the same basic legal rule that MacKinnon wanted, but for different reasons. To them, the facts alleged by Oncale constitute a classic moral struggle between a virtuous feminine or feminized man and a bunch of morally defective testosterone-poisoned coworkers. Oncale on this reading is a surrogate for actual women: his attackers would have harassed a woman if she had been there; their overall goal was to masculinize oil-rig work, and to maintain the oil rig as a province for male privilege. The consolidated masculinity of the rig after Oncale has quit not only limits women's employment opportunities but also confirms that sexuality is a, if not the, crucial vehicle for women's subordination.[8]

Cultural feminism would want Oncale to be able to sue for sex discrimination for a lot of reasons. It wants feminine men to have plenty of social stature. It wants masculine men to come under discipline. It wants the law to make official statements about gender virtue and gender vice, to send good gender-morality messages. It also wants to feminize or, faute de mieux, degender the oil rig. That would push male-dominant values out of this segment of public life; and it would clear the way for women to work there and to bring femininity with them. It's willing to desexualize the workplace,[9] either because it shares MacKinnon's structuralism, and so thinks that sex (almost?) always carries male dominance and female subordination, or because it thinks morally good sex—intersubjective, caring, respectful; alert to human dignity, human values, human sensibilities, human sensitivities— just can't happen between people as lightly connected as coworkers (only domestic monogamy is up to the challenge).

Anyone who cares about gay men or who wants to promote and protect gay identity has to regard these feminist projects, and the outcome of the case, with ambivalence. Gay rights advocates really resented the legal state of affairs before *Oncale* was finally decided, in which people harassed by someone of the same sex didn't get anywhere near as much protection as people encountering cross-sex harassment. It was for them mostly an equality and dignity harm; but they also liked the idea of homosexual predators' coming under regulation on grounds similar to Kennedy's will to punish and deter heterosexual male rapists of women. Both objected that members of their own social group were spoiling a cherished sexual scene. But there were plenty of reasons to worry.

One was a subrule, directly proposed by MacKinnon in her brief and adopted by the Court, making the homosexuality of a sex harassment perpetrator a special fact that, if established, makes the plaintiff's case easier to win. Sexual harassment law had long held that heterosexual sexual advances were sex discrimination because the male perpetrator, assumed to be heterosexual, would not have treated a man the same way. He discriminated on the basis of sex in selecting a woman for his advances, taunts, assaults, whatever. MacKinnon's brief argued that plaintiffs in same-sex cases should be allowed to prove the homosexuality of their perps so that they could get the same conclusive finding of sex discrimination (24). The Supreme Court in *Oncale* agreed, and we can now have little trials-within-the-trial to prove the homosexuality of alleged sexual harassment perpetrators.

Gay rights organizations had fought to close this route off ever since circuit courts first opened it, however, because it is also a quick and easy avenue via homophobia to false-positive liability, via the inference that because the defendant is homosexual, he probably has done this bad sexual thing. In a male-male case the inference is even richer, borrowing as it does from the feminist commitment to m > f and carrying a brief for f: because the defendant is a *male* homosexual, he is a sexual dominator.

To be sure, MacKinnon's brief counsels that courts may be institutionally unable to make findings of parties' sexual orientations, and it also indicates that courts admitting evidence of the parties' sexual orientations must prevent "homophobic attacks" (24). But a gay-identity-affirmative project would say that she entirely misses the commonsense status of the inference from a defendant's homosexuality to his character as a sexual wrongdoer. It would resent the brief's virtual invitation to the Supreme Court to indulge in this inference in the form of an entirely unnecessary footnote quoting from Joseph Oncale's deposition testimony: "I feel that they made homosexual advances toward me," Oncale opined; according to the brief, "I feel they are homosexuals" (23 n. 7). Neither lower-court opinion in *Oncale*, and none of the briefs submitted to the Supreme Court, had brought this detail in the record to the justices' attention. And the justices did not ask for it: the questions they certified for their review made no mention of homosexuality. *Oncale* made its way up the appellate ladder as an "Animal House" case:[10] the plaintiff's allegations of cruel, repeated, and unwelcome sexual assaults were persistently read as male-male homosocial high jinks gone awry—in Justice Scalia's terms, "simple teasing or roughhousing among members of the same sex" that is aberrational only in that it has become "objectively severe." Alternatively, of course, Oncale's deposition testimony could support a reading of the scene as homosexual predation. It is difficult to escape the conclusion that the MacKinnon brief aimed to induce the Court to adopt just such a reading.

A gay-affirmative mind-set reacts with horror to this state of affairs. It is quite clearly an open vehicle for antigay mobilization.

But to power feminists and cultural feminists—committed as they are to their convergentist idea that homosexuality fully resides within m > f gender—the costs aren't apparent. They're suspicious of male/male eroticism: unless redeemed by the femininity of one partner, or a thoroughgoing display of categorical-imperative respect, and the like, what men do with men strikes power feminism as a concentration of dominance, and cultural feminists as morally fraught. They would suspect that Oncale was right that his assailants were homosexuals, and would regard their sexual aggression as a textbook case of morally defective masculine eroticism. The social costs of having nasty little trials on whether or not someone is homosexual, and the possibility that plaintiffs in these cases might win more easily, are either worth it, or they're not costs at all: they might be exactly what these feminisms would want.

The overall ruling—that same-sex cases like Oncale's can be brought under Title VII—is similarly problematic. There are two bad scenarios—one antigay, the other antisex—that can now find vindication under this ruling. Indeed, none of the facts published in the various court decisions in *Oncale* (except Oncale's allegation of unwantedness) preclude the possibility that this very case embodied one or the other of these scenarios.

Before I elaborate them, allow me to reiterate that I am not saying anything about the human being Joseph Oncale, or making any truth claims about what actually happened on the oil rig. Instead, I want to show how his factual allegations can be read. I am going to put his allegation of unwantedness aside, as a mere allegation, and then connect the remaining dots. And since that heuristic produces the equivalent of a court's knowledge of a same-sex sex harassment case of this type up to and beyond summary judgment, the patterns I draw will become predictions about two alarming classes of cases that will make it to trial—

likely also leading to settlement damages and possibly also actual verdicts—under *Oncale.*

In the first of these alternative readings, we can posit, at least for purposes of contemplating what sex harassment law after *Oncale* might authorize, that a plaintiff with these facts willingly engaged in erotic conduct of precisely the kinds described in Oncale's complaint (or that he engaged in some of that conduct and fantasized the rest; or even that he fantasized all of it), and then was struck with a profound desire to refuse the homosexual potential those experiences revealed in him.

That is to say, *Oncale* might have been a homosexual panic case. It would be easy enough to generate this reading of the case out of entirely gay-identity presuppositions: in that event, Oncale is actually a gay or bisexual man, but a shame-ridden one, who reacted to his own (identity-appropriate) sexual behavior and/or desires and fantasies with remorse and a lawyer. Oncale's many television appearances in which he (I am told) affirmed his horrified heterosexuality would be taken, on this reading, as merely a closet-drama, a project in deep bad faith; my insistence on the possibility of this other reading of the case would be, then, a gesture in the direction of an outing (though note that I am reading the record, not the human being). On this, first rereading of the case, a pro-gay analysis would have to understand Oncale as the aggressor, the other men on the oil rig as the victims, and the lawsuit (not any sexual encounter on the oil rig) as the wrong.

But a more thoroughgoing queer approach would make the facts outright uncertain. Recall how Sedgwick's queered gender wanted to detach male bodies from masculinity and superordination and female bodies from femininity and subordination; how she wanted not only to celebrate but to undermine and historicize every current supersession of, and generally "get beyond," discrete homo- and heterosexual identities. Recall also that Bersani's and Kennedy's queered understandings of the power in sex wanted to notice that sexual super- *and* subordination can *both* be complex objects of desire.

It's easy to read the facts in *Oncale* in a number of ways that perform many of these queer-theoretic operations. We can imagine that the oil rig has a culture with rules, and that these rules draw not on a feminist or a gay-identity script, but on the ways in which masculine and feminine performances and gay-identified and gay-disidentified performances can diverge and converge to make the power relationships in sex expressly problematic. The rules allow Oncale to indicate a willingness to be mastered, indeed to stipulate that he is sexually accessible only if those approaching him take on the task of mastery; they submit by taking control; and something happens with a piece of soap. There's not enough in the record to say much more about how it could have been, but (assuming we are going to take Oncale's allegations about unwelcomeness as merely that—allegations) nothing I've said so far is ruled out by the record. From this starting point, the possibilities, in terms of masculinity and femininity and in terms of gay and straight, are probably endless. Mix, match, and omit as you will:[11]

1. Oncale performs a feminine man in order to signal his willingness to be mastered; it's the discrepancy between his male body and his gender that gets things going; the other guys comply with a big display of masculinity; and it's the discrepancy between their mere bodily selves and the grand controlling personae they assume that keeps things going; so "man fucks woman" but with a twist that undoes the capacity of feminism to underwrite Oncale as a victim.

2. Oncale performs a perfectly masculine man but only one kind of masculine man; it's the discrepancy between his masculinity and that performed by the other men involved that gets things going. Femininity is not important

in this version—it's just absent; the men are differentiat-
ing themselves within some diacritics in masculinity. The
terms of differentiation could sound in sentiment, age,
refinement, race, moodiness, or simply (this is important;
convergence is not mandated) masculinity itself. So "It's
a guy thing" that creates the space for a dominance/sub-
mission sexual interaction. So "man fucks man"—maleness and masculinity are important products of the interaction, but with a twist that undoes the capacity of
feminism to underwrite Oncale as a victim.

3. The other men perform a kind of femininity associated
   with power—for example, they become bitchy. There is
   no necessary gender correlate for Oncale. He could be
   the heterosexual partner of the bitch and thus masculin-
   ized, but that doesn't tell us whether he's henpecked or
   intensely phallic. He could be their lesbian partner, but
   that doesn't tell us whether she's butch or femme. Or he
   could merely play the bottom to the power on display—
   no gender at all. So "man or woman fucks man or
   woman," or perhaps "man or woman fucks," always with
   a twist that undoes the capacity of feminism to underwrite Oncale as a victim.

4. Possibly more than one of these is happening at the same
   time, or rather, perhaps, they all flicker as the scene un-
   folds. Or it could be that the sheer bodily homosexuality
   of the scene is so dominantly what it is about that any
   effort to attribute to it legible gender signification is simply doomed to defeat. In either case we would have a
   power/submission relay, but with a twist that undoes the
   capacity of feminism to underwrite Oncale as a victim.

None of the above involves homosexual panic. Indeed, a person
could pass through most of the scenes I've described without a

sexual-orientation identity; you could even do some of them "as" heterosexual; more likely homosexual and heterosexual desire would—each—be, at every moment, complexly achieved, defeated, and deferred. So to that extent the object of desire for any of the players would be some relationship to sexual orientation. Similarly, where gender is of any moment, it reads not as a property or determinant of the bodily self but as a performative language, as a means of transmitting desire. Certainly we can say that, when gender matters at all, the object of desire is not a gendered object, but a relationship to a gender or perhaps to gender more generally.

But I've made the assumption that the lead theme in the scene is power and submission. And here's the rub. The mix-and-match volatilities of gender and sexual orientation work to make the question of who is submitting to whom extremely difficult to answer. Indeed, the chief theme would have to be that the desire of the parties to any of these scenes has as its object a *mise-en-problème* of desire itself. To the extent that the decision in *Oncale* allows one participant in scenes like these to have a panic about it afterward and sue, it sets courts and juries administering Title VII a deeply problematic function.

Let me reapproach that last point from the perspective of MacKinnon's power feminism. The rereadability of the facts in *Oncale,* rather than confirming her theory, shows what's wrong with trying to understand this case with it and only it in your hypothesis repertoire. It is just too complete and too settled. Men are over there with masculinity and superordination; women are over here with femininity and subordination. Sex and sexuality are never good; they are always tools by which women are assigned subordination and men either assign or suffer it. Sexual orientation both matters and doesn't matter precisely and only to the extent that it confirms this mapping. Everything is accounted for; there is nothing left over. The model produces great certainty: Oncale transparently represents all men injured by this totalized gender system because the system frames all options for understanding his injury. But if the model doesn't apply—if homosexual panic or more complex problematicness panic is what "the case is about"; if we want to be able to notice it because we are politically, ethically, strategically concerned that it might be happening—that certainty should evaporate.

The resulting uncertainty intensifies, moreover, as we move from the homosexual panic hypothesis to the problematicness panic hypothesis. Things are bad enough under the former. Surely, on that reading of the facts, Joseph Oncale's hesitant sense that his attackers "are homosexuals" is volatile: Does his "feeling" about his attackers tell us that they are homosexuals or that he might be? That they attacked him on the oil rig or that he attacked them by invoking the remarkable powers of the federal court to restore his social position as heterosexual? If we could know the answer to these questions, at least we'd know how to judge the case: we know we're against assault, and we know we're against homosexual panic. But how, in an actual case, *would* we know? Surely we would not want Justice Scalia's "common sense" to be our guide: after all, homosexual panic *is* common sense.

Of course we could advocate putting Pat Califia on the stand to persuade juries out of their commonsense intuition that no one could want to be mastered sexually, or could take control by demanding to be mastered. But the problem in the problematicness panic rereading of the *Oncale* facts runs much deeper than that. On that reading, it was precisely the loss of certainty about wantedness that the players were seeking. That *was* their desire. It's a risky desire: acting on it places one in the way of having some unwanted sex. Things can go wrong; we need to keep one eye on the cause of action for assault. But more profoundly, if things go right, the wantedness of the sex that happens will be unknowable. The queer theoretic reading of the case reminds us that we will always do violence when we decide.

How can we think responsibly about that violence, that decision? Of course throughout we are concerned about sexual predators who make the workplace impossible for their victims. But we might also worry that Oncales who inhabit my fourth rereading contradict their own past decisions when they claim access now to a less problematic set of norms about wantedness. We might want to estop them from claiming now that then they didn't want to put wantedness *en abîme*, not only because we find this dishonesty repulsive, but also because the social forces they will gather and sharpen, if they win, bid to make Title VII a vanilla-sex regime. It might turn the normative screw in the direction of less problematic sex, making problematic sex more unwanted by more people, and increasingly more actionable. From this angle, MacKinnon's reading of the case is not a transparent translation of suppressed consciousness into the law; it's a trumping move in a culture war among leftists interested in sexuality as a dark power. There are lots of people out there—cards-on-the-table moment: I am one of them—who think the problematic of wantedness isn't just tolerable; we think it's beautiful; it's brave; it's complicated and fleeting and elaborate and human. Workplace discrimination rights to bring problematicness panic suits against it insulate a big part of the world from our political reach.

On the other hand, suppressing performances that make the problematic of wantedness explicit would not make it go away; the regulatory project would only make the problematic of wantedness more covert; indeed regulation might intensify by narrowing the vocabularies that subversion has to mobilize. After all, it's not exclusively the perverts who engage in scenes like those I've just affirmed as good who seek incoherent experiences in sex: I think most of us experience sex (when it's not routinized) as an alarming mix of desire and fear, delight and disgust, power and surrender, surrender and power, attachment and alienation, ecstasy in the root sense of the word and enmired embodiedness. Essential elements of the third Oncale scenario are enacted, I imagine, in many more sexual relationships than you would guess just by looking around the boardroom or seminar room, and the edgy experience of unwantedness in sex is probably cherished by more people than are willing to say so. Suppressing performances like my third Oncale scenario might make sex on Sunday afternoon, with your spouse, in the sacred precincts of the marital bedroom, more banal or more weird—it's hard to tell which, in a domain of experience so routinely enriched by prohibition. The queer project carries a brief for the weirdness of sex wherever it appears; it is (or should be) agnostic about where, when, and among or between whom the intensities of sex are possible. But (and this is probably the queerest reason to protect the problematic of unwantedness from regulation as sex harassment, and it is a distinctively queer *feminist* view) it would resist the redistribution of sexual intensities achieved under color of women's equality or moral virtue. Feminist queer theory resents and opposes constructions in which women become the guarantors of sexual purity: power feminism and cultural feminism promote them.

Those are some pretty striking downsides to the *Oncale* decision. They might not be worth it. Protecting feminine gay men is a good thing to do; same-sex wrongdoing should not be exempted from regulation; people should be made to worry about how their sexual desires affect other people; everybody has to work and should be able to do so without running irrelevant and acute dangers; and so on. But we can't get those social gains without the social costs. The benefits have costs. And the costs have benefits: as long as erotic masochism is a powerful position, we face the problem of infinitely unknowable preferences. Not only that; diverging various social theories of sex and identity that I've been using to articulate the costs of the benefits promotes their incommensurability: increasingly the costs are apples, the benefits oranges; women might win at the expense of gay men, or gay men who have assimilated their politics to cultural-feminist moralism might win at the expense of the queers. Or vice versa. We can helpfully recall at this point Kennedy's insistence that wildly differently interested players bargain in the shadow of the law to produce wildly complex social interactions. And finally, the decisions we face in deciding what to do about *Oncale* implicate a legal system that—as Kennedy also helps us to see—inevitably produces false negatives (the tolerated residuum of abuse) and false positives (the innocent gay man accused by a pathetic creep in the grip of homosexual panic—and held liable). Systemwide the rule manages these complexities in a dynamic world saturated with politically engaged representation, and, if we are postmodernists, in a world of constituted consciousness.

And finally, deciding not to do anything is doing something. We decide even if we refuse to pay attention to the consequences of our decisions.

Putting oneself in a position to strive to get a grip on this situation is the most important upside of Taking a Break from Feminism (and any other single theory).

THE COSTS AND BENEFITS OF TAKING A BREAK FROM FEMINISM

Inhabiting the uncertainty that lies at the heart of the *Oncale* decision, facing up to the split interests it manages and the perverse deployments of its rule that it enables, produces a disenchanted, coldly realist legal consciousness—the attitude of a responsible power wielder. It also envisions a wildly energized erotic scene, a world of many, many possibilities for sexual pleasure, and a sense that legal rules can be decided not only by sober ethical mandate but with a thrilling will to power. One way to avoid encountering this double consciousness is to wrap oneself tightly in a secure and familiar social theory—gay-identity politics, for instance, or queer theory, or feminism. Since my example in this book is feminism, it seems only right to take stock now of as many of the costs and benefits of Taking a Break from it as I can.

The Costs

People invoke several costs of Taking a Break that I think are simply not real. I consider them first, and then take up real dangers that could follow from Taking a Break from Feminism.

Getting Rid of Feminism

It has consistently amazed me that feminists of all kinds hear the words Taking a Break from Feminism as the perfect equivalent of

"Getting Rid of Feminism," "Rejecting Feminism," "Post-Feminism," and "Anti-Feminism." I doubt they would make the same mistake in any other context. If I said "Let's Take a Break from Freud," would they hear "Let's get rid of, reject Freud; let's deny any explanatory or therapeutic capacity to Freud *tout court*; let's get beyond Freud; let's be anti-Freudians"? Probably not. Something in their feminism supports the idea that any departure, topographic or temporal, from feminism constitutes an absolute rupture, an ending, a vanquishment.

I've attempted to understand this persistent misprision sympathetically, and have two ideas about the commitments which these feminists may be pursuing that make it make some sense. Neither, however, persuades me to take this accusation very much to heart.

First, the feminism of the feminists who say this may be more structuralist than they know. This would explain both the feminists who seem utterly dumbfounded by the suggestion that we might want to Take a Break—"I simply cannot imagine what you are talking about. How *could* there be an adequate analysis of sex/sexuality/gender that is not primarily feminist? And how *could* any aspect of human life *not* be pervasively structured along lines of sex/sexuality/gender?"—and the very savvy postmodernizing feminists who produce the "Rejecting Feminism" trope not with stunned incomprehension but with swift, sharp, even reflexive anger. Behind both may lie some conviction that all good things in analytic and political life eventually flow from or back to Mother Feminism. I very much doubt these feminists would want to follow this conviction to its full consequences, which surely imply a vast expansion of the ambitions of feminist convergentism. Typically that project aims simply to preserve feminism as the ground and destination of the somewhat limited range of projects involving race, class, and colonial/postcolonial subordination. The "Reject Feminism" misprision, in a breathtakingly more imperialist/paranoid mode, would preclude the idea that there could be *anything* that is not, fundamentally or ultimately, however covertly, referable to feminism.

Perhaps, however, the reaction is less conceptual than strategic. Feminists may see feminism as too weak to sustain such a departure, too valuable to be put at this risk, too precious to be put at *any* risk. They may understand feminism to need defense from threats to its very survival. I simply don't agree: there is governance feminism; and feminist theory through the 1990s, though laced with this anxiety, has actually been a vital, engaged project.

Silencing Women

It has been said of my project and others like it that they *silence* suffering women and the beleaguered feminists who advocate for them.

To be sure, saying that we should Take a Break from Feminism might have as a downstream consequence harm to women, a silencing of women, and even the complete collapse of feminism as an ongoing social and intellectual project. I might get blood on my hands. That's a real risk, and if it happens, it is a cost. I consider it under the heading "Weakening Feminism and So Harming Real Women" below.[1]

But the silencing objection does not come in the language of consequences. The accusation is that proposing to Take a Break has *already* silenced women. It's always a little odd to hear such an accusation uttered, often by a very angry woman quite evidently animated by a fierce will to power, specifically to defeat *me*! Aside from welcoming this antagonism and trying to figure out how to enjoy it, I would much prefer to inhabit these moments as ones that make sense. So, attempting to understand them sympathetically, I've derived two possible submerged logics in which the silencing accusation would be exactly right. Both, however, seem to me to be very costly analytic moves.

On one, the "silencing" objection depends on a politics of representation, quite familiar in left-multicultural postmodernizing work, in which making X audible or visible renders Y silent or invisible. If someone says that the cemetery was spread with crosses, this renders invisible the Stars of David that were also there; if someone says that women were restricted to the domestic sphere, this renders invisible the black women who never had the luxury of avoiding paid labor; if veiled Islamist feminists speak, they silence the Arab secularist feminists. Implicitly the objection envisions as the only morally adequate feminist representational practice the perpetual presentation of a complete picture of all women's interests, or all subordinated groups' interests. It is strongly convergentist, of course, and it is also committed to moral perfectionism.

The objection that Taking a Break from Feminism silences women might have another politics supporting it, however: the ethical politics of consciousness-raising. CR as a social practice required participants to respect all voices emerging within it. This was a procedural norm raised in many CR groups to near-definitive substantiveness. In CR, the accusation of silencing carried with it a charge that one had attempted to destroy the group itself, by cutting to the heart of its very mode of life, and had attempted to return the silenced party to the domination-by-false-consciousness from which she was struggling to release herself. The culture of CR treated "silencing" as a devastating accusation; it very frequently produced the effect of silencing the accused woman completely.

Whatever the merits of this norm for CR groups, when it travels outside those settings it runs into other, quite inconsistent politics. CR, after all, was a very distinctive undertaking. It was a highly ethicized practice based on commitments to small-group, face-to-face, and sustained exchange—voluntary, closed, intimate, adamantly antihierarchical, and theoretically at least quite unteleological. Query whether it makes sense to attempt more broadly contentious and institutionalized feminist politics—much less, feminist governance practices!—on rules designed for such special encounters. Let's suppose feminists dealing inside state power disagree over whether we do or do not want more protection from sexual assault, or about whether to focus on women, say, or offshore workers: should these disagreements be framed as episodes of moralized "silencing"? Perhaps we need an ethics of such engagements—I myself am highly suspicious of the will to power in all such meeknesses—but if we do, they almost certainly should not be the ones that were elaborated for CR as it was practiced in the emergence of late-twentieth-century feminism.

Indeed, when the "silencing" objection arises outside CR-like settings, it suggests (to me anyway) a political *imaginaire* in which power is thought to be total and one-sided (and to be feared and sought as such). I can't help thinking that feminists who imagine that critiques of feminism not only risk those consequences but contain and intrinsically perform them are attributing to their critics the only kind of power they can imagine for themselves. Their implicit vision of themselves and their opponents as gods capable of performative utterances on the level of "*Fiat Lux*" or "I sentence you . . ." is pretty scary.

Flight from Feminism, Imagined as Limits, to the "Queer Utopia," Imagined as Libertine, Unbounded, or Libertarian

Since Biddy Martin's "Sexualities without Genders and Other Queer Utopias" appeared in 1994, the charge of utopianism has implied a will to constrain feminism while liberating "the queer" from all conceptual rule.[2] It's not clear to me why utopianism is bad; most everybody (including feminists who want to imagine their feminism as without limit) have recourse to it from time to time. I think the gravamen of the charge is rather the allocation of limits, history, and constraint to feminism so that unboundedness, sheer futurity, and freedom can be allocated to "the queer." That is, it is a charge of definitional violence.

I do engage in definitional violence here, but not this form of it. I will discuss that problem in just a moment. But this is the place to say (again) that I'm not promoting Queer Theory as The Answer, or as the Replacement of Feminism, or as a Normative Ideal. It has been a brave Break Taker, and it has carried the ball further down certain fields. But it has its own limits; the examples of queer work that I've examined closely in Part Two are full of feet-of-clay moments; and even though it sometime wants to be about everything, it's not and can't be. Other people might idealize queer theory—for instance, the Janet Halley who started this book did—but I simply no longer think it's a good idea to collapse your theory with your utopia.

Definitional Violence; the Foreclosure of Critique; and the Reinscription of Heterosexism in Queer Theory

Any Taking a Break project, and this one is no exception, defines what it differentiates itself from. Both the definition and the differentiation are acts of violence.

Many feminist objections to Taking a Break projects say that they are bad, though, because they are violent. One version of this objection is that the prodigals have simply read feminism wrong: "I do not recognize what she's describing as feminism; that is not feminism as I know it." This objection has given me a lot of concern. Getting feminism wrong, while probably inevitable, would also be a bad thing to do. The definitional minima I've deduced—m/f, m > f, and carrying a brief for f—might indeed not be definitional. The challenge means most when it comes from postmodernizing feminists; other feminists pretty patently carry these minima on their sleeves. Here's what I hear from post-modernizing feminists: feminism without m/f, without m > f, *and* without a commitment to carry a brief for f: sure, that's possible, that's what we do, that's what we want for feminism; the horizon of feminism is justice and equality for all. It's a good idea, and I'd love to see them pull it off. But I just don't think anyone has. No feminist text that I have ever read avoids m/f, m > f, and carrying a brief for f. None of the postmodernizing entries in my genealogy comes close.

The indignant form of the objection—"And where does she get the authority to determine what feminism is?"—is itself a claim to such authority, and rests on no firmer or more extrinsic grounds than mine. I can only conclude that definitional violence is endemic to discursive engagement. Defining feminism as I've done is no more violent than claiming that feminism is so sublime that it cannot and should not be defined.

A more thoroughly postmodernizing version of this objection insists that *any* signifier that takes the form Not-X constitutes, through the form of difference, distinction, or denial, precisely and exactly X. To propose that we can actually Take a Break from Feminism, on this second objection, is to flunk Derrida 101.

This is of course exactly right. It's not clear, though, why it's a reason not to Take a Break; rather, it's a reason not to exaggerate the kinds of separation and release that Taking a Break can allow. I'm happy to admit that, as a strategy for Taking a Break from Feminism, writing about Taking a Break from Feminism has been a spectacular failure. I've read almost nothing but feminism while writing this book. My idea that Queer Theory by Men would give me a clean break from feminism was promptly defeated by the very texts I selected to study. Taking a Break projects like my reading of *Oncale* are dependent in every conceivable way on their feminist priors.

At a moment like this it might help to recall Butler's somewhat rueful rearticulation, in *Feminists Theorize the Political* and *Feminist Contentions*, of the reasons to have an internal critique of feminism. There she argued that the precipitation of a "constitutive antagonism" should be understood not to "naturalize" divisions in feminism, but to make apparent their contingency and thus to render them more available for political struggle.[3] Precisely the same critical relations pertain between feminism and its others: wherever the boundary arises, we have a series of paired terms for managing it—refusal/relation, negation/engagement, paralysis/trouble, outside/inside, disavowal/critique—that are persistently available to characterize a boundary like the one I am trying to imagine. Postmodernizing feminists can see relation, engagement, trouble, a placement inside, and critique *inside* feminism; they should, I think, learn to live with it at claimed boundaries between feminism and something else. A similar constitutive antagonism and a similar struggle should be possible. To make firm assignments of refusal, negation, paralysis, outside, and disavowal[4] is to bypass Derrida 101.

The objection that Taking a Break forecloses critique, then, attempts to foreclose critique.

The claim that Taking a Break commits definitional violence upon f and upon feminism eventually leads many making it to claim also that it reinscribes heterosexuality and thus heterosexism. Our example has been Butler's "Against Proper Objects," which concludes that queer theory that Takes a Break aims to abstract itself from m/f and thus reinstates masculinist epistemologies. It does indeed, if you must operate 24/7 within feminism. Nothing of the kind is necessary on other social-theoretical assumptions. So this objection—which I think is itself also objectionable for collapsing the heterosexual with heterosexism—begs the question.[5]

Reifying Mere Terminology

Equally disturbing, but also more exciting, is the objection that Taking a Break from Feminism exaggerates the political importance of a *mere* terminological struggle, distracts us from the real problems about sex1, sex, sexuality, gender, and sexual orientation that we really should be talking about; and will intensify rather than erode the definitional preoccupations of feminism. If the real problem is whether God requires good works or bestows salvation by grace, and if the problem emerges for you whether you are Roman Catholic or Lutheran or Presbyterian, it's a ridiculous distraction to have a war over whether to decorate the church with stained- or clear-glass windows, or whether to put the altar on the back wall of the sanctuary facing the apse or up at the transept facing the nave. Asking feminists to consider Taking a Break from Feminism can produce not curiosity but reaction, reaction *back into* feminism, which can then become more fortresslike and more assailable, producing stronger impulses to Take a Break, in a meaningless but completely obsessional spiral.

I pretty much have to concede all that. I would love to be able to transcend the problem addressed in this book, and to think outside the fieldlike forms in which the regulation of sexual pleasure and danger, sexual welfare and misery, and so on, are currently done. I won't even be able to imagine avoiding this criticism until the book is finished. I've found no way out of this problem but through it.

Matricide, Misogyny, and Male Identification

We also hear that projects that Take a Break from Feminism, and even those that merely criticize it from within, harbor matricidal tendencies, misogyny, and a bad-faith identification with men and masculinity. Biddy Martin's warning against a utopian queer desire to work "beyond gender" contains this concern. Perhaps symptomatically, Martin observes, those who seek to move "beyond gender" notwithstanding the fact of its social immanence too often manifest a conception of "gender in negative terms, in the terms of fixity, miring, or subjection to the indicatively female body" and "a resistance to something called 'the feminine,' played straight, [together with] a tendency to assume when it ["the feminine"] is not camped up or disavowed, it constitutes a capitulation, a swamp, something maternal, ensnared and ensnaring" (105).

It has even been suggested that feminist internal critique harbors some sick personal investment in aggression and/or pathos, or in sadism and/or masochism.[6]

Gently sometimes, and not so gently at other times, colleagues, friends, and opponents have lodged those criticisms as criticisms *of me*.

I was at first deeply shaken when these accusations came. For years I had worked only on gay identity, gay rights, and their critique. I was Taking a Break from Feminism when I did that, in part because I simply didn't know how to handle the experience of profound shame and anger that came over me as I shed my commitments, somewhat serially, to power feminism, cultural feminism, and convergentist feminist moralism. And it's no coincidence, I'm sure, that I began this project just before, and worked out the first angry versions of it during, the breakup of my eighteen-year relationship with a woman, the excruciatingly prolonged dying of my mother, and the formation of strong political, intellectual, and collegial intimacies with men who rejected the role-reversed masculinity that cultural feminism prescribed for them.[7] I was shaken. I was trying to be shaken.

I now think the only possible response to these accusations that could grant me any access to composure is to accept them. It always felt like bad faith to fight them. Better, I now think, to affirm that this project has for me a deeply confusing, vitally libidinal character. And once I have done that, I have a few responses to my accusers, and to the broader literature in which feminists worry that feminist internal critique and Taking a Break from Feminism are matricidal, misogynist, and/or male-identified.

First, sometimes (not always) these accusations carry an implication that such motives are too personal, too intrapsychic, too "interested." But I guess I don't want to envision or do work on sexuality while psychically disinvested; I wonder whether it's even possible. Indeed, why would *any* scholarly or critical undertaking be better if the writer ultimately didn't care about it? The contrary ideal—of scholarly neutrality, detachment, and depoliticization—is a strong force in academic life today; most appointments and promotions processes and journal editorial policies are strongly committed to it. The result is tedium and bad faith everywhere, with bad effects for the kinds of work that are beloved by every project inside and outside of feminism that I examine in this book.

Query, furthermore, whether we really want to conduct the struggle between feminism and its alternatives on the premise that an arguer who brings complex and ambivalent erotic aims to political exchange about the erotic is for that reason less persuasive. Doesn't the idea carry with it another premise, that complex and ambivalent erotic aims are less good than simple, stable ones? There's no need here for a counterclaim that they are better; simply that, at the very least, the premise that they are *worse* begs some of the questions central to sex-positive work, feminist and non-, across the board.

Perhaps (pace Martin) women *are* often deeply resentful of the feminine swamp and saturated in penis envy. If so, exactly what moral power do we want feminism to have in condemning us for it? And do we want *always* to refer this question to feminism? Of course feminism need not presuppose (as Martin seems to do) that these feelings either are politically retrograde (through a presumption of a duty of loyalty to feminine women or to the femininity of women) or manifest some species of false consciousness or bad faith (through a presumption of a duty of loyalty to oneself as a woman). To be sure, one could hold to m/ f, m > f, and carrying a brief for f without committing oneself to any of these ideas. But m > f and carrying a brief for f are loaded against my drive to affirm my involvement in such resentments, and to look inside them not only for the dangers but also for the pleasure and will to power that they may hold.

Query, finally, whether *anyone* is free of matricidal wishes, misogyny, and cross-sex identification. The idea seems implausible as description, on sheer Freud 101 grounds. To function as an accusation, moreover, this description—I'll inflect it once again as an accusation about "me"—must assume it knows that I *am* "a woman"; knows the "right" degree of masculine identification that "a woman" should undertake; knows the "right" amount of woman loving that "a woman" should do; knows the "right" degree of gratitude (and submission) "a woman" must grant to "the women" who made her physical, emotional, intellectual, academic, and/or political lives possible. Knowledges like these were precisely what Sedgwick and Butler put in question when they moved to split queer theory (without and with feminism) off from then-existing forms of feminism.

Still, matricide, misogyny, and male identification can license real harm to real women. And real harm to real women is a cost, a heavy cost, one that should not be risked without some very serious justification.

Weakening Feminism and So Harming Real Women

All the objections to Taking a Break from Feminism ultimately have to be gauged on the metric of the life-affirming, remedial, redemptive, emancipatory, safety-providing, hedonically aspirational, justice-seeking ambitions of feminism and of every related and unrelated justice-seeking project we care about. There is a high degree of theoretic incommensurability in the ways we could do that. Here I want to reduce them, rather violently, to distributive consequences lodged in the language of the "material fact" that male/female difference is of persistent importance socially and semiotically, that feminism is our most elaborated way of addressing it, and that weakening it could have consequences both for the general project of feminism and for concrete, individual women. I will assume for purposes of articulating these downsides that some people's occasionally Taking a Break from Feminism will weaken it, at least in some places and at some times.

So let me state the distributive dangers of Taking a Break from Feminism as sharply as I can. Doing so might:

   relax the epistemic vigilance that is needed to resist male epistemic hegemony;
   risk further splits among feminists at a higher conceptual location than most other splits;
   and thus risk new fissures in the intellectual, social, political, and legal endeavor;
   demobilize and demoralize feminists;[8]
   invite cooptation by the enemies of women's well-being;
   legitimate male dominance generally and specifically;
   and produce, as consequences, specific concrete harms to women that would otherwise not have happened.

All of these are big risks to run. The final consequence—concrete harms to real women—is a grave cost indeed. If, for instance, feminism is our best weapon against the constant pressure of male sexual violence, weakening feminism in any of these ways could actually result in some guy's decision to rape a woman he would otherwise leave unmolested, or prompt some woman's decision to stay married to a man she loathes rather than take her chances on independence with the risk of exposure to sexual danger. There's a chance that the arguments set forth here will circulate in such a way as to undermine a consensus that women who claim they are sexually subordinated should be believed; real women who really are sexually subordinated might become more inaudible, come into social life with men with eroded bargaining power, and be raped more often as a result. It may well be that an alert social conservative will notice my argument and use it to legitimate a paternalistic "back to marriage" agenda for women that my political allies and I seem at the moment to be unable to resist; real women might suffer their singleness or their mar-riedness more if the agenda succeeds. And so on. I am definitely risking those bad outcomes for those women.

Whether directly or through co-optation, more people's Tak-ing a Break from Feminism might, in specific instances and over-all, make things worse.

I think that the risk is real, but worth it. Some of my most important reasons for that appear below, in the section entitled "The Benefits."

Here I'll count up some of the costs of assessing the costs as feminists currently do.

I definitely disagree with the argument so often leveled against Break proposals, that advocating them belittles or discounts and even denies the harm suffered by women. Here is the objection: "Exposing the possibility that women sometimes use a posture of suffering powerfully, thus harming others, and especially exposing the possibility that they harm men, is tantamount to a denial that women suffer *and thus also* a denial that they are subordinated."

The moment repeats itself so urgently, with so little variation, that I have decided it must be a deeply embedded characteristic of contemporary feminism. It's not essential to m/f, m > f, and carrying a brief for f—but it is a basic, almost instinctive feminist defense against proposals to Take a Break—and it is, I think, delusional, dangerous, and a cost in and of itself of not Taking a Break. It may be, moreover, I will argue, that it is produced by and in turn consolidates certain antipolitical, antirealist ideas about how to engage the legal system, that it sustains them and produces and blind-spots still more harm. I'll argue all of that in the subsection within "The Benefits" entitled "Breaking with the Politics of Injury/Seeing around Corners of Our Own Construction."

Nor do I think that the co-optation objection should be cut as much slack as feminists usually cut it. The objection runs something like this: internal critique can provide opportunities to our shared enemies on the right, either to take advantage of our moments of confusion or actually to agree with the critique and mobilize it politically; *so don't do internal critique.* But the danger of co-optation does not go away merely because one falls silent: omissions are co-opted constantly. And almost none of our substantive commitments, our affirmations, are free from the danger of co-optation; critique might be our only way of foreseeing co-optation and doing something about it. For instance, we're against harm to women, but our work against it has already become the rhetorical slipstream for an amazing poster I saw in Harvard Yard while pondering this problem. The poster showed a numinous photograph of a human fetus floating in amnionic bliss, blazoned with the motto "I suck my thumb; *and I feel pain.*"[9] The right-to-life people had *already* co-opted the feminist politics of injury—before I'd even finished writing my critique of it! My anxiety about *my* work's being co-opted kind of melted away at that moment.

And, though I can't prove it, I firmly believe that one huge cost of the co-optation objection is that it has severely stunted idea production on the left in the United States. It is a mandate to stop thinking. It requires dishonesty; it asks us to deflect the logic of our ideas before we've tracked their trajectories. It has fed feminism's Brain Drain. It has inculcated in leftists the consciousness that the Right always gets the last word. So, though co-optation does happen and can be really costly, on the whole I think it's time—past time—to ramp down on the co-optation objection.

So: real women could get hurt. You really need to think about that when deciding whether it's wise to Take a Break from Feminism. But you also need to think about the women who would be benefited if you did it; and all the women who would be hurt or benefited in their capacities as something other than women; and then . . . there are the men. And all the men who live at least parts of their lives under some other social sign, in some other chain of social causation, than m. I actually think you have to Take a Break from Feminism even to *think* about how they might be hurt if you did or didn't Take a Break. When this question is squarely put to you, I think you can't answer it squarely if you're not willing to get some blood on your hands.

The Benefits

Not Taking a Break has costs; Taking one not only avoids those costs but also produces benefits. I assess the congeries of benefits I see.

Breaking with the Politics of Injury/Seeing around Corners of Our Own Construction

The objection that Taking a Break discounts and even denies the harm suffered by women, dissected and reassembled, yields a triad of descriptive stakes: women are injured, they do not cause any social harm, and men, who injure women, are immune from harm—female injury + female innocence + male immunity. Feminists often produce this triad as if it were feminism; and as if the three stakes were tied so tightly together that each requires assertion of the others.

This is the crux of the contemporary politics of injury. Women's subordination has been understood as their injury; subordination is figured as injuredness. Questioning whether the woman was injured is thought to be, in itself, unfeminist and is sometimes even said to "reinjure her." The entire discourse of the "second rape" exemplifies this turn: if women are not believed when they say they have been raped—if their testimony is challenged, if their credibility is impugned—they are not attacked and opposed; they are raped again. Moreover, the woman is "innocent" in the strict, minimal etymological sense that she "lack[s] the capacity to injure: [that she is] innocuous, harmless."[10] Attributing to her the agency, the will, the malice—even simply the capacity—to cause harm to others also sounds unfeminist and is (oddly) understood also to constitute a denial that *she* was injured. And the man, the subordinator, is understood to be immune from injury. He might have to give up his ill-gotten gains, make restitution, get his foot off our necks, learn to listen to a different voice, and so forth, but describing his suffering as a wrong done by, or even as a social cost of, the assertion of women's interests produces perhaps the most acute feminist resistance.

The pattern is pretty endemic in contemporary feminism. Prostitution is understood to harm women while or by benefiting johns and pimps; pornography degrades women to produce male sexual pleasure; and so on. It seems more *not feminist* to suggest that men are injured by women in these practices—or even simply that they are injured—than to suggest that women may not be injured by men in them.

Of course all feminism posits that female subordination is not accidental, random, buckshot. Instead, power-feminist and cultural-feminist projects insert their articulations of trauma, torture, offended dignity, pain, suffering, agony—or disempowerment, domination, deprivation, exclusion, marginalization, invisibilization, silencing, etc.—into *subordination* theories: the eroticization of domination and the degradation of women's distinctive values, respectively, harm women while benefiting men.

As I've said, this idea can be a very useful hypothesis for eager justice-seekers to have on hand. But *presupposing* that such a theory fully describes the world—refusing to Take a Break to see whether something else might be going on as well or instead—commits feminism to being unable to see around corners of its own construction.

Here would be a diagnostic test you can run on your thinking anytime (do try this at home): if someone says that we should really take into account the pleasure (some) female prostitutes take in their work; the pleasure they are able to provide for their johns; the vulnerability of pimps in the economic systems that sustain prostitution; and/or the vulnerability of johns and pimps to exploitation by prostitutes—do you have a problem with that? Are you tempted to say something like the following? "Exposing the possibility that women sometimes use a posture of suffering powerfully, thus harming others, and especially exposing the possibility that they harm men, is tantamount to a denial that women suffer and thus also a denial that they are subordinated." If so you are probably conducting at least part of your thinking and politics on the assumptions embedded in the Injury Triad.

But do you really want to think that way? Because of course we all know that some women lie, and that others are interpellated into *real* experience that is not in their "*real*" interests; some women manage to hurt other people and social interests; some men are injured by some women. What produces the intense will to blind-spot, even to deny, these obvious facts about the social world?

It's easy to understand how structuralist feminisms of the most absolute kind produce the Injury Triad: it describes the world as they actually experience it. But in many of the most interesting moments when the Injury Triad has been produced as a feminist critique of Taking a Break from Feminism—it has happened often in my presence—the accuser has been a *post*structuralist, *postmodernizing* feminist, politically opposed to most aspects of power feminism and cultural feminism. How do *they* end up producing what sounds, from outside feminisim, like such a crazily and irresponsibly limited Letraset for spelling the world?

Well, one possibility is that the categorical refusal or incapacity to Take a Break *is* structuralist. I've argued that at some length in Part Two.

But let's say that's not right, or not right all the time. Feminist recourse to the Injury Triad could be overdetermined, or alternatively motivated. I'd like to offer two additional diagnoses, arising at the contact points between feminism and the legal and political system—broadly speaking, liberalism—within which it attempts to secure its aims. Those contact points are "rights" and "policy balancing," each of which, theoretically at least, might be functioning like a little engine producing the suction that draws subordination theories back into structuralism, back into the Injury Triad. That is, rights and policy balancing—pretty much the complete set of current legal alternatives for progressive reform—provide forces outside feminism that might be propelling feminists to the (I think descriptively impoverished, blind-spotting, magic realist, and even delusional) claims entailed by the Injury Triad. Both of these possible motives for thinking in Injury Triad terms bring their own costs to the table. Getting a critical purchase on them can make more accessible the legal realist, pragmatic attitudes I've been admiring and trying to seduce you to admire too.

Even getting clear on this choice is a benefit. A more valuable benefit still would be recruiting more people to take these attitudes up.

Rights first. There are innumerable theories of rights, and many of them are embedded somewhere in our legal system. One that turns directly on the concept of harm, and has also been widely assimilated into the thought of legal actors, is that of John Stuart Mill. Mill argued that individuals are free to act in any way that does not harm others; the state and even private normative forces should limit themselves to regulation of harmful conduct; "rights" marks the boundary between freedom and regulation.[11] As Bernard Harcourt explains in *Illusion of Order*,[12] left-of-center liberals (that is, liberals with a small *l*, people opposed to conservatives) spent the major part of the last century using this argument to minimize the legitimate reach of state power in the domain of sexual life: inasmuch as neither the prostitute nor the john, neither the maker nor the consumer of pornography, neither the seller nor the user of contraceptives, and so forth, was engaged in socially harmful conduct, each should be free to do as he or she liked. To the extent Millian liberalism needed an answer to the question "Is certain conduct harmful?" the progressive/left/liberal answer with regard to matters sexual was "If it was consented to, it was not harmful." The Hart/Devlin debate blew up over a different question, to wit, whether the state could regulate where there was concededly no harm but only strong moral grounds to justify state intervention to deter and punish. As Harcourt handily shows, amid all the smoke and lightening of that controversy, almost nobody noticed that the Millian left/liberal/libertarian project involved a construction, a representation, of various sexual outcomes as "not harmful."

This plasticity should have become evident to everyone—it became evident to Harcourt—when, over the course of the twentieth century, left/progressive/liberals "flipped" their typical deployment of Mill's harm principle. With the rise of left multicultural identity politics came a sweeping and highly creative project of defining social disadvantage experienced by subordinated groups as *harm*. Not at all accidentally, now Mill's harm principle could be deployed by left/liberal/progressives operating in a Millian rights framework to justify the expansion of legitimate uses of state power to address it. A genealogy of left multiculturalist work that achieves the discursive framing of new forms of injury would be fun to write and would occupy a hefty book: it would have chapters on hate speech, pornography, abortion, battered women's syndrome, recovered memory of child sexual abuse, and the like, as sites for left reform work focused on pain, trauma, humiliation—in short, harm.

The production of the apprehendability and articulacy of pain, injury, and trauma—harm—is a central element of subordination theory working on race, ethnicity, gender, sex1, sexual orientation, nationality. In the sentimental politics[13] of this left multicultural effort, harm has a history, is plastic, can be and is created, expanded, and intensified. Seen from the social theoretic perspective of *Volume One*, this discursive production of pain may well also help to produce the subjects who experience it; feminism may be responsible for at least some of the trauma that real women really experience in their real lives. But you don't need to accept this "productivity" thesis to acknowledge that the political representation of harm may well be expanded or contracted, intensified or diluted, made urgent or chronic, inside justice projects. And so it could undergo all those operations in trends to mobilize Millian regulation or Millian liberty.

Rights discourse of the Millian sort smoothly endorses and may strengthen the feminist commitment to the particular articulation of harm that I've described as the Injury Triad: female injury + female innocence + male immunity. Here's how. The harm principle posits a harm/regulation, no harm/freedom grid for the framing of rights, something like this:

IF	THEN
Harm	Regulation
No harm	Liberty

If you do harm to me and I do no harm to you, the state must punish you and leave me in my freedom. But if you do harm to me and I also do harm to you—well, then, the grid doesn't have a third set of boxes; the harm principle would kind of run out. Rights would become irrelevant.

The system, seen not as a normative principle but as a rhetorical opportunity, thus invites rights-asserting claims that all the harm in a certain social domain runs in one direction. And it implies that, when it doesn't—when harm is shared even a little by one's social opponents—we would have to decide what to do using some other means (strict libertarian restraint on state action, deontological distributive justice, scientistic social policy, politics?) that would leave me vulnerable to raw social forces or regulatory impositions. And so if I am a social group arguing for rights-based state powers to regulate my opponents (oppressors), and if I (or the people I am determined to persuade) take the Millian harm principle as the rule of decision, I have a strong motive not only to intensify the imagery of my harm, but also to insist on my social innocence and on my opponents' immunity from harm caused by me.

If this is what has happened inside the U.S. Left to produce the upsurge of left multicultural arguments expanding a politics of injury persistently dependent on the Injury Triad, it has been at the expense of a more critical engagement with rights, a legal realist idea of their social complexity, and a clear-eyed view of all the social costs produced when rights trump competing social interests.

The Injury Triad arises again in feminist legal work that hews not to rights but to a pragmatic, instrumentalist, "conflicting considerations," policy-balancing mode of legal argumentation as well. In feminism, the lead voice advocating an embrace of pragmatism is certainly Robin West, and the lead text is her book *Caring for Justice.* You might think that the shift from rights to balancing would bring an uptick in prudence, an encompassing social vision, an alert attention to the downsides of one's preferred upsides, and so on. And indeed, sometimes it does. But the antipolitical and indeed politically paranoid character of West's feminist resort to the Injury Triad becomes even clearer here than in the rights-oriented injury politics described by Harcourt. Here we have, moreover, an opportunity to see the specific costs of the sublime ethical feminism that we first observed in *Feminist Consequences.*[14]

West argues in *Caring for Justice* that the English utilitarians of the nineteenth century and the American legal realists of the early twentieth century generated an instrumentalist jurisprudence which provides the optimal view of law for feminist and other social-movement reform efforts: "The distinctive virtues of both economic and noneconomic instrumentalism—its insistence on flexibility and pragmatism, its nondogmantic, anti-ideologic structure, and its responsiveness to the lived human condition—make instrumentalism the natural jurisprudential perspective for feminism as well as for any other liberation movement" (173–74). Seeing law not as a system of formally deduced normative commands but as a tool to be understood and used in terms of its practical effects; undertaking to use it to equilibrate competing social interests and social ends, to recalibrate the rules continually in "response to the lived human condition"; and thus, as contemporary instrumentalists are wont to say, balancing various policy objectives, their achievability, the costs of achieving them, the impossibility of achieving pragmatically inconsistent or utopian policy objectives, the desirability of compromises between inconsistent goals and of incremental steps toward utopian ones—all of these habits of mind, West argues, should be cultivated within feminism and in the legal decision makers to whom feminism pitches its arguments.

Above all, West argues, the value of the instrumentalist tradition that we receive from English utilitarianism and American legal realism is that it tied all legal decision making to the problem of *harm*. The harm caused by patriarchy is, as we have seen, the problem par excellence faced by West's feminism.

A large part of her argument is devoted to resisting the turn in legal-economic thinking away from "harm" and toward "costs"— a shift that, she argues, entails a norm of efficiency and a willingness to see all social action as expressing preferences *simpliciter*: together, she argues, these pathologies of contemporary legal-economic thinking commit it to taking into account only those "bad outcomes" that are quantifiable, and to a laissez-faire-like quiescence in the face of distributions achieved through supposedly preference-expressing behavior. It commits its users to a vision of humanity that fundamentally excludes women because it stipulates that people always make self-interested decisions (women suffer the altruistic harms and have special access to maternal altruistic love); that people cannot and do not empathize (women's altruistic love is fundamentally empathic); and that the state is either helpless before the endless preference-satisfying power of the market or dangerously threatening to the satisfaction of those preferences (feminism needs the state and law, and needs them to be seen as social goods, to undo patriarchy) (166–68).

It would be a mistake, I think, to exaggerate the degree to which the semantic shift from "harm" to "costs" drives all of this: most centrally it is the contemporary legal-economic commitment to efficiency and its family of associated ideas that West objects to.

West would root out of her instrumentalism the contemporary legal-economic deference to whatever preferences are supposedly made manifest in the bargains people actually do strike, and she would replace it with a commitment to the "objective value" of an ideal—"the *ideal* of a harm-free, good, or flourishing social world" (170). "From a *non*economic instrumentalist perspective, the law is a tool toward achieving an ideal world in which the content of the ideal can either be understood positively—as a world possessed of moral value—or negatively, as a world free from harm" (171). It is at this nexus—between the elimination of harm and the institution of moral value—that West attempts to merge her instrumentalism with her moralism.

You would think that West's instrumentalism would insulate her feminism from the Injury Triad: after all, a fully pragmatic assessment of any feminist legal rule reform would want to assess not only the harm to women it seeks to reduce but the harm it might impose on men in the process; it would want to worry about the ways in which unharmed women might even be able to deploy it to harm men; it might even ask whether intensifying the social status of women's harm creates more of it; and so on.

West sometimes speaks as though she were prepared to go there. She advocates for an "instrumental feminism" (174) partly by arguing that, despite its costs, it's worth it. Thus she can admit that feminist legal reforms in the form of women's rights to reproductive freedom, protection from sex discrimination, rape shield provisions, and so on, though they "have all improved the quality of women's lives," have also legitimated the reproductive unfreedom, sex discrimination, and rape that fall outside their narrow protective umbrella. In good policy-balancing mode, she concludes: "But there is simply no question that the gains . . . outweigh these admittedly quite real risks of legitimation" (176). She admits that her instrumental feminism would be a paternalistic ruler, a "danger" that she counterposes to the legal-economic danger of "collaps[ing] ... harm and value with 'that which is desired' ":

> Obviously, what would best serve us is a *balance* between objective and subjective conceptions of harm, objective and subjective understandings of what we do and should value; objective and subjective conceptions of the good life. We need to check our desires against our rational understandings of our best interest, and we need to continually check our rational understandings of our best interest against our present desires, and we need to use each "check" as a skeptical harness on the other. (177)

Carried through as an intellectual and political practice, this skepticism about the good life, this effort to balance objective and subjective conceptions of harm, would make it impossible for anyone to get stuck on the Injury Triad: you simply could not say that women suffer harm, men inflict it on them, and women remain innocent of any harm to men in that categorical way if you were simultaneously wondering whether you had the balance of objective and subjective conceptions of the good life and of harm calibrated just right, in attentive "response to the lived human condition."

West nevertheless does say it, again and again and again. The Injury Triad appears often in her diametricalized framings of male and female, feminine and masculine, relations to harm. I'll give a few examples.

In an argument that the state's nonrecognition of the harms that women distinctively suffer is a powerful but alterable element of patriarchy, West states that when boys accede to mature masculine sexuality, they not only become relatively safe from harm but gain full state protection from it, whereas for girls the onset of mature female sexuality inaugurates an adulthood of acute and chronic sexual vulnerability ratified by the state's failure to protect them in turn. Thus though boys may be injured at the hands of older boys—West does not wonder whether boys are ever harmed by women or girls—"[t]hey leave the playground, and the playground bully, behind them." The humiliations of boyhood "may leave scars," but the mere act of attaining adult masculinity brings with it a diminishment in the threat of male/male harm (remember, female/male harm doesn't happen) and a guarantee of state protection from it. "His mature sexuality becomes, in a sense, the *marker* of his equality with other men" (146–47).[15]

"Women experience precisely the *opposite* transformation" (147). For them, girlhood is a safe haven of female-female "placidity" (147), a web of mother-daughter relating and female friendship that is "intimate, warm, sentimental, affectionate, and above all *safe*" (130); for them, entry into sexual life is the introit to "sexual vulnerability and radical inequality." West laboriously ensures that the logic of diametricality orders the entire domain:

> *While a boy entering manhood leaves behind* the world of radical inequality that characterizes boyhood, and enters instead a world of state-created and law-created equality, *a girl entering adulthood leaves behind* the relative calm, placidity, and equality of young female companionship and enters a state-created world of sexual vulnerability and radical inequality. *While a man's mature sexuality is therefore not only a marker* of his relative equality with other men, *but also a marker* of his recognition as an equal by the state, *so a woman's mature sexuality becomes not only a marker of* her vulnerability to harm, *but also of* her infantilization by the state. (147, emphasis deleted; all emphases in this passage added)

There is but one exception to this diametricality—harmed adult men. West is not very interested in them. This is in part because men are not really harmed. Whereas girlhood injury leaves wounds, boyhood injury leaves scars: access to patriarchal power allows men to heal. But when they are injured, West, like MacKinnon, sees them as feminine: in the only acknowledgment of men's suffering that I've been able to find in the entire book aside from the playground example we've just examined, West tucks it neatly into her diametrical framing of male and female life stories: "Feminine men are also subordinated along gender lines" (18). Feminization reintegrates male injury within the terms of female injury and male immunity.

Another example: West's description of the harm women suffer because of street harassment.

> A woman harassed on the street feels not only afraid, but also chilled, humiliated, dirty, and above all *exposed*; she's been turned inside out. The fear engendered by walking past a whispered message—"Hey cunt, hey bitch, hey YOU, come sit on my face"—is compounded by the feel of involuntarily exposed intimacy—of invasion. A part of the invasion, of course, is simply an invasion of privacy: the private space of anonymity on a public street is shattered, the complicated or serious train of thought is lost, the comfortable gait becomes awkward, the light mood is gone, the feeling of comradery and equality with cocitizens is obliterated. Even more painful than the invasion of privacy, however, is the verbal and visual invasion of and exposure of the sexual body—it is that invasion which renders a woman, or at least an unprepared and undefended woman, humiliated, infantilized, chilled, and exposed. The invasion renders her a sexual amusement for others—she becomes a toy. And again, that *invasion* is gender specific. (103)

So: the street-harassed woman is harmed, and she does no harm. The street-harassing man, moreover, is immune from harm:

> A woman who is hassled on the street knows that neither the community nor the state will come to her aid. She

knows, then, that she is "at the mercy" of the harasser—he can continue or cease the harassment, with no consequence to him either way. . . . She is in the position of a truly helpless infant whose well-being is at the whim of sadistic parents. (145)

To be sure, West introduces her chapter on the concept of harm from which these passages are quoted with the proviso that she catalogs women's harms to describe them, and not to argue that they should all be made criminal or tortious—that would violate the balancing mandate of her feminist instrumentalism (99). But it's hard to imagine how her feminist law reform could omit criminalization of street harassment given the meaning she derives from its legal impunity:

The state's refusal even to attempt to criminalize these assaultive threats underscores the degree to which women exist on public streets for the [sic] visual and sexual consumption by men. (145)

Thus the Injury Triad drives West to some pretty panicky statements about women's subordinated reality and some pretty mandatory, not balancing, ideas about what feminism should seek from law to undo it.

Want to see how it happens one more time? Scanning the horizon for the ways in which the law mandates gendered harm, West observes that the foreclosure of nonmarital options for sexual intimacy and of same-sex marriage harms women more than men to the extent that marriage benefits men at women's expense (162). The extent remains to be calibrated; so far, so skeptical. Then: the rule criminalizing child abandonment requires mothers of newborns—not fathers—to care for them or relinquish them formally for adoption, whereas an absent father "will be criminally liable at most for child support"; from this "stark asymmetry" West deduces "the disproportionate *mandatory* parenting required of mothers" (162). Hello? Fathers having physical custody of their children are just as liable for abandonment as mothers; fathers without it are often absent at the mother's option and sometimes would jump to assume parental responsibility if mothers did not act to prevent them from doing so; criminal sanctions for nonpayment of child support are intrinsic to our system and increasingly enforced to a fare-thee-well, on the joint insistence of feminists and neoliberals; and a single woman who has a newborn baby and who does not want to be its parent—as long as the biodad has not manifested and even, in some states, actually shouldered the full measure of parental responsibility—can relinquish it for adoption into a very eager market: it might be emotionally painful, but technically it's not difficult to do.

West's omission of the powers held by women, of the vulnerabilities of men, and of the possibility that Holmes's "bad man" has a female counterpart draws her into the magic realism which the Injury Triad so repeatedly generates: "The message conveyed by this network of legal regimes is clear enough: women should marry, mother, and stay home. Intimacy outside marriage is unthinkable, mothering is inevitable, and working outside the home unprofitable" (164). Though some U.S. women may well encounter the network of legal rules and cultural forces in such a way that this unthinkability, inevitability, and unprofitability are their lot, the idea that this is the legal system's message to all women is—may I say it?—paranoid. And once again, it is a direct consequence of thinking gendered harms in the terms of the Injury Triad.

We've seen the effects, then, of West's adherence to the Injury Triad: but *why* does she do it, at the complete sacrifice of her skepticism, pragmatism, and realism? There's nothing in her apparatus resembling the machinelike formality of Mill's harm principle, which, as we've also seen, works quite systematically to attach distinct argumentative and justificatory advantages to the Injury Triad. It's been a puzzle to me. I think I have found the answer in the shift in West's thinking between her 1987 article "The Difference in Women's Hedonic Lives: A Phenomenological Critique of Feminist Legal Theory"[16] and her 1997 revision and expansion of much of that earlier text as *Caring for Justice*. Over the decade, over the revisions, West apparently made a shift in the direction of structural subordination of women in heterosexual sex2—and with that shift came an understanding of women's sexuality in terms that are more susceptible to moral than pragmatic or political judgment. The pattern I'll set forth suggests that her pragmatism presupposes the Injury Triad in order to remove all of its claims from the reach of balancing and a fortiori from the reach of politics. The resulting configuration gives body to her moralism and fortifies the absolutist trend in her thinking. It's not a pretty sight.

In "Hedonic Lives," West made an expansive acknowledgment that many, many women actually do derive intense erotic pleasure from sexual submission to men. She also acknowledged, and at length, that a text which MacKinnon would undoubtedly deem well within her definition of subordinating pornography—Pauline Reage's *Story of O*[17]—has genuine positive value for women who take pleasure in the scenarios of erotic domination it narrates and the fantasies of erotic domination it suggests, not only because that pleasure is genuine, but because it can become part of a redeemed heterosexual relationship in which female erotic subordination is premised not on fear but on trust (187–203).

It would be impossible to cram these affirmative understandings of women's sexual submission to men into the narrow parameters of the Injury Triad. And though many, many passages from "Hedonic Lives" are revised into *Caring for Justice*, not one iota of this argument made the cut. Instead, as we've seen in Part Two, *Caring* maps female sexuality so as to omit the possibility of a woman's pleasurable, trusting erotic subordination to a man, indeed of *any* happy heterosexuality for women: instead, the two options have become women's coerced or, even if consensual, fearful engagement in heterosexual sex2, an endless sojourn in heterosexuality under the ubiquitous conditions of patriarchal threat (and this is a soul-destroying harm), and their infantile, lesbian, entirely feminine sexuality—a sexuality of mutuality, reciprocity, self-affirming integrity, naive embodiment, empathy, and care (and this, along with women's maternal altruism, is the fount of their redemptive moral virtue and the source of their authority to rule).[18] That is, female harm, female innocence, and male immunity: the Injury Triad.

Not coincidentally "Hedonic Lives" presented an instance of West's pragmatic, instrumental reasoning that is also omitted from the intellectual style of *Caring*. For all that she insisted in 1987 that pornography can lead to genuine pleasure in eroticized subordination for women, the West of "Hedonic Lives" also insisted that it can be used to induce fear in women, fear that can cause them to consent to dominated sex which—because of its contaminated motive—cannot be pleasurable to them. She then argued that there is no logical inconsistency in holding that pornography which provides women with the genuine pleasure of fantasizing their erotic domination by men or helps them actually achieve it in conditions of trust should not be sanctioned for that reason; only the pornography that generates women's fear should be actionable. It's a pragmatic and social-descriptive question, calling for an instrumentalist deployment of legal rules: before deciding which pornography to render actionable, "[w]e need to know if there is no overlap (ideal), a great deal of overlap (worst case) or some overlap (most likely)" (206).

This is the standard protocol of policy balancing. Having gotten to this point in it, a legal decision maker needs to decide what to do when there *is* overlap. Typically at this point one is urged

to adopt a proposed rule if its benefits outweigh its costs, relative
to the existing and the realistically possible alternatives. West produced this rule of decision instead: "Whatever causes women
pleasure without causing attendant pain is something we should
celebrate, not censure" (207). It is a no-pain rule: *any* costs to
women eliminate the rule option that would produce them. And
so, even if some pornography sometimes or often or almost always causes women pleasure (and surely even if it provides pleasure to men—their interests don't count), "[t]he pornography
that should be actionable is the pornography that causes the violent expropriation of our sexuality—*that* is the injury. As the
WAVAW women insist: NO WOMAN WANTS THAT."[19] That is, if a
particular pornographic text ever causes any woman pain, it
should be actionable, no matter how much pleasure it also causes:

> *The Story of O*, no matter how erotic as text, might be proxi-
> mately causing literally untold miseries—silenced, actual,
> fearful, terrifying enslavements—and *no woman wants that*.
> If it is, then we cannot have it both ways, and as Wendy
> Williams has said in a different context, where we can't have
> it both ways we have to think carefully about which way we
> want to have it. In my own mind I have no doubt—if *The
> Story of O* is being re-enacted in real life on some farm some-
> where in the hills of Kentucky right through to the bitter
> end, then we can all live without *The Story of O*. For me, this
> is not a close question, though I know it might be for others.
> But again—this poses a choice, and even if it is a hard choice,
> that is a far cry from a disabling contradiction.[20]

"No woman wants" "literally untold miseries—silenced, actual,
fearful, terrifying enslavements": West was perfectly confident
of perfect consensus among women in that case. She shouldn't
have been: women as well as men are capable of wondering
whether the invocation of "untold . . . silenced" pain is more rhe-

torical than real, whether feminism's monopoly to speak for it should always be deferred to, and whether lurid feminist depictions of it might not both eroticize it for some men and produce the experiential capacity for it in women—that is to say, might *be* for feminists the very desire-constituting pornography they would deny to others. And it should have been astonishing to everyone to see an instrumentalist policy balancer working her way to a rule choice while leaving out of the calculus the interests of half the human race: sadly, because we are inside feminism here, that omission goes without saying, so much so that noticing it takes work.

Though this particular passage did not make it into *Caring*, those moves surely do. We've already seen how *Caring* eliminates (nonfeminized) male interests from West's normative vision. And on silent suffering, see her index, which provides sixteen entries for "silence," directing us to fifteen pages of text (354); a word search through the book for "silence" would stop on almost every page discussing women's harm.[21]

But we also see in this passage from "Hedonic Lives" some pragmatic and political gestures that didn't survive West's rethinking over the 1990s. First, she reached her judgment with a patent recognition that, if she got her way, she'd eliminate a text that brings many, many women intense redemptive pleasure inside heterosexual eroticism. She saw women's interests as divided and understood that ruling on behalf of women would require feminists to get some blood on their hands. And so she also acknowledged that women might disagree about her "no pain" rule of decision; it was not only an explicit judgment call, a choice, even a hard choice; by revealing it in this way, she framed it as a political bid within feminism. Implicitly, she issued an invitation to us, her readers and possible interlocutors, to engage with her in a political struggle about what to do about pornography.

Not only does West eliminate *these* argumentative moves from *Caring*: there's nothing in the 1997 book that remotely resembles them. To be sure, West remains a pragmatic feminist with an instrumentalist attitude to law. But she is no longer willing to engage politically with other leftists who see things differently: she concludes, for instance, that feminists *must reject* the antihierarchical democratic political vision of Roberto Unger precisely because (she says) its democratic openness reiterates patriarchy when it fails to privilege maternal altruism, women's distinctive access to the natural and the preverbal dimensions of moral life, and women's exceptional role in bringing "the human community ... [to] respond in a more nurturant, caring, and natural way to the needs of those who are weaker" (276–81). She is no longer willing to entertain the idea that women might find redemptive pleasure in erotically submitting to men and might discover this desire in feminist conscious-raising: indeed, now she argues that she can get around the dilemma of women's compliance with patriarchal desire—is it their false consciousness or their free decision?—because patriarchal harm to women is objectively knowable (174–75). She is no longer willing to risk politically engaged pragmatism all the way; indeed, she now has a moral imperative, not merely a policy preference, to guide her (and us) in feminist instrumental decision making: for Robin West has morality now—the "world free from harm" would be a "world possessed of virtue"; and any element in democracy or postmodernism which might suggest that feminism could participate in creating the discursive conditions for women's suffering is "yet another excuse for men to blind themselves to the violence of patriarchy, the destructivity of misogyny, and *the absolute moral imperative* for positive legal intervention on behalf of women" (263, emphasis added).

The Injury Triad has a very specific and distinct function in the context of this depoliticized, purportedly objective, morally

mandated pragmatic instrumentalism, and that is to predeter-
mine and then justify every decision within presuppositionally
narrow parameters of "hard choice." It's not just that it ensures
that the analytic has no stray bits that could lead it to wander off
from Mother Feminism. It also places its feminism in a position
to trump all players and all contesting visions before they can
come into conflict. Objectively verified and morally absolute, the
Injury Triad comes in as the a priori of politics.

West's move here not only manifests a deep fear of politics; it
moralizes the feminist will to supersede it. The politics of injury
in this form accomplishes something more than it might in a
Millian rights frame. We're used to thinking of rights as trumps;
and even Mill's frame leaves open an explicitly political space in
which politics (perhaps as domination) can be thought. *Caring
for Justice*, like *Feminist Consequences*, shows us the emergence of
a left antipolitics that operates through ethics *first*. Recall at this
point what West's ethics are: a program seeking through legal
change for "a political and moral, not a legal or intellectual[,]
transformation of the heart" (165), guided by the ideal of "a
world possessed of moral value—or . . . [of] a world free from
harm" (171), installing as the sine qua non for *all* judgment calls
the "absolute moral imperative for positive legal intervention on
behalf of women" (263) and reading every failure so to intervene
as a harmful ratification of the morally wrongful harm of women
(145). We have here a prepolitical moral absolute aimed at the
transformation of hearts and minds and offering to prevail whenever considerations conflict. The totalitarian tendency in the feminist politics of injury may well be exemplified here. Query
whether this tendency is itself a cost of this social *imaginaire* and
its political style.

Certainly it blocks access to a full exploration of West's pragmatism. Policy balancing is a very hard, explicitly cost-shifting
form of politics. Query, finally, whether one can engage in it bet-

ter, or worse, if one abandons West's ethical mandates and carries on with one's feminism by Taking a Break.

Seeing the Brain Drain as a Good Thing

Everywhere I go women complain to me that academic feminism has lost its zing. Many key intellectual figures in feminism have decamped to other endeavors. Sometimes they go only as far as postcolonial theory, critical race theory, queer theory; but sometimes they go much further, to the traditional disciplines, to the enthusiastic embrace of—gasp—dead white men, and to political projects parked under other rubrics of human existence.

Not facing this fact has only intensified the Brain Drain. Feminist journals accept articles only on the proviso that the authors produce the effect of $m > f$; in response authors either introduce pro forma obeisance to the subordination mantra, making the "most feminist" part of the article *also* its most formulaic and unmotivated, or publish their work elsewhere. Feminists who Take a Break and write about something else often experience their perfidy with secret joy; they relish their scholarly adultery and return to the marital bed with a new sense that it is the site of duty and routine. Then they lecture their students about how great feminism was, in the old days . . .

Faced with evidence of the Brain Drain, feminists often say they have been betrayed and abandoned, and urge one another— the saving remnant—to a renewed commitment to feminist tenets. I have even heard feminists urge one another that their academic defeat is so calamitous that they should "go underground"![22]

I think the feeling of betrayal is misplaced and the remedy has been astonishingly counterproductive.

One motive force driving the Brain Drain is, surely, the ferocious preclusion imposed on inquisitive minds and avid justice seekers by the paranoid structuralist and prescriptive convergentist presuppositions, indeed by the stricture that theory must create living space. When these impulses emerge in their more moralistic form, moreover, feminism has been not only dogmatic but notoriously *not fun*. But m/f, m > f, and carrying a brief for f are preclusive as well. For instance, if "women don't own gender,"[23] we might want to think about m and f while suspending the stipulation that subordination is always their relation, and always takes the form of m > f. And there is the hunch that many of the most devastating problems in the world might not be about m/f, not even a little.

The Brain Drain is voting with its feet. Is this a good thing or a bad thing? You'd have to look not only at the costs to feminism, in the form of depopulation, bad morale, the delegitimation of academic feminism, and the like. You'd also have to consider whether the work the prodigals are doing instead seems vital, productive in good ways, intellectually and socially useful. Never forget: no *Volume One*, no *Gender Trouble*. And how would feminism make itself capable of evaluating the work of the Brain Drain if it didn't sometimes Take a Break from Feminism?

Resisting Bad Faith

I argued in Part One that feminism now has a considerable purchase on a wide array of state, statelike, and social/cultural power; that it has a will to this power; and that, in the course of wielding its power, feminism distributes social costs among women, to men, and to other social groups and to the bearers of various social interests. I also noted that a very profound (but highly contingent) commitment among many feminists to the Injury

Triad—to seeing the world in terms of female injury, female innocence, and male immunity—not only involved them in a denial
of their will to power, and of their power, but precluded them
from acknowledging their actual social effects when these take
the form of female immunity, female aggression, and/or male injury. And I argued that even the feminist minima precommitted
feminism to disaffiliate from social groups and the bearers of various social interests that could not be converged into those terms.
That is to say, I have laid at the door of the Injury Triad feminists,
and feminists more generally, the accusation that they are exercising power in bad faith.

The Injury Triad—female injury + female innocence + male
immunity—is, I think, the positive content of governance feminism's bad-faith failure to embrace and responsibly manage its
power. Each element of the Injury Triad is necessary to hold off
the moment when feminism might say to itself and the world:
"Yes, feminism wields power; ratifies as well as critiques the experience of feminine injury; cares not whether its famous plaintiffs
are telling the truth; seeks to impose itself with vigor and sometimes with violence on the social world; rules across the board,
not case by case; and so, overall, will necessarily generate male
road kill, male scapegoats, and male objects of retributive rigor.
So be it." As long as that sounds like a thoroughly unfeminist
sentence (though of course the definitional minima could sustain
it), we might have to Take a Break from Feminism to assess the
costs and benefits—to the myriad social interests we might care
about, and indeed to feminism—of refusing to Take a Break.

Of course, operating in bad faith might actually be a good
thing. It's a way of tying yourself to the mast and making it more
likely that you'll finish a voyage you might otherwise interrupt,
possibly with disastrous consequences. But there are many, many
reasons to worry about this kind of political consciousness. Not

seeing the productive effects of one's purposive actions can cause one to intensify them. If, for instance, you don't think that young men approach heterosexuality with fear and trembling and suffer the inevitable failures of intimacy with deep pangs, you might end up imagining that male-disadvantaging statutory rape laws— which you might be advocating in your effort to protect adolescent girls—have no social costs at all, and so you might proceed, once you've got male-disadvantaging statutory rape laws, to intensify them through the addition of rape shield rules, shifts in the burden of proof, pro-prosecution presumptions, and so on. You could keep doing this until the tolerated residuum of abuse had shrunk to its practical minimum and the number of false-positive convictions of perfectly lovely, sexually animated young men had ballooned to what would be, even to you, intolerable levels. But you wouldn't notice.

At this point I often think of the time an old, otherwise not very frightening dog decided to come running at me, roaring that ominous roar and baring his teeth. I somehow knew, but realized only then, that getting eye contact with dogs who bark at me is an important part of how I influence their behavior toward me. This dawned on me at the moment I saw that this particular dog was blind. My sense of the danger I was in intensified steeply, not only because this otherwise conversable house pet could not see how effectively he was already controlling me, but because I could not communicate to him by a mutual gaze his success in that *or* the possible harm I could do to him. Feminism seeking to switch all the rules to generate feminist outcomes without regard to the costs their rules would inflict on many women, on men, and on myriad social interests that can't be spelled in the alphabet of m/ f, seems similarly blind, and similarly dangerous, to me.

Operating in bad faith can have other pretty acute downsides. It can produce rage and distrust among the unacknowledged bearers of the costs of one's activities. Alliances with them will be much harder now. As a form of consciousness, bad faith reproduces itself and blocks the radical impulse to examine the ways in which our precommitments ensure that we'll "see it because we believe it." And feminist bad faith can produce blind spots— moments when feminists do not see that carrying a brief for f might hurt *women* because, in the power situation actually in play, women are misapprehended as being the bearers, primarily, of f, power is misapprehended as being primarily >, and so on.

Suspending this bad faith might enable feminism to participate in a much more expansive political engagement with its own effects, its own imagined constituency, and other political projects it professes to care about.

Can we envision a feminist politics that could participate in such politics? Can we have feminist theory that is willing to get blood on its hands?

Minimizing Moral Perfectionism and Magic Realism

Feminists hearing this question have responded again and again with a formulation something like this: if feminism had blood on its hands, it would be because it had become a dominator; but feminism is definitionally against domination; and if it has dominated, if it has caused harm, it must chasten itself; but most likely feminism has not actually caused any harm; after all, feminism is powerless and in fact suffers harm.

This argument, for all its moral modesty, is actually quite strict: feminism (to be feminism) must be morally immaculate. It is either subordinated (and harmless) or not itself. A profound structural totalism—feminism is *the* subordination theory par excellence—subtends this formulation.

This willingness of feminism to undergo chastening in the name of its moral perfectionism is not necessarily meek all the way down. It stipulates for a binarized outcome: feminism can either assume guilt *or* deny harm. At moments when guilt has been the preferred stance, feminism has been quite acutely dysphoric. Memories of these episodes have probably done a lot to fuel the Brain Drain. The fact that denial is framed as the chief alternative has produced a certain magic realist tendency in feminism, and, as I've already suggested, it has produced a lot of distrust in allied projects (antiracist projects, pro-gay projects, etc.) whose constituencies arguably end up bearing some of the costs of the decisions made by governance feminism.

Deconstituting Women's Suffering

What if, as well as describing and opposing m > f, feminism helps to produce it? What if the politics of injury and of traumatized sensibility that have almost completely occupied the space cleared by MacKinnon's politics of domination and subordination are helping to authorize and enable women as sufferers? If indeed feminism is a powerfully constitutive discourse, it might well have a shaping contribution to make to women's suffering when, for instance, it insists that a raped woman has suffered an injury from which she is unlikely ever to recover. What if real raped women, believing this feminist line, proceed never to recover? What if some men are "guided" by this bull's-eye to target women for rape rather than fomenting other aggressions, perhaps more manageable, perhaps directed elsewhere? Feminism has trained us well that, if we ask how a particular rape might have been made possible because of the woman's own conduct, we blame the victim, revictimize her, commit the second rape: could our resulting silence on this question make rape seem more random than it is; make women more risk-averse about it than they need to be; induce women to concede more social power to the threat of rape than they otherwise would? So much feminist rape discourse insists on women's objectlike status in the rape situation: man fucks woman—subject verb object. Could feminism be contributing to, rather than resisting, the alienation of women from their own agency in narratives and events of sexual violence?

Could feminism be like the adults on the playground? Imagine: the little girl stumbles, falls, scrapes her knee. She is silent, still, composed, waiting for the kaleidoscope of dizziness, surprise, and pain to subside. Up rush the adults, ululating in sympathy, urgently concerned—has she broken her leg? Is she bleeding? How did it happen? We must not let it happen again! Poor thing. The little girl's silence breaks—for the first time afraid, she cries.

While feminism is committed to affirming and identifying itself with female injury, it may thereby, unintentionally, intensify it. Oddly, representing women as end points of pain, imagining them as lacking the agency to cause harm to others and particularly to harm men, feminists refuse also to see women—even injured ones—as powerful actors. *Feminism* objectifies women, *feminism* erases their agency—could that be right? We might need to Take a Break from Feminism to notice that the crying girl is *really* suffering; that she *really* didn't have to; and that her wails may have something in them of a (possibly successful) wish for revenge.

If we are going to think that way, we are faced with a very profound problem about the relationship between power and resistance. If a social subordination exists and an antisubordination discourse—while also pursuing its antisubordination goals—ratifies it, fixes it, creates the discursive capacity for its experiential uptake by the subordinated, all the while hanging a bull's-eye on it, then where does one intervene to attack it? This is a real question, rife with real and strategic difficulties. It has fascinated me, as I have begun to learn how to ask it, to notice the strong feminist impulse (optional, not necessary to feminism as we now have it, but recurrent) to refuse it as unfeminist. The reaction has fueled my intuition that we might need to Take a Break from Feminism precisely to be *for women* and *against this increment of injury.*

TAKING A BREAK TO
DECIDE (II)

This is the last rereading I'll offer you. I'm going to read the "facts" of *Twyman v. Twyman* against the elements of the cause of action for intentional infliction of emotional distress—and then reread them as if they were our best examples of non-feminist theories about morals, power, and sex that I derive from Nietzsche's *On the Genealogy of Morals: A Polemic*[1] and Foucault's *Volume One.* This repeats the basic protocol that produced my four readings of *Oncale.* But there I was trying to make manifest an array of fairly reified social constituencies managed by the legal regime of same-sex sexual harassment law, and to produce acute splits between them. The goal here is to read not only beyond carrying a brief for f: I am trying to get beyond m/f and m > f, and even beyond >. If you find any part of this process to be politically enabling, I think it means that at least part of your political libido wants to Take a Break.

By "facts," once again, I mean the narrative bites that we get from the various Texas Supreme Court justices whose opinions I study here. I disavow any suggestion that the resulting formulations describe the real human beings Sheila and William Twyman. But I will suggest that the rule Sheila won could be wielded by Susans and Georgettes and Lucilles who fully inhabit the alternative readings proposed here, against Sams and Barneys and Michaels who have married them there.

Twyman v. Twyman

Sheila and William Twyman were married in 1969. Sheila filed for divorce in 1985; and not too long thereafter she amended her claim to include a tort action that the trial court construed as a claim for negligent infliction of emotional distress. The factual crux of the claim seems to have been that William had "intentionally and cruelly" imposed "deviate sexual acts" on her. I work through the details below; for now it will be enough to report that the trial court found that these acts involved bondage, and that William had attempted to coerce Sheila to perform them.

The trial court awarded the divorce, divided the marital assets, and granted Sheila an additional fifteen thousand dollars in damages for her emotional distress on the tort claim. William appealed. The court of appeals affirmed, saying that negligent infliction of emotional distress was actionable in Texas and was a claim that could be sustained by spouse against spouse. Meanwhile, however, the Texas Supreme Court held in another case that no claim for negligent infliction of emotional distress was permissible in Texas. When the Texas Supreme Court took up William's further appeal, a majority of the justices, split into a plurality and several concurrences, remanded the case for a new trial on a new legal theory: *intentional* infliction of emotional distress was held to be actionable, and actionable between spouses, in Texas; and Sheila was entitled to retry her case because she could not have known until this opinion was handed down how to litigate it (619, 620–21, 624).

What this means to lawyers is that a plurality of the Texas Supreme Court thought that Sheila had already brought in enough evidence, and made enough factual arguments, that she had a very minimal number of dots left to connect between her case and the new theory of liability that had become the law. They thought her facts, so far, were within reach of winning the case under the new theory. That means that the plurality justices thought she had good enough facts to sustain findings under all the essential elements of the new claim they had adopted. Those were the following: (1) that William's conduct was outrageous, beyond all possible bounds of decency, atrocious, and utterly intolerable in a civilized society; (2) (at this point there is some legal uncertainty, so I include all the options considered important by various justices) that, when he engaged in that conduct, he *intended* to cause Sheila severe emotional distress and/or he *knew* he might cause her severe emotional distress and *recklessly* ran the risk, and/or he *recklessly ignored the risk* of emotional distress;[2] (3) and that his conduct did cause (4) her to suffer severe emotional distress. No one disputed that Sheila was "devastated," and so forth: the dicey questions seem to be these: What was the conduct alleged to be outrageous, was it outrageous, and in what sense did it cause Sheila's distress?

All the justices who give us any facts agree that William first introduced "bondage" into their sexual relationship. We learn from Justice Hecht that both Sheila and William tied each other up in those early encounters; her willing participation in those scenes, and the mobility of "top" and "bottom" roles in them, fall out of the narrative for all the remanding justices. Sheila then told William that she had been raped before they married, and that she did not want to engage in sadomasochistic sex with him any more. The justices represent this moment very differently, as we will soon see. There is no inconsistency among the justices on the basic facts of the rape, however. Sheila testified that she had been raped before her marriage, at knifepoint; had been cut with the knife; and had feared for her life.[3]

Some years later Sheila discovered that William was in psychotherapy, and, confronting him to find out why, was told that he was having an affair with a woman who was willing to engage in bondage. At this point William made some kind of link between his desire for sadomasochistic sex and the viability of the marriage. As Justice Hecht put it, he told Sheila that "if she could only have done bondage, nothing else would have mattered" (636); as Justice Spector put it, "he told Sheila that if she would not satisfy

his desires by engaging in bondage, there would be no future to
their marriage" (641). Justice Hecht further tells us that

> [f]or the remainder of the year the couple sought counsel-
> ing. On their counselor's advice, William and Sheila dis-
> cussed William's bondage fantasies, and Sheila again tried
> to participate in bondage activities with William. But she
> found the activity so painful and humiliating that she could
> not continue it. Their last encounter, which did not include
> bondage activities, was so rough that she was injured to the
> point of bleeding. (636)

Like Justice Hecht, Justice Spector understands that it is these last
bondage encounters, and not the final sexual event in which
Sheila sustained gynecological injuries, that are at the heart of
Sheila's claim to actionable mental distress:

> Sheila experienced "utter despair" and "devastation," as well
> as physical problems—weight loss and, after one encounter,
> prolonged bleeding that necessitated gynecological treat-
> ment. The *pain and humiliation of the bondage activities*
> caused her to seek help from three professional counselors.
> (641, emphasis added)

It is the bondage, not the last night of rough sex, that the justices
continually return to as the crux of William's conduct. We are left,
then, with this basic narrative configuration: faced with William's
disclosure about his affair and his statements that he could not
remain married if Sheila could not have sadomasochistic sex with
him, Sheila reluctantly but willingly engaged in sadomasochistic
sex; she decided after doing so that it was intolerably painful and
humiliating to her and went on to base her legal claim against
William on that experience. She also had some very rough sex
with him that injured her physically, but none of the justices

imagined that this event was part of her claim that William had inflicted emotional distress on her.

So there are three causal elements. One is William's desire for and solicitation of sadomasochistic sex. I'll call that the sadomasochistic solicitations. A second is Sheila's narrative to William of a rape that occurred before the marriage, and her refusal (apparently rescinded near the end of their life together) to engage in bondage for that reason. I'll call this the rape disclosure. And the third is William's inability/refusal to relinquish his kink, his pursuit of it with a lover, and his telling Sheila, when she discovered that he was seeing a psychotherapist, that the marriage would fail if she could not participate in bondage with him. I'll call this the divorce threat.

For one justice, the divorce threat and the sadomasochistic solicitations are crucial and the rape seemingly irrelevant. Justice Gonzales indicates that the element of "outrageousness" was fully met by William's solicitation of and participation in bondage activities with her, "under the rationale that such activities were necessary to the future of their marriage." He makes no reference to the claims that these solicitations, episodes, or arguments had a severe emotional impact on her because of the rape, or that William should incur liability for them because she had warned him that they would (626). He almost suggests that the solicitation of mild sadomasochistic sex with a spouse, especially if you really need it and she later finds this out, is itself outrageous and can be presumed to cause any emotional distress that follows. It's a draconian antikink stance, and not intrinsically feminist (though some feminists would no doubt endorse it, for feminist reasons that do not appear to have motivated Justice Gonzales).

For the other justices who reflect substantially on the facts, all three elements—the bondage solicitations, the rape disclosure, and the divorce threat—matter, and there are indelible marks of feminism in their understanding of their interrelation in a causal progress leading to Sheila's distress. To Justice Cornyn (writing the plurality opinion, and concluding that the action for intentional infliction should be allowed and the case remanded) "Sheila testified that William pursued sadomasochistic bondage activities with her, even though he knew that she feared such activities *because she had been raped at knife-point before their marriage*" (620 n. 1, emphasis added). (This logic must exclude from the logic of William's liability the bondage scenes that happened before William knew about the rape.) Justice Hecht (who would have rejected all infliction-of-emotional-distress actions as indeterminate and thus not capable of being brought within the rule of law) narrates the moment of disclosure thus: "She revealed to him that she *associated the activities with the horrible experience of having been raped* at knifepoint earlier in her life" (636, emphasis added). And Justice Spector (who would have endorsed a rule allowing *negligent* infliction actions because of the disproportionate harm insensitive men cause more emotionally alert women, and who would have *affirmed* the judgment for Sheila even on the stricter intentional infliction rule) basically repeats Justice Hecht's narrative here: when William "introduced bondage activities into their relationship after their marriage[,] Sheila told William that *she could not endure these activities because of the trauma of having been raped* several years earlier" (641, emphasis added).

Justices Cornyn, Hecht, and Spector (though they agree about little else) agree that Sheila's special sexual history was crucial to her claim, and the latter two (though they agree about almost nothing else) agree that it made her particularly vulnerable to harm in sexual exchange with her husband. They use a strange temporal locution—"the experience of having been raped"; "the trauma of having been raped"—that locates the moment of injury in a perpetual present. Sheila is *always* undergoing the experience of having been raped, *always* suffering the trauma of having been raped. In much feminist rape discourse, this is exactly right. Once raped, always raped. Much contemporary feminist rape discourse repeatedly insists that the pain of rape extends into every future moment of a woman's life; it is a note played not on a piano but on an organ.[4] Justice Spector's cultural feminism probably supplies this understanding; Justice Hecht, who, as we will see, attempts to reconstitute Sheila as a responsible agent with considerable powers, resorts to it in a gesture that seems almost compensatory.

At this point Justices Spector and Hecht part company, and as the latter departs from Justice Spector's cultural-feminist line, I feel strongly tempted to follow him. On the question "[W]hat did William know about Sheila's likely emotional reaction to a bondage solicitation," Justice Hecht tells us that, after the first experiments with neckties, "Sheila told William she did not like this activity and did not want to participate in it further" (636). Strong, decisive, self-knowing. An agent. But not a person with a plausible claim that her husband's desire for what she did not desire constituted intentional infliction of emotional distress. Justice Spector, however, understands the disclosure quite differently: after the rape disclosure "William understood that Sheila *equated* bondage with her prior experience of being raped"; "Sheila told William that she *could not endure* these activities" (641). Once again Justice Spector deals in standard cultural-feminist rape tropes: the deathlike pall of sexual injury, and the literal equation of every rape*like* event with *rape itself.* If bondage reminded Sheila of her rape, it was the rape all over again; and because the rape was death, being reminded of it was also death: she *could not endure it.*

And what about the divorce threat? Justice Hecht gives it a somewhat pathetic cast: "William told Sheila that if she could only have done bondage, nothing else would have mattered" (636). None of the other renditions of this fact have anything like this wistful sound. Justice Spector quotes the trial court, which

found that William had engaged in "a continuing course of conduct of attempting to coerce [Sheila] to join in his practices of
'bondage' by continually asserting that their marriage could be
saved" only if she participated in them (641). Justice Cornyn also
quoted the trial court's finding that William "attempted to emotionally coerce [Sheila] in 'bondage' on an ongoing basis" (620
n. 1). Perhaps this is where the rapelikeness of the last bondage
scenes finally emerges: the threat of divorce is like the threat of a
knife. Under threats like this, a woman loses her agency, and if
she consents to sex, it is nevertheless coerced. This, too, is a completely familiar element in much feminist rape discourse. Why so
many feminisms want women to experience themselves as completely devoid of choice when they bargain their way past a knife
by having sex they really, really don't want, I don't know. But
wait! Justice Spector has just extended this agencyless construction of women to situations involving the threat not of physical
mutilation or death, but of *divorce*. *Divorce* is represented as so
life-threatening that, faced with the possibility of it, women cannot be regarded as agents.

This image of male power and female subordination—the utter
pathos of Sheila, submitting to sex with her husband that he
wants but that they both know will humiliate and anguish her,
all to save her marriage precisely to the author of her suffering—
is of course not at all required by any particular strand of feminism. Nor, as Brenda Cossman and Dan Danielsen have shown,
need feminism endorse or seek the remedy granted by the Texas
Supreme Court in this case.[5]

But can feminism accommodate a completely reversed image
of the Twymans' marriage? Imagine it: the utter pathos of William, begging for sex he can't get from his wife, guiltily sneaking
off to have it with another woman, whipped through round after
round of psychotherapy to figure out why he is such a pervert,
and finally submitted to the public humiliation of testifying about

his hopeless intimacies and suffering a published opinion deciding that his marital conduct is very likely outrageous, beyond all
possible bounds of decency, atrocious, and utterly intolerable in
a civilized society. As against that, imagine: the astonishing powers of Sheila, laying down the moral law of the couple's sex life,
pursuing William like a Valkyrie for breaking it, and extracting
not only a fault-based divorce but possibly also money damages
specifically premised on her alliance with the state against him.
Imagine further: *Twyman* as background family-law rule that
husbands with enduring ineradicable desires for sex that their
wives find humiliating must either stay married to those wives or,
if they seek a divorce (which they might well want to do simply
to remarry and have nonadulterous sex with women who do not
find their desires humiliating), pay a heavy tax in shame, blame,
and cash. Can feminism acknowledge that women emerge from
the court's decision with new bargaining power in marriage and
a new role as enforcers of marital propriety? And can feminism
see how costly this bargaining endowment might be *to women*,
who can tap into it only if they find the sex in question painful
and humiliating? Can feminism read the case as male subordination and female domination—and *still* as bad for women?

Very possibly. There might well be a place for feminism that
carries a brief for f, but without presupposing m > f. I think this
is largely where Brenda Cossman and Tracy Higgins see the possibility of substantial gains for feminism.[6] But my project here is to
expose some of the distinctive attractions of Taking a Break from
Feminism. To do that, I'm going to reduce *On the Genealogy of
Morals* and *The History of Sexuality, Volume One*, in that order,
to a set of counterhypotheses, and offer brief rereadings of *Twyman v. Twyman* designed to exploit the explanatory power of the
resulting hypotheses. Again I hope it will be understood that I
am not making any claims about the real human beings Sheila
and William Twyman; instead, working from the obviously highly

artful constructions of them that we receive from the justices of the Texas Supreme Court, I'm going to bracket feminism and reconnect all the dots à la Nietzsche and à la Foucault.

First, let's consider the moralistic character of Sheila's project with William. She was not content to seek a fault-based divorce, and apparently did not seek damages or pursue criminal charges against him for that last night of sex between them that left her bleeding. Instead, she seeks a judge's finding that—through the sadomasochistic solicitations, the rape disclosure, and the divorce threat—William has engaged in conduct that is outrageous, beyond all possible bounds of decency, atrocious, and utterly intolerable in a civilized society. What can we say about her decision if we take Nietzsche's *Genealogy of Morals* as our theoretical ground? In the following extractions, I rewrite the "slave revolt in morals" (22) as if it were achieved not over the broad sweep of human history but by an individual:

1. The historical starting point of slave morality is the slave's perception of himself as dominated and as suffering under the will of the master. He sees his as a *passive* location in the world: the master is *active*; and in his passivity the slave suffers.

2. Though originally the slave could have understood his suffering as bad and the master's activity as good (and could have sought to be active too), this is not what happens. Instead, he translates the power relation into a moral one: he is good and the master is evil. It is now a relationship of dominated virtue and dominating vice. Morality is born as a covert mechanism of power, a sublimated form of domination.

3. This translation removes any reason for the slave to experience himself as having *a will*. Will is now evil. The rage of the slave against his suffering—his own will to power—is now denied.

4. His will and his activity don't go away, though. Instead, translated yet again into ressentiment, they are rerouted both *out*, against the master, in gestures of meek but biting vengeance; and *in*, against the slave himself, in a new form of suffering, under the whip of his own morality, the new innerness of a *guilty conscience*.

5. Slave morality wreaks itself with splendid sadism on the master, and with stupefying intensity it also punishes the slave himself for his own active impulses—impulses without which the whole terrible cycle would never have started. It establishes a third human class, the priestly class, with powers that are made more uncanny because they are waged under the sign of weakness and use not the pathetic devices of physical coercion but the intimate stringencies of conscience and inner pain. "Bad air! Bad air!" (28)

It's not hard at all to reread Sheila Twyman as the intense sufferer and wielder of slave morality. Her rapist, that blond beast, could have been her enemy but (possibly with the assistance of feminism) became her master. His power to rape her at knifepoint became *a*, if not *the*, central fact of her life. Experiencing herself as utterly dominated, she determined to oppose him with the power of the weak: he was bad not in the sense that he acted inimically to her will, but in the sense that he was evil. And her moral project of punishing him, in its ferocious will for revenge, failed to notice that William was—well—a different guy. Wielding the moral code of good sex, Sheila made William grovel; but she also suffered intensely herself. Justice Spector (of course) provides us with the gruesome details: Sheila "experienced 'utter despair' and 'devastation,' " lost weight, accepted sex with William that left her bleeding: "the pain and humiliation of the bondage activities caused her to seek help from three professional counselors." (It is an amazing detail that Justice Spector's *and* Justice Hecht's Sheila seems to find sex with neckties, but not sex that produces gynecological injuries, painful and humiliating. A Nietzschean reading of this discrepancy would propose that this Sheila was devoid of a self-preservative impulse, could not attend to the well-being of the body, so devoted was she to the quickening of her wounded soul.) She experienced her self as utterly powerless, utterly broken, and the more intensely she sought and obtained vengeance on William, the more deeply she became embedded in the stringencies of the suffering that justified it.

I can think of many reasons why Taking a Break from Feminism so as to be able to read the case in this way is a good idea. *If* this reading of her is right—and the reading itself is no empirical warrant—it brings me several important political insights I would not have without it. First, it brings strongly to my attention the possibility that Sheila Twyman is no ally of mine. Second, it warns me to think of her as no weakling, but rather as a formidable enemy who will pursue her goals with fierce drive. Third, it suggests that she nevertheless suffers terribly with every new access of subordinated sensibility. And fourth, it helps me to see that *feminism* might be responsible not only for her power, but also for the terrible suffering that grounds it.

But maybe my ressentiment of Sheila's ressentiment is torquing my reading too much. Let's look for something milder, something that suspends completely the idea that power must take the form of domination and subordination, and something that lifts us out of moralism and the temptation to fall into a moralistic rage against it. As I read *Volume One*, it offers some theoretic hypotheses that differ very strikingly from those I have attributed to U.S. feminism and to Nietzsche. In what follows I proceed as though Foucault's hypotheses about power were simple and straightforward rather than contradicted, ambivalent, and in tension throughout the text.[7] Four key points:

1. For the Foucault of *Volume One*, the task was to imagine power not as the relation of dominance and subordination, but as a highly fragmented and temporally mobile "field of force *relations*." Power could be *micropouvoir*: it could achieve vast social and consciousness effects not only by dropping down on people from on high, but also by being constantly moved about among them; and not only through physical violence but also through formations and reformations of the possibilities for organized experience. Discourses.

2. For the Foucault of *Volume One*, power was not necessarily bad. It might be pouvoir (the capacity to create effects) rather than puissance (the capacity to dominate or coerce).

3. For the Foucault of *Volume One*, sexuality emerged historically as a discourse and produced as its effect the people we are—people who think their lives crucially involve knowledge of their deepest sexual selves. There is something excruciating and "stuck" about this; a more mobile relationship to sexuality not as a truth but as a practice might be better. Foucault did not imagine liberation, but rather a perpetual search for the *rearrangement* of powers in the social and experiential fields.

4. Very few of the chief discourses of sexuality in the modern era turn in any sustained way on m/f or bear the mark of sustained male dominance. Instead, the organization of knowledge and knowledge practices are far more likely to be the way in which power constitutes sexuality. These will not oppress particular persons or groups, so much as produce differentiations within the population, spread it out in mobile but patterned arrays. Biopower.

These hypotheses would allow us to Take a Break from Feminism in both of its essential points: they analyze sexuality, m/f, and power in quite different terms.

So let's read the *Twyman* facts as if these hypotheses were the only ones available. The first thing that "goes" is the presumption, silently carried along in all the opinions of the court, that Sheila Twyman has a meaningful moral claim that William's conduct was wrong. The question addressed by the justices is whether that claim is *legally cognizable*; Justice Hecht comes closest to the claim that the power relationships between husband and wife are indeterminate, but even he fell for the "trauma of having been raped" line. Reading the case as if it were an example of how right Foucault's hypotheses in *Volume One* could be, however, allows us to give that presumption up for the moment.

One of the things that then immediately emerges is the intense, and formally almost identical, sexual pathos of both Sheila *and* William. Both are committed to the idea that they have deep, inner, injured sexual selves beyond which they cannot move one micron, and which they must enact with near-fatal completeness. William *must* live out the affliction of a perverse implantation, a deeply resisted fetishistic desire. He is a classic subject of the psychiatrization of perversions. Sheila *must* live out the affliction of rape trauma. Rape trauma is her deep inner truth, and her experiential life must make it manifest. In a terrible way, William and Sheila are perfectly matched to provoke the complete manifestation of their diametrically opposite desires; but oddly, this is because they are basically the same.

Moreover, Foucault always seems to think that this experience of deep inner truth is introduced into modern consciousness by a discourse—a power/knowledge—that imposes it on us while distracting us from the real action, the real place where power connects with sexual life. The suffering of the shamed fetishist is pathetic—indeed, it is cruel, and quite one of the terrible wrongs inflicted on the tremulous human spirit by the psychiatric discourse of sexual truth; and the suffering of the rape survivor is similarly pathetic—indeed, it is cruel, and quite one of the terrible wrongs inflicted on the tremulous human spirit by the feminist discourse of sexual truth. But both are distractions from the real game, the real place where power meets the population. (This is *Foucault's* paranoid structuralism.)

And where might we look in the *Twyman* facts for a warrant of the hypotheses of *Volume One*? We are looking for something broadly regulatory, not m/f, and capable of complex biopoweristic and micropoweristic deployments. I propose marital monogamy. Marriage provides spouses with an amazing power over each other: the power to perform (and inflict), and to prohibit (and punish), infidelity. The monogamy rule and all the possible ways of breaking it provide rich social scripts, carefully elaborated at every level of cultural detail. Those scripts provide many ways of seeing a relationship of > in the *Twyman* facts. It is very easy to say that William has breached his promise of sexual continence, indulged in gratifications inconsistent with adult self-discipline and decent regard for Sheila's dignity; that he has cracked one of the building blocks of civilization. Also easy to articulate an idea that he has unleashed the brute force of sexual yearning against the fragility of civilization. But we could see the subordination as running the other way: William enacts that immemorial figure, the Hapless Adulterer; he is the helpless bumbling dupe of a dozen trite tropes in the adultery script; the deep purpose of his affair was realized only when Sheila discovered it and gained the upper hand; Sheila as the wronged wife, the enforcer of marriage vows, fiercely restores the fidelity rule to its proper place, with the avid assistance of almost every judge involved in the case.

But let's try one more time, for a third reading without a victim and a victimizer, without dominance and submission, but *with* power. What if the struggle between the two over William's infidelity—their divorce had been pending for eight years by the time the Texas Supreme Court remanded the case *for a new trial!*—was for both of them a paroxysm of intimacy, a sustained crescendo of erotic interrelatedness, which, if it should ever end, would leave both of them aimless and lonely to the last degree?

It might be that these alternative readings of the facts recorded in *Twyman* just don't have any real-world plausibility. Maybe Sheila is never the fomenter of slave morality; maybe Sheila and William never seek love in power without domination, suffering without subordination, in the cruel coils of divorce. There is both strength and danger in framing the possibilities described by these readings. Only if we articulate and explore them will we ever look into the world and see whether it matches them. Our political desires and projects could be significantly rerouted, in very good ways, if we found a match: noticing that slave moralistic Sheila Twymans are not my allies has meant a profound reorientation of my feminism and my stance toward feminism, one I think has been very helpful to me. I admit there is danger here too, in the form of a spiral: if our axiom is "I'll see it when I believe it," theory can change reality by changing what we can notice in it; and maybe feminism is right to close its eyes. As I've suggested, I'm strongly inclined to think otherwise.

And maybe there is something terrifying about losing one's grip on a "moral compass" or in admiring a cruel marriage rule *because* people can use it for intense crazy masochistic love. Once we really do admit masochism into our vocabulary of sexual pleasure, we make it hard to know that any particular social outcome involving sexuality broadly conceived is a cost or a benefit, a good or a bad. Even there, we must—constantly, existentially, pragmatically, and in uncertainty—decide.

Very possibly this critical disorientation is an unaffordable luxury, especially in times, like these, of acute consolidation of conservative power. Again, I'm strongly inclined to think otherwise; and hope my hunch turns out to be right.

Notes

THE ARGUMENT

1. Much of this and the last two paragraphs were cannibalized from an email sent to me by David Kennedy (August 1, 2005).

2. Denise Riley, *Am I that Name? Feminism and the Category of "Women" in History* (London: Macmillan Press, 1988), 96.

TAXONOMIES AND TERMS

1. Thanks for this very useful term to Eve Kosofsky Sedgwick, "Gosh, Boy George, You Must Be Awfully Secure in Your Masculinity!" in *Constructing Masculinity*, ed. Maurice Berger, Brian Wallis, and Simon Watson (New York: Routledge, 1995), 11–20, 16.

2. See "Around 1993: Mapping Feminism and Queer Theory," 227–60, below.

3. Kelly Askin, a feminist activist deeply involved in the process, draws the following conclusion about it: "The cases demonstrate that female judges, investigators, prosecutors, translators, particularly those with expertise in gender crimes, are extremely useful in the prosecution of gender crimes. They further demonstrate that there must be political will to prosecute sex crimes, and that pressure exerted from NGOs is often indispensable to ensuring that gender crimes are investigated and indicted." Kelly D. Askin, "A Decade of the Development of Gender Crimes in International Courts and Tribunals: 1993–2003," *Human Rights Brief* 11, no. 3 (2004): 16, 19. Rhonda Copelon provides evidence of the close interaction among feminist activists, judges, and prosecutors as charges were being drawn up for the International Criminal Tribunal for the former Yugoslavia. Copelon, "Surfacing Gender: Re-Engraving Crimes against Women in Humanitarian Law," *Hastings Women's Law Journal* 5 (1994): 243, 253–54 n. 46. Looking back on his work as prosecutor before the tribunals for Yugoslavia and Rwanda, perhaps contemplating the very exchange that Copelon records, Justice Richard Goldstone of the Constitutional Court of South Africa recalled the effect of feminist NGO activism this way: "Let me start with the enormous strides that have been made by the tribunals in the development of the normative law. There has been substantial progressive development of humanitarian law as a consequence of the establishment of the ICTY. Of real

importance are developments in the law with respect to gender offenses. From my very first week in office, from the middle of August, 1994 onwards, I began to be besieged with petitions and letters, mainly from women's groups, but also from human rights groups generally, from many European countries, the U.S. and Canada, and also from non-governmental organizations in the former Yugoslavia. Letters and petitions expressing concern and begging for attention, adequate attention, to be given to gender related crime, especially systematic rape as a war crime. Certainly if any campaign worked, this one worked in my case." Justice Richard Goldstone, "The United Nations' War Crimes Tribunals: An Assessment," *Connecticut Journal of International Law* 12 (1997): 227, 231.

4. The complete story of U.S. feminism cannot be confined, as I confine it here, to the territorial shores of the United States. Governance feminism is an international event with intense local effects; it has learned to globalize itself using the mechanisms of the current globalization of U.S. legal thought. Duncan Kennedy, "Two Globalizations of Law and Legal Thought," *Suffolk University Law Review* 36 (2003): 631. One small example: Orit Kamir, who studied with MacKinnon in the United States, returned to Israel and became a prominent feminist legal activist. She writes quite engagingly about how to adapt MacKinnon's theoretical and law-reform ideas to Israeli social and legal culture: the right to human dignity rather than sex discrimination and the use of statutory rather than case law are two of the shifts. Orit Kamir, "Dignity, Respect and Equality in Israel's Sexual Harassment Law," in *Directions in Sexual Harassment Law*, ed. Catharine A. MacKinnon and Reva B. Siegel (New Haven: Yale University Press, 2004), 561–81. Working in classic new governance mode, she participated in the Knesset's 1998 codification of a sex harassment statute: "The new law was the product of a unique cooperation among women Knesset members, feminist activists, pro-feminist jurists at the Ministry of Justice, and feminist legal academics" (562). Note that Kamir's strategy is remarkably like Askin's. The Israeli statute is now ripe for invocation in the active expansion of dignity-based concepts of human rights, implantation in international human rights dogma, and reexport to national locales—including the United States— through the increasing tendency (controversial, of course) of our courts to consult foreign and international norms. For the argument that domestic courts can and should enforce international legal norms, see Harold Koh, "Transnational Public Law Litigation," *Yale Law Journal* 100 (1991): 2347; for an argument that U.S. courts should import dignity from international and foreign courts' human rights decisions, see Vincent J. Samar, "Justifying the

Use of International Human Rights Principles in American Constitutional Law,"*Columbia Human Rights Law Review* 37 (2005): 1.

5. Joseph Cardinal Ratzinger and Angelo Amato, for the Congregation for the Doctrine of the Faith, "Letter to the Bishops of the Catholic Church on the Collaboration of Men and Women in the Church and in the World," July 31, 2004. This letter can be found at http://www.vatican.va/roman_curia/congregations/cfaith/doc_doc_index.htm (last visited August 9, 2005).

6. Critical work is remarkably scarce in this domain. These exceptions stand out: Frances Olsen, "The Family and the Market: A Study of Ideology and Law Reform," *Harvard Law Review* 1492 (1983), and Philomila Tsoukala, "Gary Becker, Legal Feminism, and the Costs of Moralizing Care" (unpublished manuscript).

LIBERATION AND RESPONSIBILITY

1. See Robyn Wiegman, "Feminism, Institutionalism, and the Idiom of Failure," *differences* 11, no. 5 (1999/2000): 108–36.

PART TWO INTRODUCTION

1. MacKinnon, "Feminism, Marxism, Method and the State: An Agenda for Theory," *Signs* 7, no. 3 (1982): 515 (hereafter, First *Signs*); "Feminism, Marxism, Method and the State: Toward Feminist Jurisprudence," *Signs* 8, no. 4 (1983): 635 (hereafter, Second *Signs*); Robin West, *Caring for Justice* (New York: New York University Press, 1997); Combahee River Collective, "The Combahee River Collective Statement," in *Home Girls: A Black Feminist Anthology,* ed. Barbara Smith (New York: Kitchen Table/Women of Color Press, 1983; reprint, New Brunswick, N.J.: Rutgers University Press, 2000); Gayatri Chakravorty Spivak, "Can the Subaltern Speak?" in *Marxism and the Interpretation of Culture,* ed. Cary Nelson and Lawrence Grossberg (Urbana: University of Illinois Press, 1988), 271–313; Judith Butler, *Gender Trouble: Feminism and the Subversion of Identity* (New York: Routledge, 1990; reprint, with a new introduction, 1999); Butler, "Imitation and Gender Insubordination," in *Inside/Out: Lesbian Theories, Gay Theories,* ed. Diana Fuss (New York: Routledge, 1991), 13–31; Marianne Hirsch and Evelyn Fox Keller, eds., *Conflicts in Feminism* (New York: Routledge, 1990); Elisabeth Bronfen and Misha Kavka, eds., *Feminist Consequences: Theory for the New Century* (New York: Columbia University Press, 2001); Judith Butler and Joan W. Scott, eds., *Feminists Theorize the Political*

(New York: Routledge, 1992); Seyla Benhabib, Judith Butler, Drucilla Cornell, and Nancy Fraser, *Feminist Contentions: A Philosophical Exchange* (New York: Routledge, 1995); Elizabeth Weed and Naomi Schor, eds., *feminism meets queer theory* (Bloomington,: Indiana University Press, 1997) (originally published as *differences* 6 [Summer/Fall 1994]); and Butler, "Against Proper Objects," in Weed and Schor, *feminism meets queer theory*, 1–30. The book version of *feminism meets queer theory* differs in some ways from the journal publication; unless otherwise noted, page references are to the 1994 volume.

2. Gayle Rubin, "Thinking Sex: Notes for a Radical Theory of the Politics of Sexuality," in *Pleasure and Danger: Exploring Female Sexuality*, ed. Carole S. Vance (Boston: Routledge & Kegan Paul, 1984), 267–319; Gayle Rubin with Judith Butler, "Sexual Traffic: *Interview*," in Weed and Schor, *feminism meets queer theory*, 68–108 (hereafter, "*Interview*"); Michel Foucault, *The History of Sexuality*, vol. 1, *An Introduction*, trans. Robert Hurley (New York: Vintage Books, 1988) (hereafter, *Volume One*); Eve Kosofsky Sedgwick, *Epistemology of the Closet* (Berkeley and Los Angeles: University of California Press, 1990); Leo Bersani, "Is the Rectum a Grave?" in *AIDS: Cultural Analysis, Cultural Activism*, ed. Douglas Crimp (Cambridge, Mass.: MIT Press, 1988), 197–222 (this collection, including Bersani's essay, was originally published under the same title as *October 43* [Winter 1987]); Duncan Kennedy, "Sexual Abuse, Sexy Dressing, and the Eroticization of Domination," in Duncan Kennedy, *Sexy Dressing Etc.* (Cambridge, Mass.: Harvard University Press, 1993), 126–213 (originally published in *New England Law Review* 26 [1992]: 1309); Henry Abelove, Michèle Aina Barale, and David M. Halperin, eds., *The Lesbian and Gay Studies Reader* (New York: Routledge, 1993) (hereafter, the *Reader*); *Fear of a Queer Planet: Queer Politics and Social Theory*, ed. Michael Warner for the Social Text Collective (Minneapolis: University of Minnesota Press, 1993); Eve Kosofsky Sedgwick, *Tendencies* (Durham: Duke University Press, 1993), and Jay Prosser, *Second Skins: The Body Narratives of Transsexuality* (New York: Columbia University Press, 1998).

Before the Break

1. For an introduction to this nonce term for the physical difference between men and women, which I use throughout this part, see "A Sex Lexicon," 23–25, above.

2. For an introduction to these terms, which I also use throughout this part, see "m/f, m > f, and Carrying a Brief for f," 17–20, above.

3. Male power is, MacKinnon concluded, "total on the one side and a delu-sion on the other." First *Signs*, 542. The inequality of women is structural: "The inequality approach . . . sees women's situation as a structural problem of enforced inferiority that needs to be radically altered." MacKinnon, *Sexual Harassment of Working Women: A Case of Sex Discrimination* (New Haven: Yale University Press, 1979), 5.

4. The parallels with Black Nationalism are remarkable. See Harold Cruse, *The Crisis of the Negro Intellectual* (New York: Morrow, 1967); Gary Peller, "Race Consciousness," *Duke Law Journal* (1990): 758.

5. Second *Signs*, 638.

6. Ibid.

7. First *Signs*, 543.

8. Ibid., 536.

9. MacKinnon, *Toward a Feminist Theory of the State* (Cambridge, Mass.: Harvard University Press, 1989), 181–82 (footnote omitted).

10. Note the difference between the critical stance MacKinnon adopted vis-à-vis the state in 1982 and the following formulation a little more than ten years later: "The best thing about criminal law is that the state does it, so women do not have to. The worst thing about criminal law is that the state does not do it, so women still have to." MacKinnon, "Prostitution and Civil Rights," *Michigan Journal of Gender and Law* 1 (1993): 13, 29.

11. MacKinnon, *Toward a Feminist Theory of the State*, 155–70.

12. Ibid., 248–49.

13. Some may object to my narrative that MacKinnon published her femi-nist *legal* theory classic, *Sexual Harassment of Working Women*, in 1979, well before First *Signs* appeared. But according to MacKinnon herself, she had writ-ten First *Signs before* publishing *Sexual Harassment*. MacKinnon, *Toward a Feminist Theory of the State*, xiv. It may well be that the fallings-away from real radicalism detectable in Second *Signs*—and dramatically confirmed in subse-quent revised republications of parts of the *Signs* work like *Toward a Feminist Theory of the State*—were produced in the context of her work on *Sexual Ha-rassment of Working Women*.

14. I rely on the version of the Indianapolis ordinance published in the Seventh Circuit's decision holding it to be unconstitutional. *American Booksell-ers Ass'n v. Hudnut*, 771 F. 2d 323 (7th Cir. 1985), affirming on new grounds the prior decision below, 598 F. Supp. 1316 (S.D. Ind. 1984), and affirmed without opinion by the U.S. Supreme Court, 475 U.S. 1001 (1986) (mem.).

An edited but apparently more complete version of the ordinance appears in *In Harm's Way: The Pornography Civil Rights Hearing*, ed. MacKinnon and Andrea Dworkin (Cambridge, Mass.: Harvard University Press, 1997), 438–57.

15. For example: "In 1982, Andrea Dworkin and I advanced our equality approach to pornography through our ordinance allowing civil suits for sex discrimination *by those who can prove harm through pornography*." MacKinnon and Ronald Dworkin, "Pornography: An Exchange," *New York Review of Books*, March 3, 1994, 47–49 (emphasis added); reprinted in Drucilla Cornell, *Feminism and Pornography* (Oxford: Oxford University Press, 2000), 121–29, 121.

16. *Hudnut*, 771. F.2d at 324.

17. MacKinnon, "Pornography, Civil Rights, and Speech," *Harvard Civil Rights–Civil Liberties Law Review* 20 (1985): 1, 60; see also MacKinnon, "The Roar on the Other Side of Silence," in MacKinnon and Dworkin, *In Harm's Way*, 3–24, for a general defense of the assertion that the hearings were conclusive on this point.

18. Quoted in Paul Brest and Ann Vandenberg, "Politics, Feminism, and the Constitution: The Anti-Pornography Movement in Minneapolis," *Stanford Law Review* 39 (1987): 607, 613.

19. MacKinnon, *Toward a Feminist Theory of the State*, 248.

20. For an introduction to my use of the term "convergentist," see "Convergentism and Divergentism," 25–26, above.

21. *Oncale v. Sundowner Offshore Services, Inc.*, 118 S.Ct. 998 (1998).

22. I offer alternatives to MacKinnon's reading of *Oncale* in Part Three, "Taking a Break to Decide (I)," 290–303.

23. Brief of National Organization on Male Victimization, Inc., et al., in *Oncale*, No. 96–568 (August 11, 1997). Reprinted in *U.C.L.A. Women's Law Journal* 8 (1997): 9.

24. MacKinnon, *Toward a Feminist Theory of the State*, 248.

25. Wendy Brown, *States of Injury: Power and Freedom in Late Modernity* (Princeton: Princeton University Press, 1995), 131.

26. Gillian Rose reflects in her memoir *Love's Work* that "feminism never offered me any help" understanding her "fulfilled love relationships . . . with two younger men," "[f]or it fails to address the power of women as well as their powerlessness, and the response of both women and men to that power." She even seems to attribute her regretted decisions to end the relationships to her feminism: "Feminism does not speak of the woman with the gift and power

of Active Intelligence—to speak in the terms of Avicenna's angelology—who gives love and draws it to her, enabling and difficult. Tarrying in the negative, I accounted myself too bounteous and too restricting. And so, with much pain, I broke away, ending, not friendship, but the throes of erotic and ethical love." Gillian Rose, *Love's Work: A Reckoning with Life* (New York: Schocken Books, 1995), 140–41. Thanks to Libby Adler for drawing my attention to this mournful reflection on feminism and love.

27. Thus pornography poses a question not of morality but of power. MacKinnon, "Not a Moral Issue," *Yale Law and Policy Review* 2 (1984): 321. Similarly, MacKinnon has written that, "[i]n feminist analysis, a rape is not an isolated or individual or moral transgression but a terrorist act within a systematic context of group subjection, like lynching." Second *Signs*, 654 n. 41.

28. Virginia Woolf, *A Room of One's Own* (New York: Harcourt, Brace, Jovanovich, 1957), 76–77.

29. See "Weakening Feminism and So Harming Real Women," 316–19, below.

30. Adrienne Rich, "Compulsory Heterosexuality and Lesbian Existence," *Signs* 5 (1980): 631.

31. *Caring*, 288, quoting Ellen Bass and L. Thornton, eds., *I Never Told Anyone: Writings by Women Survivors of Child Sexual Abuse* (New York: Harper & Row, 1983), 51.

32. *Caring*, 288, quoting Bass and Thornton, *I Never Told Anyone*, 53 (emphasis added).

33. Bersani, *Homos* (Cambridge, Mass.: Harvard University Press, 1995), 103.

34. *Caring*, 289–90, quoting Luce Irigaray, *This Sex Which Is Not One*, trans. Catherine Porter with Carolyn Burke (Ithaca, N.Y.: Cornell University Press, 1985), 213. I have corrected West's page citation.

35. Gilligan, *In a Different Voice: Psychological Theory and Women's Development* (Cambridge, Mass.: Harvard University Press, 1993).

36. For a particularly interesting encounter making this disagreement manifest, see the colloquy of MacKinnon and Gilligan with Ellen C. DuBois, Mary C. Dunlap, and Carrie Menkel-Meadow, "Feminist Discourse, Moral Values, and the Law—A Conversation," *Buffalo Law Review* 34 (1985): 11.

37. This heterosexualization of feminism (and moral theory) would, by the end of the 1980s, come in for angry criticism from many feminist quarters and from emerging gay and lesbian theories alike.

38. Note that in order to do this, she also had to take the story of moral development *attributed* to men by (male) moral theory as really in fact descriptive of men's way of moral life.

39. Gilligan, *In a Different Voice*, "Letter to Readers, 1993," xiii (second emphasis added).

40. Though there is a subdifference here: MacKinnon sees the feminization of a man as an injury, while cultural feminism sees it as an instance of moral uplift.

41. For a rich description and canny critique of this move, see Amy Adler, "What's Left? Hate Speech, Pornography, and the Problem for Artistic Expression," *California Law Review* 84 (1996): 1499.

42. Though they make quite different arguments, and though neither Kennedy analyzes feminism at all, I want to acknowledge Ann Snitow, "A Gender Diary," in Hirsch and Keller, *Conflicts in Feminism*, 9–43; David Kennedy, "When Renewal Repeats: Thinking against the Box," *N.Y.U. Journal of International Law and Politics* 32 (2000): 335; and Duncan Kennedy, "Form and Substance in Private Law Adjudication," *Harvard Law Review* 89 (1976): 1685, and "A Semiotics of Legal Argument," *Syracuse Law Review* 43 (1991): 75, reprinted in *Collected Courses of the Academy of European Law*, vol. 3, bk. 2, pp. 309–65 (Dordrecht, Netherlands: Kluwer Academic Publishers, 1994), for helping me here by representing fields of thought and action as dynamic in this way.

43. The reprint of the Statement that I am using (see n. 1 to Part Two's introduction, above, for details) indicates that it is "dated April 1977" (274 n. 1). In a pamphlet republication of the Statement issued in 1986, Collective member Barbara Smith provides a foreword that gives the Statement's early publication history. The Combahee River Collective, *The Combahee River Collective Statement: Black Feminist Organizing in the Seventies and Eighties* (New York: Kitchen Table/Women of Color Press, 1986), 3.

44. "This focusing upon our own oppression is embodied in the concept of identity politics" (267).

45. Michel Foucault and Gilles Deleuze, "Intellectuals and Power: A Conversation between Michel Foucault and Gilles Deleuze," in Foucault, *Language, Counter-Memory, Practice: Selected Essays and Interviews*, ed. Donald F. Bouchard, trans. Bouchard and Sherry Simon (Ithaca, N.Y.: Cornell University Press, 1977), 205–17. Spivak provides, it seems, her own translation. Bouchard and Simon translate this passage as follows: "[T]he intellectual discovered that the

masses no longer need him to gain knowledge: they *know* perfectly well, without illusion; they know far better that he and they are certainly capable of expressing themselves" (207).

46. Spivak, "Can the Subaltern Speak?" 277. Spivak offers her own translation here as well. A slightly different version appears in Karl Marx, *The 18th Brumaire of Louis Bonaparte* (New York: International Publishers, 1963), 124. The translator of this edition is apparently anonymous. See "MacKinnon/Spivak/Warner/Sedgwick," 237–44, for a discussion of this genealogically important passage.

47. She quotes from and repeatedly cites Pandurang Vaman Kane's multivolume *History of Dharmasastra (Ancient and Medieval Religious and Civil Law in India)* (Poona: Bhandarkar Oriental Research Institute, 1962–75).

48. West, *Caring*, 19.

49. *Webster's Third International Dictionary*, s.v. "catachresis"; *The New Princeton Encyclopedia of Poetry and Poetics*, ed. Alex Preminger and T.V.F. Brogan, with Frank J. Warnke, O. B. Hardison, Jr., and Earl Miner (Princeton: Princeton University Press, 1993), s.v. "catachresis." The *Princeton Encyclopedia* defines this figure as "[t]he misapplication of a word, esp. to produce a strained or mixed metaphor. . . . a deliberate wresting of a term from its proper signification for effect."

THE BREAK

1. "Gay Rights and Identity Imitation: Issues in the Ethics of Representation," in *The Politics of Law: A Progressive Critique*, ed. David Kairys, 3rd ed. (New York: Basic Books, 1998), 115–46; also published as " 'Like Race' Arguments," in *What's Left of Theory? New Work on the Politics of Literary Theory*, ed. Judith Butler, John Guillory, and Kendall Thomas, Proceedings of the English Institute (New York: Routledge, 2001), 40–74.

2. Judith Butler, "The Lesbian Phallus and the Morphological Imaginary," in Butler, *Bodies That Matter: On the Discursive Limits of "Sex"* (New York: Routledge, 1993), 57–91; Judith Halberstam, *Female Masculinity* (Durham: Duke University Press, 1998); Richard Rambuss, "Machinehead," *Camera Obscura* 42 (1999): 96; Bersani, *Homos*.

3. Gayle Rubin, "The Traffic in Women: Notes on the 'Political Economy' of Sex," in *Toward an Anthropology of Women*, ed. Rayna R. Reiter (New York: Monthly Review Press, 1975).

4. Rubin's article was read by many feminists (not by Rubin herself) to underwrite a distinction between essential and constructed dimensions of the sex/gender system, in which the latter were seriously immutable and lawlike, and the former "merely" cultural and maintained at everyone's option or through sheer male bad faith. This confounding of the natural with the essential, and the constructed with the easily altered, became a confusing feature of the long-running debate in feminism about essentialism and constructivism. Until feminists realized that it might be much easier to modify the human body than the culture that sets the terms of its meanings, this formulation animated a brief, hectic, ultimately delusional period of feminist optimism, in which liberation seemed to be merely a matter of changing some bad conceptual habits, and in which everyone could profess radicalism without having to worry that doing so might incur a Mephistophelian price. That period ended long ago.

5. For one version, see Pamela Haag, " 'Putting Your Body on the Line': The Question of Violence, Victims, and the Legacies of Second-Wave Feminism," *differences* 8, no. 2 (Summer 1996): 23–67.

6. Lisa Duggan and Nan D. Hunter, *Sex Wars: Sexual Dissent and Political Culture* (New York: Routledge, 1995); Alice Echols, "The Taming of the Id: Feminist Sexual Politics, 1968–1983," in Vance, *Pleasure and Danger*, 50–72.

7. Rubin and Butler, "*Interview*," 78.

8. Perpetual thanks to Alan Hyde for this very helpful point.

9. "The Ethics of the Concern for Self as a Practice of Freedom," trans. P. Aranov and D. McGrawth, in Foucault, *Ethics: Subjectivity and Truth*, ed. Paul Rabinow, vol. 1 of *The Essential Works of Michel Foucault 1954–1984*, ed. Rabinow (New York: New Press, 1994), 281–301, 293, 291. Rabinow indicates that the translation has been amended, but not by whom or to what extent. He also indicates that this interview was conducted on January 20, 1984, and was first published in *Concordia: Revista internacional de filosophia* 6 (July–December 1984): 96–116.

10. François Ewald, "Norms, Discipline, and the Law," in *Law and the Order of Culture*, ed. Robert Post (Berkeley and Los Angeles: University of California Press, 1991), 138–61, 155, 156.

11. MacKinnon, First *Signs*, 537–38.

12. MacKinnon, Second *Signs*, 636.

13. Michel Foucault, *The History of Sexuality*, vol. 2, *The Use of Pleasure*, trans. Robert Hurley (New York: Random House, 1985), 7.

14. Foucault, *Remarks on Marx: Conversations with Duccio Trombadori*, trans. R. James Goldstein and James Cascaito (New York: Semiotext(e), 1991), 27.

15. MacKinnon, "Points against Postmodernism," *Chicago-Kent Law Review* 75 (2000): 687, 688–89, 691, 692–93 (italics in original; bold emphases added).

16. *Caring*, 5.

17. Foucault, "The Ethics of the Concern for Self," 283.

18. *Volume One*, 96.

19. Foucault, "The Ethics of the Concern for Self," 282–84. Elsewhere, Foucault indicates that, even if power becomes domination, it does not lose all fluidity: domination is merely a *kind* of power relation, more "incalcitrant," more "taken for granted and consolidated" than most, but even in conditions of domination one finds both "a general structure of power" *and* a "strategic situation." Caste and class domination are thus imaginable as power relations; the reciprocal appeal of power and strategy that characterizes more local confrontations reappears in them "in a massive and universalizing form, at the level of the whole social body." Foucault, "The Subject and Power," in Hubert L. Dreyfus and Paul Rabinow, *Michel Foucault: Beyond Structuralism and Hermeneutics*, 2nd ed. (Chicago: University of Chicago Press, 1983), 208–26, 226. This essay is now also available in Foucault, *Power*, ed. James D. Faubion, trans. Robert Hurley, vol. 3 in *The Essential Works of Michel Foucault*, 326–48.

20. Foucault, "The Ethics of the Concern for the Self," 283.

21. Sedgwick, "Gosh, Boy George," 16.

22. See 136, above.

23. Indeed, she almost did: in First *Signs* we find that, thanks to feminism, "[a]perspectivity is revealed as a strategy of male hegemony" (537).

24. "Is the Rectum a Grave?" was first published in 1987, and the essay states that at least part of it was being penned in October 1987 (202 n. 4).

25. *Homos*, 103.

26. I'm going to analyze "Is the Rectum a Grave?" in the present tense: the Bersani who "speaks" in these pages is the Bersani implied by the text as understood by me. Note, however, that it was written before Butler and Sedgwick nearly simultaneously produced their queer critique of feminism, and that Bersani reformulated and extended his 1987 argument in light of their work and related developments in feminism, postmodernism, and elsewhere, and also expressed a different understanding of the political stakes of his project, in his 1995 book *Homos*. And he reformulated the relationship of the self

to masochism in his subsequent essay "Sociality and Sexuality," *Critical Inquiry* 26 (Summer 2000): 641–56.

27. "Is the Rectum a Grave?" 212, 213, quoting Foucault, "Sexual Choice, Sexual Act: An Interview with Michel Foucault," *Salmagundi*, nos. 58–59 (Fall 1982–Winter 1983); and MacKinnon, *Toward a Feminist Theory of the State*, 212. A more accessible version of "Sexual Choice, Sexual Act" is now available, in Foucault, *Ethics: Subjectivity and Truth*, 141–56.

Characteristically, MacKinnon made this point in a more subtle and hypothetical way in First *Signs*: there, she poses "the feminist **question of how** female desire *itself* can become the lust for self-annihilation" (534 n. 44, bold emphasis added).

28. Bersani's images are pretty gripping. In both the Victorian representation of female prostitution and the contemporary representation of gay male transmission of HIV, "[w]omen and gay men spread their legs with an unquenchable appetite for destruction" (211); homophobia was motivated to exile hemophiliac Ryan White because it supplanted the image of his childish innocence with "the infinitely more seductive and intolerable image of a grown man, legs high in the air, unable to refuse the suicidal ecstasy of being a woman" (212).

29. "Is the Rectum a Grave?" 215. At 80, above, I noted that MacKinnon's more radical form of feminism is much less capable of assimilating to liberalism than is cultural feminism, because it lacks cultural feminism's affirmation that some sex between men and women has women's virtues. Bersani's essay notes this splitting as well: "The argument against pornography remains . . . a liberal argument as long as it is assumed that pornography violates the natural conjunction of sex with tenderness and love. It becomes a much more disturbingly radical argument when the indictment against pornography is identified with an indictment against sex itself" (214).

30. See Claude Lévi-Strauss, "The Science of the Concrete," in Lévi-Strauss, *The Savage Mind* (Chicago: University of Chicago Press, 1966), 1–33.

31. For my own etymology of "perversion" as a term of approbation, see "In Memoriam: David Charny," *Harvard Law Review* 114 (2001): 2223.

32. In *Homos*, 216–18, Bersani intensified these positions—which are only implicit in "Is the Rectum a Grave?"—reaffirming the distinctive status of male and gay male sexuality, especially with respect to the penis, masculinity, misogyny, etc., and resisting Sedgwick's and Butler's queer anti-identitarianism (31–76).

33. "Is the Rectum a Grave?" 222; quoting Simon Watney, *Policing Desire: Pornography, AIDS, and the Media* (Minneapolis: University of Minnesota Press, 1987), 126 (emphasis in original).

34. Bersani evidently came to some critique of this moment in his work; the moves I am about to describe are almost completely absent from *Homos*, which frames the relationship between the erotic and the political in much more oblique and minoritizing terms.

35. Sharon Marcus, "Fighting Bodies, Fighting Words: A Theory and Politics of Rape Prevention," in Butler and Scott, *Feminists Theorize the Political*, 385–403, 389; Butler, "Against Proper Objects," 12. See "An Experiment in Political Stylistics (do try this at home)," 192–207, below.

36. *Homos* at 37–52.

37. And of race, though Bersani is much more willing to probe and question antiracist than feminist presumptions.

38. Butler, "Against Proper Objects," 12.

39. Mary Joe Frug, *Postmodern Legal Feminism* (New York: Routledge, 1992).

40. Robin West, "Deconstructing the CLS-Fem Split," *Wisconsin Women's Law Journal* 2 (1986): 85.

41. Duncan Kennedy, "Psycho-Social CLS: A Comment on the Cardozo Symposium," *Cardozo Law Review* 6 (1985): 1013.

42. West, "CLS-Fem Split," 91.

43. Kennedy, "Psycho-Social CLS," 1020.

44. Note the exchange of danger supposed by this formulation. Shifting the line between punished and tolerated abuse toward the latter shifts the burden of taking precautions against abuse from women to men, where it becomes not only the burden of compliance with antiabuse rules, but also the burden of protecting oneself from false and mistaken accusations of abuse, the burden of desolidarizing with other men, etc.

45. Duncan Kennedy, "A Semiotics of Critique," *Cardozo Law Review* 22 (2001): 1147, 1169, 1173.

46. MacKinnon, Second *Signs*, 644–45, 655–58.

47. For the traditions upon which Kennedy's approach rests, see Kennedy, "Sexy Dressing," 236–37 nn. 9, 12. Put these footnotes together and you have a short list of classics in legal realism. For an anthology introducing many of them along with classics in other traditions of legal thought, see David Kennedy and William W. Fisher, eds. *The Canon of American Legal Thought* (Princeton: Princeton University Press, 2006).

48. Robert Mnookin and Lewis Kornhauser, "Bargaining in the Shadow of the Law: The Case of Divorce," *Yale Law Journal* 88 (1979): 950.

49. Susan R. Peterson, "Coercion and Rape: The State as a Male Protection Racket," in *Feminism and Philosophy*, ed. Mary Vetterling-Braggin, Frederick A. Elliston, and Jane English (Totowa, N.J.: Littlefield, Adams, 1977), 360–71.

50. Rich, "Compulsory Heterosexuality and Lesbian Existence."

51. To support this claim Kennedy cites a passage from MacKinnon that falls just a bit short of it: "Sex feeling good may mean that one is enjoying one's subordination; it would not be the first time. Or it may mean that one has glimpsed freedom, a rare and valuable and contradictory event." MacKinnon, *Feminism Unmodified: Discourses on Life and Law* (Cambridge, Mass.: Harvard University Press, 1987), 218. A wonderful passage, but strictly speaking it does not affirm the egalitarian possibilities of women's heterosexual experience; rather, in it MacKinnon rigorously maintains her stance of *not knowing* the difference between rape and a good fuck.

52. For Bersani's investment in Freud, see Bersani, *The Freudian Body: Psychoanalysis and Art* (New York: Columbia University Press, 1986), chap. 2, especially 38–39; for Kennedy's reliance on Ferdinand de Saussure's *Course in General Linguistics*, ed. Charles Bally and Albert Sechehaye, trans. Roy Harris (LaSalle, Ill.: Open Court, 1986), see Kennedy, "A Semiotics of Legal Argument."

53. *Volume One*, 92–96, 157, 159.

54. "A Semiotics of Critique," 1147–89.

FEMINISM AND ITS OTHERS

1. I refer readers, again, to Wiegman, "Feminism, Institutionalism, and the Idiom of Failure."

2. Kennedy, "A Semiotics of Legal Argument," 1169, 1173.

3. Elizabeth Potter, *Gender and Boyle's Law of Gases* (Bloomington: Indiana University Press, 2001).

4. "[R]epetition of a word or words at the beginning of two or more successive clauses esp. for rhetorical or poetic effect." *Webster's Third New International Dictionary Unabridged*, s.v. "anaphora."

5. Butler notes that "MacKinnon's view of feminism is one which makes free use of the copula in which causal relations are elliptically asserted through the postulation of equivalences, i.e. within the structures of male dominance, conceived exclusively as heterosexual, sex is gender is sexual positionality." Butler, "Against Proper Objects," 12.

6. MacKinnon, First *Signs*, 530–31 (emphasis added). The quoted passage sums up an even more capacious list: "If the literature on sex roles and the investigations of particular issues are read in light of each other, each element of the female *gender* stereotype is revealed as, in fact, *sexual*. Vulnerability means the appearance/reality of easy sexual access; passivity means receptivity and disabled resistance, enforced by trained physical weakness; softness means pregnability by something hard. Incompetence seeks help as vulnerability seeks shelter, inviting the embrace that becomes the invasion, trading exclusive access for protection . . . from the same access. Domesticity nurtures the consequent progeny, proof of potency, and ideally waits at home dressed in saran wrap. Woman's infantilization evokes pedophilia; fixation on dismembered body parts (the breast man, the leg man) evokes fetishism; idolization of vapidity, necrophilia. Narcissism insures that woman identifies with that image of herself that man holds up: 'Hold still, we are going to do your portrait, so that you can begin looking like it right away.' Masochism means that pleasure in violation becomes her sensuality. Lesbians so violate the sexuality implicit in female gender stereotypes as not to be considered women at all.

"Socially, femaleness means femininity, which means attractiveness to men, which means sexual attractiveness, which means sexual availability on male terms. What defines woman as such is what turns men on."

7. MacKinnon, "Prostitution and Civil Rights," 31 (emphases added).

8. Kathleen Gough, "The Origin of the Family," in Reiter, *Toward an Anthropology of Women*, 51–76, 69–70.

9. Rich, "Compulsory Heterosexuality and Lesbian Existence," 638–40 (footnotes omitted).

10. E.M.W. Tillyard, *Milton* (New York: Collier Books, 1967), 220.

11. Marcus, "Fighting Bodies, Fighting Words," 389.

12. Jorge Luis Borges, "The Analytical Language of John Wilkins," in *Other Inquisitions 1937–52*, trans. Ruth L. C. Simms (1964; New York: Simon and Schuster, 1965), 103.

13. Michel Foucault, *The Order of Things: An Archaelogy of the Human Sciences* (New York: Vintage Books, 1973), xv.

14. Rubin, "*Interview*," 76–77 (emphasis added).

15. *Conflicts* includes two coauthored essays; both are by prominent feminists carrying on disputes that they had famously originated elsewhere. The passion, aggression, pain, and self-doubt that marked these conflicts are made explicit in these continuing elaborations of them. Peggy Kamuf and Nancy K.

Miller, "Parisian Letters: Between Feminism and Deconstruction" (121–33), and Jane Gallop, Marianne Hirsch, and Nancy K. Miller, "Criticizing Feminist Criticism" (349–69). Several essays focus on the intersection of antiracism with feminism. One of them is the transcribed conversation between two women, one identified as black and the other as white. Mary Childers and Bell Hooks [I am following the typography of the text; typically hooks prefers lowercase spellings of her name], "A Conversation about Race and Class" (60–81). But paranoid structuralism and the moralized mandate to converge are not ruling norms in the volume: in another essay Evelynn Hammonds, often elsewhere identified as black, and Helen Longino, often identified elsewhere as white, coauthor an essay entitled "Conflicts and Tensions in the Feminist Study of Gender and Science" in the course of which neither of them felt any moral or lyric obligation to give herself a racial identification or to raise the question of how the "conflicts and tensions" in feminist science studies were racialized (164–83). *Conflicts* includes an essay by a man, and an essay by a woman taking serious, indeed personal, objections to it. Thomas Laqueur, "The Facts of Fatherhood" (205–21); Sara Ruddick, "Thinking about Fathers" (222–33). The editors explicitly worry over the fact that this exchange is the most bitter of all those performed by their contributors (377).

16. By comparison, *Consequences* is entirely composed of monographic essays; the sole exception is the coeditors' interview of Cornell. No apparent men appear in the table of contents. I describe Cornell's management of racial difference below. I will also show that the essays disagree, but that no one comments on that.

17. Teresa de Lauretis's contribution can be read as an attempt to produce this tension: "Upping the Anti [*sic*] in Feminist Theory," 255–70.

18. Feminists, the "we" of the volume, are "those readers/writers/thinkers/doers, engaged in different projects and struggles, who have invested and continue to invest in feminism as an enabling term" (x). Feminism is not "post": "The change marked by 'post' . . . happened while we were *doing* feminism; the change happened *because* we were doing feminism. The problem is not the death or the end of feminism, but, rather, coming to terms with the fact that its political, strategic, and interpretive power has been so great as to produce innumerable modes of doing" (xi). "[G]iven that feminism lacks a single origin as much as a single definition, it can also have no single moment of ending" (xi). "Calling this collection *Feminist Consequences* suggests that all we have to make us a 'we,' to allow us to insert ourselves into a relation to feminism, is

an investment in the history and resonances of such insertions themselves" (xii). "Being in (feminist) history means that these notions of representation, self-identity, and lived experience have been subject to criticism, and this criticism has left its indelible mark on the possible future projects of feminism itself. This collection thus seeks to reflect the way that feminism has been moving on through its own self-questioning" (xvii).

19. *Consequences,* xxi (bracketed insertion in original). Kavka quotes from Biddy Martin's contribution to the volume, "Success and Its Failures," 353–80, 371.

20. "The Subject of True Feeling: Pain, Privacy and Politics," in *Consequences,* 126–61, 148.

21. Mieke Bal, "Enfolding Feminism," in *Consequences,* 321–52; Judith Butler, "The End of Sexual Difference?" in *Consequences,* 414–34.

22. For full statements of Cornell's postmodernist convergentist liberal humanist feminism, see Cornell, *Beyond Accommodation: Ethical Feminism, Deconstruction and the Law* (New York: Routledge, 1991); *The Imaginary Domain: Abortion, Pornography and Sexual Harassment* (New York: Routledge, 1995); and *At the Heart of Freedom: Feminism, Sex, and Equality* (Princeton: Princeton University Press, 1998).

23. David A. J. Richards, *Identity and the Case for Gay Rights: Race, Gender and Religion as Analogies* (Chicago: University of Chicago Press, 1999).

24. Benhabib, "Feminism and Postmodernism: An Uneasy Alliance," in Benhabib et al., *Feminist Contentions,* 17–34, 20.

25. Scott, "Experiences," in Butler and Scott, *Feminists Theorize the Political,* 22–40. This is a shorter version of Scott's "The Evidence of Experience," *Critical Inquiry* 17 (Summer 1991): 773–97.

26. I think it's no accident that Scott and Butler included Marcus's "Fighting Bodies, Fighting Words," a classic exploration of this worry in feminism, in *Feminists Theorize the Political.* For a discussion of Marcus's argument, see "An Experiment in Political Stylistics (Do Try This at Home)," 199, above.

27. Delaney, *The Motion of Light in Water: Sex and Science Fiction Writing in the East Village, 1957–65* (New York: New American Library, 1988).

28. See "Marianne Hirsch and Evelyn Fox Keller, *Conflicts in Feminism,* and Elisabeth Bronfen and Misha Kavka, *Feminist Consequences,*" 208–21, above.

29. I draw my title, "Around 1993," from Jane Gallop, *Around 1981: Academic Feminist Literary Theory* (New York: Routledge, 1992), also a genealogy of anthologies.

30. The *Reader*, 3–61. The selection from *Epistemology of the Closet* is Sedgwick's introductory argument that the closet is a series of double-binding and paradoxically capacitating contradictions; she did not contribute her reflections on the relations between feminist and antihomophobic thought.

31. Full disclosure: I published an essay in *Fear of a Queer Planet*.

32. Without at all suggesting that Warner's more steadfast loyalty to feminism, and Sedgwick's to gay identity, are disingenuous or merely strategic, I would note that they chiasmatically mirror Warner's public persona *as a man* and Sedgwick's *as a heterosexually married woman*. Both pay homage to settled identity investments being made "over there." Query, however, why this homage seems ethically due.

33. For a more playful episode, see Sedgwick's essay "Divinity: A Dossier, a Performance Piece, a Little-Understood Emotion (written with Michael Moon)" (215–51). In this dialogue between Sedgwick and Moon about John Waters's divine (cross-dressing) diva Divine, Moon promises on behalf of both of them that they will "speak" the "subjectivities" involved in "my own experiences of divinity as a fat woman, and Eve's as a gay man" (218).

34. The list is quoted at 202–3, above.

35. See, for instance, Warner, *American Sermons: The Pilgrims to Martin Luther King, Jr.* (New York: The Library of America, 1999); and Sedgwick, *Touching Feeling: Affect, Pedagogy, Performativity* (Durham: Duke University Press, 2003).

36. MacKinnon, First *Signs*, 535 n. 48. MacKinnon quotes Marx's *The Poverty of Philosophy* (New York: International Publishers, 1963), but her page reference cannot be right. For the "class for itself" formulation, see 125, 173.

37. I am relying for dates on Robert C. Tucker, ed., *The Marx-Engels Reader*, 2nd ed. (New York: Norton, 1978), xv–xviii.

38. Etienne Balibar, "In Search of the Proletariat: The Notion of Class Politics in Marx," in Balibar, *Masses, Classes, Ideas: Studies on Politics and Philosophy before and after Marx*, trans. James Swenson (New York: Routledge, 1994), 125–49.

39. See Andrew Parker's contribution to *Fear of a Queer Planet*, "Unthinking Sex: Marx, Engels, and the Scene of Writing," 19–41. These pages also rely on Parker's presentation on *The 18th Brumaire* at a Program on Law and Social Thought *Book Trouble* event at Harvard Law School in February 2004.

40. Marx, *The 18th Brumaire*, 124 (emphasis added).

41. See, for instance, Max Weber, "Class, Status and Party," in *From Max Weber: Essays in Sociology*, trans. and ed. H. H. Gerth and C. Wright Mills (New York: Oxford University Press, 1946), 180–85.

42. Warner, *The Trouble with Normal: Sex, Politics and the Ethics of Queer Life* (New York: Free Press, 1999).

43. Warner, *Fear of a Queer Planet*, xxiii–iv. I am construing this on the assumption that Warner meant "maintain," not "contain."

44. Butler's essay "Against Proper Objects" was the introduction to the *differences* version (1994, 1); she demurs from that role in the 1997 book (1), and Weed provides the new introduction (vii–xiii).

45. Butler, "Against Proper Objects," 1–30; Rosi Braidotti with Butler, "Feminism by Any Other Name: *Interview*" (31–67); and Rubin with Butler, "*Interview*." The book contains a sustained subdebate about whether "sexual difference" feminism derived from Lacan can mediate the points of conflict between feminism and queer theory. Braidotti and Butler say yes but disagree about whether the structuralism of Lacan's "language" is a problem (21–23, 51–52); Weed says yes as long as "sexual difference" reproduces a feminist structuralist commitment to male domination (Weed, "The More Things Change," 266–91, 285); and Rubin says no, objecting to structuralist modes generally (they are "a trap") and using the term to signify something quite different—the diversity of sexual practices and subjectivities (74, 76, 83, 90).

46. Evelynn Hammonds, "Black (W)holes and the Geometry of Black Female Sexuality" (136–56); Trevor Hope, "Melancholic Modernity: The Hom(m)osexual Symptom and the Homosocial Corpse" (187–213); Braidotti, "Revisiting Male Thanatica: *Response*" (214–22); and Hope, "The 'Returns' of Cartography: Mapping Identity-In(-)Difference: *Response*" (223–26).

47. Elizabeth Grosz, "The Labors of Love. Analyzing Perverse Desire: An Interrogation of Teresa de Lauretis's *The Practice of Love*" (292–314); de Lauretis, "Habit Changes: *Response*" (315–33). The quotation is from de Lauretis (315).

48. Kim Michasiw, "Camp, Masculinity, Masquerade" (157–86).

49. Carole-Anne Tyler, "Passing: Narcissism, Identity, and Difference" (227–65).

50. See 149, above.

51. Butler's idea here is firmly built into postmodernizing-feminist resistance to the queer Break. It is repeated with formal exactitude by two comments on an article I published advocating that we Take a Break in the form

of producing and admiring Queer Theory by Men: Ranjana Khanna, "Signatures of the Impossible," *Duke Journal of Gender Law and Policy* 11 (2004): 69, and Robyn Wiegman, "Dear Ian," *Duke Journal of Gender Law and Policy* 11 (2004): 93.

52. The *Reader*'s "elision" of gender from "sex" is a "repudiation" (1994, 4) or an "erasure" (1997, 6); the *Reader* subjects the "signification of sexual difference" to "a refusal, perhaps a repudiation" (1994, 4) *and* "an elision" (1997, 6).

53. Butler poses this question at a lower level of generality than my context would suggest: she was challenging the idea that "gay and lesbian studies" could harbor Rubin's "expansive and coalitional sense of 'sexual minorities' " (14).

54. Introduction, xi.

55. "Against Proper Objects," 27 n. 8.

56. Judith Butler, *Antigone's Claim: Kinship between Life and Death* (New York: Columbia University Press, 2000); "Is Kinship Always Already Heterosexual?" in Butler, *Undoing Gender* (New York: Routledge, 2004), 102–30, and in *Left Legalism/Left Critique*, ed. Wendy Brown and Janet Halley (Durham, N.C.: Duke University Press, 2002), 229–59.

57. Judith Butler, *The Psychic Life of Power: Theories in Subjection* (Stanford: Stanford University Press, 1997).

58. "*Interview,*" 91. Citation omitted; Rubin is quoting from *Volume One* at 106.

59. "*Interview,*" 92, quoting from *Volume One* at 107–8.

60. Arguably the tradition goes back, in the West, at least as far as Tieresias. Prosser dates the first surgical transition to 1939–45, when f-to-m Michael Dillon persuaded his doctors to prescribe testosterone and conduct mastectomies and phalloplasty (10).

61. *Second Skins*, 9, quoting Carroll Riddell, "Divided Sisterhood: A Critical Review of Janice Raymond's *The Transsexual Empire*," in *Blending Genders: Social Aspects of Cross-Dressing and Sex-Changing*, ed. Richard Ekins and Dave King (London: Routledge, 1996), 189.

62. *Paris Is Burning*, dir. Jennie Livingston (Miramax, 1990); Butler, "Gender Is Burning: Questions of Appropriation and Subversion," in Butler, *Bodies That Matter*, 121–40; Prosser, *Second Skins*, 49, also 53–54.

63. Prosser is depending here on the distinction made in the early chapters of J. L. Austin's *How to Do Things with Words* (Cambridge, Mass.: Harvard

University Press, 1962), 1–52, between "constative" utterances, which designate things, and "performative" ones, which *do* things. The difference, say,
between "The cat is on the mat" and "I thee wed." Austin gradually decon-
structed and finally junked the distinction in later chapters.

64. Prosser, *Second Skins*, 25; quoting Scott Long, "The Loneliness of
Camp," in *Camp Grounds: Style and Homosexuality*, ed. David Bergman (Am-
herst: University of Massachusetts Press, 1993), 79.

65. "*Interview*," 102–4; "Thinking Sex," 303.

TAKING A BREAK TO DECIDE (I)

1. See 54–57, above.

2. *Twyman v. Twyman*, 855 S.W.2d 619 (Tex. 1993).

3. Mark Kelman and Gillian Lester, *Jumping the Queue: An Inquiry into
the Legal Treatment of Students with Learning Disabilities* (Cambridge, Mass.:
Harvard University Press, 1997). The last chapter of the book is reprinted as
"Ideology and Entitlement," in Brown and Halley, *Left Legalism/Left Critique*,
134–77.

4. Christine Littleton, "Reconstructing Sexual Equality," *California Law Review* 75 (1987): 1279.

5. For a systematic diagnosis of this pathology in feminist legal theory and
politics, and an argument about how to cure it, see Tsoukala, "Gary Becker."
Not accidentally, Tsoukala finds that Gillian Lester is almost unique in the
feminist legal theory "care/work" debate in producing a feminist intervention
that actually acknowledges the costs of paid leave and argues that it is nevertheless worth our paying them. Gillian Lester, "A Defense of Paid Family Leave,"
Harvard Journal of Law and Gender 28, no. 1 (2005). I would suggest that
Lester was able to break from the prescriptive deployment of theory that satu-
rates feminist legal argumentation in this debate precisely because she Took a
Break from Feminism in her work on *Jumping the Queue* and because, within
that, she Took a Break from >.

6. "Weakening Feminism and So Harming Real Women," 316–19, below.

7. *Oncale*, 118 S.Ct. at 1001–3.

8. One of the best statements of this view of the case is Kathryn Abrams,
"The New Jurisprudence of Sexual Harassment," *Cornell Law Review* 83
(1998): 1169.

9. See Vicki Schultz for a feminist opposition to this goal of some feminists:
"The Sanitized Workplace," *Yale Law Journal* 112 (2003): 2061.

10. For the term, and a feminist intervention against power-feminist ambitions in the sexual harassment regime, see Katherine M. Franke, "What's Wrong with Sexual Harassment," *Stanford Law Review* 49 (1997): 769.

11. A memorial moment for David Charny, who opened this avenue for me.

The Costs and Benefits of Taking a Break from Feminism

1. See 316–19, below.

2. Biddy Martin, "Sexualities without Genders and Other Queer Utopias," *Diacritics* 24, nos. 2– (Summer–Fall 1994): 104–21.

3. I am tracking the terms and argument of Butler, "Contingent Foundations," in Butler and Scott, *Feminists Theorize the Political*, 20 n. 1. The passage I am reading is reprinted in Benhabib et al., *Feminist Contentions*, at 55 n. 1. Butler reflects here on her effort to articulate a political opposition to the claim that internal critiques of feminism disable it politically; she draws on Ernesto Laclau and Chantal Mouffe, *Hegemony and Socialist Strategy: Towards a Radical Democratic Politics* (London: Verso, 1986), and William Connolly, *Political Theory and Modernity* (Oxford: B. Blackwell, 1988).

4. For examples, see Wiegman, "Dear Ian," and Khanna, "Signatures of the Impossible."

5. For my argument that the refusal suffered by feminism is delusional, and that that delusion has been bad for feminism, see "Feminism and Its Others," 187–283, above.

6. For a remarkable example, see Martha C. Nussbaum, "The Professor of Parody," *New Republic* 220, no. 8 (February 22, 1999): 37–45.

7. Not that role reversal is necessarily bad; just that requiring it as a form of masculine virtue is one of the things I most dislike in cultural feminism.

8. For a thoughtful account of the anticipatory remorse one feels at running this risk, see Duncan Kennedy, "The Critique of Rights in Critical Legal Studies," in Brown and Halley, *Left Legalism/Left Critique*, 38–79. This essay reprints, in modified form, pt. 5 of Kennedy, *A Critique of Adjudication* (Cambridge, Mass.: Harvard University Press, 1997), 299–376.

9. For some subtle reflections on this politics, see Lauren Berlant, "The Subject of True Feeling: Pain, Privacy, and Politics," in Brown and Halley, *Left Legalism/Left Critique*, 105–33.

10. *Webster's Third New International Dictionary*, s.v. "innocent." It would not be difficult, however, to show that more characterological connotations of

the word often arise in politics pegged to the conjuncture of superordinated immunity, subordinated injury, and subordinated innocence. In those politics, subordinated victims are often represented as "free from guilt or sin esp. through lack of knowledge of evil; . . . without evil influence or effect . . . ; . . . lacking or reflecting lack of sophistication, guile, or self-consciousness: artless, ingenuous, naive; foolishly ignorant or trusting: subject to being duped; . . . unsuspecting, unaware." *Webster's Third* (omitting without ellipses all numerals, capitalization, and exemplary material).

11. John Stuart Mill, *On Liberty*, ed. Gertrude Himmelfarb (New York: Penguin Books, 1985).

12. Bernard E. Harcourt, *Illusion of Order: The False Promise of Broken Windows Policing* (Cambridge, Mass.: Harvard University Press, 2001), 185–214.

13. I am borrowing the term "sentimental politics" from Berlant, "The Subject of True Feeling," 107.

14. See 208–21, above.

15. Sex-positive feminism is capable of producing almost exactly the same figure. Consider Sharon Thompson's playground image in her book *Going All the Way: Teenage Girls' Tales of Sex, Romance, and Pregnancy* (New York: Hill and Wang, 1995). Thompson, who begins her book with an epigraph from Carol Vance's *Pleasure and Danger*, aimed to show that teenage girls are "ruined" not by sex with adolescent boys but "by love." She offers a direct refutation of the sexual-dominance feminist idea that sex2 itself is the site of women's subordination. After hundreds of interviews with adolescent girls, Thompson concludes that girls, in their relentless doomed search for romantic merger with boys who are relentlessly searching for separation (diametricality again), end up with a monopoly on all the harm in adolescent heterosexuality: while girls "who staked their hopes on getting love and caring fell further and further behind," the "boys with any chance to progress raced ahead exhilarated by their sexual triumphs and near escapes" (43). This is, as far as I can tell, the only direct representation of male affectivity in the chapter from which I quote it. The claim that adolescent boyhood is this triumphal is so implausible that it can only be an ideological projection. Thompson did not interview actual boys.

16. West, "The Difference in Women's Hedonic Lives: A Phenomenological Critique of Feminist Legal Theory," *Wisconsin Women's Law Journal* 3 (1987): 81, reprinted in *Wisconsin Women's Law Journal* 15 (2000): 149. All my page citations are to the 2000 reprint.

17. Pauline Reage, *Story of O* (New York: Grove Press, 1965).

18. See "Robin West, *Caring for Justice*," 60–76, above.

19. "Hedonic Lives," 207–8. West refers here to *Women against Violence against Women*, ed. Dusty Rhodes and Sandra McNeill (London: Onlywomen Press, 1985), and to the social movement then active under the same name.

20. West refers here to Wendy Williams, "The Equality Crisis: Some Reflections on Culture, Courts, and Feminism," *Women's Rights Law Reporter* 7 (1982): 175, 195.

21. A fascinating cultural-feminist factoid: the only index items that have as many entries as "silence(s)," or more, are the following: "altruism," "feminism/feminist jurisprudence," "harm(s)," "justice," "law," "law and literature movement," "marital relationship(s)," "mother(s)," "patriarchy," "power and women" (339–56).

22. Conference titled "Why a Feminist Law Journal?" sponsored by the *Columbia Journal of Gender and Law*, Columbia Law School (April 2003).

23. Kendall Thomas, oral comments at the Columbia conference just noted.

Taking a Break to Decide (II)

1. Friedrich Nietzsche, *On the Genealogy of Morals: A Polemic*, trans. Douglas Smith (Oxford: Oxford University Press, 1996).

2. The Restatement rule does not include any requirement that the defendant knew of the risk or even that he recklessly ignored the risk of emotional distress. Restatement (Second) of Torts § 46 (1965), quoted by Justice Cornyn (621). Justice Cornyn nevertheless supposes that the fact finder on remand would have to find that William had such knowledge or was reckless when he failed to think about it (623–24). As Justice Hecht points out, the idea that the liability requires *intentional* conduct is significantly eroded by the "recklessness" proviso (630). The same view of the underlying conduct that classifies it as "outrageous" could well supply all a fact finder needed to conclude that the defendant recklessly ignored the likelihood that it would produce distress. Indeed, "outrage" *is* "distress."

3. Justice Cornyn tells us that she was raped at knifepoint (620 n. 1); Justice Hecht tells us the same thing (636); Justice Spector adds that Sheila was actually cut with the knife and placed in fear for her life (641).

4. Thus Robin West: "The woman who survives a violent, aggravated rape suffers a shattering of selfhood so profound and traumatic as to *echo throughout a lifetime*: her sexuality, her own body, her physical existence itself, are

forever objectified as that which brings on danger, injury, fear, and death."
Caring, 107 (emphases added).

5. Brenda Cossman, Dan Danielsen, Janet Halley, and Tracy Higgins, "Gender, Sexuality, and Power: Is Feminist Theory Enough?" *Columbia Journal of Gender and Law* 12 (2003): 601.

6. Ibid.

7. Thus Foucault describes power as *both* sovereign and fragmented; liberation as *both* desirable and a ruse; historical forms of power and social life as *both* superseded and enduring. For a brilliant reflection on the nonpropositional quality of *Volume One,* see Andrew Parker, "Foucault's Tongues," *Meditations* 18 (1994): 2.

Index

In this index, "m" and "f" refer to men/male/masculine and women/female/feminine, respectively. The abbreviation "vs." indicates a distinction, not necessarily an opposition or an antagonism.

Caring for Justice (West), 38, 60–77; on an ethic of care, 62, 70–72, 75–76; on child abandonment, 332–33; diametricality of (what's true for women is true, in reverse, for men), 62–63, 67, 75–76, 329–31; vs. "The Difference in Women's Hedonic Lives," 334–37; and erotic subordination of women, 334–35; on ethics, 339–40; on female injury/male immunity, 329–30, 332–33; female supremacism of, 72–76; on harms, 62–63, 67–68, 70; vs. *History of Sexuality*, 128–32; instrumentalism of, 326–29, 332, 335, 338–39; on knowledge, 128–29; on lesbian sexuality, 63–67; vs. MacKinnon's power feminism, 69–70, 76–77; on the masculine self, 65–66; on moral development of males vs. females, 69, 372n.38; on morally good vs. bad sex2, 63–64, 77; on mother-daughter relationships, 330; on patriarchy, 61–62, 64, 70, 76, 327, 338; on postmodernism, 128–29; radicalism of, 129; on rape, 388–89n.4; on silence, 337, 388n.21; on street harassment, 331–32; on Unger, 338

carrying a brief for f. *See* subordination

catachresis, 104, 373n.49

Catholic Church: on feminism, 22

child abandonment, 332–33

childhood, sexualization of, 120, 121, 123, 130, 144, 243

child sexual abuse, 20, 21

civil rights movement, 109

class-in-itself/class-for-itself, 238, 239–41

CLS (critical legal studies), 48, 167–69

"The CLS/Fem Split" (West), 194

coercion vs. freedom, 97

collapsed continuum, 163, 199

The Combahee River Collective Statement, 38, 82–90, 92–93, 102–5, 162, 210, 372nn.43–44

"Compulsory Heterosexuality and Lesbian Experience" (Rich), 64, 146, 195–99, 206

Conflicts in Feminism (Hirsch and Keller), 38, 207–21; conflicts addressed in, 209; contributors to/composition of, 208, 379–80n.15; vs. *Feminist Consequences*, 207–8, 214; vs. *Feminist Contentions*, 225–26; and the moralized mandate to converge feminism with antiracism, 208, 380n.15; as prepostmodern, 207, 208, 209

Congregation for the Doctrine of the Faith, 22

consciousness-raising, 43–44, 238–39, 307–8, 369n.4

convergentist/divergentist hybrid feminism, 81–105; and antiracist feminism, 81–90, 106; and binarisms, 92–93; and black feminism, 83–87; and "Can the Subaltern Speak?" 82, 91–105, 210; and *The Combahee River Collective Statement*, 82–90, 92–93, 102–5, 162, 210; definition of, 25–26; despair over divergentism, 187–88 (*see also* feminist paralysis); and lesbian feminism, 83–85, 87; moralism of convergentism, 90, 162–63; and the moralized mandate to converge, 233–34, 234–35; and the moralized mandate to converge feminism with antiracism, 208, 380n.15; moralized mandate to converge underlying, 188, 191–92, 193; as normative theory vs. hypothesis, 89, 90; and postcolonial feminism, 81, 106 (*see also* "Can the Subaltern Speak?"); and prodigal theory, 34–35; and socialist feminism, 81, 83–84; vs. structuralism, 89–90

Copelon, Rhonda, 365n.3

copula, 163, 193–95, 201–2, 206, 378–79nn.5–6

Cornell, Drucilla: ethical feminism of, 218–20; in *Feminist Consequences*, 208–10, 218–21; *Feminist Contentions*, 38, 221, 225–27; on the imaginary domain, 218, 220; and Latina identity, 219

Cornyn, Justice, 353, 388nn.2–3

Cossman, Brenda, 18, 355, 356

costs of making difference costless: harm to men, 288–89; incommensurability of benefits of, 288, 302–3; and learning disabilities, 285–87; and left multiculturalism, 285–86, 288; pregnancy accommodations in the workplace, 283, 287–90, 385n.5. See also *Oncale v. Sundowner Offshore Services* case

costs of taking a break from feminism, 304–19; definitional violence, 309–11; foreclosing critique, 311, 386n.3; getting rid of/rejecting feminism, 304–6; male identification, 312–15; matricide, 312–15; misogyny, 312–15; reifying mere terminology, 312; reinscription of heterosexism, 311; silencing women, 306–8; and utopianism, 308–9; weakening feminism/harming real women, 306, 315–19

critical legal studies (CLS), 48, 167–69

cultural feminism: definition/conceptions of, 58–59; disavowals of, 59–60; essentialist vs.

Managing special needs

EDITED BY
Tony Bowers

Open University Press
Milton Keynes · Philadelphia

Open University Press
12 Cofferidge Close
Stony Stratford
Milton Keynes MK11 1BY

and
1900 Frost Road, Suite 101
Bristol, PA 19007, USA

First Published 1989

British Library Cataloguing in Publication Data

Managing special needs.
  1. Great Britain. Special education
  I. Bowers, Tony
  371.9′0941

  ISBN 0-335-09257-8
  ISBN 0-335-09256-X (paper)

Library of Congress Catalog number available

Typeset by Gilbert Composing Services, Leighton Buzzard
Printed in Great Britain by Bookcraft (Bath) Limited

Contents

168855

Contributors

Glenys Andrews is Senior Inspector for Special Needs, London Borough of Ealing.

Chris Buckton is Head Teacher, Canterbury First School, Thetford, Norfolk.

Peter Caldwell is Senior Assistant Education Officer for Special Education, Bedfordshire.

David Cassar is Principal, South Lodge School, Baldock, Hertfordshire.

Terence Clayton is Senior Educational Psychologist, Wiltshire.

Fran Griffiths is Head Teacher, Sunnymede Infants' School, Billericay, Essex.

Robert Harvey is Deputy Director, Special Education, ILEA.

Mary Hope is Tutor in Special Educational Needs, Cambridge Institute of Education.

Ruth MacConville is Head of the Sensory Impaired Service, London Borough of Ealing.

Penny Platt is Consultant/Support Teacher for Children with Severe Learning Difficulties in Mainstream Schools, Bolton.

Frits Rab is Head Teacher, The Dales School, Northallerton, N. Yorkshire. At the time of writing he was Head Teacher, Hillside School, Sudbury, Suffolk.

Introduction

Management skills have always been crucial in making provision for children with special educational needs. At the individual level they have been important for the teacher in motivating children and working with colleagues to organize their learning, while vision and sensitivity to organizational structure and development have been the hallmarks of the effective senior manager, whether head teacher, adviser, inspector or education officer. Only in the last few years, however, have we begun to be aware of some of the skills, qualities and insights which teachers can acquire and how these can shape developments.

The Warnock Committee (DES 1978) shook many in-service education and training (INSET) providers by calling for attention to be paid to management training. This was intended for those in senior posts who worked with pupils with special educational needs and since that time we have seen greater emphasis given to the interpersonal and organizational components of special needs provision in both short and long courses. During the same period there have been many conceptual and practical changes in the nature of special educational provision. The movement to integration or non-segregation, the higher profile given to special educational needs in ordinary schools, curricular developments in both special schools and the mainstream and the growth of support services offered by local authorities have added to the complexity of the management challenges facing professionals in this field. This has occurred at a time when centrally and locally inspired initiatives have had their impact on the education system and have coincided with periods of teacher unrest and uncertainty and the general shift in authority and accountability

brought about by the Education Acts of 1980, 1981, 1986 and 1988.

The management of both self and others is an issue that has to be addressed, not merely by those with 'line management' responsibilities in schools and LEAs, but by the many teachers who have no formally designated role of authority but are expected to provide advice and to support the work of colleagues. The last ten years have seen a burgeoning literature on special educational needs, much of it preoccupied with curricular provision and structures designed to facilitate access to the curriculum. Less prominence has been given to the actual processes and strategies which underlie innovation and change. This book sets out to address these and to provide the reader with insights into the complexities of the jobs of those occupying a variety of management roles in relation to special educational provision.

In the first section, 'Developing services', Robert Harvey gives us his review and analysis of service provision in Britain's largest education authority. As the manager with responsibility for resourcing special educational needs in ILEA he has been uniquely placed to view and comment upon the changing social and political circumstances which have influenced services for special educational needs. Although ILEA will shortly be split up, much of what has happened there will inevitably affect educational development in the capital city for many years to come. Glenys Andrews, who has worked in outer London for some years, then provides us with a picture of the management and development of effective support services for pupils with special educational needs. Her view of an elaborated role for support teachers is extended in Chapter 3 by Tony Bowers, who examines the ways in which assumptions concerning the appropriateness of special educational provision are shaped at grassroots level and points to some of the key awarenesses and qualities which those adopting a consultant role may need. In the latter part of this first section, Penny Platt's chapter provides us with a view of her own work in enabling mainstream schools to provide for pupils with severe learning difficulties, reinforcing the notion of process consultancy in the role of the support teacher. Support teachers are just one strand of support for the mainstream, however. Over the last few years emphasis has been placed upon the provision of classroom or 'welfare' assistants to assist ordinary schools to work with special needs pupils. In Chapter 5, Terence Clayton offers an analysis of the ways in which such assistants are utilized in schools. Based on

research in his own LEA, it provides suggestions for the future management of this increasingly used resource.

The second section concentrates on the development of teams and the implementation of change in differing areas of special needs provision. In Chapter 6 Chris Buckton elaborates on the actual processes of involving everybody on her staff, including classroom assistants, in the school's task of achieving effective education for all. In the following chapter Fran Griffiths recounts some of the management issues which she encountered in bringing her infant school round to giving priority to learning difficulties and to changed approaches to overcoming them. As a head of service for children with impaired hearing, Ruth MacConville demonstrates the importance of team awareness while endeavouring to assist service members in working closely with ordinary schools. Finally in this section, Frits Rab offers a picture of the way in which management and research can operate hand in hand in a special school to change both staff awareness and staff practice.

An examination of the nature of provision in one LEA gives us an intimate impression of the changes which legislation has brought about over the last few years and of the differing forces which those managing large special needs services have to reconcile. Peter Caldwell's analysis and view of the future in Chapter 10 is followed by Mary Hope's examination of the likely impact of the National Curriculum on special schools. While nobody can, at the time of writing, be sure what this will be, she provides some useful pointers for schools endeavouring to re-gear themselves for the changes that will inevitably follow the Education Reform Act.

The twelfth chapter is written by the principal of an independent special school. Such schools have always been subject to 'market forces', and David Cassar examines their development, some current issues in their management and looks at their future in an environment which increasingly encourages the private sector. Finally, Tony Bowers's second chapter explores, perhaps contentiously, the impact which the local management of schools and devolution of financial responsibility may have on special needs provision in mainstream and special schools and on the opportunities which support and outreach services might seize. It is essentially an optimistic view, given creative and determined management; but it demands that many providers rethink their roles.

A book with twelve contributors who occupy a diversity of roles will inevitably provide differing stances and opinions. This

xii Introduction

is desirable in a book which does not set out to promote one particular point of view or ideology but to look at some of the current issues confronting those who seek to influence events in schools and services. If there is a keynote it is flexibility, for by encouraging this quality in managers and their organizations we are more likely to be able to face and deal effectively with the changes to come.

Part I

Developing services

Chapter 1

Special needs services: an overview and a view of the future

Robert Harvey

Time present and time past
Are both perhaps present in time future
And time future contained in time past.
                    T.S. Eliot, *The Four Quartets*

A view of the future must start from the perspectives of the past and present, and in special education a discussion of special educational needs services inevitably begins with the great watershed of 1978, the Warnock Report (DES 1978), which brought together different streams of development throughout the country and channelled them into clear and lucid recommendations – recommendations which found legislative expression in the 1981 Education Act. This chapter will set out the central recommendations of the Warnock Report, the response to them in one education authority and the effect on that response of current economic policies; it will also consider how development in special educational services is likely to be affected by the 1988 Education Reform Act.

The 1978 Warnock Report

Introduction

The Warnock Committee identified three areas of first priority for development: provision for those under five, those over sixteen and teacher training (19.8–19.13). The past decade has seen substantial growth in provision for special educational needs in all three areas. However, it is in three different areas

that more fundamental changes in thinking and in practice have taken place following the Committee's report:

(i) in the wider concept of special educational needs and the procedures for assessment of the most severe and complex;

(ii) in increased provision within mainstream schools on a full- or part-time basis for those children who would previously have been taught entirely in special schools;

(iii) in the drawing together of disparate advisory and support services into unified teams.

Broader concept of special educational needs

The Committee proposed the concept of 'special educational need' as indicating a more positive approach than the term 'handicap' and one which would direct attention to the help required for the child's educational progress (3.6). In doing so, they went back to the original intention of the 1944 Act, which was that 'special educational treatment' would be required for up to 17 per cent of the school population and that ordinary schools would have the major share in providing it (2.79). Planning of services was to be based on the assumption that about one in six children at any time and up to one in five children at some time during their school career would require some form of special educational provision (3.17).

The Committee recommended that the statutory categorization of 'handicapped' pupils should be abolished (3.25) and that there should be a system of recording as in need of special educational provision those children who, on the basis of a detailed profile of their needs prepared by a multi-professional team, were judged by their local education authority to require special educational provision not generally available in ordinary schools (3.31). In this way the Committee sought to safeguard the interests of the minority of children with special educational needs who have severe or complex disabilities or difficulties.

The broader concept of special education was to encompass the whole range and variety of additional help wherever it was provided and whether on a full- or part-time basis; it thus embraced educational help for children with emotional or behavioural difficulties who had previously been regarded as 'disruptive' as well as for children who had hitherto been seen as requiring 'remedial' rather than special education. The Committee tried in this way to provide a framework of special education in which it was accepted that special educational provision,

wherever it is made, is additional or supplementary, rather than, as previously, separate or alternative (3.45).

Special education in mainstream schools

The Warnock Committee are widely believed to have made an explicit recommendation that children with severe or complex disabilities should be integrated into mainstream schools. 'What are you doing about Warnock?' as a question directed at members or officers in LEAs in the early 1980s meant 'What are you doing to foster integration?' In fact, the Committee's recommendations were directed more at the question of 'how' than 'whether'. This was for three reasons: Section 10 of the 1976 Education Act was then on the statute book (though never implemented, it emerged in a modified form in Section 2(2) of the 1981 Act) (7.4); the Committee's wider concept of special education was in line with the principle that children with and without disabilities should be educated in a common setting as far as possible (2.5); and an increasing number of children classified as handicapped had been placed in designated special classes and units in mainstream schools (7.2). Importantly, however, the Committee stated, 'It follows that we wholeheartedly support the principle of the development of common provision for all children' (7.3).

Their chapter on special education in mainstream schools focused, therefore, on different forms of integration and on the conditions necessary for their success, particularly specialist training for teachers responsible for children with special needs and sustained support at a high level from the various services and suitable facilities. The Report emphasized that integration would not be a cheap alternative to provision in special schools if it were to be achieved without loss of quality (7.56). 'Parliament having willed the ends, we would expect the Government to will the means' (19.17). The question of resources for integration was to become a major issue in the following decade.

Advice and support in special education

The Committee were concerned that the various educational advisory services for children with special educational needs were fragmented, with different teachers working to different officers and little contact between them (13.3). They therefore recommended that every LEA should restructure and, if necessary, supplement its existing advisory staff and resources to provide effective advice and support to teachers concerned

with children with special educational needs through a unified service (13.3). The service would include advisory teachers giving advice to a small group of mainstream schools, peripatetic specialist teachers working with children with a particular disability, advisers and a senior adviser in special education (13.20).

The Education Act 1981

The Warnock Committee recognized that their new conceptual framework for special educational provision must be reflected in legislation. They urged that 'the necessary legislation should be introduced without delay and certainly within 18 months of the publication of our report'. It was a remarkable achievement that the Bill was in fact laid before Parliament within three years of the Report's publication in May 1978 and received the Royal Assent in 1981, the International Year of the Disabled. The Bill had been regarded as a non-controversial measure which could be subject to scrutiny by the Commons Select Committee for Education, Science and the Arts. The question of resources was a major focus of the select committee's consideration and the context of Neil Kinnock's famous remark that the Bill was like Brighton Pier, 'fine as far as it went but not a good way to get to France'.

The new 1981 Education Act set out in Section 1 the wider definition of special educational needs proposed by the Warnock Committee and in Section 2(4) laid a duty on local education authorities to keep their arrangements for special educational provision under review. Duties were also laid on governors to use their best endeavours to ensure that if any pupil had special educational needs the required special education provision would be made, that identified needs would be made known to potential teachers and that teachers would be made aware of the importance of identifying and providing for those registered pupils who had special educational needs (Section 2(5)). Children with special educational needs were to engage in the activities of the school together with those without such needs as far as practicable (Section 2(7)).

These were the clauses which referred to the broader concept of special education. Almost all of the rest of the Act is concerned with the assessment of and provision for those special educational needs which 'call for the local education authority to determine' the provision to meet them. The context, the accompanying DES Circular 1/83 and ministerial statements in

the Commons, made it clear that this group was intended to be similar to the group of children who would previously have been ascertained to require special educational treatment, the group which came to be known as 'the 2 per cent', as opposed to the wider group of Warnock's 20 per cent, who would have special educational needs at some time in their school career.

The Act included a much stronger requirement that these children should be educated in mainstream schools than had been anticipated. Adopting the intention of Section 10 of the 1976 Act, it stated (Section 2(2)) that it was the duty of local education authorities to secure that children with statements should be educated in mainstream schools on four conditions: that account had been taken of the views of the parent; that the special educational provision they required was provided; that other children's education would not be adversely affected; and that this was compatible with the efficient use of resources.

The Act also gave parents new rights in the assessment process to present their views and evidence, to see the statement of their child's needs in draft form and to comment on it and to appeal against the provision specified in the final form of the statement. These rights, taken together with the clause on integration, became a powerful lever for change in the forms of provision for special educational needs.

Implementing the Warnock Report and the 1981 Education Act

Introduction

The task of implementing the Report and the Act fell largely to local education authorities and the schools within them. This section describes some of the changes in provision and services in one education authority, ILEA, to illustrate what was attempted and the difficulties faced. Some preliminary comments are, however, necessary. These concern timescales and resources and, secondly, the nature of change in a large conglomerate body.

The Warnock Committee recognized that their recommendations would take time and money to implement.

> Our perspective reaches to the end of the century and possibly beyond. With some important exceptions we have not set our proposals against a timescale for their fulfilment. Rather, we have tried to produce a new framework within which the changes we recommend can take place progressively in step with resources.

It is unfortunate that the period since the Report's publication has seen an increasing limitation on local government expenditure.

A local education authority is often spoken of as if it were a single and indivisible entity, whereas the term is conveniently used to describe the decisions and responses of a large number of committees, groups, institutions and individuals. This is to say something more than that 'street-level bureaucrats' (Weatherley and Lipsky 1977) are the effective policy makers in their respective areas of work. Change is generated through the initiative of many different groups and individuals – elected members, teachers, parents, officers and inspectors – whose work feeds into and nourishes that of others. Development is the product of many interrelated forces.

Implementation in ILEA

In April 1981 the Schools Sub-committee received a report (ILEA 1123) outlining the main implications of the Warnock Report for special educational provision and the principal requirements of the 1981 Education Act, which was at that time still a Bill. The report suggested that the main thrust of development should be towards establishing greater cohesion between provision in ordinary and special schools, towards a greater variety in the provision for children with more severe needs and towards higher quality wherever special needs provision was made. Variety would be achieved by establishing more designated special units in mainstream schools and establishing a budgetary vote to support individual pupils with disabilities in mainstream schools.

Improved quality of provision required an expansion of the authority's very small advisory team in special educational needs in line with the Warnock Report's proposals for an advisory and support service (the Warnock Committee regarded such a service as an indispensable condition for effective special education provision in ordinary schools).

Following acceptance of the report, a small vote was established for the support of individual pupils with statements in mainstream schools. In 1981–2 it was a vote of £30,000. In subsequent years, as an increasing number of children with statements came to be supported in this way, it was expanded each year until in the 1988–9 budget it stood at £4.7 million and some 1,400 pupils were involved. This, however, already represented only a modest increase in real terms (an increase

above the level of inflation) on the size of the vote in the previous year and the effect of a further substantial reduction in the authority's expenditure limit by the Secretary of State will be that no further increase will be possible in 1989–90, the final year of the authority's existence.

Among other developments following the report were the establishment of 20 posts, two in each of the ten divisions of the authority, for advisory teachers to work with primary and secondary schools on the development of their provision to meet the wider range of special educational needs of children without statements. The work of the Special Educational Needs Support Teachers (SENSTs), as they came to be called, has received praise from schools and HMI, but the number of posts has had to be reduced because of the £100 million reduction in the authority's spending in 1988–9. Other advisory posts established in that year were two advisory teachers for special educational needs in further education and two for pre-school children.

In the following four years up until 1985, while limited growth in the budget was still possible or while new developments could be achieved by transfer of resources within it, 23 additional posts were provided for special schools staffing to enable link arrangements to be made with mainstream schools and colleges; 8 additional designated units for pupils with impaired language were established; 10 additional posts were created for peripatetic teachers working in mainstream schools with children with specific learning difficulties; and the centre at Charlton Park School for supporting children with physical disabilities and communication difficulties in mainstream and special schools was expanded. Additional posts for educational psychologists, inspectors and administrators were also established to meet the requirements of the procedures for assessment introduced by the 1981 Education Act.

During this period a major review was undertaken of the provision for young people with emotional difficulties and behaviour problems who did not have statements but received support in education guidance centres, support centres, tutorial classes or through peripatetic teams working within the mainstream schools.

The John Fish Report

These developments, though important, tended to emphasize the diversity of provision to meet special educational needs rather than its unity. There was a growing feeling that the

authority needed to have an explicit policy on the question of integration in the light of which specific decisions would be made.

In March 1984, therefore, the Chair of the Schools Sub-committee, Barrie Stead, suggested that there should be a review of special educational provision parallel to the reviews carried out by the committees of inquiry into the curriculum and organization of secondary schools, chaired by David Hargreaves (ILEA 1984), and that into primary education, chaired by Norman Thomas (ILEA 1985a). The terms of reference were to review the range, quality and coherence of provision to meet special educational needs in the authority in primary, secondary and special schools and in suporting institutions and services and in the context of post-school provision, particularly in the light of the Warnock Report and the 1981 Education Act and the authority's initiative to promote equal opportunities. John Fish was asked to chair the Committee. Though not explicitly conceived in these terms, the review was in accordance with the requirement on LEAs in the 1981 Education Act to keep the arrangements made by them for special education provision under review.

The Fish Committee's report (ILEA 1985b) began with a statement of basic principles. Part of this reads:

> The aims of education for children and young people with disabilities and significant difficulties are the same as those for all children and young people. They should have opportunities to achieve these aims, to associate with their contemporaries, whether similarly disabled or not, and have access to the whole range of opportunities in education, training, leisure and community activities available to all.
>
> 1.1.22

On the basis of this statement and their review of all aspects of the authority's services, the Committee's central recommendation was that 'the Authority adopt a policy which aims to meet all children's and young people's special educational needs within nursery, primary and secondary schools and colleges' (3.16.9). Whenever alternative or different provision was made outside mainstream institutions, it should be closely linked to them and seen as supportive and supplementary to their work (3.16.10). Plans for integration, in consultation with all concerned, should be drawn up and set within a defined timescale (3.16.13).

The committee's recommendations covered all aspects of provision in schools and colleges, in units and support services

and in assessment procedures. The Committee were particularly concerned about delegation and co-ordination. They recommended that the principle be adopted of delegating decisions about assessment, placement and the development and use of provision and services to a local level within authority-wide guidelines. They proposed that special educational needs arrangements should be based on clusters of schools to provide a continuity of concern over children's education and to facilitate links between different services and between different phases of education in the cluster. Similarly, divisional management groups should become responsible for special educational arrangements in each division and the work of advisory and support teachers of all kinds should be co-ordinated at divisional level.

The Report was published in July 1985 and was presented to sub-committees in September. Because the uncompromising phraseology of the central recommendation was seen as controversial, sub-committees called for full consultation over an extended period of time on the principles and policy set out in the Report and this took place between January and July of 1986. In addition to obtaining views, a consultation of this kind had the effect of generating discussion of the central ideas on which the recommendations were based. School and college governors and staff were asked at the same time to consider the implications of the Report for the arrangements made within their own institutions for supporting children and young people with disabilities and learning difficulties.

The consultation provoked a huge response – 694 written replies, many of them substantial documents running to twenty or more pages, from governors, teachers, health authorities and social services, voluntary organizations, parents and parents' consultative committees, consultative committees of ethnic minority communities and unions. The overwhelming majority of responses expressed support for the central policy recommendation, but many went on to say that there was a need to retain special schools. The question of resources was a major concern among respondents, some going so far as to say that they could not support the policy because there would not be resources to implement it. The consultation paper had expanded on a proposal in an appendix to the Fish Report for 'unified services' which would draw together in a division or a wider area (according to the incidence of the disability) schools, units and individual support teachers into one grouping under a head of service. This proposal was welcomed in the responses.

As a result of the consultation, sub-committees of the

authority adopted a modified version of the policy proposed in the Fish Report, aiming to meet children's needs in mainstream schools but omitting the word 'all' and acknowledging the need for a continuing but reduced number of special schools. It was envisaged that change would inevitably be slow as resources could now be generated only as a result of closures of special schools where the roll had fallen to a level which made it impossible for the school to offer a full curriculum and a reasonable peer group to the pupils. This proposed way forward caused concern and anxiety among parents of pupils in special schools and led to the formation of a parents' organization, 'Campaign for Choice'; its aim was to secure a continued choice of special school placement for parents in the future.

Present position

In the three years since the publication of the Fish Report, decision making on assessment and placement and on the day-to-day organization of services to meet special educational needs has been devolved to divisions. There has been an increasing co-ordination of services through divisional management arrangements. Though financial restraints have prevented the formation of unified services as conceived in the appendix to the Fish Report there has been an increasing drawing together of services, as in the appointment of divisional co-ordinators of support centres and teams for disaffected pupils. Special schools have continued to expand their links with mainstream schools, offering advice and extending the curriculum of their own pupils.

However, the annual reductions made in the level of the authority's expenditure and the decision to transfer responsibility for education to the inner London boroughs in April 1990 has slowed the pace of development and made structural reorganization difficult to achieve. Most serious has been the reduction in the size of special educational needs departments in secondary schools and decreased provision for special educational needs in primary schools as a result of reductions in staffing levels. District health authorities have also had to reduce the level of paramedical support to schools as a result of financial restrictions, which has meant some special schools receiving less physiotherapy and speech therapy and often limited or no provision of these services to pupils with statements in mainstream schools. It is, therefore, the squeeze on expenditure on local government and other public services which is as much a threat to further implementation of the Warnock Report and the 1981 Education Act as the Education Reform Act of 1988.

The 1988 Education Reform Act and the future

The deep concern which the 1988 Act has aroused among all those involved in special education, both parents and professionals, has related as much to its governing philosophy as to the provisions of individual clauses. The Warnock Report's wholehearted commitment to the development of common provision for all children has been replaced by a belief in the marketplace, where schools will compete for pupils and be ordered into a hierarchy of public esteem, from independent schools through city technology colleges and grant-maintained schools to voluntary and county schools, graded by their performance in national assessments; a world where local management of schools will ensure that to those that have shall be given and from those that have not shall be taken even that which they have. In this world of cut-throat competition, it is considered unlikely that schools will readily admit pupils who will make additional demands on their resources and lower their performance in aggregated test results.

In fact, of course, amendments to the Bill were made as it passed through Parliament, largely as a result of the magnificent work of the Voluntary Council for Handicapped Children at the National Children's Bureau in co-ordinating different voluntary bodies and groups concerned with children's rights in order to achieve these.

In looking to the future, therefore, it is possible to take an optimistic or a pessimistic view.

The optimistic view would be something like this. The introduction of assessment arrangements will lead to earlier identification of children's special educational needs. The tests will be formative and, as such, provide a basis for decisions about pupils' future learning needs. Because the curriculum is nationally determined, teachers will have greater scope to deploy their creativity and sensitivity in developing different teaching approaches appropriate to the individual needs of their pupils. Local education authorities will prepare schemes for delegation of the management of schools' budget shares which will (as the circular on local management of schools states that they should) include clear financial recognition of the additional cost of educating pupils with special educational needs, both with and without statements. The formulae concerned will be precisely framed and will be an incentive to schools to maintain effective support arrangements and to adopt a positive policy towards admitting children with disabilities and learning difficulties. School governing bodies will include a governor with specific

responsibility for special educational needs who will oversee and support these arrangements. School test results will be published alongside results adjusted to take account of pupil intake.

In the optimistic view of the future, advisory and support services for special educational needs will be protected by central funding from the total of up to 10 per cent (becoming 7 per cent after three years) of the general schools budget devoted to discretionary exceptions and it will be found possible to continue to maintain services at their present level or to develop them further, among other measures by taking advantage of the provision in Schedule 12 which allows authorities to make speech therapy provision. Provision for young people of over sixteen will be expanded as a result of the new duty on local education authorities to have regard to the requirements of persons over compulsory school age who have learning difficulties and the advice in the circular on governors of colleges will be heeded and at least one governor will have experience relevant to those with special educational needs.

The optimistic view would be that the new grant-maintained schools will take seriously their duties under the 1981 Education Act towards pupils with special educational needs and that the requirement placed on the governors to describe their provision for these pupils when they publish their proposals for acquiring grant-maintained status will ensure that they fully consider this aspect of the schools' provision.

The pessimistic view would be the reverse of this. There will be a continued pressure for assessment tests to be summative rather than formative and this will prevail. The new testing arrangements will result in more formal and less flexible teaching methods. Schools will devote nearly all their resources, however allocated, to providing fully for the National Curriculum, which will be their statutory obligation, and will largely ignore pupils with special educational needs. Section 19 of the Act will be deployed to put pressure on the local education authority to carry out full assessments of pupils with learning difficulties and the schools will expect that the assessment will lead to transfer out of the mainstream. The introduction of the community charge will lead to further cutbacks in expenditure and will make resourcing for special educational needs services increasingly difficult to protect. Grant-maintained schools will not admit pupils with special educational needs except children with physical and sensory disabilities of average intellectual ability or above.

Conclusion

What can be done to make the first of these two views of the future closer to reality than the second? As Philippa Russell has pointed out (*Times Educational Supplement*, 28 October 1988), the 'whole authority' approach will be increasingly difficult to sustain when schools are locally managed. But acceptance of children with special educational needs and more effective educational provision for them is not a matter only of authority policies or even only of authority special educational service provision. It is a matter of hearts and minds, of attitudes and awareness among all those working within schools and the development of appropriate teaching skills and methods. Beneath the issues of structures and resources lies the issue of how each individual child is perceived and what arrangements are made to meet his or her educational needs. This is, as the Fish Committee pointed out, a fundamental equal opportunities issue.

As the historical summary earlier in this chapter demonstrates, over the last decade voluntary organizations and parents' groups have done much to ensure that the needs of all children are acknowledged and protected, most recently in achieving amendments to the 1988 Act itself. John Fish has argued for the formation in this country of a 'disability alliance' similar to that in the USA, which was sufficiently powerful to secure the protection of Public Law 94:142 when it was threatened under the Reagan administration. This would need to include teachers' professional organizations and other professionals.

It is, of course, a much more complex and difficult task to influence 30,000 different individual institutions than to conduct a parliamentary lobby and the organization which will be required is formidable. Nevertheless, voluntary organizations are already in their advertising showing a shift towards sensitizing a wider public in their challenging of stereotypes of disability; they may be able to adapt to the new demands of the world after the 1988 Act. The basic commitment in people which informed the Warnock Report, secured ready acceptance of the 1981 Act and obtained a positive response from both Houses of Parliament to the special needs lobby in 1988, remains alive and can be constantly reactivated by well-presented information and advocacy. To achieve this will be the challenge of the next decade.

Chapter 2

The management of support services: conflicts and tensions in the role of the support teacher

Glenys Andrews

The nature of 'support'

The wider concept of special educational needs described by Warnock (DES 1978) and the 1981 Education Act signalled a change in the way in which such needs might be met. For teachers of pupils in mainstream schools who experienced learning difficulties this change related to role, to 'client group' and, for some, to name (Gipps, Gross and Goldstein 1987). The term 'support teaching' is now commonly used to describe the work of such teachers; but arriving at a precise definition of what is involved in this role has proved to be a complex task, given the often wide disparity in the expectations of the various groups with whom the support teacher interacts.

At a recent in-service training session which I conducted for a newly constituted county integrated support service, the teachers identified, in a very short space of time, no fewer than twenty such groups who might legitimately have expectations of them: pupils, parents, teachers, heads, deputies and special needs co-ordinators, governors, educational psychologists, officers, inspectors and advisers of the LEA, elected members, health and social services, voluntary agencies, colleagues within their team, team leaders and co-ordinators, and at national level, HMI and the DES. They also identified a number of sub-groups within these main categories. Following this exercise, they discussed the expectations of these various groups as they have experienced them. Clear areas of conflict emerged, either between the groups or between the teachers' own expectations and those of one or more of the groups. Major sources of tension or conflict related

to the scope of the demands made on individuals or to the focus of the service delivery: individual pupil or whole-class, whole-school development.

Bowers (1987) has referred to this as role conflict and Balshaw (1984) has suggested that the reason for such conflict often lies in the gap between policy and practice occasioned by lack of detailed knowledge of the actual job by policy makers. The importance of this link between policy and practice is emphasized by Gipps, Gross and Goldstein (1987), who further claim that it is essential that the teachers concerned are engaged in the making of the policy.

My recent experience as head of a support service in a London borough and, before that, in Scotland, both in a local authority advisory role and as a trainer and educator in a college of education, has led me to conclude that policy at school or LEA level is vital in providing a framework for a *modus operandi*, but that the details of the day-to-day working out of the support teacher's role are context bound and dynamic. The management role of the head or co-ordinator is crucial in identifying and interpreting elements of the system and the idiosyncrasies of the personalities involved in the delivery of the service.

Determining the job

In general terms the role of the support teacher can be and has been defined. HMI (Scotland) (1978) described good practice as encompassing four roles: consultancy, direct tuition, co-operative teaching and temporary support. They placed particular emphasis on the consultancy role and envisaged that it should include in its range of consultees pupils, class and subject teachers, school management teams, parents and external agencies. In terms of content it should include both matters relating to individual pupil needs and to more general issues of curriculum, organization, teaching methods and resources of a whole class or whole school nature. Direct tuition was considered to be a role with which remedial (later called learning support) teachers were already familiar and the temporary support role was considered to be one which the teachers carried out successfully as a matter of course: providing a temporary 'haven' for pupils who, for example, might be returning to school after a period of absence resulting from personal or family trauma. But the consultancy role and the co-operative teaching roles were recognized to demand knowledge

and skills not necessarily in the repertoire of teachers carrying out the remedial teaching role at the time of the HMI's report.

Blythman (1985) has described one model of partnership between a college and a local authority in designing a college-based training course to meet these demands. Such a partnership involving teachers, heads, LEA officers and advisers and college personnel undoubtedly creates conditions for coherence in the implementation of the LEA policy by the course participants. The example is one of policy, nationally initiated and disseminated, although arising from identified practice in schools, locally interpreted and supported in its implementation by joint LEA/college INSET. A similar example exists in the model described by Cowne and Norwich (1987), although the emphasis here is on school rather than LEA policy.

As head of a support service in a London borough, I participated in the evolution of policy within the service, a process by which the team of teachers involved met regularly and shared, challenged and explored views on the way in which they could most effectively deliver a service to their schools. It was important to the team to arrive at a consensus and they did this by agreeing on a range of aspects of their role which they considered to be important and effective. The result was a decision to recognize the value of a mixed mode approach, diagrammatically represented in Figure 2.1.

Figure 2.1

Thus they acknowledged, like HMI (Scotland), the complexity of the role and were concerned to maintain flexibility in their interpretation of it. They concluded that the representative circles could vary in size to reflect differing emphases, depending on the particular circumstances in which the support teachers

worked. (They might, for example, vary from school to school or teacher to teacher or both.)

Influences and limitations

The decision as to where the emphasis, if any, on particular aspects of the role will lie, will depend on:

1 Physical factors such as
 the time available in the school;
 the total number of pupils and teachers with whom the support teacher has to interact;
 the size of the classrooms;
 availability and location of tutorial accommodation;
 the adequacy, accessibility and appropriateness of resources;
 the range of other agencies involved in the school.
2 Policy and social/political factors such as
 the ethos of the school and its overall aims;
 power structures in the school;
 the willingness of teachers to collaborate with colleagues and parents;
 organization within classes and throughout the school;
 teaching styles;
 attitudes to pupils who experience learning difficulties;
 procedures within the school for identifying and meeting special needs.
3 Factors relating to the nature of the pupils' special needs such as
 learning difficulties due to lack of continuity, differentiation or pacing in the curriculum;
 physical or sensory impairment;
 emotional or behavioural difficulties related to mental or school-generated factors.
4 Factors relating to the support teacher her/himself which have a bearing on the way in which the role will be carried out. These might include
 background knowledge and experience (subject- or age-related) or interpersonal skills;
 training and actual or 'perceived' qualification to do the job;
 status within the teaching profession and relative to the local context.

The interaction of all these factors as they influence the role of the support teacher may be represented diagrammatically as in Figure 2.2.

Figure 2.2

The balance in the operation of these three overall aspects of the support teacher's role, whatever the factors pertaining to individual situations, will be affected by underlying philosophy. At meetings which I have attended, members of HMI have signalled a forthcoming report on support services for special educational needs. By the time this chapter appears, it should be available.* I shall refer to my understanding of the report here without the benefit of access to it. It appears that HMI have identified the major source of conflict as being between 'serving individual pupils' and 'the promotion of a whole school response to pupils with special needs'. Hart (1986) referred to this dilemma but asserted that the approaches need not be mutually exclusive. She writes

> That is not to suggest, however, that we should adopt a whole curriculum approach to the exclusion of work supporting particular children. Neither approach by itself is adequate to take account of the complexities involved in meeting the needs of our children and our schools at the present time . . . What is

*Subsequent to the writing of this chapter the HMI Report has been published (DES 1989).

required, therefore, is a combination of the two approaches, and it is through support teaching that this combination can be most effectively achieved. If support teachers are alert to the possibilities within their role, and allowed the flexibility to operate at the individual or whole-class level, then support for individual children can offer a way through to improving the quality of learning for all (p. 35).

The need to address both individual and whole-school needs is underlined in the HMI report referred to above. Two of its findings and recommendations are that all direct teaching by the support services did lead to improvements in the performance of the pupils and that the better support services are helping schools across a broad front to make more effect provision for all pupils.

Managing support

If, then, the support teacher's role is to encompass all three aspects referred to in the diagrams above, what are the management implications for the tensions and conflict surrounding these roles?

On the consultancy/advisory role, HMI (Scotland) (1978) suggested that the kind of help offered might include:

(i) alerting class and subject teachers to the full range of differing causes of learning difficulties;

(ii) alerting class and subject teachers to the need for revision and reiteration of work with quite sizable numbers of pupils;

(iii) alerting class and subject teachers to the key part to be played by probing discussion with individuals and with groups of pupils to arrive at a recognition of the cause of any difficulty;

(iv) advising teachers on the reading and language levels in the resources used in their courses;

(v) advising teachers on the problems faced by individual pupils;

(vi) being available as consultants to staff at points where individual pupils have to make subject or course choices.

Another aspect of the role, referred to by Hockley (1985) and Visser (1986) is that of in-service education and training (INSET) delivery. This was certainly an increasing part of the role of teachers in the support service of which I was head and HMI have recorded that 60 per cent plus of the services in their survey were

providing some form of INSET for teachers. But as the consultancy/advisory role develops dilemmas emerge, associated with appearing as an 'expert', with the result of distancing the support teacher from class teacher colleagues, of 'deskilling' the class or subject teacher and of marginalizing pupils with special needs as a group whose needs can be met only by a specialist. This issue of the expert role of support teachers is looked at again by Tony Bowers in Chapter 3. We now find a movement away from the person who takes away problems: thus Dessent (1987) argues that support work should 'reaffirm, reinforce and reassure teachers in ordinary schools that they have the potential as teachers to meet the majority of the special needs which confront them' (p. 91). This description of consultancy most closely exemplifies the 'process model' described by Conoley and Conoley (1982) and referred to by Wolfendale (1987) as a co-operative approach to support.

The head or co-ordinator of a support service needs, then, to consider:

1 The clarification of both the schools' and the support teacher's expectations of the consultancy role. Galloway and Goodwin (1987) refer not only to an initial potential mismatch of expectations, but to the possibility of the support teachers becoming socialized into accepting group norms and thus, in the absence of a clear brief or service policy, adopting idiosyncratic approaches.
2 The training required to enable the support teacher to adopt the most appropriate model of consultancy to the demands of a situation. A useful analysis both of the range of possible models and of their relative training demands is provided by West and Idol (1987).

The co-operative or collaborative teaching role, often referred to as 'in-class support', is one which requires clearer definition. HMI have highlighted this and, in my experience, there is too often a lack of focus to the work. I have outlined (Andrews 1987) a range of purposes for which a co-operative teaching approach was adopted by teachers in the Fife region of Scotland. What is important is that a purpose is established, whether it be to support a particular teacher, or area of the curriculum, or group of children.

The purpose having been established, planning must then take place which involves:

(i) setting clear goals and defining roles for the teachers and pupils;

(ii) drawing up a timetable which includes space for consultation between the teachers;
(iii) deciding how many classes or subject areas can feasibly be targeted by one support teacher at any one time;
(iv) ensuring that the classroom organization and ethos are conducive to co-operative teaching;
(v) the preparation of resources.

At the implementation stage it is vital to ensure that there is constant monitoring of the kinds of issues which may arise and which can contribute to the success or failure of the exercise. We need to ask:

1 Do teachers get on well together or are there conflicts of personality or approach which impede real collaboration?
2 Are there clearly defined strategies for ensuring, for example, that the pupils do not play one off against the other?
3 Are both teachers thoroughly familiar with the aims and content of each lesson, of what has gone before and what will follow?

Successful implementation will also depend on the quality of evaluation which may take place at two levels, formal and informal. Formal evaluation may include assessment of pupil progress and recording by the staff of their effectiveness in meeting specific targets. Informal assessment may include collecting samples of pupils' work to monitor progress; a discussion with pupils about their work; discussion among the staff involved as to the effectiveness of the co-operative teaching. It is this kind of dialogue which provides the context for the kinds of co-operative consultation referred to above.

Action approaches

The extent to which the individual direct teaching role is carried out will depend both on the needs of the pupils and the approach adopted by the support teacher. Gross and Gipps (1987) have drawn attention to the effectiveness of direct teaching of special needs pupils and HMI in their survey found that all forms of direct teaching by the support services did lead to improvements in the performance of the pupils. What they found to be unsatisfactory, however, was: (i) the poor working conditions in which this teaching tended to take place; and (ii) the lack of continuity in content between this teaching and the overall curriculum of the school. This latter problem was also highlighted by HMI (Scotland) in 1978. Where direct tuition

takes place, it is vital that it does not result in the physical and curricular isolation of the pupil, that it has a clear purpose for pupil, parent and teacher and that it has an agreed time limit relating to that purpose.

In deploying support service staff, a number of heads or co-ordinators whom I have talked with recently are moving towards a flexible approach whereby, rather than spreading staff around on a numerical or geographical basis, they are drawing up contracts between schools and the support service. This may mean that a support teacher who would traditionally have visited two or three schools on a peripatetic basis may alternatively spend a fixed period of a term or a year, or whatever is appropriate, in each of the schools with an agreed remit and set of goals. This can in some way help to resolve some of the conflicts and tensions referred to above at the level of individual schools. It has implications, however, for policy at school, support service and LEA level and reinforces the need for agreement of philosophy in the role of the support teacher.

Perhaps the most significant area of conflict facing managers of support services in special educational needs in the 1990s is the potential effect of local management of schools under the Education Act 1988 (see DES Circular 7/88). Among the questions this raises a major one must be whether support for pupils with special needs, but whose needs are not the subject of statements under the 1981 Act, should be administered centrally or devolved to the schools.

One aspect of this is not a new issue for support services and relates to the dilemma of whether support should be internal or external to the school. Bowers (1987) has explored this question in terms of the demands both on the school and the support teacher of each approach. My experience in Scotland was of support internal to the school; in London it was of an external support service. Clearly there are merits and demerits in both approaches. This experience and recent experience of joint initiatives involving support teachers and school-based special needs co-ordinators leads me to believe that the most effective way of innovating and of consolidating strategies and structures to enable schools more effectively to meet the needs of all of their pupils is for both to work together. The special needs co-ordinator within a school is in the best position to facilitate the on-going development of a whole-school approach; the support teacher coming in to the school can be a catalyst for change and can provide helpful, enriching links with the authority and with other schools.

The competition for resources

If, then, some level of support is administered centrally – and it is my view that it has to be in order to protect this group of pupils from the effects of the pressures on schools concerning the deployment of resources (Wedell 1988) – how should it be distributed? HMI have found in their survey that the number of pupils directly helped by the support services varied considerably between authorities. They also found that policies directing the work of support services were explicit in only a few LEAs. The dilemma facing administrators seems to me to relate to the question of whether schools which are successful in making provision for pupils with special needs should be 'rewarded' for their commitment by being given additional, external, support or whether they are penalized by being denied support. The converse applies to the less 'successful' schools. The solution is not a simple one, but it must involve the deployment of support services in a co-ordinated LEA inspectorate and advisory service where the special needs of pupils are recognized as the special needs of teachers. By extension, what support services must address are the special needs of schools and this needs to be done in the context of identification of need by the schools themselves and in collaboration with other agencies involved with them, including psychologists, advisory teachers, advisers and inspectors.

It appears that HMI have recognized that the administrative demands on the senior management of support services are considerable. I have referred here to some of the issues relating to the management of support services. I would also suggest that the task could become even more complex as schools are placed in the position of competing for resources. The role of the head of service in deploying staff on the basis of 'need' will be even more fraught than it has hitherto been. Further, the maintaining of a policy of directing efforts to curriculum reform, rather than to individual 'failing' pupils will, I suggest, come under increasing pressure as schools and teachers are concerned with published test results. More than ever it will be vital to the effective operation of the role of the support service to have a clear LEA policy on the way in which it should be deployed. It will then be possible to evaluate and monitor its effectiveness in individual schools and to ensure that schools which use it well are rewarded and thus encouraged, not only to admit but to provide the best possible education for pupils with special educational needs. Governors, too, will be partners in this process and the role of the

head of service, among all of the other aspects discussed here, may become a marketing one. Some notions of marketing are explored in Tony Bowers's chapter on this topic in this book. For the purposes of this chapter, marketing does not necessarily imply selling the service – although that too could become a reality should LEAs in the future decide to devolve this support to schools' budgets – but selling its approach and demonstrating its effectiveness in tangible terms.

The challenge of the 1990s to special needs support services is clear; the challenge to managers of these services is equally clear. The task is to secure the protection of rights of pupils with special educational needs in mainstream schools where their needs, in spite of the goodwill and intentions of teachers, may be sacrificed in the struggle for success and survival. Like Robert Harvey, I believe that there is an optimistic view where pupils' special needs may in the future be identified earlier and where there may be more pressure to ensure individual success and progress. Such an ethos provides opportunities for support services and the sensitive and enterprising head of service will be able to exploit this to the benefit of a wide range of pupils. Whichever view becomes reality, and for some support services it may be both, the demands on the head of service are such that it will be vital for LEAs to recruit, train and reward appropriately those who will be expected to carry out such a role in the next decade.

Chapter 3

From support to consultancy

Tony Bowers

Marian Keech of Lake City, USA, received messages from outer space which she recorded in automatic writing. She acquired a circle of true believers who hung assiduously on every word she passed on to them; when, therefore, there came to her from the planet Clarion the prediction that Lake City would be destroyed by a great flood on 21 December, there was a deep and shared commitment to the prophecy. The beings that spoke to Mrs Keech from outer space told her that her group of believers, the Seekers, would be spared in the great flood. At midnight on the twentieth they were to stand by to be picked up by a flying saucer. Some had already left the area, but ten of them gathered at Mrs Keech's house and waited for the arrival of the hour. It came and went, but there was no knock on the door. There was no flying saucer to be seen. Not only that, but the flood did not happen either.

You are probably not surprised by this. After all, there is a long tradition of calamitous events predicted by eccentric prophets failing to materialize. What does take a little getting used to is that after the event Mrs Keech's supporters, the Seekers, were actually more committed to their belief in her and her special powers than they were before that fateful 21 December. Looked at logically, we might have expected them to reject her, blame her and generally denigrate her capacities. Mrs Keech, of course, had to change her story to fit in with events: the essence of it was that because of the impressive faith of a small group of the believers, the city – perhaps the world – had been spared the predicted cataclysm. The remarkable thing was that this adjusted story was not merely accepted by the followers in her house but that

the events of that night strengthened their faith in the credibility of their chosen prophet.

Every so often someone like Mrs Keech comes along and invariably time and events demonstrate that they have miscalculated. Faced with the facts they have to admit this but, just as Festinger *et al.* (1956) found in Lake City, they actually gain in status among those who have closely followed their creed. Rather than being ignored, any new pronouncements from what we might call the 'guru' figure carry even more weight than they did before.

The 'guru' effect in special educational thought

Writing in the middle part of the 1980s, one leading author has observed that 'when the history of this period comes to be written it will probably be recognised as a time of considerable changes in special education' (Ainscow 1985, p. 38). Seen from the present, 1985 appears to be quite static. What we need to beware of, however, is the tendency for us always to see our immediate time as one of particular turmoil and to associate 'change' most strongly with our current experiences. A glance back just forty years before that quotation will show the major alterations which have occurred in attitudes and provision within education, and certainly within special education, since implementation of the 1944 Education Act was begun. Since then we have seen the raising of the school-leaving age, two major reforms of school-leaving examinations, widespread moves to comprehensive reorganization, the merging or closure of many schools and numerous curricular initiatives and innovations, both centrally and locally inspired. Within the sector of special educational provision alone, a glance at the state-of-the-art review in the Underwood Report (Ministry of Education 1955) demonstrates how much change we have seen in the intervening period. Change, it seems, is a given factor in education in general just as it is in the education of children with special needs. It is the one thing that we can be certain of: we can be quite sure that whatever the situation is now, it will be different in ten years' time. Not only that, but if the past is any guide then the ways in which we conceptualize special educational needs and provision are also likely to be at variance with the ways in which we see them today. A prophecy of change is always the safest prediction.

Special education in this country has always had a tendency to throw up 'guru' figures. These have, of course, been associated with the received wisdom of the day. In the 1960s there was a

movement from what might be termed a non-systematic form of curricular provision in special schools and in what were then remedial departments of mainstream schools; the notion of diagnostic–prescriptive teaching became particularly fashionable. Essentially, the assumption was made that academic problems, particularly those related to reading and language development, result directly from inadequate neuropsychological development or are the product of intrinsic perceptual or perceptual–motor difficulties. Many examples of attempts to identify strengths and weaknesses in learning-disabled children, and to devise suitable training programmes based on these, abound. In this country, visual perceptual training, auditory perceptual training, perceptual motor training, neural patterning and psycholinguistic training all played their part in approaches to learning difficulties. Works such as that of Tansley (1967) became influential in shaping practice and those who had worked with that author tended to achieve prominence in the literature of that time (e.g. Nicholls 1970; Brennan and Jackson 1972).

The received wisdom of the day became increasingly questioned, however (e.g. Hammill and Larsen 1974; Robbins and Glass 1969), and a new orthodoxy arose. In this, assumptions concerning causality were viewed as irrelevant; emphasis was placed upon addressing those aspects of instruction which the teacher could control. Strongly influenced by the general acceptance of behaviourist views of learning within the field of special education (e.g. Jeffree *et al.* 1977), those committed to this approach leaned upon such notions as task analysis, 'precision' teaching and – of course – behavioural objectives. Despite his earlier connection with the diagnostic-prescriptive perspective Brennan (1979), in his report of his Schools Council project on slow learners, outlines seven essential teacher competences, all of which see effective learning in terms of the achievement of objectives. The objectives approach was by no means new in the world of education and training (e.g. Mager 1962), but to the world of special education it presented a new technology of instruction which largely discounted internal processes in the child; in many ways it paralleled the decline in psychodynamic explanations of emotional disturbance and the widespread acceptance of behavioural explanations and treatments highlighted vividly by, for example, the contrast between two works of Martin Herbert (Herbert 1975 and 1978).

No one in the UK has probably had as profound an impact on the curriculum for pupils with special needs as Ainscow and

Tweddle. In 1977 their suggestion that all teachers should establish carefully graded sequences of objectives in their programmes and that the statement of explicit objectives was a 'fundamental responsibility' of the special needs teacher, was the prelude to many LEA special schools overhauling their curricula to meet these specifications. Subsequent works, such as Ainscow and Tweddle (1979), embraced the philosophy more firmly. Paradoxically, much curricular thinking outside the special needs field had long since rejected so narrow a view; Stenhouse (1975) had already effectively summarized the arguments against objectives and had crystallized these by writing 'Education as induction into knowledge is successful to the extent that it makes the behavioural outcomes of the students unpredictable' (p. 82).

Despite this, the use of structured objectives flourished, not only in work with pupils with severe learning difficulties but also with pupils with minor learning problems who attended mainstream schools (e.g. Williams and Muncey 1982). As Swann (1983) has observed, the approach received a boost from the notion of the individualized education plan (IEP), which in the USA must by law list objectives for each child with special educational needs. The use of objectives does not, of course, determine the content of what is delivered, although they do tend to fit most easily within the framework of basic skills teaching. In 1978, however, Ainscow and Tweddle seemed to see them as a general panacea: 'where appropriate objectives are chosen and stated explicity *all* methods and materials will be used in a more effective fashion' (Ainscow and Tweddle, 1978, pp. 142–3).

Many schools, particularly special schools, have as a consequence of the impact of behaviourist thinking geared their teaching towards the use of instructional objectives and have developed individual learning programmes to assist pupils to move forward at their own pace. However, the very exponents of such approaches are now pointing out their shortcomings. In a chapter enumerating the weaknesses of special schools 'as we now know them', Ainscow (1989) sees as a fundamental deficiency 'the emphasis that has been placed on determining precise objectives in so-called basic skill areas of the curriculum' (p. 10). Perhaps forgetting the developments in mainstream schools in the past ten years or more, he goes on 'One of the trends that is so influential in curriculum development in ordinary schools at present is towards greater pupil involvement in decision-making. It is based on a belief that schools should be helping pupils to become autonomous learners' (Ainscow 1989,

p. 13). Planning with objectives, though, is now seen to 'lead to the production of lists of objectives which define in detail those aspects of the curriculum which are most easily measured. Other aspects of learning are left unrecorded and, by implication, defined as requiring less attention' (Ainscow 1989, p. 10). Some thirteen years after Stenhouse's analysis, then, the model has effectively been abandoned.

Interestingly, another criticism of the objectives model comes from Tony Dessent, who was at one time a major exponent of Portage, itself heavily dependent on the achievement of structured developmental sequences of objectives (Cameron 1982; Dessent 1984). Dessent (1987) sees behaviourally based approaches to intervention placing undue emphasis upon 'normalizing' pupils or making them 'successful'. By leading to expectations that we can somehow maximize the academic attainments of children with learning problems, an objectives-based approach draws attention away from the Dessent's 'major requirement' for non-segregated provision: that mainstream teachers accept the relative failure in traditional educational skills of some of the children whom they teach. While running counter to the now entrenched view spawned by Rosenthal and Jacobson (1968) that high and low expectations will be self-fulfilling, this normative view of 'success', and Dessent's assertion that support services should assist schools in re-defining it, provides us with an alternative, if transitory, philosophy. As this chapter is written, all the indications are that the National Curriculum, age-based assessment and the publication of schools' results will render the attainment of key objectives a major priority within the operation of most classrooms.

The bandwagon effect in special education

The preceding section by no means provides a digest of changes in special educational thought in recent years. Oracy versus signing for severely hearing-impaired pupils, dietary measures for the control of hyperactivity, 'holding therapy' for children with autism, 'instrumental enrichment' for the development of cognitive flexibility and the use of coloured spectacles to overcome dyslexia are just some of the controversial innovations in intervention which have risen and (sometimes) waned in the general consciousness. In their analysis of the reasons for adopting particular intervention strategies for meeting chil-dren's special needs, Ysseldyke and Algozzine (1982) see what

they term the 'bandwagon effect' as the most powerful deciding factor. In looking, therefore, at why particular approaches are popular, and why particular opinions hold sway at any given time, we need to be aware of how potent this phenomenon can be. Another author has described the bandwagon effect as the tendency

> to produce hastily conceived, poorly implemented innovations or programs, the failure to achieve anticipated goals, and consequent disillusionment with the original idea, or backlash. In turn, backlash may lead to equally precipitant abandonment of meritorious programs which have not been adequately conducted or sufficiently tried.
>
> Trachtman 1981, p. 141

I am not arguing, of course, that all changes are the result of this effect; however, it is important that we should be aware of the forces that operate to cause us to take on new approaches. Nobody wants to appear to be left behind, or to seem out of date. Pressures may come from outside groups, often encouraged by the media. Whatever our view of the efficacy of conductive education for children with cerebral palsy, and however we consider the procedure to harmonize with current notions of general curricular access for special needs pupils, its championing on television and in certain newspapers provides a vivid example of the bandwagon effect.

Which brings me back to Marian Keech. On the face of it, she was fairly dotty: who in their right mind would believe somebody who says she gets messages from outer space? You would surely have to be very gullible to do so. The fact remains, though, that a substantial number of people did follow her, did pack ready for the spacecraft and were still right behind her when she was forced to change her story. The lesson from this is that there seems to be a need in many of us to have faith in a particular person's judgements and to modify our thinking and practice accordingly.

Of course, the cult of the 'guru' or expert extends well beyond the boundaries of education, impinging on such diverse areas as sport, politics and most occupations. It operates locally, nationally and internationally. Why do I dwell on it here, in a book concerned with children with special educational needs?

There are two main reasons. First, it is important for those who occupy management and consultancy roles in this field to be aware of the ways in which their thinking, and that of those with whom they work, is shaped. Why people believe in particular

methods or procedures, how they come to develop commitment to them and how their views on the nature of childhood disabilities and the way they should be dealt with are shaped, should be of central concern. Without taking note of these factors, we remain blinkered and locked into the concerns and constraints of what goes on immediately around us. Secondly, the nature of 'experts' and expert knowledge needs looking at critically, particularly by those who seek to peddle their own expertise. Ysseldyke and Algozzine (1982) have used the term 'doctor-tested' to describe many of the methods of working with special needs pupils. They draw on the analogy of medical products which are recommended by physicians: if enough high status people urge their use then they must be all right. There will always be pioneers and opinion shapers; there will always be those who maintain a high profile in the literature, at conferences and through the media. But this does not necessarily make them correct in any absolute sense. Interestingly, we may be seeing an 'anti-expert' trend emerging within the field of special needs support; Dessent (1987) has drawn our attention to what he views as the popular myth of expertise on the part of special education professionals. Perhaps this is the bandwagon of the day. I shall attempt to explore this issue further later in this chapter.

Support for special needs

The word 'support', as I have pointed out elsewhere (Bowers 1987), is one which has gained general use and acceptance over the last few years among those concerned with attempting to meet children's special educational needs. We have seen the advent of the 'support teacher', the 'support team' and the 'support service' both within schools and in the wider context of LEAs. My own experience is that the term is used indiscriminately, that everyone seems to assume that their own perception of 'support' is shared by others but that so many meanings are attached to the word that it is effectively rendered meaningless. Usually relating to special educational needs in mainstream schools, the notion of support can attach to the allocation of a part-time unqualified classroom assistant to, say, a child presenting behaviour problems; it may apply to a visiting specialist teacher who has a caseload of children placed in a number of schools; it may be something provided by a teacher working in the same room as a regular teacher in the primary or secondary school; it may constitute advice or special resources

provided by somebody designated as a special needs co-ordinator. These are just a few examples. In their research in LEAs, Gross and Gipps (1987) looked at what members of peripatetic teams actually did. In one borough they found that support staff taught basic skills, 'usually in withdrawal sessions, but sometimes in the classroom'. They also saw that the general approach was 'to use highly structured teaching materials based on an objectives approach' (1987, p. 12). In another LEA, Ruralshire, they found a mixture of approaches to the support role, ranging from the provision of a testing service, through in-service training, to the facilitation of problem-solving self-help teacher groups. In their analysis of another authority (Newtown) they are quite specific: 'the role of the support team is one of advising rather than teaching' (p. 84), while in another, which they name Midshire, support for the class teacher is identified as taking the class while the teacher takes out a child for special help. The researchers never actually saw this happen, however; they only observed individual tuition on the part of the 'supporter'.

Dessent (1987) has criticized the notion of support services because he sees them broadly expecting to 'advise', 'train' and 'raise the level of expertise' of ordinary teachers. Within this framework they are operating from a superior position – what exponents of transactional analysis (Berne 1964) know as an 'I'm OK – you're not OK' position. However, the analysis in the foregoing paragraph reveals that many of those offering support do little more than take away some of the problems of the regular teacher: they actually act as supplementary teachers, carers or minders. In such a context, they do not necessarily claim – or need to have – greater knowledge or more skills than other teachers; they provide another pair of hands for a limited period of time. In working on the development of relevant skills in in-service sessions in a number of local authorities, I have introduced the notion of the special needs consultant (Bowers 1987). With some groups this is readily accepted; others respond 'But we're not consultants, we're supporters'. On further examination, this turns out to be true; most of what they do can be categorized as direct teaching, usually with single children or small groups. The term 'consultancy' implies engagement at a different level, and requires awareness and skills which transcend those of the supporter. I shall explore these further in the ensuing sections.

Consultancy

A reasonable working definition of consultancy is that it is a helping relationship which is provided by individuals or groups who have a particular range of skills. These skills will assist those with whom they work to understand more clearly what they are trying to do and how they can become more effective.

Summing up the main issues for consultants, Morris (1988) sees them attempting:

(i) to achieve results;
(ii) to show concern for people and relationships.

If we accept this analysis, we can assume that the first indicates a management orientation while the second is really about counselling. Consultants are not managers, however, because in any management situation there will be some form of hierarchical relationship between people; put crudely, somebody is 'the boss'. While they may not rely on formal authority in everything they do, managers – head teachers, deputy heads, heads of department, team leaders and so on – have that designation. A consultant still has to attempt to get things done, through other people, just as a manager does. The difference is that the consultant has no formal power over the others with whom he or she is involved. Leadership skills may be useful, but a true consultant is not a manager or even a surrogate manager.

Perhaps the consultant is more like a counsellor. After all, Morris's second category, above, would appear to reflect this orientation. The term 'counselling' itself is a vague one, but the approach generally taken in this country reflects a humanistic value system (cf Rogers 1951). Within such a framework the counsellor aims to assist his or her clients to determine the nature and direction of their own development. This is where the distinction lies between the counsellor and the consultant: anyone who has taken on a consultancy brief will know that they have to work within relatively narrow confines and, most importantly, that their client system is usually considerably more complex than that of a counsellor. However, counselling skills undoubtedly help, as Murgatroyd (1988) has eloquently explained.

Having said what consultancy is not, I had better try to say what it is. Basically it is what occurs when one person is asked to influence the behaviour or actions of an individual, group or organization, but has no direct power to make changes or put programmes into action. Consultants can operate internally, when they are on the same staff as those whom they seek to

influence, and externally, when they come into a school from outside and will probably work in a number of schools during the same time period. I have looked at some of the main issues for the two kinds of consultant elsewhere (Bowers 1987): for both, though, most of the processes which I will outline are relevant. Most special needs consultants working either internally or externally will, I assume, not always adopt such a role. At times they will have a direct 'service delivery' function; in other words, they will work as teachers. We depict the distinction diagrammatically in Figure 3.1; the first situation reflecting direct teaching, the second a consultancy relationship.

Figure 3.1

In the consultancy mode, then, the special needs teacher works through other people; his or her success depends on their actions. This is where the problem of 'expertise', already touched upon, becomes apparent. Dessent (1987) has remarked that for the support teacher to be perceived as an expert can 'undermine attempts to provide support' (p. 82), and it is certainly the case that an approach which offers to deal exclusively with problems will tend to deskill the person who is helped. To draw on a familiar situation, if a plumber deals with my sink when it becomes blocked, then I will be no better equipped to sort out the sink the next time: I will probably send for the plumber again. However, should the would-be consultant demonstrate no particular skills in dealing with problems confronting teachers, or claim no special knowledge of ways of overcoming learning or behaviour problems, then his or her services will probably never be sought. If we retain the domestic analogy, I will not want to use the plumber if I think he knows nothing about sinks.

The essential dilemma for special needs support teachers who wish to operate in a consultancy mode is how they should use

what expertise they possess. Organizations and individuals ask for assistance because they need it; when they need help they are inclined to dependency. If you do not provide assistance, you are not meeting their needs and in the increasingly consumer-oriented climate of education they will probably be in a position to go elsewhere to have these needs met. I look more at this in Chapter 13. If, though, you take over the problem for them, then they may well lack the capacity to deal with similar problems on future occasions. A good working premise is that initially, at least, you should expect to provide some of the help that is asked for. In doing so, though, there is the danger of becoming sucked into a 'doctor–patient' relationship in which you are seen to have 'cures' in the form of diagnostic procedures and teaching methods and materials. This is particularly seductive because it reinforces the consultant's view that he or she is needed and, indeed, indispensable.

The consultant role

At this stage it may be useful to look at different ways in which we can legitimately view the consultant role. First, consultants have clients; these are the people with whom they work and who ask them to perform their work, although there may, as we shall see later, be distinguishing features between these types of client. In examining relationships between consultant and client, Schein (1987) has distinguished three main types.

1 The purchase of expertise, in which the client determines what the problem is, what kind of help is needed and who to go to for that help. The consultant is thus approached to provide the help. Within a special educational needs context, this is the kind of model which we see operating when a school asks an adviser or some other expert to run in-service training sessions on the 'whole-school approach' to learning or behaviour difficulties. On a smaller scale, the model is operating when a child is defined as having specific learning difficulties and a specialist teacher, perhaps part of a support team, is asked to work with him or her.
2 The doctor–patient approach to consultancy is a variant of the above model. In this the client gives the consultant the additional power to find out what is wrong and recommend treatment. It is the relationship which educational psychologists traditionally enjoyed with schools; a child or group of children were failing, the reasons were diagnosed by the

consultant and suggestions were given for effecting a solution. The model still holds good for many support services, where a head teacher of a primary school may express concern that a number of children in a given class are failing and ask a member of the service to look them (and the teacher) over and recommend changes as a result.

3 The process consultation view of the consultant–client relationship is quite different. It can, and probably will, start with a client's attempt to use the consultant in one of the two ways described above. It differs from them in that within this model the consultant ensures that the client *retains responsibility* for whatever problems there are and *continues to take responsibility* throughout the time of the involvement. Instead of saying 'leave it to me', the process consultant will effectively communicate 'it's still your problem, but I'll try to work on it with you'.

The third model, that of the process consultant, is the one which I shall pursue further. In Chapter 4 Penny Platt analyses some of the stages in carrying out the role of such a consultant with teachers who have children with severe learning problems in their classroom. It is, though, in this mode that the paradox of expertise becomes most apparent. Unless a parent, a teacher, a school or someone sees the support teacher as an expert – a person who has skills to deal with the issues which concern them – then they are unlikely ever to approach that person. Credibility is vital, and credibility stems from a perception of expert knowledge or skills. However, to demonstrate such skills may disempower the client, leaving the consultant operating in one of the first two models above. In short, it does matter for support teachers operating as consultants to know how to tackle reading problems, to understand why children become difficult to manage, to recognize difficulties in teacher–pupil communication, to be able to formulate a wide range of responses to the 'sticking points' encountered by colleagues. It matters because they are unlikely to gain entry to a consulting relationship unless they have qualities which are seen as valued. However, if expertise is put into play, either in the form of advice or direct teaching, the client is unlikely to be left better able to deal with similar difficulties in the future. The essential assumptions of process consultation are that (i) the client is capable of learning to diagnose and solve his or her own problems, and (ii) ultimately, the only one who knows what will work in his or her situation is the client.

The idea of advice and support in meeting special needs in ordinary schools is not a new one. Topping (1986) has stressed the importance of experience and abilities in dealing with pupils presenting behaviour problems but has then provided a rather traditional model of consultation which starts with the specification of the problem, passes through the specification of objectives and ends with evaluation and exit of the consultant. Somewhat earlier, Smith (1982) produced six points for the consultant which encompassed the teacher's feelings of incompetence, fear of lack of confidentiality and worries about an already heavy workload becoming heavier. In particular, he stressed the need to provide some immediate practical advice alongside a more 'in-depth' approach to the problems encountered. While not actually advocating a process consultation approach, Smith has provided a view of the support teacher's role which steers carefully between the 'prescriptive' and 'non-expert' positions.

Effective consultancy

I started this chapter with a look at the way in which slavish adherence to a particular viewpoint or philosophy can permeate views of special educational treatment. Anyone setting out to offer help to teachers or to schools, certainly within a process consultation framework, needs to be aware of the ways in which their own views of the educational process and of ways of providing for children's special educational needs have been shaped and coloured by the views of others. This does not make them wrong; it does not necessarily make them right either. What should be remembered is that it is only human to believe that one approach is better than another and to try to persuade others to that view.

The consultant needs to be constantly aware of the potency of the guru effect. This can operate at two levels. It can permeate the thinking of the consultant, influencing his or her judgements of situations; it can also lead to those in the school expecting quick and easy results for which they do not have to expend energy. The consultant, in the shape of visiting expert can readily be given – or adopt – the mantle of guru.

Effective process consultation involves assisting others to solve their own problems. To start with, the support consultant should therefore ask him- or herself how the problem is viewed by other parties, leaving his or her own value system as much in abeyance as possible. Colin Smith's (1982) first question, 'Will

you listen, really listen?' (p. 75) is a critical one here. It is important that the consultant should be someone who can tease out the concerns of others without trying to put his or her own viewpoint across. A good listener is someone who avoids finishing others' sentences, interrupting or guessing the outcome of what they are being told.

I have written elsewhere of the essential differences between internal and external consultants (Bowers 1987). Within a special needs context the former are likely to be permanent members of the school's staff, while external consultants are those who operate as part of a wider service and will visit a group of schools. In Chapter 2, Glenys Andrews looks at the differing roles of support teachers and remarks that one important quality of both internal and external consultants is that they should be capable of crossing boundaries. In the case of external consultants such boundaries are only too evident; for internal consultants, however, the boundaries between departments in the school may be equally marked. I do not refer to physical boundaries, but to psychological ones. A good consultant will be able to discern the differing roles which operate in particular schools or teams: the subtle distinctions concerning what is and what is not openly discussed, how conflicts are dealt with, how people support one another, what they expect in terms of standards of behaviour and performance in pupils. If the consultant appears to be out of sympathy with these 'rules', he or she will probably not be able effectively to cross the boundary. On the other hand, unconditional acceptance of those ways of operating should not mean that the consultant falls into following them or there is little chance of them becoming modified. A fine line has to be trodden between accepting another group's values and standards and actually adopting them.

The external support teacher must also be aware that his or her own team's culture may in certain ways clash with those existing across the various boundaries. This is inevitable, because priorities will obviously differ between the support team and those charged with meeting the varying demands of mixed ability teaching. Placing children with special needs first, and assuming that children's learning failures stem from inappropriate teaching, come naturally to many support team members. For many ordinary school teachers, on the other hand, these may be alien values. An effective support consultant will need to remain aware of the norms and expectations of the culture from which he or she stems, while acknowledging that they are not universally held outside that culture.

Identifying clients

Consultants have clients. So do solicitors and estate agents, but their relationship with their clients is clearly defined; they tend also to work with simple client systems. By contrast, the special needs support consultant operates with a more complex nexus of clients. Some or even much of their role will involve them in direct teaching of children either within the ordinary classroom or in specially withdrawn groups. At such times they do not strictly speaking fulfil a consultant role; they will, though, still have a 'client' or 'clients' – the children whom they teach. In a consultant mode, where they are working through a teacher, a group of teachers or an entire school, to influence what goes on with one or more children, they are likely to have a multiple client system.

In every case, the first client encountered will be the person who makes the consultant aware of a need for his or her involvement. This may be through a telephone call from, say, a head teacher, through an informal chat in the staffroom with a colleague or through a formal approach from a school medical officer. There are many ways for this to happen. This first client has been termed (Schein 1987) the contact client.

There is likely to be another stage beyond the contact client. For an external support consultant, contacted by the head of a primary school over a child with learning difficulties, the next person to be seen may be the school's special needs co-ordinator. For an internal consultant, where the contract client may be a head of year, the next person to be seen may be a head of department. This person, integrally involved in the process of meeting children's special needs, may still not be the individual with whom the consultant will finally work most closely. In such a case, this is the intermediate client.

The person – or group of people – whose problems form the focus of the consultant's work can be termed the primary client. Having talked things over with the intermediate client, the external consultant in our example may elect to work most closely with the child's class teacher. Similarly, the internal consultant may decide to focus upon one or two teachers as his or her primary clients. This is often the case, but not always so. The contact client can be the primary client as well. It may be that the head teacher has general problems of communication with staff which have led to a clash of expectations between him or her and the class teacher; the head may become the primary client because of this. The question of where to place the focus of consultation can only lie with the consultant.

Making contracts

A consulting contract is not, unlike a contract to purchase a house or a marriage contract, legally enforceable. Like a legal contract, though, it needs at least two parties and mutual consent if it is to work. Fortunately the notion of a contract is not a new one in the special needs field. Behavioural contracts and learning contracts with pupils have been used for some time to clarify expectations and outcomes on the part of teacher and taught. Like them, consultancy contract is actually an agreement concerning what will be done, by whom, and when.

Anyone adopting a consultancy role needs to understand the vital importance of the negotiation of a contract with a client and of the links between that contract and those made with other members of the client system. There are some fundamental competences which anyone negotiating with clients has to possess. These are abilities to:

(i) ask direct questions about the client's expectations of the consultant;

(ii) tease out the client's position in relation to other members of the client system;

(iii) state in clear and simple terms what the consultant is prepared to offer and how he or she is prepared to work;

(iv) probe non-threateningly the client's underlying concerns about not being adequately in control;

(v) give verbal encouragement to the client;

(vi) where necessary discuss with the client just why the contracting meeting is not going well.

Issues like these are not always easy to discuss, but by directly addressing anxieties over control and vulnerability, the client's and the consultant's wants, the prospects for success and the sticking points which arise, the probability of problems being encountered later is considerably reduced. They do not have to be discussed; some consultants tend to shelve them with the rationalization that they can be addressed later if it becomes necessary. However, by bringing them into the open at the beginning, the consultant lays the ground for an authentic and non-collusive relationship.

What are the specific implications of the above for the special needs consultant? They are relatively simple: do not get involved in any project until you have talked to each person, clarified his or her expectations and made sure that your clients are broadly in agreement with one another on what they hope to achieve and how they see your role.

Such agreement may not always be easily achieved. Consider the case where a local authority inspector or educational psychologist (the contact client) has a generally negative view of a primary school head teacher's capacity or willpower to implement effective policies for children with learning difficulties within the school. The support teacher is given a general brief of sorting things out there. On meeting the head teacher (the intermediate client), the support teacher is told of one class teacher who has a large group of children whose progress in reading is poor and whose written work is not of the standard of those in the parallel class. The head teacher has tried to discuss changes in teaching strategies with the class teacher but has just met arguments and defensiveness; indeed, early retirement of the teacher is being considered. In the meantime, the head hopes that the class teacher will report on what are the deficiencies in that classroom. The class teacher (primary client) is pleased to see the support teacher. It is about time somebody came along who could sometimes take off the less able, and often naughty, children for extra remedial help. The support teacher, on the other hand, sees her role as that of a facilitator, committed to creating equal opportunities for all children within the classroom and to generating team commitment to meeting special needs in the school.

Expectations and attributions

It is not uncommon for a consultant to encounter this kind of clash of expectations. There are three options: to try to comply with everyone's wishes but covertly work towards the achievement of the consultant's own desired goal; to have no more to do with the situation; or to follow the six pointers already given, making a decision, after generating sufficient information, as to whom to work with and what the purpose of that work will be. It is easy for the support teacher to be seen as somebody who 'does things to people', whether those people are head teachers, class teachers or children. An open and frank attempt at establishing effective contracts with clients will reduce the risk of this.

At the start of this chapter we looked at the ways in which beliefs about the nature of children's learning and behaviour difficulties are shaped. The contracting meetings with potential clients provide the opportunity for the consultant to tease out, from the mass of content which he or she will receive, the beliefs and attributions which each one holds and makes. In our example, the contact client will see the problem as one of

management: ineffective leadership and poor communication on the part of the head teacher. The intermediate client, though, sees it in terms of an intransigent staff member who is inflexible and not prepared to listen to advice. The potential primary client, on the other hand, views matters in terms of inability or unwillingness to learn and also in terms of priorities of time allocation in a crowded classroom. Within each person's terms of reference, the consultant will be able to discern an underlying theory of cause and treatment. To fail to spot these, or to ignore them, will make the task of intervention more difficult.

Earlier in this chapter we also looked at what I termed the guru effect: the tendency to ascribe particular credence to the views of one favoured individual or group of like-minded *cognoscenti*. There are two levels of the operation of this effect for the would be consultant to keep in awareness in the contract-forming stage:

(i)   the extent to which his or her own opinions have been subtly shaped by the received wisdom of the time;
(ii) the extent to which the client wishes to endow him or her with qualities of knowledge and competence in an attempt to shrug off the personal responsibility implicit in the process consultancy relationship.

In short, gurus promote dependency relationships and these are what the consultant should seek to avoid, whether they involve him- or herself or the clients in the system.

The elements of a contract

In any contract with any client at any point in the system there are a number of areas which a consultant needs to clarify and make plain. Contracts do not have to be in writing; but if they are it helps. They do not have to be formal: often a letter after the meeting, setting out the consultant's perceptions of agreements made on both sides, will actually embody the contract. Ideally such a letter should allow the client to disagree with or modify any points made.

More formal forms of contract can also be used. Figure 3.2 shows one widely used by a comprehensive school's special needs support team. Because of the close bonds formed between the team and the other staff members, this is not seen as in any way threatening and actually provides a framework for negotiation of roles. Whatever structure is used, though, there are certain areas which any contract's contents should attempt to cover.

Copies to: Key teacher (Coordinator/Dept, Records)

Support contract

Support teacher: Subject teacher:

Tutor group:	Lesson:	Subject:
Target for support	Needs of pupils (if appropriate)	Purposes of support

Agreed duration of support:

Nature of support:

Any relevant information to facilitate support:

Agreed arrangement for liaison
(meetings, support diary, etc.)

Outcome of support
(report, resources, etc.)

Figure 3.2

1 The boundaries of your involvement
   This is the problem you are going to focus on. It may be a very
   limited one, such as modifying materials for one child in one
   area of the curriculum or reducing a particular child's
   aggressive outbursts in one teacher's lessons. Alternatively it
   may be broader in scope, encompassing the work of a
   department or the behaviour or performance of a group of
   pupils. Whatever the boundaries are, they should be specifically stated. When everyone understands what a consultant's
   involvement will and will not encompass there is a greatly
   increased chance of that involvement being acknowledged as
   successful.

2 The purpose of your involvement
   Here the contract will make plain what everyone involved is
   trying to achieve. This may become modified over time -
   through a renegotiation of the contract - and should not be
   confused with a blinkered objectives approach. However, it
   provides a mutually agreed starting point for initial action.

3 The kind of information you need
   Any consultant needs access to key people and to information.
   Most clients try to limit that information to what they see as
   relevant. When you ask for it later, they may be 'too busy' or
   reluctant to talk. This is the stage to emphasize what you will
   need to know and from whom.

4 Your role and what you will deliver
   You will probably not be able to spell out all the ways that you
   and the client(s) will work together. However, as we have
   already discussed, there may be a number of expectations
   concerning the way you will work and the responsibilities you
   will take on. This is the point where, if you do not expect to be
   directly involved in teaching or if you will only do so much of it
   or if you see the best way of working as being in the classroom
   at all times, your way of working should be pointed out and
   clarified. Clients may not like it; it may be that you will be
   prepared to make concessions or you may decide to change the
   level of your involvement. Whatever the outcome, effective
   negotiation at this stage will remove the risk of shattered
   expectations later. What you will deliver will include the
   above, but it may relate also to advice, equipment, teaching
   materials, written reports and so on. Once again, you can
   avoid recriminations later by being specific at this stage.

5 The support and involvement you need from client(s)
   Here we have the heart of any process consultancy contract.
   This is where you make plain what you want from each client

to make the project successful. It may involve the clients in making more effort in reading about and finding out new ways of working with particular children; it may involve energy in them communicating with one another or with 'outsiders' such as parents or inspectors. It may involve them in trying again in situations which they can no longer tolerate or it may involve them in just giving more time to planning or to particular activities.

6 The time schedule

This is very important. It may, like all other areas, be subject to later renegotiation but from the outset time factors should be accounted for. When will you review your involvement? After a month? At the end of the term? In a year's time? How often will you visit the client(s)? Once a week? Daily? And for how long on each occasion? All too often we hear from teachers, 'I was promised help, but then I hardly ever saw anybody'; 'I think they just ride round in their cars and pretend to be busy'. From the outset, your time involvement should be made explicit.

7 Confidentiality

We often take our own confidentiality for granted. Clients, though, may not and it is as well to make plain what will and will not be reported or discussed with your own line manager or with the client's boss. For a teacher to be open about his or her concerns or problems in dealing with children, there must be a guarantee that only with that teacher's agreement will any of your findings be disclosed to others. Many projects fail or limp along because the clients feel that they cannot trust the discretion of the consultant.

Implementation

The constraints of this chapter obviously do not allow a detailed analysis of the various ways in which a special needs consultant will work. There are so many factors which will influence their activities, not least of them the nature of the special needs which they encounter and the ages of the pupils with whom the consultation process is ultimately concerned. Others include whether the focus of the project is an individual child, a classroom, a department, a school, a parent, a family and so on. Finally, the outcome of the contracting process outlined in the previous section will be of crucial importance in determining what is to happen and how the parties to the contract expect it to happen.

Looking at the kinds of approaches to intervention and change which a consultant can use within schools, Murgatroyd and Reynolds (1984) provide a useful selection for consideration. It is worth noting, though, that they write as high status consultants: people who are called in by senior management and who have established reputations which extend well beyond the boundaries of any school in which they work. My own involvement with internal consultants in schools – people designated special needs co-ordinators or their support staff in comprehensive schools – has revealed that for many of them there are often frustrations which can be summarized as: (i) limited access to top management; (ii) a lack of priority given to their own areas of interests and skills; and (iii) the politics of the school, which can seriously hamper their work in certain areas. Because they are often in less senior positions in the school's hierarchy than many of their clients, the maintenance of credibility can use a lot of energy and at times cause insecurity.

With these points in mind, it is still worth looking at the suggestions made by Murgatroyd and Reynolds (1984). They list a number of tactics available to the consultant:

1 The promotion of conflict – not fostering arguments, but encouraging people to voice their differing viewpoints.
2 Sharply marking out power boundaries, which can mean spelling out just how the consultant sees groups and sub-groups forming and people combining to keep things the way they are.
3 Sharply marking out individual boundaries, where the consultant ensures that individuals' needs – children, teachers, parents, classroom assistants or anyone else involved in the project – are not ignored or discounted in the pressure for some particular form of action.
4 Creating new alliances and coalitions: through the creation of planning teams or small groups with a particular task, such as attempting to provide consistent handling for a child, fresh relationships in the job can be created.
5 The notion of consensus management is widely espoused in schools. By bringing the differences between individuals' attitudes and wants to the fore, the consultant brings senior management to face the fact that 'consensus' almost invariably involves rejection of the ideas of some people.
6 Confronting, where the consultant directly addresses issues which others tend to skirt around. 'Blockages' are often caused by anger between colleagues over past events, by dissatis-

faction with aspects of the way people are regarded by senior staff, by unspoken fears of what may happen if new approaches are adopted and so on. Often people know why others behave in a particular way, but do not wish to mention this. The consultant may choose to break the rules of politeness in a group and bring the blockages directly into focus.

7 There are times when the consultant may see fit to provide certain advice or demonstrate new strategies as a means of developing the resources of those with whom he or she works.

This does not in any way provide an exhaustive list of possible interventions, as Murgatroyd (1988) acknowledges; it does, though, point to some of the processes and possibilities which need to be in the awareness of any consultant.

Schein (1972, 1985) has adopted the widely held view of social change as a model for consultant intervention. The three stages of the change process – unfreezing; changing through cognitive restructuring; refreezing – are seen as overlapping but conceptually distinct. While the consultant is not likely to make the nature of the stages explicit to clients, it is important to retain an awareness of what stage he or she is working in.

Unfreezing any system means creating a readiness to change. Schein (1987) sees that readiness often involves 'unlearning' rather than learning something new and it is the unpleasantness of this which causes resistance on the part of clients. There are three conditions which have to be met if resolution of this first stage is to be achieved.

1 Disconfirmation or lack of confirmation
   Here the consultant, perhaps using information from outside – from colleagues, from children and so on – assists the primary client to recognize that what he or she is doing is not achieving the desired results (disconfirmation) or does not provide psychological support for that client in the actions which he or she is taking.

2 Induction of anxiety
   This involves connecting the disconfirmation with issues that the client cares about. We can experience disconfirmation without anxiety when, for example, a TV programme turns out to be less interesting than we had hoped. The consultant needs to connect a disconfirmation of, say, such a general statement as 'We're wasting our time with children like him' with the experience that an important goal or ideal is not being met.

3 Creation of psychological safety

Disconfirming information is likely to be rejected as part of natural defensiveness if it involves any sense of humiliation or loss of self-esteem. Even if his or her goals or ideals are disconfirmed, the client needs to feel worthwhile. If a teacher is failing to help a child in developing reading skills, for example, the consultant has to ensure that after disconfirmation of the child's essential stupidity, with ensuing anxiety, the teacher does not experience feelings of uselessness. Often an assurance that he or she has problems, but that these are not unusual, is sufficient to meet this condition.

In the second stage, change through cognitive restructuring, the consultant can look to two mechanisms in assisting the client to create new patterns of thinking. The first, identification, involves wanting to be like another person in certain ways and thereby beginning to see things from that other person's point of view. Some consultants deliberately utilize this process, and having 'unfrozen' a client they set out to provide a model themselves for the way things should be done. We are back, however, to the guru effect, with its attendant perils. Other approaches may involve finding relevant role models within the client's situation – a colleague, perhaps – with whom the client can work more closely or actually emphasizing that how others see and deal with a problem situation provides another possible solution. The client must decide whether or not this is suitable for him or her.

An alternative mechanism is scanning. In this the client, recognizing that a problem exists, looks for sources of information on which to base a solution. This may involve talking to others, reading, attending courses and various other ways of gaining new ideas, concepts and skills. The consultant may act as a resource here but should also stimulate the client to act on his or her own behalf. The important thing at this stage is to recognize and harness the client's motivation which has been triggered during the first stage.

Finally, in refreezing, the consultant's attention turns to embedding the new perspectives and approaches adopted by the client and influencing the client's relationship with others. Personal refreezing, Schein (1987) argues, will occur best when the client selects and accepts those new learnings and behaviours that most suit him or her. Where a doctor–patient model of consultancy is adopted, the consultant's suggestions may be eagerly adopted but then applied in a way which makes them unsuccessful, actually setting up disconfirmation of the consul-

tant and his or her ideas. This has been the fate, for example, of many advocates of behaviour modification who have eagerly put across their views to teachers experiencing classroom management difficulties (Bowers 1986). Their ideas have been good, but their suggestions have often become distorted upon implementation, leading to clients' rejection both of the underlying principles and their advocates.

In relational refreezing, the client(s) may have to come to terms with the fact that old alliances and social contacts are not quite the same as before. Adoption of new ways of working may actually damage some earlier relationships with colleagues. While trying to avoid this, the consultant may have to take a role initially in sustaining and reinforcing the new approaches in order that they are maintained.

These stages sound relatively simple; however, they may at times overlap and they require practice to identify with any certainty. There is a temptation for the consultant to believe that he or she can make them happen and, as I have suggested, they can certainly be facilitated. However, it is no good trying to dictate the pace: to do so may in fact arrest or reverse the process.

When clients resist

On the face of it, most of the interactions that a consultant has with clients are rational, logical and intellectually based. Yet beneath this may run an emotional reaction against the process of being helped and against having to face up to issues that cause discomfort. This is the essence of client resistance. It does not always appear, but when it does it can be both puzzling and frustrating for anyone in a consultancy role. What is important to remember, when encountering client resistance, is that it is a natural phenomenon and that to understand its nature, deal with it and pass through it can actually assist clients and strengthen the process of change.

How can resistance be identified? It can take quite subtle and elusive forms and will usually be denied if confronted too soon. While occurring at all points in a client system, resistance is more likely to be observed in the primary client. Here are ten indicators to look out for:

1 Asking for more and more detail – the client keeps probing the consultant for more and more information concerning either a particular child or a 'condition' such as dyslexia or hyperactivity, on the grounds that detailed knowledge is necessary before any action can be taken. Because not

enough detail is ever forthcoming, not a lot gets done.

2 Flooding the consultant with detail – here the client actually bombards the consultant with a huge amount of information, much of it irrelevant, claiming that all of it is necessary for a full understanding of 'the difficulty' to be arrived at.

3 The client would like to be involved and to work on the issues with the consultant. Unfortunately, so many other matters are pressing him or her and they have to take priority.

4 Impracticality – the client lives in the 'real world' and has seen all these airy fairy ideas before. They never work – and are never allowed a chance to do so.

5 Despite all the best endeavours of the consultant, the client seems at a loss to know which path to take. Early confusion is a natural experience for the client; when it persists, it may indicate resistance.

6 Passivity – the client appears compliant and seldom says anything to question or challenge the consultant. The consultant needs to ask if an absence of enthusiasm or any form of involvement, while apparently not blocking his or her path, may be a sign of resistance in the client.

7 When phrases such as 'those people' or 'they ought to' – about anyone who is not present – occur, a front of superiority may be being used to act as a defence against self-understanding or the taking of personal responsibility for a problem.

8 The client has a theory, or perhaps a number of them, about the way things are. 'A lot of research shows that pupil disaffection is linked to early maternal deprivation', or 'there appear to be conflicting views of the importance of visual tracking in the reading process' are examples of intellectualization which can actually be blocking getting on with the task in hand.

9 The client presses for solutions and demands an 'expert' role of the consultant, with prescriptive answers. If these are not immediately forthcoming, then the consultant's competence is called into question.

10 Suddenly, after the consultant has begun to work with the client, there is no longer a problem. It has just gone away, or is minimized to the point of irrelevance. Immediate 'cures', usually expressed by the client, often indicate an unconscious desire to terminate the relationship and therefore to return to the status quo.

Consultancy and support: the future

Being a 'remedial teacher' was never a high status activity,

whether school-based or peripatetic. With the advent of the Warnock Report (DES 1978) and the 1981 Education Act, attention became focused on meeting children's special educational needs within ordinary schools. It was a Cinderella which, if not a princess, at least had a ticket to the ball. Instead of special classes or pupil withdrawal, new ways of working became developed and the concept of 'support' became widely accepted. Now, though, there are powerful forces in education which may shift schools' priorities away from meeting special educational needs, as Robert Harvey points out in Chapter 1. Coupled with these, the pressures of 'market forces' are likely to be brought increasingly to bear on services which lie outside the direct delivery of the National Curriculum. In Chapter 13 I look at some of the implications of such pressures.

It is therefore vitally important that those in support roles should develop levels of awareness and skills which, until now, have not been strongly in evidence in the teaching of children with special educational needs. Dedication, commitment, a capacity to care and faith in others' pronouncements and prescriptions are not enough. Indeed, at times they may actually get in the way of doing an effective job. In this chapter I have touched on some of the insights and skills which are needed by a competent consultant and which, in the training workshops in which I have been involved, we endeavour to assist participants to acquire. As I pointed out earlier in this chapter, the one thing we can be sure of is change. As changes occur in our education system, then competencies which have previously not been expected become vital in those charged with support for the less advantaged pupils in our schools.

Chapter 4

Consultancy in action

Penny Platt

I work with children with severe learning difficulties. Traditionally, such pupils have been seen as presenting too many problems to be effectively integrated into ordinary schools; my job is to make it possible for them to start at and stay in the mainstream. Before I go further, perhaps I can draw you a picture of a couple of pupils with whom I am concerned.

Jenny

Jenny is seven years old. She is shy on meeting strangers, but has a wide smile for her friends. Her brown eyes twinkle from behind the large prettily framed glasses which perch on her snub nose. She is a small child, popular for the warmth of her personality, and works hard in the Infant 3 class of her local primary school, where she is doing very well. Jenny enjoys school enormously. She loves to read and to work on associated phonic activities and study skills. She is reading the Gay Way yellow books in school. Her work books are full of lively drawings and her own writing – both news and class topics. She loves to help other children with their spellings. Jenny is working through the Peak Infant Maths Scheme, Section 3, and will soon be ready for extra, preparatory activities for Section 4. Her favourite lessons are PE and music and she enjoys the weekly speech therapy sessions held in school to encourage her language development.

William

William is only five, but he is very tall for his age. Like Jenny he is

reserved at first but he quickly warms and becomes friendly and chatty. His face lights up as he talks about his family and his toys. He loves to play with cars and when he has finished his school work, he chooses to make little vehicles out of Lego. Sometimes his friends help him to snap the pieces together, for he has difficulty in getting the pressure right, but the designs are all his own. William is in the first class of his local primary school. It is a small, mixed first and second year infants class and he is in his second year. He, like Jenny, is working his way through his school's reading scheme, although more slowly than she. He has learned recognition of quantity to 6 and can also form the numerals, although he has physical difficulty with the movements. The infant curriculum develops early concepts of size, colour, shape and comparison and William has acquired, and uses, quite a range of knowledge. Perhaps his greatest difficulty is that his co-ordination and motor control are very poor, part of a condition with which he was born.

Educational opportunity: the 1981 Education Act

Both Jenny and William were born with genetic disorders which include the prognosis 'mental handicap'. Ten to fifteen years ago that would have been sufficient to make theirs a birthright of segregated education, of specialist schooling for 'mentally handicapped' children. For William and Jenny, however, life was to be quite different. Their parents were able to take advantage of radical new rights embodied in the 1981 Education Act. They were able to share, with the professionals, in the decision making about their children's abilities and needs. They were able to give serious consideration to the advantages and disadvantages of mainstream, local, peer group schooling for their cognitively impaired children, as well as for their siblings. They had good contacts with their neighbourhood schools, which already knew the families and had both known Jenny and William from their baby days.

They were also fortunate in being part of a network of similar families in the area, all of whom were convinced that their children would gain most, developmentally as well as socially and emotionally, from education in mainstream schools. Some were members of a mutual support group known as the Children's Opportunity Group (COG) and all had had considerable pre-school input from a multidisciplinary community mental handicap team. The children themselves had also benefited from the experience of nursery school or class. Some were older

than Jenny and William, some much the same age, but all had 'identifiable mental handicap', to quote the words of medical practitioners.

A support service for children with severe learning difficulties

By September 1987 eight such children were in full-time mainstream primary education in schools throughout Bolton, where they all live, with other younger children placed in nursery schools, classes and day nurseries. The ages of the eight ranged from 4 to 9 but none of them had ever known anything other than mainstream education. The older children had previously had nursery nurse (NNEB) support on a temporary basis and it had become apparent that with at least that level of support and some extra teacher input to help the schools to resource their needs, other children too would benefit from mainstream schooling. There was also a hope among parents, professionals and the local education authority (LEA) that such a resource commitment would not only enhance the existing integration but also provide an incentive for expansion to meet and encourage increased demand from parents.

Thus, in September 1987, Bolton Metropolitan Borough became one of the first LEAs in the country to establish a support service designed specifically to enhance the full-time, local, mainstream placements of children with what is commonly known as severe learning difficulty (SLD). That such a commitment to mainstream opportunity for children with SLD is in the vanguard of current educational thinking may be seen from the literature (ILEA 1985b; Mittler and Farrell 1987; Bowers 1987; Wolfendale 1987). However, my LEA is not alone in offering such opportunities, although its particular form of provision is still quite new. There are other similar children elsewhere who have known only local community, peer group schooling and the first of them are now going through secondary schooling.

They are all pioneers, pushing back barriers of 'It's never been done, therefore it can't be done' every step along the way. Their achievement is considerable, no less because often there has been little help. The role and achievements of the schools and individual class teachers in this should not be underestimated or worse still patronized. Their spectacular success to date with children like Jenny and William has been achieved largely through the determined efforts of child, school and home to learn and teach a mainstream curriculum despite the constraint of few extra resources.

Changing needs: changing the response

LEAs are now, however, beginning to respond to pressure for those extra resources. The support service for which I am responsible is due to double in size from September 1989. It will support 16 children seen to have severe learning difficulties, all in their own local primary school. There will be two teachers and the equivalent of eight full-time nursery nurses.

Those teachers who are being appointed to resource children with 'specified handicap' in full-time, neighbourhood schooling represent something relatively new in the annals of supported learning, as they do not derive from any existing structure. They are not supporting children partially integrated from other special schools or special units. Nor are they derived from those well established services which have traditionally supported the 18 per cent of the school population identified by the Warnock Report (1978) as having learning difficulties of a less severe or temporary nature. Some of the new support for the 2 per cent with statements of need under Section 7 of the 1981 Education Act will, to be sure, be provisioned from within existing generic support services; but some will be charting new waters.

The visiting teacher offering this new provision will nevertheless, like her more traditional colleagues, have an expertise to offer. For children with severe learning difficulties, for example, this expertise will be in the cognitive curriculum, hidden for most children within their developmental pattern but needing identification and teaching to this client group. She will need to be able to share this expertise with the schools, to encourage modification of the curriculum for all to take it into account, but what she will most need to avoid is the 'expert' role. To date, schools have succeeded spectacularly without such help. Aware that the mainstream curriculum ahead of these children is increasingly complex, staff in many schools are asking for help in addressing future issues well in advance. They should not be seen as asking for help to put right a problem but as looking for a pooling of ideas in order to continue to provide a supportive and effective learning environment. The person to whom they turn for help will need to be able to offer far more than 'adequate child-related teaching skills'. She will need what Tony Bowers (1987) has described as competences in adult human relationships which can be placed under the broad umbrella of consultancy skills.

The consultancy role within my own work, for example, seems to have been seen by the education authority, by the schools, by the families and by outside agencies who have looked at the

development of the service over the first year as being an important and useful extension to traditional support. It is increasingly taken up by the schools as a valuable resource, offering help and advice in the shared planning and management of a continuingly effective learning environment for the child with SLD and for her peers.

The resource needs of schools, or their need for up-to-date specialized information or access to specialist contacts, are constantly changing. They alter in response to the shifting dynamics of the needs of the children with learning difficulties, the other children and the internal and external influences shaping the nature of the school (e.g. changes in personnel or the implications of new legislation). There is a constant process of metamorphosis and it is on ways to bring about the most effective change out of all these interactive influences that consultancy is sought and achieved. Furthermore, such dynamics are mirrored in the home lives of the children and in their changing medical or paramedical needs. Home and school interact and interrelate even more than they do for most children.

The consultant's role includes extending the parent–professional partnership already in existence and ensuring continuing good relations and open dialogue. Working with children who have, or who are being assessed for, statements of need, she will have certain contributions of her own to make (written reports, joint consultative meetings to attend etc.), either to the educational advice for statement or to the annual review. She needs also to be aware of her potential use to parents as an advocate. They may wish to take advantage of her specialist knowledge of the workings of the 1981 Education Act (or indeed subsequent Education Acts) to guide, advise or inform their own actions. It is the consultant, too, who may be best placed, through her specialized network of contacts, to liaise between the school and the medical support services used by the child.

Those of us working in this field, particularly where we are external to the day-to-day dynamics of the individual schools, are not unaware of the magnitude of the task ahead in advancing the role from that of support teacher is that of change agent. There is a long established tradition of simply providing remediation to overcome, a tradition of an extra adult teaching the same curriculum a different way. Schools with a child who not only needs a carefully designed and modified individual version of the classroom curriculum, but who also comes pre-packaged and neatly labelled as offering 'difficulty', may look for more of the

same sort of help. There is a familiar form of help which can be assimilated without too much reconstruction of the norms or organization of the school. If the school is reassured by the title of the bearer of that promised help and sees it as the old familiar teaching help but highly specific to the perceived difficulty, then there is a danger that its staff will breathe a sigh of relief and mentally or physically pass the 'difficult' child across to her highly specialized and therefore 'expert' helper. Some schools may well be unaware of other possible forms of help, such as consultancy, and despite their success to date may be consequently expecting input of a traditional nature.

Defining the consultancy role

Even before the consultant meets her new colleagues and begins to define her boundaries for a contract, she may be at a substantial disadvantage. If her job title is that of 'support teacher', 'advisory teacher' or 'home tutor', the receiving school may consider that it knows her job parameters and have already begun to define the boundaries within which she will be required to work. In setting out her own stall, the consultant who finds herself in this position has not only to sell her own analysis of the situation, or even the right to be invited to make an analysis, but also to persuade head teachers that their preconceptions of her role are perhaps inaccurate. This is crucial to making the transition from traditionally passive support to active change. It is, however, probably the largest, most difficult task facing the hopeful consultant. For it is now, right at the start of a complex and delicate series of negotiations to establish a right to the role of consultant and to develop that role to the mutual satisfaction of all parties, that the consultant comes face to face with the management of power.

This is where in-school consultancy may well differ from business consultancy, at least until LEAs or other agencies of formal control are prepared substantially to back and redefine special needs help as consultancy. In the business world, the consultant is invited into the workplace to consider a problem. Management and consultant meet as partners in negotiating a contract to analyse the problem and to consider how best to help the organization to decide upon and implement change. For the purposes of this exercise they both have equal power. The consultant does not have the formal authority of the manager, but as her agent, is given devolved power or influence.

Client systems

The support teacher or head of service, working alone as a consultant without a framework of formal authority, is not working as an equal in the power stakes. The head teacher has formal authority derived from her status and influence. The consultant does not. Neither does she have devolved authority until the head chooses to confer it. Working only from the 'status' power conferred on her as 'expert' she has to convince the head that she would receive more satisfactory long-term help by using her to help change the organization than by using her merely as a support teacher. Small wonder that most teachers, finding themselves in this position, baulk at the task and settle primarily for the head's definition of their role while still hoping to effect wider change from within.

What of the consultant, however, who chooses to proceed with her perception of that role? Without formal recognition of her consultancy role to give her direct authority, she will need to enter into negotiations from as equal a power base as she can muster. This means looking at those agencies or clients who confer authority on her and knowing what amount and type of power each confers. In all probability her authority will derive from four key clients. Her contact client, the one who appointed her to be the person to whom the school would turn, will almost certainly be the local education authority, via an intermediary agent such as a special needs adviser or education officer or head of service. The person with whom she will have most contractual dealings will be her intermediate client – in this case, and almost certainly in a primary school, the head teacher. Her primary client will be the person(s) with whom she will work most closely; ideally the whole school, but possibly a class teacher or an individual child. (In getting away from the support teacher role, however, the latter is less likely.) The child, or her parents on her behalf, is best seen as being the ultimate client, i.e. the person(s) on whose behalf the consultant is ultimately working. It is the parents who, albeit indirectly, first approached the LEA with the need for help. With this network of important and influential clients, therefore, the consultant has increased her power and influence, by taking advice from contacts unavailable (or less available) to others.

It is probable also that the consultant has a back-up team of some status who would help in compiling a creditable and workable framework within which to operate. Again there are bound to be variations from service to service and differing

degrees of influence. In my own service I am fortunate in having considerable autonomy and freedom of action and I also have the benefit of access to several key individuals with any one of whom I can discuss a proposed action or derive greater authority, if I so wish. Together we form a semi-formal joint management team. It comprises myself, the education officer for special needs, the head teacher of the special school (SLD) where the service has been based and the educational psychologist for 'pre-school' and 'mental handicap' who worked with the children in their nursery setting and who helps to identify future clients. I also have direct access as required to a multidisciplinary network of service managers: the senior educational psychologist, the consultant community paediatrician, the assistant director of community nursing services and the education adviser (general) who has a specific interest in education in the early years. This network is in turn further strengthened by the fact that the service is seen as part of a tripartite thrust of local provision for the mentally handicapped (*sic*), which is currently under review in the context of opportunities for 'normalization'. The service thus finds itself scrutinized and supported by the various forums held under the review, including parents and local councillors. It is possible, therefore, to see a variety of contact clients, all with an interest in encouraging the consultant to develop her role to meet the needs of the ultimate client.

Managing contractual relationships

This alone is not enough, however. No amount of back-up authority can compensate for the management skills required of the consultant, particularly in managing relationships. She will, for example, need skills in establishing contractual relationships, both to persuade the head to listen to her point of view and to be able to offer openings for negotiation and exchange of which the head can take advantage without being seen to lose any of her formal authority. Equally, the consultant will need to be able to recognize openings which are offered to her by which she may be able to 'trade' for outcomes. She needs a cool-headed but none the less assertive ability to recognize and play power games equally as well as the head teacher (but never being seen to play these better, for that carries a high risk of alienating the head). A more experienced consultant might at this point consider it advantageous to take that risk, but risk management is a finely tuned skill which develops with experience. It is not to be recommended too early in a consultant's career!

With a combination of a clear sense of her own authority and effective skills in human relations, the teacher consultant ought to be able to overcome her apprehension. This may not come easily at first, particularly for the many teachers who have never before considered themselves to have any formal power. They may need to look carefully at the ways they have in fact exercised power in the past in order to gain confidence for the future. Because the consultant may be having to establish her right to be there, rather than having been invited in and given power to help effect organizational change, it is a fearsome task.

However, many heads are committed to constantly reviewing their organizational procedure and adapting the school's philosophy to new influences upon it. They themselves may be looking for someone externally based to help them effect such change and feel constricted by the narrowness of having 'support teaching' imposed upon them. Such a head teacher's first question might well be 'How can you help me?' This is not aggressive, but represents a very real opening up of genuine discussion, negotiation and, ultimately, consultancy.

The support teacher/consultant who is not prepared with broad aims for her consultancy role ready in her mind, if not in a 'sales brochure', puts herself yet again at a disadvantage. She needs to maintain a positive view of the successful outcome of her task and to be sure of her ground, not to be dogmatic but to know when to give way and when to pursue a point. In this way she is able quickly, competently and confidently to reassure the head teacher that she really is going to be an asset to the school in effecting change.

Negotiating a contract

At this point both partners are ready to negotiate a contract for the role the consultant will play. Again, there may be an imbalance of expectations at the outset. The head teacher will probably have a long list of requirements which she expects her consultant personally to implement. These are very likely to be child-centred rather than related to broader issues such as curriculum design or classroom management within the school (the issues the consultant might later identify). The head may ask for design and implementation of an individual curriculum, remedial reinforcement of certain teaching areas, diagnostic assessment, record keeping, report writing and parental involvement, among others. She may also confide that help would be

appreciated in modifying the class teacher's attitude or approach to the 'problem of special needs'.

The consultant, however, should resist the temptation to accept such a list as her final task description. To do so would be the normal reaction of a subordinate to the instruction of a superior; but the consultant is not a subordinate. It is not for her to own the problem. The school has to acknowledge that it is theirs. The consultant's role is to assist certain people there in resolving it, sharing and using her experience in order that they can take it back to themselves, no longer as a problem, and move on (Bowers 1987). She will need, therefore, to define her boundaries very firmly and clearly.

Her first commitment needs to be to an analysis of the situation. From this she will produce a report for the head teacher summarizing her findings and outlining proposals for how she can offer help. This is likely in turn to lead to further renegotiations before the contract begins. It is worth noting that her analysis will almost certainly encompass all the points noted by the head teacher but with a different perspective, for her concern is how best to help the school to achieve each of those for itself.

Once it has been agreed that the consultant will not automatically take up the empty seat adjacent to the 'problem child', but is in fact to assume the role of observer, the next step is to establish a timetable. For this she needs skills in the management of time. She will need to allow sufficient time to get a feel for the organization's norms, methods and 'hidden agenda' without becoming too familiar a part of it. She will need to be able to reconcile this with the head's need to be seen to be doing something as soon as possible. An important part of the contract now being negotiated is the frequency and duration of visits and the date of the preliminary review meeting with the head. Having established boundaries, and the timetable, it is advisable to run a final check on how the head teacher now sees her own terms of reference, as well as the consultant's role. The consultant might also find it valuable to follow up the discussion with a written résumé as soon as possible. This acts both as her own safeguard and as a basis for renegotiation if either party is unhappy at this stage. When work begins on the analysis, both parties will define areas of involvement more tightly, so a preliminary review meeting is essential.

This review meeting is the time when the contract is most tightly defined and at which both parties make and discuss proposals for areas of change and methods of action. From this

meeting come the consultant's job description and the support, resources and organization required of the school.

The contract should include details of frequency, time and duration of meetings and with whom they are to be held. The role of the consultant at each of these meetings needs to be clearly established and explained to all participants. If the consultant has agreed to take on some specialized teaching input for a specific child, it is now that her contribution to statementing, or more importantly, review procedures must be clearly understood, agreed and documented. Consideration needs to be given to the wish for written reports and for whom they will be produced, by whom and with what frequency. This is particularly important when the consultant considers herself to be working ultimately on behalf of the child and her family. She may wish the parents to receive specific, periodic, written reports from herself. The fact that she intends to maintain close communication with the families and the implications that that will have for the school's own organizational links with home need to be thoroughly discussed and clarified. This is in fact an issue which may become a major item on her agenda for change.

Meetings with staff

Although, inevitably, every contract will be as unique as the individual's needs, and the circumstances defining it, it may be possible to identify some common considerations. Firstly, if the consultant is to help the organization to re-order itself and assimilate a new special needs perspective, she will have to become very involved with all of the staff, not just the teacher(s) of the problem child(ren). This will mean a clearly defined and explained role at certain staff meetings. It may mean the consultant suggesting that certain types of meeting be called, with specific agendas. They may be meetings at which the head teacher has a natural leadership role. They may be meetings in which the staff need to be encouraged to become much more involved in discussion and brainstorming than they are now, in order to become more interactive and take responsibility for their own collective decisions. There may need to be meetings without the inhibiting presence of a head teacher (Hanko 1985). The consultant may feel it appropriate to suggest certain forms of school-based INSET or useful external 'workshop' leaders whom the school might wish to 'buy in' as part of an INSET bid. All of these issues need to be identified and

resolved when the head teacher and consultant negotiate the contract.

What of the staff? They were not involved in the actual contract negotiation. They do not, therefore, have a contract with the consultant and yet they are the people whose classroom organization, methodology and attitudes the consultant has contracted to help change. It is important, therefore, that not only has the idea of using a consultant arisen from interactive staff discussion, but that the head teacher reports back to the staff on the proposed involvement of the consultant. At the earliest possible opportunity, before beginning her observational analysis in school, the consultant needs to meet with the staff and explain her brief and to negotiate a contract with her primary client, the staff themselves. Such discussion should serve not only to inform and clarify ideas about her presence and role but also to redefine it. This in turn might entail renegotiation with the intermediate client on the overall contract, for it is now that she will pick up not only useful suggestions thrown up by the exchange of feelings among the staff, but also elements of the hidden agenda of the tensions and conflicts within the organization. Hanko (1985) suggests that the preliminary meeting with staff is so important as ideally to take place with the head's sanction but before she herself speaks with her staff.

Resistance

Another common factor likely to be encountered is client resistance. It will take many forms, some instantly recognizable, some more subtle. Tony Bowers, in his work on consultancy has described resistance as:

> a reaction to an emotional process taking place within a client. It is not a reflection of the interaction we are having with the client on an objective, logical, rational level. Resistance is a predictable, natural emotional reaction against the process of being helped and against the process of having to face up to difficult organisational problems.
>
> Bowers, 1988, personal communication

Teachers are used to being offered lack of resources (time, material, human) as a reason for resistance to curriculum innovation but there are other less instantly recognizable defences. There are the stalling tactics of the colleague who may wish to help effect change but be unsure of what is expected of her or how the changes will affect her personally in the short or

long term. There are many forms, ranging from persistent requests for more and more detail, to silence, which should not be taken as consent. The important thing for the consultant to remember is that resistance is part of the change process and should not be taken personally or as an attack upon her competence. Recognized and worked through it is a valuable part of the interactive process.

It is never easy to introduce change. A multiplicity of skills are required to manage its many dimensions. It is even more difficult when the change agent, in this case the consultant, is not only new to the challenges involved but has not had the benefit of a role model set by the example of predecessors or seniors. Consultancy in schools is a new idea. Those who take it on may make mistakes but they may also achieve worthwhile change in others and in themselves.

A theory of interactive consultancy

The following section examines the consultancy role from a theoretical perspective. It looks more closely at the nature of interaction within an organization and contrasts that with another organizational model, that of reaction or passive intervention (in sociological terms, the functional model). It considers the demands on support teachers and the difficulties and conflicts which can arise from the dual role of teacher and adviser (Bowers 1987; Wolfendale 1987; Moses *et al*. 1988). These conflicts are examined within the context of the organizational models and contrasted through the use of a case study with the development of a consultancy role within an interactive framework.

The interactive school

An organization which is interactive is an integral and dynamic whole, constantly metamorphosing to allow enlargement, development and change. It consistently shifts its own dynamics in response to internally and externally imposed change, absorbing and adapting its shape and performance, generating and regenerating internal growth.

The head of an interactive school involves all her staff in discussion of all elements of change. Her communication skills enable all members to feel that they have contributed to, and participated in, identifying and creating constructive change.

This is the school where there is communality of purpose and understanding, derived from those shared discussions which contribute to decision making; the school where thoughtfully evaluated feedback enables each member to feel that he or she is a valued participant. In such a school, special educational needs do not present a problem. The term represents one of many elements in the lives of the children, who are the life of the school. The individual with learning disabilities is recognized as being an important element within this social dynamic. Clements (1987) sees that person as having an equal contribution to make to it, influencing and being influenced, a source of change as well as an object of change.

The teaching appropriate for each child in the school comes from its interactive framework, for it is this framework which defines the classroom organization and approach. The school constantly reappraises the influences on its development. It will identify the help it needs in understanding and accommodating each new influence. Here the consultant (or advisory) role is dominant. The school will have sought out that particular form of help.

The consultant will be introduced to all staff and her anticipated role offered to her on the basis of prior discussion and agreement within the organization. After negotiation of an appropriate role, the framework for interaction is established. With the role of each participant thus defined, the school, with the help of its consultant, is able to look at itself and its needs and propose its own redefinition, ultimately internalizing the change. The consultant is a resource available to the school which is looking to adapt to a changing environment and happy to seek help in so doing. She will almost certainly be asked to bring with her into the discussion her expertise, knowledge and experience of the external factors which are further influences for change. She will work alongside her new colleagues, sharing with them the exploration of the dynamics influencing the need for change. Together they will reach conclusions about outcomes and ultimately the school (in particular the intermediate and primary clients) will use those conclusions to make its decisions and create a new appropriate environment. If it has been considering special needs, for example, it will have adapted to provide for the difficulties likely to be encountered by the youngster(s) under consideration, as I illustrate in the case study below.

Before looking at this case study, however, it is important to consider another more common approach to special needs

support in order to be able to contrast the two positions. Furthermore, it is a contention of this chapter that it is the contrast between the two perspectives which underpins many of the difficulties currently being experienced by support teachers with an 'advisory teacher' brief.

Functional organization and reactive support

Learning difficulty is commonly perceived as a problem in need of treatment. The remedy proposed has varied over the years, most recently evolving from a remedial to an environmental or ecological mode. The problem child with a learning difficulty was formerly withdrawn from the classroom environment and given extra and different practice in a curriculum area in which she was considered to be weak, in the hope that such intensive treatment would make the child better. This view became unpopular as it was seen as unrealistic to remove a child and her difficulty from the context in which the difficulty was experienced. It was also considered to be socially divisive.

The currently prevailing ecological perspective on special educational needs support stresses the need for extra help to be given to the child within her normal classroom context and to the class teacher in the form of advice on how to 'access' the curriculum for the child. Despite this changing emphasis, the child and her needs are still seen as problematic. This derives from the structuring and organization of many schools within a functional framework.

An organization run on this model is a system with a number of different components (branches, departments etc.) each of which functions independently while still being co-ordinated by the manager or director. It runs as smoothly as the skills of the management allow. Change, innovation and conflict are dealt with as functions of the department or component which they affect but with reference to their impact on the continued efficient functioning of the whole. The manager of the relevant sector identifies the problem and proposes a solution or a need for help. The problem is isolated and reacted to in a manner considered to be least disruptive and most beneficial to the system.

Using this model in relation to schools, we see various components including (not exhaustively) departments, classes, children and children with special needs. 'Special needs' here is quite clearly a separate component, its very description indicating a problem in need of a special and different approach.

A child with special needs in a functional system is potentially a dysfunction. She is a problem, a faulty part which, without treatment, poses a threat to the continuing efficiency of the remainder.

From this perspective, the support teacher may be seen to be the expert, the mechanic, called in to service the dysfunction. Formerly called upon to remedy or even to remove the faulty part, she now models, or advises upon, possible modifications. She shares her expertise but she is none the less still the problem solver. Hers is a reactive role. The school presents her with its problem and she reacts to it, attempting to solve the problem or to make it as little a nuisance as possible, perhaps offering the school advice on how to minimize it but nevertheless accepting the brief to handle the problem on behalf of the school.

Advisory teacher: a conflicting brief?

We have looked so far at two different organizational models and at the nature of the support input appropriate to each. Many of today's support teachers have assumed the designation 'advisory teacher' in line with the recommendations of the Warnock Report (13.24). They are experiencing conflict and difficulty within their role, both in terms of their own interpretation of it and in the expectations others have of them. This conflict may be seen to arise essentially from the differences between the two organizational models.

The Warnock Report called for the traditional role of the support, or former 'remedial', teacher to be widened to emphasize in-class support and co-operative working with the class teacher. The use of the term 'advisory' reflects demand for special needs staff to advise colleagues on a variety of possible organizational and curricular approaches. Its juxtaposition with the title 'teacher' underlines the insistence on retaining the child-related teaching role.

Many advisory teachers will find themselves working within a functionally organized school, given and accepting a brief to take over the management of the 'special needs problem'. Asked to be expert support teachers they will employ their specialized teaching skills to interpret the curriculum to the child or children and attempt to teach appropriate strategies for mastery of areas of difficulty. They have a skill for sale – attending to problem parts – and the school has need of the practitioner of such a skill. There is harmony, not conflict between the expectations of the two parties.

The addition of an advisory capacity, however, introduces potential for disharmony or conflict because it arises from an intrinsically different model. It derives from an interactive, not a reactive, model; from an interactionist perspective not a functionalist one. To superimpose so active a model of structural change on to such a diametrically opposed foundation is bound to create tension, uncertainty and misunderstanding. The functional school's expectations will vary fundamentally from those of the advisory teacher who is looking to share in bringing about change within the organization. The essence of the conflict in the role of the advisory teacher is to be found here, in the dichotomy between passive problem solving *for* the school and offering help *to* the school in adapting itself to provide a supportive learning environment. The functional school's management team may consider that it is not the place of the mechanic to offer advice but rather to get on with sorting out the problem and it may resist such an approach. Alternatively it may consider that some advice on alterations to the area creating or exacerbating the problem might be beneficial in helping to reduce the problem but there might be a breakdown in communication between the advisory teacher and management team or class teacher. She may experience resistance from class teachers, for by perpetuating the idea of special educational needs as problematical the functional school perpetuates the idea of the support teacher as an expert problem solver. The further designation 'advisory' implies therefore that expert advice on problem solving will be forthcoming. This will almost certainly engender either resistance from teachers, who consider it in turn to imply a failure on their own part in not solving the problem or a total devolution of the 'problem' to the 'expert'.

There is bound to be conflict for the advisory teacher whose training (post-Warnock) or instinct will be towards seeing herself as a helper and change agent. It is probable that the advisory teacher considers herself already to have a consultancy role with a brief to help effect change. If she is developing that role within an interactive environment she will have a productive part to play within a receptive interplay of ideas, views, strategies and advice. If, however, she is developing it within the 'It's your job to solve this problem' environment of the functional school, she will find many instances of clashing expectations or culture shock. These create disorientation and conflict within her own perceptions of her role in theory and practice and lead to the sorts of difficulties for advisory teachers identified by Bowers (1987). An organization cannot be both

functional and interactive; yet we expect our advisory teachers to be both. If we are to resolve this conflict, we need to offer external special needs supporters a clearly defined role as one or the other. This chapter proposes the adoption of an interactive consultancy role.

Cassie

The story of Cassie, a child with special educational needs, illustrates the advantages offered by such a consultancy.

Cassie had been taken into her local church school as an enlightened and even Christian gesture on the part of governors and staff. The school was popular with parents not only for its emphasis on religious teachings and family unity but also for the formality of its teaching approach. Its organization was predominantly functional although the head was prepared to consider any way open to her of meeting Cassie's needs within her school. As Cassie grew up, her need for an individualized curriculum and for help with interpreting much of the classroom curriculum ('real' and 'hidden') became ever greater, until at last her school was given an advisory teacher.

The advisory teacher intervention

'Too late', cried the despairing head and staff, 'You're too little too late. We can't solve this problem and nor will you. Oh what shall we do? . . . It's all yours!' Now the difficulty for the advisory teacher was threefold. Firstly, this was a functionally organized school and secondly, the cry for help was, she felt, clearly a manifestation of client resistance and not an opening for negotiation on how to provide the most supportive learning environment for Cassie within that school. Thirdly and importantly, she was ambiguous about her own role and saw herself being asked to offer expert advice to the school on how she would solve their problem. She accepted the premise that there was a problem in need of an externally derived solution.

For months she grappled reactively with the problems Cassie and the class teacher were having. She devised and taught individual and remedial programmes. She reviewed and restructured work in consultation with the class teacher, offering her best advice. Cassie's behaviour became increasingly inappropriate, so the advisory teacher wrote a behaviour modification programme. She contributed to reports and case conferences as the situation moved uncomfortably on to its seemingly predestined outcome of alternative provision in a special school.

The problem was getting worse. The only solution appeared to be to take the problem out before everything around it broke down. No one was happy, but no one could see any alternative.

The consultant intervention
Before that decision was taken, however, the head teacher and the advisory teacher both remembered something. They remembered that the head had said she would try anything. They remembered that she had asked the advisory teacher for help. They decided that if they forgot the 'problem' and considered instead how they could work together to effect change within Cassie's learning environment throughout the school, there was perhaps still a chance of keeping her. So the advisory teacher offered a consultancy relationship. She and the head discussed internal organizational changes which were then implemented. These involved managing resources (human, time, material) in a more effective way, for example redistributing the 16¼ hours of nursery nurse support to gain an extra session. At the consultant's suggestion, the adults concerned with Cassie's learning environment were allocated meeting times to work out a curriculum methodology which would not only meet Cassie's individual needs but also adapt the learning style of the rest of the class to take those needs into account without detriment to the other children. The head and consultant met regularly to discuss progress and resource the on-going changes. The consultant was a facilitator, helping the school to adapt to meet Cassie's needs from within its own resources. Her help was sought and encouraged but above all the school was taking back its own problem and seeing it no longer as a problem but as an internal challenge to be adapted to and reprovisioned in order to continue to meet Cassie's needs.

The decision on whether or not alternative schooling would be necessary was deferred as everyone became aware of a change. Cassie was much happier. She was more manageable and found herself enjoying her work. Her adult helpers were happier and more responsive to her needs. Her timetable had been restructured to manage human resources in a more supportive way and her class curriculum was devised and presented in such a way that not only could she now join in but the other children, too, responded more productively. Cassie's parents were delighted with the change.

Cassie's story is not unique; we can derive generalizable principles from it. By taking on the school's definition of a 'problem', the advisory teacher found herself confused and

distracted from what she perceived as the fundamental need. Once the change was made to a consultancy role, in collaboration with the head teacher and staff, she gained a clearer definition to her work. The school too had its role clarified in the redefinition. It took back its 'problem' and looked again at its frame of reference. The consultancy relationship helped the school to provide a supportive learning environment for a child with special educational needs.

By adopting the approach outlined here, the consultant herself becomes more at ease in her professional persona. She is not an advisory teacher, given vague and conflicting briefs to help solve a problem. She is not a support teacher shoring up a deficiency. She is an interactive resource available to help the school to meet its needs.

Chapter 5

The role and management of welfare assistants

Terence Clayton

Welfare assistance as a developing resource

Increasingly, local education authorities are using welfare assistance as a resource to help mainstream teachers with the management and education of children with special educational needs and, as Hodgson *et al.* (1984) have pointed out, this is more likely to occur in primary than secondary schools. Evidence of this trend comes from the recent London University Institute of Education survey (Goacher *et al.* 1988) which showed that some 64 per cent of metropolitan LEAs and 90 per cent of shire LEAs recorded a 'substantial increase' in the number of welfare assistants/non-teaching auxiliaries employed and 65 per cent of LEAs indicated that this was an area of priority funding. Nevertheless, fewer than one in three offered any training for these staff. In the author's own authority the number of hours of welfare assistance allocated to named children with special educational needs has almost trebled since the implementation of the 1981 Education Act.

What are the reasons for this increase? Is it that local authorities have been impressed by the arguments put forward by Plowden (DES 1967), Duthie (1970) and Warnock (DES 1978) or has it occurred, as Hegarty (1987) suggests, as a response to pressure or representations made? While not wishing to minimize the desire of some LEAs to fulfil the spirit of the act and promote policies of integration, we cannot dismiss the feeling that financial considerations and outside pressures have played their part and that development has often occurred in an *ad hoc* fashion. Welfare assistants are also used, as Kolvin *et al.* (1981)

noted, because of the lack of trained specialists. The financial benefit of employing welfare assistants is highlighted by the example given by Dale (1979), who demonstrated that the cost of integrating a partially hearing child by supporting her in the mainstream with an assistant worked out at three-fifths of the cost of special unit provision.

Whatever the reasons, numbers are clearly increasing quite rapidly. This makes it more important than ever that we gain a better understanding of the variety of welfare assistant practice within our schools. The author agrees with Thomas (1987) that, if sensible change and progress are to occur, those in a position to influence policy and planning should know what is actually happening in schools. Unfortunately, the whole field of welfare assistance is poorly researched. Several of the studies frequently referred to in the literature, although offering useful insights, had issues other than welfare assistance as their main focus. Others with a direct focus, however, have generally been small scale and limited in their scope. It was for these reasons that the Wiltshire study, described later in this chapter, was carried out. However, before considering this, it would be helpful to look at three of the more substantial and important studies, described in the earlier literature – those by Anderson (1973), Hegarty *et al.* (1981) and Hodgson *et al.* (1984), as these provide useful insights into the role of welfare assistants.

Recruitment and role of welfare assistants

The three studies referred to above all draw attention to the fact that, where LEA recruitment policies exist, these vary considerably, with some LEAs appointing only qualified personnel, usually holders of the Nursery Nurses Examination Board certificate, whereas others are content to employ women who have had experience of bringing up their own children. Further, the majority of those appointed hold few formal qualifications and have little experience of handicap. Once appointed they are poorly paid, generally have little job security and their duties seem to be wide ranging.

Anderson (1973), through a number of case studies, was able to illustrate the welfare assistant's varied but mainly care role with physically disabled children. The assistants' duties included general supervision, which was also described as 'being around' all the time; physical care of the children which involved helping with toileting, movement, dressing and feeding; individual help, particularly during such things as music and movement, PE and

games; individual help in class, especially with basic skills, under the class teacher's supervision; and taking children for special exercises as directed by the physiotherapist. Anderson noted that the assistants worked not only with allocated disabled children but also helped others in class. She referred to instances of good practice and emphasized that sound preparation was essential, noting one instance where the assistant had been well briefed by the assistant education officer (special education) and head teacher, had visited the infants school where she spoke to the child's previous assistant and had also visited a school for spina bifida children so that she had some initial understanding of her child's difficulties. The study also described a group of 15 incontinent children, noting that the help that these had received from their assistant had proved so successful that only in two cases did these children's teachers regard toileting as a problem. It was clear that the majority of teachers in this study welcomed the provision and Anderson concluded that the more skilled the teacher the better such help could be utilized.

Hegarty *et al.* (1981) noted that most of the schools in their study opted for an assistant role which involved group rather than individual work not only in order to avoid the child becoming too reliant on the assistant but also to maintain the special child's social interaction with his or her peers. They also noted that there was no general agreement about which activities assistants ought to engage in or how their time should be allocated between activities. Four main roles were identified which they described as care, educational, para-professional and general.

Two aspects of caring were noted: physical care which included dressing, toileting, walking and feeding; and promoting independence, particularly with regard to feeding and mobility. The educational role usually amounted to freeing the teacher from routine and mundane classroom activities or carrying out direct instruction under the teacher's guidance. The para-professional role focused on the carrying out of speech and physiotherapy programmes and included such activities as walking exercises and helping children transfer from their wheelchairs to splints. The general role was a mix of less tangible duties of which acting as a mother figure or friend seemed to be central.

Hodgson *et al.* (1984) took a similar view but concluded that two main educational roles predominated: (i) working alongside specific children; and (ii) general duties coupled with a 'watching brief' on a particular child with special educational needs. It seemed that the former often gave way to the latter once the

child became more established and confident in mainstream but inevitably this depended upon the subject, requirements of the mainstream teacher and the child's special needs.

The Wiltshire study

Studies to date provide only an impression of welfare assistant practice and what is now needed is a larger-scale survey which is wide ranging and will provide a data base for service planning as well as a springboard for further much needed research. The Wiltshire study, which investigated welfare assistant practice by means of a questionnaire, interviews, work records and case studies, was planned as a first step in this process. Central to this study was the self-administered questionnaire which was sent to all primary schools which, at the beginning of the autumn term 1986, had one or more welfare assistants working with named children with special educational needs. Only one of the 73 schools failed to respond; the response rate was thus very high and completed questionnaires were received from 72 head teachers, 81 class teachers and 100 welfare assistants. In addition, records of duties were provided by the assistants and follow-up interviews and case studies were undertaken to check the reality of practice and provide as comprehensive a picture as possible of the assistants' background, role, training and support needs.

The questionnaire consisted of three autonomous but related sections for completion by head teachers, class teachers and welfare assistants. Confidentiality was ensured as each participant completed his/her part independently and returned it in a separate sealed envelope. The head teachers' section of the questionnaire provided mainly background information about how the assistant had come to be appointed, the children receiving help and the special needs resources available both within the school and from outside agencies. The assistants' section focused on their background experience, training and qualifications, the role and specific activities undertaken, as well as their perceptions about different aspects of that role. The class teachers' section elicited information about organizational factors such as timetabling, programme preparation, direction and monitoring of assistants' work and also asked about any difficulties encountered. All three sections asked for opinions about assistants' support and training needs. The overall purpose of the study was to provide baseline information about welfare assistant practice and needs from which to generate further

essential research, develop training programmes and, where necessary, modify and improve administration and management practices. The head teachers' section provided useful background information about both the material and quite substantial human special needs resources available to schools and these are discussed below.

Head teachers and their resources

The Warnock Report (14.32), in considering the integration of children with special educational needs, made the point that, 'the help of an ancillary worker is often crucial to the effective placement of an individual child with a disability or disorder in an ordinary class'. It is no less true that vital to the successful employment of a welfare assistant in this capacity, indeed essential to the success of the school as a whole, is the effectiveness of the head teacher in organizing resources and encouraging and enabling staff to response positively. As the force of the 1981 Education Act continues to be felt, many head teachers find themselves in a position whereby they have to identify not only the ordinary but also the special educational needs of their pupils. Organizing the whole school's approach and deciding the balance between ordinary and special needs is never easy. Once identified, special needs have to be resourced. Good practice, to my mind, entails looking to within-school resources first and only when these have been fully exploited seeking help from the out-of-school support services available from the local authority, district health authority and social service departments. In some cases, of course, it will become obvious quite quickly that such support is required. In other instances, the school itself may have at its disposal members of staff who can offer preliminary assessment and advice as well as specialist teaching. A school may also have its own suitable materials, facilities and equipment. As more and more governing bodies and head teachers become responsible for their own delegated finances, this initial within-school approach will probably become more attractive.

In the Wiltshire study, head teachers were asked to indicate: (i) how they acquired their welfare assistant; (ii) the availability of resources of the kind just described; and (iii) the nature of any outside support received. Their responses show that in just over half the cases welfare assistance was automatically allocated by the LEA either following the issue of a new statement or, in some cases, because a special needs child who had already received

welfare assistance had transferred from an infant to a junior school. When priority requests from head teachers were also taken into account, it became clear that the LEA had responded positively and promptly to these requests for help in over three-quarters of all cases. In other instances, head teachers had acquired their welfare assistants by seeking the support of other professionals, mainly educational psychologists.

As far as their own resources were concerned, very few schools had qualified special needs teachers on their staff and fewer than one in five had teachers with special experience. All those who did, however, were appointed to designated posts of responsibility and in almost every case were employed in a school which also had special unit provision. One-third of the schools had ready access to their own specialist equipment and materials, mainly for physically disabled children; but few offered special teaching programmes.

Help from the support services was wide ranging and quite substantial and only one head teacher claimed that she received no help of this kind. About half the schools received materials and equipment, mainly from advisers, and approximately the same number said that extra teaching, usually of a specialist nature, was available to them, most of it from area support teachers working primarily with children with literacy problems, often on a weekly basis. In addition, 17 per cent of schools reported that they also received physiotherapy and speech therapy, again on a regular basis. Most head teachers said that they could call on a wide range of professionals for assessment and advice. Although educational psychologists were the most frequently mentioned providers of this service, there was also a substantial investment of time by specialist teachers, school medical officers, physiotherapists, speech therapists and audiologists. District health authority services were available to 60 per cent of the schools in this survey. Less readily available was training, with only 15 per cent of schools receiving such support from the LEA and 7 per cent from the district health authority.

Thus, apart from in-service training, we have here a record of substantial and, in some cases, regular, support to schools which have integrated their children with special educational needs. When finance is delegated, the 'buying-in' of such substantial human resources could prove very expensive, particularly if the limited level of special needs expertise within primary schools shown in this study occurs elsewhere. If only 7 per cent of primary schools have teachers with special needs qualifications on role either extensive training programmes will be needed or expertise will have to be purchased.

Organizing and managing the welfare assistants' work

Turning now to the welfare assistants themselves, the study showed that, despite the LEA's general expectation that those appointed would work, if not solely, at least primarily with named children with statements, only 4 per cent actually did work solely with the child(ren) to whom they were allocated. Slightly more than half said that they were also working with other children with special needs, although not necessarily ones with statements, and 96 per cent also worked with 'normal' children. Just over a half also undertook a variety of other duties unconnected with the special needs child(ren) to whom they were allocated. The list of such duties seemed endless and included 'housework' type activities such as tidying classrooms, replenishing toilet paper and towels and making refreshments for staff and visitors; medical and health duties such as dealing with all cases of first aid, sickness and incontinence in the school and contacting the parents of sick and injured children; general administrative and clerical duties such as collecting registers, photocopying and duplicating and acting as the school secretary; supervisory activities such as playground duties and accompanying children on outings; and a variety of broadly educational duties such as recording radio programmes, preparing displays and assembling project work, assisting with swimming, art and craft groups, covering and numbering books and organizing the schools resource area. In addition, two assistants reported that they filled in when the general welfare assistant was absent and several that they did 'whatever was needed' at the request of the head or class teacher.

As far as the duties specifically connected with the special needs child(ren) were concerned, individual and small-group instruction under the direction of the class teacher and general care and supervision took up most of the assistants' time, whereas least time was spent on cleaning and administration and recording.

Forty per cent of the class teachers involved in the study said that their assistants were working to a written, and often quite specific, timetable which either they or the head teacher had prepared. As far as planning the child's programme with the assistant was concerned, 68 per cent of the teachers said that they had sufficient built-in time for this and another 17 per cent, who did not have the advantage of such an arrangement, found time out of school or used their break and lunch hours. A few said that they directed the assistant as necessary during class time and only two teachers did not plan at all. A similar number also

had sufficient time allocated for monitoring but, again, 17 per cent had to do this outside normal school hours. The few who did not monitor, said that this was because either they or the assistant had too many other duties or because they were unable to arrange a mutually convenient time as the assistant was employed on a part-time basis. The importance of adequate preparation and monitoring is emphasized by the fact that 94 per cent of class teachers felt that their assistant needed direction, one in five describing this need as 'a lot'.

Welfare assistants frequently worked both with individuals and small groups of children engaged in educational activities set by the teacher. This also entailed relating the child's progress to the teacher. There was general agreement that the assistants were doing what was expected of them, with only two teachers complaining that their assistant was engaged in more general duties than they had expected. Only four of the assistants felt that they were engaged in inappropriate activities, one complaining that she had too large a group to work with and too many activities to do at once, and another that she had been appointed to work with a particular child on a one-to-one basis but then found that she had to help with a class of problem children. Another felt that the physiotherapist expected too much from an unqualified helper like herself and one, who was a qualified teacher, said that she was actually being used as a teacher and not as an assistant. It should be noted, however, that this is not an arrangement that the LEA would either expect or support. Very few assistants indeed felt that there were other activities which they could undertake although two were convinced that, with appropriate professional advice, they could contribute more to the well-being of physically disabled children and another wanted to write progress reports and be involved in any discussions that took place about her child.

The survey revealed very few relationship difficulties and teachers made only two complaints about their assistants, one of whom was described as being 'insensitive to quiet' and another who was said to have poor grammar, did not adhere to the school's handwriting style and did not encourage the children to tidy up after activities. The overall impression was of an harmonious, co-operative and mutually supportive working situation.

Specific activities undertaken

A checklist of 37 specific welfare assistant activities was compiled (Table 5.1) based on an existing job description as well as

Table 5.1   A checklist of welfare assistant duties

Code	Duties
M.1	Administering basic first aid and seeking the advice of teachers on more serious injuries.
M.2	Looking for sores, bruises, etc. and reporting all such ailments to teachers.
M.3	Placing children having fits in recovery position ensuring that breathing passages are not obstructed, comforting and reassuring children and notifying teachers.
M.4	. Fitting and adjusting surgical and similar appliances, e.g. calliper and special shoes.
M.5	Administering medication as directed by doctor.
M.6	Carrying out programmes of physiotherapy laid down by physiotherapist, e.g. stretching, balancing and walking children.
M.7	Carrying out programmes of speech therapy as laid down by the therapist.
PSH.1	Toileting of children including, if necessary, cleaning and changing them.
PSH.2	Dressing and undressing children ranging from complete removal or fitting of clothes to assisting children with shoelaces and buttons.
PSH.3	Washing children incapable of washing themselves.
PSH.4	Supervising children capable of washing themselves.
PSH.5	Applying and training girls in the use of sanitary towels.
PSH.6	Helping children with their feeding, e.g. fitting bibs, cutting and mincing food, spoonfeeding, cleaning up messes.
I(d).1	Supervising and assisting small groups of children engaged in educational activities set by the teacher (e.g. listening to reading, writing, number work, practical and creative activities, games and PE, cooking, needlework).
I(d).2	Assisting individuals undertaking educational activities set by the teacher.
I(d).3	Relating child's progress to the teacher.
I(d).4	Implementing teacher-directed schemes and instructional programmes (such as Distar and Data Pac).
I(d).5	Adapting and/or interpreting lessons and instructions to children with learning difficulties and/or sensory problems, e.g. use of Makaton and other forms of signing or merely explaining lessons and instructions to less able children.
I(d).6	Assisting children with or supervising their use of micro-computers.
I(p).1	Making and maintaining work cards, wall displays, apparatus and other teaching aids at the direction of the class teacher.

Code	Duties
I(p).2	Helping class teacher/head teacher to set up, catalogue and maintain a special education resource.
B.1	Helping class teacher with the general management of behaviourally difficult children. This may include general minding, supervision or ensuring a child's concentration.
B.2	Implementing structured behavioural programmes under the direction of the class teacher and/or educational psychologist.
B.3	Physical restraining or removal of children who are seriously misbehaving, a risk to others, etc.
C.1	Cleaning wet and/or soiled floor and furniture.
C.2	Washing wet and/or soiled clothing and nappies.
C.3	Maintaining, setting out and cleaning up of materials, apparatus, and equipment required for use by pupils and teachers.
AR.1	Keeping a daily diary of events including work completed, behaviour, general comments.
AR.2	Maintaining a home/school liaison record.
AR.3	Taking part in discussions with parents if required.
AR.4	Distributing and checking library books and other school-based materials.
GCS.1	Escorting children at school, e.g. between bus and school, around school, wheeling children in chairs.
GCS.2	Supervising children during break periods.
GCS.3	Organizing and participating in games, children's parties and other leisure activities.
GCS.4	Escorting children outside school premises, e.g. to swimming pool, on educational visit etc.
GCS.5	Accompanying and supervising children on outings.
GCS.6	Giving encouragement to children by offering appropriate attention and by showing interest in their activities.
O.1	Other activities (if any, please list below).

Instructions

Respondents were asked to indicate for each of the above duties whether they were performed frequently, sometimes or never.

The codes listed on the lefthand margin refer to the following categories of activity:

M	Medical	C	Cleaning
PSH	Personal self-help	AR	Administration and recording
I(d)	Instruction (direct)	GCS	General care and supervision
I(p)	Instruction (preparation)	O	Other activities
B	Behaviour		

activities identified from the literature and from the author's own observations. The assistants were asked to say whether they engaged in these activities frequently, sometimes, or never, with frequently being defined as an activity occurring at least once a day. Activities were categorized as medical, personal self-help, direct instruction, preparation for instruction, behaviour management, cleaning, administration and record keeping and general care and supervision. Direct instruction and general care and supervision were the two activities which took up most of the assistants' time. Well over 90 per cent reported that they helped individuals and small groups of children engaged in educational activities set by the teacher and related the children's progress to the teacher. A similar number also made and maintained teaching aids and materials, escorted and supervised children out of school and, in class, engaged them through appropriate attention and by showing interest in their activities. Almost all also had some first-aid responsibilities. In addition to these activities, 50 per cent of the assistants were involved in dressing and undressing children, escorting them around school, supervising them during breaks and organizing and participating in games, parties and leisure activities. The same percentage also looked for sores and bruises and reported such ailments to their teachers, assisted children who were working on micro-computers, kept daily events diaries and helped the class teacher with the general management of behaviourally difficult children.

Thus, the welfare assistants undertook a great variety of duties and of the 37 listed on the questionnaire, 23 were undertaken by at least half the assistants, quite often on a frequent basis.

Class teachers and their assistants were in agreement about the usefulness of particular activities, both regarding direct instruction and general care and supervision as the most helpful contributions to meeting the children's needs. Both also regarded these as the two activities most helpful to the class teacher. Interestingly, the welfare assistants also enjoyed these two activities most and felt most competent in them. They least enjoyed cleaning and personal self-help duties and felt least competent in carrying out physiotherapy exercises and helping children with microcomputers. The latter was an activity frequently engaged in and therefore represents a priority area for training. Follow-up interviews and discussions with the assistants confirmed their anxieties about working with compu-ters and, in an attempt to remedy this, the LEA responded quickly by arranging for them to accompany their teachers on its

recently introduced microcomputer-user courses. Training assistants to carry out physiotherapy exercises is a much more difficult proposition as this involves relying on the good services of health authority personnel and the exercises have to be tailored to each child's particular needs. However, physiotherapists within the county have responded to individual needs as far as they are able and now also contribute to the LEA's welfare assistant induction courses. Thus, despite the constraints of time and finance, improvements are steadily occurring.

Training and support requirements

The questionnaire also asked heads, class teachers and the assistants themselves about the kind of additional information, advice, support and training that they perceived necessary to enable the assistants to carry out their work more effectively. It was interesting to note that 98 per cent of the assistants, on taking up their appointments, had been briefed about their general duties and the child's difficulties, mainly by their head teacher but in some cases also by the class or special needs teacher, parents and professionals involved. Despite this, almost half of them felt that they needed more detailed information about the child, as well as advice about how best to help. Nearly 40 per cent also requested more general information about the actual problem or handicap affecting the child.

As far as training was concerned, about half the assistants felt that they would have benefited from an induction course that focused on their general role but also included areas such as first aid, behaviour management, speech therapy, learning difficulties, child development and psychology and general methods and approaches to teaching and classroom support. Two-thirds also felt that they needed more substantial training in specific skills, quoting first aid, behaviour management, physiotherapy and computer studies as particularly important.

The heads and class teachers agreed closely with each other and with the assistants in their perceptions of welfare assistant training needs, both listing knowledge of classroom approaches, behaviour management, first aid, special needs, speech therapy and communication, and physiotherapy exercises and general co-ordination, as important constituents of courses. In terms of priorities, the teachers rated a knowledge of classroom approaches highly, together with behaviour management and first-aid training, whereas the latter two were priorities for the assistants.

Some conclusions

Local authority recruitment policies, where they exist, vary enormously but, in general, it seems that few of the assistants appointed have relevant qualifications, that their experience of special needs is limited and that, once in post, they have little job security. On the positive side, however, the Wiltshire study showed that many had substantial *general* experience of children of different ages and in various settings. Many of the assistants had also worked in schools both in voluntary and paid capacities and this experience represents a strength which should be recognized. Despite their limitations, our assistants undertake a wide range of duties, including some which are clearly educational. In fact, irrespective of the main reason for their appointment, most nowadays undertake a variety of educational and instructional activities, albeit under the direction of the class teacher. Indeed, they do so frequently and feel most competent with activities of this kind. They also derive the greatest enjoyment from educational activities, suggesting that they form an important component of the welfare assistants' job satisfaction. This also represents a clear progression from the earlier view of the assistant as a domestic helper to their present position as direct contributors to the educational process.

Given the range of care, educational, para-professional and other duties which welfare assistants now undertake, it is essential that those employed receive clear job descriptions which cover their specific duties as well as their general role and the way the work is organized. Such a safeguard is needed not only for the individual assistant but also for the child and the local authority. This is particularly important when we note that most of the assistants in this study, although technically allocated by the LEA to a specific child, in reality also worked with other children with (and without) statements and performed other general duties in school not directly related to the children's education. The appropriateness of this is a matter for the LEA to decide but it does point to the need for clear job descriptions to avoid abuse of provision and to ensure that the needs of a child, as described in the statement, are fulfilled. It also suggests that independent monitoring by the authority's educational psychologists and special needs advisers is important.

Considerable thought also needs to be given to training, for if these Wiltshire findings are typical of the situation nation-wide, courses will be required which address not only the specific training needed for the job but which also offer continued general education. There seem to be various alternatives:

1 LEAs could try to recruit better qualified personnel. This is only likely to be successful if higher salaries, improved conditions of employment and better career prospects are offered.

2 The development of large-scale pre-employment training of the kind envisaged by Plowden and Duthie. This could possibly be based in teacher training or further education colleges, and might include continued general education as well as specific training for the job. There are no indications that initiatives of this kind are likely to occur in the near future.

3 We can continue as at present without imposing entry qualifications and train those appointed through in-service initiatives. From my discussions with colleagues in other authorities this seems to be happening but, as Goacher *et al.* (1988) have shown, it is not widespread and more than two-thirds of LEAs still do not provide training of any kind.

One way forward might be to offer brief induction courses, supplemented by more substantial follow-up training which focuses on specific areas of knowledge likely to be of benefit to the assistants and on the particular skills that they will need. As the reader will recall, over two-thirds of the assistants in this study felt that they needed training in specific skills and were explicit in what they thought to be most important, namely, first aid, behaviour management techniques, assisting with physio-therapy exercises and computer studies. When you add to this the teachers' requirement of a knowledge of classroom teaching approaches and practices, we have a core of essential in-service training for welfare assistants working with children with physical/medical, behaviour and learning difficulties. Whatever the content of either in-service or pre-employment training, should the latter ever get off the ground, there will always be a need for induction courses which orientate newly appointed staff to the authority's way of working and to the specific needs of individual children and their schools.

As far as information about the children is concerned, issues of confidentiality might occur, although if they are carefully handled by the head teacher they need cause no real problem. The wise head will check with parents and professionals to ensure that the assistant has adequate, but not unnecessary, information to enable the child to be supported effectively. Advice about the nature and likely effects of children's difficulties is a matter for the specialists concerned and in many cases this can be provided by educational psychologists, advisory teachers and relevant health authority staff. In their question-

naire responses, many assistants said that, although they had been briefed, they felt that they needed more general information about the child and about the child's specific difficulties or handicap. This is something that could be provided during an induction course in the form of well prepared information packages which, ideally, should form part of the school's general special needs resources and be readily available to all members of staff.

Welfare assistants will also continue to require advice and guidance about various aspects of their job from the professionals and the class teachers with whom they work. The main management burden, at least on a day-to-day basis will, however, inevitably fall on the shoulders of the class teacher. Most in this study felt that their assistants needed direction regarding what to do and when to do it and there seemed to be insufficient built-in time to prepare individualized programmes with the assistant and monitor these. The number of teachers who were using their free time for management duties of this kind was striking. This is clearly an unsatisfactory situation as it deprives them of rest periods and interferes with other essential duties. The lesson to be learned here is that just as you cannot have integration on the cheap you cannot have effective welfare assistance without adequate secured preparation time for both the assistant and the teacher.

The Wiltshire study, which is probably the first substantial investigation focusing specifically on the work of welfare assistants, has provided useful information about their role and current management practices. We are, however, about to enter a period of considerable change and uncertainty in education and there is undoubtedly something to be gained by looking ahead.

The imminent future

Among the major provisions of the Education Reform Act, local management of schools and opting out would seem to be the issues most likely to affect welfare assistants, for the clauses describing these (i) provide for financial delegation to individual schools and for a greater measure of devolved management to the governing bodies of these schools; and (ii) allow existing maintained schools to opt out of local authority control and into a new grant-maintained status. As far as the primary sector is concerned, these provisions will apply to all schools of 200 or more pupils and to those with fewer than this if the LEA so wishes. Thus, schools within the local authority system will

receive an 'aggregated budget' from which they will have to meet the costs of such things as staff salaries, both teaching and non-teaching, and generally deploy their resources according to the particular needs and priorities of the individual school. Staff costs are likely to use up most of this budget for, according to the national figures recently provided by Jeff Austin (1988), 67 per cent of a school's direct costs relate to teachers' salaries and 11 per cent to support staff. As with all other areas of delegated finance, the head teachers and governors of individual schools will have to decide what percentage of their budget to set aside for welfare assistance. No doubt within their remit they will also wish to determine the qualifications and experience which they require of candidates and specify the requirements of particular posts. Head teachers should have greater flexibility, and once a need has been identified, will be in a position to appoint without delay. Theoretically, they can also appoint a generous number of non-teaching staff with a *general* as well as a 'special' brief so that, as situations arise, assistants can be redirected from their ordinary duties to help children with special educational needs, returning to the former when appropriate. Head teachers could also, of course, use some of their delegated budget to train their assistants. What the future holds is a matter of speculations; but there is no reason, given the cost effectiveness of welfare assistants. What the future holds is a matter of speculation; but part of the scene as they are now. However, then as now, they will need adequate advice, support and training in order to work effectively and contribute to the general improvement in educational standards.

Turning to the local authority and district health authority support services, the evidence from the Wiltshire study suggests that the advice, assessment, specialist teaching and therapy currently being provided is extensive. Such substantial support is therefore likely to prove costly whether provided centrally by LEAs or delegated. In future, LEAs will also be empowered to employ speech therapists and other similar specialists who are always much in demand in schools. At present the district health authority provides these services free but we cannot assume that this state of affairs will continue, for they too are becoming more accountable and conscious of costs.

The future of special education in the United Kingdom may not be as bleak as some fear and welfare assistants could have much to contribute. However, rather than simply speculating, it is important that we can carry out some preparatory work, first of all identifying what is currently happening in our classrooms.

What kinds of activities do welfare assistants undertake and how can their work be organized most effectively? What training, advice and support do both they and their teacher colleagues require and who should deliver it? We also need to know something about the relative costs of different types of special educational intervention. These are some of the issues that can be tackled now and which are likely to have some bearing on the way special education is approached in the future. The Wiltshire study makes an initial contribution to these areas of investigation.

Part II

Teams and leadership

Chapter 6

Teamwork in the primary school

Chris Buckton

The background

Three years ago I was appointed to the headship of a first school serving a 'severely disadvantaged' London overspill estate. Although it is surrounded by trees and grass, in many ways it has starker problems than those I have confronted in Islington where I had worked as a class teacher. Extended families are not close at hand. There are few local meeting places. Stress and suspicion isolate single parents still further.

The ethos of the school I inherited was 'traditional benevolent'; the care, though real, was coloured by disapproval and patronage. There was a separate 'remedial class', rather ominously called 'West Wing' (shades of the asylum?), where the teaching was dependence creating, disenabling and joyless.

Throughout the school the teachers perpetuated in the children a general feeling of inadequacy. The parents felt inadequate too. They were kept very firmly at arm's length. The children's reading books were allowed out only to 'nice homes' and only 'nice parents' were selected to work in school, in traditionally restricted ways.

The teaching was formal, even for the rising fives: chair-based, passive, repetitious rote. In the staffroom recurring phrases emphasized deficiencies. 'It wouldn't work with our children.' 'They get too excited/aren't used to it at home/can't listen/can't talk.' 'The parents aren't interested/don't care about their children/won't come in.'

Changing attitudes

Nobody seemed to be enjoying school very much. The adults escaped from their sense of hopelessness by holding tight to complicated school routines – the day seemed to be swallowed up by changing shoes/administering tuck/moving to and fro to watch schools TV, as if that might protect them from examining too closely the reality of the children's learning experiences.

Many of the children were markedly hesitant when talking with adults. Most of the adults, similarly, hung back during staff meetings. I found myself bleating anxiously into the silence, needing some response but not knowing how to encourage it. Not only was there a lack of joy, there was also no expectation of excellence. 'These children' had so many problems, what could one expect?

Ainscow and Tweddle (1988) have observed that 'whenever learning difficulties occur, it is assumed that there is a deficiency within the pupil . . . Instead of focusing on the pupil's limitations, let's concentrate on those things which we can do something about – namely *our own teaching*' (p. 1). This strikes a poignant note. Although the home problems concerned us and affected us, (and although I certainly believe that schools *can* do something by really involving parents in school) we were clearly not going to get anywhere if we allowed ourselves to feel helpless despair or cynical resignation. We needed new impetus.

Somehow as a school we needed to change our teaching, changing our focus towards what Feiler and Thomas (1988) call an 'ecological view', in which learning difficulties are seen as context-bound, dependent on particular circumstances. This approach emphasizes the human factors of the system – relationships and interactions. We would start from the premise that the school could change.

A person-centred approach would act on the belief that people, and that includes children, like work and find it a natural activity, enjoy responsibility and learn best when the task has personal meaning and when relationships are collaborative.

At first there seemed to be no way of building a whole-school team until attitudes changed. For instance, how could I disband the remedial class when the mainstream children were taught in formal 'lock-step' with few allowances made for individual differences? How could I tell parents they were welcome if the teachers did not feel confident about their presence in the classroom?

Children as catalysts for change

As it turned out, a staffing cut precipitated the disbanding of the remedial class and I discovered that the children with learning and behaviour difficulties became the catalysts for change. It is not until we are jolted out of the expectation that children will do what we say that we are forced into looking at our own purposes. It is the child who resists that moves us forward as teachers.

Gary, for instance, simply could *not* merge into lock-step. He crouched in the coat rack, sat white and dumb and baleful when everyone else sang, hurled belongings across the room, rushed relentlessly round the school unable to bear the pressure of work that made no sense to him. He insisted that we paid attention to his truly desperate needs. Everyone quickly got to know him because the only way his teacher and his class could survive was to lend him out to other classes from time to time. He was not shut away in West Wing where his yells would not be heard.

Painfully, we had to stop insisting that 'he must learn to fit in', or 'we can't make exceptions', and move towards acknowledging Gary's and every child's unique perceptions and learning experiences. Instead of striving for conformity and uniformity, perhaps we could dare to consider self-realization?

Not, I hasten to emphasize, *not* Gary's self-realization at the expense of everybody else's. Freedom for the individual has to be negotiated by everybody, and we had to work hard to help Gary 'fit in', and be fitted in with, in a two-way process.

Staff development

It was clear that with so many walls tumbling down, there was a need for shoring up elsewhere – to reassure, support and comfort during a period of acute stress. Now that the children with special needs were integrated, the support teacher and special needs welfare assistants spent the bulk of their time in the classroom. This had implications for the relationships between the adults, the relationships the children had with the different adults and the relationships between the children themselves.

It was essential that other adults in the classroom should be experienced as supports not threats – so time to talk to each other in a safe and trusting setting was a priority for INSET provision. With this in mind, we attended a local course which used the OU materials *Making School-Centred INSET Work*. We began to be able to declare (sometimes!) how much we needed each other and to release for more positive ends the energy that had been spent on

defending ourselves. Our decreasing sense of isolation from colleagues helped us to be less defensive with parents – and they rewarded us a thousand-fold with enthusiastic help and the unfolding of hidden talents as their confidence grew.

Our sharing of difficulties has led to working with the midday supervisors on a county INSET project, *One Step At A Time*: *Responses to Children with Behavioural/Learning Difficulties*. The project aimed to enable schools to identify their own areas of need and to develop strategies to tackle 'their' problem. Several of the midday supervisors had dual roles in school, as welfare assistants, parents and/or cleaners and their inclusion as full members of staff helped to blur boundaries.

As another INSET project we organized a stress management course in school run by the educational psychologist. We learned (or started to learn) that we could change our responses even if we could not change the 'stress factors'. It provided a time to be open about the worst moments with children we found hard to handle. It was a great relief to be listened to instead of competed with and it was especially helpful for myself as head to confess to panics, dreads and failures. We have made many resolves to take more care of each other now that we know more about our frailties. I am quite sure that our behaviour towards each other has been a major influence in changing the children's behaviour.

The part played by outside agencies

The involvement of outside agencies has been crucial – in particular that of the area educational psychologist. He helped us to abandon the culture of the expert ('teacher knows best' at whatever level in the hierarchy) in favour of individual *expertise*. Expertise is context-specific: it will be lodged in different individuals depending on the circumstances.

The educational psychologist very explicitly abdicated his own role as expert. We responded with flurried outrage, which changed in time to a really liberating sense of our own competence. Or – if that sounds too rosy – we had a sense that together, with our shared knowledge of the individual children, *we were as competent as anyone else*. Thus our anxiety became a strength – it created propitious conditions for collaboration.

We benefited, too, from working with the behaviour support teacher and other members of the educational psychology team. I think one of their most important contributions was the positive reinforcement they gave to the teachers. We felt that our efforts to accommodate *all* children were recognized and appreciated, as well as our hurt and anger when we felt we were failing.

Increasingly we are learning to provide this reinforcement for each other and even to risk observing each other now that we are often not the only adult in the classroom. We wanted, and I think have at least partially achieved, a highly flexible classroom structure that was sensitive to the changing needs of both child and adult.

Problems and dangers

To be steadfast about offering an open and flexible environment means being prepared to face particular problems. Parents, once they feel truly welcome, can in their enthusiasm be unaware of the unspoken limits, both physical and emotional, that may exist for staff. For instance, the need to let off steam sometimes about an individual child can be inhibited by the presence of parents in the staffroom. And confidentiality can be a concern in an office where there is frequent parental help, on an estate where secrets are not easily kept. Sensitivity to others' needs, and discretion are sophisticated skills which need practice.

Bad moments included the time when a parent reorganized our stock cupboard and then told teachers they must see her before taking anything out; the time when I found two drunk dads using the girls' toilets; the time when an over-zealous helper gossiped on the estate about a neighbouring child's 'difficult behaviour' in school; disagreement with the authority over 'suitable' and 'unsuitable' parent helpers. (The requirement for police vetting can complicate this issue.)

But these moments are only aspects of learning to communicate honestly with each other and to negotiate roles. We are much more relaxed now about emotional upsets and see them as normal – they are bound to be part of working closely together if we all really care about our work, but we are managing to avoid some of them now as assertion takes over from aggression.

The parents' needs can be as pressing as their children's and certainly as head I have to be prepared to spend a large part of my time listening and counselling. For a lonely parent, sometimes we are just providing a warm building and some company. But perhaps in the future that parent will be able to offer something in return.

The blurring of boundaries between teaching and non-teaching staff can be difficult, too. One teacher who was unable to yield to change (and who finally left the school) felt very strongly that her professional credibility was being destroyed by the presence of non-professionals. She could not accept that as a manager of other adults her professional status was increased.

There is a special need to agree and respect each other's roles and strengths in a shared classroom. In our attempts to break down the old hierarchy we must not ignore differences and we have to make sure that there is enough time to talk so that we can understand each other's perspectives. When I am appointing SEN staff it is important to pay especial regard to temperamental compatibility.

Other boundaries that can be confusing are those between home and school. Attitudes and expectations in the school can conflict with those on the estate – a familiar problem for many teachers and parents; but when we meet face to face every day it is one that must be urgently addressed. The most common area of disagreement is the attitude towards physical violence. I do not think we will get anywhere if this is not discussed in depth. Parents can see us living an alternative if they come into school – we do not have to preach.

The SEN welfare assistant's job is a paradoxical one – to be successful means working oneself out of that job, often out of an intense relationship with an individual child. It is difficult, too, for the welfare assistant to keep a balance between her 'special charge' and the needs of the whole class. Inevitably she sees the situation through the eyes of the child she is closest to and this parental position can lead to friction with the class teacher. In turn the class teacher may almost unconsciously distance herself from the SEN pupil in order not to trespass on another's relationship; or else she may compete for the child's affection.

Sometimes the assistant may interfere with pupil interaction by creating a dependence in the 'special' child or perhaps she may offer too much help for children who need to work out a problem themselves.

There is always the need for an overview. Although this is the major responsibility of the class teacher, we have found it easier to achieve if *all* the adults are involved in general discussion. The welfare assistant or parent works with a changing group within the classroom in a variety of capacities to extend her viewpoint (and incidentally to encourage the independence of her special charge). The child with learning difficulties benefits from sometimes working with 'successful' peers and *every* child can benefit from extra attention.

Practicalities

On the days when there is extra help available (parents, students, friends from the local community, head teacher) our most

successful classroom organization follows that outlined by Wolfendale (1987) and Ainscow and Tweddle (1988). The adults can work in the following ways:

(i) as individual helper, concentrating on working with individuals for short periods;
(ii) as activity manager, looking after the class as a whole;
(iii) as mover, keeping the flow going by protecting the other two from interruptions and distractions.

These roles are not rigidly adhered to and work best when there is a natural flow growing out of a shared awareness of the needs in the class.

Our team now is the result of two years' hard talk, trial, adaptation and negotiation. It is fragile because the SEN welfares' posts are insecure, tied to individual children, not the school. I wish it was otherwise. Currently we have two full-time assistants and one part-time who each have groups of children. They work closely with their class teacher and the part-time support teacher. They attend case conferences and parent interviews, share the writing of children's records and forecasts of work, with suggestions going in both directions. Ideally the teams are complements to each other, not clones.

The part-time support teacher used to work as a supply teacher in the school so she knows everybody well and is sensitive to the very different teacher styles. She worries about not being 'specially qualified' but this has meant that she has been much more easily accepted by class teachers. She has a base – a small room adjoining a central classroom, where she can sometimes work separately with small groups without becoming isolated. We want this room to be tempting to enter, with special games and activities and work imaginatively displayed. Next to it is another group room with a 'lonely box' – an up-turned table screened with a blanket where children can retreat if the going gets too tough. (Adults have the same right even if they cannot fit into the box!)

We also have at least one voluntary parent helper for every class, some of whom are virtually full-time. Among other things they provide a pool for future welfare assistant or midday supervisor appointments. To attract regular helpers the school must be fun and the helpers must feel valued. Nobody is allowed to say 'I'm only the welfare' or 'dinner ladies don't count'. Everyone must have a share of the treats and the thankless tasks. The feeling of strength and stimulus is worth the extra effort we demand from everybody, including the children.

Essential ingredients for successful co-operation

To sum up, we have found the following ingredients essential for our recipe (but of course there are many other models):

1 A school where relationships are the priority, not the afterthought, on the curriculum.

2 A climate of trust and confidence – although a pinch of anxiety is more likely to encourage collaboration than any amount of complacency.

3 A situation where adults and children have flexible interchangeable roles and can experience different perspectives.

4 A readiness in those with authority to gladly abdicate their roles as experts and instead to share expertise.

5 The involvement of sympathetic outside agencies – 'outside' becoming 'inside'.

6 Time ... and the willingness to spend it on exploratory talk, on planning and reviewing.

7 Genuine valuing of *all* contributions, child or adult, teacher or helper.

8 A clear consensus about what we are trying to do and where we are trying to go.

9 Explicit guidelines (e.g. written handbook and repeated discussion) as to what we expect of each other in our working relationships. In-service training and time spent working as an apprentice with an experienced teacher helps here.

10 An emphasis on self-assessment and self-discovery rather than on judging and testing, for adults as well as children.

There are other seemingly trivial matters that make a great deal of difference: remembering birthdays, writing notes to those who are ill, arranging treats when morale slumps – and in all these evidences of caring for each other the children play their part too. A warm and loving secretary is vital – the first voice or face that greets newcomers.

We are still far from achieving all we hope for, but the growth in everybody's self-esteem indicates that we are on course. When you walk into the school it is often quite difficult to distinguish teachers from parents, welfares, students. A parent said recently 'It used to feel like us and them but now it feels like just us'. It is difficult to pick out the children with statements of SEN. We are all just the people who share the school. And so far I believe we would all say it pays to be human.

Chapter 7

Who is good at reading?

Fran Griffiths

I was appointed head teacher of an infant school with eight teaching staff in a highly desirable commuter suburb nearly three years ago. I feel that a brief description of the infant school in relation to the junior school and the school community is imperative here to put the place of special needs in our school in perspective.

The infant school shares the site with the junior school which has a widely known and respected reputation in the locality for its pupils' success in the eleven plus grammar school selection examination, which the county still retains. As a consequence the infant school receives many 'out of catchment' area children whose parents are anxious to enrol them into this selective system at the earliest opportunity.

The credibility of the infant school centred on the appropriateness of its curriculum in preparation for the junior school. At the infant level reading accuracy was the yardstick by which teachers assessed a child's potential and it was used as an indicator and predictor of a child's future success at eleven plus. The answer to the question 'Who is good at reading?' spoke volumes.

However, children with learning difficulties are still to be found in areas like this and their failure to perform noticeably well is often more marked and stigmatized than in less advantaged areas. In this area of high expectations the parents are very supportive of fund-raising events organized by the Parent Teacher Association but many were happy to abdicate responsibility for their child's success in reading. A few parents helped in school with a number of tasks from accompanying school trips to cutting up paper, but only a very few, those with

qualified teacher status, were allowed to help with reading.

The staff felt little or no obligation towards children with special needs and this was reflected in their lack of awareness of each other's individual needs. Despite having been a long-serving and stable staff over a number of years, they demonstrated a quiet reserve with each other and almost all disappeared in different directions at lunch-time.

Staff meetings were irregular and lines of communication had been hampered by a personality clash between my predecessor and my deputy head. Most communication was effected by pieces of paper being sent around the school on which the staff ticked their initials to show they had read the missive.

I came to the school with a strong commitment to the involvement of parents in education and to meeting the needs of all children, especially those who, for one reason or another, were failing academically. My commitment to children with special needs was confirmed by my background as a part of the county's special needs support service. I did not accept the 'deficit/failure' model (Wolfendale 1983) widely held within the school as a reason for the child's lack of progress in reading and I found that my attitudes clashed markedly with those of other staff in the school.

I propose now to recount the changes made in relation to reading development and special needs and the role of parents in the reading process and how these linked closely with the management issues which I encountered as a new head teacher.

Reading development and special needs

Most of the children in our school who have learning difficulties are actually children with reading difficulties. There has been a good deal of research into why some children read well and others have difficulty. Hewison's (1985) review of research suggests that what most poor readers have in common is a particular type of home background and in her research in the Dagenham area (Hewison 1982) she found that 'the factor which emerged as most independently, as well as most strongly, related to reading performance was whether or not the mother reported that she regularly heard the child read' (p. 158).

Research in Haringey (Hewison 1982) and Rochdale (Jackson and Hannan 1981) has demonstrated that children who have experienced reading difficulties make significant improvement over time when their parents are involved in a shared home/school reading programme in which they agree to hear

their child read regularly and that all children benefit from parental participation in reading. Before arriving in my present school my own experience in a similar socio-economic area further substantiated this evidence.

Parental involvement

Several government reports from Plowden (DES 1967) to Warnock (DES 1978) and, more recently, the Education Reform Act 1988, have emphasized the importance of collaboration between parents and teachers to maximize children's learning opportunities. There is a general awareness of the many advantages of involving parents, not least as a valuable human resource, and I sought to utilize this resource in the management of all children's reading development and especially those with learning difficulties.

The introduction of a shared reading programme using 'real books', with the active involvement of parents, exemplifies the process of change within our school. It also has implications for the management of staff morale and the development of decision-making structures and team building in the school.

The initiation of change

The initiation of change was hugely influenced by opportunity in the first instance! My commitment to effecting change in the reading policy by involving parents meshed with my deputy head's dissatisfaction with the reading schemes used. She had written widely on the subject of the inclusion of non-fiction in a child's reading programme for *Reading and Learning* (Paice 1985), and was a keen exponent of reading with 'real books', but had been frustrated in her ambition to implement this policy by lack of support and an inadequate forum for the discussion of new curriculum initiatives. The initiation of a changed reading policy necessitated the implementation of a proper forum for debate and I arranged a whole school staff meeting one lunch-time for this purpose. (This curriculum meeting was separate from the weekly business meetings at which we discussed daily organizational matters.) It was addressed by my deputy head who outlined our proposal for effecting a change in school policy which she hoped all the staff would agree to. We had agreed all the following points in our planning sessions before this meeting.

Shared reading – organization

In essence, we were going to involve parents in their child's reading development and move away from a very teacher-directed and structured pathway to reading which had used reading schemes in a numbered sequence from Book 1 to 76, to an individualized pattern in which the child became the director of his or her learning. He/she would be free to choose any book from a broad-banded selection comprised of our brightly coloured and attractive 'real books', e.g. *The Enormous Crocodile* by Roald Dahl, as many new 'real books' as we could afford and some of the better books in published schemes. I explained that we had agreed not to colour code the books, as we felt this would be replacing one imposed sequential structure with another. In organizational terms we would decentralize the reading scheme books from their central resource area in the corridor. The better scheme books would be shared between the classes and the remainder disposed of. Each broad band, three in each classroom, would be stored in bright strong plastic containers and would represent the following gradations of difficulty: picture story books with little or no text; picture story books with more difficult texts; bridging books between picture story books and paperbacks. They would all be available for all the children and while some teacher direction would be involved in guiding a child to a particular band, no child would ever be denied access to any book on any grounds. Children with reading difficulties, who had previously been confined to scheme books in the predetermined sequential order, would now have access to exactly the same books as successful readers.

Role of parents in shared reading

The success of the system would depend to a very large extent on the approval and willingness of parents in agreeing to hear their children read. We discussed a home/school contact book and agreed that each teacher would write a comment and that the parent would be encouraged to respond. The parents were to be asked to attend an informal meeting arranged for one afternoon directly after school so as to learn about their involvement. Any mother who could not attend would be approached individually and another appointment made. It was important that all parents were involved. The parents were to be asked to share a book with their child each evening, if they liked, but at least three times a week. 'Sharing' meant reading the book to the child, or the child reading to the parent, or a combination of both, depending on the

match between the child's level of fluency and difficulty of text. The teacher would provide guidance in the home/school contact book. In order to impress upon the parents the importance of the book going home, we were anxious for it to be carried in a specially designed 'bookbag'. We did not want, nor could afford, the books to be lost or damaged in the sandwich box or swimming bag and so we had approached a national company for financial sponsorship and they had agreed to provide the finance for the purchase of our own specially designed 'bookbag'.

At this point I felt it important not to stress my concern about children with special needs. I was conscious of not wanting to alienate and overburden staff and felt that much of the change I was planning had to do with developing awareness and changing attitudes and that this would take time. However, this meeting had laid the foundation for on-going curriculum meetings and the formation of smaller working parties to discuss the implementation of shared reading in our school. This format for curriculum innovation and change has become a part of our school policy and has proved to be especially important in the light of the impending implementation of the National Curriculum.

Initial staff resistance to change

The staff's response to the proposal to change the reading policy ranged from the stance of 'rational adopter' through 'Stone Age obstructionist' to 'the pragmatic sceptic'. The implications of change in terms of taking away security evolved through practice and the support of the tried and tested method led to responses which fitted the model provided by Day *et al.* (1985).

The 'rational adopter' was prepared to look at the proposal strategically. She wanted further clarification of our aims and reassurance of an evaluation of the outcome before agreeing to implement the policy. The 'Stone Age obstructionist' neither responded to the invitation to be involved nor saw the need for change. The 'pragmatic sceptic' looked for a pay off for herself: 'I will go ahead with this proposal but what do I and my pupils get out of it, and how much extra time will be involved?' In practice, though, all eventually asked to be involved in the first year.

Management of change

The management of this initial resistance had to be dealt with sensitively and it was clear that the whole-school involvement in

a shared reading programme from a single starting point was not appropriate. It would be better implemented class by class as each teacher showed a commitment to becoming involved and asked to join in. Insisting that all took part immediately despite their misgivings would clearly not be workable, partly because some staff were not convinced of the validity of shared reading for developing reading accuracy and partly because of the sheer lack of suitable reading resources. The management of the second point was easier to deal with than the first in terms of time. I had planned that the purchase of suitable reading material would have priority in our expenditure of capitation, curriculum development funds and other private funds and anticipated that it might take over a year to establish an adequate base from which to operate. I was aware, however, that it can often take a great deal longer to change attitudes. How to move people on a pace from the point of believing that reading is only about accuracy to believing that reading is also for fun and can be enjoyable, became a priority. This was especially important for the self-esteem of children with special needs who are always seen to be failing at the level of reading accuracy but hardly ever at the level of enjoyment. All children can enjoy books.

Parental involvement and attitudes

Parental attitudes towards our policy of shared reading differed over time. At first there was a good deal of suspicion about this new method. They had not, not surprisingly, heard of the national projects in shared reading and I think they felt that I had plucked this idea out of the air. Many were prepared to believe that it was the new head's whim and one parent was overheard saying to another on the train, 'I don't know what's happened at that school. They don't seem able to teach the children to read any more. We've got to do it.'

In spite of these feelings almost all parents were willing to be involved – my deputy head's involvement gave it the credibility that I, as a new head, lacked. However, there were deep rumblings for a long time over the issue of reading accuracy and how it would affect children's chances of success in the junior school. Parents were fairly vocal in their criticism of our choice of books. One of my tasks as a manager was to initiate parent education through greater involvement in the everyday life of our school and to make myself available for parents to call in for reassurance and guidance.

Support during the process of change

My support role in relation to my deputy head was on two levels. On one level I supported her in the mechanics of implementing the policy by taking her class on a regular basis to enable her to share books with individual children in her class (a very time-consuming activity – changes in organizational strategy were eventually discussed in order to cope with it). On another level, I supported the principle by sharing her success with other members of staff and outside agencies. We became involved in the production of *Book Policy in the Primary School* (Essex Education and Library Service).

My role in relation to the staff during this year moved from that of initiator to supporter and enabler. The actual process of change served as a unifying force among the staff as they looked to each other for support in setting up the system and monitoring it. In an enabling role, I took their classes while they visited an area special needs exhibition, local resource centres and each other's classes. I invited sales representatives from educational publishing companies to visit us at lunch-time by prior arrangement with the staff and we selected and purchased reading resource material together. This also served to keep staff in school at lunch-time and by the end of the year we were nearly all having lunch together and lunch-time became a valuable opportunity for informal discussion. We were beginning to feel dependent upon each other and developing an awareness of each other's individual needs.

Evaluation at the end of the first year

We were beginning to feel like a team. We began to celebrate each other's birthdays with a card and sometimes a buffet lunch and we had begun sharing ideas and passing on useful information. We had reached the second stage of development in team building, identified by Knight and Bowers (1984). Things were beginning to come to life; but the staff were still dependent on a leader for guidance.

The establishment of regular staff meetings for discussion of everyday organization and curriculum initiatives had set in motion a forum for the implementation of decision-making structures. Staff were beginning to feel that their views were useful and staff morale was noticeably higher. This was also reflected in the staff's awareness of children with special needs and in recognition of my concern and expertise in this area, I was

beginning to be asked for support and advice in managing resources. Support networks for children at the top infant level were discussed and negotiated. Classroom support in the adaptation of resources was provided by a member of the authority's special needs support service and I initiated a weekly parent and child group to provide support through 'guided observation' and counselling. In these sessions I taught the children with special needs while their parents observed their child's response. We spent some time at the end of each session discussing our observations and planning the next learning task.

Overall the children demonstrated a willingness to read and our monitoring of the shared reading programme showed that they had read a larger number of books than we would have expected. When my deputy head asked her class, at the end of the year, 'Who is good at reading?', all the children immediately raised their hands, including those children who were still at the pre-reading level of development.

Conflict

I started my second year in the school with the management of conflict as a reality and a priority. On the surface, all appeared to be going well and yet closer observation just below the surface revealed a growing resistance. In my informal conversations with staff I found that anxiety levels were raised for some and one particular teacher became the focus of all our concern because of her difficulty in accepting change. There was also growing resistance from the parents who, despite all our reassurances, were still worried about reading accuracy and the time differential between being a non-reader and becoming a fluent reader.

The conflict stemmed from a growing disparity between the parents' aims and those of the school for the teaching of reading and was fuelled by a chance remark from one of the teachers at the nearby junior school who was overheard saying that the reading ability level of the new intake was noticeably lower than in previous years and that they may have suffered as a result of our shared reading policy with 'real books'. There was no evidence for this, but rumours do spread quickly. Matters were further exacerbated by a large turnover of staff. One of the longest serving teachers, a 'folk hero' in the eyes of the parents, retired and my deputy head was promoted to a headship in the same county. A little later in the term one member of staff applied for early retirement and left soon after on the grounds of

ill health, perhaps as a result of anxiety induced by the implications of change.

Coping with conflict

Bowers (1984) quotes Karp whose strategy for coping with conflict is based on the ability to fight creatively. Karp argues that the most important skill in handling conflict is not the ability to get on well with people but to fight them well. I am not sure that my management style supports the notion of 'fighting creatively', but I am attracted to the ideology of conflict management as a means of problem solving and effecting change.

In managing this conflict issue, I sought to confront and analyse the tensions by initiating communication between myself and those parents who were reputed to be most anxious about our reading policy. I encouraged a more open and honest dialogue with the staff through confrontation and positively discriminated in favour of recruiting replacement teachers with a background in special needs. I also attempted to set up a network of liaison with the junior school, which was not entirely successful in the first instance. However, we began to have a dialogue to prevent further rumour and discord.

An analysis of the underlying cause of the conflict centred on the lack of security felt by both parents and staff in using 'real books' to teach reading. They would have felt happier and more secure using published scheme books as a core, around which 'real books' could be slotted, to teach reading. In the light of this experience we revised our policy for the selection of reading material and sought to purchase some attractive scheme material as a yardstick by which a child's progress could be measured. The process by which we arrived at this decision involved a compromise on my part but enabled me to demonstrate my willingness to listen to both parents' and staff views. Dealing with the conflict openly had served to enhance my relationship with both groups.

In conclusion

Almost three years later, we have established a series of support networks for children with special needs, based on a collaborative team approach to development. We have the status of a mature team based on shared leadership and collaboration not only within the school but within the wider context of the

community: parents, potential parents and the governing body. Our shared reading policy has become a part of our accepted practice and parents' anxiety is raised if and when a child fails to take books home regularly. Annual reading tests administered to all top infants throughout the county show that our results are above average for the area. Most importantly, we have developed structures for decision making and dealing with change which will be essential in the light of impending external forces for change in the form of teacher appraisal, the National Curriculum and local management of schools.

Books have a very high profile in our school. We take care in evaluating new books and time in sharing them with the children. Their enthusiasm for the books is measurable by their success, and we no longer ask 'Who is good at reading?' The child would be puzzled by such a question. Instead, we simply ask 'Who enjoys books?'

Chapter 8

Service management for hearing-impaired children

Ruth MacConville

The content of this chapter has developed from my work in hearing-impaired units in inner city comprehensive schools, as an advisory teacher and from my work as an organizer of services for sensory-impaired children in a London borough.

One of the most significant developments in the education of deaf children over the last decade has been the increasing number of them being educated in their local school. In this chapter I intend to reconsider a number of issues which arise for a small service in responding to the increasing trend for integrated provision.

Firstly, what is a service? In my experience it is a very complex organization, perhaps more complex than a school because of the expectations laid upon it, because it struggles to reconcile many competing and often contradictory forces without any formal or easily recognized structure. Peters and Waterman (1982) suggest that an organization can be described in term of a 'Seven S's' conceptual framework; and this in my own service's context looks like this.

1 Strategy – our key tasks and the constituencies they serve; providing for the needs of children whose educational and social emotional development may be affected by sensory impairment.
2 Structure – the work to be done; organizer; peripatetic (visiting) teacher; teacher in hearing-impaired units; attachment to mainstream schools.
3 System – the ways we have of monitoring what is going on.
4 Staff – recruiting the right people and keeping them excited and committed.

5 Skills – training and developing the competences required for our work.
6 Style – developing the best way to lead and relate to the people we encounter.
7 Shared values – establishing a sense of mission and a common set of beliefs.

The management of a service, like that of a school, is becoming more difficult. Technological, cultural and structural changes in society mean that the general level of education and of expectation in the population is rising. The remainder of this chapter focuses on how to respond to these pressures and to manage the changes.

A service must be responsive to a changing society. In addressing two of the issues which arise out of the increasing trends for integrated provision, for partnership with parents and working with mainstream colleagues, it is worth noting that services for hearing-impaired children have led the way in the provision of integrated educational opportunities and pre-school guidance, both areas with long established traditions. The inherent danger is that experience can lead to complacency and rigidity of thought. There is a need to be responsive to the new context within which we work.

The Warnock Report (DES 1978) and the Education Acts of 1980/1981 have had a considerable effect upon educational thought and practice, particularly with regard to attitudes towards integration and, closely linked with this, the relationship between parents and professionals. Subsequent Education Acts, in 1986 transforming governing bodies and in 1988 extending parents' rights to choose schools, have given parents new opportunities to be involved in decision making. Parents now have rights to information and consumer rights to determine the level and type of professional services. They also have a right to active involvement in the activities undertaken with their children by professionals. The 'rights' approach firmly places parents in a central position and demands that the professional provides a service and is responsive to consumer needs and demands.

Parents are central

My experience has been that there is usually unanimous agreement within a service that the key task is to work with parents at the pre-school stage of their child's development and

that work should commence as soon as possible after the child's deafness has been diagnosed. As Outsan, Brown and Constable (1989) have observed, the greatest time priority should be given to the pre-school child together with those school children with a more severe hearing impairment. The fact that this level of agreement exists, despite the fact that peripatetic teachers have notoriously large caseloads, underlines the importance with which work at the pre-school stage is viewed.

Furth's (1973) analysis of the anxieties and necessary readjustments of parents when they discover that their child is deaf is an important one to bear in mind. The aim of the parent–teacher relationship following diagnosis of hearing impairment in the child is the realistic acceptance and understanding of the child as deaf by the parent. The slogan 'Parents as partners' wrongly implies that such a relationship is easy to establish and too easily leads to the assumption that such a relationship exists because the professional says so. By definition, anyone meeting a member of the service for the first time will not feel at their best; initial insecurity and anxiety are what we must expect.

Ineffective ways of handling a parent's confusion and grief can too easily result in the parent being cast in the role of patient, with his or her own problem, in this case having a deaf child, which must be dealt with via the professional relationship. Alternatively the parent can be cast in the role of unqualified assistant to the professional – a passive one of being expected to learn certain skills in order to be able to cope. The three most frequent sources of complaint made by parents are: (i) the giving of inadequate information; (ii) unrealistic advice; and (iii) that what they say is ignored. The importance of establishing a constructive working relationship with parents at the early stages is crucial, not only to enable the parents to overcome first reactions and find acceptance and understanding of their child as deaf but because the early stages of parent–teacher partnership are inextricably linked with the on-going support required in the education and development of the child.

One of the major implications of the 1981 Education Act is the central role parents are to play in contributing to the assessment of their child's special educational needs. The teacher who does not achieve a working relationship with the parent is unlikely to help the parent form a realistic understanding of the child's needs. This is likely to have long-term consequences. Partnership needs to be based upon respect for the differing roles of parent and teacher. The professional who does not recognize the

wider demands on the parents, or their particular expectations for the child, is not likely to establish a partnership with the parents.

It is necessary not only to constantly evaluate the content of any advice we may give to parents; it is also as important to consider how we work so that relationships with professionals are not a source of stress, guilt and dependency. The move to a more considered way of working is not easy. Professional training is not in most cases a preparation for working with parents and parenthood is not a preparation for working with professionals.

Our clients at one level are the parents; at another they are the children with hearing loss. Here we are talking of a vast range of disability, ranging from minor losses for which hearing aids are prescribed, through the middle ranges helped by amplification, to severe and profound losses. Most deaf children develop spoken language skills but again the variation in these will be great. Competence in spoken language will be gained by some, enabling them to operate in the hearing world; but for many of them it will never be a free and easy means of communication.

It is not surprising that services such as mine offer a range of provision to hearing-impaired pupils, in schools for the deaf (frequently paid for outside our own LEA), in hearing-impaired units attached to mainstream schools or individual placement in local neighbourhood schools.

Pupils and provision

There are now, and have been for a number of years, far more hearing-impaired children being educated in their local neighbourhood schools than receiving education elsewhere. While this is and has been in the past appropriate for the vast number of pupils, the most significant aspect of recent change is that previously placement in a local school was largely for pupils whose language and speech skills were not too significantly below those of the class group and whose social/emotional maturity was more or less equal to that of their hearing classmates. What was once regarded as an appropriate starting point – nearness to an age-related norm for expressive language, communication skills and general level of maturity – is in an increasing number of cases no longer the rule. This situation has serious implications for the management of a service.

While there is a steady number of profoundly deaf children entering schools for the deaf, there is a trend away from unit

provision for less severely impaired children. Parents who in a different climate have been happy for their deaf child to attend the nearest hearing-impaired unit are now no longer agreeable to their child travelling to attend a unit and are requesting 'the school next door' with support.

In some ways it must be viewed as unfortunate that what amounts to a hierarchy of placement has evolved, a continuum that has at its peak the local mainstream school and at its base the residential special school. The range of special educational needs which are found within the population described as 'hearing-impaired' requires a diversity of response in terms of educational provision. No single form of provision can meet the spectrum of needs and it is necessary to provide an appropriate range of placements. The current trend puts at risk some aspects of a service, most notably the hearing-impaired unit.

At its best a unit can provide a consistent, varied network of support across the mainstream curriculum. The teacher of the deaf can support the deaf child in the mainstream classroom, enhance the skills of mainstream teachers with regard to a range of children with special educational needs and can act as a specialist resource to the school as a whole. In short, the teacher of the deaf working in a unit has the possibility of operating as an internal consultant, having time to develop relationships and trust over time with mainstream teachers and time to do successful work and projects in the school and thus be regarded as effective by colleagues.

It would appear that the skills that are required for supporting individual deaf children in their local schools are the same skills that some teachers working in units have developed: working closely with mainstream colleagues on the curriculum and classroom management, providing and preparing materials that class and subject teachers can use, working directly with a child within an ordinary lesson, giving intensive help on an individual or small-group basis for a particular purpose related directly to the mainstream curriculum. The teacher working in a unit has learnt how to adapt to the needs of a class or a class teacher. The peripatetic teacher as external consultant (Bowers 1987), with a large case load, has not usually had to adapt to the mainstream in the same way. This is borne out by the findings of a study of severely and profoundly deaf children integrating into mainstream schools which concludes that a different model of integration is required from that of individual integration with occasional support from a peripatetic teacher (Gregory and Bishop 1989).

The challenge for a service in supporting the individually placed deaf child is ensuring that the child has access to an appropriate curriculum and has the opportunity to participate actively in the learning process. Integration must be viewed as a means to an end, not an end in itself. Gregory and Bishop (1989) have emphasized that exposure to the normal curriculum does not necessarily imply access to that curriculum. After all, equality of opportunity implies more than the same thing for everyone: it involves the same chance to seize the opportunities that everyone should have.

Pressures of the job

The traditional split of teachers in a service between units and peripatetic duties is often unsatisfactory in meeting the needs of the severely deaf child in an individual placement. This has resulted in parts of a service being overburdened and has caused individual teachers to experience the stress arising from role ambiguity, role conflict, role overload or underload. Needless to say, this is unhealthy for the service as a whole.

For the peripatetic teacher, there is often uncertainty over what his or her priorities should be. With a severely deaf child to support in a mainstream class, the task may easily seem overwhelming because there is so much to do: relationships to build with child, class teacher, school, parents, issues of appropriate curriculum to organize and perhaps the need to attend to the child's use of hearing aids and his/her own management of deafness. Within a small service, each member of staff has a caseload and the time available to discuss individual situations is very limited. It is likely that the task has not been laid down in sufficiently precise terms. To the strong-minded teacher the situation, and about others' expectations. Enriching or over-confident teacher it may easily be experienced as threatening and produce feelings of uncertainty – uncertainty about how the task will be evaluated, the extent of the teacher's responsibility in the situation, and about others' expectations. Enriching or over-whelming? It depends on a frame of mind but also on how much real support is available in the service, perhaps not only in terms of individual discussion of caseloads but also the sense of security and freedom that exists for individual teachers in knowing that the only valid answers are those formulated by each individual teacher working in a specific context.

The fact of belonging to a team can benefit teachers not only by providing a support and a sounding board but by bringing an

awareness of strategies that may be useful in organizing their work. We have worked on our consultancy skills, in particular on the use of contracts in work with colleagues. Contracts can provide an explicit statement of mutual, positive expectations about working together. They help prevent disappointments, frustrations, anger and disillusion on both sides. Contracts encourage both parties to think clearly, to talk and verbalize any confusion that is felt.

A written contract that is renegotiable allows each teacher to ask for clarification and to talk through the inevitable uncertainty. Contracts provide a useful record of intent and of progress. In Chapter 3, Tony Bowers looks more fully at the process of contracting, developing ideas which an effective consultant can usefully employ. Penny Platt, in Chapter 4, also explores ways in which the consultant can negotiate contracts with clients.

Closely related to the pressure of role ambiguity is that of role conflict. Peripatetic teachers in a service experience this when they have to divide their attention between a number of difficult tasks and feel that one is stealing time and importance from another. New demands such as a new referral can be challenging; but if this conflicts in time or priorities with existing responsibilities then it can produce conflict.

Teachers in units often experience role conflict because they belong to a mainstream staff and to a service. Galloway (1985) points out the anomalies created by the parallel systems of special and mainstream schools, the divisive salary scales and the notion of special education which he sees running counter to developing a whole-school approach to special educational needs.

Is it possible to belong to two teams? The question often arises. A sense of mission and shared values would seem to be the factors that link teachers in a service and create a team, but only when responsibilities are shared and the act of working together enhances the work that is done can a team be said to have formed (Knight and Bowers 1984). We have to concentrate on making ourselves a cohesive and caring team since the team can provide the strength and sense of mission required to go and work in other situations. Here we need to distinguish ourselves from a work group. A work group is of a lower order than a team: it exists whenever people are brought into relationships with one another by virtue of their work. Teachers in a service may belong to one team but several work groups and the distinction between them is important. We have to ensure that our own service base retains an identity as a team.

Unfortunately the role overload which is frequently experienced by peripatetic teachers – too much to do and not enough time – does not make for job satisfaction. Quantitative overload results in advice for teachers which is prescriptive and seeks to direct their behaviour. Another form which we may unconsciously generate for others is informative overload: giving new knowledge, usually based on a deficit model of what the child cannot hear and superficial advice regarding hearing aids. Mainstream teachers are more likely to respond to a facilitating style which is supportive to their individual situation. Peripatetic teachers with large caseloads seldom have the opportunity to work in sufficient depth with colleagues to meet a child's needs. This is unfortunate because it is potentially a source of satisfaction for all concerned and is productive in terms of meeting the child's needs.

Teachers working in units often experience the pressure of role underload when the numbers of children attending are low. The problem here is that the task is not conducive to an energetic and productive self-image. In some situations it has been possible to avoid role underload by involving teachers in other areas of work, particularly peripatetic duties. This has proved to be very satisfactory. Supporting an individual child in a mainstream class can also potentially be a cause of role underload if the teacher of the deaf does not feel involved with the class as a whole. This is a situation which usually improves, given time, but the head of service needs to keep an eye on the ways the two teachers see and share their work.

In conclusion

The increasing tendency for individual deaf children to be placed in mainstream schools poses many management questions. Cutting across the traditionally neat boundaries of unit/peripatetic work, it has resource implications which cannot be ignored in times of shrinking education budgets. It also highlights the importance of working closely with parents so that they are able to make informed choices. The changing demands which face teachers of the deaf have implications for training and in-service training in terms of developing the skills required to work effectively with parents and mainstream colleagues and the evaluation of current local provision to which the whole service can contribute.

There has been a great deal of discussion recently about the 'whole-school' approach. It would seem that for teachers

attached to a service the way ahead is also to develop a 'whole-service' approach which moves away from fragmented provision. The increasing demands which are being made upon teachers of the deaf are largely concerned with working effectively with mainstream teachers and this feature of the work will become more crucial with the introduction of a National Curriculum.

Webster, Scanlon and Bown (1985) have remarked that as a profession, teachers of the deaf have often clung to a particular ideology and methodology and have been accused of being inward looking. It is time to turn our attention to developing our listening skills and improving our communication between one another and with our colleagues in the education service as a whole. An outward view, while retaining team identity as a centre, is what I constantly aim for.

Chapter 9

Teacher–parent communication in the special school: the head as manager and researcher

Frits Rab

The account and discussion which follows is based on my work as head teacher of Hillside Special School, Sudbury, Suffolk. At that time Hillside had approximately fifty pupils whose ages ranged from two plus to sixteen. One or two remained at the school beyond the age of sixteen; most had severe learning difficulties. The school had six groups including nursery and special care classes. As well as the head teacher there were six class-based teachers and a deputy head teacher who was not class-based. Much that took place during the school day was fairly typical of this sector of educational provision. This had been verified by staff visits to similar establishments. The demands of the day were many and varied. More recently, requirements for self-appraisal and accountability had been added; staff development and work towards improving school management were also included. Our joint endeavour was to provide a comprehensive service.

Recent legislation has, of course, stimulated educational debate in an unprecedented manner. Many, it would appear, feel swamped or highly defensive regarding the implementation of the reforms. However, I have generally attempted to turn the new requirements into a positive focus for change. The extent to which I have been successful is, of course, open to debate. The responsibility for creating a positive school atmosphere and of fostering constructive responses to outside demands lies with the head teacher, a view supported by many authors (e.g. Dowling 1988; Barton and Moody 1987). This expectation was enshrined in Sir Keith Joseph's now famous remark in which he described the head teacher as the nearest thing to a 'magic wand'

for a school (quoted by Dowling 1988). Many of my colleagues may very well feel less than well disposed to such a remark. In at least one sense, they would be justified, for a school is far more than just a head teacher. A tremendous responsibility rests with class teachers. However, the head teacher is in a highly privileged position. The response to demands, both internal and external, will largely depend on the manner in which he/she influences staff development. For this purpose the notion of a 'magic wand' is hardly sufficient.

In addition to what may be regarded as common sense and the basic processes of informed and appropriate planning and organization, which are very much part of any head teacher's role, I would maintain that research activities can be of great assistance in establishing authoritative and respected management. Action research, for example, is a widely used and highly regarded means of development which can relate very closely to the needs of an establishment such as a school. In their aptly titled book, *Becoming Critical: Knowing Through Action Research*, Carr and Kemmis (1983) present well argued reasons for using this type of research methodology. They note that the aim is to establish 'self-critical reflection which helps the practitioner to emancipate him or herself from the dictates of habit, custom, precedence and coercive social structures' (p. 168).

Carr and Kemmis (1983) emphasize the need for collaboration, for a dialectical approach and for the implementation of democratic principles. Action research, as described, shares many similarities with ethnographic studies but its distinguishing feature lies in a cyclical spiral of planning, action, observation and reflection. Those involved are very much practitioners in their field and are seeking to improve their practice. Free discourse, open communication and informed decision making are essential. These principles are, of course, very briefly stated; but the current demands for greater accountability, for integral evaluation as part of most school activities and for the more efficient use of resources will surely require the rigorous investigation associated with such research principles. Action research can, I feel, maintain and foster the supportive relationships which must exist in a successful school, for as Sandow *et al.* (1987) have stressed, it is important to keep teachers informed and involved.

I have found that many colleagues, both past and present, have been keenly concerned to improve the effectiveness of educational provision. Expressions of frustration at not being able to meet their own standards and expectations have been frequent.

Such difficulties are, however, often attributed to external factors. Although this may be justified, such accusations must be supported by informed research into existing circumstances and practice. In addition, I would maintain that if teachers are engaged in critical or research processes as an integral part of their everyday work, they will be in a strong position to meet the requirements of internal and external evaluation. They will also enhance their status as professionals and become more proactive.

Home–school liaison

The need for the emancipation quoted in the introduction supports the view that there is frequently a lack of definition concerning roles. The purpose of engaging in certain activities can easily be lost. This applies as much to educational establishments as to society as a whole. Home–school liaison is, of course, also prone to these omissions, yet there is a strong feeling that working in partnership with parents is an essential part of a teacher's role. The much quoted Plowden, Taylor and Warnock Reports (DES 1967, 1977, 1978) supported this view. In the area of special needs alone the literature is extensive and much has been written concerning various approaches. In this regard Wolfendale (1986) represents a most useful starting point for anyone interested in this work. Current developments are outlined, both social and legal, and she notes that 'as expectations alter regarding a realignment of home, community and school, so professional skills required to work with parents need to be identified' (p. 37).

Wolfendale (1986) has been instrumental in such identification and her findings are summarized in this article. However, the problems of developing these skills within schools are considerable and will require a great deal of attention even though evidence supporting the need for this work is now unequivocal. McConkey (1986), for example, notes that 'the evidence from national studies in Western countries is pretty unanimous: the home has more influence in a child's learning than does school' (p. 21). If schools aim to compensate for influences which are regarded as being a hindrance to educational progress or enhance those which are felt to be conducive, then this would suggest that a well developed form of home–school liaison is required.

The position of the teacher, especially during the early years of education, has traditionally been one of acting *in loco parentis*. General concern for the welfare of children is regarded by Hirst

and Peters (1970) as a necessary condition for education, as well as being required by what is described as the more diffuse role of the teacher. They highlight the need for common social experiences or mutually acceptable reference points; these are regarded as essential to educational achievement. It is argued that there is a very strong link between education and development, in fact, they are considered by Hirst and Peters to be synonymous. It is also stressed that education is a highly value-laden activity. These assertions, which have received general support, also point to the need for close working between schools, the local community and parents.

For children who have severe learning difficulties, the problems of the relevance and generalization of learning are particularly acute. This has resulted in extensive work on home-school liaison in this sector of educational provision, a point recognized by Moses and Croll (1987) in their general outline of developments and concerns regarding this issue. The work which takes place within SLD provision is not without its difficulties. Barton and Moody (1987) stress that there is often a great deal of difference between the rhetoric and what occurs in practice. However, this particular area of education, perhaps more than any other, cannot take place effectively in isolation from family and social factors. For children with severe learning difficulties, development does not occur prior to what will be demanded but is related to the whole functioning of the child within what, it is hoped, will be an appropriately managed and stimulating environment, including both home and school. In this respect, Harris (1983), for example, feels that it is a natural progression to use parents to bridge the gap between the clinic, hospital or school and the home in the development of programmes for developmentally disabled children. In the light of the arguments so far presented it is surely an essential requirement. The extent to which this condition can be met within or through a school is, of course, another matter. The implications are considerable.

For the reasons outlined above it was decided, admittedly out of personal concern and interest rather than through any process of consultation, to establish a research project into home-school liaison and by implication teacher-parent communication. As already indicated a large degree of responsibility rests with the head teacher of a school to generate appropriate evaluative and research processes. The skill in management lies in enlisting the co-operation and support of colleagues, or others who may be involved, so that outcomes are both relevant and corporate. The

details which follow describe how this process was set in motion at Hillside.

Directed time

With the advent of teachers' directed time, further thought had to be given to the allocation of hours for specific school activities. By and large this was done in such a way as to facilitate current practice where desirable patterns of meetings, preparation time and curriculum development had already been established. Home–school liaison was ill-defined in this regard. Home visits were made, parents visited the school but policy statements about this work tended to be somewhat vague. There were many unanswered questions and unchallenged assumptions. For example, how did existing home–school links function in practice? What did parents and teachers feel about what occurred or about what was expected? How were school policies interpreted? Did parents actually want links with the school? If so, what forms should these take? Did teachers feel prepared and confident with regard to the demands of this work?

Despite colleagues' willingness and regularity in reporting to me, either for advice or information, I was frequently left with insufficient information to assess the seriousness or significance of what was being described. Consequently it was difficult to know what action might be appropriate, if any. This, I felt, reflected poorly on the nature of our involvement and on the way in which the work was carried out. It appears that there was a need for a more systematic approach and for more detailed information. What this approach might be and the extent to which information could be sought and recorded had, therefore, to be determined.

During the academic year 1987–8 it was agreed to allocate up to 37 hours for home–school liaison. It was suggested that, for a class of eight pupils, this could mean up to one visit per term per child with the teacher going to the home or the parent visiting the school, whichever was mutually acceptable. It was agreed that time outside the normal school day would be used for this purpose, though exceptions might be necessary; there would be a need for flexibility. It was requested that notes be kept concerning home–school contacts. Each would record the length of the visit, where it took place, under what conditions and the main points discussed. The purpose of this record was not to make sure that colleagues were carrying out their instructions but to help clarify what home–school liaison actually involved

and how this fitted into the total role of the teacher. I was also anxious to assess the appropriateness of the number of hours allocated. Generally, it was left to the teachers to arrange where and when meetings would take place, in consultation with parents. Both I and the deputy head teacher were also involved in some of the meetings.

A duplication of work had, of course, to be avoided. For example, where a pupil's special eduçational needs were due for reassessment under the provisions of the 1981 Education Act, which would necessitate contact between parents and the professionals involved, meetings were arranged under that auspice rather than for a termly or annual review. Similarly, where pupils were due to be reviewed at a full multidisciplinary meeting involving parents, this also served as part of the home–school liaison programme, although a different form of minuting and administration was used. Where no statutory reassessment or multidisciplinary review was due, it was stressed that the meetings arranged should also refer to the annual review report for general discussion. This has since, of course, become a legal requirement. The LEA defined the purpose of the annual review of a child's statement of special educational need and provided a specific form for completion. However, this statutory requirement could not be regarded as sufficient when circumstances can so often change from week to week and when support or liaison is seen as an on-going process.

In brief, the purpose of the contact between home and school, apart from facilitating statutory requirements, was described as being to discuss the child's work and progress at school and any issues concerning the parents and teachers involved. The importance of establishing a consistency of approach was stressed.

Towards action research

The general plan for the academic year 1987–8 had, therefore, been outlined. The spiral of planning, action, observation and reflection had been set in motion, though with what can only be described as minimal preparation. Most of the conditions necessary for true action research had yet to be established. Does too much of our planning within schools remain at the level described above? Protests and comments by teachers had been few; but then the discussion time allowed had been very limited.

With hindsight, several management issues and certain questions are highlighted by what took place. Had my somewhat

directive approach blocked open debate or do issues need to be identified more clearly before discussion, at least of an informed nature, can occur? If the response to a request is largely a reflection of the manner or terms in which that request has been made, then the way in which it has been interpreted needs to be explored. This had not been considered to be necessary at the time. Is sufficient time ever allowed for this type of clarification? When this line of enquiry is pursued, are defensive reactions an inevitability? How is information to be gathered and analysed to facilitate further development of this work? Clearly, there was a need for action research.

Initial data

By the end of the school year 1987–8 an almost complete set of notes had been submitted concerning the meetings which had taken place between teachers and parents, including the details stipulated above. Once these had been studied, the first cycle of the action research process was regarded as having been completed. It was clear that the 37 hours had not been exceeded. In most cases far less had been used, at least as far as the records submitted were concerned. Two questions occurred to me. Would teachers have used more time if they had been provided with a more detailed framework for this work? Had the use of the 37 hours been interpreted too narrowly?

It was clear that the notes represented only the bare bones of what had taken place. It was generally not possible to evaluate the work any better than before. The problems of the 'dilution' of data, as it can be described, are considerable. This can be seen in a study by Seed (1988) in which parents were asked a series of questions concerning their views of the school for children with severe learning difficulties which their children attend. Their answers are represented on a five-point scale on which 1 equals very satisfied and 5 equals very dissatisfied. In many cases Seed had to resort to describing parents' actual comments and circumstances to attempt to make valid inferences. Similarly, further evaluation of home–school liaison at Hillside would require much more detailed data. It was, of course, recognized that colleagues had been given very sparse guidance as to what was required. The term 'brief' had, it would appear, been taken literally. Had I really meant 'relevant'? If so, by what criteria is relevance judged? The importance of considering how language is used and interpreted is, of course, another important issue relating to both management and research. This has been

emphasized by Bandler and Grinder (1975), who have argued that much communication is characterized by generalizations, distortions and deletions. Before effective communication can occur these have to be identified and resolved.

Despite the limitations outlined above, it was possible to identify four key issues relating to home–school liaison. These were: (i) the situation in which the discussion between teachers and parents took place; (ii) the exchange of information between those involved; (iii) the planning of strategies and responses to requests; and (iv) parents' expressed wishes and anxieties. In addition, I was concerned to explore colleagues' perceptions of their role in this work and the philosophical basis upon which it is founded. I decided, therefore, to devise a simple question schedule, based on these issues, to put to colleagues, on an individual basis. The questions upon which our subsequent discussions focused were as follows:

1 Where do you prefer to meet parents?
2 What have you found to be the most conducive times?
3 Which conditions or settings for the meetings do you find most worrying, if any, or most conducive?
4 What information do you think parents should have about school?
5 What information do you think they want?
6 What are your personal feelings about home–school liaison?
7 Do you feel that you are prepared for the work?
8 What difficulties, if any, are there in following up the plans and strategies made during home–school discussions?
9 Are you sufficiently briefed regarding the medical or welfare matters which may arise?
10 How would you define the role of the teacher regarding home–school liaison?
11 What differences are there between a teacher and a social worker?
12 What do you consider to be the place of home–school liaison within directed time?
13 What skills are required by the teacher?
14 How would you summarize the general philosophy of home–school liaison? Why do we do it?
15 Have you any specific suggestions regarding our current practice?

To help in retrieving and examining responses, the discussions which took place were recorded on tape.

Analysing the results

Guidance for the analysis of the recorded data comes from Strauss (1987), who outlines the main principles and application of what is known as grounded theory. His brief summary of what this entails can be paraphrased as the generation and testing of theory by means of a particular style of qualitative analysis of data. The analysis of the data includes the identification, coding and categorization of what are identified as the more significant factors which are influences on, or determinants of, the phenomena being studied. The depth of analysis achieved will, to a large extent, depend on the knowledge and experience of the researcher concerning the phenomena under scrutiny. This type of approach is, therefore, particularly applicable to action research, especially when the sample is small and there is a wide range of variables which are difficult to control, as is the case with home–school liaison in many special schools.

Five interviews were recorded in September 1988. The detailed analysis of what was said will take some considerable time to complete. At the time of writing, however, a number of what are termed generative questions have been identified. These will eventually lead to the codes and categories necessary for more detailed analysis. Strauss stresses that each coded item must be referred to a coding paradigm which he has divided into four sections: (i) conditions; (ii) interaction among the actors; (iii) strategies and tactics and (iv) consequences. The generative questions or issues which arise can also be related to this coding paradigm. This is demonstrated by the examples below. Both constructive and destructive factors are listed though the ways in which these relate to each other is complex. Although these examples are somewhat limited, they illustrate the process of thinking which is involved in the earlier stages of analysis outlined by Strauss. He refers to this initial stage as open coding. Once exhaustive analysis has taken place, the key issues which have been identified will need to be verified. This can be done by further data gathering or by going back to the original data.

Example 1
Conditions   Home visit by teacher
                           TV left on
                           Pupil present
Interactions   Lack of concentration
                           Interruptions

Interactions (*cont.*)   Lack of focus to discussion with pupil in same room

Pupil referred to in third person

Strategies and tactics   Avoidance of issues

Include pupil in discussion

Ignore pupil

Effect change in conditions

Consequences   Positive or negative involvement of pupil

Unable to focus on objectives

Need for better preparation before meeting

Need for clarification of aim of meeting

Example 2

Conditions   Teachers' judgements, about for instance, parents' ability, appropriateness of home environment, parents' willingness or otherwise to follow suggestions

Interactions   Less than committed interest, by teacher, in home–school liaison.

Unhelpful attributions, unless very carefully verified and resolved

Differing perceptions concerning child's need

Strategies and tactics   Avoidance of contact

Antagonism

Sensitive identification of issues and discussion of concerns

Involvement of other agencies

Establishing of agreed approaches

Consequences   Complicated situations

Exposed limitations of professional skill in communication

Improved progress of child

Better understanding between home and school

Example 3

Conditions   Different terminology used by those involved

Careful attention to words used

Mutual exploration of meaning entered into

Interactions	Based on confused discourse
	Seeking clarification of detail and working towards understanding
	(Examples of actual words which have been interpreted differently are: topic, firm, records, partnership)
Strategies and tactics	Questioning
	Defensiveness
	Explanation
	Rejection
Consequences	Better understanding
	Confidence
	Poor communication

Staff uncertainties

From the discussions which took place between myself and colleagues, it was clear that there was a large degree of uncertainty regarding home–school liaison. To the question relating to teachers' preparation for the work (7), two teachers replied that they did not feel at all prepared. There was a general agreement that it was beneficial to meet parents in a pupil's home and several parents said that they felt more at ease in their own surroundings. As with so many issues relating to this topic, flexibility and sensitivity are called for. It was also recognized that the more formal atmosphere of a school-based meeting could help to focus attention more directly on the issues which might be causing concern. With regard to the information which is imparted to parents, there was guarded approval for an open policy. There was general agreement that working with parents was a good thing. There was, however, a great deal of expressed uncertainty concerning the skills which might be involved. The answers to the question concerning the difference between a social worker and a teacher (11) reflected a definite feeling that there are limits to what can be done, though these were not clearly defined. In general, there was a tendency for answers to suggest that teachers saw their role as providing information to parents concerning their child's work and progress at school and giving advice. Answers did not tend to reflect a sense of partnership. The infrequency of contact, other than through the home–school diaries, and the problems of a rural catchment area were two reasons given for this.

The practicalities associated with establishing a true partnership between parents and teachers are discussed by Marra

(1984), who maintains that in many circumstances this will remain an ideal. It is suggested that a more realistic aim would be the establishing of greater involvement by parents in their child's education. The particular difficulties described by Marra relate to the significant gap which often exists between parents and teachers, educationally, socially, economically and with regard to attitudes and values. This is particularly true of a school for children with moderate learning difficulties. Although this factor exists in a school for children with severe learning difficulties, it is generally less acute and the causes of the children's disabilities are frequently more obvious. Educational aims and objectives also tend to be more easily defined. However, the measures adopted by Marra to improve home–school liaison would, I feel, be effective in any special school. These include the passing of regular information to parents through an attractively produced newsletter and school magazine, the forming of small parent groups, the establishing of a parents' room and, above all, the promoting of a clearly defined school policy on home–school liaison. It is clear that such a policy must include an outline of the expectations and boundaries of such liaison. Conflict with the other professionals involved in schools must also be avoided. The content of communications, both within school and between parents and teachers will also need to be given careful consideration. Practical issues such as choosing an appropriate venue, timing and transport are other factors to be considered. Clearly the issue of home–school liaison is very complex. Wolfendale (1987), for example, lists 29 different ways in which this can take place. The implications for staff INSET are considerable. One of the main points raised by colleagues during our discussions based on the questions listed above was that better guidance is required. The aim of the project is that this should be generated by the staff as a whole in line with the principles of action research. For teachers who are ill at ease about home–school liaison, appropriate support may be required on an extended basis through a liaison teacher or senior colleagues.

Turning to staff attitudes, Marra (1984) asserts that 'staff can be directed and guided towards examining themselves critically in their approach and judging regarding the objectivity of recorded comments in reports etc' (p.135). The way this is achieved is not described and was perhaps beyond the scope of his chapter. However, this is very much the intention of the present project, based on the premise that the best means of examining the processes involved in home–school liaison is

through what teachers and parents actually say to each other. The development of skills in communicating must form an integral part of INSET concerned with this work. Although teachers will need to demonstrate their professional competence, the rather one-sided means of communicating indicated in answer to the questions above must be replaced by a more reciprocal dialogue if we are to come closer to the aim of true partnership. We need to consider how we listen to parents and how we encourage them to talk about their feelings, expectations and concerns. We need to be aware of the type of language we use and of our own prejudices and assumptions. Can we modify these without being condescending? Are we able to convey real concern and warmth in our contact with parents? Can we create a positive outlook with clear and mutually acceptable objectives? Can these be followed through to their conclusion?

Field data

As already indicated, home–school contact takes many forms and what is said is only part of what occurs. Yet it is through dialogue that most communication takes place. It is dialogue which is the most accessible for the purposes of research. Therefore, from September 1988, recordings were made of actual discussions between parents and teachers. These were largely carried out under the auspice of the annual reviews, either at home or at school. In my original planning for this project I had envisaged that separate meetings between parents and teachers could be arranged to facilitate the recording of discussions. This was both unrealistic and naïve as such meetings would have created extra work for teachers and would have been an unnecessary duplication. In addition, such contrived meetings could not be taken to represent what would have happened as a matter of course during the school year. The need for more naturalistic data collection is highlighted by Stratton *et al.* (1988).

It was not possible to record all discussions which took place between teachers and parents. A cassette recorder is inappropriate where a sensitivity to certain stresses is necessary. Discussions are often unplanned, they may occur through a visit to the school by a parent on business. The discussions which take place in this way often commence with the enquiry, 'How are you? However fruitful such meetings may be, it is generally inappropriate to reach for a cassette recorder. Confidentiality and the basic requirement of anonymity with regard to the use of data had to be confirmed in each instance. Parents must feel

confident that these conditions will be met. With this proviso, colleagues and parents were happy to meet my requests for the recording of discussions and their co-operation was very much appreciated. However, the extent to which they were coerced by the fact that it was the head teacher who was making the request and the extent to which this influenced the data will need to be considered.

Into action research

Once the analysis of the initial and field data has been completed it will be important to outline the issues to both teachers and parents, either individually or in small groups. Much of this could be included under the heading of in-service training but it will be important to stimulate open discussion and a frank exchange of ideas. In this way it will be possible to establish a new cycle of planning, action, observation and reflection. As this will be on the basis of a joint venture, the conditions necessary for action research, as defined by Carr and Kemmis (1983), will become more of a reality. The outcome, it is hoped, will be better communication, a clearer idea of what can be achieved and greater confidence in its implementation.

Part III

Provisions and providers

Chapter 10

The Education Act 1981:
a current view

Peter Caldwell

In educational administration there is a need to survive; the alternative is not acceptable. The challenges of modern legislation, commencing with the Education Act 1980, have progressively made it more difficult but, at this stage, LEAs are still afloat. Whether they will stay afloat remains to be seen. My brief is in relation to special education and I want to look at the changes brought about by the Education Act 1981 now that we have had a period of six years of living with this new legislation.

The history of special education is well documented elsewhere and particularly well presented in the Warnock Report (DES 1978). For many people it will be hard to realize that our famous Warnock Report is itself becoming part of history. It was, after all, published over a decade ago. At the same time it still represents a major contribution to the development of special education even though the 1981 Education Act did not represent the Report in the way the Warnock Committee might have hoped.

This chapter attempts to compare special education over a five-year period in one county. Clearly it has to be said that I must offer much of what follows as my analysis of the position and it cannot be assumed that my view is shared by my Chief Education Officer or by the Education Committee.

The medical model

It was the Education Act 1944 which introduced the term 'special educational treatment'. This referred to children who suffered from any disability of mind or body. For the purposes of

ascertainment, authorities were empowered to require parents to submit their children for medical examination.

The Handicapped Pupils and School Health Service Regulations 1945 defined 11 categories of pupils:

Blind
Partially sighted
Deaf
Partially deaf
Delicate
Diabetic
Educationally subnormal
Epileptic
Maladjusted
Physically handicapped
Those with speech defects

In 1953, diabetic children ceased to be a category and these were included in the category 'delicate'. The regulations at the time prescribed that blind, deaf, epileptic, physically handicapped and aphasic children were seriously disabled and had to be educated in special schools. For many, this inevitably meant residential schools.

In 1971 the Education (Handicapped Children) Act 1970 was brought into force and all children were deemed to be educable; the term 'educationally subnormal' was divided into two categories—moderate and severe. Until this time, the children we refer to as having severe learning difficulties had been deemed 'ineducable' and were the responsibility of the health authority.

Many readers will remember and understand the medical model and will require no further comment. However, bearing in mind my introductory comments about Warnock fast becoming history, there will be those who would not have known of the importance of the role of the school medical officer in 'ascertaining' what 'treatment' was required. This was eroded a little by DES Circular 2/75 which introduced a number of changes, not least strengthening the professional role of the educational psychologist. However, it still left us with the school medical officer certifying that a pupil needed special educational treatment if there were a dispute with the parents.

The Warnock model

In 1978 we had the Warnock Report which favoured the concept of special educational need and the abolition of categorization of

handicapped pupils by disability. The Warnock Report also introduced the term 'children with learning difficulties'. It actually recommended a system of assessment based on the 'SE' model:

(i) SE1 for head teacher's report;
(ii) SE2 for medical report;
(iii) SE3 for educational psychologist's report.

New SE forms were suggested for social services to report and for parents to be involved in the assessment process. Thus essentially Warnock was proposing a development of the existing concept of special education as set out in DES Circular 2/75 and finally abandoned the medical model in favour of an educational model.

Under the Warnock proposals, a further form would be produced which would be a summary of the various forms giving a statement (4.66) of and a prescription for meeting the child's needs. The Warnock Report had thus introduced the word 'statement', although there was no special emphasis on it; indeed, much more was made of the term 'recording', the idea being that an authority would 'record' all of these pupils who needed special educational provision.

For those who were around at the time, it will be remembered that the publication of the report was followed by massive governmental silence. The Labour government of the day had other more immediate problems, including trying to stay in office, and it was something of a surprise when a Bill was eventually published. It is not unusual for an official report to gather dust and not lead to legislation. As we all know, the Report led to the Bill which led to the 1981 Education Act. There then followed a series of announcements about when the Act would be brought into force.

Finally and, ironically, with precious little notice, the Act was brought into force with effect from April 1983. The transitional provisions were thoroughly inadequate but I will comment no further on that aspect and go on to assess the changes brought about.

The Education Act 1981

The Warnock Report also recommended the stages of assessment which, duly amended by the Act, are by now very well known. To remind the reader I will now attempt to summarize the important elements of the Act.

Section 1

'A child has "special educational needs" if he has a learning difficulty which calls for special educational provision to be made for
him' (1.1). Immediately, then, in the very first section, the Act
abandoned the old system of categorization. We had a new
concept of special educational needs which finally abandoned the
medical model of special educational treatment. Further, it was
agreed that the definition included that larger group of pupils,
thought in the Warnock Report to be about 20 per cent of the
total national school population, who might have special
educational needs at some time in their school career.

The significance of the first section of the Act is quite simply
breathtaking. Not everyone fully understood this section when it
was first published – and for good reason. There was a problem
about definition and many were caught up with the Act's circular
definition of special educational needs and learning difficulty.
But the Act had abandoned the medical model, had given us an
educational model and conceded that 20 per cent of all children had
special educational needs at some time in their career.

Section 2

Section 2 then gave us integration.

> Where an LEA arrange special educational provision for a
> child...it shall be the duty...to secure that he is educated in
> an ordinary school subject to the following:
>   (i) the views of the child's parents
>   (ii) the ordinary school being able to provide for the child's
>   special needs
>   (iii) the provision of efficient education for children with
>   whom he will be educated
>   (iv) the efficient use of resources

At first sight, Sections 1 and 2 of the Act had gone a long way
towards implementing the Warnock recommendations and local
authorities had no difficulty in turning to the stages of assessment as set out by Warnock and setting them up professionally
and procedurally to 'fit' with the requirements of the Act. The
structure is shown in Figure 10.1

However, the steps required by the Act under Stage 4 were
significantly different from what had been proposed by
Warnock. The term 'statement' had been promoted beyond the
Warnock usage. Indeed Warnock had used the term in the
traditional sense but now we were into a world of *agreed*
statements. Not only were we producing a document required by

Flow chart of assessment procedure
Education Act 1981

Stage 1   Class teacher → Headteacher   → Resolved
                             ⇕
                             Parent

unresolved proceed to
↓
Stage 2   Class teacher ⇌ Teacher with expertise in
          Head teacher   special education   → Resolved
          Parent

unresolved proceed to
↓
Stage 3   Class teacher
          Head teacher   ⇌ Educational psychologist
          Parent   and/or   → Resolved
          Specialist   School doctor
          Teacher

unresolved proceed to
↓
Stage 4   (i) Letter to parent under Section 5
                  Assessment – educational advice
                               medical advice
                               psychological advice
                               nursing and social services advice where
                                  available
                               parental advice
            (ii) Letter to parent under Section 7
                  Statement agreed
           (iii) Arrangements made for special provision

Figure 10.1

law but it had to be agreed with the parents; if the parents were
dissatisfied they were left with avenues of appeal via local
committees and the Secretary of State. There is little doubt that
parents had gained far more than they ever had imagined. All of
this, of course, was handed to local authorities with the
government advising that there were no financial implications.
The careful reader will note that there is a set of new demands
here, but no resources with which to meet them.

The Education Act
1983 to 1988

Before we go on I must offer an explanation. The Act has
discontinued the old system of categorization of special
educational needs. However, from an organizational point of
view, we have needed to retain a system of categorization. There

is no point in knowing how many children there are who are the subjects of statements and not knowing, for example, how many need radio hearing aids or speech therapy or are immobile. Special education, particularly, has to be organized and the manager of the service needs to know about the client groups, their size and their needs. If the manager does not know then there may not be the necessary finance in the budget for a particular group of children with particular needs.

We will now look at what has happened in my own LEA, Bedfordshire. I will consider the special schools in the county and provide a comparison of numbers in 1983 immediately before the Act was implemented and five years later (Table 10.1).

Table 10.1

Categories			January 1983	January 1988
Old	New			
ESN(M)	Moderate learning difficulties (MLD)	(6)	668	668
ESN(S)	Severe learning difficulties (SLD)	(5)	351	306
Physically handicapped (PH)		(2)	131	130
Maladjusted	Emotional and behaviour difficulties (EBD)	(2)	63	57
		15	1,213	1,161
Total school population		April 1983		90,294
		April 1988		84,548

(Numbers in brackets indicate number of schools)

Only in our SLD schools have we 'lost' pupils. In fact at the time of the survey we had a small number of pupils with severe learning difficulties in mainstream schools (usually nursery or primary schools) but, quite simply, our SLD population has decreased.

I will now turn to special units and other designated special provision (Table 10.2).

In 1974, local government reorganization was effected and the new Bedfordshire County Council was established. This strengthened special education, bringing together a number of special schools and special services and making the whole service much larger and, quite simply, more of a force. The authority closed some special units, set up the special education support service from the money made available as a consequence and

Table 10.2

Type of provision	April 1983	April 1988
Provision for physically handicapped	14	24
Maladjusted/EBD	35	48
Visually impaired	0	15
Hearing impaired	94	73
	143	160

established new provision with the emphasis on integration. This philosophy was developed before the introduction of the 1981 Act and one large comprehensive school in Luton was purposefully modified to accommodate physically disabled pupils. Other provision was established for visually impaired pupils and pupils with emotional and behavioural difficulties, with an emphasis on integration.

The figures show a marginal change which can largely be accounted for by the establishment of new provision for visually impaired pupils. Interestingly, our numbers in this category (I know the Act abandoned categories) quite simply increased.

Finally, our out-county provision, indicating pupils placed in schools run by other LEAs and in independent schools (Table 10.3).

Table 10.3

Categories		September 1983	September 1988
Old	New		
ESN(M)	Moderate learning difficulties (MLD)	8	10
ESN(S)	Severe learning difficulties (SLD)	38	22
Maladjusted	Emotional and behaviour difficulties (EBD)	39	22
Blind/Partially sighted	Visual impairment (VI)	17	14
Deaf/Partially hearing	Hearing impairment (HI)	15	7
Delicate		11	8
Epileptic		8	4
Autistic		11	11
Physically handicapped (PH)		9	3
Dyslexic		7	17
		163	118

Our numbers here have progressively decreased as provision within the county has been improved. There is, of course, one interesting growth area.

When we look at our figures presented in the three tables it looks very much as if not a lot has changed. Overall we have slightly fewer pupils although the balance between out-county and children in integrated provision has changed.

There are further figures to present, on teacher numbers, and these *do* reveal significant change.

In September 1988 we had
- 100 children with additional teaching assistance in ordinary schools; and
- 104 children with additional non-teaching assistance in ordinary schools.

During the last five years our allocated resources have increased by
- 8 teachers in schools with units or special provision
- 20 teachers to help in relation to integration
- 25 non-teaching assistants (NTAs) to help in relation to integration
- 1 teacher plus 4 NTAs to help particularly with SLD pupils in relation to integration
- 4 teachers for visually impaired pupils
- 1 additional educational psychologist
- 3 teachers and 1 NTA for EBD pupils
- 4 teachers for pre-school provision
- 5 teachers for MLD schools to help with integration
- 5 teachers (and 5 NNEBs) for language provision.

This produces a total of 50 extra teachers along with a sizeable number of non-teaching staff.

The challenge

Remember that we were told in 1983 that additional resources were not required! In fact the message from the DES was at that time, that if resources were required to support integration they might be formed by closing special schools. Our evidence in Bedfordshire is that:

1 We are not going to be closing any special schools in the near future (see Table 10.1: our special schools overall are no less full).

2 The special schools are demanding additional resources in order to help them link with mainstream schools.

As indicated, additional resources have been required and, indeed, in the financial year in which I write we have been allocated an extra 20 teachers and an extra 25 non-teaching assistants to continue to develop our integration policy. This is quite clearly an indication that the demands of the Education Act 1981 are not being met and that we have not yet got on top of it in terms of managing our necessary human resources.

Let me try to define the problem.

1 We have to meet the special needs of pupils with learning difficulties. The Act defines pupils with learning difficulties in a circular way: 'a child has a learning difficulty if he has a significantly greater difficulty in learning than the majority of children of his age' (1.2.a). Obviously this is no help at all and every mainstream school can argue that there is a significant number of its pupils in this category who need assessing under the Act.

2 Parents have rights. They can ask for an assessment. Invariably we have to do it. They have a right (and are encouraged) to put forward their parental evidence. They can hire independent private experts – psychologists, doctors, teachers or whoever.

The parents have rights to demand meetings and can talk to everyone involved in the assessment. They can use up a lot of professional and officer time and at the end of it all have the right to appeal. If they are still not happy they have the right of appeal to the Secretary of State for Education.

So in considering all of this from a management point of view we have:

(i)   schools (understandably) bidding for more resources via statements for pupils with special educational needs; and

(ii) parents (understandably) bidding for more resources via statements for their children.

All this has to be seen in a context of no end definition of what is meant by special educational needs. In summary, then, schools consider themselves to be under-resourced and parents are expecting and demanding more for their children. There is no doubt that the resource question is now 'up front' and until we have all schools adequately resourced in order to meet a 'whole-school' approach we will remain in this position.

Interestingly, the Warnock Committee (DES 1978) argued for

three areas of priority: under fives, 16–19 provision and teacher training (p. 336). Progress has been made in all three areas in my own LEA. It appears to me that our in-service training has heightened awareness and led experienced teachers to push even harder for more resources for their children with special educational needs. The annual reviews of statements are also proving a challenge to the system. Rarely do we hear that the additional provision is no longer required. Frequently we hear it must continue and even at school transfer we find it virtually impossible to discontinue the provision. In short, planning is difficult! How does one advise an education committee about the resources required for the next year except on the basis of the previous year?

Sadly, the Select Committee of Enquiry (1981) into the implementation of the Education Act 1981, having identified the issues, concluded:

> we have drawn attention to areas where problems have arisen in implementing the 1981 Act. For the most part we have not proposed particular solutions ... but have instead pointed to directions in which further reviews might go. We trust that these will be taken up by the Department in its review of the Act in the course of this year
>
> paragraph 19.9

But within their report the Select Committee have said that the most common difficulties experienced by parents are 'a lack of weight being given to their views in the assessment process....' and 'a lack of choice from a range of forms of provision' (paragraph 16). This, if anything, adds to the difficulties. Let us try one further and last complication. It is this. We issue draft statements of special educational needs regularly, providing five hours' additional teaching, one hour per day on a one-to-one basis. This might apply to a child in a primary school or a secondary school. These five hours do not represent the only special provision made for the child. The total package presented by the school will be adapted in some way to meet the pupil's special needs. Consequently, all of this should be detailed in the statement and the drawing up of the statement will be time consuming. Some of the parents require a highly detailed statement. One particular voluntary organization encourages the parents to demand details such as:

(i) the qualifications of the teacher(s);
(ii) what experience they have in SEN;
(iii) what methods they will use.

Some parents go further and, in effect, demand a guarantee. Unfortunately there is no guarantee with the education service and some parents will then use this at appeal either at the local level or with the Secretary of State in order to try to secure a place at a 'specialist' boarding school which appears to some to offer more than local provision. Thus, in this situation we have a small number of parents using the Act to good effect to deny the authority's integration approach and opt for a segregation approach; and this, of course, runs counter to the philosophy of the 1981 Act.

Finally, two other associated problems are rapidly emerging. One relates to health service provision and the other to the recruitment of teachers. In Bedfordshire we have enjoyed a good working relationship with our colleagues in two district health authorities. However, some of the staff are rapidly finding that time spent in assessments – as required by the Act – takes away time available for treatment. Secondly, time spent in assessment invariably indicates a need for some form of treatment. If the budget is strictly limited by government control then the health authority simply gets into further difficulties with the consequence that treatment becomes increasingly difficult to obtain. And as we all know, health authorities are also struggling financially.

A growing problem in relation to delivery of an education service is that of recruitment of teachers. There is no doubt that it has become increasingly difficult to recruit a part-time teacher to assist a particular pupil and so again the increasing demand will not be met by the local supply. There are not enough teachers to go round and this problem is likely to become worse in the next few years.

Summary of the problems

The reader may feel exhausted, so I have tried to summarize the main problems as I see them.

1 We have a financial system which is structured and is organized but was not given any additional finance when the 1981 Act was introduced.
2 The parents were given rights far above and beyond what was suggested by the Warnock Report and are starting to use them.
3 There is no end definition of special educational needs.
4 The Act gave status to the 20 per cent of pupils with SEN and then nothing further.

5 There is a certain pressure on local politicians when considering matters of special education.
6 Health services are in considerable difficulties in their delivery in accordance with the Act.
7 There is a real problem developing in relation to the recruitment of additional teachers.

Was there a way forward?

Bearing in mind that the Select Committee have thoroughly researched the position in relation to the Education Act 1981 and have clearly identified all of the shortcomings and avoided recommendations to improve the position, it is really quite hazardous for an education officer to enter the arena and set about putting matters right. There is no simple answer, of course; but without doubt answers could have been found.

Before we had the 1981 Act, we had a system of special educational treatment which was roughly in balance. By and large the provision was available for those who needed it. Choice was limited and much of the provision was in special schools and a significant proportion was in boarding schools. The 1981 Act disturbed the balance. The concept of special educational needs was progressive, the notion of the rights of parents was a radical change and the general move towards integration brought about a shift in the system which will take some years to achieve a new balance. The lack of resources has been a problem which is obviously not beyond resolution. The fact that, one day, 20 per cent of pupils would benefit from this legislation was inspirational and again, given the resources, a service could be provided.

A social reform such as this Act embodied had, inevitably, growing pains in association with the stress and the strain of the system. As part of the strain, the more articulate parents would be able to use the legislation; but there would be the consolation that they would bring the pressure to bear which would help education authorities improve the services and eventually everyone would benefit.

Having had five years of the Act we can, in fact, see where we are going but, assuming no other changes, it could well take us another five years to get the system back into balance. One thing, looking back over the five years, is abundantly clear. Had the government funded this initiative at the same level as the TVEI project our problems would have been minimal. But they did not see special education as having the same priority as TVEI.

The new way forward

We have at present a system which is underfunded and not in balance. The balance can be found, given funds and time. However, neither is available. We have the 1988 Education Act which applies *to all schools* and in some respects almost denies the existence of the 1981 Act. Remember that all schools have responsibilities under the 1981 Act. Herein lies the potential for further storms and the question is now on everyone's lips: 'Will education authorities stay afloat?' If the 1981 Act threatened a storm then there is no doubt that the 1988 Act threatens a hurricane.

The 1988 Act is, according to the government, aimed at improving the teaching and learning process in schools. In order to achieve this, there has to be the maximum delegation of financial and managerial responsibilities to heads and governing bodies. As part of the new system, each authority will have to produce a formula for allocating finance to the schools. The concept of formula funding will produce a certain amount of money per pupil. So far as special education is concerned there are three groups of pupils: a group on statements, the larger group, 20 per cent with special needs and the remainder with no identified special needs. To arrive at a formula which is attractive to schools to meet the special needs of all of its pupils and which will not persuade schools to over-react and seek more statemented provision appears to be an impossible task. This is particularly so when the governing body will be responsible for school-based decisions and the parents will still have rights to make demands of the authority under the Education Act 1981.

Bearing in mind the mandatory requirements in relation to the education psychological service, the 1988 Act then fudges the issue by including this service as a discretionary exception subject to the 10 per cent limit. This is particularly disappointing when the independent report by Coopers and Lybrand (1988) urged that school psychological services should constitute a mandatory exception within the DES Circular 7/88.

There is the issue of the National Curriculum. Will parents accept that their child should not have access to the full National Curriculum if the child is the subject of a statement? This is obviously another possible source of dispute between parents and the authority. If a child is to be denied full or partial access to the National Curriculum, this will have to be indicated in the statement. Someone will have to spend time detailing this, so

there is an increased administration cost which, presumably, is not going to be funded.

Finally the new Act allows education authorities to provide services hitherto provided by health services. Education authorities now have the power (but not the duty) to provide certain paramedical services but have been given no additional money to provide the services. Inevitably, some parents will take issue with a lack of service somewhere and present the argument (in the courts if necessary) that the education authority must provide. Parental rights and expectations when not matched by funding do not seem to make for harmony.

DES Circular 7/88 suggests that the funding of special units might remain under central control but overlooks the integration component of good unit provision. Special schools are seen as a separate entity by the same circular, so how do we preserve their links with mainstream schools when hard cash now comes into the equation?

There is a real danger that the hurricane will be fierce and authorities may not stay afloat. There is, I think, a sequence of events to be followed as the ship goes down which includes manning the pumps and then lowering the boats. Somewhere along the line it might be possible to find a buoyancy aid; but after that it is a case of swimming.

I believe that most swimmers learn by one of two methods. Many are taught, some are thrown in and learn. If we are honest, most of us opted for the first method. But so far as special education in all schools is concerned, we are about to jump in at the deep end and some will learn by the second method and some, of course, may not learn in time.

Chapter 11

The introduction of the National Curriculum: implications for management in special schools

Mary Hope

The Education Reform Act 1988 introduces radical changes in the education system and in the structure of the power that governs it. For many teachers the most immediately significant part of the Act appeared to be the chapter establishing the National Curriculum and its associated programme of testing. This chapter is relatively brief in the context of such a huge piece of legislation and the concept of a nationally prescribed curriculum is in some ways at odds with the political philosophy that apparently lies behind other changes embodied in the Act. The full significance of those other changes is gradually becoming clearer. Nevertheless, teachers' recognition of the importance of the National Curriculum's potential influence on their working lives is well founded. The task confronting schools is that of implementing it in a way that utilizes any potential for good and minimizes the inherent risks of divisiveness among pupils and professional devaluation. This is an urgent task that requires rapid preparation and skilful management.

Although moves towards a centrally determined common curriculum have been under discussion for years, the introduction and passage of the legislation was comparatively abrupt. Few teachers expected it to take quite the form it has taken or to be set within a framework of testing such as the one now laid down. The arrangements for pupils with special needs appear to have been determined as an afterthought with little understanding of the continuum of needs and its complexity. Special schools as well as mainstream will be required to teach the National Curriculum. Perhaps officials drafting the original Bill thought that special schools would scarcely be affected because a

substantial proportion of their pupils would be largely exempted. The integrationist cause has become too firmly established to allow that to happen without protest. Considerable pressure is being brought to bear to ensure that children with special needs participate as fully as possible in what is being prescribed for the general school population even though special educators are by no means entirely happy with the prescription.

Heads and others responsible for the management of the National Curriculum's introduction in special schools will have some advantages over mainstream, particularly secondary, colleagues. These include smaller pupil numbers and staff sizes, less complex timetables, less scope for invidious comparisons between pupils, recognition by parents and the community that the school has a special function and the fact that they will not be simultaneously grappling with the introduction of full local financial management. However, they will have to cope with diverse patterns of exemptions and modifications resulting from the heterogeneous nature of pupils' disabilities. They will also have to struggle to maintain the confidence and self-image of pupils and the morale of staff and parents, perhaps in a position of growing isolation from an educational mainstream that will be developing an increasingly competitive ethos.

As originally presented in 1987, the Education Reform Bill contained only a brief section regarding the application of the National Curriculum to children with special educational needs. Clause 10 declared that 'a statement…of a pupil's special educational needs may direct that the provisions of the National Curriculum shall apply…with such modifications as may be specified in the statement'. By the time the Bill had passed through its various stages and emerged in July 1988 as the Education Reform Act, a long and complicated section (number 19) had been added, permitting the disapplication of the National Curriculum to some pupils without statements for temporary periods. The section on statemented pupils, now numbered 18, is the one most relevant to special schools and runs as follows:

> The special educational provision for any pupil specified in a statement under section 7 of the 1981 Act of his special educational needs may include provision –
> (a) excluding the application of the provisions of the National Curriculum; or
> (b) applying those provisions with such modifications as may be specified in the statement.

The Secretary of State has been empowered to make further

orders and regulations that will affect pupils with special needs and these are still awaited. A special educational needs task group was set up early in 1989 and its findings and advice will presumably have an important influence on the regulations.

Local authorities are making progress in preparing staff for the impact of the introduction of the National Curriculum. By the time this book is published teachers will have acquired a new vocabulary, with particular specialized meanings attached to such terms as core and foundation subjects, key stages, attainment targets and programmes of study. Yet another set of acronyms – SEAC, TGAT etc. – will have become part of the currency of education discourse.

General awareness raising may be well advanced but more detailed planning will not be easy. The gradually phased introduction of the National Curriculum is more feasible than an attempt at comprehensive sudden change would have been. However, it means that schools face a long transitional period during which some areas of the curriculum will be more clearly regulated than others. The fact that many of the procedures for modifying the National Curriculum and for testing have yet to be made by the Secretary of State in the form of regulations gives rise to uncertainty, speculation and insecurity. It seems that even the distinguished panels of experts formed into working groups and councils to advise the Secretary of State have not yet had the opportunity to think through all the later stages and long-term implications. The situation is, at one and the same time, more tightly controlled and more uncertain than it has ever been within the experience of most currently practising teachers. Keeping up with developments has become both time consuming and anxiety producing.

Wide disparities between local authorities in the provision, including curricular provision, made for children with special needs have long been deplored by professionals working in this field. It may therefore seem perverse of them to object to the imposition of a National Curriculum. However, making pupils with special needs fit in to a curriculum model designed for a – perhaps hypothetical – majority school population is not what special educators had intended when calling for centrally determined requirements. There has always been a tension between, on the one hand, the desire to enable children with special needs to participate as fully as possible in a broadly based curriculum in common with their peers and, on the other, the desire to provide each child with a programme based on careful assessment of individual abilities and disabilities. Ideally the two

approaches can be reconciled, but only people with very limited experience of the extent and diversity of disabilities can pretend that no dilemma exists. Policies in favour of one approach or the other have often been made on the basis of current fashion, strongly influenced by economic considerations. The dilemma will continue to exist in relation to exemptions from the National Curriculum. We must be vigilant to ensure that children are not excluded mainly because their inclusion would be inconvenient, requiring extra effort and alternative methods from teaching staff, or unpopular, lowering class and school aggregates for test results. On the other hand, we must ensure that children are not consigned to years of miserable struggle with an inappropriate curriculum and failure in a series of unsuitable tests.

Although schools will not be directly responsible for determining the disapplications and modifications recorded on statements, their advice and their policies when referring and reviewing pupils will clearly be influential. A major concern will be that of keeping a balance between pressures towards the normal (i.e. national) and pressures towards the specialized in providing curricula for pupils with statements.

Coverage of the National Curriculum

Under section 10(2) of the Education Reform Act it is the duty of every head teacher of a maintained school to secure the implementation of the National Curriculum within that school. In the opening sections of the Act such a curriculum is described as one that is balanced and broadly based which 'promotes the spiritual, moral, cultural, mental and physical development of pupils at the school and of society;' and which 'prepares such pupils for the opportunities, responsibilities and experiences of adult life'. These are extremely ambitious aims. Some might argue that it is unrealistic, indeed unfair, to expect schools to accept such heavy and wide ranging responsibilities, particularly when we take account of the possible implications of the phrase 'and of society'. (Speculation on the significance of that phrase in relation to the education of children with special needs would generate a long and interesting discussion for which, unfortunately, there is not space in this chapter.)

Demanding as these aims are, the concept of a curriculum designed to meet the needs and promote the development of what is sometimes referred to as 'the whole child' is not at all alien to teachers in special schools. In such schools it has never been appropriate to make many assumptions about what the

children will have learned before entering school or what they will acquire incidentally in the home or community. Such teachers have always had to concern themselves with basic functioning in self-help and social skills, with rudimentary understanding of right and wrong and emotional control. Incorporating contributions to a child's development made by physiotherapists, speech therapists and others is a familiar aspect of their curriculum planning. In most special schools now there is consciousness of the importance of preparation for adult life. Training schemes explicitly designed to foster vocational and life-skills have been established in many. The idea of a curriculum which aims to promote all aspects of development is one that might well find acceptance most readily in the special school sector.

Traditionally, however, special schools have not addressed themselves to their curricular aims in terms of clearly demarcated subjects. Some special school staffs include a few subject specialists, particularly physical education, music, art and home economics. In recent years special schools have been officially encouraged to appoint co-ordinators for curriculum areas such as language and mathematics; but much of the teaching they co-ordinate is done by their colleagues and they themselves often have class responsibilities that cover other subject material. Special school staffs are accustomed to teaching content drawn from a wide range of subjects including those in which they have no specific training. Faced with the possible need to demonstrate that they can offer the full National Curriculum, heads of special schools may feel themselves constrained to make changes in the deployment of their staff. They may consider it expedient to maximize the use of any subject specialisms the staff have, even when this runs counter to their personal views about the forms of organization and time-tabling that best suit their pupils. When vacancies arise they may be tempted to appoint applicants with qualifications in subjects not otherwise represented among the staff rather than applicants with the best general ability to work with pupils with special needs.

Reappraisal of staff deployment will not necessarily be bad. Some schools will benefit, particularly if full participation of staff members is encouraged, and some teachers may gain opportunities which have positive value for themselves and the children. Nevertheless, it is important that head teachers should resist pressures to change what is working well in their staff organization merely in order to show that the school can provide

the National Curriculum. It is officially recognized that, at least in the first stages, many subjects can readily be taught by good teachers without specialist subject qualifications. Indeed as the draft proposals appear, many teachers in primary, as well as special schools, are gaining confidence in this respect. It is also acknowledged that teachers with specialist qualifications will not be available in some subjects even in large mainstream schools and at more advanced levels of work.

The prospect of the National Curriculum is already causing some special school staff to look more closely at the way in which mainstream secondary schools structure a subject-based curriculum and at what mainstream colleagues regard as the key features of their subjects. In so far as this process of consultation leads to increased understanding of each other's work it is beneficial. It would be very unfortunate, however, if special school heads felt under pressure to imitate a curriculum framework that many educators find questionable even within the mainstream.

As the programmes of study are issued, careful reappraisal of a school's current curriculum content and its relation to the officially stipulated content will be required. There will always be value in reviewing the curriculum on offer and some schools will benefit greatly from this exercise. Many special schools, however, have recently been through radical and time-consuming reviews of curriculum. Staff could well be dismayed or resentful at the prospect of having to go through the process in detail again, particularly if it puts at risk an agreed curriculum with which they are happy or indeed if the whole idea of a National Curriculum with accompanying tests is incompatible with their approach to educating children with special needs. As in the case of staff deployment, it is important that what is good in current practice should not be jettisoned. A good deal of the existing curriculum content in special schools can probably be matched to the programmes of study and with a little ingenuity most can be classified under subject headings. The particular heading under which a topic or activity is classified may depend to some extent on a school's perceived need to demonstrate that it is giving sufficient time and attention to a particular subject area; but head teachers should have the confidence to argue for their school's own considered forms of organization. In the next couple of years, when everyone will be seeking appropriate ways of applying national regulations to special education, there is likely to be a welcome for ideas contributed by schools with the courage of their own convictions who can demonstrate their effectiveness.

When the draft proposals for attainment targets and programmes of study began to appear, many special educators greeted them with relief. It was clear that at the first levels there were a number of items that even pupils with quite severe learning difficulties could and do achieve. A greater problem arises, however, over progression to higher levels. The targets soon begin to include operations that involve complexities and a degree of abstract thinking. In special schools we are familiar with the problem of trying to make the jump from the early stages of reading and number schemes which our pupils can master to the next stages which seem too quickly to reach a level of difficulty beyond their competence. It may be that some children who are initially assessed as being capable of participating in the National Curriculum will become stuck at the lower levels, with consequent disappointment and frustration for themselves and parents. Conscientious conduct of annual reviews should enable schools to accumulate valuable evidence on this issue, which does not so far appear to have been adequately addressed.

During the coming period of change and uncertainty one vitally important management task will be that of allaying the anxieties of staff and of maintaining confidence and morale. Staff who have been teaching general classes satisfactorily for years may become insecure about their lack of subject qualifications. The fact that for some children they have to work towards externally laid down attainment targets that will be assessed by national tests may make them uneasy. Although for many the objectives model is not their preferred model of curriculum design, most special school teachers are at least familiar with working to objectives. However, these objectives are formulated on an individual basis by people who know a child intimately and they are continually reviewed. Working towards nationally imposed attainment targets in conformity with study programmes classified under subject headings is an unfamiliar and perhaps less acceptable task. The fact that some pupils in an age group are to participate in the tests and some are not could also give rise to conflict. Even teachers who are confident in their own ability to teach effectively may feel vulnerable to challenge from governors and parents for whom the introduction of the National Curriculum has created new expectations.

It is important that those in management positions should equip themselves with adequate knowledge about the curriculum changes to be able to give informed reassurance and that there should be opportunities for staff to discuss anxieties on an individual basis as well as sharing concerns. A sound programme

of in-service training should help to allay worries; but it cannot be assumed that talks and seminars about the National Curriculum and its assessment will automatically do so. Staff can emerge from such sessions with more anxieties than before, particularly if those providing the sessions are not fully attuned to the problems at classroom level. The Secretary of State has authorized two extra days for staff training during the year after the National Curriculum begins to come into operation. After that any training on the topic must be covered within the basic number of five days annually. This is a pitifully small amount of time for the task and, clearly, heads will want to release some staff members for additional training. Wise use of the time is vital. This requires forward planning, ideally with collaboration from schools, about the most suitable input and the requirements for supply cover and resources.

Some special schools may find that the National Curriculum is disapplied to nearly all their pupils with regard to certain subjects. Decisions then have to be made as to how far it is ethical and feasible to provide coverage of them for very small numbers if this has resource implications and cannot be managed simply by individual timetabling. Since heads may be open to challenge from parents, it is to be hoped that the Department of Education and Science will provide guidance on this issue.

In the days when handicapped pupils and the special schools they attended were classified by categories of handicap, a simplistic solution might have been to exempt children from specified subjects according to these categories. Since the Education Act 1981 embodied the recommendations of the Warnock Report on this issue, there has been more widespread appreciation of the diversity of the patterns of disability and the fact that each of the former categories included a wide range of impairments and degrees of severity. Any attempt to return to crude categorization as a simple mechanism for determining disapplication and modifications should be strongly resisted.

Commitment to a special curriculum

Many special school staff are wondering whether attention to the requirements of the National Curriculum will leave adequate time and resources for all the other areas of teaching that currently form such an important part of their work. The most basic skills of communication and mobility, the opportunities to experience and control emotions, the acquisition of early self-help skills are prerequisites to meaningful participation in more

advanced education. It would be unrealistic to expect attainment targets for normally developing children to be set in all these areas; yet in special schools they may be relevant up to the school-leaving stage. Work is currently going on to develop programmes preparatory to entry to the National Curriculum and it is hoped that in many cases these will be accepted as more positive alternatives to disapplication. Even when disapplications are recorded on statements, those responsible will be expected to specify alternatives to demonstrate that a child's curriculum will still be broad and balanced. This may provide another way of giving statutory force to some of the more specialized curriculum. Schools must safeguard these vital areas. It is essential that the most effective teachers should not be directed towards those areas where the children's progress is to be officially tested, leaving the teaching of areas outside the National Curriculum to less experienced or less competent teachers or to classroom assistants. Many classroom assistants are excellent at teaching the skills appropriate to early development and their contribution should be adequately valued; but role demarcation between them and teaching staff should not be made on the basis of what is included in the National Curriculum.

Special schools are also places in which new approaches must continue to be developed. There is still a great deal to learn about the most effective ways of working with pupils with various impairments and difficulties. In some schools what is generally called the sensory curriculum (Longhorn 1988) is being adopted and built up. Others are trying out aspects of the system of conductive education which originated in Hungary (Hari and Akos 1988; Cottam and Sutton 1985) and which, largely in response to the demands of some British parents, is now the subject of a government-sponsored research project. Feuerstein's instrumental enrichment programmes (Feuerstein 1980) are being used as part of the curriculum in a number of special schools, particularly with pupils with moderate learning difficulties. A curriculum based on observations of interactions between normal infants and their care givers is being explored for some young people with profound learning difficulties (Smith 1988). While some of these initiatives currently concern only the most severely handicapped pupils who are unlikely to be included in the National Curriculum, they may well have elements that could beneficially be adapted for use with those whose problems are less severe. It is important to ensure that initiatives of this type are not inhibited by the advent of the

National Curriculum requirements. Section 16 of the Education Reform Act allows schools to claim exemptions on the grounds of experimental or developmental work. There is no indication as yet that special schools will not be eligible to put forward claims under this section, although the total number of schools to which such exemption is granted is likely to be very small indeed.

Effects on links with mainstream

Another area of development which special educators fear may be particularly threatened is that in which links have been formed with mainstream schools to initiate and expand schemes of partial integration. Since the passing of the Education Act 1981 rapidly increasing numbers of such schemes have been set up. Not all have been entirely successful. Some have been inadequately thought out and prepared for or inadequately resourced. Sometimes the tasks involved have been delegated at too early a stage to staff who do not have the management skills and experience to handle the sensitive liaison work necessary.

Conversely, sometimes too little has been delegated and decisions have been taken by those too far removed from the classroom realities with little practical experience of special needs. Nevertheless, much understanding has been gained even when mistakes have been made. In many cases all those involved have been surprised and heartened by the high level of success. This seemed to offer a challenging but promising way ahead. Now mainstream schools are confronted with the need to demonstrate their effectiveness by maintaining good aggregate scores on national tests, to rely on the support of governors for decisions involving the allocation of finance and to be ever-mindful of the possibility that parents may opt for grant-maintained status. It would hardly be surprising if, in the midst of so many pressures and with so many changes to implement, even well disposed colleagues in mainstream schools gave a lower priority to the development of partial integration schemes.

On the other hand, schemes whereby special schools act as resource bases and special school staff spend part of their time supporting special needs work in mainstream may be strengthened. In this way local authorities could fulfil certain obligations to pupils with special needs in mainstream while keeping financial control over the resources involved. Whatever the short-term effects of the legislation it will be important for special school management to maintain an interest in curriculum developments in their local mainstream schools if any prospects of future integration are to be kept alive.

Assessment and testing

From the moment the *Consultation Document* was issued in July 1987 (DES 1987a), one of the aspects of the National Curriculum that worried special educators most was the fact that it was tied to a programme of regular testing. Pupils in special schools have been subjected to many tests of different types throughout their lives. Their experience of testing has seldom been a happy or even a neutral one. For many a series of bewildering or humiliating experiences has left a lack of confidence in themselves generally, an unwillingness to engage with any challenging task, a reluctance to commit care and effort even in areas where they have adequate ability. One of the major functions of a special school is often to repair a pupil's damaged confidence and one of the contributing factors to the damage has often been repeated failure in test situations. In those cases where children are too severely disabled to show awareness of their failures, it may be the parents who have felt the humiliations most keenly and who need to be supported and encouraged to have confidence in their child's ability to develop.

In the context of a national programme of testing, there is no easy solution. It will be possible for pupils with statements to be exempted from taking the tests even in cases where they have been assessed as capable of following parts of the National Curriculum. The *Task Group on Assessment and Testing* (DES 1987b) also recommended that heads should be allowed to use professional judgement to exempt in cases where testing would exacerbate a medical condition or emotional disorder. If this occurs, however, great care will be required to ensure that pupils who follow the curriculum but are not tested are not deprived of a sense of achievement or that their parents do not feel they have been cheated of an opportunity to show, and obtain some recognition for, what they have attained.

The *Task Group* recommended that tests should be designed so that a teacher could curtail a test discreetly without the child being aware that this was being done or could give assistance and record the amount of help. This might be easier to carry out in a special school than in the more competitive atmosphere that will be generated in mainstream, where we can see the alarming potential for accusations of unfairness. Even in special schools, however, careful judgement would be required. Pupils with special needs are often erratic in performance and their patterns do not always conform to those of normal development. They are sometimes able to succeed on items rated as more difficult, having failed some of the items normally regarded as easy. For

some pupils, particularly those with sensory impairments and specific communication difficulties, there will be statutory modifications to the tests and schools will need to make arrangements to ensure that they can comply with the requirements involved. The problem of progression has already been noted in the earlier discussion of curriculum. It will be difficult to devise tests that register the very small, but nevertheless important, amounts of progress that some pupils make. Agencies have been commissioned to work on the development of tests and procedures that will be 'sufficiently wide-ranging and sensitive to respond to the needs of these children'. As yet we do not know how successful they will be nor whether the results of their efforts will be acceptable to the government.

There are therefore still many issues to be tackled about the suitability of different types of test and the procedures for their administration. Attention to the programme of national tests should not, however, be disproportionate. It is envisaged that most of the assessment of a pupil's progress in the National Curriculum will be carried out through continuous monitoring by teachers. Special schools may well have useful ideas to offer in this respect. Whether they have adopted an objectives model or not, careful monitoring and detailed recording of the progress of individual pupils is a feature of practice in most special schools. As with curriculum organization, the immediate task is to improve and demonstrate the effectiveness of what is good in current practice as this may help to forestall the imposition of more restrictive systems.

The moderation process should provide schools with valuable feedback about their standards and an opportunity to consult with others about the results of any modifications they have made to the normal procedures. It is not as yet clear how the moderation of results from special schools will take place. The *Task Group* report (DES 1987b) makes a general recommendation in favour of group moderation. If this method were adopted, representatives of a number of schools would meet together to compare the distribution of results in their schools with the distribution of results on the national tests. This would provide opportunities for them to discuss, justify or adjust their distributions and find interpretations for departures from the expected patterns. The difficult position of special schools is immediately obvious. If all special schools in a geographical area were grouped together they might lose touch with the standards in mainstream. They would also be cut off from the reciprocal

benefits of discussion with teachers dealing with special needs in mainstream. In any case, the heterogeneity of their pupils' needs would mean that they could not be looking for a common pattern of distribution of attainments. If, on the other hand, a special school were included in a group with neighbouring mainstream schools, it might find few common reference points, little understanding of issues specific to pupils with special needs and therefore very limited opportunity for meaningful discussion of possible interpretations of idiosyncratic results.

The *Task Group on Assessment and Testing* has recommended the use of records of achievement as 'a vehicle for recording progress and achievement within the national assessment system'. This is an encouragement to those who have recently been devoting time and effort to devising ways in which pupils with even quite severe special needs can contribute to the compilation of their own records. In their interesting submission to the *Task Group* the Steering Group for Records of Achievement emphasized the importance of pupils' involvement in their own assessment, the fact that their records are expressed in terms of positive achievement and the fact that pupils retain ownership of their records. In these respects the emphasis of records of achievement differs from that of the National Curriculum assessment, though perhaps not irreconcilably. The emphasis on pupil involvement and ownership accords well, however, with the aims of the self-advocacy movement which in recent years has had considerable impact on attitudes towards physically and mentally disabled young people and adults. If the Education Reform Act is serious in requiring that the curriculum should prepare pupils for 'the opportunities, responsibilities and experiences of adult life', it is important that pupils with special needs should be encouraged to express their own views and participate in identifying and evaluating their own achievements. Some governors, parents and, indeed, teachers may find difficulty in crediting special school pupils with the ability to do this to any significant extent and patient effort will be required to build up a body of evidence to convince them.

Handling information

The introduction of the National Curriculum and testing will confront head teachers with the task of reading, digesting and processing a great deal of additional information. It is to be hoped that the DES and LEAs will make every effort to keep their documentation clear and straightforward. In their turn, heads

will be required to pass on much of this information to staff, to governors and to parents. It seems that the ability to present information clearly and succinctly in both written and oral form is an increasingly important attribute in a head teacher. Report writing has long been recognized as a significant part of a head's job but since the Education (No.2) Act 1986 the extended obligation for formal reporting to governors and parents has added to this aspect of the work.

Some of the transmission of information requires not only clarity but also considerable tact and sensitivity. This will certainly apply to communications with parents about the curriculum and test results. It may also apply to communications with the local press who in some areas may consider test results an interesting source of material but who may not appreciate the complexities of this topic in relation to children with special needs. Where local authorities have not made such arrangements, head teachers as a group may find it useful to request or organize training to promote their skills in processing and presenting information and to familiarize themselves with relevant technological advances.

It may also be possible to make more effective use of any particular aptitudes for communication that staff members show. While responsibility for what is communicated must ultimately lie with the head, there is no reason why some of the work should not be delegated to those who have a flair for writing and may enjoy the challenge if their efforts are appreciated and acknowledged. It will be important for head teachers to impress on local authorities the necessity for adequate clerical help and to give a high priority to maintaining the morale of secretaries and clerical assistants at a time of growing pressure of work.

Relations with parents

One of the government's declared aims in bringing in the 1988 Education Reform Act was to increase parental choice. In effect the Act's first chapter on the National Curriculum restricts the extent of the choice parents have in curriculum matters unless they decide to send their children to fee-paying schools. There is, however, encouragement for them to monitor the delivery of the nationally prescribed curriculum in their child's school and, in later chapters of the Act, there are measures which foster a climate of consumerism and competition between schools for the favour of parents.

In the field of special education, awareness of parents' rights and the importance of their role in the education of their children steadily increased in the 1960s and 1970s, culminating in the chapter entitled 'Partnership with parents' in the Warnock Report (DES 1978). Parental rights figure prominently in the Education Act 1981 which constitutes the legislation governing most aspects of the education of children with statements. Although the rhetoric of partnership is by no means always matched in practice, most special schools have a high level of awareness of the importance of co-operation with parents and some have excellent relationships and well developed frameworks for consultation and parental participation. It would be very sad if these existing good relationships were jeopardized because of the growing encouragement of a confrontational approach between schools and parents. Where children with special needs are concerned, dissatisfaction with National Curriculum arrangements could well provide a source of friction. Some parents may be worried about additional pressures being placed on a child who is expected to follow the curriculum and take the tests, while others may be resentful if a child is excluded from a subject which they consider him/her capable of following.

A number of well organized parental pressure groups, active on behalf of the families of children with disabilities, maintain effective representation of their views to politicians at national and local level. Most teachers appreciate the need for these groups and recognize the useful functions they perform; indeed some teachers are active members or supporters. Nevertheless occasions arise when there is confrontation between a school and such a group and this can present a head teacher with a threatening situation, especially if the local press becomes involved. Sometimes the head does not have the resources or the local authority backing to accede to the pressure group's wishes. Sometimes the school staff believe that the group is not speaking on behalf of the majority of parents and that it is therefore the duty of the school to represent the less articulate. Head teachers would be well advised to acquaint themselves with any policy decisions taken by pressure groups with regard to the National Curriculum. Foresight over possible issues of contention might enable schools and parent groups to avoid unproductive conflict and to co-operate in the development of procedures that will be seen as serving the interests of all pupils.

For parents, one of the most worrying aspects of current procedure is the length of time involved in the carrying out of

assessments and the compilation of statements. Part of the delay is attributable to the statutory requirements allowing parents time to make their own representations and comments at various stages in the process. Much of the delay, however, is said to be due to the pressure of work on professionals contributing advice and officials collating it. Whatever the reasons there is no doubt that their experiences during this anxious waiting period can antagonize parents and sour their initial relationships with the special school. This situation is hardly likely to improve. Currently few statements carry much detail about the kind of curriculum recommended. From now on statements will also have to specify details of disapplications of, and modifications to, the National Curriculum and testing, plus indications of the kind of alternative curriculum appropriate if the child is not to follow the nationally prescribed one. This makes it incumbent upon those carrying out assessments to know a good deal about the curriculum being offered in the schools and the way in which it is taught if they are to make judgements on its suitability in the case of each child who requires a statement. It seems unlikely that this can be done without increasing the delays. Many special schools can probably expect either to receive more pupils for whom the process has not been completed or more who have been kept waiting for considerable periods of time.

There are also widespread fears that the desire to show good aggregate test results will cause mainstream schools to refer, and press for statements on, more of their pupils who are experiencing difficulty. This would also add to the delays. Under the arrangements for local financial management the number of pupils with special needs is a factor to be taken into account when an authority determines a school's budget share. Whether any additional funding will be enough to counteract a tendency towards more referrals and whether authorities can resist pressures to issue more statements and admit more pupils to special schools is not yet known. Parents of pupils whose difficulties are moderate, and who suspect that their children have been referred because their performances on national tests would depress the mainstream school's averages, are likely to be particularly resentful and unhappy about their placement in a special school. This is another situation that would call for skilled and sympathetic handling by the special school's management.

Support for the managers

Throughout the difficult period ahead the school management

team will be required to provide support for teaching, welfare and clerical staff and for parents and pupils. Who will offer support to management? The effect of various aspects of the Education Reform Act on local education authorities is not yet known. If many of its schools opt for grant-maintained status, taking their financial allocations with them, an LEA will find itself with less money to spend on maintaining its advisory services. In these circumstances advisers will have even less time than they do at present to visit schools and provide heads with opportunities for an exchange of views, encouragement or backing in their requests for practical help.

Even if very few of their schools opt out, LEAs' control over their finances will be dramatically reduced by the introduction of local financial management. Some may find their continued responsibilities for special and small primary schools a rather inconvenient nuisance since they will involve maintaining an administrative structure for what they see as an insignificant remnant. They may be anxious to have special schools included in the local financial management arrangements as soon as possible. Others may regard special schools as important because they remain a sphere in which the LEA can exert financial power and influence. Since LEAs retain their financial responsibilities under the 1981 Education Act, they may decide to channel relevant resources through special schools. In these circumstances special schools may find themselves the focus of more, not less, LEA attention.

Whatever the general reaction of the local authority, the backing of a well informed and sympathetic governing body will be invaluable to the school management. Some LEAs have established courses to familiarize governors with the implications of the National Curriculum. A good deal of the educative work, however, will fall to head teachers. They will need to help governors to understand the implications for the particular type of work being carried out in the school and why in certain respects it is, or is not, appropriate for the National Curriculum to be followed. Frequent visits from governors and their participation in school activities are an accepted feature in some schools but in others they may require additional encouragement. As with all the tasks discussed this is time consuming and heads will need to consider how much can be delegated to teacher governors.

In the past in special schools, which are relatively small, it has not always appeared necessary for heads to delegate managerial responsibilities to any great extent. Now, faced by recent

legislation with the need to review curriculum organization, assessment and recording arrangements and staff deployment; to allay staff anxieties, to secure appropriate INSET; to process all the extra information; to keep governors and parents acquainted with developments and maintain good relationships with them, head teachers will require a well considered framework of delegation if they are not to be overwhelmed.

At present the introduction of the National Curriculum in relation to pupils with special needs is a frustrating topic for writers and readers alike. It is easy enough to speculate about the possible implications but not at all easy at this stage to offer practical suggestions for tackling the problems that may arise. So much is still unclear that any attempt to advise seems presumptuous and perhaps misleading. Those responsible for managing special schools will need to accumulate and share experiences as the National Curriculum and testing become realities. Support for colleagues working with pupils with special needs in mainstream must also be kept in mind, for in many ways their problems will be more complex and more intense. Time to meet, discuss and plan with colleagues in other schools may not seem a high priority in a busy schedule. However, in the coming era of competitiveness it will be vital for those throughout the special needs sector to resist the prevailing pressures towards isolation or rivalry and to sustain a spirit of co-operation and mutual support.

Chapter 12

The independent residential special school for emotionally and behaviourally disturbed pupils

David Cassar

In this chapter I intend to show that independent special schools for emotionally and behaviourally disturbed children are not a new innovation or a replication of the state system. Neither are they cashing in on the 'loads-a-money' mentality in this present climate of profit and privatization. They have been a necessary part of the system and much innovation has come out of the independent special school sector. The management of such schools could be a model for state special schools and the future of independent special schools is, I believe, secure no matter what political colour central government might be.

A historical overview

The early history of special education was dominated by the provision of special institutions or schools for categories of handicap. These categories were determined by 'medical' diagnosis. Training and education was developed to meet the needs of groups supposed to be homogeneous on the basis of their medical classification. The 1944 Education Act enshrined this approach and categories of handicap were defined based on a medical examination; there was an implicit assumption, at the time, that educational methods would be developed in each category.

Before the 1944 Education Act those young people, now referred to as emotionally and behaviourally disturbed, were referred to as 'delinquents' or 'problem children'. The Act classified these young people as 'maladjusted'. There were many people who now saw the need for an all-embracing educational

treatment centre for maladjusted children. Generally education-alists were uneasy about schools that were 'environmental' as well as educational, spurred on by a suspicion of psychiatry and psychology. The word 'integration' at that time meant that teachers were going to be mixing with other disciplines; with psychiatrists, psychologists, psychotherapists, social workers, speech therapists, play therapists and others. The teacher's independent assessment was now being questioned; there was to be an interchange of ideas and opinions, knowledge and observations would be shared between a multidisciplinary team and children were not only going to be educated, they were going to be 'treated' as well.

Bredinghurst School was the first special school after the 1944 Education Act which dealt solely with maladjusted boys. It was opened in 1948 and Wilfred F. Kemp was the headmaster. Bredinghurst marked the fruition of ideas that had been shared between Kemp and Colonel E. Eton in 1943 when Eton was education officer for special services for the London County Council. Even though Kemp had tremendous enthusiasm and concern he was still a little suspicious of his new venture. Shields (1962) quotes Kemp:

> Though we were enthusiastic, full of ideas, equipped with some knowledge and experience, it was nevertheless correctly called an experimental school. The limitation of a purely educational and environmental set-up had been exposed to me, but as an educator I was suspicious of psychiatry.
>
> Shields 1962, p. 9

Kemp was a pioneer, for Bredinghurst School in Peckham, South London, was the first school for maladjusted children in England to incorporate into its structure a full psychiatric unit, thus bringing into close association teachers, child care staff and a psychiatric team. Before Bredinghurst, schools or communities for difficult children were often regimes operated by individuals with their own idiosyncratic way of life. A few of them were teachers, others were doctors or therapists and some were from other walks of life that one would not normally associate with caring and educating children. Bridgeland (1971) summed it up rather well.

> Some, like Leila Rendel and Barbara Docker-Drysdale came from secure upperclass background; others like N.B.C. Lucas, from difficult or broken homes. Many rejected their own backgrounds and sought, like A.S. Neill and Homer Lane, to

build new order, while others endeavoured, as did Leila Rendel, to preserve the virtues of an older and more settled order of things. For many, school had been, as it was for Norman MacMunn, a place of terror, or, as it was for Lane, Fitch and Neill, a stimulus to rebellion. A few were happy in school and tried to communicate their happiness to others. Religion was to David Wills, Father Owen or Edward Seel the essential foundation of their work; others like Bill Malcolm or Lucy Francis rejected it as something essentially injurious to mental health.

Bridgeland 1971, p. 24

Before Bredinghurst, almost all schools for the 'maladjusted' were residential. Day schools for 'maladjusted' children developed later and were the product of state rather than individual action. These schools evolved largely from remedial and observation classes for children who were seen to be underachieving in school, whereas the independent school derived its residential form from many different ways in which treatment away from home was implicit. Much of the work of early pioneers was derived from the needs of individuals, many of whom would otherwise have been either potentially, or in fact, the responsibility of the poor law or child care authorities. These children were usually quite desperately deprived socially and for them a residential placement was either desirable or essential. If the work with children was not to be wasted by 'unhelpful home backgrounds' it seemed essential to provide a residential setting.

As stated earlier, most, if not all, early 'experimenters' usually had an individual style and techniques developed by them were reported either by other people who studied them in action or by themselves through published papers or seminars. Practice almost always preceded theory and until the Underwood Report (Ministry of Education 1955), there was little official attempt to see practice in terms of anything other than the, often unwelcome experimenting of a number of independent individuals.

The 'new' approach to educating, caring and 'curing' those who were recognized as 'unhappy' rather than as 'naughty' children were essentially addressed by individuals. Given the nature of local authority red tape and central government bureaucracies, individualism takes quite a knock and it becomes difficult to experiment within the 'safe' state school system. Individualism then, as Bridgeland expresses it, is perhaps one of the characteristics of pioneering in any field. Shields writing in 1962

about the education of maladjusted children, remarked that 'Up to the present, virtually all the pioneer research work in the treatment of maladjusted children has been done in private or independent schools' (p. 182).

Growth and development

The years of the Second World War actually provided the biggest opportunity for the development of residential schools for children who were emotionally and behaviourally disturbed. When war broke out in 1939 a number of children, previously manageable at school and at home, were evacuated to reception areas. This move proved damaging to a large number of these children and they were found to be 'unbilletable' as they had become emotionally disturbed following their arrival in an alien environment (Hurt 1988). Special hostels for such children became part of the government evacuation scheme. Where possible staff attached to existing child guidance clinics practised in them. By this means and by the war-time dispersal of staff, the number of clinics had increased from 17 in 1939 to 79 by 1945. Under the Education Act of 1944, the Minister who now had a specific responsibility for 'maladjusted' children approved some of these hostels as schools.

After the war, grave doubts grew about the provision being made by the Ministry of Education, particularly as the independent sector was growing and making pioneering strides into new methods of work. In 1950, D.H. Stott's *Delinquency in Human Nature* was published and reinforced the conviction that if maladjustment in childhood could be properly treated, juvenile delinquency would diminish. As is usual in these circumstances, the lure of cost effectiveness finally produced a government committee, the Underwood Committee. Five years after it was appointed the Underwood Report (Ministry of Education 1955) found such a severe shortage of public sector accommodation that LEAs had to make extensive use of independent schools.

Independent special schools flourished and with their growth came the good, the bad and the ugly. Potential educational imperialists came and went. Educational gymnasts jumping from one educational theory to another, juggling with behavioural modification practices, found it a hard world in which to survive and quickly disappeared. However, many independent schools still exist and a large proportion of them, now 'approved' through sections 11 and 13 of the 1981 Education Act, are excellent institutions offering sound education and care, operating outside

the mainstream sector's propensity for cautious advances, short staffing and inadequate resources but operating within a system whereby they are regularly and thoroughly inspected by Her Majesty's Inspectorate and have to maintain very high standards to remain on the 'approved' list. Remaining on this list means that LEAs would continue to refer statemented children to a DES 'approved' school when unable to provide appropriate resources in their own area to meet an individual child's needs.

At the same time as special schools for 'maladjusted' children were being developed through the independent and state systems, a curious development within the penal system was also emerging. The historical background to the changes that took place in the whole field of child care and more specifically in approved schools, can be briefly traced through a number of pamphlets, white papers and committee reports which span a decade of discussions (Rose 1967 and Carlebach 1970). These culminated in the Children and Young Persons Act 1969, which had the effect of altering the legal framework for the treatment of juvenile offenders.

Approved schools for young offenders came into being with the amalgamation of the previously existing reformatory and industrial schools by the Children and Young Persons Act 1933. The Act incorporated the belief that delinquency was caused by faulty training and approved schools, therefore, were encouraged to produce good citizens by a process of good physical and moral care, coupled with training in basic skills. Approved schools were subject to and organized on lines set out in the approved school rules subject to both the 1933 and 1963 Children and Young Persons Acts. The Government department responsible for the schools was the Home Office and the schools were part of the penal system for juvenile offenders.

The pre-1969 approved schools were primarily regarded as resocializing agents and their social and educational objectives were clearly defined by the Home Office. As in the development of 'educational' institutions for emotionally disturbed children the emphasis in the approved school system was placed on emotional and social readjustment; but whether this had to be at the expense of educational advance is less clear. The educational needs of the children attending both types of institutions were not their foremost needs and the young people were obviously admitted because of their personal and social needs, as attention to these frequently had to take priority over the attention given to their educational needs (Laslett 1977).

The main provision of the 1969 Children and Young Persons

Act led to the integration of approved schools into the locally provided system of children's homes and hostels for children in care. Thus, approved schools moved from a centrally controlled system under the Home Office (financed by central government funds), to control by the social services departments of the local authority (funded from the rates). The abolition of the approved school order – to be replaced by a care order – avoided the concept of a fixed sentence with remission for good behaviour and upheld the philosophy that anti-social behaviour required treatment, that social handicap required care and that either, if injurious to society or the individual, may require control.

Perhaps the most important requirement of the Children and Young Persons Act 1969 was the abolition of the power of juvenile court magistrates to make an order committing children to approved schools. Young offenders were now committed to the care of the local authority whose social workers had the delegated responsibility for deciding the form of care appropriate for each child according to his needs; this could be a placement in an ex-approved school, now designated as a community home with education on the premises, i.e a CH(E). These changes, however, removed the distinction between deprived and delinquent children, since it had now become the duty of the local authority to place a child committed to care to any one of a number of residential establishments, each providing different forms of treatment, education and care depending on the needs of the child.

This fitted in well with the many independent institutions that had now developed in different ways to treat emotionally disturbed children. Many of the independent hostels became independent CH(E)s and in turn developed into boarding special schools; some have received DES approval since the implementation of the 1981 Education Act.

It will be apparent from the foregoing that changing attitudes, reflecting society's concern for the underprivileged, neglected and deviant child, have resulted in radical changes in legislation and methods of educating, treating and caring for such children. It is within such changes and developments that independent boarding special schools have emerged as an integral and important part of the total provision for children in Britain.

The management of the school

The changes and developments outlined have also meant that independent schools very often receive a very mixed client

group. As an example, my own school has at present on roll pupils that have been referred to us for any number of reasons. Any one of our pupils would meet one, some, or all of the following criteria:

(i) Statement of special educational need
(ii) Abuse;
    sexual
    physical
    mental
(iii) In care because of;
    family breakdown
    delinquent behaviour
    being beyond the control of the parent/guardian
    school truancy
    exposure to moral danger.

The first management issue in such a school relates to the problem of cementing and directing teaching and non-teaching staff and in so doing attempting to create a homely environment and not just a formal school. The school must be designed in order that the child, as the centre of the process, is given the opportunity of seeing realistically the opportunities and limitations of the future. It should also be designed so that all the professionals involved continually strive to attain high standards of 'service delivery'.

It is not suggested that it will be possible to meet all the child's needs or restore all the damage and compensate for handicaps, but an attempt at least should be made to present an understanding of the situation and give sufficient strength of purpose to enable each individual to make the best of his/her life. In order to do this it is essential for multidisciplinary professionals to be formed into a cohesive team. Within a special school the one thing that could cement these professionals together is the establishment's curriculum, and in a boarding special school this was to be seen as a 24-hour curriculum (accepting of course, the limitations of stimulus and control once the pupil is asleep). It is important here to distinguish between the 24-hour curriculum that my school may offer and the subject-dominated National Curriculum that may not necessarily be appropriate to an emotionally disturbed client group. In my view the residential school curriculum has to be defined in the way that Kerr (1968) has conceptualized it as all the learning which is planned and guided by the school, inside or outside the premises.

The staff

The two professional groups that are likely to be together most and which are essentially the mainstay of the residential special school are teachers and residential social workers. The teacher is, of course, responsible for the classroom experience, the time for formal education. Teachers should offer carefully planned educational programmes containing a careful mixture of therapeutic situations whereby the child is given experience of new relationships with adults in a new setting. The residential social worker should be responsible for two main areas and these are: (i) social skills training, including health and hygiene, environmental awareness, interpersonal relationships, intra-personal relationships; and (ii) organized leisure activities, which should include a potentially extensive range of varying activities that should cater for the needs of the pupils.

The link between teachers and residential social workers within a residential setting is the common function of making and using relationships towards the rehabilitation and full development of the children in their care. With this in mind, all staff must be in a position to contribute, on an equal basis, as members of the 'treatment' team. Opportunity for this can be provided by organizing the school on group-work principles.

It is unlikely that either teachers or residential social workers will have much conceptual knowledge of learning theory and even less of group dynamics. Organization, particularly of the curriculum, along small group lines, however, offers the opportunity initially for working with fewer children than is customary in most traditional settings. As the knowledge and expertise of the group worker increases more therapeutic dimensions can be added via the medium of the group activity. Most professionals have experience of some group work through seminars, group tutorials, conferences and discussion work. It is the opportunity presented by the use of a small group that enables a choice of appropriate learning methods to be made and the smallness of the group enables the bias of the group work to change when it is felt necessary.

When focusing on these areas it is important to keep the demands of the 1981 Education Act in mind. Essentially the Act centres on the individual needs of the children in our schools. It is important that the entire staff group of a school are continuously observing and assessing the needs of each and every child. Only when this is done successfully can we attempt to meet the needs of the child by responding with an appropriate curriculum. Only when we in our individual establishments are

satisfied that we are continually improving our observation and assessment techniques can we write a curriculum to suit the individuals in our care.

Communication in the team

Other than cementing or 'bonding' teachers and residential social workers through an organized curriculum it is also essential, in a residential school, to use staff meetings for more than just school business or in-service training. The staff meeting is an excellent vehicle for bonding these two professional groups. It is therefore essential to have 'joint' staff meetings in order to facilitate this. The management of these meetings should be such that the staff should be given important and concrete issues to discuss in order that between them they can have ownership of the outcome of these discussions. It is also important that decisions made at the staff meeting are implemented by the head teacher with the minimum delay.

These meetings need meticulous planning and execution, particularly because the two sets of professionals usually have very different backgrounds and training. Very often the majority of residential social workers are not formally trained to the same degree as teachers and unless care is taken a divide between the two groups can evolve. In-service training at staff meetings can help individuals to understand and develop supportive roles towards each other. The training of staff is centrally related to the concern for the quality of their work and the amount of importance any school gives to directing its staff to its particular way of doing things. Training can therefore reinforce the bonding links between the two sets of professionals by highlighting common ground. Teachers and social workers can experience success and failure together, share frustrations and reach a point of mutual respect for the difficult jobs they do with difficult children. Children whose experience has generally given them sophisticated defence mechanisms and a high level of mistrust for adults obviously have an impact on all the adults working with them and this, therefore, can be a common denominator for professional bonding because even at the simplest level the staff concerned can see that they share common problems.

Administration

The head teacher of an independent school has no administrative support from any local authority and therefore has to make sure

that the added load of administration does not in any way hinder the smooth running of the school. The school's therapeutic purpose can be upheld only by a firm and sustained administrative structure. Even the more mundane and monotonous administrative tasks contribute to this purpose; therefore the head teacher should not hesitate in giving time and attention to routine matters. Poor administration can rapidly cause a build up of frustration amongst both pupils and staff, while good administration is a major factor in creating the structured environment necessary for emotionally and behaviourally disturbed children. In saying this, it is essential to retain a balanced perspective at all times, as an overorganized school would create an equally unsuccessful extreme. Laslett (1977) sums it up quite succinctly when he writes that 'The children need to be sustained by evidence of forces in the school environment which are in alliance against the destructive tendencies within themselves, and sound administration forms part of that alliance' (p. 88). Good administration should be part of a well structured environment.

In the residential setting a structured environment indicates a place in which boundaries of acceptable behaviour are clearly delineated and enforced. Hoghughi (1978), sees this as essential but very difficult to attain. However, it is vital to attempt to build a structured environment in order to reduce the ambiguity of expectations from the pupils and to facilitate adequate adaptation to demands made on pupils as well as enforcing the limits that mark the boundaries of what may and may not be done. In short, a well ordered, structured environment can greatly facilitate the quality of life for 'maladjusted' children in a residential setting.

The quality of life which exists in any residential community for children can be perceived within minutes of entering the school. Our human sensitivity gives an immediate intuitive assessment of the warmth, or lack of warmth, while a myriad of tiny clues are given out as to the existence, or non-existence, of authority and control. An overall impression of the degree of individualism tolerated or encouraged will be apparent almost immediately and will be equally evident to children coming to live in at that school. This will affect their expectations of help and trust in the future; therefore the staff must put a high priority on the ambience they create. It follows that success in creating group and individual education/therapy programmes can only be triggered by our success in this basic concept of a constructive rather than a destructive community.

The Future

As I indicated earlier, virtually all the pioneer work with difficult children has been carried out in the private sector (e.g. Shields 1962, Bridgeland 1971). Concerned practitioners such as A.S. Neill and Homer Lane attempted to meet the demanding needs of disturbed children without the external pressures, bureaucratic systems and political change within the state sector. More recently, in setting up programmes within independent residential schools, there has been a good deal of emphasis placed on the need for an affective–artistic approach rather than a cognitive–intellectual approach for those children who show little aptitude for the cognitively based curriculum (cf Bantock 1971).

It is likely that within the UK state system there will always exist a group of children with highly specialized inventories of need who will not be able to be placed in local authority provision due to economical and political restriction of adequate resources. This is primarily because of policies developed from the Warnock Report and the 1981 Education Act.

Although neither the 1981 Act nor the accompanying circulars and regulations use the term integration, the major new duty on LEAs to make special educational provision in ordinary schools, and to secure where practicable that children with special educational needs engage in the activities of the school together with children who do not have special educational needs, leaves no doubt over the thrust of the legislation. Furthermore the DES urges LEAs and voluntary bodies, when considering schemes for school organization, to examine the issues of falling roles and integration together to determine whether the opportunity may be taken to accommodate children with special needs in ordinary schools.

While the emphasis of the 1981 Act supports the trend away from segregated provision, the continuing role for special schools is recognized. The majority of children on whom LEAs maintain statements are educated in special schools and this is likely to continue for a number of years. However, sooner or later and probably over a period of years, most maintained special schools will disappear in their present form. Existing practice, where the majority of head teachers of special schools recognize the spirit of the legislation, requires a re-examination. Social links with mainstream schools have been generally practised for some time now, and increasingly the curricular and practical facilities of mainstream schools are sought to provide opportunities for children with special needs attending special schools.

However, although we may be witnessing the demise of the

special school as we know it, I believe most strongly that one particular client group having special needs will always be excluded from mainstream schooling and that this group is the emotionally and behaviourally disturbed. This is the group that very few teachers have time for and have little sympathy with when their class of 30 pupils is being disrupted by possibly one or two very determined, difficult children. Very few mainstream schools that I know of have developed structures and strategies for dealing with those difficult pupils and the end result is usually exclusion from school.

The new initiatives in maintained secondary schools will also mean that it is very unlikely that head teachers and governors will want such children in their schools. After all the school will need to build a 'good' reputation and publish 'good' examination results showing that a high percentage of its pupil population is doing well socially and educationally.

It would seem, therefore, that some special provision will always have to be provided for this group of children and if LEAs integrate all other special provision it may well prove to be too expensive to school the emotionally and behaviourally disturbed in special provision within a local authority. If this were to happen then I can foresee these children being schooled in independent special schools, if for no other reason than political and economic pressures.

If special schools do eventually disappear and become part of the mainstream structure, it will mean that the children who are not part of this system and who are schooled in separate establishments will be labelled and stigmatized more than they are now or have ever been. The gulf between 'special' and 'mainstream' will become wider. The 1988 Education Act has done nothing to help this inevitable separation. Indeed, it has made it more difficult to manage local authority special schools because of their present exclusion from the new schemes for financial devolvement. It must also be noted that the National Curriculum will not have to be taught in independent schools and that this could be a liberating feature for such schools. The advantages of not teaching the National Curriculum are that independent schools could offer an alternative curriculum which could include more therapeutic work. This in itself could be a valuable marketing feature. The 1988 Act does not seem to engage with the problems of special schools at all. It has almost totally excluded special schools from the National Curriculum debate and where debate has taken place it would almost appear to have set back any interesting

development within the curriculum of special schools already taking place. Because of the neglect by central government in taking a lead and giving direction in these matters, it seems inevitable that local authority special schools will close, leaving a gap that will be quickly filled by the independent sector. As this happens it will be essential that a sensitive response is made by everyone involved in order that the correct, possibly a corporate, approach can be adopted in the formulation of policy, planning, development, co-ordination and monitoring. At the moment there are thousands of young people in special units and schools, very few of which are maintained by local authorities. Mittler at the 'Warnock Plus Ten' conference in London in May 1988 said there was a 'conspiracy of silence' on children with emotional and behavioural difficulties. These are the young people for whom integration has not meant anything at all.

It is unlikely that any but the most damaged children will be considered for residential placement before a battery of non-residential alternatives has been tried. This means that the children urgently requiring the structured support of a residential setting are already approaching their early teens. It is noticeable, too, that many will need to acquire skills to enable them to live independently of their families and will need continued professional support for some considerable time.

This situation has highlighted the need for specialized forms of education and residential care outside the state system; for both economic and practical reasons these are likely to continue to develop rather than diminish over the next decade. Because of the very nature of some children's special needs these establishments are likely to be small in size, accommodating 30 children or less. This presents unique problems of curriculum (programme) organization. The introduction of a National Curriculum is also likely to lead to a good deal of negotiation and compromise before programmes to meet the individual needs of children can be instituted. Mary Hope's chapter explains such issues more fully.

However, this situation is not without parallel: residential resources for children in the USA have gone through similar reorganizational systems. For example, the closure of state institutions in Massachusetts gave rise to a number of independent and private bodies setting up programmes for emotionally and behaviourally disordered children. Following their establishment, growth and a good deal of experimentation the federal government have been able to select and publish a

number of so-named exemplary programmes indicating those programmes showing outstanding merit in coping with specialized problems in certain circumstances with particular groups of children.

It may well be, therefore, that with the undoubted growth within the independent special school sector there will be need to set up some collection of programmes under a recognized prospectus for use by authorities in selecting suitable placements for the children for whom they maintain responsibility. Additionally, in some ways comparable with the London Boroughs' Children's Regional Planning Committee, there will be set up some national system able to inspect, advise and be informed of the national resource of independent establishments available to all local authorities.

As Tony Bowers's chapter on marketing points out, there is a climate within society, reflected in recent legislation, which favours competition, financial accountability and, in particular, consumer choice. In these times, there is great scope for the entrepreneur to develop new services, just as there was forty years ago in the wake of a world war and new educational thought. Interested and determined professionals will have the opportunity to advance methods of meeting children's needs and the way forward would seem to be to establish a wide range of highly specialized, small units, thereby avoiding the uneconomic (and often wasteful) necessity of local authorities attempting to meet the needs of all their children. These small units will need to establish links with mainstream schools, industry and other 'special' units in order that the pupils placed in them are not disadvantaged and have as many curricular opportunities as their peers will have in mainstream education.

Chapter 13

Marketing services

Tony Bowers

In a totally unchanging world, there would be no requirement for management at all. I sometimes find it strange that people run courses, write articles or even books on 'the management of change' as though it were a sub-element. Management is about change. It may be concerned with achieving change within an organization – in the context of this chapter a school or a service – or it may be primarily aimed at minimizing or reducing the impact of changes going on around these organizations. The management issues may concern small changes in the system when, say, somebody becomes ill or leaves; or they may be much larger, reflecting regional or even national influences. In a totally unchanging world we would not need managers: there would simply be the requirement to administer routines and procedures and to keep things ticking along.

The emphasis of this chapter will be on the larger issues of change confronting those working with pupils with special educational needs. We have already looked, in Mary Hope's chapter, at some of the implications of the National Curriculum, and other contributors have given us their views of some of the general implications of the 1988 Education Reform Act. What we should not lose sight of is a phrase which was much heard at around the time of the Warnock Report (DES 1978) and the passing of the 1981 Education Act. These two events were frequently prefaced in debate by 'The spirit of . . .', implying that we had to remember the motivating forces and general intent of those preparing the Report or enacting the legislation. I do not propose here to dissect the latest extensive legislation but the mood which appears to underlie it is one which embraces

individual and organizational accountability, community involvement in decision making and, crucially, the introduction of market forces to the public sector of education. Present concerns with content issues – curriculum, assessment, financial management, appraisal – should not be allowed to draw our attention from this 'spirit' of the Act. In this chapter I shall try to look at some implications this may have for the work of those responsible for offering services for children with special educational needs.

The components of management

I have already expressed the view that management is about effectively initiating, progressing or dealing with change. Perhaps the most striking features of management, however, are that it is necessary because of the existence of organizations and that it involves working through other people. While there are discernible differences between special schools and local authority support services, and between these and mainstream school special needs teams, they all qualify as organizations and all involve their leaders in delegating tasks to others and depending upon the skills and performance of those others. Much of what follows will be of equal relevance to those given the task of managing any of these organizations, although there will obviously be distinctions between their circumstances at certain points in the discussion.

If we accept that much of the task of management relates to change, then the manager can be broadly reactive, responding to circumstances which mean that change has to occur or to be brought about, or proactive in looking forward and ensuring that change has been set in motion before events dictate it. In the latter case, an organization is likely to be well placed to take advantage of the environment in which it subsequently finds itself. Examples of this are those special schools which developed themselves as 'resource centres' for children with learning difficulties in other schools ahead of the post-Warnock rush to do so, those peripatetic remedial teams which rejigged their ways of working to be consistent with notions of 'support' for teachers as well as children and those mainstream remedial departments which restructured their ways of working to facilitate movement towards school-wide responsibility for special needs pupils.

Clearly there will be occasions when organizations are forced to be reactive: the responses of schools and local education authorities to their new statutory obligations under the 1988

Education Act provide examples. However, there are some organizations which are predominantly reactive, waiting for things to happen, and some which seem to go out and actually make things happen and be at the forefront of events. The latter are entrepreneurial, their leaders entrepreneurs. This is a word which permeates our times and which underpins the notion of market forces and therefore reflects the spirit of current legislation.

What does entrepreneurship entail? Minkes (1987) specifies three components of entrepreneurial management:

(i) the effective determination of the mission or basic direction of the enterprise;
(ii) the selection of strategy for meeting its perceived purpose;
(iii) the creation of the organizational means for both devising and implementing strategy.

Put more simply, to know where you are going – the first component – and how you will get there – the second – is not sufficient without the third, which involves building teams and decision-making structures, establishing motivation and ensuring that team members have the necessary skills to carry out what is expected of them. A further feature of entrepreneurship, of course, is the willingness to take risks, building upon the positive consequences of risk-bearing actions and coping with any negative results.

In this chapter, I shall not of course attempt to deal with all aspects of entrepreneurial management. We are concerned here with the notions of marketing. However, marketing itself requires looking at the product which we will deliver and that entails looking outside, seeing opportunities and seizing chances: some of the qualities associated with the entrepreneur. It might be argued that entrepreneurs are born, not made; that it is no good asking people to change from one sort of manager to another just because the climate of opinion or government decree makes such a shift necessary. However, the work of Hayward and Everett (1983) suggests that it is possible for individuals to change. Looking at the qualities of 'adaptation' (the tendency to be cautious in decisions, careful of others' feelings and to follow set rules and routines) and 'innovation' (the tendency to take chances, to risk offending some people and to set up new ways of working), they found that a major influence was not fixed individual features but the climate, culture and general traditions of the organization in which people functioned. It would seem reasonable to infer that the longer you work in a setting where

little prominence is given to ideas, to starting off new projects, where growth is not encouraged and where people stay away from risks, whether personal or financial, the less likely you are to demonstrate entrepreneurship. As the climate changes, so behaviour may also be expected to change; the problem is, which comes first?

Marketing in the wake of the 1988 Act

Just two years before this chapter was written, I tentatively introduced the idea of selling and its associated skills with these words: 'Within the caring professions generally it is unfashionable, and for some even abhorrent, to look at commercial practices in developing models for service delivery' (Bowers 1987, p. 95). Now such ideas are more readily accepted, particularly in relation to self-promotion and, by implication, the gaining of relative advantage over other organizations offering similar services. The LMS Initiative, a conglomerate of influential professional bodies, has recently emphasized that the local management of schools is not simply concerned with financial decisions but actually represents a major management challenge. 'Management decisions will be required on virtually every aspect of running schools including staff appointments, dismissals and the marketing of the school to the community at large' (LMS Initiative 1988, 1.2). The message is clear. If everybody else is doing it, those associated with special educational needs will have to ensure that they take up the same challenge.

Let us look briefly at the implications of LMS for special schools and support services as well as for special needs services within mainstream schools. As most readers will know, the Education Reform Act 1988 requires that LEAs must devise a formula by which they allocate the bulk of their funds to each of their primary and secondary schools. For all secondary schools and for primary schools with over 200 pupils, the LEA must also delegate to their governing bodies the responsibility for determining how the allocated funds should be spent. For primary schools with fewer than 200 pupils, and for special schools, the LEA may, if it wishes, also delegate responsibility for financial management.

Full details of the situation at the time of writing are set out in a 53-page circular (7/88) from the Department of Education and Science. Briefly, by looking at the costs of running the primary and secondary schools in its area, the LEA arrives at what is termed the general schools' budget. It then has to deduct the

costs of certain items, which include central administration, the LEA advisory or inspection service, and grants of various kinds: education support grants, training grants, Section 11 grants, TVEI grants and travellers' children grants. After that, the LEA has the discretion to spend up to 10 per cent of the general schools' budget on a number of areas. Among those relevant to the topic of this book are education welfare services, educational psychologists, the costs of special units attached to ordinary schools, the direct resourcing of individual statemented pupils (looked at quite extensively by Terence Clayton in Chapter 5) and the costs of peripatetic and advisory teachers. These last will include support services for children with learning difficulties, behaviour difficulties, sensory impairment and so on and will not simply relate to salary costs but to overall expenditure on such items as travel and materials.

This is by no means an exhaustive list of the items which the LEA may or may not choose to include within the scope of delegation to schools. If it does not include them, the overall discretionary cost must not exceed 10 per cent of the general schools' budget, a figure which reduces to a maximum of 7 per cent after three years. If it includes them within the scope of delegation of responsibility to schools, then their services will have to be charged for directly. Under these circumstances the schools will presumably be able to choose whether or not to use those services. They will have to bear in mind their responsibilities under the 1981 Education Act for learning difficulties and meeting pupils' special educational needs, but might choose to do much of this by spending the money available to them elsewhere: perhaps using a nearby LEA's service, an independent service or using their own staff to resource much of the work which would have been done by the LEA's support or psychological services.

There are a number of issues which make it impossible to make general statements about what outcomes will occur in relation to pupils with special needs. The formulae of different LEAs will not all be the same; the weighting given to discretionary items will not be the same; some may choose to dispense with some of their services, such as peripatetic music teachers, to give financial weight to other direct services which they prize more highly. But the message is clear. If they want to spend their entire 10 per cent, then in three years' time further cuts will have to be made. Who knows what more stringent limits may be placed on LEAs' discretion after that time? Who knows whether the restrictions set out in Circular 7/88 will be tightened if they do not appear to be achieving their intended purpose? And who knows what the

size of the general schools' budget will be if significant numbers of schools opt for grant-maintained status? After all, 10 per cent (reducing to 7 per cent) of an overall LEA sum for schools may look much smaller in a couple of years' time. The squeeze has surely begun. What are the implications for services and their marketing in the three groups that I distinguished earlier in this section?

In the mainstream

Although many pupils' special educational needs are met from normal resources within ordinary schools, statemented pupils often come with additional provision. This may be the full- or part-time allocation of a classroom or welfare assistant, or it may mean that additional money is made available for temporary or supply teaching for a specified period of the week. Paragraph 115 of Circular 7/88 allows for some flexibility in LEAs' arrival at how the final sum to be distributed to schools (the aggregated schools' budget) should be shared among them. One factor which may be taken into account is the incidence of 'special needs', which include both statemented and non-statemented pupils with learning difficulties, but also encompasses notions of social deprivation and giftedness. That flexibility, up to 25 per cent of the total aggregated schools' budget, has to incorporate other factors which may or may not relate to special needs, such as the size of the school, the type and condition of the school premises and the area in which they are situated.

Mainstream schools, whatever the extent of provision within their own resources, are at present net consumers of services for children with special educational needs. A visually impaired child, for example, attending an ordinary school will usually have some form of resource and specialist support provision built into his or her statement. Similarly, a child showing behaviour problems, almost certainly if the subject of a statement, will be there with some form of additional provision. That provision may take the shape of additional staffing and in many cases involves advice and consultancy from a visiting member of the LEA's staff, usually an 'advisory' or 'support' teacher.

If the LEA chooses not to delegate any of the sums available for the provision of such services or additional resources, things may stay as they are. However, it is possible that in not delegating, the LEA may still, because of cash limits, reduce its overall provision. A general experience of frustration and diminishing service and support would be the result.

An alternative scenario is the full delegation of the sums available for statemented pupils and for advisory and support teachers. If the school's share of the aggregated budget were commensurately larger, this would leave that school, probably through its special needs co-ordinator, the capacity to purchase the help that it has previously received. There are a lot of implications for management should this come about – too many to explore within this chapter – but they will need to be addressed if any such system is to operate to the advantage of pupils with special needs. Not least of them will be the advocacy role of special needs staff in ensuring that the financial resources meant for pupils with learning difficulties are actually allocated in that way within the school. On the assumption that they are, the choices will be clear: whether to 'buy in' the services of existing LEA support staff, to extend the school's staffing on a permanent or temporary basis to meet existing needs or to 'shop around' for services from other providers, perhaps from other LEAs, from other schools or from what may become a burgeoning private sector.

We should not lose sight of the possibility that an increasing number of schools may opt for grant-maintained status. Where they do, they will still have pupils within them who have special educational needs as defined by the 1981 Act. For them it will be as if all the delegation described in the previous paragraph had taken place and the choices outlined there will have to be made. We should not lose sight of the fact that such schools do not necessarily have to be 'service consumers'. They may be in all cases, or they may be only in cases where a child has highly specific needs calling for specialized resources. It is entirely possible for those with already well developed special needs teams actually to become 'service providers', offering skills or expertise which are unavailable in other schools – and charging for them.

Special schools

As I write, most special schools are not likely to be included within their LEAs' formulae for LMS. Their allocations will therefore fall outside the delegated schools' budget and will not therefore be subject to the limitations – or opportunities – provided by the new financial initiatives. Their existence outside the overall system of LMS has provided some LEAs with the option of offsetting a proportion of the time of educational psychologists and advisory and support teachers, usually on a

generously notional basis, against work with them; this allows a proportion of the costs of those services to be set outside the upper 10 per cent limit defined for discretionary items in paragraphs 63–89 of Circular 7/88. Such a device, if it is to have any ring of genuineness, will require a redirection of much of the existing energies of school psychological services and support services. It will probably also be of limited duration, for two reasons: the requirement set out in paragraph 97 of the circular that LEAs must review their excepted items within three years and set targets for their reduction, and the power given to the Secretary of State in Section 43 of the Education Reform Act to create regulations 'to allow or require schemes to cover some or all of an LEA's special schools' (Circular 7/88, paragraph 40). The implications of this last provision are fairly clear: special schools will probably at some point all have delegated budgets. This may particularly be so if they provide a haven for excepting LEA services for the general schools' budget. Given the limited flexibility provided for arriving at the allocation of finance to schools without direct regard to pupil numbers, however, it is almost certain that some form of special formula will need to be allowed to protect the necessary staffing levels.

A special school with a delegated budget would be in an interesting position, provided that its own staffing was of sufficient size and adequately competent to offer 'outreach' services to mainstream schools. Many special schools do this already, of course: in the climate created by LMS, there is no reason why a special school should not enter the marketplace as a net provider of services to other schools.

External support services

Many LEAs have over the past few years developed quite extensive, and in some cases sophisticated, external support services for children with special educational needs. Their intention has been, through one means or another, to assist schools in integrating or retaining children with identified special educational needs within the mainstream. In some cases they have acted as trainers or consultants in developing 'whole-school' policies for special needs, their staff often acting in lieu of local authority advisers. In some cases, their very size and the cost of their associated travel makes them vulnerable, particularly when the 7 per cent ceiling on discretionary exceptions is implemented.

If LEAs except the provision of support and advisory teachers

from delegation to their schools, then of course the central service can be retained. Provided that this can be done within the quite generous overall 10 per cent limits, it would at first seem the most obvious solution. I have, though, pointed out already the pitfalls of counting on the ability of an LEA to continue financing support services at the level at which they start doing so. An alternative strategy might involve, as the amount which can be excepted decreases, charging an amount to schools which use the service which makes up the shortfall but does not reflect its true cost. The final solution is effectively to 'privatize' an LEA's support services for special needs by delegating its finances to schools but ensuring through adequate monitoring and inspection that those schools meet their obligations under the 1981 Education Act, at the same time offering relevant services to them at their actual cost.

The last strategy sounds the riskiest. After all, why should a service allow the cold winds of the marketplace to blow through it when it can find a warmer place to stay? To expose a support service to the vagaries of schools finding their way through the National Curriculum, through new methods of assessment, through appraisal of its staff and through the financial tangles of LMS would seem at first sight sheer foolishness. However, it seems fairly safe to predict that the legislation, regulations and orders which we have on hand at present are not all that we will have to deal with in the future. What will be there, ever present, is an ascendant market-force ideology.

An entrepeneurial service will seize the opportunities presented by the changes which the education system is currently encountering, trimming and refining its offerings to meet the requirements of schools and the needs of their pupils. We can make a useful distinction between 'domestic' and 'wild' organizations. The former are protected, cared for and fed regularly; the latter have to fend for themselves, compete with others and rely upon their wits and capabilities for their rewards and survival. It seems likely that eventually all support services will lose their domestic status; to be out in the wild earlier is actually to gain an advantage.

How is this so? Consider the support service which eventually has to charge schools for its activities within them, having staved off that time until it can be delayed no longer. It has had a protected market share within its own LEA boundaries, although this has been eroded to some extent by schools opting out for grant-maintained status. Within its boundaries, two independent consultancies have been operating in independent schools, one

run by staff of the local polytechnic and another by two educational psychologists. However, they have made little impact on the existing LEA schools because they have to charge for their services at an economic rate whereas the LEA support service comes 'free'. Now, though, they are all on the same terms. In a neighbouring LEA, the support service has had an aggressive policy of issuing new contracts from opted-out schools across other LEAs' boundaries, and has already generated an effective way of communicating its offerings to heads and governing bodies.

In this setting, the newly 'wild' service is likely to be seriously disadvantaged. It has relied on a captive market share, it may not have developed a clear statement of its mission, it has not developed the strategies necessary to win new contracts in a competitive environment and, perhaps most importantly, its members do not think in economic terms about their time, their travel and the way they apply their skills. Its relations with its former client schools are reasonable but because its staff have often had too much to do, they have chosen to concentrate their efforts where they are appreciated. As a result, the connections with some schools within the LEA are not as sound as they might be; in short, the pool of loyalty is not as deep as it could be. It does not take a great leap of imagination to see that such a service will have to work very hard simply to retain the status quo, that other services will be well placed to replace it and that schools may choose to spend their increased delegated sums on alternative resources.

Notions of marketing in a changing environment

Some of the issues which I will now address apply equally to a support service for special needs, to a special school or to a well resourced special needs team in a mainstream school. Clearly they may differ in the kinds of service which they offer and the nature of the learning difficulties with which they feel competent to assist other schools. Until now their nature and function has been manifestly different but there is no reason why this should always be so. In the same way that distinctions between building societies' and banks' services are less easy to discern, so we may see the demarcation between service providers for pupils with special needs becoming less distinct.

Until a few years ago, it would have been unheard of for professionals such as dentists or solicitors to actively seek clients. A brass plate on their door and discreet word of mouth was all

that was permitted them in expanding the scope of their activities. Now it is increasingly common to find them promoting their services and although this is ostensibly not supposed to be at the expense of their colleagues, one person's achievement will inevitably spell a little less success for another. Competition has begun: professionals are now marketing the services which they offer.

Marketing as a separate, identifiable component of management has grown out of the philosophy which recognizes the importance of the customer to any enterprise. The assumption of any free market is that without clients or customers no undertaking can exist for long. Of course, many educational enterprises, formerly not particularly consumer-oriented, are now turning their attention to marketing. Higher education establishments have had seriously to reappraise their overall strategies in attracting clients; many teachers will have observed the significant changes in policy and approach which INSET providers have undergone since the introduction of GRIST and the subsequent local education authorities training grants scheme (LEATGS). In many cases, though, their marketing ignores the wealth of established research and literature in the field, simply involving a problem-solving approach which runs along the lines of 'how can we attract more customers?'

So, what pointers does the established 'science' of marketing hold for special needs service providers? Indeed, what does it consist of? Chisnall (1985) sees marketing as a management function involving 'the vital tasks of identifying marketing needs, of anticipating trends in demand and of planning to supply . . . acceptable products and services. As an entrepreneur, the marketing manager must be seeking new market opportunities' (p. 7). If this sounds too business-orientated, Chisnall goes on to explore the relevance of marketing methods to service provision in health, welfare and education. In another recent analysis, Woodcock (1987) reminds us of the four 'p' principle: product, price, promotion and place. From this we can see that anyone offering a service has to be quite clear about what they can offer, how much they will charge to make their service viable, how awareness will be raised and maintained in potential clients or consumers of the service and in what locations that service will be delivered.

Better marketing

All this may sound alien to some readers. It may even sound far

fetched to the members of many special needs support services. Usually they have too much to do already. It seems an irrelevance to talk about marketing their services when they are spreading themselves too thinly among too many schools. But for the reasons which I have already pointed out, now is the best time to give marketing serious attention.

The primary route to better marketing which Courtis (1987) outlines involves improving contact with existing customers. This has a number of components:

1 Ensuring that the present job is done properly. Here, many of the constituents of effective consultancy (Chapters 2, 3 and 4) may need to be attended to.
2 Ensuring that clients understand that previous jobs are done properly. It is not sufficient to evaluate your own efforts favourably; the client has to be satisfied that a good job was done.
3 Gaining more information about the client and his or her needs. This means taking the time to understand the concerns and expectations of the client.
4 Occasionally reminding clients that you exist – keeping up contacts even when there is no job in hand.
5 From time to time offering further service or a new service.

The second route entails doing substantially the same with potential customers. Here a job of management will be to establish and maintain links with schools where previously there were few. And a further route lies in ensuring that any new enterprises are dealt with efficiently. It is easy for members of a service inadvertently to appear cool or unconcerned when approached for the first time. In a free market environment, this may quickly lead to a client going elsewhere. Courtis (1987) explores other routes, all of which may be worth while bearing in mind. What comes across strongly is that marketing is not just about preparing brochures or advertising in the right journals: it is about doing a good job and making sure that others recognize it as such.

Advertising – or spreading a message – is of course an important element in any marketing strategy. It is often said that half of all advertising is wasted; the trouble is that we do not know which half. When we can easily identify clients such as schools, it is probably profligate to advertise in journals. Direct mailing of literature outlining services is usually far more efficient. The imponderable is who reads it and who they pass it on to. Webster and Wind (1972) have identified five important

roles in any organization's decision to buy which they label 'the gatekeeper', 'the influencer', 'the user', 'the buyer' and 'the decider'. While these roles may be combined in some cases, we have to ensure as far as possible that advertising material gets past gatekeepers to potential users, buyers and deciders.

Other notions related to advertising include branding. It is actually something that happens already: we all know of the names of certain schools or certain LEAs which have a strong reputation for excellence in a particular field. 'She used to work at . . . School' may convey a particular implication of experience or expertise. Services which acquire a particular brand image are more likely to be approached when difficulties seem to be appropriate to them arise.

An element of the branding process, discussed separately by Courtis (1987) but in an educational context almost inseparable from it, is that of employing editorial in journals. An article in the *Times Educational Supplement* or an account of your work in a professional journal read by potential clients is of greater value than most advertising – and it is free. Since most services operate at a local level, an article in the local paper, preferably with a photograph, can effectively raise the public profile of what you are doing. Press releases which are brief, newsworthy and, if possible, exclusive can often work; but keep them clearly and simply written.

What is manifestly true from our own experience as consumers it that the quality of the products we buy or the services we receive are of major importance in our decisions to purchase them again or to recommend them to others. You will be unlikely to revisit a restaurant, however cheap or well advertised, if the food is bad or the service unfriendly. Quality is not just about how well something is done, however; it relates to other factors such as speed of response and interest shown in consequent results. In defining the 'quality' of any service we need to be aware of our own standards of what is good and what constitutes an effective way of working, while still being sensitive to customer requirements and expectations. To give too much weight to the first may isolate a service from the clients it seeks to serve, while to concentrate solely on the second may produce an opportunist ethos which lacks substance and integrity.

Marketing people

Any special needs service is ultimately offering others the skills

of its own personnel. Potentially they are themselves the best promoters of themselves and the team to which they belong. In an earlier work (Bowers 1987) I have suggested that a number of qualities and skills found by earlier research to make people a success at selling to others are likely to influence effectiveness in the consultancy role. These include:

  (i) showing and generating enthusiasm;
 (ii) paying attention to customers' needs, feelings and require-
      ments;
(iii) showing integrity and professionalism;
 (iv) planning and organizing ahead;
  (v) working steadily with little supervision;
 (vi) devoting time and energy over and above the minimum
      requirements;
(vii) making effective contacts with new and prospective
      customers;
(viii) showing mood control.

Investigations as yet unpublished, researching data derived from managers with responsibilities for special needs in special schools, ordinary schools and support services, indicate that many of the interactive profiles which they demonstrate are consistent with the above characteristics. Over two hundred profiles on the *FIRO* 'B' (Schutz 1978) have been analysed, with particular reference to two dimensions 'inclusion' or the extent to which people find it easy to – and want to – relate to groups of people and 'control', which indicates the extent to which they can work independently and need to organize and influence others. Although the research is in its early stages, it seems that the profiles of more than half the special needs managers are consistent with those which should make effective independent or entrepreneurial consultants. The role is not in any way alien to the nature of many of our managers, even if it is one to which some of them are as yet unused.

In conclusion

The notion and reality of competitive tendering is already with us. The Local Government Act 1988 requires local authorities to seek outside tenders from private contractors rather than simply handing over many of its functions, such as buildings main-tenance and refuse collection, to its own direct labour force. This issue impinges upon schools under the new arrangements for LMS, and is addressed in DES Circular 7/88 (paragraphs

192–208). It does not require an enormous leap of the imagination to envisage similar provisions being made in the future for many of the discretionary exceptions to the general schools' budget. Already we have the Circular stating that 'Where a school wishes to organize its own staff to compete for the contract for any defined activity, it should be free to do so' (paragraph 201).

As we move away from central financial decision making and into the climate of the free market, it is vital that there should be the structures available to fit into the environment which meet the special needs of children and which match the new powers of schools as consumers. Special education has always had its entrepreneurs, but they have frequently been looked at askance and attempts made to marginalize them. In the coming years, it is to be hoped that a new breed of entrepreneur will move closer to the centre of the stage to ensure that the pessimistic view (see the end of Robert Harvey's chapter) does not become a reality.

References

Ainscow, M. (1985). 'New directions in meeting special needs', *Pastoral Care*, 3, 38–45.

Ainscow, M. (1989). 'Developing the special school curriculum: where next?', in D. Baker and K. Bovair (eds), *Making the Special Schools Ordinary*? London, Falmer.

Ainscow, M. and Tweddle, D.A. (1977). 'A fundamental responsibility', *Remedial Education*, 12, 36–7.

Ainscow, M. and Tweddle D.A. (1978). 'Overcoming learning problems: teaching to objectives', *Remedial Education*, 13, 141–3.

Ainscow, M. and Tweddle, D.A. (1979). *Preventing Classroom Failure: An Objectives Approach*. Chichester, Wiley.

Ainscow, M. and Tweddle, D.A. (1988). *Encouraging Classroom Success*. London, Fulton.

Anderson, E.M. (1973). *The Disabled School Child*. London, Methuen.

Andrews, G. (1987). 'Putting policy into practice in primary schools in Fife', in T. Booth, P. Potts and W. Swann (eds), *Preventing Difficulties in Learning*. Oxford, Blackwell.

Austin, J. (1988). 'Bringing accountability to schools', supplement to *Local Government Chronicle*, 10 June, p. 76.

Balshaw, M. (1984). 'Mainstream support work – what is it all about?', in T. Bowers (ed.), *Special Educational Needs and Human Resource Management*. London, Croom Helm.

Bandler, R. and Grinder, J. (1975). *The Structure of Magic*. California, Science and Behaviour Books.

Bantock, G.H. (1971). 'Towards a theory of popular education', in R. Hooper (ed.), *The Curriculum: Context, Design and Development*. London, Oliver and Boyd.

Barton, L. and Moody, S. (1987). 'The value of parents to the ESN(S) school: an examination', in J. Bastiani (ed.), *Parents and Teachers*. Windsor, NFER-Nelson.

Berne, E. (1964). *Games People Play*. New York, Grove.

Blythman, M. (1985). 'National initiatives: the Scottish experience', in

J. Sayer and N. Jones (eds), *Teacher Training and Special Educational Needs*. London, Croom Helm.

Bowers, T. (ed.), (1984). *Management and the Special School*. London, Croom Helm.

Bowers, T. (1986). 'Interpersonal skills and conflict management', in D. Tattum (ed.), *Management of Disruptive Behaviour in Schools*. Chichester, Wiley.

Bowers, T. (1987). 'Internal and external support: roles and definitions', in T. Bowers (ed.), *Special Educational Needs and Human Resource Management*. London, Croom Helm.

Brennan, W.K. (1979). *Curricular Needs of Slow Learners*. London, Evans/Methuen (for the Schools Council).

Brennan, W.K. and Jackson, J. (1972). *Look Visual Perceptual Materials*. London, Macmillan.

Bridgeland, M. (1971). *Pioneer Work with Maladjusted Children*. London, Staples.

Cameron, R.J. (1982). 'Working together: the Portage model', *Community Care*, 409, 18–19.

Carlebach, J. (1970). *Caring for Children in Trouble*. London, Routledge and Kegan Paul.

Carr, W. and Kemmis, S. (1983). *Becoming Critical: Knowing Through Action Research*. Victoria, Australia, Deakin University.

Chisnall, P.M. (1985). *Marketing: A Behavioural Analysis*. London, McGraw-Hill.

Clements, J. (1987). *Severe Learning Disability and Psychological Handicap*. Chichester, Wiley.

Conoley, C. and Conoley, J. (1982). *School Consultant: A Guide to Practice and Training*. Oxford, Pergamon.

Coopers and Lybrand (1988). *Local Management of Schools: A Report to the Department of Education and Science*. London, DES.

Cottam, P.J. and Sutton, A. (eds), (1985). *Conductive Education: A System for Overcoming Motor Disorder*. London, Croom Helm.

Coupe, J. and Porter, J. (1986). *The Education of Children with Severe Learning Difficulties*. London, Croom Helm.

Courtis, J. (1987). *Marketing Services*. London, Kogan Page.

Cowne, E. and Norwich, B. (1987). *Lessons in Partnership*. Bedford Way Papers, 31. London, University of London Institute of Education.

Dale, D. (1979). 'Integration on an individual basis', *Special Education: Forward Trends*, 6, 2, 22–4.

Day, C., Johnson, D. and Whitaker, P. (1985). *Managing Primary Schools: A Professional Development Approach*. London, Harper and Row.

DES Central Advisory Council for Education (England), (1967). *Children and their Primary Schools: A Report* (Plowden Report), Vol. 1, London, HMSO.

DES (1977). *A New Partnership for Our Schools* (The Taylor Report). London, HMSO.

DES and others (1978). *Special Educational Needs: Report of the Committee of Enquiry into the Education of Handicapped Children and Young People* (Warnock Report). London, HMSO.

DES (1987a). *The National Curriculum 5–16: a Consultation Document*. London, DES.

DES and Welsh Office (1987b). *National Curriculum: Report of the Task Group on Assessment and Testing*. London, DES.

DES (1989). *Report by HM Inspectors on a Survey of Support Services for Special Educational Needs*. London, DES.

Dessent, T. (1984). *What is Important About Portage?* Windsor, NFER-Nelson.

Dessent, T. (1987). *Making the Ordinary School Special*. London, Falmer.

Dowling, M. (1988). *Education 3 to 5: A Teacher's Handbook*. London, Chapman.

Duthie, J.H. (1970). *Primary School Survey: A Study of the Teacher's Day*. Edinburgh, HMSO.

Essex Education and Library Service (1988). *Book Policy in the Primary School*. Harlow, Longman.

Feiler, A. and Thomas, G. (1988). *Planning for Special Needs*. Oxford, Blackwell.

Festinger, L., Riecken, H.W. and Schachter, S. (1956). *When Prophecy Fails*. Minneapolis, University of Minneapolis Press.

Feuerstein, R. (1980). *Instrumental Enrichment: An Intervention Program for Cognitive Modifiability*. Baltimore, University Park Press.

Furth, H.G. (1973). *Deafness and Learning*. Belmont, California, Wadsworth.

Galloway, D. (1985). *Schools and Persistent Absentees*. Oxford, Pergamon.

Galloway, D. and Goodwin, C. (1987). *The Education of Disturbing Children*. Harlow, Longman.

Georgiades, N. and Phillimore, L. (1975). 'The myth of the hero innovator and alternative strategies for organisational change', in C.C. Kiernan and F.P. Woodford (eds), *Behaviour Modification and the Severely Retarded*. Amsterdam, Associated Scientific.

Gipps, C., Gross, H. and Goldstein, H. (1987). *Warnock's Eighteen Per Cent: Children with Special Needs in Primary Schools*. London, Falmer.

Goacher, B., Evans, J., Welton, J. and Wedell, K. (1988). *Policy and Provision for Special Educational Needs*. London, Cassell.

Gregory, S. and Bishop, J. (1989). 'The integration of deaf children into ordinary schools: a research report', *Journal of the British Association of Teachers of the Deaf*, 13, 1–6.

Gross, H. and Gipps, C. (1987). *Supporting Warnock's Eighteen Per Cent*. London, Falmer.

Hammill, D.D. and Larsen, S.C. (1974). 'The relationship of selected auditory perceptual skills and reading ability', *Journal of Learning Disabilities*, 7, 429–35.

Hanko, G. (1985). *Special Needs in Ordinary Classrooms*. Oxford, Blackwell.

Hari, M. and Akos, K. (1988). *Conductive Education*. London, Routledge.

Harris, S.L. (1983). *Families of the Developmentally Disabled*. Oxford, Pergamon.

Hart, S. (1986). 'Evaluating support teaching', *Gnosis*, September, 26–31.

Hayward, G. and Everett, C. (1983). 'Adaptors and innovators: data from the Kirton Adaptor-Innovator Inventory in a local authority setting', *Journal of Occupational Psychology*, 56, 339–42.

Hegarty, S. (1987). *Meeting Special Needs in Ordinary Schools*. London, Cassell.

Hegarty, S., Pocklington, K. and Lucas, D. (1981). *Educating Pupils with Special Needs in the Ordinary School*. Windsor, NFER-Nelson.

Herbert, M. (1975). *Problems of Childhood*. London, Pan.

Herbert, M. (1978). *Conduct, Disorders of Childhood and Adolescence*. Chichester, Wiley.

Hewison, J. (1985). 'Parental involvement and reading attainment: implications of research in Dagenham and Haringey', in K. Topping and S. Wolfendale (eds), *Parental Involvement in Children's Reading*. London, Croom Helm.

Hewison, J. (1982). 'Parental involvement in the teaching of reading', *Remedial Education*, 17, 157–62.

Hirst, P.H. and Peters, R.S. (1970). *The Logic of Education*. Oxford, Oxford University Press.

HMI (Scotland) (1978). *The Education of Pupils with Learning Difficulties*. Edinburgh: Scottish Education Department.

Hockley, L. (1985). 'On being a support teacher', *British Journal of Special Education*, 12, 27–9.

Hodgson, A., Clunies-Ross, L. and Hegarty, S. (1984). *Learning Together: Teaching Pupils with Special Educational Needs in the Ordinary School*. Windsor, NFER-Nelson.

Hoghughi, M. (1978). *Troubled and Troublesome: Coping with Severely Disadvantaged Children*. London, Burnett.

Hurt, J.S. (1988). *Outside the Mainstream: A History of Special Education*. London, Batsford.

ILEA (1984). *Improving Secondary Schools*. London, ILEA.

ILEA (1985a). *Improving Primary Schools*. London, ILEA.

ILEA (1985b). *Educational Opportunities for All?* (The Fish Report). London, ILEA.

Jackson, A. and Hannan, P. (1981). *The Belfield Reading Project*. Rochdale, Belfield Community Council.

Jeffree, D.M., McConkey, R. and Hewson, S. (1977). *Teaching the Handicapped Child*. London, Souvenir Press.

Kerr, J.F. (1968). *Changing the Curriculum*. London, University of London Press.

Knight, R. and Bowers, T. (1984). 'Team development', in T. Bowers (ed.), *Management and the Special School*. London, Croom Helm.

Kolvin, I., Garside, R.F., Nichol, A.R., MacMillan, A., Wolstenholme, F. and Leitch, I.M. (1981). *Help Starts Here*. London, Tavistock.

Laslett, R. (1977). *Educating Maladjusted Children*. London, Crosby Lockwood Staples.

LMS Initiative (1988). *Local Management in Schools: A Practical Guide*. London, The Local Management in Schools Initiative.

Longhorn, F. (1988). *A Sensory Curriculum for Very Special People: A Practical Approach to Curriculum Planning*. London, Souvenir Press.

Mager, R.F. (1962). *Preparing Instructional Objectives*. Palo Alto, California, Fearon.

Marra, M. (1984). 'Parents of children with moderate learning difficulties', in T. Bowers (ed.), *Management and the Special School*. London, Croom Helm.

McConkey, R. (1986). *Working with Parents: A Practical Guide for Teachers and Therapists*. London, Croom Helm.

Ministry of Education (1955). *Report of the Committee on Maladjusted Children.* London, HMSO.

Minkes, A.L. (1987). *The Entrepreneurial Manager.* Harmondsworth, Penguin.

Mittler, P. and Farrell, P. (1987). 'Can children with severe learning difficulties be educated in ordinary schools?', *European Journal of Special Needs Education*, 2, 221–36.

Morris, G. (1988). 'Applying business consultancy approaches to schools', in H.L. Gray (ed.), *Management Consultancy in Schools.* London, Cassell.

Moses, D., Hegarty, S. and Jowett, S. (1988). *Supporting Ordinary Schools. Disability, Handicap and Society*, 2, 75–84.

Moses, D. Hegarty, S. and Jowett, S. (1988). *Supporting Ordinary Schools.* Windsor, NFER-Nelson.

Murgatroyd, S. (1988). 'Consultancy as counselling: the theory and practice of structural consulting', in H.L. Gray (ed.), *Management Consultancy in Schools.* London, Cassell.

Murgatroyd, S. and Reynolds, D.R. (1984). 'The creative consultant – the potential use of consultancy as a method of teacher education', *School Organisation*, 4, 321–35.

Nicholls, R.H. (1970). 'Children with learning difficulties', *Forward Trends*, 14, 90–2.

Outsan, S., Brown, R. and Constable, H. (1989). 'A strategy for helping children with mild hearing loss in the mainstream', *Journal of the British Association of Teachers of the Deaf*, 13, 22–4.

Paice, S. (1985). 'Reading and learning', in C. Moon (ed.), *Practical Ways to Teach Reading.* London, Ward Lock.

Peters, T.J. and Waterman, R.H. (1982). *In Search of Excellence: Lessons from America's Best-Run Companies.* New York, Harper & Row.

Robbins, M. and Glass, G.V. (1969). 'The Doman–Delacato rationale: a critical analysis', in J. Hellmuth (ed.), *Educational Therapy*, Vol. 2. Seattle, Special Child Publications.

Rogers, C. (1951). *Client-centered Therapy.* Boston, Houghton Mifflin.

Rose, G. (1967). *Schools for Young Offenders.* London, Tavistock.

Rosenthal, R. and Jacobson, J. (1968). *Pygmalion in the Classroom: Teacher Expectations and Pupils' Intellectual Development.* New York, Holt.

Sandow, S., Stafford, D. and Stafford, P. (1987). *An Agreed Understanding?* Windsor, NFER-Nelson.

Schein, E.H. (1972). *Professional Education: Some New Directions.* New York, McGraw-Hill.

Schein, E.H. (1985). *Organisational Culture and Leadership.* San Francisco, Jossey Bass.

Schein, E.H. (1987). *Process Consultation*, Vol. 2. Reading, Massachusetts, Addison-Wesley.

Schutz, W. (1978). *FIRO Awareness Scales Manual.* Palo Alto, California, Consulting Psychologists Press.

Scottish Education Department (1978). *The Education of Children with Learning Difficulties.* London, HMSO.

Seed, P. (1988). *Children with Profound Handicaps: Parents' Views and Integration.* London, Falmer.

Select Committee (1981). *Third Report of the Education, Science and Arts*

Committee, Special Educational Needs. London, HMSO.

Shearer, A. (1981). *Disability: Whose Handicap?* Oxford, Blackwell.

Shields, R. (1962). *A Cure of Delinquents.* London, Heinemann.

Smith, B. (ed.), (1988). *Interactive Approaches to the Education of Children with Severe Learning Difficulties.* Proceedings of a conference held at Westhill College, Birmingham, April 1987.

Smith, C. (1982). 'Helping colleagues cope – a consultant role for the remedial teacher', *Remedial Education*, 17, 75–8.

Stenhouse, L. (1975). *An Introduction to Curriculum Research and Development.* London, Heinemann.

Stott, D.H. (1950). *Delinquency in Human Nature.* Dunfermline, United Dominions Trust.

Stratton, P., Munton, T., Hanks, H., Heard, D. and Davidson, S. (1988). *Leeds Attribution Coding System Manual.* Leeds, Leeds University Press.

Strauss, A. (1987). *Qualitative Analysis for Social Scientists.* Cambridge, Cambridge University Press.

Swann, W. (1983). 'Curriculum principles for integration', in T. Booth and P. Potts (eds), *Integrating Special Education.* Oxford, Blackwell.

Tansley, A.E. (1967). *Reading and Remedial Reading.* London, Routledge.

Thomas, G. (1987). 'Other adults in the classroom: opportunities or problems?', *Links*, Autumn, 19–21.

Thomas, G. and Feiler, A. (1988). *Planning for Special Needs.* Oxford, Blackwell.

Topping, K. (1986). 'Consultative enhancement of school-based action', in D. Tattum (ed.), *Management of Disruptive Behaviour in Schools.* Chichester, Wiley.

Trachtman, G. (1981). 'On a full sea', *School Psychology Review*, 2, 138–81.

Visser, J. (1986). 'Support: a description of the work of the SEN professional', *Support for Learning*, 1, 4, 5–9.

Weatherley, R. and Lipsky, M. (1977). 'Street-level bureaucrats and institutional innovation: implementing special educational reform', in W. Swann (ed.), *The Practice of Special Education.* Milton Keynes, Open University Press.

Webster, A., Scanlon, P. and Bown E. (1985). 'Meeting the needs of hearing-impaired children within a local education authority', *AEP Journal*, Supplement to 6, 5, 2–10.

Webster, F.E. and Wind, Y. (1972). *Organisational Buying Behaviour.* Englewood Cliffs, New Jersey, Prentice-Hall.

Wedell, K. (1988). 'The new Act: a special need for vigilance', *British Journal of Special Education*, 15, 98–101.

West, J. and Idol, L. (1987). 'School consultation (part 1): an interdisciplinary perspective on theory, models and research', *Journal of Learning Disabilities*, 20, 388–408.

Williams, H. and Muncey, J. (1982). 'Precision teaching before behavioural objectives?' *AEP Journal*, 18, 116–24.

Wolfendale, S. (1983). *Parental Participation in Children's Development and Education.* London, Gordon and Breach.

Wolfendale, S. (1986). 'Involving parents in behaviour management: a whole school approach', *Support for Learning*, 1, 4, 33–8.

Wolfendale, S. (1987). *Primary Schools and Special Educational Needs.* London, Cassell.

Woodcock, P. (1987). 'Marketing', in D.M. Stewart (ed.), *Handbook of Management Skills*. Aldershot, Gower.

Ysseldyke, J.E. and Algozzine, B. (1982). *Critical Issues in Special and Remedial Education*. Boston, Houghton Mifflin.

Index